The Improv Handbook

The Improv Handbook

The Ultimate Guide to Improvising in Comedy, Theatre, and Beyond

Second Edition

TOM SALINSKY AND DEBORAH FRANCES-WHITE

FOREWORD BY MIKE MCSHANE

methuen | drama

LONDON · NEW YORK · OXFORD · NEW DELHI · SYDNEY

METHUEN DRAMA
Bloomsbury Publishing Plc
50 Bedford Square, London, WC1B 3DP, UK
1385 Broadway, New York, NY 10018, USA
29 Earlsfort Terrace, Dublin 2, Ireland

BLOOMSBURY, METHUEN DRAMA and the Methuen Drama logo are trademarks
of Bloomsbury Publishing Plc

First published in 2008 by the Continuum International Publishing Group Inc.
Second edition published by Bloomsbury Methuen Drama, 2017
Reprinted 2019 (twice), 2020 (twice), 2021

Cover design: Louise Dugdale

A catalogue record for this book is available from the British Library.

Library of Congress Cataloging-in-Publication Data
Names: Salinsky, Tom, author. | Frances-White, Deborah, author. |
McShane, Michael, writer of foreword.
Title: The improv handbook : the ultimate guide to improvising in comedy, theatre,
and beyond / Tom Salinksy and Deborah Frances White ; foreword by Mike McShane.
Description: Second edition. | London ; New York : Bloomsbury Methuen Drama, 2017. |
Includes bibliographical references.
Identifiers: LCCN 2017008514 | ISBN 9781350026162 (pbk.) |
ISBN 9781350026155 (hardback)
Subjects: LCSH: Improvisation (Acting) Classification: LCC PN2071.I5 S27 2017 |
DDC 792.02/8–dc23
LC record available at https://lccn.loc.gov/2017008514

ISBN: HB: 978-1-3500-2615-5
PB: 978-1-3500-2616-2
ePDF: 978-1-3500-2614-8
eBook: 978-1-3500-2617-9

Typeset by Integra Software Services Pvt. Ltd.
Printed and bound in Great Britain

To find out more about our authors and books visit www.bloomsbury.com
and sign up for our newsletters.

For my parents
For Mother and Dad who encouraged me in all my endeavors.
And for Patti Stiles, our mother in improv.

CONTENTS

FOREWORD

Mike McShane

Tom and Deborah have done it again. They've revised their already widely read and well-received book on improvisation. This revision is important because it omits their origin story, and therefore the history of the invisible pleasure planet, Orgiius-5. The official uniform designs for their all Janet Jackson troupe of Improv Stomp Queens have also been excised, much to my personal disappointment.

What they did keep, however, is all that made their book a superior practical guide for everyone with an interest in this great art form. Improvisation has become a sophisticated and rich way to create entertainment, a philosophy grounded in real time contact, akin to a sport, confirming what Brecht said, that artists are "athletes of the soul." It has found its way into the think tanks of businesses and boardrooms, as well as garnering awards on the West End.

Its prominence as a form of expression also comes with some stranger facets; there is pedantry, sexism, dogma and misinformation as well. This is what happens when you try to wrestle down an angel. It's a seductive, humane pleasure and its joyful cooperative spirit wants for absolute rules.

Thankfully, Tom and Deborah are enthusiastic and knowledgeable guides, offering their vast experience and concise observation, and reminding you all the time that a place where failure is fearless, and having another go is your goal, is ideal for your art, your spirit and, really, our planet.

Which kind of puts Orgiius-5 on the back burner.

INTRODUCTION TO THE SECOND EDITION

Publishing *The Improv Handbook* was an absolute joy. Apart from the fun of putting it together and the thrill of seeing it in bookshops, the feedback from the improvisation community has been amazing. No doubt some readers took issue with our stance on various topics, but on the whole we have been immensely gratified to read or have been told about people who have enjoyed reading it and found it useful.

Going over the material again has been a curious process. A lot is very familiar, but sometimes on reading the manuscript we were struck by a particularly striking phrase or brilliant analysis and had no memory of having written it. Just as often, we came across something clunky, inappropriate or just inaccurate and equally it felt like it had been written by another person.

So now, eight years later, we have the chance to do the one thing which improvisers never get to do: refine, iterate and improve. We've added new sections, updated others, revised some awkward language and deleted material which no longer applied. If we've removed your favorite bit, we apologize, but hopefully the new sections will make up for the loss.

In the intervening time, we have been as active as ever in the improvisation community, continued teaching and delivering some of the same insights in the corporate world, but we have also diversified even more. Deborah's career as a stand-up comedian has flourished, not just in live shows but also on BBC Radio 4 where she won a Writers Guild Award and in her podcast *The Guilty Feminist*. Tom has written four stage plays and five Big Finish audio dramas with Robert Khan and continues to pursue this career as well as producing *The Guilty Feminist* and Deborah's spin-off podcast *Global Pillage*.

None of these things would be possible if it weren't for the lessons we learned through improvisation. Returning to improvised comedy always makes us feel nostalgic and grateful and that goes for this book too.

Tom Salinsky and Deborah Frances-White
July 2016
London

INTRODUCTION

What follows is a personal account of the state of the art of comedy improvisation. In writing this book, we have tried to serve two masters. On the one hand, we want to give as broad an overview as possible. We have tackled questions like: Where did improvisation come from? Where is it going? What is it good for? Who are the major leaders and how do they differ? Can you make money at it? How?

But, on the other hand, as practitioners of the art with many years of experience between us, we have also formed some pretty strong opinions about what works and what doesn't, what's helpful and what's destructive, what's positive and what's negative. Our experience in improvisation has mainly been with the school of thought associated with Keith Johnstone and Calgary, although we have also made it our mission to go to Chicago and train with people associated with Del Close—notably Charna Halpern—and Deborah is now an Artistic Associate of the Chicago Improv Festival. And this book also covers work influenced by Viola Spolin, ideas we have developed ourselves, and some material that doesn't neatly fit into any of these categories. Does our longer experience with Keith make us biased? It depends on how you look at it. On the one hand, yes, we think that we have found a productive methodology and we acknowledge the enormous debt we owe to Keith in discovering that. On the other hand, we don't feel any particular intellectual loyalty to Keith, and will be happy to accept, use, and apply ideas from anyone. Our mantra is simply: whatever works.

Our hope is that this personal viewpoint will be appealing and interesting. This book, for better or worse, is *our* account of what improvisation is, has been, will be, and should be. It is shaped by our experiences and our history, and if we come across as opinionated, then we hope that you will be either overjoyed to have found like minds or stimulated by an opposing argument, or at least made pleasantly aggrieved to have found people you can entirely disagree with.

The core of this book is Section Two: "How to Improvise." Before that, we will briefly look at "What Is Improvisation?" and after that we will look at "How to Improvise in Public," "How to Make Improvisation Pay," and also hear from some of the current leading lights of the art form (Del Close and Viola Spolin are both sadly no longer with us).

Section Two is modeled on our improvisation workshops, which have been enormously popular almost since the day they began. We are tremendously pleased and proud to have trained hundreds of improvisers since then, and to have been invited to teach at British institutions such as The Actors Centre, RADA, The Central School of Speech and Drama, and as guests of other improvisation companies the world over.

Improvisation has a tremendous power to liberate, inspire, and enthuse—which is why we still love it after all these years. Agree or disagree, seasoned improviser or trembling neophyte, we hope this book is an enjoyable and stimulating read.

A glossary of terms is included at the back of the book, which may be helpful for those new to improvisation. When we use "terms of art" in the text, we will often render them in SMALL CAPS.

Tom Salinsky and Deborah Frances-White
October 2007
London

SECTION ONE

What Is Improvisation?

1.1

What Was Improvisation?

Overview

Where did improvisation come from, and who are the main and most influential practitioners today?

ANTIQUITY

Almost any book on improvisation will tell you that improvised theatre began with the Commedia Dell'Arte—and for once, "any book" is right, although possibly not for the reasons supposed.

A moment's thought about how theatre came to be will reveal that the notion of re-enacting events for an audience almost certainly came before the notion of writing a script to be memorized, but it isn't really accurate to describe this kind of proto-theatre as "improvised" despite the fact that it was necessarily re-created fresh at each performance.

As the writer, very swiftly, assumed dominance of the theatre, the script became of paramount importance. The reason for this is also clear to see, and applies not just to theatre, but to all "temporal" art forms. Mozart was thought to be an astonishing improviser, but it is only his "premeditated" music which remains, since—by definition—his improvisations were not recorded for posterity (although they may have inspired music which he later set down). Scripts, books and music manuscripts can *travel* and *endure* in the way that a brief moment of inspiration cannot.

The Commedia Dell'Arte arose in Italy in the fifteenth century and specialized in bawdy comedies built around standard situations and populated by stock characters, often played by actors who had played them for many years, or even decades. In contrast to almost all the theatres which preceded it—at least from the ancient Greeks on—there was no definite script. Instead, Commedia Dell'Arte performers were free to improvise around the familiar situations, creating extemporized comic set-pieces, dialogue exchanges and even plot details as the fancy took them. No doubt this was a highly successful methodology, as it endured well into the eighteenth century and its influence is still felt today.

So, we don't feel as if the term "improvised" can be applied to primitive proto-theatre. "Improvised" to us implies a *rejection* of the process of scriptwriting and rehearsing. The Commedia Dell'Arte players could have written scripts but they chose not to. Thus, they were the first practitioners of improvised theatre.

VIOLA SPOLIN

The next major innovation in improvisation had to wait almost five hundred years. Viola Spolin began her theatre work in the late 1930s. Like Augusto Boal after her, she was working in community theatre, and in trying to stimulate the children she was working with and make the process of theatre easy for them to grasp, she invented dozens of what now seem like fundamental improvisation games and exercises. Like Stanislavski and later Lee Strasberg, she viewed improvisation as essentially a rehearsal tool, rather than a performance piece. Despite this, in one public demonstration of her methods, she asked for a suggestion from her audience, and improvisers have been doing this ever since. To many, the process of getting audience suggestions is the bedrock of improvisation, and many groups use a description of that process to encapsulate their whole show ("all based on your suggestions"). It is, however, easy to overuse and abuse.

In the 1950s, Spolin's son Paul Sills fell in with an exciting group of young actors in Chicago, headed by producer David Shepherd. Initially organized under the name the Playwrights Theatre Club, many of them followed when Shepherd and Sills began a new enterprise—the Compass Players. Sills and Spolin taught the Spolin games to this ensemble, and Shepherd hit upon the idea of using outlines of dramatic action—a contemporary version of the scenarios of the Commedia Dell'Arte—to act as the bases of plays whose dialogue was developed improvisationally by the company during rehearsals.

The owner of the bar where they performed asked if they could make the shows longer. Not having time to rehearse more material, they followed Spolin's example and began improvising directly from audience suggestions. This proved so popular that the improvised plays went by the wayside in favor of performances entirely devoted to the shorter improvised scenes. What started as a theatre company became a cabaret entertainment.

A schism develops right here, which we will return to again and again in this book, between content and process. The problem which this creates is sometimes known as the SKATEBOARDING DUCK. For the Commedia Dell'Arte players, extemporization was simply the most effective method of channeling their inspiration, of creating the kind of comic energy which their scenarios demanded. Likewise, Shepherd and the Compass Players were initially seeking a fresher, more truthful acting style within a predetermined plot structure.

As soon as the audience is made aware of the process, however, then a second point of interest emerges. There is something *daring* about beginning with a random suggestion from the audience, which makes much of public improvisation about taking a *risk*. The potential problem with this approach is that the audience may be encouraged to admire the process rather than being engaged in the story. Like a duck riding a skateboard, they are astonished that such a thing is possible, and are thus distracted from whether or not it is done well. Taken too far, this is a recipe for both mediocrity and a thirst for novelty—problems which often bedevil the form to this day.

That isn't to say that process should be ignored, or even de-emphasized. We don't regard an acknowledgment of process as evil—in fact, we regard it as essential—but we want to be aware of the dangers and drawbacks as well as the advantages.

The Compass ran sporadically from 1955 to 1963 and counted among its alumni Alan Alda, Jerry Stiller, Mike Nichols, Elaine May, and—of course—Del Close. In 1959, some of its members founded Second City, about which more in a moment.

KEITH JOHNSTONE

At around the same time, in London, Keith Johnstone, a one-time high school teacher now working at the Royal Court Theatre in London, was beginning to direct plays for the first time. Despairing of the "theatre of taxidermy" which he saw in the West End and remembering how his own teachers had (seemingly) done their best to stifle his creativity and self-expression, he pinned up a list of things his teachers had told him not to do and used it as a syllabus. Not having had any drama training himself, he found himself constantly questioning his actors' preconceptions and the prevailing wisdom of the day—notably Stanislavski.

As he developed more and more exercises intended to keep his actors in the "present" and aware of each other, and to wreck their concentration, he found that he and the rest of the group were laughing prodigiously. Their improvised performances seemed much more alive, fresh, real, and inspired than the play they were supposed to be rehearsing. Was this some vast untapped reservoir of comic inspiration, or were they fooling themselves with colossal self-indulgence? The only way to find out was to go public, and pretty soon, Keith's "Theatre Machine" was touring all around Europe, with Keith himself acting as a sort of ringmaster, setting tasks for the actors and trying to keep order (ideally without quite succeeding). Keith, too, used audience suggestions, although sparingly.

In the 1970s, Keith moved to Calgary and developed Theatresports, one of the most popular ways of "packaging" improvisation for public performance yet devised. He founded the Loose Moose Theatre, which was an ideal home for the energetic young Canadian improvisers he was teaching, and although Keith has now stepped down from the Moose, it still presents his formats and runs an annual summer school which attracts improvisation practitioners from all over the world. Keith published the book *Impro* in 1979, a collection of his thoughts and ideas about improvisation. Continuously in print ever since, it is now regarded as a classic. This was followed by *Impro for Storytellers* in 1999.

IMPROVOLYMPIC

At Second City, the schism previously mentioned was dividing the company. Some practitioners held that using improvisation to develop terrific cabaret was certainly possible, provided it was understood that improvisation, whether in public or in private, was fundamentally a writing tool: excellent at developing inspiration and finding new ideas, lousy at delivering those ideas with economy and focus. Others, including Del Close, held that improvisation was a uniquely exciting process which audiences would be thrilled to witness.

In the 1980s, Del and his partner Charna Halpern left Second City to found ImprovOlympic, now generally known simply as iO. Today, iO is a major force in improvisation, especially in Chicago, whereas almost all of Second City's public performances are of scripted sketch material. Both institutions teach improvisation, and each has become a training ground for many familiar faces from American TV and movies, including Bill Murray, Chris Farley, John Belushi, Tina Fey, Amy Poehler and countless others. Today, Chicago is home to dozens of improvisation companies and annually hosts the Chicago Improv Festival, probably the largest improv festival in the world.

THE SPONTANEITY SHOP

And this is where we come in. Tom and Deborah met attending improv classes in London and, inspired by Canadian improviser and teacher Patti Stiles, decided to start putting on their own weekly show in a basement in Earl's Court which smelled slightly of damp (or as the owner put it, history). That company became The Spontaneity Shop which still presents improvised comedy shows, improvisation classes, stand-up comedy shows, plays, podcasts, corporate training sessions and corporate seminars. Improvisation gave us both a living and a wonderful creative outlet, and of course the opportunity to write this book.

1.2

Improvisation in Performance

Overview

A quick summary of some of the most popular ways of "packaging" improvisation for public consumption.

KEITH JOHNSTONE AND COMPETITIVE IMPROVISATION

In the 1950s, Keith Johnstone was trying whatever crazy ideas he could think of to liven up his improv classes, and he found that pitting one team against the other brought out some of their competitive spirit and spurred them on to try and outdo each other. It was obvious that the unpredictable nature of improvisation meant that the sporting analogy was apt, and Keith was further inspired by the reactions of crowds at wrestling matches. In Keith's eyes, wrestling was a form of theatre since the fights were quite carefully planned. But this was theatre which energized and inflamed the (generally working-class) audience. By contrast, middle-class audiences at the Royal Court, watching plays about the struggles of the working class, would simply clap politely. Keith longed for a way of presenting theatre which would engage the audience in the same way that wrestling seemed to, and was convinced that improvisation was the answer. This vision was thwarted by the Lord

Chamberlain, who forbade any play being performed without prior script approval.[1]

In the UK, Keith got around this restriction by presenting the Theatre Machine's improvisation as "public comedy workshop demonstrations," but any competitive element would have given the game away and so, Theatresports was kept in the rehearsal room until the 1970s, when Keith arrived at the University of Calgary and found an ideal space for it. That first generation of Calgary students also contributed ideas, and now the basic structure—two teams, issuing challenges, three judges, an MC and points for the teams—is seen all over the world (under various names, and with various modifications).

The idea of competitive improvisation seems to have also occurred independently to David Shepherd in New York (giving rise to ImprovOlympic) and to Robert Gravel and Yvon Leduc in Quebec (giving rise to Le Match and the Canadian Improv Games, which are still in action today, although they haven't seen the wide geographical spread enjoyed by Theatresports). It seems more obvious that ComedySportz is directly "inspired by" Theatresports, as it was created by Dick Chudnow who saw a performance of Theatresports and encouraged Keith to franchise it, a suggestion which Keith declined. Chudnow's own show debuted shortly thereafter.

Ironically, the franchise structure of ComedySportz, which specifies exactly how the show should be run, does a better job of preserving the integrity of the format. Licenses to perform Theatresports are fairly easy to obtain and since the International Theatresports Institute has not the resources to very closely monitor the activities of most of its licensees, Theatresports tends to be performed very differently by different groups, with few of the alterations groups make to the format sanctioned by Keith or likely to meet with his approval.

Theatresports is very popular for international "tournaments," not only because the competitive format is an interesting "hook" for the audience, but also because it's a great way for teams who have never played together to share a stage (since players generally improvise scenes with their own teammates). However, care should be taken that the competitive spirit does not get the better of some teams who believe that national pride is on the line. The judges are improvising too, and should feel free to give low scores for arbitrary reasons if it will make the show better. Within a single company, fixed teams have the advantage that those teams develop an

---

[1] Hard as it is to believe today, Keith suffered the embarrassment of visiting theatre companies from the Soviet Union asking him how he put up with such terrible censorship. Legend has it that Keith wrote to the Lord Chamberlain suggesting that he send an emissary to sit at the side of the stage and ring a bell if anything happened which he disapproved of. The Lord Chamberlain's response is not recorded.

identity and a style, but may start taking the competition too seriously. True competitiveness on the stage is unpleasant for audiences to watch and kills the happy spirit of improv, and so "scratch" teams may be preferred.

At our international tournament, we made a great show of recording all the scores from the "heats" (while actually expending no effort at all to make sure the same number of challenges was played each night) and then, on the last night, presented four out of the six teams as the "finalists" whose names had in fact been pulled out of a hat backstage. Some matches are secretly decided on the toss of a coin, with the judges given target scores to try and reach—*anything* to remind the players that the competition is for the audience's enjoyment, and that's the only thing which really matters.

It is useful for the improvisers to be seen to treat the mechanisms of the competition with some respect, however. The temptation for improvisers to treat all aspects of the show as opportunities for witticisms is strong enough already, and so the scores should be treated as a fiction, which the improvisers believe in enough that it looks like something is at stake, but not so much that it wrecks the feeling of good nature which the best improv shows conjure up.

Not quite as popular outside Calgary, but more favored these days by Keith, are his more recent inventions: Micetro Impro and Gorilla Theatre. Micetro[2] is an elimination game created by Keith when a very large group of students all wanted to play Theatresports at the end of a workshop in Utrecht. Realizing that if they all played, then no one would get very much stage time, Keith nevertheless decided to let them all enter, and looked for some mechanism to whittle down the field as the show progressed. He assigned each player a number, and he and a fellow director sat in the front row and pulled numbered discs out of a hat to get random combinations of players whom they would then set up in a scene. At the end of each scene, he decided to ask the audience to give the scene a score from 1 to 5. Every player in the scene receives the same score and they cross to other side of the stage. When every player has had a go (more usually these days, two goes), those at the bottom of the scoreboard are eliminated and round we go again with those who remain. At the end of the night, a single player is crowned "Maestro."

Micetro proved to be a very successful format, with skilled directors able to generate variety and keep the standard of work high. In Micetro shows, the audience generally gets to see a cast that decreases in number but increases in ability as the night goes on, so the show tends to get better as it goes on (good!). This is not only because the more talented players (or at any rate the players having the best night) tend to get higher scores, but also because the experience of surviving elimination after elimination boosts their confidence. They start to think "I can do anything!" which becomes

---

[2]Pronounced "Maestro."

a self-fulfilling prophecy. The eliminations may sting at first, but players should be reminded that since all players in a scene get the same score, the scoring system is not very fair, and that excellent players can be eliminated very early. However, the scoring system is not entirely unfair either, so if you play Micetro every week and you never get past the interval, that's good feedback (or you need to invite more friends).

Whereas Micetro works best with a group occupying a wide range of experience and ability levels, Gorilla Theatre is designed for veterans. Three to six players take turns directing each other in improvised scenes and games, with successful directors (again by audience voting) receiving a (foam) banana to pin on their shirt, and unsuccessful directors having to pay a forfeit (make up a limerick, buy drinks for the front row, be insulted by an audience member, etc.). The most successful director wins "a week's quality time with the resident gorilla," who may or not be present corporeally.

The mechanism of having players publicly direct each other—as in Micetro—keeps the quality of the work high and the audience enjoys it if directors boldly announce their intentions, since it gives them a yardstick by which to measure their success. The competition aspect also gives the show an automatic "shape" and a climax in the form of the announcement of the winner. It can also be argued, however, that these devices are safety nets which improvisers should learn to do without.

Keith's other well-known format, although it's harder to get the license for this one nowadays, is Life Game. Not a competitive format, this takes the form of a chat show with one guest (not necessarily, but often, a celebrity) revealing stories from their life, aspects of which are then improvised by a resident cast. Life Game was recently toured very successfully by the amazing company Improbable Theatre, and was also turned into a cable television program in the United States. As with Theatresports, the idea seems to have occurred to more than one practitioner independently, as Playback Theatre has been performing a very similar show since at least 1975.

DEL CLOSE AND THE HAROLD

Whereas Keith Johnstone latched on to a sporting metaphor to liven up his improvised theatre games, in Chicago, Del Close was trying to make a piece of improvised cabaret more theatrical.[3] The Harold was designed to accomplish this, but eschewed a traditional narrative and instead presented a number of apparently unrelated strands which then connect together,

---

[3]Despite the name "ImprovOlympic" and the frequent reference to Harold "teams," there is no longer any element of competition in a typical Chicago-style improv show. The idea is retained in "Cage Match" shows, but these are the exception, not the norm, and the scores are generally decided by anonymous audience voting after the players have left the stage. Thus, they do not form a part of the theatrical entertainment.

revealing fresh insights. The odd name was apparently a joke which stuck: "What should we call this format?" "Harold!"

The Harold, as described in the book *Truth in Comedy*, has a tight, three-part structure, but this has largely been abandoned at iO, and everywhere else, in favor of a more open exploration of a single suggestion, with connections made throughout and lots of elements coming together at the end—at least in theory. Once the initial suggestion has been taken, there is no longer any audience interaction, with improvisers "editing" (ending) their fellows' scenes and starting new ones "from nothing." This approach puts less emphasis on the narrative of any one scene, and more on the way the scenes relate to each other, although this varies from group to group. In some instances, the audience simply sees a series of scenes, each flowing into the next, with nothing from past scenes ever referred to again. Sometimes this unstructured version is referred to as a Montage. One other significant variation is the Armando, in which one improviser's monologue, usually personal in nature, is threaded throughout the Harold. A variation on this variation, also incorporating elements of Life Game, is David Shore's show *Monkey Toast* which has been performed several times at the Edinburgh Fringe and elsewhere.

Despite the fact that Harold is often described as "long-form" and competitive formats such as Theatresports as "short-form," neither attempts to tell a continuous narrative for the length of the piece, and a particularly disconnected Harold (this is not uncommon) could have much less unifying it than an ideal Theatresports show. Even in these supposedly short-form shows the audience quite frequently sees ideas, themes and personalities continually developed and amplified over various otherwise unrelated scenes, as well as in the interactions of the judges and the players in between those scenes.

Rather than having to pick one of exactly two labels to apply, we feel that it makes more sense to observe that an improvised show can...

- consist of many self-contained and unrelated sections or be one long, unfolding narrative
- constantly self-reference and acknowledge the format, the audience and the players in between scenes (as in Theatresports) or keep the fourth wall more or less in place throughout (as in a Harold)
- be biased toward games or scenes
- and that the players can put their focus on characters, stories and situations or on jokes, teasing and playfulness.

These are independent decisions, and almost any combination is possible, save that an emphasis on games usually brings with it an emphasis on self-contained sections and especially an emphasis on audience and format.

Many other shows exist, but most can be described as existing somewhere along each of these lines. The Spontaneity Shop's most popular and successful show, DreamDate, tells a single story from beginning to end, but between each scene, we consult audience volunteers for their input, and often play games in order to advance the story. The show Triple Play, from Unexpected Productions in Seattle, takes the pressure off having to sustain a complete narrative with no time to pause for breath, and allows the players to show off their knowledge of genres, by "shuffling up" three different improvised three-act plays, so the audience sees act one of a western, followed by act one of an unrelated Shakespeare play, followed by act one of an unrelated kitchen sink drama. Then we see each of the second acts, and finally each of the third acts.

In Edmonton's improvised soap opera, Die-Nasty, the forward-seeking narrative drive of the best Johnstone work is combined with the freedom that Harold gives the improvisers to cut to something new. Having multiple storylines and a fairly large cast of well-defined characters, each show contains a lot of variety, but audiences come back to see the next episode because—just like with a real soap—they want to know what happens next. That's virtually the definition of story.

In Chicago, on those occasions where Harold has been eschewed in favor of something with more continuity, again story is usually avoided or minimized, putting the emphasis back on the cleverness of the performers. In Joe Bill and Mark Sutton's BassProv, two bass fishermen from Indiana sit in a boat, drink beer, fish and talk about life, much in the way that Peter Cook and Dudley Moore did in art galleries and pubs forty years earlier. A typical BassProv show lasts forty-five minutes instead of the five to ten minutes of a Pete and Dud sketch, so some stories about their private life inevitably creep in to sustain the effect. At the Loose Moose, the scene would last four minutes and end with one fisherman drowning the other!

Also in Chicago, the innovative Annoyance Theatre created Modern Problems in Science, starring Rich Fulcher, Phil Gronchy and Dick Costello as three college professors who would "prove" an absurd hypothesis suggested by the audience over the course of a fifty-minute comedy lecture. In many ways, this show exemplifies Del's approach: fiercely intelligent, terribly funny and containing nothing whatsoever in terms of plot. The show was very successful and toured for many years.

A brilliant Chicago improviser named Andy Eninger had been working with a double-act partner who was suddenly unable to perform in a planned run of shows. She jokingly told him he should continue to perform the show without her. His solo improvised show, the Sybil, is now his signature piece, and he performs and teaches it all over the world. It typically contains pieces of stories which he feels free to abandon in favor of something new, if that's where his inspiration takes him.

Back at The Spontaneity Shop, our workshopping with Andy led to the creation of a format we call TellTales, wherein an improvised play is performed entirely in monologues. Our definition of "monologue" is very broad—we just insist that there only be one improviser on stage at any one time. A typical cast of five will play five principal characters whose lives are all intertwined—and may play other characters as well. The aim is to involve the five main characters in one story, possibly with one or more subplots, and to avoid the effect that Andy creates where new stories can begin at any time, even five minutes before the end.

Tom developed a stripped-down improv show called *Horse Aquarium* (nobody can remember why) in which three improvisers get three suggestions from the audience at the beginning which are written down on cards. The improvisers create short-form scenes from nothing, based on the first suggestion, each one ending with a blackout, until a third of the way through the show, when they switch to the second suggestion in mid-scene. By the end of the show, there are usually lots of reincorporations and running jokes, and the playing style is very playful and silly—quite unlike the usual narrative-based Spontaneity Shop show.

On both sides of the Atlantic, genre-based narrative long forms have become very popular. Using an existing concept or name helps enormously with marketing (a version of what Hollywood calls a "pre-sold franchise") and the emphasis on narrative helps to distinguish this kind of comedy theatre from the more familiar game-based shows. Some companies focus on a single genre, like the UK's hugely popular and successful Austentatious in the style of Jane Austen or *Showstopper! The Improvised Musical* which recently enjoyed a West End run. In Los Angeles, veteran improviser Dan O'Connor has been leading his company through a tour of different genres and styles, offering seasons of improvised Twilight Zone episodes, Shakespeare plays, Sondheim musicals and—again—Jane Austen novels, among many others.

Also worth mentioning is a productive trend of strong improvisers like Paul Foxcroft and Cariad Lloyd, Katy Schutte and Rachel Blackman and most famously TJ and Dave (TJ Jagodowski and Dave Pasquesi) staging two-person shows, often with a strong narrative flavor but a Harold-like quality. At their best, these shows can be as funny as any short-form show, but the focus is on character and truth—and of course only two players means no one can get caught slacking.

Improvisers need to discover what the medium can do for them, and pick the format which will exploit their talents to the fullest, never forgetting to ask the question, "Would this be better if it were scripted?" That should be the end to those interminable Internet debates over which is "better," short form or long form.[4]

IMPROVISATION ON TV

Clearly, the medium of improvisation is wounded once cameras enter the picture. As soon as the audience knows that mistakes could have been

---

[4]It won't be, of course.

edited out, a lot of the risk evaporates, and risk is a primary reason for an audience to see an improvised show.[5] But the wound doesn't have to be fatal. One could make a very similar argument for magic on TV, and yet many magicians have become very successful through the medium of television.

But it isn't the case that risk—as important as it is—is the only reason to prefer improvisation over writing and learning a script. On the television show *Curb Your Enthusiasm*, improvisation is used to provide a naturalistic acting style. The scripts include all the details of the plot; they just don't include the dialogue. On the other hand, *The Office* (in both its British and American incarnations) is often assumed to be improvised, but is for the most part very tightly scripted, despite the naturalistic acting style.[6]

Some comic minds simply find greater expression on the spur of the moment rather than when sitting in front of a typewriter. In the 1940s, Groucho Marx looked like a relic of an earlier age. The Marx Brothers began their careers in vaudeville in the 1910s and made a string of successful films throughout the 1930s, but the partnership all but broke up following 1941s *The Big Store*. Groucho, especially, was still a well-known celebrity and was often asked to guest on radio and TV shows. On one such radio broadcast, in 1947, Groucho's disdain for the scripted material he had been given made itself felt as he and Bob Hope ad-libbed their way through a hilarious ten minutes or so of wisecracks. A bright producer named John Guedel realized that this was the way to tap Groucho's gift for spontaneous verbal comedy[7] and installed him as the host of *You Bet Your Life*, a quiz show which ran on radio for three years and on TV for a further twelve. The quiz structure was a thinly veiled pretext for Groucho to chat with contestants and make jokes at their expense, much as today's TV comedy quiz shows, such as *Have I Got News for You*, use the quiz structure as a vehicle for the personalities of their panelists.

Less joke-oriented is the filmmaker Mike Leigh, who uses an extended improvisatory rehearsal process, during which actors explore aspects of

---

[5]One solution to this problem is for the show to go out live, but it's hard to imagine any TV boss sanctioning that in the current climate. It was not always so, however. In the BBC's wildly influential 1960s satire show *That Was the Week That Was*, which did go out live, Lance Percival was given a slot to improvise topical calypso numbers based on audience suggestions. Percival has made it clear in interviews that he was very well prepared for these impromptu numbers, but equally that the audience suggestions were genuinely spontaneous and unplanned.
[6]Ricky Gervais himself would sometimes ad-lib, especially the comments to camera, but this was the exception rather than the norm where the rest of the cast was concerned. Any alterations to the script tended to be made in rehearsal rather than on camera. Despite the preponderance of improvisation actors in the superb American version of the show, the same seems to be true there as well: material is improvised sometimes, but rarely on camera, and not more than about 10 percent of any given show. Michael Scott's kiss with Oscar was apparently improvised on camera by Steve Carrell, but, again, this was exceptional rather than typical.
[7]Groucho also had an astonishing gift for making dialogue sound spontaneous. This is a key reason for actors to learn improvisation.

their character and their relationships, until a script emerges. But that script is replicated as faithfully as any other once shooting starts. This is much the same conclusion that was reached by Second City, as previously discussed. In each case, improvisation facilitates the writing process, but is largely ignored in the delivery.

The movies of Christopher Guest, such as *A Mighty Wind* and *This Is Spinal Tap*, use improvisation on camera, combining both aspects. These films tend to follow simple plot lines which allow characters simply to talk to each other or the camera. Improvisation allows the actors to find the moments of vulnerability and (with a significant editing process) allows a script to be developed which makes terrific use of the spontaneous wit and insight of the actors involved.

Another trend worth mentioning is the recent profusion of comedy films featuring performers who cut their teeth doing improvised comedy in Chicago or Los Angeles, and who graduated via *Saturday Night Live*. On these movies, especially those associated with producer/director Judd Apatow, the cast is encouraged to shoot multiple takes of every scene, ad-libbing different responses and attitudes. In one case, *Anchorman 2*, there was so much left on the cutting room floor that an entirely different cut of the film was circulated, telling essentially the same story, but substituting different jokes throughout. The unsung hero of these movies is the editor, who needs not only the taste to select the funniest lines and line-readings, but also the skill and sensitivity to control the rhythm of the scene as a whole. Much the same principle is at work in TV shows such as *Veep* or its UK progenitor *The Thick of It*, both produced by Armando Iannucci.

The key difference between all of these forms and a typical live improvised comedy show is that the contribution of improvisation is a "behind-the-scenes" detail rather than an essential (and ostentatious) feature of the performance. You do not have to know that detail about the process in order to enjoy the results. The same could not be said of *Whose Line Is It Anyway?* which replicated many of the features of a typical live improvised comedy show for ten years on Channel 4 in the UK, and a further eight years on ABC in the United States, having begun life as just six half-hours on BBC Radio 4. In *Whose Line*, all the emphasis is on the *fact* of the participants' improvising and their verbal (and sometimes physical) wit. The development of the show sheds some interesting light on the ever-present issues of risk and failure.

In the first couple of series, *Whose Line* featured an eclectic assortment of contestants. As well as seasoned improvisers from London's Comedy Store Players (*Whose Line* made stars of Comedy Store players Josie Lawrence and Paul Merton), the shows also included writers, actors, comedians and other personalities, some of whom had never improvised in public before. Often, when faced with the constraints of the games or their own choices (electing to improvise in rhyme when asked to pick a particular author, for example), the outcome would be a failure—which delighted the audience and which the producers elected to keep in. This also reflects the loose, happy atmosphere generally associated with The Comedy Store Players.

In subsequent series, American performers with a more physical style were recruited. Stand-outs during this period were Mike McShane, Greg Proops and Ryan Stiles. The failure rate plummeted and very few new games were introduced. Gradually the producers found what worked, both in terms of games played and performers to play them. By the end, the shows had become essentially indistinguishable, offering exactly the same games, exactly the same performers (and in some cases exactly the same jokes), week in and week out. By this time, the American influence was so dominant that the shows were being recorded in the United States. Ryan Stiles was instrumental in getting the ABC version off the ground, hosted by Drew Carey, on whose sitcom Stiles had been a supporting player.

This new American show locked down the format even further. The original radio series had featured Stephen Fry and John Sessions as permanent team captains. For the first Channel 4 series, there were no teams, but John Sessions was in every single show. In each episode of the second and subsequent series, four contestants would be selected from a fairly large pool, with no one appearing in every show except the non-improvising host Clive Anderson. The American series by contrast installed Stiles, Colin Mochrie and Wayne Brady as the three regulars, with only the fourth spot open, and this usually filled by one of Greg Proops, Brad Sherwood, Jeff Davis or Chip Esten. A very limited palette of games was offered, many of which were little more than devices for the players to indulge in shtick (Crazy Newsreaders) or tell jokes (Scenes From a Hat).

But while the limited pool of players meant that the shows suffered from precisely the sameness as its UK progenitor, having four people working together every week also had advantages. Over time, a relaxed, mischievous atmosphere began to pervade the show, as running jokes developed between the performers and their mutual teasing began to be as entertaining as the improvised games themselves. This gave the show an excitement and a freshness which—for some years—few other shows could match. Most theatrical improvisers would look in horror at the easy laughs, lazy shtick and scene-killing gags which paraded across their television screens on a Thursday night. But most theatrical improvisers would also give their left leg to have the kind of ease and charm these four demonstrated.

And the formula keeps on working. Theoretically canceled in 2007, the American version was reborn in 2013 with a new host and on a new channel, but otherwise pretty much identical to the previous iteration, with a slightly increased emphasis on the starriness of the players in the fourth chair which also helps guard against staleness. Guests in the 2016 season have included Yvette Nicole Brown from *Community*, magicians Penn & Teller, Keegan-Michael Key of Key & Peele and even Kathie Lee Gifford, host of the *Today* show. Meanwhile, in the UK, the format has been resurrected as a live show with Clive Anderson back in the chair for both an Edinburgh Fringe and a West End run with stalwarts Josie Lawrence, Greg Proops and the rest.

The legacy of *Whose Line* for those of us continuing to work in the live improvised genre has been threefold. First, people now know what improvised comedy is. This is tremendously useful. Second, people now think they know all that improvised comedy can be, and so it can be hard to persuade people that what you're doing is anything other than *Whose Line Is It Anyway?* Third, anyone now hoping to get a "pure" improvised show on TV has to do something more than point a camera at their cast and get suggestions from the audience. The bar has been raised. Most attempts to solve this problem have failed to take account of the issues discussed here, although Dan O'Connor's *World Cup Comedy* on cable channel PAX is worthy of note, as we thought it was particularly successful in balancing all of these potentially conflicting elements.

Another show to mention is the 2006 Australian television series called *Thank God You're Here* which ran for four years. It managed very successfully to "package" the challenge facing improvisers while preserving something of the scene-work which can be seen in the best improv theatres. It also makes excellent use of the resources of the television studio. Whereas the contestants on *Whose Line*, except on some of the earliest British shows, are presented as experts, and typically owe their fame to their ability to improvise well, *Thank God* uses celebrity comedians and actors not known for their improv skills, and shoves them through a door into a situation they have no prior knowledge of. A "rep company" of improv actors then involves them in a scene, making life difficult for them or setting them up for jokes, depending on how confident and experienced they are.

Part of the show's success lies in the fact that Theatresports is so popular in Australia that almost any Australian actor or comedian working today will have done improv at some time. The celebrities on the American version tended to be rather more panicky and crude, which perhaps accounts for its lack of success over there. In the UK version, the improvised scenarios were far more tightly controlled which meant the show was neither as exciting to watch as the best improvisation, nor as cleverly constructed as the best sitcom and it was canceled after a single season.

Attempts to repeat the success of *Whose Line* continue, with producer Dan Patterson launching both *Mock the Week* (in 2005) and *Fast and Loose* (in 2011). The former combines elements of both *Whose Line* and *Have I Got News For You* and has proven to be very successful. *Fast and Loose* introduced TV audiences to some marvelous new improvising talent, and had a couple of brilliant innovations, notably the Sideways Scene shot with an overhead camera, but didn't quite manage to find a unique style or focus.

INTERMISSION

"What Should Improvisation Be?"

#1 "From Innovation to Art Form"

By Deborah Frances-White

Overview

The first of two answers to this important question, this is Deborah's personal summation of where improvisation came from and where it is going.

Improvisation is not simply ad-libbing or extemporizing. It is a form of theatre. It can create comedy or drama, but tends toward comedy when performed. Opinions vary as to why this is should be so, but it is probably a by-product of the fact that improvisation tends to be performed as a series of scenes or sketches which stand alone, despite sometimes being connected or revisited later. Short-form sketches are usually comedic in scripted work as well, as it is difficult for an audience to take short scene after short scene of misery or pathos, though they will accept it as the climax or turning point of a longer story.

This is why it's quite common for sitcoms to do a seasonal "Remember the time…" clips show where they edit together lots of funny moments on the same theme and then cut back to the characters reminiscing about them. It would be unusual to see this sort of convention used on a show like *24*. "Remember the time my wife died?" "Sure, it reminds me of the time you thought your daughter was dead but it turned out she was just horribly injured." It would be too much to see a montage of moments of high tragedy, but we can easily take "Remember the time you got your head stuck in the turkey?" "What about the time you got trapped in bathroom without your trousers?" Well, we can take it for a short time, anyway.

We have found that, when doing an improvised story of forty minutes to an hour, the audience will accept genuine emotion, sometimes even tears, because they have invested in the characters and care enough to allow themselves to feel for them. The improvisers, too, can feel more for a character they have embodied for a while, and can more easily allow some emotional authenticity without being self-indulgent. This is not to say these longer improvised stories have not chiefly been comedic—they have—but they have benefited from the variety that comes with allowing the audience to feel other things, like fear or sympathy.

If you are looking to begin improvising or are already an experienced improviser, you are probably chiefly interested in improvisation as a tool for comedy. There are lots of different styles and choices to be made. Some companies want to be fast and funny and are only interested in performing the sort of games they have seen on *Whose Line Is It Anyway?* Other groups are only interested in performing some variation on the Harold and they tend to dislike games and find them constraining. Still other groups are most comfortable using formats they and their audiences are familiar with, such as Theatresports. Some groups will not work with audience suggestions and others will not work without them. Some try to conquer long stories, feeling that short-form is unsatisfying. Others feel long stories lack variety and that once you are locked in, you and the audience will be trapped in something that runs the risk of being tedious.

There are often arguments between improvisers about which of these styles are better, more valid, more likely to produce work of substance, more entertaining for the audience and more satisfying to deliver. We have been to many international improv festivals and have engaged in these discussions ourselves. There are often surprisingly heated opinions expressed on social media about the way improvisation is presented on stage, what truly constitutes long-form or short-form improvisation and even what improvisers should wear on stage. Almost invariably these discussions seek right ways of operating and suggest the elimination of variety in the pursuit of theatrical purity or finding some ultimate entertainment zenith. It seems to me that there is room for all styles of improvisation and, rather than narrowing our opportunities, since the art form is so new and green, we should be doing everything we can to experiment with as many different styles as possible—and discover new ones in the process—while still respecting groups' rights to their own preferences and tastes.

As Viola Spolin generally kept her work in the rehearsal room, performance improvisation dates back to the 1950s when Keith Johnstone began developing his techniques in London, and at around the same time in Chicago, the Compass Players were staging plays with improvised dialogue around a predefined scenario, and later performing improvised cabaret. That means the art form is currently around fifty years old.

Keith developed Theatresports (still his most popular format) with actors in Calgary in the 1970s, based on ideas that he had developed in London in the 1950s and 1960s. The Harold, Del Close's famous format, was developed in the late 1960s. So, the period of greatest development for improvisation, when most of the seminal work was being done, was between the 1950s and the 1970s. Since then, improvisers have mainly spent their time arguing over which work done between the 1950s and the 1970s is the best, and re-creating it without much progress. Most groups still present some version of Theatresports or the Harold, rarely deviating from these in any significant way. They may find a different way of beginning the Harold or of presenting Theatresports games, but essentially the form is the same and the quality of the work has not improved from all accounts.

This compares very unfavorably to, say, the film industry. The first films— for example, *Workers Leaving the Lumière Factory* or the famous *Arrival of a Train*, made in 1895—were little more than a demonstration of the medium. Forty-six years later, in 1941, Orson Welles made *Citizen Kane*. The following year, *Casablanca* was released. In 1945, exactly fifty years after *Arrival of a Train*, Hitchcock released *Spellbound* and Billy Wilder won the best picture Oscar for *The Lost Weekend*. All this despite the fact that there was a war on. If filmmakers were improvisers, one wonders if in 1950 they would still have been arguing over whether the British Robert William Paul or the French Lumière Brothers truly invented cinema and whether it was best to re-make a two-minute film about two men carrying a ladder or a horse winning a race.

The question is: Why did film, in fifty years, take such astonishing developments though silent cinema—including Chaplin and Keaton, the talkies, the golden age of the musical, animation (Disney's *Snow White and the Seven Dwarfs* was released in 1937) and film noir, just to name a few extraordinary movements? Such bold, creative, risky steps into the future could only have been made by people who were not looking back to early mentors but were prepared to take the medium with both hands and explore every avenue—and when they had run out, invent avenues for others to explore. Cinema has never stopped progressing. Every year, films break molds and buck trends in terms of form, tone, subject matter and technological advancements. Television similarly continues to go through extraordinary changes. Look at the difference between *The Lone Ranger* (a popular 1950s show) and *Breaking Bad*, or between *I Love Lucy* and *30 Rock*. It is not just the desire for creative expression but the need to find a new commercial success that keeps cinema and television professionals innovating.

As much as those in the cinema and television industry complain about the commercial demands made by studios and networks, it is possible that we as improvisers are hampered by the fact that no one is pressuring us to come up with something new that they can sell. Improvisation is the only art form that I can think of that has an unlimited budget. The only restriction is our imagination. Once we have a space with a stage and basic lights, whatever we tell the audience is in that space they will believe is there. If we mime a screwdriver which takes us back in time every time we turn a screw, the audience will buy it if we commit to it, no CGI necessary. If a 21-year-old man in an AC/DC t-shirt acts like a puritanical old priest, the audience will suspend their disbelief. Casting and costumes are not paramount. Whether we wish to create lengthy real-time stories or a series of startlingly short scenes with lots of quick cuts, the audience will keep up. No time is required in an expensive editing suite. While this is an astounding and often overlooked advantage, it can lead to the work being treated casually, as if having an unlimited budget means it is an art form of little value.

It is fairly easy to be cast in an improv show and, if no one you know will cast you, it is no great feat to mount one of your own. You are unlikely to make any money performing in an improv show. Most performers work for free and most of those who are paid are paid little. Even those who are paid well are unlikely to be able to live on the proceeds, and instead are using improv to leverage other work. Some people have an idea that performing regularly in improv shows will help them with a career in sketch comedy or sitcom, and this might even be true.

All of these attitudes, while understandable, probably contribute to the fact that there is little quality control in improv. A lot of talented people leave improvisation for other art forms because they find a resistance to innovation or have to work with people who are poorly trained or who have bad habits, because the group is functioning more like a social club than a place for great creative expression or a home to develop great spontaneous comedy. It is possible that most of the innovators among us get dragged into the endless arguments over the purest form of the Harold and eventually leave, frustrated, to make a short film or write a play.

I think it is time that the international improvisation community decided to create quality improvisation regardless of their tastes for style or format. I also think it is past time that we as individuals and groups, regardless of our school of thinking, seriously begin to build on the work that was started by Johnstone and Close in an intelligent and exciting way; not by creating outlandish new games with no point, not by changing things for the sake of them, but by asking ourselves what we love about improvisation, why it is exciting and interesting to us, and exploring those qualities in performance—and by making more of the wonderful advantage of it being fairly free of commercial constraints. It costs little to do no matter how we do it, so let's risk trying to do it differently. It might be wonderful.

There are of course many around the world who are making developments, but part of the reason film and television have changed so dramatically is that so many practitioners sought new ways of doing things and shared their methods. For a movement, improvisation does seem to be surprisingly stationary.

#2

"Two Stories"

By Tom Salinsky

Overview

Tom tackles some of the same questions and tries to answer the SKATEBOARDING DUCK conundrum.

Improvisation is a very peculiar way of entertaining an audience, and contains a number of traps for the unwary. If no emphasis at all is placed on storytelling, improvisation can quickly dissolve into slurry. If this is good-natured slurry, then the audience may still be charmed, and if it's funny, then so much the better, but this is almost guaranteed to provide nothing that the audience will remember the next day. Worse, the improvisers may be seduced into believing that the fact that they are improvising gives them a "free pass" from the audience—that the audience has no expectation of intelligence, story, character, logic or even coherence because "it's just improv."

Worse, the lack of any narrative framework compels improvisers to try to be funny at every opportunity. Improvisation is very attractive to the amateur performer. Compared to stand-up comedy, one has the support of one's teammates, and standard games are available which can provide some of the entertainment value "for free." Compared to sketch comedy or theatre, improv is much more low-commitment, and much less like hard work. There are no lines to learn, no moves to remember and if you can't make a given rehearsal—or even show—someone else can probably take your place. A group of amateur performers trying their hardest to be funny, and assuming that the audience will swallow their nonsense because "they are just improvising," is a recipe for a horrible show. If the performers stay happy and pick games that they are suited to, it might be watchable, but more than likely it will be a train wreck. Even on a good day, however, this is still SKATEBOARDING DUCK theatre. "Don't worry about how entertaining the content is—applaud us merely for making the attempt."

And so, in many places, teachers, directors and improvisers bang a different drum. "Improv," they tell us, "is *theatre*." These groups place *all* their emphasis on telling the story, getting the audience to care about the characters and to buy in—to forget that they are watching an improvised piece. Some companies remove absolutely all of the trappings of improvisation. At a recent international festival, I saw a show which had been getting a lot of attention and praise from other attendees for the commitment of the improvisers and the power of the performances. Having seen several improvised long-form narrative plays, with no interaction with the audience after getting an initial suggestion or two, and finding that they tended to be a little long-winded and unengaging, I was a little trepidatious.

The audience gives very direct feedback to improvisers but this needs to be treated with a certain amount of caution. If you start thinking "They're laughing—I must be on the right track," then you'll panic if there's even a few seconds of silence and start doing anything for a laugh—and now you'll be presenting the same sort of slurry described above. When I'd only been improvising for about a year, I remember doing a scene in which I played a love-struck pupil hopelessly infatuated with my French teacher. The audience found it very funny, even though both of us played it straight, as she tried gently to let me down and as I made feeble advance after feeble advance. I had brought her a crystal vase as a present (mimed obviously) but she had refused to take it from me, so I had been carrying it around for the whole scene. When she finally rejected me in terms too straightforward to ignore or misinterpret, I was so shocked and disappointed that I dropped the vase—and the audience gasped. Of course, there was no vase for me to drop. I simply opened my fingers, looked down and made a "chhkksssh!" noise with my mouth, but the audience believed in that vase and they believed in my plight. I marveled afterwards at how much more satisfying that gasp was than any laugh. It meant we had them.

But if your attempt is to engage the audience in an improvised drama, you don't even have the rather unreliable feedback of laughter. A bored audience sounds very similar to a rapt one, and so it's terribly easy to end up in self-indulgence. What I expected from this show was largely what I got. Lots of melodramatic moments, but a plot that advanced very slowly and which often didn't make sense. Improvisers who are surprising and delighting each other will find it very easy to generate comedy, which may very well be funnier than anything they could sit down and script. But it's much less likely that improvisers fighting their urge to be funny will come up with a better-structured drama which delivers the requisite doses of tragedy, irony and revelation at the right times.

With this show, unless you knew the people on the stage, or had talked to them about the show, you would have no way of knowing it was improvised. People came out in costume, with characters already apparently predetermined. There were no suggestions, or interactions with the audience of any kind. But by presenting the work as indistinguishable from straight theatre, the producers of this show invite the public, who don't understand the mechanisms of improvisation, simply to compare this show to scripted theatre they might have seen and it's very, very unlikely to compare favorably, so what's the point? What happened on the night that I saw it was that one plot twist in particular which should have been an absolute game-changer was entirely ignored by all those onstage who didn't in the moment realize the implications of what had just been said—even though they must have heard the audience gasp a little (only a little, it's not like anyone dropped a crystal vase). It was not a great start to the festival for me. Is this really what was considered the must-see show, the state of the art?

After a while, I realized that this show was receiving so much praise largely because we were at an improv festival. Improvisers who have been successful onstage by goofing around will often be disproportionally impressed when their buddies improvise straight scenes or stories and resist the urge to go for the joke.

A little later in the festival, I was talking to Patti Stiles about her new show. Patti was our first really formative improv teacher and we take any opportunity we can get to work with her and talk to her about improv so I was fascinated to hear what she was planning. Patti's new work-in-progress was an improvised Western, and as with the earlier show, there was very little in the way of audience interaction to let the audience in on the process. As with the earlier show, the improvisers show up on the stage with characters ready-to-go. This means that much more time can be spent watching the story and less times need to be spent on walking the audience through the mechanisms of the show, which is certainly good. But once again, there's the risk that this will just look like a stage western in which the plot doesn't quite work and the characters are thinly drawn. Patti had another bullet in her six-shooter, however. At the beginning of the show, she explained, each improviser drew a poker chip out of a bag and looked at it without showing anyone else what they had got. Only people who drew red poker chips had the power to kill. But only Patti knew how many red chips were in the bag and only the people who had drawn out a red chip knew they had it.

As I watched the show, I saw some of the same problems as before, but fewer. Yes, there were some narrative cul-de-sacs which, had this been a scripted show, would have been removed in the second draft, or which would never have made it past the planning stage. But the *fact* of their improvising seemed much more relevant and apparent, and when one improviser pointed a gun at another, there was genuine tension. Nobody, including the person with the gun to their head, knew whether this person could pull the trigger or not. The gimmick of the poker chips, combined with the story so far, combined with the moral choice facing the character holding the gun made for electrifying theatre, not least because the uncertainty of the improviser about their fate was exactly aligned with the uncertainty of the character.

I congratulated Patti after the show and said it would have been great for the audience to have seen at the end who had been holding the red poker chips (they give the *power* to kill; after all, they don't compel you to kill). I found Patti's reply astonishing—she said that was the first time they'd done the show and had the poker chips drawn onstage in front of the audience. Previously, it had been a covert operation performed backstage. This meant that the audience would be more focused on the morality of the story and less on the mechanisms of the show, and while this is certainly a strength, it is also a weakness.

Let's take a step back for a moment and look at how improvised shows have been successfully presented in the past. If the framework of your show includes a mechanism which is constantly reminding the audience of its improvised nature, then it doesn't rob the show of anything if the improvisers choose to commit to story and character the rest of the time—in fact, it adds to it, because there's a greater likelihood that they will generate something of power and impact. This is why forms such as Gorilla Theatre, Micetro Impro and especially Theatresports have been so successful. Being apparently competitive, these shows have a built-in mechanism to deal with failure. If a Micetro Impro scene or game falls apart, the audience will give it a low score and those players will be more likely to be eliminated. By telling the audience up front, "Some of these scenes are going to be better than others," the players are freed to be daring and to take risks—which means the actual hit-rate goes up. Without such a mechanism, players must adopt "stay-safe" tactics or try to convince the audience that they were proud of even the most hopelessly incompetent work. Such players confuse success at achieving a goal with success at being entertaining.

Thus, competitive formats tell *two stories*: The first is the story the improvisers are telling within their scenes and games. The second is the story of their struggle for glory. But it's important to recognize that improvisers are *always* telling these two stories, and that the art of developing and performing a good improv show is identifying which of the two is the more interesting at any one moment, and therefore where the emphasis should be placed. Attempting to eliminate the second story altogether, removing audience suggestions, any hint of breaking the fourth wall, any temptation to sell out the narrative, results in a rather peculiar and unsatisfactory form of theatre with all of the flaws of improvisation and none of its virtues.

But this doesn't mean that competitive formats are necessary, nor even are gimmicks like Patti's Poker Chips of Death (as brilliant and successful as that is). There is a fashion at the moment for presenting genre improvised long forms. Some of these get plenty of audience suggestions and include an onstage director who can keep the improvisers on their toes, such as the amazingly slick and stunningly successful *Showstopper*. But many groups get one or two suggestions at the top and then never explicitly acknowledge the fact that the show is improvised, and yet manage to keep the sparkle of improvisation alive just through the playfulness of their interactions. Get it right and you can combine the playing of strong characters, the creation of clear plots, and just enough cheeky bouncing off each other to prevent the show from collapsing under the weight of its own good intentions.

This, then, is the real *point* of improvisation. Not because it's easier, more fun to do, creates better comedy or tells better stories. The point of improvisation is that it's fun and engaging for an audience to *share in an artist's moment of inspiration*. Reacting to a location shouted out by an audience member is one way of "surfacing" that so that the rest of the audience can see it, but there are many others and not all of them are anything like so overt. Attempting to hide that process altogether removes almost everything that's worthwhile about improvising in public. If they can't *see* you being inspired, you may as well prepare your content offstage—at least then you can take the time to refine it.

SECTION TWO

How to Improvise

2.1

How to Use This Section

Overview

Who are we trying to teach here, and what should be borne in mind while reading this section?

If you want to learn to improvise, you should go and take some improv classes. There, we've said it. Put down this book, go on Facebook, or do a Google search, and find some. It almost doesn't matter how good they are. Even if you're saddled with a moon-faced fool who blathers endlessly on about "truth" and lets turgid scenes waffle pointlessly on forever, or a ruthlessly cynical comedian who tells you with no trace of enjoyment which tricks "always make 'em laugh," you will gain far more from the experience of actually working with other people, without a script, in front of even an informal audience than you can ever learn from passively reading a book.

But that doesn't make this section of the book useless or pointless. Over the pages which follow, we have described what would happen if you were in one of our workshops, often with a little more detail about what is going on "under the hood" than might be apparent if you were simply attending the class. Our hope is that this will be a useful manual for teachers and students, experienced improvisers and novices.

If you are reading this book as someone who is new to teaching improv, we also highly recommend reading *Impro* by Keith Johnstone (a life-changing book for anyone). Having an open mind and a genuine desire to see the students improve would also be excellent. You could then adapt the exercises given here into a syllabus for your students, tailoring them as necessary to suit their particular requirements, but we hope not confining them entirely to a classroom or rehearsal room. This stuff was meant to be staged.

If you are a more experienced improvisation teacher, you may be reading this for fresh inspiration, some contentious viewpoints to get you charged up and questioning again or just for some new exercises to cherry-pick from to freshen up your classes.

Alternatively, you might be a school teacher looking to liven up a dreary syllabus or trying to avoid staging yet another production of *West Side Story* with under-fifteens. You may work at a drama school and see how scared the students seem—especially of improvisation—and wonder if that fear can really be helping them. You could use some of the exercises in this book to alleviate their anxiety and remind them why they wanted to become actors in the first place.

You could also be an experienced improviser looking for a fresh take on the nuts and bolts of improvisation. You may find new games and new exercises here, which you can bring back to your group, but if you're craving novelty and new games, you are likely to be frustrated by the emphasis here on craft and process. We're more interested in what games teach improvisers about the business of improvising for performance than in learning a wide variety of "hoop" games.

You could be one of a group of people starting an improvisation company from scratch. The exercises described here begin at the beginning, with no prior knowledge or experience assumed, so the designated director could work through this section of the book, chapter by chapter, coaching the group as they go. Or you could take a chapter each. At some point, however, you'll probably benefit from having a more experienced coach take a dispassionate look at what you're doing. The act of teaching can itself be fraught with anxiety, especially when working from someone else's syllabus, and that will cloud your vision.

Finally, we imagine that there will be members of the improv and theatre community who want to read this book, and this section in particular, not necessarily to go out and put it into action, but just to be stimulated about the challenge of improvisation and listen to our take on various topics.

We welcome all readers (including those not mentioned here) and hope you enjoy the book and find it of practical use.

2.2

Teaching and Learning

Overview

We examine what happens during an improvisation class—or any class—in the minds of the teacher and the student, and tackle the ever-present issue of anxiety.

Whether you are attending improvisation classes or teaching them, it is important to know that the words "Can I have a volunteer?" often ignite feelings of fear and anxiety. People who have paid to be at the class, or have sometimes paid for three years of drama school, will often avoid eye contact with the teacher when this request is made.

It is not always like this, however. On some occasions, if a volunteer is asked for, every single person puts their hands up and some actually rush forward. That's when those people are *children*.

Children approach playing games, or doing exercises, or being given the chance to try something new, very differently from adults. Children approach these situations with one mission, and that mission is to *have lots of goes*. They sometimes actually rate their success that way: "I had four goes and you only had three—I win!"

Adults are very different. We want to sit back, assess—from our seats!—whether we'd be any good at the task in question. If we think we'd be successful at it, then and *only then* will we want a go. If we think it is something we would not be good at, we would usually prefer to have no go at all.

Children want lots of goes, but adults want *one perfect go*.

As adults, we've already decided what we're good at and what we're bad at, and we only want to have goes at things we're already good at. We've met lots of people who've told us they can't draw, but none of them was seven years old. All children think they're brilliant artists and want their drawings displayed on the refrigerator. As adults, even if we secretly think we can draw, we hide our sketches away under the bed: "Don't look at those—they're just some silly things I was doodling." The thing is, we all were those children. We believed we were great artists, we sang and danced when we were happy and acted out cops and robbers for hours. No one ever stopped and said, "I'm not a very good robber. I've run out of ideas. I think I need to research my character." We always had *endless* ideas. Endless positivity. Endless faith in our own talent. What happened to us?

One answer is: our education. We hope at least that your education was free because, wherever you got it, it has screwed you over and transformed you from someone who volunteered fearlessly and believed in your own creative abilities into someone who is unwilling to get up at all in case "you make a fool of yourself," and who claims they "can't" sing, dance, draw, act or speak in public and who has no imagination.

When you're at school, if the teacher tells the class to write an essay and everyone else is writing, and you're just sitting there, all Zen and relaxed, thinking about your essay, what will happen? The teacher will shout at you. She'll say, "You! You're not even trying." She would know if you were trying because trying looks like something. If your shoulders are hunched and you look worried and a little ill, then the teacher will probably come and do it for you. We learn to look anxious before we do things—like we're not up to it.

We also tend to punish ourselves *after* we do things. Two adults will volunteer for something, and after they finish they'll make a physical gesture of apology which says to the room: "No need to mention it—we know it wasn't very good." Maybe this is because we teach our children to punish themselves if they suspect they've failed. When you're a kid, if you're washing dishes and you break a plate and you say, "Well, never mind, everyone drops things from time to time," and you clean it up in a relaxed and happy fashion, your mother will shout at you. That in our society is a "bad attitude." A "good attitude" is to cry and feel worthless. Then your mother will say, "Never mind, darling, it was only an accident," and clean it up for you. Therefore, as adults, we anticipate this; we've learned to. We look anxious before and after everything we do to avoid punishment from others.

This means we come to any learning opportunity, like an improv workshop, feeling tense and anxious. If that was a good state for learning or creativity that would be great, but unfortunately you're less likely to be good at learning—or any creative pursuit—with a gun pointed to your head. The fact is you're the most able to learn, create and improvise when you're most yourself. Think about it: are you more witty, sparky and full of ideas when you're with your oldest friends and a bottle of wine or when you're on a job interview? Your inner improviser is far more likely to be with you when you're relaxed.

It follows that the people who are most successful at learning to improvise are those who are most relaxed. We tell our students that their only mission is to have lots of goes and see if we're worth our money. We say, "I'm the only one who's shown up claiming to be an expert and therefore I'm the only one who should be nervous." If they can already do everything we show them very well, that makes our job very difficult. As teachers it's our job to find things the students can't do and show them how to do them. Education is not coming to the workshop pre-educated. We tell them "I'm hoping for a very high level of failure in this workshop, otherwise how can I take your money in good conscience?" We say if they can do everything we show them perfectly, they should ask for their money back because it means we're not teaching them anything new.

On the other hand, we say that if they're no better at the end of the workshop, they should ask for their money back as well, because that can't possibly be their fault. It must by ours. We really believe that if we're taking the money we absolutely need to take responsibility for what happens in the workshop. If there's someone who's not getting any better, it's our job to find a way to get through to them, and if we can't, we should be prepared to offer them their money back. Too many teachers blame their students and get frustrated with people they see as talentless. We really don't think anyone is talentless, especially at improvising. We all have our experiences to bring which will inspire stories worth telling. Some of us may be more natural performers than others, but others will be better storytellers or more happily collaborative. As a teacher, try and see what your students are bringing with them. As a learner, the best advice we can offer is to listen to what your teacher says, have lots of goes and see if they're worth their money.

This is not to say that you should go into the room with a "prove yourself" attitude toward the teacher. Be positive and open and contribute to the kind of supportive environment you want to learn in. Be supportive and interested in other improvisers' work. Just don't take the burden of responsibility for learning onto your shoulders. Let your teacher do that.

Teaching at RADA, we've talked to the students about their hopes for the course. It's a big honor to go to RADA and so most people go there with the hope that their whole three years will be filled with classes where they will be the star. Their hope is that all their goes will be wonderful ones and the teacher in each class will say, "That was a wonderful go. I wish all the rest of the students could have a go as wonderful as that one." No one comes to RADA hoping to fail. We think that this is a strange attitude to bring to a learning experience (despite the fact that it is overwhelmingly common), because it means the student is hoping not to be educated but validated.

Compare this to taking your car to a mechanic because it's making a strange noise. It's frustrating if the car won't make the noise when the mechanic's there, because then they can't diagnose it. So you drive away and there's that damned noise again. If you go to drama school or improv classes and the teacher only sees your very best work, they will never have an opportunity to diagnose you and help fix your weaknesses. You will then go on stage and your weaknesses will come out. Sadly, all your goes in class were so good that your weaknesses went unnoticed. We say to the students we teach at RADA, "Some days you'll be great all day and the teachers will only be able to praise you. If that happens, it happens. Never mind. Maybe you'll have a worse day tomorrow." We usually get groups to say, "We suck and we love to fail!" in order to get them into the right counterintuitive headspace. This was something that Patti Stiles invented for her time in London (we were all obviously terrified) and left here when she went. We had t-shirts made, because it was such a liberating sentiment.

2.3

Spontaneity

Overview

First steps in learning to improvise: getting "out of your head" and abandoning control of the future.

We are now ready to begin the main work of this book: our improvisation workshop in text form. Whereas we have elsewhere referred to ourselves as "us" or "we," when talking about our teaching experiences we have chosen to refer to ourselves in the first person singular, "I" or "me." This is because we almost never co-teach and so the plural seems inappropriate. Tom and Deborah can be assumed to share all the opinions and all the approaches described, however. Well, almost all. We regularly have spirited debates with each other, other members of our company, our students and improvisers we respect and learn from when we travel internationally or when we invite overseas teachers to teach in London. We don't always agree with Keith Johnstone or Patti Stiles, who taught us how to improvise. It's really important for the development of the medium that we think differently and engage in passionate discussion and well-reasoned arguments, so take nothing here as absolute and feel free to email us if you just have to tell us why we're wrong.

POINTING AT THINGS

The first game is very simple. You could do it while reading this book. You don't need a partner, you don't need any props, special equipment or any public liability insurance. Presenting it to a group, we stress how easy and how trivial it is. The game is called Pointing At Things And Saying What They Are. Try it now. Put the book down and spend sixty seconds marching around the room, pointing at things and calling them by their correct name. "Sofa, carpet, wall, wallpaper…" and so on.

Welcome back. So far so easy? Let's play game number two. Game number two is called Pointing At Things And Saying What The Last Thing You Pointed At Was. Start off by pointing at the floor, but don't say anything. Now point at the ceiling and say "floor." Now point at something else and say "ceiling." Keep going like that. We'll see you back here in sixty seconds.

Are you ready for game number three? Game number three is called Pointing At Things And Saying What They're Not. This time when you point at the floor, you can call it anything in the world except "floor." Okay? You've got sixty seconds. Away you go!

Now, everyone's experience of these games will be different, but in a group, some fairly typical patterns tend to emerge, and you can tell a lot about how the group is getting along just by listening to the volume and looking at the general level of activity in the room, even though you probably can't pick one person's words out of the general din.

Let us ask you, the reader, some of the questions that we ask of all groups playing these games and try to anticipate some likely responses. First of all, you'd probably agree that these games vary in difficulty. The first game presents very little difficulty at all—it's what you've been doing ever since you first learned how to talk. It's trivial, so let's ignore that for now, and consider the second and third games. Of these two, people often express a strong preference for one or the other—not surprising since they test different parts of your brain.

Game number two tests short-term memory. Some people quickly pick up the knack of "banking" the current object in short-term memory while retrieving the object they had previously "banked." Others find the procedure more challenging, but they generally find the game—as you might expect—tends to get easier as it goes on, regardless of how difficult it is to begin with.

The third game is rather different. Since there are no naming rules to follow, each object becomes a creative act, albeit a fairly minor one. About half the people playing generally report that this game is more difficult than the previous one. But observing and listening to the group tells a story closer to 90 percent. Almost everyone plays the third game *more slowly* than the second game, even those who say they prefer it. The result is that, often, it is only in the third game that there are moments of silence, even with twenty-odd people in the room. Even more mysteriously, this game actually seems to get *harder* as it goes on. Many people can rattle off three or four or five objects fairly rapidly and easily, and then they get "stuck," at least for a moment. It feels like you've run out of words, at least temporarily.

What is odd about this is that playing the second game, it is *possible to be wrong*. If the last thing you pointed at was the door and now you're pointing at the light switch, the only right answer is "door." Every other response is wrong. Playing the third game, it's almost impossible to be wrong. Provided you don't actually say "light switch," you can't fail. So why should this third game be difficult at all? People in our workshops offer many solutions to this conundrum, and the fact is that this apparently trivial game brings up a great many issues.

One of the first solutions offered is often "too many choices," and this is indeed a good answer. Psychologists call this Option Paralysis. If you're on a plane and the flight attendant says "Do you want the chicken or the fish?" it won't take you very long to come up with an answer. On the other hand, if you're dining in a fancy restaurant and there are forty pages of menu, you may hardly know where to begin. But in that fancy restaurant, there's a cost to making the wrong choice. You may pick something you don't really like or which isn't as nice as what someone else is having. What is the cost to saying the wrong word here? What even is the wrong word? The real problem is not that we have too many options; it's that we have lots of options and *no criteria*.

Ever since you first went to school you were taught that the world is divided into Right Answers and Wrong Answers. Right Answers earn you ticks,[1] and Wrong Answers earn you crosses. Your job (in life!) is to see how many ticks you can earn at the cost of how few crosses. But here's a situation where you have no satisfactory criteria—you don't know whether calling the chair a "beehive" is the right answer or not, so you don't know if it earns you a tick or a cross. The second game, albeit a challenge for some, feels like a *familiar* challenge. We take comfort from knowing we are getting the right answers, and even from knowing that we are getting the wrong answers from time to time. We take comfort, in general, from being able to accurately judge our own performance.

Playing Pointing At Things And Saying What They Are Not, people are apt to invent their own rules to fill the void. Many people refuse to repeat a word, although there is nothing in the instructions which forbids this. It would be boring to call everything in the room a "battleship," mind you, but an occasional repeat is not a problem. (Note that playing the second game successfully is also playing the third game successfully but in a more restricted way, which makes it even odder that people are slower playing the third game than the second!)

Some people play the game in order to show off how clever and imaginative they are. If they point at a window and find the word "dog" on their lips, they will censor this out as "unimaginative" and wait until they've dredged up "aquifer" or "dirigible" or "centripetal force." Or they look for

---

[1] "Checks" for our American readers.

opportunities to crack jokes, pointing at friends and saying "nice person," for example. (It's not a bad idea for teachers to try and head this off in advance when giving the instructions for the first game, by asking players to avoid pointing at other people, "they might find it distracting.")

Other people play the game in order to show how *dull* they are. Terrified of revealing anything about themselves, they will make sure that each word seems nice and safe and mundane—they often restrict themselves to other objects in the room—so as never to risk saying anything remotely sexual, scatological or in any other way interesting. However, as improv teachers, what we are interested in is *not* the quality of words chosen (this isn't Scrabble and you don't get extra points for using a Q) but *fluency*. It's an essential skill for improvisers to come up with not the perfect choice after careful deliberation, but *a* choice right now. So, can you play this game with the same pace and fluency that the first game has? Can you get the gaps between the words as small as possible?

Trying your hardest to come up with good words only makes the game harder, but *trying your hardest isn't always your best strategy!* Trying your hardest means you are just piling the anxiety on yourself. You have already admitted that the task is beyond you. Imagine a plank of wood lying on the floor. If you had to walk across it, you'd probably just march across it first time without any difficulty at all. It doesn't seem like a hard thing to do, you wouldn't try your hardest and you would certainly be successful.

Now imagine the same plank of wood lying between two very tall buildings. This time, if you had to walk across it, you'd probably feel very differently. If the plank of wood is securely fastened so it doesn't move when you step on it, then the task is identical— it's exactly the same as if it was lying on the floor. But the penalty for failure is very different this time! This time, if you had to walk across it, you might start thinking about every moment of balance and imbalance, every muscle, every tendon, every joint, and the harder you tried to stay on that plank, the greater the likelihood you'd go plummeting to your death (which is why this is only a thought experiment).

Likewise with this game, instead of trying your hardest to play it well, try this: point at the first object, with no particular idea in mind as to what you are going to call it. Open your mouth, and be mildly curious as to what word emerges, but pay no more attention to it than that. Then *immediately* move on to the next object. Don't give yourself time to praise yourself for your excellent choice or punish yourself for your feeble choice—just keep moving. Even if it's a word you've said before, or it's a word you just heard someone else say. If you really feel there are no words left, that your "word well" has run dry (impossible, as you know thousands upon thousands of nouns, but it can feel like that), try starting with a sound, try starting with a letter. Point at the carpet and pick a letter at random. Start saying "Mmm…" until a word or phrase emerges—"Mmmmacaroni and cheese!"—and then go straight to the next object. Go!

If you are at all typical, you will have found the exercise a great deal easier than last time. Listening to the group this time around, fewer gaps, if any, can be heard and it will be less likely that there will be a trailing off in volume after about thirty seconds, as was the case last time. For yourself, you may have noticed that the gaps between words got shorter and less frequent. If not, well, this is a rather weird thing to ask your brain to do! For some people, this requires time, so if you observed no improvement at all—practice! Even people who struggle at this game can get quite good at it after practicing just five minutes a day for a week.

Your brain, of course, prefers to link items together (a very useful preference which we will exploit later on) and so you may find yourself naming six or seven fruits in a row, or half a dozen animals. That's fine at first, but as your confidence with the game grows, try to nudge yourself onto something fresher after the first couple of similar items. Choosing to name fruit is *one* creative act. We are hoping for a whole succession of creative acts.

With most groups we work with, these instructions do increase fluency but this is very often at the cost of volume and energy. There's no trailing off in the sound level over the course of this iteration, but the overall volume in the room is generally depressed, comparing this try to the last one. This is easily fixed and provides other advantages.

Play the game again (this will be the last time, honestly) with the same mental attitude: point at something, open your mouth and be mildly curious as to what word emerges. See what word your mouth wants to say, what word your unconscious hands you in that split-second. But this time, as it emerges, pronounce it with great joy and energy and at the top of your voice. Pronounce it with a big smile on your face as if it is the best word anyone could possibly have come up with and you are absolutely delighted with yourself—even if it's a word you've said before or a word you just heard someone else say. Play this game loudly, brightly and boldly! (As teacher, I may demonstrate at this point, parodying someone whispering out a random word shyly, and then demonstrating what we actually want, bellowing out another random word, while wearing a lunatic grin. By playing the game rather more crazily and loudly than most of the group would dare, I set the bar a little higher, I give them more permission.)

Most people discover that the game is easier played like this than played meekly. But it would be rare indeed to discover a person who, surrounded by others playing the game quietly, would experiment with playing the game loudly and boldly. Not one student in a thousand would do that (we can't remember it ever happening). We've discussed that adults are reluctant to volunteer early on, but even if people do volunteer, they don't always behave like they're happy to be there. In fact, that apparently willing volunteer—who looked perfectly healthy when safe in their seat—is likely to start looking a little ill, a little feeble, as soon as they are isolated from the rest of the group. This might be conscious or unconscious, but either way, they are doing their best to send the signal to the rest of the group: "Don't expect too much. This isn't going to be very good." Which, of course, becomes the truth.

But the reality is that attempting any kind of performance with energy and focus and enthusiasm dramatically increases your chances of success. So why don't students typically volunteer with a big grin and an attitude of "Ah, this is going to be fantastic! What is it?"[2] The answer is that by so doing they abandon control over the size of the gap between what they advertise and what they deliver. There is less shame in failing at something you are ill-equipped to do, so by making themselves seem not up to the task, they absolve themselves of the failure they "know" is coming. Despite the fact that they are pretty much guaranteeing failure by their own actions, they take a large degree of comfort from the fact that the failure is under their control. The safety of a certain failure is more rewarding than the possibility of success.

The bold advertising of success, by contrast, is terrifying! Despite the fact that students would be upping their chances of triumph considerably by doing this, they would not then be able to control the size of the gap between what they advertise and what they end up delivering, and this is a horrifying prospect. What's peculiar about this game is how readily it demonstrates that your ability (talent) is related to your attitude. Want to be better at this game? Play it with an attitude of mild curiosity instead of trying your hardest. Want to be even better? Play it with the same mental attitude, but wear an expression of joy and play it loudly and boldly. (Want to be even better? Play it while *running* from object to object—but don't crash into other people.)

The reality is that people are very "body-led"—much more than is generally realized. We're all used to the idea that as the situation changes, our emotions change, and then as our emotions change, our behavior changes and now anyone looking at us can see we are anxious or uncertain or whatever. But you can also reverse the causality. Play this game like "this is easy and fun for me," and that becomes the truth. Your body can tell your mind what to think. Researchers in Germany in the 1980s showed three groups of people cartoons. One group held a pencil in their lips, another group clamped it between their teeth and the last group just held the pencil in their hand. The second group found the cartoon funnier on average. Why? Clamping a pencil between your teeth forces your face into a smile. And now your unconscious starts thinking "Well, we're smiling at this so we must be enjoying it," and that becomes the truth. (Holding a pencil with your lips makes you frown instead.)[3]

---

[2] Later in the session, or in later sessions, students often volunteer with exactly this attitude, which presumably means that we're doing a good job of managing their mental states. They could just be doing it to please the teacher, but it will work in either case.

[3] F. Strack et al., "Inhibiting and facilitating conditions of the human smile: A nonobtrusive test of the facial feedback hypothesis," *J Pers Soc Psychol*. 54(5) (May 1988): 768–77.

The other benefit you get from playing the game loudly and cheerfully is that it turns off your internal censor. Pretty much everyone over the age of seven has one of these—the little mechanism inside your head that likes to check what you say before you say it. This is a very useful thing to have. It stops you from saying "fuck" in front of your grandmother. But when improvising, it can be a nuisance, so it's helpful to discover mechanisms which will temporarily silence it. If your attitude is one of cheerfulness and delight, you will fool your censor into thinking that there's nothing here that needs checking. And so, if you do happen to point at a candlestick and say "penis" there's no harm done!

What's also surprising about this game is how easy it is to trigger the learning-anxiety response. This is an utterly trivial game; it cannot possibly reflect on your ability to broker stocks, cure diseases, design buildings, program websites or seduce a potential lover, or however else you tell yourself you are marvelous. Yet very few people initially approach it with anything like the relaxed, positive attitude which it requires, and almost everybody punishes themselves bitterly for what they perceive as a failure. People will often report that on their first attempt, they realized they were saying only names of fruits, or animals, and then they tried to correct this shortcoming, which meant that they couldn't think of anything else.

Many adults have simply stopped being creative, so those muscles are tired and atrophied. The imagination is like a scared animal—it needs cosseting and encouraging. One negative remark—even from oneself!—is enough to cause it to shut down altogether. On the other hand, one positive remark—yes, even from oneself!—is enough to open the valve a little wider and let a torrent of ideas flood out. Think about how great you feel when someone tells you you're talented—it can lift you for weeks. As this game demonstrates, you can do this to yourself.

From the point of view of training improvisers, this is step one: can we, on demand, generate any number of arbitrary ideas without stress? It is a game well worth returning to, since the ability to control when your mind generates arbitrary ideas and when it generates connected ideas (as well as deciding which mode is appropriate) is crucial for your success.

In a more general sense, what we are talking about is the importance of BEING IN A GOOD STATE. When you are in a GOOD STATE, everything is easy. We can all be charming, funny, quick-witted and charismatic having a drink with our oldest friends. Standing on a stage with an audience staring at you, it's not so easy. But why should this be? You are still the same person, with the same talents, experience and abilities. But in this more challenging context, your state changes and when you're in a BAD STATE, even trivial tasks like coming up with random names for different objects can seem amazingly difficult.

The ideal improviser has no fear of the stage and experiences very little change in state when moving from sitting on the sidelines (or in the audience) to being on stage about to play a scene. This is not true of very many beginners, but it's vital for the coach to make allowances for this and to continue to remind the group of this key fact and provide exercises which help them to close the gap.

WHAT ARE YOU DOING?

Depending on the needs of the group and the time available, we may also play this next game before moving on to the more technical section which follows. This is a game which could easily be included under a round-up of random warm-up games (which we have also included at the back of this book!) and, in fact, there are probably several similar games which would serve our purpose just as well. We just use this one out of habit. This exercise works best with a fairly large group—at least twelve.

> *Everybody get into small groups of three to five. Choose the two people from your group who are going to go first. One of them says to the other, "What are you doing?" Their partner responds with an arbitrary activity—"I'm brushing my teeth" or "I'm piloting a plane" or "I'm stroking a kitten"—whatever you like. The first person now mimes the activity named by the second person. The second person asks, "What are you doing?" and the first person, while continuing their activity, names another arbitrary activity, which the second person then acts out. Now the first person asks again, "What are you doing?" and so on. If either person makes a mistake, one of the people watching gets to "tap in" and replace them.*

These instructions are a bit confusing, and if I get a lot of perplexed looks I may demonstrate the game, but I don't want to over-explain it. As they start to play, I notice that some groups are working very hard to get the game right. There are plenty of furrowed brows and tight shoulders, but very little laughter and very few smiles. If these do occur, it will be when somebody makes a mistake. Often there will be one quite happy group where a lot of mistakes are being made and people are laughing quite a lot. There may also be one or more very serious groups, where the game is being played nice and slowly, with plenty of concentration and next to no mistakes, to the total boredom of those who are standing and watching.[4]

---

[4]This game is not recommended for use with corporate groups, especially male-dominated ones. As it is, a certain "last day of school" spirit can dominate these events, which can get between the attendees and their learning. In this game, it's far too easy for groups to use this game to humiliate each other by making each other perform scatological or sexual tasks—a form of PIMPING. Most groups of strangers wouldn't dare do this to each other, and drama students generally wouldn't want to.

After three or four minutes, I call order and ask them what they think the point of this game is. Students hazard various guesses: "Spontaneity?" "Concentration?" "Doing one thing while saying another?" None of these is wrong, but there are better games to work each of those muscles. Finally, I explain that what I'm wondering is how much *fun* they will have. The real point of this procedure is that it is rather difficult to do—it screws up your ability to plan, which is also helpful for improvisers—and so a mechanism is built in to deal with what happens if the players get it wrong. However, it's a rather tedious spectator sport, so the game only has any interest while it's impossible to sustain. This is quite a profound demonstration of the importance of failure. Here's a game which has no function when people stop failing at it.

Again, it's interesting to contrast the way children and adults play this game. Adults are very concerned to get the rules right, and consider not being "tapped out" to be a great success, cursing themselves bitterly if, despite their best efforts, they do get "tapped out." Children will tap out joyfully at any excuse and will invent new rules if the game isn't moving quickly enough: "We've had 'combing my hair' already, you're out!" "You said 'er,' you're out!"

At this point, I mix up the groups and have them play the game again, this time just to see how fast and furious they can go. If I'm feeling daring I may even tell them that if they feel they aren't getting enough goes, that they've ended up in a group that isn't much fun, and that they're still spending too much time watching—then they have my permission to quietly leave and go and join a group which looks like it's having a better time. If a group gets down to two, it has self-destructed and both players should find another group.

In practice, almost nobody abandons a group—the problem of making the group a happy one is shared by everybody. But it's good for everyone in the group for me to not only claim but to demonstrate that I've "got them." That they are allowed to reject each other in this, fairly minor, way and that nothing bad will happen as a result. Compare this, for example, to Keith's Teenage Nightmare game in which four improvisers play four friends and three of them have to, by complicity, agree to socially exclude the fourth, each trying to ensure that they are not the one excluded. This kind of rejection is mortifying when it happens for real. Introducing the possibility at this early stage of the training helps embolden anxious students and builds trust in the teacher. But you need to present the idea with a lot of confidence and enthusiasm. Treat the idea of abandoning the group with any hint of gravity or solemnity and it ceases to be a game.

2.4

Saying Yes

Overview

Key concepts and a classic improvisation game. About the only things common to all practitioners (although terminology differs).

Everybody find a partner, someone you haven't worked with before. Introduce yourselves. Now, you and your partner are going to go on a picnic together. You are going to take turns suggesting things you could do or things you could bring on a picnic—but you are also going to kill every idea your partner comes up with.

I wander around the room, hoping to hear sequences like this:

> **A:** I've got champagne.
> **B:** Eaurgh! Yuck, I hate champagne. It's disgusting. I refuse to attend any champagne-infested picnic. Here, have some cucumber sandwiches.
> **A:** With my cucumber allergy? Are you trying to kill me? If they're even in the same basket, I'll break out in hives. Er... let's have our picnic on the beach.
> **B:** Beach picnics were made illegal months ago. We'll be arrested and shot if we even set foot on a beach carrying as much as a single sandwich. Um...

Even though coming up with new ideas will be a struggle, and even though none of these picnics are ever going to get anywhere, many people may be relishing the "permission" that I've given them to squash the other person's ideas—and their "killing" of ideas may be quite creative. Correct anyone who merely discards or dismissed their partner's idea. ("Let's bring a thermos of tea." "No thanks, let's..."). Insist that ideas are genuinely engaged with—and then exterminated. Also correct people who defend their ideas—they may spend the whole game arguing about idea number one—or those who leave it to one person to come up with all the ideas. It may be worth demonstrating the game to avoid these misunderstandings.

After a couple of minutes of this, I call the group to order and we do "take two."

Start again, but this time I'm going to "reprogram" you. Again, you're going to go on a picnic. Again, you're going to take turns suggesting things you could do or things you could bring on a picnic. This time, however, I want you to accept every idea your partner comes up with— but without any enthusiasm. I want you to be a bit grudging, maybe even a bit pissed off. But you do accept your partner's ideas, their suggestions do make it into the basket, you are going to do them.

This time, I hope to hear something like this. A demonstration, again, is sometimes useful:

> **A:** Do you want some chicken drumsticks?
> **B:** Chicken drumsticks? Really? Well, I know you like them. I think they're horribly greasy, but I suppose I could have a bit of one. What about playing Twister?
> **A:** It's a bit childish isn't it?
> **B:** So?
> **Me:** *You must accept the idea.*
> **A:** Okay, maybe later, but I don't promise to play it for very long. Er...

And so on.

Again without comment, we move on to a third iteration.

Start again from scratch. Take turns suggesting different things you could do or things you could bring on a picnic. This time I want you to greet every idea your partner comes up with great enthusiasm. Respond as if it is the best idea anyone could possibly have come up with and you can't wait to put it into action.

This time, I don't demonstrate the game—this is the "real" version and I want them to make their own mistakes, if any. I am likely to hear sequences like this:

> **A:** Let's put up a parasol to keep off the sun.
> **B:** Yes! And if it's hot, we can strip and go skinny-dipping in the lake!
> **A:** Yes, and let's put on our water wings so we don't drown!
> **B:** The ones that make us look like idiots?
> **A:** Yes, the enormous ones, bigger than we are!

The group will be much more active this time—their use of gesture more extravagant, almost Italian—and they may start acting out the events of the "story" they are now inventing. Silencing the group (and it may be a struggle this time!), and soliciting feedback on all three games, some or all of the following are likely responses.

> – It's much easier to say yes.
> – It's much more fun to say yes.
> – I didn't like the first one.
> – I *did* like the first one, but I didn't like the second one.

They are likely to agree that there is a *momentum* present in the third version which was entirely lacking in the first two. In the first two versions, nothing is developed, but the third one often flows very easily, and can even start developing into something like a story.

This exercise and the one that follows it are endlessly applicable. We use both Pointing At Things and this Yes game very regularly to open sessions with people of all kinds: actors, improvisers, adults, children, drama schools, community centers, corporate groups. Between the two exercises, they cover all of the most fundamental elements of improvising. When improvisation is boring or uncomfortable to do or to watch, the problem can often be traced back to these key concepts.

It's safe to assume that the more noise a group makes, the more fun they're having. Playing this game the first way is likely to generate quite a lot of noise—because killing other people's ideas is fun! Playing this game the second way is likely to depress the volume considerably. This is generally considered the least fun. But the volume goes through the roof with the third iteration, and even supposedly reserved Brits become voluble and expressive. Their eyes sparkle, their faces gleam and some will be charging around the room or collapsing in laughter or both.

Any new idea brought to the stage (often a line of dialogue but also a gesture, mime, change of expression and more besides) we call an OFFER. Offers can be either BLOCKED, which is what happened the first time around, or ACCEPTED, which is what happened the third time around. In general, we prefer improvisers to accept offers, because what the audience hopes to see is people cooperating with each other to construct a world in which a story can take place. If they spend their time instead fighting for control of that world, the story can never get started. The audience may be diverted—and may laugh—at the sight of one person thwarted by another, but all of these mutual blocking scenes will be the same and the sight of them will soon become tedious.

What's particularly fascinating is that the second game is often cited as the least fun and the least productive. In this version, *technically* you could be said to be accepting your partner's offers—their sausage rolls or whatever *will* make it into the basket—but everything else about your reaction *screams* "That's a dumb idea, you're a fool for having suggested it and I'm only saying yes because I have to." We want to say yes to our partner's ideas, at least in part, in order to *inspire* our partner. If we can find a way to say yes to them without inspiring them, that entirely defeats the purpose!

The same principle—offers which can be blocked or accepted—is common to every school of improvisation we have so far encountered. Del Close prefers to use the words "initiate" for offer (or for a certain class of offers), "yield" for accept and "deny" for "block," but the principles are the same.[5]

You may be unlucky enough to know people who are so defensive, so negative or even so aggressive that talking to them is most like playing the picnic game the first way. You may be lucky enough to know people who are so unguarded, so open and so positive that talking to them is most like playing this game the third way. But you've certainly had plenty of conversations which most closely resemble the second option, despite the fact that the second option is the least fun and the least productive. These conversations probably happened with people you don't know very well, maybe people you have known for some time, but not people you feel close to. And they probably happened at work.

Why on earth should this behavior be so prevalent? The answer, we think, is again in our schooling. Whereas the needing-to-get-the-right-answer behavior exposed by Pointing At Things is something we learn pretty much on our first day at school, this "yes, but" behavior we learn a little later in life. This is behavior we learn as teenagers.

If, as a teenager, someone asks you "Have you seen this movie?" "Have you played this game?" "Have you heard this band?" and, in an unguarded moment, you respond with honest enthusiasm: "Yes, it's fantastic!" Oh my god—what a risk! You have just made yourself vulnerable. You can now be held up to public ridicule as the loser who likes the stupid movie, the sucky game, the lame band. But equally, if you fire back with "Ugh, such rubbish, I hate it," well that too could be the wrong answer. Your friends will all look at you, puzzled and say, "Well, we all like it. We've just formed a fan-club. Oh, well we won't be seeing you on a Wednesday night, then," and once again you're the outcast, you're the loser. Very quickly, you learn to say of *everything*: "S'alright," with a dismissive shrug. Now you cannot be wrong.

---

[5]We prefer the term "block" because it implies that someone is trying to get an idea past you and you're blocking it, like you might block someone getting a soccer ball past you. A bad improviser is like a goal-keeper—"No idea is going to turn into a story on my watch!"

And the blessed safety of this behavior is very rewarding, so we continue to adopt it in other areas of our life.

As in the previous chapter, and the previous game, *people adopt behavior that feels comfortable*, regardless of how successful or unsuccessful it is in meeting other objectives. Feeling comfortable is overwhelmingly important to a great many people, who will sabotage any number of other goals in order to hang on to it. To learn to be a good improviser, you need to maintain a positive, happy attitude in the face of failure. Often the prospect of discomfort is far worse than the actual discomfort. So, while almost nobody objects to the experience of playing the Yes game, nobody would be likely to discover it for themselves if just asked to plan a picnic with a partner.

This establishes what is for us the Golden Rule of improvisation, and possibly the only principle which we are prepared to give that label to. If improvisers can't tell themselves "I must try my hardest to be good," what can they tell themselves? They will be facing an audience of strangers who have paid good money to be entertained. The improvisers want to give them a good show; they want to be interesting, witty and funny, and tell good stories. But as soon as they tell themselves that, their talent will flee like a frightened cat. Instead, they should focus on *being good to work with*. Go on stage to give your partner a good time, to make them look good. If your partner does likewise, the process will be good. If the process is good, the results will be good. Almost any behavior on stage, almost any flouting of a sacred improvisation principle, can be justified in furtherance of this ideal. Improvisers who are genuinely invested in finding out what other people want will get amazing work out of the other players, and that work will be like nothing else either person is capable of on their own.

Let's return to the workshop and take this game to another level. This version of the game will probably be familiar to anyone who has ever taken an improv class of any kind, but it contains some subtleties which are sometimes overlooked.

Find a new partner and this time, instead of a picnic, plan a vacation. The first person to speak will say "Let's go to..." and they will name a destination. "Let's go to the beach." "Let's go to Paris." "Let's go to the Bahamas." Wherever you would like to go. The second person, with that same spirit of positivity and enthusiasm as before, responds "Yes, and..." and they add an idea of their own. So if you began by saying "Let's go to Paris," your partner might respond, "Yes, and let's climb up the Eiffel Tower." Then you respond "Yes and" again and add another detail, and so on and so on until all the details of your vacation are established.

If the group is in a good mood, I might add this extra wrinkle.

When you played the picnic game, I don't know how you decided who should go first. Maybe it just happened, or maybe you had a little conversation, a little negotiation about it. Who cares, it's in the past. I care a little bit this time. This time, let's take this principle of being good to work with and apply it from the word go, the literal word go. This time, when I say "Go!" I want there to be no conversation and no negotiation about who goes first. This time, just turn to face your partner, look them in the eyes and try to figure out what they want. Then give it to them. Do they want to go first and name the destination, or would they rather that you had that responsibility? Bear in mind that no partner wants a long awkward silence, so if your partner doesn't say anything, that means you have to go first. And if you both speak at once—I don't know, figure it out. Away ... you ... go!

After a (noisy and joyful) couple of minutes, I silence the group and get a few pairs to tell me where their vacations have taken them. Quite often I will hear something like this: "Oh, we're going to Miami for snorkeling, and then we're going to Canada and we're going to have marshmallows, and then we're going skiing in the Alps..." This is full of life and ideas and positivity—but it's no significant improvement on the Yes game.

If one person begins by making the offer "Let's go to Paris," and their partner responds "Yes, and let's go up the Eiffel Tower," and then the first person responds "Yes, and let's go for a boat ride on the Seine," then that first person is being as positive as you could wish for. But how does their partner know that they even heard what they said? The boat trip has nothing to do with their Eiffel Tower; it YES ANDS Paris, which was the *first person's* idea. So as far as their partner is concerned, they could be standing there[6] while the other person is coming up with their Eiffel Tower nonsense thinking to themselves "Yeah, yeah, whatever, skip to the end, is it time for my idea again yet?" The idea of Yes And is to build a *chain* of ideas, each linked to the previous one—not to continue one's own chain, or start a new chain. Here's a quick Yes And sequence, improvised at the keyboard by way of demonstration, again using the vacation idea.

> – *Let's go to Australia.*
> – Yes, and let's go on safari in the bush.
> – *Yes, and let's hunt kangaroos.*
> – Yes, and let's disguise ourselves as sexy female kangaroos to lure them in.
> – *Yes, and let's end up falling in love with one particularly hunky kangaroo.*
> – Yes, and let's raise a family of little bouncy kangaroo-people.

In this way, some quite bizarre material can emerge quite rapidly—again, playing it loudly and boldly, and getting positive reinforcement from your

---

[6]These games *must* be played standing, by the way, never sitting.

partner serves to silence your censor. But this still feels like a (reasonably) logical chain of ideas. By contrast, some people just end up making a shopping list of ideas, all connected to the first idea, but not connected to each other.

> – *Let's go to Australia.*
> – Yes, and let's go on safari in the bush.
> – *Yes, and let's go surfing.*
> – Yes and let's visit the Sydney Opera House.

Or, they keep starting new chains…

> – *Let's go to Australia.*
> – Yes, and let's go surfing.
> – *Yes, and let's surf in shark-infested waters.*
> – Yes, and let's go to Berlin.
> – *Yes, and let's see the Brandenburg Gate.*

This needs to be corrected, since saying "Yes, and" to your partner's ideas, accepting and building, is the fundamental mechanism of all improvisation. In some cases, it may be weeks or even months before students again achieve the pure joy and creativity of their first experiences of playing this game. Saying yes to your partner's idea represents a risk. You have to let an alien idea in and, if you have to build on it, you have to let it influence you. You can't plan your response in advance, it depends on what your partner offers. If this is your only focus, it isn't hard to do. The trick is hanging on to that process when other forces are also acting.

In the previous game, Pointing At Things And Saying What They Are Not, we observed that your "talent" at the game changes according to your attitude toward it. In this game, your *partner's* "talent" changes according to your attitude toward *them*. Want a partner who is a genius? Treat them as if they are a genius. It is far, far easier to come up with "good" ideas when all of your previous ideas have been greeted with enthusiasm. When the "go" order is given for this game, some people clap their hands with glee and bounce around to face their partner when offering their first idea *in anticipation of the positive response they know is coming!*

So, in this game, your most vital job is to reassure your partner that they are doing a good job and that you like their ideas. What better way to do that than to make your responses dependent on theirs? How better to demonstrate that you actually heard them and were pleased by their idea? Perhaps this is what is meant by the term "active listening." (What else could this phrase be describing? Nodding?) This same idea can be generalized to any number of other situations. In a job interview, instead of struggling to give the best possible account of yourself, just try to make the interview pleasant and fun for the interviewer. In a networking event, try to take the pressure off the other attendees and play the role of "host" (regardless of your actual function at the event).

Despite the ostentatious success of these strategies, they are quite hard to develop and sustain in some situations. A corporate brainstorm should be a joyful YES ANDing process, but is more often than not a bitter clash of egos. A facilitator who understands this may offer the observation that "There is no such thing as a bad idea," but may also be oblivious to the cynical reaction this statement may silently receive. Clearly, there must be such a thing as a bad idea. What would a world look like in which there were no bad ideas? Every business would be as successful as every other business, every investment as sound, every relationship as happy. Good brainstorming isn't about having ideas which are all equally good, it's about *treating* all ideas as equally good—at least for now.

The problem is that the habit of immediately analyzing ideas and finding them wanting can be very deeply ingrained. Arrogant people find security in trashing other people's ideas. People with low self-esteem find security in trashing their own ideas. Senior people in an organization may be subconsciously visualizing themselves as "filters" whose job it is to stop bad ideas from progressing further. Controlling improvisers (who may also be very funny, but who define themselves primarily by their intelligence) similarly filter out "bad" ideas by blocking or ignoring them, and then can't understand why their "brilliant" ideas are blocked or ignored by their partner.

The real question that should be asked is: When is it appropriate to sort and filter ideas and when is it appropriate to simply gather and build on ideas in an uncritical way? A director shooting a movie should not take the editor out on location. It may very well be that the location is only available for a few days, that it is time-consuming and expensive to get the cast and crew there. Returning for more shots weeks later may not be an option. And so, a good director will aim to get as much "coverage" as possible, shooting the action many times and from many different angles. Directors do not need editors tugging at their sleeve telling them "Don't bother with this angle, I won't need it." If they heed this foolish advice, when the time comes to cut the film, weeks later, they will discover they do not have all the shots they need, that they have reduced their choices quite unnecessarily. Brainstorming sessions should be regarding as gathering ideas in *quantity*— shooting footage—with the editing saved to a later stage. This is the right time to discard ideas, to say no. Creative endeavors often fail either because people didn't say "yes" enough at the beginning, or because they didn't say "no" enough at the end, and the finished product is a compromise between a lot of different ideas which don't fit well together. This should make sense to (and pacify) those who can't bear to let a bad idea go by without comment.

Learn to accept ideas without fear, embrace the possibilities that other people's ideas open up in your mind, and you will discover that people are drawn to this positivity. Learn to do it on stage, and you can become a great talent. Notice that friends are people who YES AND each other naturally. Adopt the procedure yourself and (with a little practice) you can make almost anyone treat you as a friend.

Finally, it must be pointed out that in a slab of improvised narrative, a BLOCK is killing an *idea*, denying the audience something they thought they had been promised, whereas ACCEPTING an idea develops it, continues it, pushes it into the future. The distinction is not dependent on the words "yes" and "no." If I come into your shopkeeper scene waving a mime gun around and yell "Give me all the money in the register!" and you beam back at me and say, "Yes, and would you like my watch, too?" you have BLOCKED my offer that this is a dangerous situation, that you would want to protect your money and so on. Playing games like "first to block loses" or "one blocks, one accepts" can sharpen students' minds as to what is and is not a block, although there is bound to be a gray area. Sometimes neither response is a block. "Will you marry me?" is not blocked by the response "No," since we now have a story about unrequited love. Nor is it blocked by the response "Yes," since now we have a story about a wedding.

One question a coach has to consider is whether an apparent block is made out of fear or out of confidence. When teaching, we are likely to correct trivial blocks, such as insisting on tea when coffee is offered, if the improvisers are inexperienced. We have more faith that happier improvisers will refuse coffee to make a character choice or to be playful, and so will let it through. Sometimes it is essential to block stupid or destructive offers, but we don't have to teach beginners how to block, so we emphasize accepting in the early days.

2.5

What Comes Next

Overview

This theoretical game is an excellent way of teaching key storytelling concepts to a new group, as well as diagnosing weaknesses in a more experienced group. The group learns to build one story idea on another, to create a stable situation rather than plunging the hero into disaster straight away, to be obvious, to add information, to raise the stakes and to reincorporate ideas to provide structure.

Telling stories is something human beings are essentially compelled to do. Not a day passes when we don't exchange stories, and we cannot escape prepackaged stories of all kinds—not just books, movies, TV shows and plays, but simpler stories like newspaper headlines, billboard advertisements and snatches of overheard conversation on the bus.

Stories are not social constructs. Stories don't have the shapes that they do because of tradition, culture or history. The fundamental aspects of stories are the same, and always have been in every human society the world over. As soon as a theatre practitioner stands an actor on a stage, audiences start inventing stories. Who is she? Where is she? What is she waiting for? What mood is she in? Whom will she meet and interact with? The hunger for story is almost impossible to sate.[7]

---

[7]Our show Imagination started exactly like this, with one improviser sitting alone in the middle of the stage. We would ask the audience "What is she waiting for?" and get loads of great ideas for scenes. Because the audience thought they were guessing, there was no pressure on them to be creative.

That's not to say that story is the only thing which audiences go to the theatre for. It is possible to distract audiences away from their need for story; a spectacular song-and-dance routine will hold their attention even if the narrative is suspended temporarily to make room for it.[8] A wonderful piece of physical theatre, a marvelous scenic illusion, a hilarious piece of comedy shtick all have the same power. But the hunger for narrative returns as soon as the "set piece" overstays its welcome—and if you have achieved the trick of getting the audience to wonder "What will happen next?" then you betray the trust they have placed in you if you don't have, or appear not to have, an answer to that question.

The game What Comes Next (and some of its variations) is described in detail in *Impro for Storytellers*, but we wanted to include some of our personal experiences teaching it. It's a very pure game, and in typical Keith style it's absolutely to the point. It's also not without its pitfalls. We've found it very difficult for teaching teenagers and hopeless for teaching children because it's too theoretical (although children tend to be good storytellers anyway, because they aren't *trying* to be good at it). We'll describe the game first and then discuss some of these issues as they come up.

> *Can I have one volunteer, please? Thank you. Your prize for volunteering is that you are responsibility-free! All you have to do is ask the audience: "What comes first?" and they'll give you something to do. You do it and then you ask "What comes next?" and they give you something else to do. Do what you're told and only what you're told—don't embellish!*

Depending on how much they've heard about the game before we play it, it may not even occur to the group that this is a story game, so we get sequences like this:

> *What comes first?*
> – You stand on one leg.
> *What comes next?*
> – You jump up and down.
> *What comes next?*
> – You wave at us.

---

[8]If there is no promise of a narrative, then this isn't a problem. If you go to a concert, you don't necessarily expect a storyline because the songs are all you came for. And on rare occasions, a storyline can even become intrusive. It's said that Al Jolson would sometimes get bored of the dialogue in whatever musical comedy play he was in, and after about forty minutes, he would say to the audience, "Okay, I'll tell you how it ends. The guy gets the girl. Now do you want to watch the rest of the show, or do you just want to hear me sing?" And then he'd just sing songs for the rest of the night.

Some groups, especially corporate groups, discover the game of "make them do things they don't want to do." (See What Are You Doing? under "Spontaneity" on page 44.)

> *What comes first?*
> – You do ten push-ups.
> – No, twenty! (*everybody laughs*)

If necessary, I suggest to the group that we make the volunteer the hero of the story. The results are usually either INSTANT TROUBLE:

> *What comes first?*
> – You get out of bed.
> *What comes next?*
> – You fall out of the window.
> *What comes next?*
> – You break your legs.

Or a purely random sequence:

> *What comes first?*
> – You get out of bed.
> *What comes next?*
> – You sing opera.
> *What comes next?*
> – You eat an ice-cream cone.

I ask the audience whether they would be surprised if a film started in this (disjointed) way, and there is general agreement that they would be. "Have to be a French film," I say. Of course, there is an audience for disconnected narratives or for stories about inexplicable disasters visited on people we've never met, but they tend not to have broad appeal.

The power of this game is the ability it gives the coach (and the rest of the group) to analyze a story idea by idea, suggestion by suggestion. This is why it is vitally important that the actor does what is asked *and only what is asked*. When the actor starts embellishing, the group (who are making the suggestions) can't help but be influenced by what they see, and it becomes difficult to tell where the audience's inspiration was coming from.

If this comes up, I explain that this is a theoretical game, and that we don't really need the actor there at all (see The Problem With Theory later in this section). However, it's helpful to have a visual indication of what our suggestions look like in action, and it also removes ambiguity—we're all visualizing the same thing. Depending on the size (and mood) of the group, I may ask that as and when extra characters are created, additional actors jump up to play them. This also instills the virtue of jumping up to support your fellow improvisers. The same actor always asks "What comes next?" but the audience can give instructions to anyone.[9]

When the group presents the teacher with an unsuccessful sequence, it's up to the teacher to explain what went wrong and to suggest a remedy. And early on, it's important to suggest one remedy at a time, which sometimes means overlooking interesting or significant points (they can always be referred back to later). Take this sequence, which we'll imagine is only the group's third or fourth try:

> *What comes first?*
> – You're driving your car.
> *What comes next?*
> – Someone jumps in front.
> *What comes next?*
> – You swerve to avoid them.
> *What comes next?*
> – You hit a lamppost.
> *What comes next?*
> – They come and see if you're okay.

The word "someone" here is a dead giveaway. This a WIMP, a failure to define. We don't know who has jumped in front of your car. The story plays very differently if it's your sister than if it's a policeman or a nun. However, the more serious problem (for now) is that it's still INSTANT TROUBLE. So I'll remedy that first and make a mental note of the WIMP to bring it up later.

We'll describe a typical journey that a group might go on, but as coach you need to respond to what they give you and not look too hard for these things in this order. If they stumble on a really good story early, then praise it, but don't go into too much detail about why it succeeded. It's likely a fluke and they'll get back to screwing stories up before too long.

The first challenge is to get the group telling *coherent* stories. I remind them of the Yes And game and encourage them to YES AND each other's

---

[9]Another minor controversy surrounds un-actable offers. When the group says "You put on your gloves," that's very easy for the actor to portray even if they aren't a skilled mime artist. What about "You feel nervous"? That's a bit harder. What about "You're at the beach but you can't swim"? That's essentially impossible to convey on an empty stage through behavior alone. But it is information which an audience would benefit from knowing. So if this comes up, we generally say to beginners that they can make any offer at all, even if it doesn't provide anything for the actor to physically do, because it's more important that they act on the instinct to supply answers to questions like "Where are we?" Later, it may make sense to make it a rule that only actable offers are allowed because by now they will actively want to provide information such as where a scene is taking place, and this will force them to find more elegant ways of putting it across. "You spread out your towel." "You liberally apply sun cream." "You glance apprehensively at the breaking waves…"

ideas. I might also tell them that their only responsibility is for "the next obvious idea," and before long, we'll get a sequence like this.

> *What comes first?*
> – You're riding your bike.
> *What comes next?*
> – The wheel comes off.
> *What comes next?*
> – You discover it's a unicycle.
> *What comes next?*
> – A clown sees you.
> *What comes next?*
> – He pushes you off the unicycle.
> *What comes next?*
> – You fall on a mattress.
> *What comes next?*
> – Somebody's peed on it.

This is still lurching from idea to idea in a rather haphazard way, but there is at least some "connective tissue" between the offers. The biggest problem is that it presents a battle between two forces: positive and negative. The group is seemingly split into two tribes, one determined to be positive and one equally determined to be negative (although in fact, the same person may be responsible for positive and negative offers). Between them, they tear the story in two. The group knows instinctively that for the story to be interesting, the hero must be made to suffer (and actually their instincts are dead right) but they are also trying to YES AND each other. The result is that every positive idea is destroyed by a negative idea and vice-versa. This is a cousin of blocking, called CANCELING. CANCELING undoes the effect of the previous offer.

> *What comes first?*
> – You light a fire.
> *What comes next?*
> – It rains.

The rain CANCELS the fire, so there will be no toasting of marshmallows, prolonging the scene-setting or a forest fire raging out of control to begin the story proper.

I suggest that the group tries again and makes every idea positive. Pretty soon, we get a sequence like this:

> *What comes first?*
> – You're combing your hair.

What comes next?
– You find a knot.
Me: No you don't! Remember, every idea has to positive. Try again.
– Your hair looks wonderful. (*everybody laughs*)
What comes next?
– You put on some lipstick.
What comes next?
– You put on some eyeliner.

By this stage, anyone watching knows that she's getting ready to go out, but not one group in a hundred will commit to where she's going, or get her out the door. No matter—we proceed.

What comes next?
– You put your new necklace on.
What comes next?
– You admire your reflection.
What comes next?
– There's a knock at the door.

This could be an attempt to SIDE-TRACK away from the story. Beginners love having knocks on doors or ringing telephones, although they rarely know who's there (sometimes nobody is). It might be necessary to ban these two offers entirely in an effort to keep the story focused. But we'd like our hero to interact with someone at some point, so provided *somebody* comes in, this isn't too bad.

What comes next?
– Your husband says "Are you ready, dear?"
What comes next?
– You say, "Nearly."

By this time, the group is desperate to have something bad happen to the hero. "Can you feel a sort of black force welling up inside you?" I ask them, and they laugh happily. But this story is no less interesting than the unicycle or the lamppost. In fact, despite the lack of incident, it's doing a far better job of drawing us in. Let's see what happens if they are now allowed to be negative.

What comes next?
– You go to leave and your dress catches on a nail.
What comes next?
– You put your foot through a floorboard.
What comes next?
– The roof falls in.

Any thought of "Yes, and" or "the next obvious idea" goes out the window and we just get TROUBLE SALAD, but at least we've delayed the trouble long enough to build some sort of platform for the story to stand on. What we want ideally is THE RIGHT TROUBLE FOR THE RIGHT HERO (this will be discussed in more detail later).

THE IMPORTANCE OF PLATFORMS

If you read about a natural disaster on the other side of the world, in which hundreds, maybe thousands of people have been injured, lost their homes, possibly lost their lives, then you think to yourself "Oh, how awful," and you go about your day. It's just a headline. But if your best friend falls downstairs and breaks her leg, that's a tragedy, and you'll rearrange your week to look after her. The difference is that you *know* your best friend, so her accident affects you in a way which the newspaper headline doesn't.

A storyteller is playing an evil trick on an audience. First, we establish a hero and make the audience care about them and like them. Then, we torture that hero. But we have to do it in that order, or there's no effect. If I were an evil demon, and I knew that you were going to be hit by a joyrider and badly injured on Tuesday, I might take you to a party on Monday to meet a whole gang of new people. I might make you particularly charming and likeable at the party, just so that your new friends would feel devastated when they learned about your accident. Storytellers must learn to do exactly the same thing. In the "make-up" story above, the dress catching on the nail plays much more strongly than the car hitting the tree in the earlier story (although everything after was botched). This is very surprising information for beginners, who imagine that interesting stories are composed of interesting incidents. However, without the proper structure, the most interesting incidents in the world count for nothing.

The PLATFORM is the stable situation which precedes the "start" of the story. It shows the hero in the right place for them and shows us what normal looks like. Having very interesting platforms can make the storyteller's job harder; if you begin by having your hero lowered into an erupting volcano, you have to think of something more interesting than that to sustain the audience's attention. If you begin with a walk on the beach, finding something more interesting is far easier.

This doesn't mean that platforms are imagination-free zones, however. Insisting on making everything positive means sometimes students will try to get away with this kind of sequence:

> *What comes first?*
> – You're walking your dog.
> *What comes next?*

> – You feel great.
> *What comes next?*
> – It's a lovely sunny day.
> *What comes next?*
> – Your dog barks happily.

This achieves the first aim of building a platform—it allows us to spend time with the hero before disaster strikes—but the details are bland and there's nothing here that is likely to inspire the imagination. This isn't as egregious an example of WIMPING as saying "You hit *someone* with your car," but it still shows a lack of willingness to add information (presumably for fear of being "wrong"). This makes life harder, not easier, because it's difficult to be inspired by such vague offers. Encourage the group to be a bit more specific and the story starts to want to tell itself.

> *What comes first?*
> – You're walking your new puppy for the first time.
> *What comes next?*
> – You put on her new collar which reads "Treasure" and has a bell on it.
> *What comes next?*
> – You pull twice on her leash like the dog trainer taught you to.
> *What comes next?*
> – Treasure obediently walks forward.
> *What comes next?*
> – You enter the park.
> *What comes next?*
> – You see a large Alsatian coming toward you.

The details in this platform make the audience want to know what happens next. The name "Treasure" implies that this is a much-loved lap dog. The tag with the name and bell implies that you think you might lose her. Seeing her be obedient to the commands she learned under a dog trainer promises that something will make her disobey and you will not be able remember the right command, or that Treasure will ignore you to her detriment. Finally, the presence of the Alsatian promises a scary or violent interaction—Treasure out of her doggy depth, and our hero in trouble, trying to protect her. Contrast this to a story in which the first suggestion is the bland "You are walking your dog," and the second is "You see an Alsatian coming the other way." Before we know anything about what makes this dog or dog walker different from any others in the world, the trouble enters. It's like turning on a television drama twenty minutes in (see our comments on Starting in the Middle, under "The Rules and Why There Aren't Any" on page 305).

Improvisers who are about to complete an action feel a terror of being uncreative. They panic and try to wreck the action so as not to complete it. Thus, cars run off the road, wheels fall off bicycles, dresses get snagged on nails. However, the audience doesn't much mind a few completed actions early on—they just think "Okay, this is still the introduction." Interrupting a routine feels like action, but if the interruption is too arbitrary, it doesn't feel as if it has any point. Interrupting or BREAKING A ROUTINE with something "obvious" provides the point of the action.

Here's a nice illustration of this process, based on an example we saw Keith give in a workshop.

> *What comes first?*
> – You wake up.
> *What comes next?*
> – You work on a farm.
> *What comes next?*
> – You get dressed.
> *What comes next?*
> – You go downstairs.
> *What comes next?*
> – You eat breakfast.
> *What comes next?*
> – You go out and start your chores.

This is all introduction, for the reason that every action begun has been successfully completed. Our hero has successfully got up, successfully got dressed, successfully eaten breakfast. Since we know what farms are like, the platform can be assumed, so if he successfully completes the first chore, we'll go out of our minds with boredom. The whole story feels pointless. It's a diary entry, or a day in the life, nothing more.

In Keith's version, the routine of the first chore is brilliantly broken:

> *What comes next?*
> – You start milking the cows.
> *What comes next?*
> – The first cow says "I love the way you do that."

And suddenly the audience is in love with the story. "That's the point!" they cry. "That's the point of having him work on a farm! That's the point of having him milk the cows!" What's surprising about this procedure is how important BEING OBVIOUS is, not just for the improvisers' state of mind, but for the choices themselves as well.

A proposed BREAK IN THE ROUTINE can be too feeble to get the job done. Having the cow knock over the bucket might temporarily disrupt the routine, but there's nothing so far to stop the hero from righting it and starting again with greater care. More typically, routines are broken arbitrarily. If you're milking cows and an alien spaceship lands, that would stop you from milking the cows all right, but it wouldn't satisfy the audience's need for a point. The entirely unexpected alien spaceship is too ORIGINAL, whereas "I love the way you do that," exploits the latent sexuality which was already present in the action of manually milking the cow. Improvisers who are desperate to be interesting take a long time to learn the importance of being OBVIOUS, whereas improvisers who are desperate to be dull (equally common) can hide behind being "obvious" as an excuse for being boring, or for WIMPING.

Exploring breaking routines is also an excellent way to give improvisers' JUSTIFICATION muscles a workout. Arbitrary breaks in routines can be salvaged, if you make them relevant to the original routine. If you're milking a cow when aliens land and blow up the dairy, that's confusing. If you're milking a cow when aliens land and say, "Give us the milk," or the ramp of the spaceship lowers and alien cows come out, or the aliens talk to the cows and ignore the humans, presuming the cows to be the dominant species—then the story starts to make sense again.

Having introduced the idea of breaking routines, I describe a routine and have the improvisers break it. If you're reading this book by yourself, get a piece of paper and try this now. Write down six different ways to finish this sentence. "You're practicing the piano when…" Try and finish it in such a way that the routine is broken. In other words, nothing purely arbitrary has happened, but we know you aren't going to just carry on playing the piano. You should find this a rather easier challenge than "Think of six amusing incidents which might happen to a piano student."

Here are some ways in which students have met this challenge:

- The stool breaks. (*This feels a bit like abandoning the action, because it just curtails the action without make any new promises.*)

- The piano says "You're not very good, are you?" (*That's more like it!*)

- The composer knocks on the door.

- The notes you are playing create a resonance that starts shaking the house to bits.

- Your neighbor bangs on the wall. (*Better if you're sexually attracted to your neighbor, then you're conflicted.*)

- A mouse runs across the keys.

The following don't successfully break the routine, but rather than reject them, I encourage the students to help me salvage them:

- There's an earthquake. (*This has nothing to do with the piano and could have been presented to break pretty much any routine. If the earthquake only affects the room with the piano, that's much better! Or if the ground shudders with each note you play.*)

- You feel a bit tired. (*Not enough.*)

Also, breaks in routines can be positive:

- You realize you are playing better than you have ever played before—you are improvising a wonderful sonata.

Now let's try the same exercise again with a new routine. "You're reading a book when…" Again, get a piece of paper and see how quickly you can write down six completions of this sentence.

Some common responses include:

- You realize it's your life story. (*And turn to the last page?*)

- Money falls out from between the pages. (*Why?*)

- One page is missing. (*Which one? The last one, obviously! Tony Hancock[10] got thirty minutes out of that idea.*)

- The light goes out. (*Wrecks the routine and feels arbitrary.*)

- You get tired. (*Meh.*)

In general, this routine is rather harder to break than the previous one. "You're practicing the piano when…" paints a very clear picture. Students will generally imagine a piano, a living room, sheet music, a stool to sit on, no one else around and so on—lots of things which aren't specified. But "You're reading a book when…" leaves out a couple of crucial elements. Not only is the location not named, but most importantly, the book is left undefined. To see why this is so important, compare "You're reading a book when the lights go out…" with "You're reading a horror novel when the lights go out… and you hear a strange knocking coming from the basement."

Now, try breaking the routine "You're reading a *fantasy* novel when…" (you look up and realize you are in the fantasy world/one of the characters appears in front of you/the book levitates out of your hands in a cloud of pink smoke). As soon as you identify the type of book, that detail inspires your imagination and certain next steps become "obvious"—and therefore "right." It takes no great talent to arbitrarily name a genre of book and it makes everything else so much easier. Despite this, it may be months before some beginners wean themselves off the comforting habit of being vague.

---

[10]Hugely influential sitcom star on British radio and television in the late 1950s, most successful when working from scripts by Ray Galton and Alan Simpson.

LENGTHS OF PLATFORMS

How long to sustain a platform is a more subtle and difficult question. The accurate (but useless) answer is that a platform should be sustained until just before it gets boring. The longer the platform, the more material the story has to sustain itself. But the story doesn't start until the first break in the routine, and the audience may get impatient waiting for that moment to arrive.

A more helpful answer is that platform length varies according to how long the story is and how familiar the platform is. Longer platforms support longer stories. A sketch about a superhero needs only to establish one superpower before breaking the routine. A movie about the same superhero may spend forty minutes on back-story before spending another ten on the present-day platform, and only then introduce the villain.

The other factor is the familiarity of the platform. *The Lord of the Rings* takes the whole of the first half of *The Fellowship of the Ring*—350 pages of novel or almost two hours of movie—just setting up the rules of the world of Middle Earth. It takes that long to establish what "normal" looks like, and only then can we appreciate what "out of the ordinary" might be. Similarly, *Gosford Park*—a movie which is obsessed with detail and barely interested in plot at all—spends almost two-thirds of its running time showing us tiny variations on business-as-usual in this unfamiliar world before somebody finally has the good grace to be murdered and something resembling a conventional narrative can begin. By contrast, *Die Hard III* can get away with having a department store explode as soon as the credits have faded away, because not only is the location (contemporary New York) very familiar, but this is the third film in the series and so both the hero's and the movie's methods are well known to the audience. The platform here isn't so much omitted as assumed. We don't have to take the time to set up subway stations, Central Park, the NYPD, the character of John McClane and so on. The audience already knows them.

On the other hand, look at how carefully and how elegantly the original *Die Hard* sets up its platform. A famously violent film, a watchword for modern action gun-slinging, yet it is seventeen minutes into the movie before a single shot is fired. Until then, much of the movie plays like soap opera, but there are tiny hints (PROMISES) of what is to come: Bruce Willis's gun peeking out from under his jacket, his background as a New York City cop and the intercut shots of a mysterious truck powering through the LA streets, underscored with sinister music.

One other technique from movies and TV is worth mentioning, that of starting *in media res* before flashing back to events earlier in the narrative. This is a similar, but more elegant, ploy to the long-standing tradition of James Bond movies starting with a self-contained action sequence which may have very little to do with the rest of the movie. It's a way of delivering on the promise of violence and spectacle early, thus earning the right to do some potentially less thrilling, but nonetheless vital, platform-building subsequently. The beginnings of movies like *The Hangover* or TV series like *Breaking Bad* begin with the heroes in massive jeopardy, which makes the everyday platform which follows seem more loaded, a version of Hitchcock's bomb under the table.

But this is a mechanism which is very easy for writers to accomplish. Even if the storyline wasn't initially planned like this, it's trivial to cut-and-paste the most exciting moment of Act Three and drop it into page one at a very late stage. Improvisers don't have this luxury, as they have to create all of the content of the world, while acting it out for the first and only time. So, this kind of structure is certainly not for beginner improvisers, and might not even prove to be productive for experts as it goes against the grain of how improvised narratives are constructed. (See the game First Line Last Line on page 275 for a discussion of some related issues.)

KEEPING PROMISES

The group now understands that for a sequence of ideas to feel like a story, it will usually be necessary to build some sort of platform to provide a context before the suffering starts. They are also beginning to appreciate the value of being obvious to prevent the story from lurching off in unexpected directions, although many will take some time to become entirely convinced of the importance of this.

Unnecessary originality crops up in (at least) two different situations, and this game highlights both. Sometimes, as we've said, improvisers may panic and introduce a knock on the door or a ringing telephone which SIDE-TRACKS away from what was being developed—but these aren't the only means by which side-tracking can be achieved.

> *What comes next?*
> – You're cooking a meal.
> *What comes next?*
> – You taste it.
> *What comes next?*
> – It needs salt, so you add some.
> *What comes next?*
> – Your girlfriend has brought you a present.

Even if the girlfriend has brought a ladle, this improviser is almost certainly trying to prevent the (unnamed) meal from moving into the future. New improvisers imagine that they won't have enough ideas to sustain them, but the truth is that most improv scenes collapse under the weight of too many ideas, all jostling for attention. Anxious improvisers play a private mental game we call THAT'S NOT GOOD ENOUGH—hopping from idea to idea in the hope of finding the "right" one—whereas the audience is usually happy with any idea that is moving the scene into the future.

In other cases, improvisers simply don't believe that obviousness is a virtue and work hard to show off how imaginative they are. But being arbitrary is trivial and, while very useful to avoid wimping, has little to do with keeping a story on the rails.

> *What comes next?*
> – You're cooking a meal.
> *What comes next?*
> – You kill another rat and add it to the pot.
> *What comes next?*
> – You stir in marshmallow.
> *What comes next?*
> – Er…

This pointless absurdity means no one else is remotely inspired. Some groups (and some famous comedians) value absurd juxtapositions for their own sake, but more commonly these are JUSTIFIED. Eating your own shoe might seem absurd, but it makes sense for Charlie Chaplin to eat his own shoe *because he is trapped in Alaska with nothing else to eat*, and a leather shoe is the nearest thing to meat which he can find. Rat-and-marshmallow stew has no such justification, and while one could now be provided, it's going to be uphill work to draw the audience in.

A combination of both factors is at work when improvisers try to delay the obvious, a strategy known as BRIDGING.

> *What comes next?*
> – You're fishing.
> *What comes next?*
> – You feel a tug on the line.
> *What comes next?*
> – You start to reel it in.
> *What comes next?*
> – It struggles.
> *What comes next?*
> – You pull a little harder.
> *What comes next?*
> – You don't want to break your rod, so you give it a little slack…

And so on, *ad infinitum*. This *can* be used to provide suspense, especially if the audience knows what's coming but the characters don't. Here, alas, the improvisers are just spinning their wheels.

If they substitute the obvious action with an original action, they may momentarily feel very creative, but just like the rat-and-marshmallow stew, they'll often end up killing the story.

> *What comes next?*
> – You're having a romantic meal with your girlfriend.
> *What comes next?*
> – You get down on one knee.
> *What comes next?*
> – You open a small box.
> *What comes next?*
> – You take out a peanut.

Presumably the thought process here is "Anything but a ring!"

Here's what we sometimes say to groups or individuals who don't believe that giving the audience what they want is worthwhile:

> *The audience is constantly one step ahead of you. As soon as you make your first offer, they are imagining what will come next and anticipating possible futures. That means that when you make your second offer (and all subsequent offers), you have exactly two choices: give them what they expect, or give them something else. I maintain that if you give them what they expect (without making them wait for it), the story will make sense and they will be pleased. If you pick the other path and give them something other than what they expect, then again there are exactly two possibilities. What you give them will either be better than what they expected or not as good as what they expected. Most of the time it will not be as good as what they expected.*

Another way of thinking about this is in terms of PROMISES made to the audience. We've used this word before, but let's try to be absolutely clear about what we mean. When Little Red Riding Hood is asked by her mother to take a basket of cookies to Grandma, this PROMISES the audience that a trip to Grandma's will take place. Anxious improvisers will do anything to sabotage or delay this trip, because KEEPING THE PROMISE makes them feel unoriginal. But BREAKING PROMISES strains the trust between audience and storytellers. Mother also tells Little Red Riding Hood not to stop and pick flowers on the way (or some variation on this). This, more subtle, PROMISE tells the audience that Little Red Riding Hood *will* stop to pick flowers on the way, and that this will be her undoing. See Everything for a Reason under "Go Through an Unusual Door" on page 104 for more on this topic.

Of course, if you are convinced you've got something better than anything the audience is anticipating, go for it. In Quentin Tarantino's *Pulp Fiction*, John Travolta has to take his boss's new wife, played by Uma Thurman, out for the evening. Thurman is flirty and the audience knows as the end of the evening draws near that Travolta will get into trouble by reciprocating her advances. However, while he is in the bathroom wrestling with his libido, Thurman discovers the heroin in his jacket pocket and snorts it like cocaine, precipitating an overdose. Now Travolta's problem is not keeping his hands off Uma Thurman, it's keeping Uma Thurman *alive*! Notice that this still pays off the general promise that Travolta will risk his boss's wrath, while substituting a more high-stakes reason. The problem is that beginner improvisers tend to lower the stakes rather than raise them.

PROVIDING FEEDBACK

Now that the group has an idea of how this game—and stories in general—work, it's a good time to shake things up a bit. Coach the group to shout "Yay!" for suggestions that they like and "Boo!" for those they dislike. They may need some encouragement to boo at first, but stress that they won't learn anything by being polite to each other. It's not uncommon for the first suggestion with this feedback mechanism in place to take a little longer than usual, but this is a great moment to remind the group about "I suck and I love to fail" and the low-stakes situation. So you kill the next story? Great! That puts you one sucky story closer to being an expert storyteller. Tell the group a majority of boos means that you will give them another chance to come up with something more pleasing.

It's often hard to get a group to respond quickly enough in unison. As ever, people would rather consider their response. It may be necessary to cue them after each suggestion.

> *What comes next?*
> – You pull out a gun.
> **Me:** (*Quickly*) Yay or Boo? On three: one, two, three!
> **Group:** Yay!

As a coach, you have to be on your toes here. Provided the group is responding "Yay" or "Boo" as an audience would (they aren't trying to consciously apply "the rules," they're just giving voice to their instinct), you don't have the power to say, "That response was wrong according to such-and-such a principle." The audience knows what it wants, and it's the improviser's job to find out what that is and provide it. So as a coach, you may sometimes find the audience's responses initially confounding, but ask people why they responded the way they did and you'll generally find a sound rationale there. This can be a good moment to explore the difference between improvisation rules (which don't really exist) and principles or tools (which can be learned and applied, but aren't inflexible and dogmatic).

In particular, the audience will likely not "police" INSTANT TROUBLE (unless it's very absurd). They will roar with delight when your car skids out of control at the second or third suggestion, the problem of the lack of platform only becoming apparent later in the story.

FEEDBACK

I remember playing What Comes Next in this way with the RADA graduate group in 1999. The group was lackluster and unwilling to give feedback for fear of seeming critical. I explained that those playing the game were dependent on the yays and the boos. Imagine that your friend needs to park in a very small parking space and they're afraid of hitting a car, so you get out of the car to guide them in. You're giving them directions because they can't see. You wouldn't say "Keep coming, keep coming, keep coming," until they hit the car and then say, rather embarrassed, "I thought it would be rude to tell you to stop. I thought it would imply that you were a bad driver." I told the group: "If the improvisers crash, it's your fault." The group then got excited about the game and realized their power and the importance of their role. They could create great stories just by giving feedback about what they did and didn't want to see.

I divided the group into girls and boys and told the boys they had to tell a story the girls would want to see, and the girls would boo and yay. The boys started off with a girl getting ready to go on a romantic date. The girls loved it and cheered every suggestion. One of the boys suggested that the date who turned up was unattractive. The girls booed. Suddenly the boys found a game to play: every third suggestion, they deliberately provoked the girls into booing by making a suggestion they knew the girls would hate. The boys roared with laughter every time, and then fixed their deliberate mistake. That's a good atmosphere. When the group is separating themselves from the work to the extent that they're deliberating soliciting bad feedback, they're really in a great state to learn and to improvise.

—Deborah

THE RIGHT TROUBLE FOR THE RIGHT HERO

We've said already that some groups figure out how to prolong the trouble, but then when it arrives, it arrives from multiple sources, none of which feels "right." We call this TROUBLE SALAD. The "obvious" trouble, on the other hand, is "right" for a given hero. We don't care whether or not Hamlet gets to go to the ball and we don't want to see Cinderella avenge her father's death—although her father *is* dead! Certain platforms promise certain kinds of trouble, and good improvisers, improvisers happy to be obvious, deliver that kind of trouble—and then look for ways to make it worse.

Let's put together a more ideal version of this game, exploring a couple of blind alleys along the way. A bright young improviser jumps up and the group starts giving him suggestions.

> *What comes next?*
> – You're weeding the garden.
> **Me:** Very hard to be wrong with the first suggestion!
> *What comes next?*
> – Your boss has told you to pay particular attention to the roses.
> *What comes next?*
> – You pick one to give to your girlfriend.

We've sketched in quite a lot of platform here, and so while it's early to BREAK THE ROUTINE, it wouldn't be INSTANT TROUBLE.

> *What comes next?*
> – You prick your finger.

This is perfectly obvious, but a bit feeble. Unless you're a hemophiliac, there's going to be nothing to stop you from putting a Band-Aid on it and carrying on. Let's try again.

> *What comes next?*
> – The rose dies as soon as you've picked it.

This is better, but will need some justification to back it up. It's also much more appropriate for a gardener picking their own flowers, since that would be experienced as a personal loss, or indictment of their skills. But that's not who our hero is. His job is to weed someone else's garden.

> *What comes next?*
> – Your boss sees you.

Provided the group doesn't lower the stakes now ("Your boss says 'Take all the flowers you want—it is Valentine's Day, after all.'"), this is paying off all the promises and being obvious and getting the hero into trouble. You can do all this in a more absurd or cartoon-y register if you choose to.

> *What comes next?*
> – An alarm sounds and ten-foot-high bars shoot out of the ground,
>   trapping you.

But either way, you have a story that knows exactly where it's going. Finding the right trouble for the right hero hinges on knowing who the hero is. Once you know that, it's far easier to deliver the right trouble. Once you've done that—stop adding new ideas. Develop that idea rather than adding new sources of unrelated trouble (THAT'S NOT GOOD ENOUGH).

SOLVING PROBLEMS

Here we see how middles (getting the hero into trouble) depend on beginnings for their effectiveness (who is the hero?). Endings likewise depend on both beginnings and middles. Once the group has developed a couple of stories following this template—platform, break in the routine, get into trouble—and have done it without lowering the stakes, bridging or otherwise faltering, then they may stumble again. Another unhelpful instinct kicks in: to solve problems. Continuing the previous story...

> *What comes next?*
> – The boss sees you.
> *What comes next?*
> – You hide the rose.
> **Me:** Where?
> – You stuff the rose under your jumper.

Hiding the rose threatens to CANCEL the effect of being spotted by the boss, so the boss *must* see through this ploy. But the boss spotting the rose will CANCEL the offer of us hiding it. Provided we continue to raise the stakes and we don't solve the problem, however, either plan will work. No audience would be satisfied with this:

> *What comes next?*
> – You apologize and give the rose back.
> *What comes next?*
> – Your boss accepts your apology.

This cancels everything, no one is made to suffer and the stakes return to ground level. Let's try again.

> *What comes next?*
> – You hide the rose under your shirt.
> *What comes next?*
> – Your boss comes over and demands to know what you're doing.
> *What comes next?*
> – You say you are just weeding.
> *What comes next?*
> – One of the thorns sticks into your chest.
> *What comes next?*

> – Your boss says he thought he saw you pick a rose.
> *What comes next?*
> – You deny it.
> *What comes next?*
> – Blood starts trickling down your chest.

Notice that now being stuck by a thorn *is* the right trouble. We now have a story which is in excellent shape. The "point" has been established, we know who our hero is, we know what he is trying to achieve (so many characters in improv have no purpose that they are trying to achieve; so many heroes in fiction do), he is suffering in pursuit of that goal and he has been forced to make a moral choice—also something that audiences find very interesting.

This is also a simple example of the power of REINCORPORATION. Rather than searching forward into the future for a new idea, the improvisers make use of something already mentioned. We've just stuck a thorny rose under our shirt. A possible consequence of that is being stabbed by it, which not only hurts, it gives the game away.

JOIN THE DOTS

To develop and expound on this skill of reincorporation, I set the following pair of exercises.

> *Everybody find a partner. Call yourselves A and B. Now I want A to start telling a story and for B to call out a random word every ten seconds or so. A, you have to include that word in your story at the earliest possible opportunity.*

> **A:** Once upon a time there was a little boy named Tony who loved to play with toy soldiers.
> **B:** Strawberries!
> **A:** He would feed them strawberries on special toy soldier picnics and dress them...
> **B:** Matchsticks!
> **A:** ...in little uniforms made of matchsticks that he got from the shop on the corner.
> **B:** Pocket watch!
> **A:** One day, Tony was looking at his pocket watch when...

And so on. Get people to do it both ways round, so that everyone experiences both roles. Most groups find that neither role presents any great difficulty; since A is continually inspired afresh, having to JUSTIFY B's random inputs keeps the story moving into the future. In fact, sometimes the game gets *harder* for A if B is "asleep at the wheel" and enjoying the story so much that they stop calling out random words. But as fun and easy as this procedure is, it has a huge drawback for telling satisfying stories. Because new material keeps being introduced, *these stories will never end.* Here's a related exercise which is less about ideas and more about structure.

> *Find a new partner. This time A will tell chapter one of a story and B will tell chapter two. Chapter one consists of a piece of* PLATFORM, *followed by the word "Meanwhile..." and then another, unrelated piece of* PLATFORM. *B has to join the two platforms up, justifying their juxtaposition.*

A: Once upon a time, a farmer was struggling to mend his broken tractor. He needed to get his field ploughed by the end of the day or he would have no harvest at all this year. Meanwhile, in the river, two fish were setting out on the long journey upstream to spawn.

B: As the farmer worked on, the heavens opened and it began to pour with rain. The river burst its banks and the field flooded. Standing up to his waist in water, the farmer cursed his luck, but then saw two plump fish swimming past. "Forget farming, I shall become a fisherman!" he declared, scooping one up and wading home with it.

This feels like the end of *something.* Maybe Act II has the second fish plotting revenge on the farmer. Now get the groups to switch and try the same game with *three* platforms.

A: Steve, a nervous fifteen-year-old, was preparing for his first date ever. Any minute, Carol would arrive. They were going to go and see a movie together. Meanwhile, Sam, a composer, was struggling to complete her latest work. The orchestra was assembling that night and she was entirely uninspired. Meanwhile, in Russia, Secret Agent 009 was preparing his incursion into the KGB with his high-tech laser-cutter.

B: Carol was late and Steve was beside himself with worry. Eventually, he called his father for advice. His father, Secret Agent 009, had mistakenly left his mobile phone on and it went off at the critical moment, leaving him surrounded by guards. Upstairs, Sam the composer has her ear pressed to the carpet and is listening to every word. As Carol arrives, Steve hears the awful sound of his father being captured by the KGB. He falls, weeping, into Carol's arms, knowing that this is all his fault. It's all too much for Carol, who just wanted a night at the movies, and she runs away, leaving Steve feeling utterly alone. Sam is filled with inspiration and turns the events she has overheard into a magnificent opera. Weeks later, with his father returned home safely, Steve receives free tickets to the premiere of Sam's opera. He takes Carol to see it, and when they hear Sam's sweeping, romantic music, they kiss for the first time.

This time B has to expend so much effort joining up all the bits that it sounds like a complete story. For ordinary scene work, this is too intricate and too difficult a structure—but it's very useful to know about for narrative long-forms. The important lesson is that REINCORPORATION provides both structure and endings. Try getting the group to create a story through building a platform and breaking a routine, then when they come to the point where they might be tempted to start solving problems, pause and have them "audit" the story. What elements do they have in the platform? Now encourage them to REINCORPORATE those elements to provide an ending. If our gardener had had a trowel, he could have used it as a weapon or to fling soil in his boss's eyes. If he'd been wearing an apron, he could have shoved the rose into his pocket. So, building platforms doesn't just mean delaying trouble until we've gotten to know the hero a bit. All of the arbitrary details later become useful, you just have to remember to use them.

Inventing extra elements only as they are needed (retrospective platform-building) can be done, but it's harder to get right and you run the risk of *deus ex machina* endings, which audiences tend to find very unsatisfying. *Goldfinger* director Guy Hamilton understood this. Q's scene introducing James Bond to the Aston Martin was originally a page shorter. The producers wanted the car's gadgets to be surprises, but Hamilton thought that the audience would feel cheated if it were suddenly revealed that the car possessed the perfect feature for a given situation. He wrote extra dialogue for actor Desmond Llewellyn to perform, pointing out all of the abilities of the car, so that the audience would remember them with satisfaction when they were used "in the field," instead of being surprised and confused by their appearance. This went on to be the pattern for James Bond films for the next forty years. (If you watch the film, you can clearly see when the scene was originally planned to end!)

Compare Hamilton's decision on *Goldfinger* to the need of many improvisers to seem surprising or original and to subvert the audience's expectations for the sake of it. One way to think about the business of storytelling is to imagine that you, the storyteller, are exploring a country lane late at night with a flashlight. Each step you take reveals just a little more of the path ahead. In the same way, each idea you add to a story suggests possible ideas about what should happen next, although the end of the path may still be shrouded in darkness. And of course, you also remember everything that lies behind you, so you can reincorporate previous ideas to add structure.

COMMITTEES

You can continue developing the themes of What Comes Next and storytelling, and raise the stakes for the students again, by asking a small number of improvisers (three is about right) to become a committee, seated between the audience and the actor. Only these improvisers will answer the question "What comes next?" but the whole audience roars "Yay!" and "Boo!" A majority of boos means that the committee has the *option* to substitute a new suggestion—they may think: "No, we know where we're going with this." If the committee looks anxious, remind them that if they get honest feedback from the audience, they will always know if they are on the right track or not. And remind the audience that this means they are responsible for quality control. I usually ask the committee for a series of six to eight suggestions, just enough to begin the story, to take the pressure off a little bit. If it's going well, the next committee can carry the story on for another series of six to eight suggestions.

The bizarre and glorious thing about playing the game in this way is that the experiences of being in the audience and being on the committee are so hugely different. Being in the audience is easy. You almost always know when to say "yay" and when to say "boo." Ideas about what should happen next come easily and unbidden. Sometimes the committee will seem stumped or will miss what you wanted and it will seem so obvious to you what is required, you'll want to shout it out. In fact, it's very common for the audience to volunteer suggestions at least once, forgetting that they aren't on the committee.

Being on the committee is vastly different. Now, the weight of expectation presses down on you like an anvil. You stare stupidly at the improviser in front of you, whose "What comes next?" rings in your ears like an accusation, a definitive damnation of every creative thought you ever had. You dredge up an answer and it sounds like the stupidest idea in the history of the world. Yet the same person, watching the next three committee members suffer through the same fate, will be as fecund, as obvious and as relaxed as one could want. It's amazing the difference five feet of floor makes!

Many people will struggle with the experience of being on a committee, but the experience of effortless creativity *with the pressure off* contrasted with complete cessation of creative thought with a modicum of pressure applied is an immensely valuable one. Trying your hardest is not your best strategy. We suck and we love to fail.

The other vital thing to recognize is that what is "obvious" to one person may be entirely overlooked by everyone else—although they will see how "obvious" it is once they've heard it. Striving for originality means that stories lurch from arbitrary idea to arbitrary idea in a very unsatisfactory way. Even more important, everyone's "original" version of the story will seem disconnected and bizarre in much the same way. What's surprising and delightful is that with the "obvious" story, sometimes an "obvious" idea is unique to one individual. Being obvious means you are tapping right into your unconscious creative processes. It is the most direct route to your talent. Your obvious is not the same as mine, and *your obvious is your talent*.

We believe that creative geniuses are people who have learned to TRUST THEIR OBVIOUS. Lewis Carroll said "I pushed a girl down a rabbit hole and followed her to see where she would go." Mozart's manuscripts are said to have contained no amendments. Coleridge dreamed *Kubla Khan* but, on waking, was interrupted before he could write it all down. This is effortless creation, not sweating over every line. They are inspired geniuses in tune with their instincts. If we could learn to trust "our obvious," who knows where it might lead us?

ENDINGS

Endings are the hardest things to work on. This is partly because a group can improvise isolated beginnings all day, but endings don't make any sense—they don't really exist—out of context. Additionally, a story may already have failed in numerous ways by the time you have flogged your way through a beginning and a middle and so a satisfactory ending may not in fact be available. Finally, endings are intrinsically harder than beginnings or middles. Wise novelists, playwrights and screenwriters rarely begin work without knowing how the story will end, and it's not just longer forms that face this problem—plenty of comedy sketches are great until the punchline. Quick—what's the last line of the Parrot Sketch?

Even scenes which start strongly can often end up stuck, with the improvisers "spinning their wheels" or the energy draining away toward the end. This is highly regrettable, since audiences remember scenes that end well as terrific and those that end poorly as awful—they don't take accurate averages. While it is certainly true that if the middle or end of a story is soggy, the problem often lies in the beginning; it is a striking fact that a lot of improvisation manuals and teachers put all their emphasis on the beginning and just seem to trust that the middles and ends will take care of themselves. No wonder that the Harold allows the improvisers to abandon a scene as soon as they get bored of it: that means they never have to worry about middles, let alone ends.

In practice, improvised scenes often end before the story does. Not just because (as in Harold-like forms) they get "edited" prematurely. Sometimes something so funny will happen that it's pointless to continue, because the scene has already peaked. Making this call can be tricky—you don't want to bang the lights down on every big laugh, especially if there are promises which have yet to be kept—but it's essential to the rhythm of short-form shows to keep the energy up and not let scenes limp on past the point where the audience has grown tired of them and the improvisers have run out of inspiration.

So, a brilliant GAG (specifically a laugh you get *at the expense of the story*, not something funny which happens naturally as a result of the story) can be a fine way to end a scene and move on to the next one, but GAGGING is a particularly pernicious disease among improvisers. Since the main point of an improvised comedy show is to make the audience laugh, some beginner improvisers who are funny and witty offstage (and a few that aren't) will seize upon anything as an opportunity to crack jokes. But attacking your partner's mime skills (or your own), their ability to sustain an accent (or your own), deliberately lowering the stakes or punning for the sake of—all these things will kill the story because how can the audience continue to suspend their disbelief? This doesn't mean you can't be funny, but if you focus on telling the story, then you will always be interesting and making the audience laugh becomes a happy by-product. If you insist on GAGGING, and the audience doesn't find your joke funny, then you've got no laugh and no story.

But ending scenes often involves breaking rules which are intended to keep scenes alive. At the end of a James Bond film, the threat presented by the villain is thwarted and so the villain is canceled. When that happens two minutes in, it's a disaster, but at the end of two hours it's is exactly what's needed. Similarly, COMPLETING ROUTINES can bring stories to a close, as can JOINING (see Being Changed, page 137).

In general, stories end when all promises have been kept and all questions have been answered, but this is a hard principle to apply when onstage. Reincorporating earlier elements helps to signal that a story is moving to a close, and a bold punchline can act as a suitable cue for the lighting improviser. If nothing else is working, keep building the energy of the scene, and it may be possible to fade the lights slowly over the mounting hysteria— but you can only do this once or twice per night.

THE MAGIC FORMULA?

What we have established here is a general structure that is very useful. Build a platform, break the routine, get into trouble, raise the stakes, reincorporate. It isn't the be-all and end-all of storytelling, and it would be easy to find counterexamples—famous stories which omit one or many of these elements, or use them in a different order. However, something like this structure will enable you to tell an infinite number of satisfying stories, while eliminating many of the most common failings of improvised stories. Once you've mastered this, you can play around with it a bit more, but now you'll be "breaking the rules" intelligently. Feted scenic improvisers TJ and Dave are known for starting their improvised plays *in media res*. They begin in the middle of the action and part of the fun for the audience is watching the improvisers figure out the details of the PLATFORM as the story continues into the future.

The truth, of course, is that there are no rules. There's a whole essay about this later in the book, but for now, suffice it to say that BEING OBVIOUS, BUILDING PLATFORMS, RAISING THE STAKES, REINCORPORATING and so on are all tools that create certain effects. That's true of BLOCKING, CANCELING and BEING NEGATIVE too of course, but first we don't need to teach beginning improvisers to do those things and second, they tend to have *destructive* effects. Typically, at the beginning of the story you want to establish both a hero and what normality is like for that hero. BREAKING ROUTINES feels like the start of a story and REINCORPORATING feels like the end of the story, so typically BREAKING ROUTINES will happen early and REINCORPORATING late. But the most important thing is to understand what the effect is on the audience and where you are in the story. Then you can do what you like.

THE PROBLEM OF THEORY

The very fact that What Comes Next is a theoretical game also presents certain problems. We want to stress that the kind of analysis presented here is a means of learning intellectually what stories are built from, and possibly also a way to analyze improv scenes that have gone awry. Not one improviser in a hundred can analyze a scene *in progress* in this fashion without obviously pausing for thought and/or missing half of what the other improvisers are saying. An education in improvisation should retune your instincts, not substitute analysis for inspiration. It is also true that this kind of "story Sudoku" will only appeal to around half of any given group. Those who prefer thinking and planning will delight in discovering the hidden structures, while the doers and feelers will eventually get frustrated by not being able to experience making up a story for themselves.

In another lesson, the thinkers and planners will be disconcerted and confused by the lack of structure, while the doers and feelers get to plunge in, and ultimately the thinkers will need to feel a little more while the feelers will need to think a little more in order to become great improvisers. We recommend teaching both Word At A Time (see "Working Together" on page 118) and What Comes Next to beginners in session one. One game stresses instinct, the other intellect. We can't reject the idea of telling stories, nor blindly accept the absurd notion that the first idea to spring to mind is always the best idea, but we also need to avoid getting bogged down in structure and concept and allow inspiration through.

All of the same storytelling "machinery" is covered in the chapter "Go Through An Unusual Door" (page 102) and it's perfectly possible to omit What Comes Next entirely. However—as noted—different people have different learning preferences, and since in our experience many of these negative behaviors are very persistent, it may be well worthwhile to deliver the same concepts in two different settings.

A big advantage of learning to play What Comes Next is developing the skill of post-improv analysis. If you learn to play this game then after an improv show you know which scenes went wrong and why, and you also know when and why they went right. If you can analyze your work, you can get better. You can say: "We're really lacking platforms at the moment—next show, positive platforms." Or "Scenes weren't ending tonight—where were the reincorps?" Or "That was great, Pat, finally somebody broke the routine. We were spinning our wheels until then." This means you can establish a syllabus for yourself and your group so you can improve. Without this, you just have to sort of trust that experience accumulates and that you aren't developing bad habits.

2.6

Status

Overview

Maybe Keith's most profound contribution to improvisation and theatre. We provide some new takes on some old games and talk about how this work fits in to a general improv "education."

Deserving of a whole section (one of just four) in *Impro*, Keith Johnstone's work on status alone should ensure his position in the theatre hall of fame. Right at the beginning of his theatre career, Keith began analyzing transactions in plays (and in life) in terms of *dominance*. He also realized that people often very clearly display how dominant or how submissive they feel in their *behavior*, and so this was an ideal way for improvisers in particular to create characters, since your behavior is always in the present. Our approach includes a number of classic Keith games, which we'll just sketch in, plus some exercises and insights of our own.

It's also worth mentioning that we prefer to teach status *early*. This is for two reasons. First, it reinforces our core belief that improvisation can and should be about great stories, rich characters and believable interactions. Second, after the formal, technical exercise of What Comes Next, it's nice for the students to get their feet wet by jumping up and doing improvised scenes. In the status exercises, the effort of maintaining a status leaves less mental space available to worry about story, failure, acting and so on. For all our love of theory, the truth is that if you get the status right (and, as we'll see, the environment), the story often takes care of itself.

INTRODUCING THE CONCEPTS

Can I have two people up please? Great, just sit on these two chairs facing the audience. I'm going to give you a number of pieces of direction which will change the way this audience perceives you. Don't worry if you forget any of them, I'll prompt you if need be. Start by sitting neutrally and symmetrically. Now bring your whole body forward so you are perched on the edge of the chair rather than sitting back in it. Turn your toes in just slightly and let your shoulders fall forward. Now bring your chin up and forward and tuck the back of your head into your shoulders. Can you smile so that your top teeth are over your bottom lip? Try a goofy giggle to go with the smile. Now start touching your face intermittently. One hand or the other always wants to go to your face for some reason— to scratch your nose, adjust your glasses, brush some hair back—but it's only ever a very brief touch. Now try and look at the other person, look at their face. If you make eye contact, look away immediately and giggle, but try to shoot a glance back as soon as possible.

If your volunteers follow the instructions, by the time you get them smiling, the audience will be laughing happily, and when you start managing their eye contact, often the audience will be a little hysterical. All of these directions are designed to make the volunteers look like LOW STATUS clown characters. The eye contact instruction is particularly powerful, since it not only contributes to lowering their status in a profound way, but it also yokes the two performances together. Now the actors have to respond to each other, and so we get all the pleasure of cooperation games, as well as seeing each character's instantaneous *reaction* to the other.

Get these two characters to improvise a little bit of dialogue. Maybe Sheila is bringing Ken back to her place for coffee after their first date. You may have to intervene to keep the action moving forward and remind them to keep touching their faces, look away if they make eye contact and so on. The instinct to block will likely still be present, so if Ken asks for coffee, Sheila will only have tea. Take the opportunity to correct this, unless the volunteers are really struggling with the status behaviors. You only need about ninety seconds of material to demonstrate the principle: come in, have a seat, nice place, put the kettle on, talk about the film they saw is ample. If you want to stir things up toward the end, have one of them say, "Where's the bedroom?" or "I liked the love scene best." Obviously you should end the scene before they start groping each other!

Okay, relax guys, relax. I want you to play the same scene again with as much of the same dialogue as you can remember. It doesn't have to be absolutely word-for-word the same, but I don't want you to make any deliberate changes either. This time I want you to forget about all of that twitching and fidgeting and instead just focus on this. Find it easy to make eye contact and keep your head absolutely still when you're actually speaking. Not solid like a rock or rigid like a board, just still like a pool of water.[11]

Most people move their head to a certain extent every time they talk, and few people realize just how much they're doing it, so it's a good idea to have the two volunteers practice just saying "Hello, my name is…" while maintaining eye contact and with a still head. Despite this, I will often end up saying "Say that again with a still head," multiple times as we retake the scene.

This instruction is designed to create HIGH STATUS characters. Depending on the energy and chemistry of the performers, this second iteration of the scene will come across as either a smoldering seduction or a bitter battle for dominance.

After these two scenes, I'll point out to the group that the story told is very different the second time around, although the dialogue is almost the same. I may ask the group to describe the first pair and I'll generally hear answers like "awkward," "anxious," "geeky," "nervous." If I ask them to describe the second pair, they'll tell me things like "sexy," "confident," "mature," "intimidating." But I point out that I didn't tell the volunteers to be any of those things. Instead I gave them specific *behaviors* which I thought were likely to create those effects. I also ask the volunteers if giving them these behaviors made them feel nervous (the first time) or confident (the second time), and they almost always agree that they did (because people are very body-led). Interestingly, even though the dialogue was generated by low status characters, when spoken by high status characters it still works, but it now comes across differently. If you say, "I am sorry. I seem to have spilled coffee on your carpet," while looking someone in the eye with a still head, it will read as if you've done it deliberately and are anything but sorry.

It's generally a good idea to give everyone a chance to experience these different modes of behaving and the individual behaviors that make them up. You could divide the group into A's and B's and have them interact at a party, with the A's displaying high status behavior and the B's low status behavior. Give them jobs in the same company, the A's very senior and the B's very junior, then switch the statuses while keeping their positions in the corporate hierarchy the same. Here's a quick list of useful instructions (this is not intended to be comprehensive).

To Be More High Status...

- Gesture infrequently but purposefully
- Make the middle of your body (throat to belt) bigger and taller

---

[11]This excellent instruction, which seems to prevent students from stiffening up like the Tin Man when asked to keep a still head, is due to Alex MacLaren.

- Invade someone else's personal space
- Speak in very short sentences
- Pause and comfortably sustain the silence
- Hold eye contact
- React minimally to the physical presence of others (don't be reactive)
- Place your feet a little wider apart than normal and then don't move them for a while
- Think about touching the other person's head (but don't do it!)

To Be More Low Status

- Touch your face briefly and intermittently
- Use long rambling sentences, fragmenting your speech
- Make the middle of your body smaller
- Try to keep a distance from other people
- Want to look at others but hate to make eye contact
- Giggle nervously
- Shift from foot to foot or make purposeless repetitive movements with your hands
- Answer quickly and say "er" before you speak
- Stand with your feet very close together, perhaps with one foot crossed over the other

Notice that none of these instructions includes *what you say* or *your situation in life*. Status has nothing to do with class, upbringing, accent, job, salary, dress sense or grooming, and has less to do with dialogue than you might think. Students will often want to demonstrate being low status by talking about being poor or uneducated and try to be high status by being wealthy, snobbish or upper class. When we have a status party where the janitors are high status and the managing directors are low status, the students start to understand that these things are not necessarily related. (Some of the improvisers who play high status janitors talking to low status bigwigs love this experience. Someone once said to us, "It feels like being a cleaner *on your last day*.")

WHAT IS STATUS?

If students ask for a definition of status (or even if they don't), this is what we tell them:

> *In different circumstances or at different times, you will feel more or less powerful, more or less confident, more or less in control. But ultimately how you feel is private knowledge. Only you can know for certain how powerful or confident you're feeling. But it's also true that we make guesses all the time about how other people might be feeling, and those guesses are often right (just not all the time). Status can be thought of as anything somebody does which you would use to base such a guess on.*

Most people's sense of status is extremely acute, and even very subtle cues carry a lot of weight, but this sense is generally subconscious. If two students play the same tiny scene fragment—a couple of bland lines each—with a variety of different status relationships, the rest of the group can generally make good guesses about who these two characters are. One person will say, "She's waiting outside the headmaster's door to be punished" or "They've come for the same job interview, but he's going to get it." Others generally agree that this looks right, even if they "saw" something else. From the improvisers' point of view, this means they can communicate a great deal of interesting information very rapidly by means of these techniques, sustaining and enriching the platform. What students also need to appreciate is what different status behaviors look like on *them*.

For example, if the group is coaching someone to be higher status, it's not uncommon for them to suggest folding arms. On most people, arms folded closes the body off and suggests defensiveness rather than high status—truly high status people have nothing to hide. However, certain individuals, especially taller men with broader chests, can fold their arms loosely and look comfortable and relaxed. Improvisers should experiment to see what works for them personally.

Body language theorists purport to understand motive through physicality. For example, they say, "If you cross your arms it's a sign you are defensive." While sometimes that's true, it may also be that you are crossing your arms because you are cold or because it feels comfortable. We can never really know for sure why people do things, but we can determine how others generally perceive certain behaviors, and this can be very important information. If you are hosting a show or setting up an improv game, and you're bobbing your head up and down as you speak, the audience is likely to subconsciously think "If you're not even in control of your own head, are you really in control of this situation?"

It's also true that status behaviors *clump together*. Look back at the "still head" version of the "back to my place" scene and you'll probably notice that—without being told to—the improvisers eliminated "ers" and "ums," made fewer unnecessary gestures, sustained long pauses and so on. All of these behaviors arose in response to the still head quite unconsciously. Determining what is a strong and a weak STATUS TRIGGER for an individual will help them become truthful at any point on the status spectrum, since they will only be consciously altering one aspect of their behavior, while their body unconsciously—and therefore truthfully—adjusts to match.

STATUS OFFSTAGE

The person running the History department at most universities may well be lower status than their most outgoing first-year student. You might know janitors who enter a room and say, "Why is this rubbish on the floor?" in a very high-handed way. Where we live in Camden Town, London, there are a lot of homeless people, and this fact tends to polarize their status. They tend to be either far higher status or far lower status than other people, and this is very evident in their physicality. This is no doubt because it's tough to live on the street and you need a very strong defense mechanism to keep other people at bay. That's really what is at the heart of status. It's a way of keeping others at a distance by being someone who can intimidate others away if necessary, or someone others are unlikely to be threatened by, who will therefore go unnoticed.

It's a technique we learn in adolescence to get people to like us or bullies to leave us alone. You can no doubt think of girls at your school who were coquettish and low status to attract boys and those who took a more high status "Rizzo from *Grease*" approach. You can probably also remember a time when you stood up to a bully to get them to back down and another time when you scurried away with your head down. When students understand that status has far less to do with what they say and far more to do with what they are doing when they speak, they are usually turning a corner of understanding. While it is possible to talk meaningfully about high and low status dialogue, it is important to recognize that we get more status information from the body, so if the status of the dialogue and the body are not congruent, the body will tend to win. This is wonderful for improvisers who have to create interesting characters (the low status policeman trying to arrest the high status shoplifter, for example) and also for actors who are working on text. Playing a line or a scene against its implied status can sometimes give it a fresh new life, especially if it's a role that is well known or associated with an iconic performance.

In high-stakes situations, gaps in status tend to be widened. Look at the outward signs of status that exist in the military. Physical submission and dominance are constantly being demonstrated because if there is any doubt about the chain of command in a battle, lives will be lost. Saluting, standing at attention and marching are all ways of marshaling status and keeping it in absolute clarity. Likewise, hospitals have clear chains of command and broad status gaps which are exacerbated during a doctor's internship, when they are most likely to put a patient's life in danger. We see the same sort of status gaps in Gordon Ramsay's kitchen, but while there are no life-threatening situations there, there are heavy time pressures which can create a similar atmosphere. If we saw someone in a sandwich shop or family accounting firm behaving this way, we would conclude that they were crazy and they would not be able to retain staff. Where the ramifications for mistakes are less consequential, the status gaps are likely to be quite narrow.

When society wants to bestow status on someone they often give them a title. The "Very Right Reverend Spacklington-Smythe" is a higher status name than "Bob" because it takes all day to say. If the Very Right Reverend invites you to his house for drinks, he'll probably say, "Call me Bob," because it's a status leveler. Some people who are endowed with status by others are comfortable with it, and some are not. Think of the Queen as compared to Prince Charles on the red carpet. Which one looks like they "belong"? If you watch a reality show like *American Idol* you will see the contestants grow with confidence as they are given more and more status. One year after the show, if they are performing in big arenas and selling lots of albums, they will be unrecognizable in status terms from the nervous person who first auditioned and cried with gratitude when they were put through to the next round.

Some people who are normally very high status can lose it suddenly in certain situations. Watching the coverage of a James Bond premiere on television, we recognized everyone in the line of people meeting the Queen, but there was one person we couldn't place. Then one of our friends texted: "Did you see Madonna without her status?!" Apparently, Madonna, a well-known Anglophile, couldn't sustain her status in the presence of royalty. This transformed her so much, we didn't know who we were looking at.

STATUS AND ANIMALS

Once I was standing in my friend's kitchen looking into the garden and I saw a fox creep in. The family cat, which wasn't very big, stood up and made itself as large as it could (size equals high status). It looked the fox dead in the eye and stood totally still. The fox looked left and right, then turned and ran, surprised by the cat and then intimidated by its high status signals. It was the cat's garden and cats stand up for their territory. Even though the fox was twice as big as the cat, with teeth and claws that could rip up a sheep, the cat won the status battle. This is also true of people. We've developed an instinct about status so we can avoid battles we don't think we can win.

—Deborah

STILL HEADS

Keeping your head still while speaking is a tremendously powerful high status move—too powerful for most normal purposes. Its effectiveness may stem from the fact that the head, and especially the face, is a particularly rich source of status information. By refusing to move it when you typically would, you cut off the flow of status information, thereby giving yourself the upper hand.

Maybe because it's such an extreme ploy, many students find it tremendously difficult. Sometimes we will arrange them into twos and have one person say a line of dialogue to their partner while maintaining eye contact and keeping a still head. Something like "Go ahead, make my day." Their partner can then coach them and let them know if they did in fact move their head without knowing it. Then swap roles and have the other person say, "Hasta la vista, baby."

These are both famously threatening catchphrases, although both are perfectly pleasant things to say. What makes them interesting is the juxtaposition between the apparently pleasant sentiment and the context and attitude with which they are said. To make the point pretty much unarguably, get both people to say "Hasta la vista, baby," while moving their head. If you say "Hasta la vista, baby," and waggle your head around, you don't look like the Terminator, you look like Austin Powers!

This does not mean, despite a wealth of misguided claims to the contrary, that 93 percent of what you communicate is how you behave rather than what you say. If what you are saying and the way you are behaving are congruent—you are saying the same thing with your words and with your body—then your message will shine through loudly and clearly. But if what you are saying is apparently being contradicted by your behavior, then—and only then—your behavior will be assumed to be "the truth" and now much of your verbal message will be ignored or disregarded. In life, it's important to be aware of when you are undermining your verbal message and to take care that status "tics" are not preventing you from landing a sale, inspiring your team or getting through to your spouse. On the stage, we can be more flexible, delivering more subtle information that someone is out of their depth, or lying or trying to hide something. Good improvisers will know how to YES AND these subtle offers just as well as overt verbal ones.

STATUS LADDERS

To demonstrate how effectively status relationships can be used to sustain a platform, as well as giving the group a further chance to practice these skills, I ask four people to enter a scene one at a time and form a Status Ladder, with each person who comes in being higher status than those who preceded them. Perhaps I ask them to play co-workers going for a drink after work. The scene should last about two or three minutes and will likely be largely GOSSIP (talking about events in the past or the future or otherwise offstage) but the characters will be revealed very strongly and the audience will enjoy seeing them interact. Despite the virtual absence of plot, it would be very unusual for the group to find the scene remotely boring. To start a story here, try prompting one of the group to say, "I've got something to tell you all," or some other such open-ended routine-breaker.

If, as sometimes happens, people are arranging themselves up a corporate hierarchy which matches the status, have the last person to come in do a menial job, but have a high status attitude.

We often follow this Status Ladder with the same exercise but in reverse. Another four people get up and this time each person who enters has to be lower status than those who went before. Maybe this time, pick one person to be the host of a party and have the other three knock on the door to come in as guests. Often it will be the case that in the first Status Ladder exercise, the four characters were fairly evenly distributed across the status spectrum, with the first person playing fairly low status and the last person playing quite high status. Before the Reverse Ladder exercise starts, I point out to the host of the party that it doesn't have to be like that. She *can* start quite high status if she wishes, and create lots of "space" under her, but since it should always be possible to play *even lower* status, she may prefer to start already quite low status and watch the others crush in "underneath" her. She gets to set the bar. This instruction tends to result in a low status first character, and thus a rather unhappy, neurotic party which is nevertheless great fun to watch. Wretched characters apologize for not having brought presents, curse themselves for tiny errors of etiquette, become desperately shy in front of members of the opposite sex and so on, to great comic effect. Once, the final character crept up to the "door" at the side of the stage, and tapped feebly on it but was ignored, and then fled into the night—to gales of laughter from the delighted audience.

Two things are worth noticing about this. First, extremes of status usually lead to comedy where small status gaps tend to lead to drama. Second, the first person's status tends to *creep up* over the course of the exercise. It's almost as if the presence of so many other lower-status people forces up the status of the first person. There's nothing wrong with this, but notice that status is a two-way street, especially as we consider the next exercise, which is slightly trickier and confronts some of the more interesting aspects of status, particularly as it relates to improvisation.

Okay, four more people up. In both the previous exercises we built a status ladder—once from the bottom up and once from the top down. In either case we could have assigned each character a number according to status, 1 for the highest status, 2 for the second highest, then 3 and then 4 for the lowest status. This time around, again I want you to

construct a status ladder, but in a random order. So you have to keep an
open mind about where you are going to fit in. The first person on can
play whatever status they like. The second person to come on makes the
choice: higher or lower? The third person on has a more complicated
choice: higher than both, lower than both or in the middle? And the
fourth person on has the most complicated choice of all: higher than all;
higher than two, lower than one; higher than one, lower than two; or
lower than all? Give each person a chance to interact with the others on
the stage before entering.

Again I'll pick a bland scenario for them to meet and talk in. I'll probably
have them all know each other so we can see the status relationships clearly,
and I'll probably have them all be friends so it doesn't get too negative.
Maybe they are meeting up at the movies, or in line for a ride at the
fairground.

At the conclusion of the scene, it's very likely that there will be a degree
of confusion about who is what number. I'll often ask the audience if anyone
can put them in the right order, as well as asking the actors themselves.
In about one group in ten there is general agreement as to who is number 1,
2, 3 and 4. This makes it harder for me to make my point, but I can always
tell them they were "too good," which they like hearing.

In about three groups in ten, there is a "collision" on the number 1
spot. What has likely happened is that one of the improvisers, typically
a confident man, has entered the scene as number 1. He may even have
successfully been number 1 for a while, while there were only one or two
other players on stage. However, when another player (again, usually
another man) enters, hoping to be the new number 1, the previous player
does not accept his new role as number 2 and instead a STATUS BATTLE
is waged. This is a particularly pernicious form of blocking. Once we've
trained improvisers to be fearless, they may never show vulnerability on
stage, even if a scene is crying out for it. Teaching improvisers never to ask
questions may exacerbate this tendency. Note that the game Fight For Your
Number (see page 463) depends for its effectiveness on a status collision
of this kind. The point is not that status collisions are bad, it's that one
occurred here when it was not called for—in fact, when it was explicitly
forbidden!

What is usually the case is that there is a clear number 1, much more
high status than the rest, and a wretched number 4, the ultimate victim, but
it's hard to decide who is higher out of the middle two. (A collision on the
number 4 slot can occur, but it's very rare.) Let's assume this is the case:
probably there were moments when Sam was higher than Chris and other
moments when Chris was higher than Sam. In all probability, the scene
will still have been interesting to watch, and arguably it's more truthful
that statuses shift, they ebb and flow, over the course of an interaction.

However, this still suggests a weakness in technique: Sam was aiming to be a number 2 and yet we couldn't decide if they were a 2 or a 3 (some "Sam"s will sheepishly admit that they'd forgotten what number they were trying to be).

The key to this is to realize, as we've been hinting at for a couple of pages now, that *status is relative*. With only two people on the stage, all we can say is that one is higher or lower than the other (and how big the gap is). We have a number 1 and a number 2 and that's all. We don't know if they will be the eventual 1 and 2, 1 and 4, or 3 and 4 because we don't know where the others will go. It's always possible to find a gap. Number 1's are easy to spot because *they dominate everybody*. Number 4's are easy to spot (assuming there are four people on the stage) because *they submit to everybody*. To be a number 2 you need *a number 1 you can submit to and a number 3 you can dominate*. Rather than try and summon up an ineffable sense of number 2-ness, it's therefore recommended that the improviser aiming for number 2 shows a different side of themselves to number 1 than they do to number 3.

Here's a quick sample showing some of these features at work.

> **Adam:** Hi Barbara
>
> **Barbara:** Hi Alex. Don't you look nice? (*Barbara's tone is patronizing and she invades Adam's space, making a play for number 1.*)
>
> **Adam:** Oh, er, thanks. (*Adam fidgets and stammers, accepting the offer and becoming number 2.*)
>
> **Barbara:** Where's the rest of the gang? Late as usual. (*Barbara becomes arrogant, securing her position as number 1.*)
>
> **Charlie:** Adam, Barbara, how you guys doing? (*Charlie sweeps in, filled with confident charm, aiming to be the new number 1.*)
>
> **Barbara:** (*Looking at her shoes*) Fine, Charlie, fine. (*Then, sharply, to Adam*) Say hello to Charlie. (*Barbara solidifies her position as number 2, deferring to Charlie but still being dominant over Alex.*)
>
> **David:** Hi everyone, sorry I'm late. (*David is aiming for number 4, creeping in pathetically.*)
>
> **Adam:** Hello David. (*Adam will find David easiest to talk to, but Adam tries to see if he can be number 4 and bump David up to number 3.*) I've got your ticket, just like you asked.
>
> **David:** Thanks. (*David accepts Adam's offer and brushes past him, approaching Barbara with lust in his eyes.*) Hello Barbara. Maybe we can sit together? (*This is hopeful, rather than seductive, maintaining his position as 3 to Barbara's 2.*)
>
> **Charlie:** I'll be assigning seating, if you don't mind. (*Charlie reminds everyone that he is number 1.*)

The final order is (from highest to lowest) Charlie, Barbara, David, Adam. Note that both Charlie and Barbara were aiming for number 1 when they first entered, and David was aiming for number 4. It takes a certain amount of sensitivity—plus the willingness and the courage to make bold, unambiguous and definitive offers—to get this right. You have to be completely aware of everything your partner is doing and make your own offers subtly but clearly.

That status is relative, and that this game is as difficult as it is, shows the folly of the popular high school drama game wherein students adopt statuses based on a randomly selected playing card—the higher the number, the higher the status. In some versions, the card is worn on the forehead so everyone else can see a person's card except that person. In other versions, a card is privately looked at and then returned to the pack. In either case, the game is built on two dubious premises. The first is that people generally know how to adopt high and low status behavior. Most *actors* need to be trained in it, let alone most schoolchildren. The second is that there exists a state of being which is characterized as 6 out of 13 on some cosmic status scale.

Status describes how we interact *with others*. It is meaningless to talk about "absolute" status. Which isn't to say one can't have status on stage by oneself—one can have a status relationship to a space and that can be quite independent of the relationships one has to the other actors. The dynamic way in which we share space with others is called the KINETIC DANCE. It's the absence of this kinetic dance which makes actors look stiff or awkward. Adding status, to text or improvised pieces, is an excellent way to get it back.

HIGH STATUS COMPETITIONS

In order to explore high status behavior further, I ask two students to volunteer to play a scene. Let's say Abi plays a homeowner and that her roommate has moved out. She needs a new roommate so that she can pay the mortgage. Bob needs to rent a room, he has read a classified ad in the newspaper about this one and has arranged to come and look at it. Abi has to try to be more high status than Bob and Bob has to try and be more high status than Abi.

It's important that one person isn't trying to sell the flat or sublet it. If this person moves in they'll be roommates, which evens the status out. Coming to look at someone's house to judge whether it is "worthy" of living in can give you status, but so can deciding whether or not you will allow someone to move into your home. We tell them it's a competition and that the audience will decide who's more high status. We can usually tell when someone's "lost" the status battle because a quick drop in status is generally funny and will tend to get a big laugh.

STATUS AND SLAPSTICK

'Man slips on banana peel" is the archetypal joke. It's a quick drop in status. If a frail old man slips on banana peel, though, we'll rush to help him up. This is not funny because his physical status is already very low. But if the Pope slips on a banana peel and his hat falls off, this is very funny—despite the fact that he's a frail old man—because of the status his position and costume endow him with. This is why *Monty Python* and lots of other sketch groups deal with politicians and arch-bishops so frequently. They're socially high status so it's fun to bring them down. You will even see comedians raise their status immediately before a fall to maximize its comic potential.

One of the funniest things I ever saw was during a RADA summer school. I came into the room to teach the class and the students were joking around. One of the girls declared loudly in an accusing tone to someone: "Who's the loser now?" Immediately afterwards, for no apparent reason, her chair fell out from under her. The class didn't stop laughing for about an hour. Now, if she'd been a shyer member of the class just sitting there quietly, and her chair had fallen out from under her, people would have rushed to help her up, concerned, wanting to make sure she was okay. It was the juxtaposition between her mock self-aggrandizing and her sudden physical demise that created comedy. A drop in status over three hours and five acts, though—that's tragedy.

—*Deborah*

People employ all sorts of strategies to win the competition. They're normally very rude. If they're looking at the flat, they talk about how small and dirty it is. If they own the flat, they talk about how expensive the rent is—implying that the person looking at it can't afford it. They rarely look like strangers meeting for the first time. They often look like they're in a Pinter play. There are lots of awkward pauses and pointed remarks, which makes the audience feel that the two players shared the same lover years ago and for this reason play out some kind of annual charade in the flat where they slept together. Otherwise it tends to look like the beginning of a porn film, and when one of them says "Where's the bedroom?" the class will laugh hysterically. Interestingly, because they're trying to "win", their goal is not to be entertaining or do a funny improv scene—and for this reason they are often hilarious. Even total beginners do wonderfully entertaining scenes which you could put in front of any audience.

This is all a great process to go through. Let the students explore all the places it can take them. Whether or not they're successful at appearing high status or winning the competition, they'll learn a lot about different status relationships and the effect they can have on another actor or character in a scene. Sometimes I show them how if you come up very close to someone face-on, you can make them recoil. It's like a sort of human physics. Only an extremely high status person can hold their nerve. If they're actors, I ask them "Wouldn't it be wonderful to have this sort of effect on other actors, so instead of remembering their blocking, they couldn't help moving when you moved?"

HAPPY HIGH STATUS

After they've played around for a little while and had some fun, I ask them "Would you want to live with any of the people you've seen in these scenes?" They all agree that, while we've seen lots of people who we would consider to be high status, if someone turned up to see our spare room and behaved this way we definitely wouldn't let them have it. Likewise, we wouldn't move in with someone who was rude and high-handed. I point out that high status people have to rent flats and get jobs and buy cars all the time, and no one would deal with them if their only strategy was to be rude and spiteful.

We play the status competition again, but this time I tell the person coming to view the flat that they've been looking for a flat all week and they're really hoping to rent this room or they'll have nowhere to stay. I tell the improviser who owns the flat that they can't find anyone to take the room and they really hope the next person is okay because otherwise they'll have trouble making the mortgage payment. Neither party is desperate, but they both want it to work out.

This time we get to see some far more subtle signals of status which underlie the characters' primary desire to get what they want out of the transaction. This is far closer to how people operate in real life. Sometimes people make a big deal out of something small, like the ideal location for the office coffee machine, when actually they don't care about the coffee machine nearly as much as they do about winning the status battle. Sue puts it in one place. Neil moves it. Sue puts it back, justifying it to herself and others as a location issue, but really she just doesn't want Neil telling her what to do. These sorts of arguments are nearly always about status and dominance but they don't exist in a vacuum—there's always a coffee machine of one sort or another.

When a few people have played it this way, everyone agrees that this looks far more like real high status people making a transaction—while they're not actively rude, they don't tend to be warm either. I ask again "Would you want to live with them?" and the class usually answers "Not really." So I ask them if it's possible to be *both* likable *and* high status. A few people usually boldly shout "Yes!" and so I ask them to show us.

Together the group has to solve the problem of how to be both charming and high status by jumping up, trying new strategies and giving feedback. People who were terrified of volunteering in the morning, and thought all the attention would be on them if they did so, have forgotten their fear because the focus is entirely on solving the problem, and they've just come up with a theory that they have to try. Reinforce to the group that during our exploration we will accidentally discover many wonderful transactions, moments, ways of dealing with people and comedy that will be very far from our goal. It will all be immensely valuable. Each class will stumble over different things and each class will get there through a different route. You are just there to guide them toward success—but not too quickly, unless you are pressed for time. Otherwise they and you will miss this process of discovery.

BACH

My high school music teacher told me that when he was learning composing, his tutor would always say that our contemporary rules of harmony were established by Bach. In other words, if Bach did it, you can do it. He said many students pored over Bach day and night to find an example of what they had in mind. The tutor told my teacher one day that actually the students could do what they liked, but what they would learn from the hours of studying Bach would be far more valuable than anything he knew about composing. As a teacher, it is advisable not to rush the students to your conclusions—although if you set a problem it is good to have an answer, or you may frustrate the students.

—*Deborah*

The method we discovered to be both charming and high status came about when we were doing corporate training. We wanted to show people how to be more confident, and when we taught them high status techniques, we discovered that they were invariable defensive or aggressive. So we started to study what people like Bill Clinton, Oprah Winfrey, Helen Mirren or George Clooney did to give the impression of always being the most confident person in the room while at the same time being eminently likeable. We discovered that they used all the high status body language and married it with smiling, charming behavior. They complimented others, never defended themselves and raised the status of others, crucially, while maintaining their own.

Such people can afford to be generous. The Queen wouldn't come into your apartment and say, "It's terribly small isn't it? I live in a palace, you know," because she can afford to be generous. She's far more likely to find something in your flat to admire or to find a common interest with. Her position and upbringing have given her lots of status, so she gives it rather than takes it. A happy high status person usually wants the coffee machine where you want it. They feel it's more important to you. If they do really want something, they prefer to get it in a way which makes you feel good about it.

I tell the students this, and people are very eager to have a go at maintaining their status while raising the status of others. But at first it's not easy. Mostly the group will agree that in any given scene, one person succeeded at being high status and the other succeeded at being likable, but neither were both. I tell the students not to worry, that most people who are naturally happy high status are making twenty million a movie, which makes them laugh. We always manage to coach one or two people to find it, and then I tell the rest of the group to practice when they buy their newspaper in the morning or in the bar after the class. I tell them that if they can go to the bar, order a round of drinks and then tell the bartender they've left their money at the table and the bartender lets them *take* the drinks without paying, they have successfully made themselves seem happy high status. The bartender likes them and trusts them enough to let them go and believes they will come back with the money (which of course they should do!).

Once they've discovered this, they realize that high status behavior is not inextricably linked with wealth and importance. I've been saying this all along, but it takes ages for it to sink in. They can then have fun saying "I'm unemployed," or "I can't afford it," with high status body language and realize the power. Someone who can admit that without physically apologizing must *really* be confident, whereas anyone can boast about a Porsche and maintain their status. Alex Lamb, who is now a successful novelist, came to a workshop we taught years ago and played this game opposite a woman who was boasting about her wealth and looking down her nose at him. "What do you do?" she sneered. He looked her in the eye and said "I clean lavatories. You've never cleaned a lavatory, have you? Never mind." He leaned forward and gave her a patronizing pat on the knee. She nearly exploded with rage. We often use this as an example when explaining status to students. Notably, it was because the woman *reacted* that she lost the exchange. You can never really win a status competition— you can only lose and let someone else win. If you don't let it show that your partner has affected you, it doesn't really matter what they say.

Of course, once people are used to "losing" the status competition, I point out that "losing" is exactly what an audience is looking for. Remember, that's when the audience laughed and often gasped. I play this game with them to teach them how to *maintain* status, so their status doesn't just drift back to neutral. They need to be able to maintain it, but they also need to know when to hold it and know when to fold it. (See Status Exchange under "Working Together" on page 142.)

For much more about the kinetic dance and all aspects of status, see both of Keith's books.

BEING ANDREW WILLSON

When I was teaching high status competitions at the RADA summer school, there was one student, Andrew Willson, a twenty-year-old American, who simply couldn't be beaten. Everyone who came up against him looked either defensive and annoyed, or low status and keen to please him. He always looked effortlessly in charge but likable. Eventually, he retired from the competition undefeated and we replaced him with Saskia. Saskia had a much more difficult time facing the same opponents, and I was encouraging the group to coach her. Another student, Pete Schilds, suggested that she try and be more like Andrew, so I asked him to coach her to be like Andrew. He side-coached her enthusiastically throughout the scene to do the things he thought he'd seen Andrew doing—"Slow down," "Relax your hands," "Pause before you answer"—but although Saskia tried to do these things, she really didn't change very much. So I tried, thinking perhaps the job required a more experienced coach or that she would listen better to my instructions because I was the teacher, but the results weren't much different. Eventually, I realized that we had an expert on "being Andrew Willson" in the room—Andrew Willson himself. So we asked him to coach Saskia.

Andrew's coaching was very different from ours. When the other person knocked at the door, Saskia hurried to answer it, and Andrew said "You're not in a hurry. I'm sure they'll wait at the door for a minute. You have all the time in the world." When the other person swept past Saskia into the space, Andrew said, "They seem very eager to look at the apartment. Why don't you let them do that while you go and relax?" When the other improviser started playing Saskia's piano without asking, she became anxious and tried to stop them. Andrew side-coached: "Why do you care? I'm sure it'll be fine." He wasn't telling her what to do. He was telling her what he was thinking!

Suddenly she slowed right down and relaxed. She smiled at the person who was busily looking into all the rooms and criticizing them. She didn't rise to their bait. Without being told to, she did all the physical things that Pete and I had tried to coach her to do without success. She had the thoughts of Andrew Willson, who was naturally happy high status, and so she seemed happy high status.

Saskia was instantly transformed, and we knew we had something good on our hands. But I didn't know if it would work without Andrew. Could anyone transfer their status to anyone else by telling them what they were thinking in any given situation? It seemed too good to be true. I took the exercise to my advanced students who'd formed their own company, Dance Monkey Dance, through our Level 3 workshop program. First I got them doing high status competitions. I asked Alexandra to coach Claire in the ways of being Alexandra if confronted by a defensive high status person, who was played by Ece. Alexandra is known as a very positive, charming person who puts everyone at ease, so I was keen to see how she'd react under these circumstances.

Before Ece even knocked on the door, Alexandra said to Claire "You're really looking forward to meeting potential new roommates but you're also just really enjoying the experience of having random people come to your house." The audience laughed. None of us could imagine feeling like this. When the doorbell rang, Alexandra said "Tidy up on the way to the door," but almost as soon as Ece was inside, she said "Confess that you've just tidied up." Suddenly we had an insight into Alex's mind and some absolutely brilliant character traits. To tidy up and then confess to it is a lovely thing for a character to do—so human. The status cues were more subtle but still wonderfully obvious to the audience. When Ece's character became rude, Alex said "Okay, you want to get rid of her now, but don't let her know that. Be nice about it."

When James played Ed, he told him that he was annoyed by the intrusion of people coming to look at the flat but that he should try not to show it. When Claire turned up to look at the flat, Ed told James to be "very tired but enthusiastic." Suddenly James had Ed's physicality and a rather defensive low status manner. (This is unusual—people are generally happy low status or a more guarded high status.) When James made a joke about Claire staying the night, Ed quickly added "Oh no! Now you're worried she thinks you want to sleep with her." James said "My girlfriend will be here soon."

What was interesting was that if the "coach" gave the improviser their real thoughts, they automatically knew what to say and would not need to be fed lines of dialogue. They never stopped and said "What do you mean?" I think that's because they were *real thoughts*, not improviser/director thoughts. In other words, they were obvious and human. At the same time they were hilarious, and the audience's reaction was a combination of "Wow! Is that how Ed thinks? I'd never think that!" and the laughter of recognition of those things we all think but never talk about. It was astounding how often there was a dichotomy between what an individual said they were thinking and what they asked the improviser to show. The scenes were a far cry from the presentational work improvisers often perform that audiences find so hard to relate to.

Next Joanna wanted to be Claire and vice versa, so I got them both up and developed a new game. When Claire wanted advice on how to be Joanna, she raised her hand. Joanna, who was also Claire's scene partner, would then give Claire a "Joanna thought"—"Come in tentatively but trying to make a good impression." Claire would do so. Then Joanna would put her hand up and Claire would give her an instruction: "Apologize, because you feel like you've messed up already and you should already have shown her the flat." Joanna would start apologizing.

We found this game was fun to watch and do and flowed much better than we thought it would, but the improvisers felt they had missed out on seeing themselves in a scene. So I told Joanna she knew how to be Claire now, so she could be in a scene without direction. If she needed direction she could put her hand up, and Claire would give it to her from her seat. Malcolm then trained Ece to be him from his seat, giving frequent direction, with Joanna only getting direction occasionally through a hand signal. We found that once people had been trained to be someone else, they only needed direction when they encountered a situation they hadn't been in before and didn't know how to truthfully react.

We then did first date scenes, crossing genders to see if that would create interesting effects, but Ed pointed out that all the setups we were using were situations where you would try to make a good impression, so we weren't really seeing people at their most natural. We decided to get the improvisers to be roommates on a Sunday morning. Ece instructed Claire to be her and James instructed Ed to be him. Ece said on a Sunday morning she'd normally be obsessing about something that had happened the night before, and James said he'd be wanting to watch a documentary about Buddha that he'd recorded during the week. A very funny scene ensued in which Ece and James each coached their alter-egos to pursue their own agendas. As Claire talked more and more about whether her friend had implied she was an alcoholic the night before, James told Ed to "agree, but don't get drawn in," "Put the DVD in," "Press play," "Turn up the volume." Eventually, Ece told Claire "You're going to have to confront him now." Throughout the scene, the characters both pursued their own action, their own agenda, until with perfect timing, they turned on each other and something happened.

What was interesting was that the improvisers in the scene, far from being hampered by the outside direction, seemed freed by it. They were imaginative, funny, emotional, physical—and they were even able to reincorporate specifics from the platform. My fears that the mechanism of taking direction from outside voices would slow the action down were unfounded; if anything, it seemed to speed it up. The improvisers looked very natural, but each interaction seemed meaningful. I think it's because it made the job of improvising a scene easy. You just had to listen to the voice in your head. It would tell you how it was feeling and you would base your actions on that. It was liberating as well; the voice gave them permission to do all sorts of things they may not have done otherwise.

Finally, it was personally revealing and consequently very good for bonding. We all did it and were slightly surprised how aware we were of our own faults and duplicities. Claire's "Rush to the door. You need approval," or my "Tell an anecdote but then worry they're not interested," made everyone laugh—we've seen each other exhibit these behaviors before—but also bonded us. I would recommend that you play this game with any group who wants to learn about each other. Compare this game to Characters From A Hat under "Playing Characters" (page 187).

—Deborah

2.7

Go Through an Unusual Door

Overview

This exercise stresses the importance of building platforms and uses the frequently overlooked power that improvisers have to build the physical environment to generate story, character and comedy.

This game sets a simple challenge that allows us to study the fundamental mechanism which drives all stories, whether comedy or drama: two people interacting. However, that's not where we put our emphasis. Typically, this game would come after at least one session working on What Comes Next and another working on Word At A Time (described under "Working Together," page 118), and even though it covers much of the same ground, the same errors tend to crop up here as well. For teen groups or younger, we might teach this first and eliminate What Comes Next altogether.

Set up a few chairs to resemble a living room, or use a sofa if one is available. Ask two improvisers to play the beginning of a scene. Chances are, this will be their first time improvising in front of the rest of the group without the support of either a game or a task to achieve, such as sustaining a given status. Tell them that they are work colleagues, and one of them is taking the other back to their house for the first time, maybe because they are attending a conference together and have to catch an early train together in the morning. Usually the scene will go something like this:

> *They enter.*
> **Brian:** Come in.
> **Walter:** Thanks.
> **Brian:** Do you want a cup of tea?

> **Walter:** That'd be great.
> *Brian goes into the kitchen and comes back with the tea almost immediately.*
> **Brian:** I can't believe how late we're having to work.
> **Walter:** I know. It's so unfair. Ever since Sheila left we've been crazy busy.
> **Brian:** I heard she was fired for stealing.
> **Walter:** Really? Wow. I never trusted her.

This is standard. Occasionally they give some details about the flat, but almost invariably they go on to gossip about a colleague or a roommate who's out. This always ends up feeling unsatisfying. The audience starts to think "I wish *we'd* been there that day when the drunk brother came home with four Labradoodle puppies or when all the staff at Evergreen College went on strike because they got food poisoning in the cafeteria." But they know they never will. They'll just hear about it second-hand from people who aren't personally affected by it.[12]

When the improvisers start to look uncomfortable, like they're running out of ideas, I finish the scene. I ask the audience if it was entertaining and they are usually encouraging and say the actors did a good job but that they were waiting for something to happen. I ask the couple how it went and usually they say it was fine at first but then they started to feel a bit like nothing was happening and that they had no ideas. I ask the audience what they know about the flat the improvisers were sitting in. They usually say: "They were sitting on a sofa." "The kitchen was to the right." "Er, that's it." I tell them that the improv flat comes standard. It consists of a sofa or two chairs in the middle of the stage, sometimes a television downstage, a front door at one side of the stage (opening straight into the living room), and if you go off to the other side of the stage, possibly after a brief moment of hand waving passing for mime, you can come back straight away with two cups of tea. Teaching in other countries reveals that this is also the Global Standard Improv Flat, although in Australia we noticed that the cups of tea were replaced by tins of lager.

I point out that improvisation is the only art form which has an unlimited budget; if we tell the audience we are in a hut made of mud and straw, clinging to the side of a mountain in the Andes—and we commit to the idea—they will believe it. The same is true if we say we have a view of the Eiffel Tower or a pool table or a home cinema or a collection of Monet paintings or a time machine. Whatever we tell them, they'll believe.

I get Brian and Walter to do another scene. This time I tell them that rather than talking about more interesting things elsewhere, they should

---

[12]This kind of GOSSIP can be useful, however, if it becomes a mechanism to deliver a status transaction or something similar.

show us what's right there in front of them. It's the same setup of one work colleague bringing another back to their flat for the first time. The truth is if you do visit a friend's flat for the first time you'll probably comment on it, admire something, look at the view, etc. To help them out I give them an instruction to go through an *unusual door*. That door will inspire the flat or house they enter. Just in case they now start planning the door, I tell them to "let their hand decide." They can just reach out, have their hand close on the doorknob or some other feature, and that will "tell" them what is unusual about the door. I might also instruct them: "Whatever is in your head, keep it there. But it's not what you're going to do. At the last moment you're going to do something else and surprise yourself." (This is a technique we learned from Patti Stiles to avoid planning in any scene.) I remind the improvisers to start positive.

Brian fiddles with the lock and apologizes because the door sticks a bit. He forces it open with his shoulder. Walter looks around. "Wow, it's lovely. And so big!" There's a pause for a moment, so I say, "Walter, what's at your feet?" "Tell me about this rug," he says, "it's gorgeous." "Yes," says Brian, "it's real buffalo. I shot it myself." If they get stuck I move them on to a new object, but usually once they're on their way they start to enjoy it.

Pretty soon we have a painting of Brian's father over the fireplace, a remote-controlled lighting system and a panoramic view of St Paul's Cathedral from the balcony. Both improvisers seem effortlessly imaginative and inventive. The audience members usually say that they looked like different people from the improvisers who were running out of ideas and talking about other people in the previous scene. The improvisers themselves are often surprised by how easy it was.

Now it's time to take it up a level. Although the flat was full of *stuff*, there weren't any clear promises made because everything was disconnected. It was an imaginative, eclectic place, but it didn't give us much insight into the sort of character who might live there. Let's go back to the beginning. "What was the first offer?" I ask. "The rug?" "No, before then." "The door!" "What kind of flat is suggested by a door that has a fiddly lock and that sticks when you open it?" "Run-down," "Falling apart," "Dilapidated." But when the actors were inside, that idea was abandoned, and each offer seemed unrelated to the last.

EVERYTHING FOR A REASON

Another important principle is developing here: The audience assumes that *everything you do you do for a reason*. This is because they are used to watching premeditated art forms where this is (or should be!) the case. As an example of this, consider that in real life speech errors are common. In plays and films they are vanishingly rare, since any misspeaking would be assumed by the audience to be very significant. Likewise, people frequently cough and sneeze in life, but in stories it almost always presages a fatal dose of consumption or plague, or gives away the presence of someone who is trying to hide.

When Brian fiddles with the lock and the door sticks, the audience assumes that this is a necessary element of the story—which indeed it would be, if the promise were kept and the flat revealed to be equally in a state of disrepair. When the flat is revealed in fact to be rather grand, they assume that *this contradiction* has been introduced for a reason. When no reason is forthcoming, the audience starts to lose faith in the narrative abilities of the players, and everything becomes much harder. Now, *we* know that Brian had no grand plan in mind when he made the door stick—it was just an arbitrary detail. But if Walter assumes that there was a reason, he will naturally develop the idea. And indeed, Brian should assume that his subconscious has a reason, too. In improvisation, it's desirable for reasons to follow actions, for causes to follow effects (otherwise improvisers would always be planning), but causes must eventually be established or the logic of the story will fall apart completely. For more on this, see Master/Servant Dubbing (page 128).

Now we ask another pair to come up and have a go at the game. They will probably have been planning something from their seats, so I remind them to let the hand decide. Veena puts her hand out and places her palm against a mime panel, and the "door" beeps and swishes open. Her scene partner Danny reacts with surprise and admiration. This time, as they explore the flat, they apply the *theme* of push-button technology. The television glides out of the wall. The couch reclines at the touch of a keypad. The lights go on and off by voice command. This is more satisfying for the audience, and it is also *easier* to do for the actors. One offer inspires the next.

Soon, without any effort on the part of the improvisers, promises are made which the audience wants to see fulfilled. Danny asks Veena how she can afford all this stuff when they're on the same wage. She says she builds it herself. He asks how she has time, and she admits she has built the robots who build the technology. She asks if he wants to see the robot room. Of course he does. She takes him into an underground factory where hundreds of robots are making state-of-the-art equipment. Some of them are making more robots. The improvisers build this picture together, one offer at a time. (I might have to encourage other improvisers to jump up and be the robots.) Danny is a little amazed and unnerved by all this. He asks why she needs so many robots and Veena replies that she's making an army. Danny says he needs to leave.

This is a break in the routine, so I usually stop the scene here and ask the audience what promises have been made and what they guess will happen. The audience can't wait to guess: "He's not going to get out!" "The army is going to turn on him!" "He's going to be turned into one of her robots!" I ask them what they know about the front door if he tries to escape. They say, "It only opens with her palm print so it won't respond to his! He's trapped!" I ask how other things from the platform could be reincorporated if he was trying to escape and they say, "He can plunge her into the dark with the voice control lights," or "He can trip her up by pushing the button on the reclining sofa." Suddenly anything reincorporated seems purposeful. The improvisers seem so inspired and talented. It all seems easy. The story is telling them, and every little thing they put in their platform will later on become a good idea when they need it. (I don't always get this far; just a good platform is far enough, but it's nice to see a couple that start to turn into stories so the students can feel how easy it is and how much they, as audience members, want promises fulfilled.)

Everyone seems to have fun playing this game, and the scenes are usually very funny. I get everyone in the group to play it, and every scene is different. Once we've had a few good scenes, sometimes people feel they have to compete and that the pressure's on. Usually that means they'll plan a submarine or something specific and come in and drive through three or four ideas quickly, and it won't have that feeling of inventiveness. It will usually not be very entertaining either, so I stop it and say that it doesn't have to be a "good house," which takes the pressure off.

Another thing to watch out for when teaching this is that improvisers will often disconnect themselves from the flat. The flat is really only interesting so long as it enlightens us to Veena's character. If Veena says "This was all here when I moved in," or "It's my uncle's apartment," then why do we care that it's high tech? They do it to stay safe. If their scene partner finds a blowup doll, then it's not theirs. They don't have to own it or even know about it. Interestingly, improvisers always refer to uncles and cousins and distant relatives in these circumstances. They never say that it's their dad's apartment. That's because their dad reflects on them and their upbringing in a way that their cousin doesn't. Make them own or rent the flat and have decorated it themselves, otherwise it won't feed the scene and they'll stay safe.

MAKING ASSUMPTIONS

It's acceptable to make a BLIND OFFER, introducing a new object by saying something like "Wow, this looks like it's a hundred years old," or "I've never seen a couch like that," provided it is understood that a blind offer is an *invitation to define*. The improviser making the blind offer, which leaves certain information conspicuously unsaid, *must* be willing to do their own defining if their partner does not. If this is not understood, then instead of being an excellent way of sharing the fun of defining the world and for getting over the need to have a "good idea" prepared and ready to go, blind offers can become a pretext for WIMPING. More experienced improviser can make open-ended blind offers, trusting that one or another of them will supply the necessary definitions before it becomes a wimp.

Thus, MAKING ASSUMPTIONS needs to be taught as a skill at the same time as blind offers, so that improvisers are happy to contribute ideas as they are needed. You can introduce this skill by encouraging the improvisers to fill in a more detailed back-story for themselves. Hopefully, we get exchanges like this, enabling the improvisers to make further discoveries quickly:

> **Paul:** Hey, thanks for putting me up for the night.
> **Dan:** No, problem. It's cool that I get to help you out for a change.

This has led some improv coaches to the conclusion that you should *always* know the other person in a scene (so no scenes about job interviews, first dates, weird strangers and so on, but lots of opportunities for that dreary improv cliché "Didn't we go to school together?"). Quite apart from automatically doubting the veracity of sentences which include the words "always" or "never"—especially where a subtle art form like improvised storytelling is concerned—we're entirely unconvinced that this strategy achieves what is claimed for it. Yes, exposition sucks, but characters that know each other are more likely to make their dialogue sound awkwardly expository precisely *because* they already know so much about each other.

> **Paul:** I'm really glad to see you, brother of mine, especially after Dad cut you out of the will like that.
> **Dan:** That's okay, Steve. I'm just glad I've still kept my hair, and I'm not bald like you are.

Strangers have a legitimate reason for asking questions and getting personal answers, which obviates the problem of how to deliver this kind of information naturally and elegantly. However, MAKING ASSUMPTIONS about the other character is the key strategy, whether you choose to have a prior relationship with them or not.

Using this terminology often makes the task seem easier and makes the exchange of information between improvisers seem more natural, but make no mistake, it is essential that they learn the skill of being able to happily define the world which they are inhabiting. The downside of an art form with no budget and no sets is that everything which exists will have to be created out of the players' own imaginations as the audience watches. Improvisers who reject obvious ideas or who claim that they "can't think of anything" (by which they generally mean that they can't think of anything "good enough") will attempt to push a story forward through a fog of vague non-definitions. The reason this game produces such good work so early on is that it's immediately obvious when one or other player "refuses the jump" which makes it easy for the coach (or the other player) to correct the error.

So—to be clear—the audience doesn't much care who does the defining, as long as it makes some kind of sense (the owner of the flat is much more likely to know the provenance of the object in question, but that doesn't stop the other improviser from describing it). And, if they're paying any kind of attention to the process, they will enjoy seeing the ball passed back and forth, so when I'm teaching I will make sure that neither is "carrying" the other and prompt offers like "Let me show you this lamp," or I'll say, "Notice something about the rug." And I'm very happy for either player, but especially the new visitor, to ask questions. This is an excellent way of prompting information which needs to be supplied, but which wouldn't be credible coming from someone who hadn't seen the flat before.

But take care that this isn't used as cover for WIMPING. That doesn't just signal that one player is in a BAD STATE; it can totally wreck the logic of the scene. If I produce a mime object and don't myself define what it is, then I present my stage partner with a problem to solve—but not a very difficult one. Really, it's just a version of Pointing at Things and Saying What They Are Not. Anything which roughly fits the shape I'm making with my hands will probably do. Or even if it doesn't fit the shape I'm making with my hands, we can probably yes-and our way out of it.

> **Sofie:** Here, I got you this.
> **Chris:** Er, an elephant?
> **Sofie:** That's right! Well, it's a paperweight, but in the shape of an elephant.
> **Chris:** Because I miss Nairobi so much?
> **Sofie:** Of course.

"An apple" would probably have made Sofie's life easier, but no real harm has been done, and if Chris doesn't define the object, then Sofie understands that it's now up to her to name it.

> **Sofie:** Here, I got you this.
> **Chris:** Oh you shouldn't have.
> **Sofie:** It's just an apple. I know how hungry you get when you work these late shifts.

But, what if Chris, in a really bad state, stares panicked at Sofie's empty hands and asks "What is it?" Hasn't he just tossed the ball back to his scene partner? No. The problem he is presenting Sofie with is a far more complicated one. The puzzle he had to solve is, "What object fits this shape?" which has dozens of answers (a cricket ball, a cream bun, a pet mouse, a hair scrunchy, a hand grenade—it's almost impossible to be wrong). But the new puzzle which Chris gives to Sofie is, "What object fits this shape *which you couldn't tell what it was just by looking at it?*" If Chris asks, "What is it?" and Sofie responds, "It's an apple," the audience will be thinking, "Couldn't you see it was an apple? What's going on?" and the reality of the scene will collapse.

STRATEGIES FOR BREAKING THE ROUTINE

We wouldn't generally provide this list for students, but as we do multiple iterations of this exercise, it's useful to be able to break the routine in different ways. Sometimes the students will break routines without trying, sometimes you'll have to encourage them to do so. Having this list in the back of your mind may help you to coach them through the process.

Up the Absurdity Curve

Sometimes students will find a sequence which they can accelerate. Play even a few iterations of this game and before long, one student will open a door with dozens of locks on it. This is a bit of an improv cliché, but maybe it's something that every group has to discover and then discard. They may take the general theme of "security conscious" or "bad neighborhood" from this, or they may be more literal and put dozens of locks on *everything*. "Want a drink? Hang on, I'll open the fridge…" (seven locks later) "Beer? Hang on I'll open it…" As the number of locks increases and the absurdity of their placing builds, the audience laughs more and more, and they may laugh so much you can just end the scene (chastity belt?). Compare this to Finding The Game (page 228).

The absurdity curve can also be used to check improvisers who want to be very bizarre right away. Invite someone into your home and say, "Come in, sit down, oops, mind the French Revolution Fully Working Guillotine!" and you've broken the routine instantly, have a ton of justification to do and the scene may never recover. Instead, start by saying "I've always been interested in the French Revolution." Then later, point out "That's a map which, it's said, belonged to the Scarlet Pimpernel himself." After that: "This is a cloak worn by a doomed aristocrat. In fact, here's a death certificate. Would you like to see the basement?" Now, you've *promised* a guillotine, or something like it, and the audience will be delighted when you deliver.

One very important idea here is that an absurd offer is really only as absurd as the reaction it generates. If you (unwisely) show off your fully functional guillotine almost as soon as you cross the threshold, this is clearly an attempt to break the routine. But when your partner responds with "Oh, yeah cool. Is it the 9000 model? I just got the 9080, with optional head basket," and refuses to be affected, then this is still platform. Now the story takes place in a world where having a working guillotine in your living room is normal. This isn't forbidden, but it makes life a great deal harder, since in order to break the routine you now need to have a *more interesting* idea than the guillotine! A much better strategy is to have one ALICE and one Mad Hatter.

BEING ALICE—playing a sane person in an insane world—generates story much faster than just having a gang of crazy people running around. Improvisers who always want to be the funny one need to recognize that they will make their partner funnier, and the show funnier, by BEING ALICE, rather than trying to out-do the Mad Hatter.

Obsess on One Object

Beginners will also sometimes need to be coaxed away from objects they discover early on, because as you provide more information about each new thing, the audience gets more and more interested. Get them too interested in any one thing and they won't like it when you move on to something else. You will have broken the routine early, or at least made it clear what the story is about, and you'll discover later that you don't have enough material to reincorporate. However, if you and your partner have built a nice, coherent environment and you think the time is right to break the routine, just keep YES ANDing one object. Eventually, you'll discover something you can use to break the routine.

Add an Object That Doesn't Fit

In the first example of this game, the buffalo skin rug, the door in a state of disrepair and the remote controlled lighting all seemed to belong to different flats. However if you add *one* object that doesn't fit, *after* the theme has been established, its presence will likely break the routine. For example, Geoff's apartment is a vile, squalid pit. He and Stan have to pick their way through the debris to walk around. Stan discovers week-old pizza under the cushion. A broken floorboard is nearly life-threatening (they're on the seventh floor). However, the TV (revealed behind a curry-stained panel) is a gleaming 60-inch behemoth. Now Geoff is not just a scummy student-type, he lives in reverential awe of his TV screen, his devotion to it leaving no time to cook, clean or even sleep.

Have a Strong Reaction

This is really how to break all routines, all the time. If Stan has seen Geoff's flat before and knows just what to expect when the TV is revealed, there is no break in the routine. And the same is true of all the other examples. When one character is emotionally affected by the other, we get the sensation that "something has happened." Refusal to be changed is a form of BLOCKING. So if, instead of taking it all in his stride, Stan is progressively more revolted by Geoff's squalor, maybe things will reach a crisis and the arbitrary giant

TV won't be needed. Perhaps Stan will refuse to stay the night as agreed and Geoff can then become offended, or remorseful or angry, and you'll have a great scene going. The audience is delighted not just by the way the characters affect each other, but also by the richness of the context and the way in which they have been able to share in the improvisers' process of discovery.

As well as reinforcing the other strategies, having a strong reaction can be used in isolation. This is another form of BLIND OFFER. Just decide that the next thing you see will be something shocking (or surprising or revolting or exciting—anything "big"). Glance behind the sofa, open a cupboard, pick a book off the shelf and cry out in alarm "Oh my god!" Between you and your partner, you should be able to YES AND your way to a definition. "Something's moving." "That's probably Simon." "Simon!?" "My pet snake." It is now vitally important that the "guest" is afflicted with a crippling fear of snakes!

This brings up another issue which will be discussed at more length under "Being Changed" (page 137), but for now, notice that not only can a break in the routine be killed if you refuse to be affected, and not only can a break in the routine be contrived by *deciding* to be affected, but both improvisers have then to capitalize on this discovery. If your scene partner has been nice enough to show you how to hurt them (by being afraid of snakes, for example) then you *must* be sadistic enough to take advantage of this. There *must* be a whole "snake room" next door, or you should start shedding your skin and hissing. Your partner of course must equally be masochistic enough to submit to the suffering and secretly relish it!

Reincorporation

Continuing the previous scenario, if the "guest" whips out a gun at this point and shoots the snake through the head, we still hope that the owner will be changed by this. If you say "Oh well, I can get another at the pet store tomorrow. Beer?" you've got nothing. What the audience is hoping for is remorse, guilt, grief and so on (all of which can be very funny if the absurdity of cradling a dead snake in one's arms is kept at the forefront). But the gun seems arbitrary and promotes a whole host of other questions (unless the characters have been previously identified as gun enthusiasts or Secret Service agents). The audience's attention is torn between the emotional content of the story and the need to justify the plot choices. However, items reincorporated seldom need any additional justification. If the guest beats the snake to death with the heavy doorstop established earlier, the audience will love it. "Oh, so *that* was the point of the doorstop," they think. The truth is more subtle. Fill the environment with arbitrary things at the beginning of the scene and at the end of the scene, they magically turn into good ideas, and all you have to do is remember them and pick them up.

VARIATIONS

This exercise is a microcosm of what happens in pretty much any two-person improv scene (and most stories are fundamentally about two people, at least at any given moment). Two characters meet, we sketch in their relationship and the environment, we discover why today is different from any other day and we watch one or both of them suffer as a result. Depending on the group, it can be helpful to broaden the parameters as we go on. As mentioned, we may make the improvisers decide for themselves what the nature of their relationship is—and they may balk at this initially. As ever, the audience is often several steps ahead of the improvisers and will have spotted the little cues that let them know how intimate or distant these two people are, cues that the improvisers will be entirely oblivious to. Keep repeating: if you define quickly enough *you can't be wrong*. Put off the definition and you may end up in a situation where no object exists which fits all the vague criteria established for it.

As the improvisers' confidence grows, you may like to play essentially the same game in other situations. Coax them to define their relationship and the space they are in to create a platform, and trust that an opportunity to break the routine will present itself or can be contrived. See the Shoe Shop game on page 190 for another example.

THE CJ SWEEP

One technique for getting students to imagine their environments more, so they won't be stuck in a void with just a couple of chairs, is called the CJ SWEEP, after long-standing member of The Spontaneity Shop performing company, Chris Harvey John. We noticed that Chris had a richer visual world than the rest of us. He always saw and created (usually through mime) an extraordinary environment, which would feed any scene he was in. We realized that instead of inventing stuff, he would look around and "see" what was there. If he walked onto the (empty) stage in a scene set in an office, he would look around and see an expensive desk, a black leather couch and a view of Manhattan through big windows—or a dingy cluttered desk with a slow ceiling fan and an old photocopier. If another improviser came in and endowed the office as being tiny and shabby or not an office at all but a waiting room, Chris would simply sweep his eyes around the room and see what was there now.

Try it now. Decide you're in a ballroom. Look around. What's there? Is it empty or full of dancing couples? What color are the walls? Are you in the center of the room or hiding behind a curtain? If you're behind a curtain, is it heavy red velvet or white chiffon? All of these things can give your scene huge imaginative scope. Even if the audience never sees or hears about most of these things, knowing they are there will inspire you. You'll look and act like you're really there. When you're stuck for an idea you can just look around the space: "Can I put some music on?" "The kettle's boiling." "Wow, an indoor fountain!"

When we've taught this technique, it seems to come easily to most people, but here are some exercises which are fun to do and can make a workshop really memorable and useful. Divide the group into pairs and have one person shut their eyes and the other ask them questions. "Where are you?" "In a French café." "How big is it?" "About ten small tables." "What can you smell?" "French coffee." "What's on the counter?" "An old-fashioned cash register." The questions are better if they are open questions that make assumptions—"What can you smell?" rather than "Can you smell anything?"

Next, get a student up in front of the group and get them to enter a space onstage. Side-coach questions in a similar fashion. When they've established a space, let them play a scene in it, using as many things in the environment as facilitate the scene. Over time, this process of imagining the space around you and continuing to enrich it becomes ingrained.

TILTING

One technique for creating stories by breaking routines, which Keith writes about extensively in *Impro for Storytellers*, is that of TILTING. The principle is that improvisers sustain a normality—a PLATFORM—for some time before introducing one idea which, while it could not have been predicted from the platform, does not contradict it either, and which is designed to immediately and massively change the other character. For example: two strangers meet on a park bench. They share sandwiches, feed the birds, discuss how much the park has changed in recent years, watch a small boy playing football, etc. Then one says to the other "Yes, this was my favorite place to come when I was still alive." The tilt can be wrecked if the other party JOINS ("It's a shame we're both dead isn't it?") since the *point* of the offer is to massively change the other person.

And this doesn't fly in the face of BEING OBVIOUS either. It's not that audiences hate to be surprised, it's that surprising them for the sake of it is often confusing, and therefore becomes boring. Refusing to give them what you've promised for the sake of being original is crazy, but just as crazy is to pass up great offers because they don't slavishly obey the rule "Thou shalt always be obvious." Saying "This was my favorite place to come when I was still alive," doesn't deny the audience anything it has been promised, and it will pay off the latent promise that one of these people will be changed by the interaction (or at least it should).

When BEING ORIGINAL is a problem, it's usually because an improviser has made a low stakes, trivial, random offer which hasn't been reacted to by the other player. If you are in a pet store, the audience will expect you to come in and ask for a pet, or pet-related products. They will not expect the pet store owner to say, "We don't have any dogs but we've got ice cream." This is *both* trivial *and* confusing for the audience. They've never been to a pet store that sells ice cream, so it looks like the improvisers are panicking and denying their environment to try and get a laugh.

If the second improviser playing the customer goes along with it—"Great! I'll have pistachio."—the audience will not relate to them. If they were in a pet store and were offered ice cream, they'd be surprised and they'd question it. However if the scene is set in a pet store and the owner offers to perform an exorcism for the customer, or if the pet store turns out to be a front for a hit-man operation, then the audience—although not having anticipated this development—will accept it and be interested, especially if the improviser playing the customer is affected or changed in some way. This is because audiences come to a theatre *expecting* drama, so a high stakes offer that's out of the ordinary and which receives a truthful, emotional reaction plays very differently from a low stakes, out of the ordinary offer that affects nobody.

Tilts can also be useful to teach PLAYING A RESISTANCE. If the other improviser says: "When you were still alive? Don't be ridiculous," that isn't a block. It's a truthful reaction. Now the audience will have the fun of watching them become convinced.

But for all their virtues, Keith quickly discovered that the pattern of "build a platform, add a tilt" got old after a few repetitions. The same structure served up again and again will always get tiresome eventually, and good improv troupes and directors look for ways to provide variety over the course of an evening. Plus, the ideal tilt scene has elements of the platform reincorporated to justify the tilt or achieve a resolution (or both), but time and again we've seen the tilt line hijack the scene, rendering the platform irrelevant. And this is all without mentioning the problems caused by the list of tilts given in Keith's newsletter and also in *Impro for Storytellers*. Throwing in a "standard" tilt is a great way to teach beginners the values of being affected and playing a resistance, and is very useful for Gorilla Theatre and Micetro Impro directors, but in our opinion, tilts are fundamentally training wheels for beginners. More experienced improvisers should look within the scene and discover offers which will deliver equally profound reactions—the right trouble for the right hero. Or let the reaction come first (see "Jumping and Justifying").

WHAT'S IN A NAME?

Tom: Audiences love details, but some details are more easily remembered than others. Details which have little bearing on the plot are easily forgotten, especially by improvisers in the heat of the moment. Particularly when people are starting to improvise, I'd much rather they called each other by their real names, instead of having to stop and think up a name which they (and the other improvisers) are only going to forget a minute later. Obviously, I don't object to improvisers coming up with names for other characters (or their own character), and in a show it would certainly be advisable. But I'd never side-coach a beginner, or even an intermediate player, to take back the real name that they'd just used and make up a new one instead. There will be plenty of time for that once they can get through a three-minute scene without panicking, trivializing, being stupid or being boring.

Deborah: I encourage students to make up names. Using their real names restricts them to thinking like themselves. After all, what Neil the accountant would do is very different from what Igor, Pierre or River would do, and even just calling Neil "Tony" will give him more permission to seduce you or shout at you. In real life, Neil is married and gentle. Tony can be an obnoxious guy who fancies himself a matinee idol. Also I've seen wonderful scenes where a forgotten name has generated plot—"You just called me Sandra. Are you having an affair?" (This depends on the improviser taking it as a serious offer, not using it as a gag to point out their scene partner's mistake to the audience.) It's true that the audience will obsess for a moment if you're called Chris at the beginning of the scene and Kelly at the end and no one onstage picks up on it, but it will happen from time to time and in my experience, if the scene's full of life and heart then the audience will forgive and forget very quickly. When we did TellTales, an improvised play in monologues, we put an extra improviser in the wings with a whiteboard who wrote up the names (and other details) so this wouldn't happen. But as we got more used to it, we found the format itself trained us to listen and care about the characters, so after a while we didn't need the whiteboard.

Tom: Actually, at a recent show, I saw one very good reason to invent new names for each other. A fairly inexperienced group was playing the Standing Wave game where the actors keep "tagging-out" each other, so the same character is played by different actors as time goes on. On this occasion, one actor kept calling the other character by the name of the current actor, spoiling the illusion that she was interacting with the same person throughout the scene. Also, If you have given a character a new name, both you and the other improvisers should try repeating the name a few times as this will help it to stick. With more experienced improvisers, I would also give the advice to try and give other characters exotic names. It's pretty easy to get confused about who was Phil, who was Paul and who was Peter. If instead the characters are called Egbert, Montague and Crazy Abe, you'll get much less onstage amnesia.

2.8

Working Together

Overview

What most drama teachers think improv is all about—and a vital skill—but it needs to be taught hand-in-hand with storytelling, or improvisers will accept even the most ludicrous offer in order to be seen as someone who is "good to work with."

In bad theatre, self-absorbed actors are stuck within their own "bubble," desperately concerned to show how much work they've put into their "motivation" and their "character." In bad relationships of all kinds—business, creative, personal—people exist in their own space and expend a great deal of energy insulating themselves from other people's ideas and insights. In bad improv, players alternate between "shining" and "outwitting," and a poisonous competition for superiority dominates the stage.

Learning to work together means happily giving up the initiative and either looking to your partner for guidance or trusting that an idea will emerge from "nowhere." Many people will resist this—it feels unsettling to take off so much of your social "armor"—but it's essential to get the best out of your partner, to create a happy atmosphere on the stage and to keep the audience engrossed in the process of creation.

One way to introduce the concept is to get everyone to find a partner and play Tug of War with a mime rope.[13] Have people get into pairs, with

---

[13]We first saw this at the Loose Moose Summer School, and I don't think we would have believed this outcome if we hadn't witnessed it ourselves (and done it ourselves, too!).

plenty of space around them, and to each pick up one end of the mime rope. Call "One, two, three, go!" and let the pairs compete for twenty seconds or so.

In all probability, most pairs will struggle and strain, the rope will stretch (which spoils the illusion), but nobody will win because nobody will want to lose. Point this out and remind them "It's not a real test of strength if there isn't a rope." Chances are everyone will laugh as they realize what has happened.

The process of learning to improvise involves learning to "turn off" a lot of instinctive behavior—behavior which has proven to be very useful in achieving most people's top priority: maintaining a feeling of comfort and safety. The work on status confronts some aspects of this, but this section on working together does so even more profoundly and directly.

PLAYING TO THE DEATH

Some people take this competitive nature to extremes. I once brought home a chess set from a holiday and my then-roommate and I played a game of chess, which I won. Neither of us are particularly accomplished chess players, but we both have quite a high opinion of our general intelligence, and my friend was most aggrieved to have lost. His reaction was to insist that we play at least one game every single night from then on, during which time he kept a running tally—and abruptly halted the contest as soon as he was one game ahead. That was over twenty years ago and we have not played a single game of chess together since.

—*Tom*

Playing the Mime Tug of War game feels very much like a real competition (even though with no rope it can't possibly be a test of anything—except your good nature) and so the need to win, the need to be in control, the need to be successful, all kick in and the game goes on forever.

Here, however, the loss of control is pure illusion. In order to bring the game to a close, somebody must choose to lose, and whoever does that seizes the initiative. Stress to the group that you want the illusion to look good. The rope should *not* stretch; it isn't made of rubber. But this time, instead of trying their hardest to win, players should look into their partners' eyes and try to give them what they want. Do they want to win or do they want to lose? Give the group three or four goes so that everybody wins and everybody loses. Barking "Give in!" at pairs who continue tugging miserably away at nothing while the rest of the group is falling down and giggling can be very effective.

Encourage the group to remember this image. The story may require someone to be the loser, and that person may be you. Don't tug away at empty air when the audience wants to see you vanquished! The actor playing Hamlet has to choose to die. It's not a weakness; it serves the story. The actor or director who changes the ending so that Hamlet "wins," lives and becomes King of Denmark misses the point, and so does the improviser who must "win," live and triumph in every scene.

When improvisers collaborate to build a satisfying story in which a hero is getting into trouble, sometimes there will be two characters with opposing goals. Improvisers will often confuse their character straining to achieve their goal with making strong story choices. A NEGOTIATION will frequently be very unsatisfying if it is sustained for more than about a minute, since it will often degenerate into an endless restatement of each character's point of view, with no further development. Skilled improvisers know how to break the deadlock and discover what comes next. Often this can be done by abandoning the goal—although this must then be justified. See Twitching, Topping and Paperflicking (page 171) and Shoe Shops (page 189) for much more on this.

WORD AT A TIME

Like What Comes Next, this is a fundamental game and one which improvisers who are trying to improve their technique should return to often. Unlike What Comes Next, progress will often be less swift early on, and care is needed to make sure that new improvisers don't become discouraged. If you stick with it, no game will teach you more. As a rapid, instinctive, seat-of-the-pants game, it is also a good counterpoint to the thoughtful, theoretical What Comes Next, but both are story games. Word At A Time is also greatly enjoyed by audiences, if done well—or at least joyously.

First, a couple of caveats. The mechanism of speaking one word each at a time, while at the heart of the game, is not the only important element. In our preferred version, two people collaborate to create one character who narrates the events that happen to them. However, it is far more common to see this mechanism used for (yet another) "expert" scene. In this version, often called Three Headed Expert, three people sit down in a row and answer questions. This "expert" is created by having the three people speak one word each at a time, while the questions are put to them by a host who is under no such restriction. Let's look at what is lost in this version.

Physicality: The original Word At A Time is a physical game. Three Headed Expert is just talking heads, which makes for a slower game as well as a less visually interesting one.

Risk: Since the host can always make sense of pretty much anything the expert says, the risk of the scene degenerating into nonsense is much reduced. But risk is an essential point of the game (and a big part of inviting an audience to watch you improvise). Also, the expert will talk for around half the time, and because three people speaking one word each at a time speak more slowly, the expert will probably say about half as much as the host in the same time. So three-quarters of what is said isn't dependent on the game at all!

Variety: All of these Three Headed Expert scenes will resemble each other, whereas almost any story can be told one word each at a time—and if you're bored of that, you can have two or more Word At A Time characters interacting with each other, or use a genre.

State: Because this version of the game is fundamentally limited, players are in a much worse state. The expert *has* to say funny things or the game is of no interest whatsoever, so any attempt to work together and be obvious goes out the window as the three players desperately try to make *their* word be the funny one.

The "Arms" game has been castrated in much the same way. For more— *much* more—on why games exist and why good games are in short supply, see "Playing Games" on page 254.

Teaching the Game

Get the whole group to stand in a circle, and announce that you will attempt to create a new proverb or wise saying by contributing one word each at a time, proceeding around the circle. You can either dictate that the saying is composed of exactly one word from each person in the circle (if you have a suitably sized group), or just let them end when they sound like they've ended. In either case, a particularly wise saying can be celebrated by a thoughtful "*ahh…*" sound from the group, maybe accompanied by some chin-stroking.

Some people will contribute the word that naturally comes next without any apparent fuss. Others will panic and seem unable to come up with anything. Still others will wreck the sense in order to seem "clever," but usually the group as a whole will start to see that saying the next obvious word is all that is important.

When you have done half a dozen proverbs and/or your sentences are generally making grammatical sense, you can expand the scope of the game to telling stories. Suggest that the first story begins "Once" "Upon" "A" "Time," and stress the importance of ending one sentence and beginning a new one, otherwise groups tend to get lost in endless clauses and sub-clauses. Also point out that the game has two possible endings: one in which the story reaches a profound and satisfying conclusion and the group feels tremendously pleased and proud; and another in which the story gradually wanders into nonsense. Should the latter happen (and it's far more likely), tell the group to just kill the story and start again.[14]

This is an excellent time to introduce the idea that improvisers are creating "disposable theatre." Good improvisers are risk-takers, but not all risks will pay off. There will be work that you do in pairs in a workshop which will make you think "I wish an audience of a thousand had seen me do that!" On the flip side, there will be work you do in front of an audience which will make you think, "I wish no one in the world had seen me do that." But you don't get to choose. You have to treat the failures and the successes with equanimity. The instinct to kill a story that isn't working and try again is a good one, especially, but not only, in a workshop. The need to be successful will prevent many students from doing this, but what's so "successful" about flogging away at a story that stopped making sense about two minutes ago? What's most important is that the groups are enjoying the process.

This presentation has only limited dramatic potential, so let's now present the game as it is usually played.

> *We are now going to play the game just in pairs. You might think this will be harder, because you will have more responsibility for the story, but actually it is often easier. With ten minds on the job, your story can end up being pulled in ten different directions. In this version, you only have to worry about you and your partner.*
>
> *We can also make it a bit more theatrical with just two people. Stand near your partner, with your body turned somewhat toward them. Check in with the audience from time to time, but give your partner most of your attention. Tell your story about you, have it happen to you right now and act it out.*

A few quick technical details.

Pronouns: We have no strong views about whether people refer to themselves as "I" or "we," but it must be clear that everything that happens in the story happens to both players. One player may try to feed their partner to the monster in order to escape, for example, but since you never know which of you will get to say the pronoun, this will just garble the sentence. You are one person, regardless of which pronoun you use to refer to yourself.

Tense: The present tense makes the most sense, and it is especially useful in reminding the players to act out what is happening. "I *am* walking

---

[14]You can usefully get students to celebrate stories which lurch unhappily off the rails by having one or more players joyfully cry "Again!" while flinging both arms in the air, yet another contribution from Keith Johnstone.

through the *forest* when *I* hear *my* mother *calling* me…" However, since most stories are written in the past tense, we don't object too much to an active past tense. "*I* walked *through* the *forest* then *I* heard *my* mother…" Digressions about what *might* happen in the far future or what *may* have happened in the distant past should be avoided.

Act it out: Players should act out *their* role. They are the hero. Also, they should mirror each other's physicality, with their bodies turned toward each other. So the person standing on the left brandishes a sword with their left (outside) hand, and the person on the right mirrors them. (If they use their inside hands, they will create a physical barrier between themselves.)

Voice: Some players keep getting locked into a dialogue with a nonexistent other. This is very limiting and needs to be nipped in the bud early, and a narrative voice substituted instead. "*Shall* we *go* and *look* for…" is not the voice of a narrator and this approach limits what can be described. "*We* are *looking* for…" is much better and more flexible.

The Proto-Story

Get the whole group into pairs and have them act out and tell this story, in their own words and speaking one word each at a time. "You go into a forest. You meet a monster. You run away. The end." Have them do it two or three times with different partners just to get the hang of the procedure. You are looking for pace, physicality and gusto! This is a big, energetic game, and BEING GOOD TO WORK WITH means pumping enthusiasm and energy out. If you play the game feebly, you send a signal to your partner that says: "Oh dear, this isn't very good," as a result of which your partner will also rapidly become discouraged. Played with enthusiasm, the game becomes much easier and your partner is reassured.

Actions should be acted out together, and as their skill with building up sentences one word at a time improves, you can encourage players to make the actions bigger, and you can emphasize mirroring each other precisely. Do take care that the physicality isn't leading the dialogue—you can't mime the word you want your partner to say next! As a teacher, try to avoid pointing out problems like this while the game is in progress as it will ruin the flow. Save it for the end.

Once the group has begun to get bored of the proto-story, move them on to phase two: "Go into a forest. Meet a Monster. Do something *other* than run away from it." Let the group play this out for a few minutes, then stop and ask each pair in turn what kind of interaction they had. The results may surprise you. Pair after pair will likely tell you that they cuddled the monster, had tea with it, danced with it and so on. Maybe one pair in ten will have engaged in some kind of fight with the monster, and one pair in twenty will have killed it. No one will have been seriously injured.

Human beings come pre-equipped with a range of defensive instincts which will often be the exact opposite of whatever is required of them as improvisers. Asked to play two roommates, the audience will like them more and they will find it easier to build a platform if they are positive. But in fact, you'll find that they start low-energy and miserable, and can't wait to have an argument over some trivial thing or other. Given a monster to fight, which every child realizes must be a terrible threat, they find a way to drain the story of all interest by having the monster be cuddly and cute. The audience assumes that everything you do you do for a reason. The reason you meet a monster in the forest is not to cuddle it!

What's going on here? Well, it seems as if improvisers *treat imaginary dangers as real*. They won't go down to the cellar to investigate the strange scraping noise in real life and so they won't do it on the stage either, even though by refusing to confront the imaginary danger, they face the completely real danger of being dull while an impatient audience watches them. On the rare occasions that the monster does attack them, it will almost always go for an extremity—a toe or a finger. Bolder, more experienced, improvisers will have the monster slash open their abdomen, and keep fighting while holding their guts in with their free hand.

Get everyone to play the game again—go into a forest, meet a monster and this time *kill it or be killed by it*. Neither is necessarily the end of the story! Kill the monster and its hundreds of friends may come pouring out of the forest, desperate for revenge. Or discover that its blood is infecting you and turning you into a monster. Or meet a scientist who tells you it's an endangered species. Be killed by the monster and emerge from the battle simulator to face the wrath of your captain. Or wake up in heaven to discover it's run by monsters. (See page 200 for another version of this story.)

The difference in energy in the room is often extraordinary as pairs happily fall to the floor screaming in mock-pain or plunge imaginary swords into the monster's eye. Very often, the energy and momentum of the story obscures or even entirely removes any grammatical stumbles, even with improvisers for whom English is not their first language.

Beyond the Proto-Story

One of the virtues of Word at a Time is that it's a *story* game, with all the limitless possibilities that implies. Once players have exhausted the possibilities of the proto-story, get them telling a wider range of stories. Initially, just coach the *form*. Are they maintaining a brisk rhythm and are they acting the story out? Are they using intonation to tell their partner where they think they are in the sentence? Are they playing the game with enthusiasm? (Audiences would far rather watch this game—or any game—played rather incompetently by enthusiastic, happy improvisers than played technically well by restrained, stiff improvisers who are TRYING THEIR HARDEST.)

Once the challenge of the form recedes, start coaching the stories themselves. Often, Word At A Time sentences begin with a verb, and this is a very useful way to start subsequent sentences too because it gives you something to do right away: "*Leaping* over *the* body *of* my *opponent*..." But you must work your way around to the pronoun "...*I* sheathe *my* sword *with* a *flourish*." "Suddenly" is a useful word with which to start a new sentence, if the story lacks interest. When coaching, prompting the players to start their next sentence with "Suddenly..." will often kick-start a story that isn't going anywhere.

Another way to begin the story is to start with the phrase "*I* am *a*..." and then say what you are. Typically, this will lead in to a number of generic sentences describing what you do every day. This is good platform-building. To break the routine, begin a sentence with "Today..." Beginners will sometimes want to be inanimate objects, but "I am a surgeon" or "I am a wolf" both have many more possibilities than "I am a pencil." Encourage them to be a profession or an animal.

You can also try setting exciting tasks for the heroes of Word At A Time stories to complete. Get one pair to rob a bank, get another pair to jump out of an airplane. With luck, the excitement of the situation will spill over into the enthusiasm of the performance, and people will stop trying to be clever. People know there needs to be a shoot-out in a western or violence in a bank robbery. The more we convince new improvisers to act out the robbery or cowboy scene like they did when they were kids (using accents, big physicality and really imagining the bad guys) the more they automatically include drama and forget to keep themselves safe. They understand the conventions of the genre and it liberates them, freeing them to plunge joyously into dangerous situations.

You can also try something like a Jane Austen-style Word At A Time. The improvisers will understand that this is not an area for violence and large physicality, but instead an opportunity for subtle movements and strength of feeling hidden beneath polite dialogue. The genre will still impose an automatic sense of drama—one person changed by another. Then try a Shakespearean one, or whatever you think will inspire and be fun for the people in your group.

Other Things to Watch For

Adjectives: Some players, usually those who want *minimal* control, will insist on inserting extra adjectives. This can result in a string of adjectives which simply serves to delay the story. "*We* see *a* huge, *green*, scaly, *slimy*, ugly..." and so on. This even occurs when telling one of the proto-stories and is a variation on THAT'S NOT GOOD ENOUGH.

Too much too soon: Players for whom *maximal* control feels most comforting will adopt the opposite strategy. They may say two or three words when it's their turn (although the stop-and-apologize does far more damage than the mere fact of saying an extra word or two) or mangle the grammar in order to be the person who says the key word. "*We are going to MOVIES!*" (implication: "I'm not going to give you a chance to screw this up").

Peculiar pauses: Sometimes many seconds will tick by before a player eventually volunteers a word like "then." This is a clear indication of a player who cannot commit to even a little filler word without first mentally constructing the whole of the rest of sentence—an obvious waste of time, since whatever sentence you may be imagining, your partner's next word is likely to destroy it.

Pointless originality: "*We are* washing *our* car *because* we *like* our ... *octopus.*" The player who said "octopus" is terrified of being thought unoriginal. In all probability they will resist any attempt to be controlled by other players and will find it very hard to discover their true talent. If they really think they don't need another person's input to show off their creativity to its best potential, then they should pick a less collaborative art form.

When faced with a new group of improvisers who have some preexisting experience but who haven't worked with one of us before, we will often get them to play this game first, especially if they already know it or some version of it. It ruthlessly exposes weaknesses in technique and approach, because it runs on pure instinct. Improvisers can't paper over the gaps with shtick. As such, it is a marvelous diagnostic tool for both player and coach alike. It is also an audience favorite.

STANDING WAVE

Get about half the group up, say seven or eight people, and from their number, persuade two volunteers to step forward. Explain that you are about to ask them to improvise a scene. We've found it helpful to start with something that includes a very obvious transaction, like a doctor and patient scene, so that the first few lines of dialogue take care of themselves to some extent. Explain to the whole group that the way this game will work is that although the two volunteers begin playing these roles, their parts can be taken over at any time by other people standing in the lines. The procedure is that people in the line step forward, tap one of the current actors on the shoulder, and at that moment replace them, continuing the scene as seamlessly as possible. The original actor returns to whichever is the more convenient line.

This game should not be confused with the more well-known but much less useful "Freeze Tag" in which players start a *new, unrelated* scene, inspired by the physical positions which they inherit (see Appendix One: Games). In Standing Wave, the scene carries on, from the same point in the same situation with the same characters—only the cast changes.

If necessary, demonstrate the procedure. Then let the game run for about ninety seconds, or until either plenty of people have tapped in and had a go, or—much more likely—nobody or only one person has tapped in and the two volunteers start to look very uncertain.

Assuming, as is typically the case, that almost nobody tapped in, we can start to apply a couple of familiar concepts to this new game. The first is BEING IN A GOOD STATE. It should be apparent that the people still in the audience are in a perfectly good state. They're fine—for the time being. The people who jumped up to play the game are in a worse state, but it's tempting to conclude that the two people who started the scene are in the worst state of all, but that doesn't tend to be the case. After all, those two have done it now. They've stuck their heads above the parapet. Come what may, they are definitely going to spend some time in harm's way. But for the people left behind it's totally different. For them, tapping someone out so they can contribute to the scene is a *choice* and for many people it's a terrifying one. For them, coming forward now almost smacks of arrogance: "I don't *have* to be in this scene, but I've got an idea that's *so good* it has to be heard. Out of my way, here I come." No wonder it's these people who are often in the worst state of all.

But now, I ask the whole group: "What does 'being good to work with' mean in the context of this game?" If they need prompting, I find someone in the line who looks fairly confident, but who did not tap in at any point, and I ask the original two volunteers "Was this person good to work with?" I'll probably get blank looks, but some people may be starting to understand: you can't be good to work with in this game, or any other, if you *refuse to take part*. The two volunteers may have felt very out of their depth, and yet nobody, or next to nobody, stepped forward to help them out. Of course, it's possible that the original two volunteers were thinking to themselves, "thank goodness we're getting such a nice, long go,"—but the chances are against it.

People in the line, who are in a very poor state, will often want to wait until they have thought of a good idea before going in, but this is a losing strategy. First, it means they probably won't go in at all! Second, by the time they have formulated the idea, assessed its worth, decided that it definitely is worthwhile acting on, and have started to cross the floor and tap out the person in question—their idea may no longer apply, the moment may have passed. So, rather than waiting until you have thought of an idea, it is far better just to go in because the time is right, or because one of the people on stage looks like they need help, or just because you feel like it. Then react to what is actually happening when you get there. It should be possible to get a rate of one substitution about every five or six seconds, and still keep some sort of coherence. If that rate is achieved, then nobody will be out there for more than seven or eight seconds, and *anyone* can survive for seven or eight seconds—you might not even get to say anything in that time.

Despite appearances, this is not a game for two people to play at any one time. The whole group is responsible for all of its members having a fun and stress-free experience. So no one should be standing back thinking, "my work here is done." Everybody is either listening to offers and saying "yes and," leaving because they have been tapped on the shoulder, or they are about to go back in. There are no other states.

We play the game again and this time people are much more willing to go in (or if they're not, I yell "Switch!" or clap my hands and then point at someone to make it clear that it's their turn). Inevitably, their worst fears are never realized. Paradoxically, leaping in without pre-planning is putting them in a far better state. This is partly because they have so little time to plan for the future or fret about the past. They are genuinely IN THE MOMENT, attending to what is actually happening *right now* and not drifting off into their own thoughts. This is an ideal state for an improviser, albeit one which is hard to sustain. The combination of higher-energy performers and being in the moment makes the *procedure* more interesting to watch but also raises the level of the content, sometimes quite dramatically. People in this state make much bolder offers and are much more willing to take risks. I also tend to "load the dice" by giving them a scenario which promises a bit more conflict the second time around (a child in detention, or trying to get out of a parking ticket perhaps), but this probably isn't necessary.

As they get bolder and happier playing the game, I can start to be a little stricter. Whether consciously or not, people will often try to pinch a little control back and this can be damaging both for their training as improvisers and for the enjoyment of the audience watching. Recall that the true purpose of improvisation as a performance art form is to witness a moment of spontaneous inspiration. This game enforces and surfaces that by making one player continue where another player left off, but beginners will sometimes insist on finishing their sentences before they leave and very often ignore half-finished sentences when entering, preferring instead to roll out the offer they thought of moments before.

So when doing this game a second or third time, I start to clean it up a little bit. Sometimes the hand-overs aren't quite as crisp as they could be. Improvisers who dither, who advance toward the players and then back away again will "behave" themselves into being in a bad state. Worse, the onstage improviser who sees them coming out of the corner of their eye may think, "whew, the nightmare is over," and leave prematurely, unaware that the other player has had second thoughts and retreated to the presumed safety of the back line. I insist instead that new players coming in, march across the stage boldly and deliver a smartly confident tap on the shoulder; and that the players onstage should not leave until they feel that tap—but when they do feel it, they should stop talking and leave instantly. Now the player coming in should attempt to finish their sentence for them, proving (if need be) that they aren't coming in with some would-be clever offer which they've cooked up off to the side. They are genuinely in the moment and responding to what their fellow player has started.

These instructions need a tiny bit of care. If you don't seem like these details are important, and you can't make the players understand why, then they may ignore you in favor of the joyous pell-mell of the previous iteration. But if you overemphasize the importance of finishing other people's sentences, people may be futilely trying to time their entrances to make sure they are *always* cutting someone else off and this is quite unnecessary. Continue to stress the importance of *rapid* substitutions and plenty of opportunities to finish sentences will present themselves.

This game is worth spending some time over, and it's worth playing in front of the rest of the group (the difference between the uncertain, bold, and truly in-the-moment versions is often easier to appreciate from your seat than on the stage) and in groups (so everyone gets lots of goes). I generally demonstrate it with around eight people, depending on the total size of the class (people are more likely to go in the first time around if the team is small—a version of the Bystander Effect[15] very likely) but get people to practice it in groups of five or six so that people have little choice but to go in.

This game can also be related to a situation which crops up often in front of audiences. Your team is in mid-scene, and you are on the sidelines. Should you enter? Regrettably, improvisers tend to crash scenes which are going well, in order to share the glory, but stay off the stage when the scene is getting stuck. Better players know when to leave well enough alone and when they have to jump in to perform a rescue (or at least share the pain).

Good friend, comedian and improviser Justin Rosenholtz told us a wonderful story about an improviser who jumped on stage to save his teammates from a scene that was going nowhere, despite having no idea about how to save it. Rather than entering as a new character or adding a new plot element or trying to "narrate" it to safety, he mimed throwing down a rope ladder from a "chopper" and told the improvisers that he would airlift them out of the bad scene. The improvisers gratefully climbed up the "ladder" and the audience cheered at this good-natured play. It was an acknowledgment from players and audience alike that the scene was bad, and they were delighted not to have to watch it or be in it any more. This improviser didn't know how to fix the scene but wanted to be good to work with, so he got his fellows out of trouble in the way that seemed obvious to him in that moment.

---

[15]The finding from psychological research that the more people who are available to help someone in distress, the less likely it will be that anyone actually will help since everyone presumes someone else will do it.

MASTER/SERVANT DUBBING

Slightly superior to the usual two-people-on-stage-with-two-people-dubbing-their-voices-from-offstage version, and vastly superior to the Four Way Dubbing game (which is almost always a train wreck), we often use this game to introduce the concept of the Master and Servant, as well as to continue to explore how working together can enhance improvisers' skills and the work itself.

Sit one improviser in a chair and get another improviser to stand near them—close at hand but without invading their space. Masters are not always high status to Servants—Jeeves played high status to Bertie Wooster, Blackadder played high status to the Prince Regent, John Gielgud's Hobson played high status to Dudley Moore's Arthur—but the Master always plays high status to the space. Thus Blackadder stands neatly at one side of the room, while Prince George sprawls across the cushions. However, down in the kitchen, in his own space, Blackadder reclines in a chair with his feet on the table, while Baldrick cowers in the corner. To reinforce the relationship, ask that Masters call their Servants by their first names (or at least invent a name of some kind for them) and have Servants call the Master "sir" or "ma'am," as appropriate. To make life easier, improvisers should begin by playing their own sex, despite the fact that the English language is not equipped with a gender-neutral term for "Master" ("Mistress" has all the wrong connotations).

The Master is asked to change their voice, usually adopting a gruffer, deeper tone (even the women). Once we've heard that demonstrated, the Master is then asked to change their voice again, this time to a high-pitched, squeak (take care that volume isn't overly reduced and that the words are still intelligible). This is the Servant's voice. The two improvisers have to work together to sell the illusion that the Servant is responsible for their own dialogue. When the Master speaks in the high-pitched voice, the Servant must make their lips move (boldly, but without even attempting word-for-word synchronization) and fit their facial expressions, actions, gestures and so on to the words provided for them. Likewise, if the Master sees the Servant's lips moving, they have to provide words for them—and without hesitation. "Call your Servant in and interact with them. Try not to send them away," I tell them.

Initially, I am just trying to get the illusion to work. Masters who don't look at the Servant will find it impossible to provide appropriate dialogue for them (it's amazing how common this is). Servants who can't bear to have dialogue invented for them will pantomime furiously in order to get the Master to say the "right" thing (which is bound to wreck the illusion, whether the Master correctly interprets their gesticulation or not). Masters who believe that the Servants' actions are a puzzle to be solved will stare stupidly at the Servant's flapping gums, not knowing what to say. Some also will struggle with separating the two characters and forget to get angry with an insolent Servant—even though they made the offer of insolence themselves!

Anxious Masters who can't provide dialogue quickly enough need gentle handling. They have become convinced a long time ago that their ideas are worthless and believe that inspiration and/or right answers come only after careful thought. Sometimes (rarely) I will play the Servant myself and make a very obvious offer of happiness or anger so that they can appreciate the difference between *inventing* dialogue for the Servant (too slow) or trying to solve the puzzle of what the Servant *wants* to be saying (irrelevant), and instead just learn to *see* and *respond* in the moment.

The fact is that the unconscious mind is *better* (and certainly faster) at this task and others like it than the conscious mind, but the conscious mind clings to the steering wheel and won't be pried off. Not only that, but the conscious mind is already revealed in other art forms: acting, writing, painting, many forms of music. Audiences come to an improv show to see the improvisers reveal their unconscious processes. And people come to improv workshops to discover them (or if they don't, they should).

Once a number of people have been able to create successful interactions (a useful test is: where is the audience looking when the Servant is speaking?), I pose the following question: "Who has more control here?" People generally think that the Master has more control, since that improviser is responsible for their own physicality plus both sets of dialogue, leaving only a quarter of the equation left for the Servant. This is true as far as it goes. But, I point out to the next volunteer Servant, there is a certain amount of freedom in the servant role.

If the Servant does something unexpected—throws the Master's dinner in the fire, strangles the dog, begins a soft-shoe shuffle—then even if the Master roars "Sandy, what on earth do you think you are doing!?" it will be that same improviser who has to answer the question! The Servant is responsibility-free. If the time is right, and if the improvisers in question are not threatened by the technical requirements of the game, a lot of very bold, playful behavior can be released. In fact, it can be a problem to rein the Servant in and prevent the scene from collapsing under the weight of a lot of unrelated physical offers. The Servant *must* give time for the Master to justify one arbitrary offer before going on to the next one. Above all, both improvisers must continue to make the illusion convincing.

Different servants adopt different strategies, and you can suggest some of these. Have servants refuse an order, have them produce mime objects (which the Master will have to name, or at least use in a way which makes their identity clear[16]) and—best of all—have them be emotionally affected.

---

[16] An audience engrossed in a story may forget from time to time that it is improvised, and this need not be (arguably should not be) the most interesting thing about it. For that reason, the audience simply will not care which of two improvisers happens to be the one who names a new mime object. It need not be the person who first introduced it. The only thing that will worry the audience is being kept waiting. But note our earlier comments about asking "What is it?" under Go Through An Unusual Door on page 108. This is a particularly useless strategy here, since the Master is passing the buck back to themselves.

This procedure makes the Master very observant and very in-the-moment. The Servant enters hurriedly, although this wasn't a deliberate, thought-through choice on the part of the improviser. "Late again," growls the Master, and then—seeing a flash of panic across the Servant's face—supplies the falsetto dialogue "Yes, sir, please don't beat me, sir." No one in the audience is sure who initiates the action, but suddenly the servant is producing a mime object from about her person as she is made to say, "Look, sir, I've brought you your favorite pet to play with." The Servant looks down at her hands in horror. "What have you done to Fluffy!?" roars the Master. When the scene is brought to a stop, both players—and most of the audience members—are helpless with laughter, not because of the wit of the players but because of the sheer pleasure of seeing them collaborate so instinctively and with such complicity.

This game has a lot of incidental pleasures. A drunken audience who laughs (quite naturally) at the sight of one player thwarting another will quickly teach improvisers bad habits.[17] This game can provide a less destructive version of this.

> **Master:** You have been thoroughly insolent, Jeremy.
> **Servant:** Yes, sir, sorry, sir.
> **Master:** Jeremy—fetch me the gun. (*Indicates offstage*)
> **Servant:** (*Looks where the Master is pointing, suspiciously*) That gun, sir?
> **Master:** Yes, Jeremy, that gun. Fetch it for me please.
> **Servant:** No, sir.
> **Master:** What?
> **Servant:** No, sir. If I fetch you that gun, sir, you'll shoot me.

This scene was performed by a group of improvisers whom we taught during an international improv festival. They had come to feel that saying "no" was automatically a block, and so their scenes were often lacking conflict. Just as too much conflict early on eliminates helpful platform, too little conflict toward the middle of a scene makes it dull. These improvisers knew better than to try and outsmart each other for laughs, but they hadn't realized the importance for narrative of GETTING INTO TROUBLE. What the scene above gave us was the joyous sight of one improviser *thwarting himself*, and there was a marvelous sense of discovery in the room!

---

[17]At a Theatresports show which Tom guest-hosted, he was horrified to see a very charming, experienced and successful improviser respond to their teammate's opening offer, clearly establishing the situation as a mad scientist in a lab, with the pointless block: "I only came in here to deposit a check." What made it worse was the fact that the scientist-cum-bankteller was sitting down, and the experimental-subject-cum-customer was standing up, so the physical relationship was all wrong for a bankteller's window. The rest of the scene was nonsense, and the audience gave it a low score, but they had laughed at the initial block, so the improviser in question must have thought they were giving the audience what they wanted.

Ultimately, the Servant was coaxed into procuring the gun, the Master smoothly convincing him that no harm would befall him. As soon as the gun was in his hands, he pointed it at the Servant and announced: "Jeremy, this was an exercise in trust." Then he pulled the trigger, ending the scene.

If both improvisers are paying attention, and both are working to pick up on each other's offers, the story almost takes care of itself. It seems very easy to play the part of the Master—all you have to do is react to what the Servant does. It also seems very easy to play the part of the Servant—you can do what you like, you never have to justify anything. This JUMP AND JUSTIFY method is an excellent way of freeing oneself from the awful prospect of always needing another new idea. The "jump" part of the equation requires merely boldness; it needs no skill at all. And justification is innate. It's part of the way in which we make sense of the world. Nobody comes home from work, hears voices in the living room and thinks "Pixies!" We think "Ah, my roommate is home and has the television on." We simply need to learn to make use of this familiar skill in an unfamiliar situation, and judge *how much* justification is required.[18]

OVER-CONFESSING

Another Master/Servant game, described briefly by Keith and further developed by Patti Stiles, is of tremendous use in practicing these skills. This time, both Master and Servant are responsible for their own voices. I get my two volunteers on to the stage and ask the Servant to wait off to one side. I remind them of the correct modes of address, and then I set the scene for them.

Josie, you are the Master, and you're going to call in your servant, Malcolm, to discuss some trivial matter with him—a piece of silverware wasn't polished properly, a picture was hung incorrectly, something like that. But, Malcolm, what she doesn't know is that today has been a catalogue of disaster for you. Everything that could possibly have gone wrong has. So when she says "There's something I want to discuss with you," you think you've been found out. And because Josie is a particularly quick-tempered and sadistic master, you think your best course of action is to confess. Whatever Malcolm confesses to, Josie, will be news to you. So you'll be horrified, furious. You'll ask whatever questions you may have, to get the complete picture, and then you'll get your anger under

---

[18]Sometimes the difference between a feeble justification and a satisfactory one is nothing more than length. A rather unconvincing explanation can grow in power as the improviser keeps talking and sometimes you can almost see the audience moving from furrowed brows and the internal monologue "That doesn't sound at all right to me…" into a much more relaxed state and a sense of "Oh now, I understand, okay, fine, fair enough."

control and say "That's not what I wanted to talk to you about." And then, Malcolm, you confess to something else.

The scene that emerges will probably have some pleasures—it's a rich comic situation—but it's unlikely to live up to the promise of hearing the situation described. Very likely, the Servant will be nowhere near terrified enough, nor the Master furious enough. The Servant may also attempt to shift the blame onto others ("It was the cook, ma'am, she was drunk and...") because, as we've just discussed, improvisers treat imaginary dangers as real. Both improvisers—but especially the Servant—will be trying to think of "good ideas" to keep the scene moving. The Servant is likely, on some level, to have misheard the instructions as "think of a number of highly amusing disasters" and will er and um and hem and haw their way through the scene—their waffle simply frustrating the audience, whose hunger for detail and definition is very hard to satiate.

I congratulate the first two volunteers and point out some of these difficulties before offering to show two other people a better and easier procedure. Over four or five iterations, we gradually build up a pattern that uses the JUMP-AND-JUSTIFY method to not only free the improvisers, but generate better ideas, too.

In the next iteration, I get the Servant to begin the confession with a JUMP. Instead of dredging up a comic disaster after a lengthy internal monologue ("I battered the children instead of the fish? Too silly. I broke a plate? Not good enough. Oh, er, um...") I get them just to name an item. Managing the tone of both characters is important to get best value out of this and to make sure that the illusion of cause and effect is maintained.

"Ah, Malcolm, there's something I wanted to discuss with you," says the Master, firmly but pleasantly. "The car, ma'am!" blurts out the Servant, eyes wide with panic, voice filled with guilt and fear. "The car?!" responds the Master in sudden alarm. In this version, the Servant doesn't have to worry about inventing something, all that's required is to name an object. A once daunting game is reduced to Pointing at Things and Saying What They Are Not. Note that it's fatal in this game to let the Master keep talking initially. If the Master spits out the trivial matter in question, the Servant is off scot-free and the scene is over! The interruption must come promptly!

This second version plays with much more energy and brio than the first version, and the audience has a much better time. They enjoy the risk that the improviser has taken, and it also helps that improviser to play their part more convincingly—part of the panic is genuine! However, at least one problem may present itself right away. We would ideally want the stakes to rise over the course of the scene, but if you are just blurting out the first word that comes to mind, there's no guarantee that this will happen. You may begin the scene with "The dining room, ma'am," and then later volunteer "Your handkerchief, ma'am." As well as being an anti-climax after the tale of the demolition of the dining room due to a runaway wrecking ball, it isn't at all clear why the Master should be at all bothered by *anything* having happened to her handkerchief.

But, the Servant's fear and guilt makes it clear that this must be a very precious handkerchief. To say "Why should I care about that?" or "I've got lots of handkerchiefs," would be a BLOCK (everything you do, you do for a reason). A better strategy (which I now suggest for our third pair of volunteers) would be for the Master to automatically RAISE THE STAKES on whatever object happens to be named by the Servant. The Master should JUSTIFY the Servant's guilt and fear by adding details to the named object, making it more valuable, more personally precious, more urgently needed and so on.

If the Servant says "The East Wing, ma'am," very little raising-of-the-stakes is required (although it doesn't hurt), so the Master can simply say, "That's my favorite of all the wings! I spend more time there than in any other wing." She will have to work a little harder if the Servant says "Your handkerchief, ma'am." For example: "My handkerchief!? Not the silk one? Not the one given to me personally by the First Lady herself—the only memento I have left of our forbidden love for one another?" Some Masters have a taste for the absurd: "...containing the only remaining genetic material of her, from which I hoped one day to produce a clone?" which is great, but the *real* raising of the stakes happens when the Master first hears what the object is and reacts. We know *how* important the object was when we hear her gasp of shock and disbelief. Certainly we want to know *why* it's so important but (up to a point) any old nonsense will do if it's said with commitment.

This third iteration will likely be far more successful, with Master and Servant working together to establish what each item is and what its importance is, but the waffle and the need to blame others may still occur after this point as we get into what actually happened. The fourth and final part of the puzzle is for the Servant to JUMP one more time.

"My spectacles!?" gasps the Master, "my laser spectacles which I wear at nights to fight crime in my secret alter-ego as the Bespectacled Barnacle!? What's happened to them!?" Rather than searching for an entertaining story, the Servant at this point, should simply say, "I [BLANK]ed them," filling in the blank with whatever verb seems appropriate: I crushed them, I lost them, I sold them, I blew them up, etc. This structure means that the audience gets the information in the order they want it: What has been damaged? Why is it important? What has happened to it? It also means that the Servant is forced to take full responsibility and it's another opportunity to JUMP AND JUSTIFY. Now the Master can ask whatever questions would be in the mind of the audience.

> **Master:** You crushed them? But how? Why?
> **Servant:** I was testing your new vice, ma'am, for the workshop.
> **Master:** With my spectacles?
> **Servant:** They were the nearest thing to hand.

> **Master:** But they never leave the Barnacle Case except when I'm fighting crime!
> **Servant:** I tried them on, ma'am. I'm sorry. I was curious. I'll get you a new pair.
> **Master:** You certainly will! But that's not what I wanted to talk to you about.
> **Servant:** Your books, ma'am!

Some Masters need a great deal of coaching before they know when to move on. They will tend to end the interrogation with obvious questions unanswered, or keep repeating information unnecessarily. The audience, of course, always knows exactly when they want more information and when they have had all their questions answered and are ready to hear about the next item.

It's worth setting this as an exercise in pairs once everyone is clear on the structure, although it's also worth stressing that the point of the structure is not to learn it and replicate it in front of an audience (although I suppose you could if you kept it short). Rather it is to give improvisers practice at JUMPING AND JUSTIFYING, since the crucial ingredient one needs to successfully deploy this technique is the courage that comes from having used it successfully many times in the past. Improvisers sometimes describe what they do using the metaphor of jumping out of a plane and trying to construct a parachute on the way down. This overlooks just how scary your first parachute jump must be. When the door of the plane opens, your whole body is going to scream at you, "For god's sake, stay inside, there's nothing down there." But on your first jump you will learn that physics works, that your parachute will open, will slow your descent, you will remember how to land safely, and so on. Then subsequent jumps will be easier. It's just that sometimes you have to pry people's fingers off the fuselage the first time!

EVERYTHING IS AN OFFER

While the structure is designed to keep improvisers jumping and justifying and stop them from thinking up clever ideas, there is one moment where an improviser could mentally withdraw from the scene and think up an offer—but please don't do this. Some Masters raise the stakes at great length: "My whip? Not the whip with which I fought off that pride of lions in the African Savannah? I was there in 1943 as part of the India Corps—we were hopelessly lost, you see, and my Bat Man told me..." While the Master drivels on, the Servant starts planning different responses. "When he stops speaking," he thinks, "I'll say 'I ate it.' That'll be funny." Meanwhile he hasn't heard a word the Master has said. While very lengthy justifications of this sort should be discouraged, they are offers. The truth of this was brought home to me in a workshop, where I had the chance to revisit this game as a student, having taught it for years. Working in pairs with another improviser, the following exchange occurred, which I have never forgotten (this was around fifteen years ago).

> **Me:** That's not what I wanted to talk to you about.
> **Him:** Your son, sir!
> **Me:** My flaxen-haired, blue-eyed boy with the voice of an angel?
> **Him:** Yes, he's bald, blind and mute, sir!

The memory of this exchange still makes me smile. What was perfectly "obvious" to this (excellent and experienced) improviser was that *I was telling him how to hurt the object he had named*. Servants who aren't listening will miss this information, and it may be crucial! If you say, "Your bear, sir!" and the Master says "My ferocious fighting bear, which has developed a taste for human flesh and must never be unchained under any circumstances?" then you must have released it and it should be chomping its way through the kitchen staff or the villagers. If, on the other hand, in response to "Your bear, sir," the Master says "Mr. Happy? My teddy bear? My childhood friend which cuddles me to sleep every night?" then you must have thrown it in the furnace, or fed it to a horse, or used it as an archery target.

—Tom

Versions done in front of the group are generally ended by me when I've seen my point demonstrated, or when the scene has reached a suitably hysterical pitch. So, another question students have asked in the past is "How do you end it?" It's not an unreasonable question. The structure is quite tightly regimented, so it's not impossible to imagine a standard ending, but in fact no so such ending exists. I now set this as an exercise: do three iterations (i.e. confess three times), then find an ending. This can provoke a very useful discussion about how to end scenes in general.

Common endings include: the Master firing the Servant, one or the other character dying (heart attacks are common in Masters), a disaster turning out well for the Master ("We can claim that on the insurance! Well done, Matthew!") or the Master finally spits out the trivial request ("All I wanted was to remind you to change the cat litter!"). Generally, endings will include one or more of the following: a JOINING of the protagonists (they now agree and are in the same state), the completing of a lengthy routine, or a sudden lowering of the stakes. As before, when looking for an ending, reincorporate. If either the Master or Servant reincorporates the first thing, the audience will feel like we've gone full circle and so expect an ending. For more on endings, see "What Comes Next" (page 78) and "Twitching, Topping and Paperflicking" (page 171).

UNDER THE GUN

The best ending to this scene I ever saw was performed in a show by Deborah and Chris Gibbs. "That's not what I wanted to talk to you about," barked Chris. "Er, your impending assassination, sir?" hazarded Deborah. "My what!? Ugh!!" responded Chris, as he mimed receiving a bullet in the chest and collapsing on the floor. Lights.

—*Tom*

OTHER GAMES

Most improvisation requires a degree of cooperation and a willingness to abandon control of the future and instead embrace your partner's offers. Improvisers who want to be in control will resist this, and so games which enforce instant cooperation and being in the moment are very useful. It's also one of the things improvisation can do which other forms of theatre can't (though some physical theatre can). Hence a great many games exist which exploit this and which can be used to teach this skill. Examples include: Arms Through and Hypnotist/Magician (described in 2.14, "Control Freak") and Speak In One Voice, Pillars and He Said She Said (described in Appendix One: Games).

2.9

Being Changed

Overview

The fundamental component of drama, but often overlooked by improvisers, who see in it a tremendous risk. In fact, it can be the most useful tool in their toolbox, and very often the best way to accept offers of all kinds.

At a visit to the UK, Keith Johnstone recalled attempting to solve the problem of what dramatic action was. He and his colleagues at the Royal Court in London in the 1950s knew that in some plays there seemed to be a great deal of action—wars, death, plague, destruction—but they were left feeling that nothing much had happened; whereas in other plays (fewer), there seemed to be very little action, but they left feeling that they had seen something of tremendous power. The answer, Keith recalled, was just *too simple* for them to see: "A changes B." If one character is altered by another, we perceive this as action. If characters remain unaltered, we get the feeling that nothing is happening. We saw this idea in action when we looked at changing environments into stories in Go Through An Unusual Door, and it may be worthwhile to discuss this general principle a bit more thoroughly before we further discuss how to develop this habit in improvisers.

Once you look for it, it becomes very obvious that reactions, emotional changes, are the heart and soul of stories, but oddly they are often not the most conspicuous features. When we talk about stories, we often focus on the *plot*, on what happens, and may eliminate how the events affect the characters altogether.[19] "Macbeth, told that he is destined to be King, and egged on by his wife, decides to take matters into his own hand and murders his way to the throne before being murdered himself," is a perfectly accurate, if very brief, account of Shakespeare's famous play—but it's the plot, not the *point*! The play is a study of ambition, pride, guilt and humiliation. Without the emotional content, the story has very little to recommend it.

Among the most famous sequences in the play is the appearance of Banquo's ghost. This has a negligible impact on the plot. The scene could be removed entirely and the rest of the play would still make sense. But this justly famous scene sums up the entire play, since it very effectively dramatizes the *cost*, in emotional terms, of Macbeth's murderous actions. The same can be said for the scene in which Lady Macbeth hallucinates bloodstains on her hands and wails "Out, damned spot!"

The same principles crop up in more lightweight drama as well. The famous twist in *The Empire Strikes Back* (and stop reading if you haven't seen the film!)—that Darth Vader is Luke Skywalker's father—is famous (at least in part) because it was hard to see it coming. What also makes this twist so effective is the bitter irony of Luke's mortal enemy also being his beloved father, but what really makes it succeed is the internal conflict and *anguish* which Luke experiences when he finds out. His response to hearing the news is to *howl* with emotional pain, and that's what makes the episode so resonant. Were he to say, "I don't care, I'm going to kill you anyway," all the drama would drain away.

Even comedies, which often treat serious subjects in a flippant way in order to make them palatably funny, rely on this same principle. Treating gigantic events with little or no emotion is a joke, but it's only one joke, and it's actually a rather tricky one to do well. Most drama involves people having big reactions to big events. Most comedy involves people having big reactions to little events. It's a staple of situation comedies like *Friends* or *Fawlty Towers* that a trivial event like reading a book or hanging a picture will be the catalyst for an eventual hysterical outburst. Improvisers, unproductively, spend most of their time inventing ludicrous events to which they barely react at all. While this can be effective, it squanders the one thing an audience is really there for more than anything else—A changing B.

As situations get less and less realistic, emotions often run higher and higher. Jane Austen characters in love are famously repressed, sitcom characters camp outside the object of their affection's front door for days,

---

[19]This recalls E. M. Forster's observation that "The King died, and then the Queen died" is far less effective than "The King died, and then the Queen died of a broken heart." Weirdly, Forster calls the first of these "story" and the second "plot," which seems the wrong way around to us, and doesn't really reflect the way these words are used today. We gratefully borrow his insight, but switch the labels.

sketch characters literally cling on to the leg of the adored person as they are dragged from place to place, and when Tex Avery's cartoon wolf sees a woman, he leaps four feet in the air, his tongue unfolds like a staircase and his eyes bug out on stalks. What makes the difference, what RAISING THE STAKES really means, is how much the characters care about the plot— whether or not they happen to be wearing their hearts on their sleeves. Once the characters *care* about something, it's easy to change them. Give them what they want and you make them happy; take it away and you make them sad (or angry). Improvisers who are desperate to seem "cool" won't care about anything (see the "teenage" version of the Yes game on page 49).

Since different things are extraordinary in different worlds (different PLATFORMS), if you fail to react to an extraordinary offer, you squander an opportunity to start the story, since you send the signal "This is just the introduction—the story hasn't begun yet." If this happens early in the story, it creates problems because the *real* break in the routine has to be even more extraordinary. If this happens late in the story, you'll likely lose the audience altogether. An audience, which has become invested over many minutes in the plight of an anxious teenage boy trying to ask a girl out, is unlikely to be pleased if she reveals herself as an alien and he reacts with a shrug and bored indifference.

Let's look briefly at a couple of potential counterexamples, again from "premeditated" narratives. In adventure stories, such as those featuring Rambo or James Bond, there is typically very little in the way of emotional change. We would be very surprised to see James Bond anything other than cool, calm and collected. First, let's acknowledge that this is exactly the criticism which is often leveled at these stories: that they are thin, characterless and survive on spectacle and gloss alone. This is a specific instance of the general rule that an audience can be distracted from their hunger for story by something spectacular. However, it can be argued, in this case, the stunts really are what the audience is there for. The plot just has to set them up. But the best action films make us *care* about the outcome of the chase, and films that spend all their money on stunts and forget story often fail at the box office.

Second, while we don't necessarily need to see James Bond "learn" and "grow," it is entirely false to conclude that the average James Bond film does not involve characters being changed by each other. The villain will get more hysterical and eventually be humiliated. Q will be annoyed by Bond's mere presence. The female lead will be initially aloof until she finally surrenders to Bond's charms. The better actors to play the Bond role give us *tiny* changes all the way through. This is a version of small reactions to big events, but it makes it all the more important that the whole thing is played and realized with verisimilitude. If we believe that this man routinely skis off mountain tops and lands by parachute, then we may believe that he does it with little more than a raised eyebrow. And then, if he *is* shocked or surprised—even for an instant—the effect is even more powerful.

The problem for improvisers is—once again—anxiety. Faced with a lot of nameless eyes staring at us, we are flung back to our evolutionary past on the African savannah, where that situations means we are *prey*. We are therefore likely to want to display very consistent behavior, so that anyone who looks at us can look away and then look back and see the same thing. Thus we become boring, we fade into the background, and we cease to be of interest. Frustratingly for the coach, improvisers who think they are doing their best to be *interesting* by coming up with all sorts of bizarre offers are subconsciously doing their best to be *dull* by refusing to be affected by anything that happens. The following exchange, which we saw performed by experienced and feted improvisers at an international festival, exemplifies the worst excesses of this approach, topped off with a dose of horrible misogyny and bigotry for good measure.

> **A:** Hey, I saw your wife the other day. She looks really retarded.
> **B:** Yeah, I hit her in the face with a baseball bat. You want a sandwich?

What other art form would introduce issues of extreme domestic violence and consequent disability, only to throw them away for what is barely even a joke? The improvisers in question looked relaxed and calm, but a certain degree of panic or desperation surely must have been driving them.

In life, if we are changed by what is said to us, this may be perceived as weakness or loss of control. With close friends, we laugh at their jokes, crinkle our faces in sympathy on being told bad news, and in general make our emotional reactions to them very obvious. However, if we are in a tricky situation, if our ideas are being challenged or if we are among strangers, often we will work very hard to keep our impassive mask in place. We daren't let the opposition see that they have affected us. A similar reaction is in place here— and is heightened as soon as the improvisers attempt to out-funny each other.

We had a few lengthy debates at the Chicago Improv Festival with improvisers from various parts of North America about the responsibility that improvisers should take for their scenes. One scene we saw during the festival was a matter for contentious discussion. It was set in a record store and went like this:

> **Boy 1:** Hey, I saw a deaf girl in the soundtrack section.
> **Boy 2:** What's a deaf girl doing in the soundtrack section? She can't hear.
> **Boy 1:** I know!
> *Girl gets up and mimes looking at CDs.*
> *Boy 1 and 2 come up behind her and start clapping their hands and laughing because she can't hear and doesn't know that they're mocking her.*

Our argument was that every story has a moral. The audience will always unconsciously go away with a message about why you chose to show them these particular characters on this particular day. Of course in drama and comedy we can—and often must—show people behaving in objectionable ways, but the problem is that these characters are never foiled, enlightened or changed in any way. Even though the show was a Harold, and the characters could have been reincorporated, we never saw any of them again. This meant we were left with the impression that the improvisers thought that this was desirable behavior. The moral of the story seemed to be that it's funny to mock deaf people without them knowing. There are many ways that the improvisers could have developed this scene into something more interesting that would have left the audience with a different impression. Here are some alternative developments which change the moral of the story:

- The deaf girl turns around and says: "We're facing a mirror, morons—I can see you," which embarrasses them.

- In another scene, one of the guys starts working with the deaf girl and becomes her friend. He realizes that his behavior in the shop was immature and callous. Maybe he asks her out and she turns him down because she's looking for someone more grown up.

- In a later scene, she and her deaf boyfriend mock the hearing boys in sign language and they can't understand what's being said about them.

- Another customer in the store says to her "How do you put up with it?" She says "Why do I care about these jerks? I'm an attorney and I earn $200,000 a year. I happen to know they work in the Dairy Queen."

The people we argued with about this scene (and others like it) claimed that improvisers couldn't possibly be asked to think about the content of their work, otherwise they'd be censoring themselves. While we agree that beginners might need to be told not to censor, once you are performing work on stage, you need to take joint responsibility for the show. We feel it is patronizing to improvisers to say that they are the only artists who cannot be aware of the messages they are sending. Racist, sexist or other unpleasant or insensitive work performed for a quick laugh and never revisited is beneath us—unless these are the real views of the improvisers and this is the message they wish to propagate. Sometimes it seems like merely *including* a subject matter like disability is seen as somehow daring or edgy, but if it's not explored from the deaf girl's point of view, if it remains just teenagers laughing at hearing impairment without understanding anything about deaf culture, then surely it's just something we can see in any school yard.

The creators of *South Park* and *The Book of Mormon* are among the edgiest comedy writers currently working in mass media. No one is safe and often their observations are vitriolic, but they are brilliant satirists who are always making some kind of point. Whether they're making fun of politicians, left-wing liberal celebrities, even environmentalists, they are saying *something*, and they know what they're saying even if lots of people won't agree with them. When we asked the improvisers who were performing these sorts of scenes what they were saying, they said that they didn't know. They were just "in the moment." This doesn't seem like edgy, dark satire to us. It seems like relinquishing responsibility for the content we generate. It seems unlikely that improvisation as an art form will grow or develop in this environment.

And this, ultimately, is the point. Creating an amoral character and having them vanquished is not just a better thing to put into the world, it is also likely to be *more interesting theatre* than creating an amoral character, chuckling at them and then moving on to something else, unrelated. Let's take this idea and see how we can make it happen.

STATUS SWITCH

Over-confessing is an excellent workshop game, but we don't recommend performing it in public, or at least not often. It will seem too pre-meditated which won't be as much fun for the spectators who may feel they are missing out on something. This next procedure seems almost mechanical in its simplicity, but the effects are so excellent (on both improvisers and audiences), the mechanism so easy to hide and the core idea so profound that you could easily do three or four of these in an hour-long show and no one watching would never even notice it.[20]

The basic idea is to start with one improviser high status, the other low status and, over the course of the scene, switch the statuses. Two important principles of storytelling come into play here, *in this order of importance*:

1   When you are changing, you are interesting.
2   Story is about cause and effect.

Here, we use JUMP AND JUSTIFY so that, if necessary, the effect (a shift in status) can precede the cause. But the cause must be present—the shift in status must be justified or the illusion of one person affecting another is destroyed.

---

[20]Typically, this would be a discovery onstage: "Aha, I can play this as a Status Switch," rather than a premeditated choice.

Here's how to teach it. An excellent scenario to use is that of a job interview. There are a couple of reasons for this. First, it raises the stakes automatically but it doesn't give the improvisers too much of the plot (compared to, say, "ask her to marry you" or "tell him he's fired"). Second, it requires the improvisers to make two fundamental decisions and stick to them, rather than having to constantly invent. They must make a decision about what the job is, or they will have nothing to talk about. Human nature being as perverse as it is, it feels far safer not to name the job at all (because you can't then name the "wrong" job), even though as soon as you (or your partner) does name the job, the whole scene becomes much easier. The other decision is when to change.

So, stick a couple of chairs in the middle of the stage—at forty-five degrees to each other and to the audience, as is traditional. Get a couple of improvisers up and invite one to take a seat and the other to wait offstage.

> *This is a job interview. Sue, I'd like you to be the interviewer. Ted, wait over there, you're going to enter as the candidate. Sue, I want you to play super high status. Use all the tactics that we studied when we looked at status, and any others which you think will work for you. But go for broke: I want you to be the job interviewer from hell. I want you to do everything you can to make his life a misery: be rude, dismissive, arrogant, aggressive. Ted, I want you to play super low status. You were quite anxious about this interview when you got up this morning, you've gotten more anxious in the waiting room and now everything she says and does makes you feel worse. One of you should name the job or you'll have nothing to talk about, but I don't care who. Okay, Sue, call the next candidate in.*

With any luck, your two improvisers will take these instructions and run with them. Sue will bark "Come in!" and Ted will creep through the door. Sue will snarl "Faster!" and Ted will throw himself at the chair in a sudden panic, then freeze and look up at Sue's disdainful face, while nervously touching his own. The characters seem rich and vibrant. As soon as they name the job (it really doesn't matter who gets it out first), ideas suggest themselves, although watch out for wimp jobs like "my assistant" or "manager." If this occurs, get one of them to name the business.

As is usually the case, it isn't the idea, it's what you do with it. Improvisers who name "funny" jobs like "lion tamer" or "particle physicist" may find they've backed themselves into a corner if they in fact don't know anything about those professions. Improvisers who are trying to show off how original they are by naming absurd jobs that they then struggle to YES AND should be encouraged to start with a simpler job and then YES AND their partner to discover the specifics which will bring the scene to life. Improvisers who are desperate to be dull should be encouraged to pick less "safe" options, and interview someone for a job with a bomb disposal squad instead of at a supermarket.

Once the scene begins, I coach them to maintain the statuses, if necessary, and make sure that the low status player is reacting in a low status way and not just saying low status things. Some low status candidates give perfectly good answers—"How long were you in your last job?" "Six years"—but say them so feebly that they can't be taken seriously. This is fine. Others give wretched answers: "An hour. I was fired for cutting off a customer's finger." But these *must* also be delivered in a wretched fashion or they will sound like insouciant arrogance.

After a couple of minutes, if they look inspired, I freeze the action.

The big status gap creates rich characters which inspire the improvisers and makes it easy for them to come up with telling details. This means the platform will sustain for longer. But we need to break the routine before the platform becomes boring. Ted, keep doing what you're doing. Sue, ask him a couple more questions with that same attitude. But be a little bit impressed by one of his answers and let your status drop a little. That doesn't mean it has to be an impressive answer, Ted.

If they are really on a roll, I might just jump in and side-coach: "Sue, be a bit impressed by that," and then explain this later.

> **Sue:** So, which is your favorite animal to butcher?
> **Ted:** Er, I don't know.
> **Sue:** You must have a favorite—pick one.
> **Ted:** Um, rabbit?
> **Sue:** (*dropping her status slightly*) Rabbit? Interesting choice. You like game animals, do you?
> **Ted:** Yes, yes, I do.
> **Sue:** Tricky to butcher neatly, rabbits. Very sinewy.
> **Me:** *Ted, you like talking about this, get a bit more confident.*
> **Ted:** The trick is to work down the backbone first, and to have a really sharp cleaver...
> *Sue shudders a little.*

I keep directing them, so as to lower Sue's status and raise Ted's. Probably after quite a lot of prodding by me, it will transpire that Sue can't stand the sight of blood and Ted will terrify the life out of her by casually waving his butcher's knife around before Sue shrieks in hysterics that he can have any job he likes if he leaves now. It can be useful to direct the person trying to raise their status into more dominant postures—standing up and so on. The other person can abase themselves on the floor as the scene nears its close. The teacher may need to work quite hard to get the interviewer to keep lowering their status. Possible reasons for this will be discussed shortly.

Now you can explain the whole strategy.

Set up the platform: one very high status and one very low status. Establish who these people are, keep the statuses constant for a while. Before inspiration runs dry, one of you needs to change, and it's usually easiest for this to be the high status person. We want to create the illusion of one person being changed by another, so you need to lower your status as a reaction to something the other person said, but you don't need to wait for a cue from them—you can just decide to change. Then you need to justify the reaction. Keep reacting and keep justifying, one slowly lowering their status, one slowly raising, going at about the same rate, until you meet in the middle. From there you can send your status through the floor, and you can send your status through the roof.

The scene that results will almost always be very satisfying, and will feel like a story (albeit a simple one). Note that it maps almost perfectly on to the pattern we have already established. One high, one low: that's your platform. Add detail: what's the job? Break the routine: begin to change status. Now the high status person is in trouble. If you can end with a reincorporation, so much the better, but the switching of statuses is the completion of a routine and often feels like a reincorporation in a peculiar way.

Here's a slightly abbreviated and idealized version of this scene, based on a version improvised at a workshop Tom ran for the improv group NSN24. It will help you to picture the scene if you bear in mind that Claire is in reality about eighteen inches shorter than Dom, who is very tall and lanky.

> **Claire:** Next!
> **Dom:** (*From outside the door*) Sorry?
> **Claire:** Next!!
> **Dom:** (*Making appeasing gestures, big smile*) Hello!
> **Claire:** Sit. (*She begins shuffling papers and ignoring him. Dom looks more and more awkward.*)
> **Dom:** Um…
> **Claire:** Quiet, please.
> **Dom:** Sorry.
> **Claire:** (*Eventually giving him some attention.*) So, you're here for the bakery job, are you?
> **Dom:** (*Eagerly*) I am, yes.
> **Claire:** Experience?
> **Dom:** Ooh, yes, lots. And I brought some samples.
> **Claire:** Samples?
> **Dom:** My cookies. (*Dom pulls a mime container out of his pocket and opens the lid.*) Here, try one.
> **Claire:** I don't usually like cookies.

Dom: Your receptionist thought they were lovely.

Claire: (*Takes a cautious bite*) Mmm…hey, these are *good.*

Dom: (*Relaxing a bit*) Told you.

Claire: (*Stuffing the cookie into her mouth.*) Oh, that's delicious. Mmm. Oats, honey…

Dom: Yes, and something else…

Claire: Butter?

Dom: Obviously butter, but what else?

Claire: Oh…er…

Dom: Oh, come on!

Claire: Er…

Dom: (*Leaning back, hands behind his head*) Even your receptionist got this!

Claire: I…I…

Dom: Almonds, of course.

Claire: I was going to say almonds!

Dom: Hmm…

Claire: Give me another one.

Dom: (*Sealing the lid and standing up*) Well, that depends.

Claire: (*Throwing herself on the floor and wailing*) Give me another! Give me another!

Dom: Quiet, please.

Claire: Sorry.

At this point everyone knows the scene is over, not just because of Dom's reincorporation of Claire's line, but because the characters have been transformed and because we understand why. We are left with the impression that a profound and irrevocable change has taken place.

Once you've got one of these working, try some variations. The scene works just as well with a high status candidate, swaggering in as if the job is already theirs, faced with a pathetic, incompetent interviewer who has never conducted an interview before and has very little idea of how to do it. Or let the interviewer pick their own status and have the candidate wait and watch and pick the opposite. It's also a great scene to play in silence (the improvisers move their lips, so it looks to the audience like they are watching TV with the sound turned down). See the section on gibberish which follows this for some ideas about what makes this work.

Some improvisers will offer a certain amount of resistance to your direction. This resistance will usually take one of these forms.

- The shifts in status will not be justified (sufficiently).

- They will start playing THAT'S NOT GOOD ENOUGH and leave the butchery techniques that prompted the initial shift in status to talk about which counties have the best cows.

● The high status person will not drop their status, or it will start creeping back up again.

If the shifts in status are not justified, this is a failure of technique and, to some extent, nerve. Improvisers need to understand that JUMP AND JUSTIFY only works if both parts of the equation are deployed (at least by somebody). Games like It's Tuesday[21] can be very useful to give improvisers permission to explore different emotional states, but their emotional overreactions must then be justified or the game is just a couple of people shouting at each other. Remember, justifications don't have to be *good*, they just need to be comprehensive; a feeble justification can become convincing as more and more detail is added.

THAT'S NOT GOOD ENOUGH is a function of anxiety. It is easier for the interviewer (especially a high status interviewer) to control the interview, and some interviewers may discover the (excellent) trick of saying "So, tell me about..." whenever inspiration runs dry. This will be a marvelous way of building the platform, but it should usually be resisted once the routine has been broken. The audience perceives the candidate's answer as having found a chink in the interviewer's armor, so even if the interviewer would logically want to move the interview on, between them the two improvisers must not let this happen. Just as in Go Through An Unusual Door, if your fellow improviser has been nice enough to let you know how to hurt them, you must not shrink from your task!

The last of these three is the most important here. We've discussed at some length why improvisers might find it difficult or uncomfortable to be seen to be affected by other people's offers onstage. But the problems are much worse when it comes to getting people to lower their status! As we've seen, it's a general problem that improvisers treat imaginary dangers as real, and may therefore continue to fight for what their character wants, even as the scene descends into repetitive boredom. Thus, scenes in which characters compete for status are commonly seen and easy to do—people are used to fighting to raise their status. There are almost no instances in life where people will willingly lower their own status, and so people are often very reluctant to do it on stage (compare the Tug of War game discussed under "Working Together" on page 116).

Many people turn up to improvisation workshops with this kind of baggage. They are unlikely to want to lower their status on stage because they don't want to lower their status in life. What has their prior improvisation training done to prepare them for this? Very likely it has made matters worse! We want improvisers to be bold and fearless, we want them to snap out confident offers, to JUMP AND JUSTIFY and to happily define without hesitation. We don't want

---

[21]Keith Johnstone's game of over "over-accepting" wherein mundane offers are greeted with instant overreactions. The Emo-Roller game (page 474) is possibly a degenerate version of this.

to see them baulk onstage. We want them to relate to the audience happily and self-assuredly. One negative outcome of this is that some improvisers—especially young male improvisers—are gradually trained never to play *vulnerable characters*, since they have been taught never to display the vulnerability they feel about the business of being onstage in front of an audience and without a script.

This *must* be addressed or we will be right back at the kind of repetitive, frat boy, out-clever-each-other nonsense which rapidly outstays its welcome. Audiences can effortlessly tell the difference between a genuinely uncertain actor and a confident actor deliberately choosing to play vulnerability and low status. The improviser choosing to lower their status is taking the initiative when it comes to determining the direction of the scene, and this will likely be rewarding for the improviser who wants to "shine." They need to discover the pleasure of being defeated!

Partly for this reason, in this exercise the high status character *must* be defensive or aggressive. They have to be someone that the audience hates, but if the improviser is playful, the audience will love to hate them. The only thing the audience will love more is seeing them humiliated.

BEING A BASTARD

I can't think of anything more fun, as an improviser or as an actor, than swaggering on stage as a complete bastard, knowing how much pleasure the audience will get out of my eventual downfall. That's why the villains are always the best parts.

Irving Thalberg, the MGM *wunderkind*, understood this. Worried that Lassparri, the chief villain in *A Night at the Opera*, was receiving too much of a drubbing at the hands of the Marx Brothers, and that the audience would see them as persecuting the poor man, Thalberg inserted a scene at the beginning of the movie wherein Lassparri is seen to physically beat poor mute, defenseless Harpo. Following this, the audience would laugh happily and without the least bit of sympathy as Lassparri was dangled out of portholes, clobbered with sandbags, had his costume ripped to pieces and eventually his part in the opera taken away from him and given to another singer. They had already decided they didn't like him and so anything was fair game.

—Tom

Hopefully, by this stage, the students are starting to understand that when they are changing they are interesting, and so by changing just a little—

but always in the same direction[22]—in response to everything that's said to them, they can make this status exchange scene fascinating, funny and convincing. ABC: Always Be Changing.

Always Be Changing

Change is interesting, especially emotional change. If you're sitting in a café and the couple at the next table start to argue, you will try and look away, but it's hard. You want to look. You want to know what's going on. If one of them starts to cry, it will become even more difficult to look away. You will start to make guesses about what's happening: maybe they're breaking up. If nothing changes for a while and they continue to argue and cry at the same level, you will soon be able to go back to your own conversation because it looks like no further changes will occur. As soon as we are reassured that we have seen everything there is to see, we lose interest. If the man suddenly stands up and storms out, we look, because something has changed again. We also want to look if the couple appear to kiss and make up. We want to know how the story ends. If you want to be riveting on the stage, keep changing. If you argue, the audience will be interested for a while, but if you *keep* arguing, they will feel they have seen all they're going to and stop watching. Start to cry and they'll look back again. Not because crying is interesting, but because *change* is interesting.

Actors who shout through a whole scene do so because they believe the audience wants to see emotion, but audiences only want to see the same emotion for so long. Then they need to see something new. If you want to be watchable, always be changing. It is not uncommon to see improv shows where characters come and go and are never changed or affected. Why is this so difficult to do onstage?

Well, if you're shopping in a supermarket and see someone suddenly crouch down on the floor and weep uncontrollably and then start to scream, you will call the authorities. Someone from a hospital will probably come and take them away—unless they are three years old, and then you will think nothing of it. Erratic, mutable behavior is standard in a toddler. They will scream if they're angry, sing if they're happy and cry if they're sad. They will swing between these emotions with startling rapidity. By the time you are an adult, you must have learned to curb these quickly changing displays of emotion or you will be committed.

We teach our children to look sane. We encourage them to display consistent behavior, no matter what they are feeling. We say to our children:

---

[22]Sloshing back and forth on the status spectrum doesn't allow the audience to get a handle on what the story is about. It's a version of THAT'S NOT GOOD ENOUGH.

"Don't make such a fuss. Pull yourself together. Be quiet." And as they get older, we expect that their behavior, at least in public, will be more and more consistent. Eventually, they will probably only display inconsistent behavior or quick changes of emotion in public if there is some kind of personal tragedy or national disaster.

The only other socially acceptable way of behaving inconsistently in public is to be drunk. Alcohol is something we use to regress to this childish state. Many people only sing when they're drunk. It also gives adults an opportunity to shout loudly in the street, express emotions to friends, cry, steal traffic cones and dance wildly. It gives us an opportunity to *play*. This is probably why it is so popular. It is the only opportunity that society allows us to express how we really feel moment to moment. The next day we can distance ourselves from the behavior by claiming that it was the alcohol that was responsible for the emotions, as well as the abandon it allowed.

No wonder then that it is so difficult for improvisers, who are not merely in public but *onstage*, to fight the instinct to look sane and instead make large emotional changes. We have spent our whole childhood learning not to do it and, if we do not have the excuse of drunkenness, we are far more likely to stand and talk, to be emotionally consistent, invulnerable and glib. In an improv scene, if someone tells us they've just totaled our car, we want, above all things, to look *sane*. If we realize we've lost our job, or the pictures of us in a compromising position have just been released to the national press or our partner has left us for someone younger, we will probably reach for a funny line rather than a new, raw emotion.

Some people are genuinely terrified of strong emotions, possibly rightly so. A leading theory from the new field of evolutionary psychology suggests that powerful emotions are "doomsday devices," which serve no purpose of their own except to be so unpleasant that we take action to avoid triggering them in ourselves and others. They are also hard to fake (like laughter), which is why acting is so difficult. You can't fight evolution! In a setting like an improvisation workshop or show, where comedy is rewarded, this fear may manifest itself in making jokes, just as some people crack gags as a coping mechanism at times of great stress or sorrow. Making jokes about strong emotions belittles the emotions and reassures the joke-maker that he or she is still in control. However, it makes for lousy drama and usually fairly poor comedy, and a sensitive coach will encourage the improviser to treat the situation seriously and make sure to heap (detailed) praise on them when they manage to sustain it.

It might help to start seeing improv like alcohol. It's a healthier, more socially acceptable way to show emotion, and it will leave you with no hangover. Try playing someone who is drunk in a scene and see if your reactions are bigger. Then play someone who isn't drunk but shows the emotional fluidity generally associated with excess alcohol. Start to feel what it's like to have big responses in scenes. Justify these responses and you will be an improviser who drives scenes forward. Make offers that will illicit big emotions in others. If they don't respond, be emotional about their callous lack of emotion. Fight the urge to look sane.

A Quick Counter-Example

Let's do another one with a really high status interviewer, and make them a really nasty piece of work. You basically just get people in here to humiliate them—maybe there isn't even a job here at all. And I want a completely pathetic candidate with no qualifications and even less confidence. And I don't want you to alter the statuses unless or until I tell you.

With any luck, the improvisers will be very inspired by these instructions and we will get a hilariously crazy scene with a horribly aggressive interviewer and a desperately vulnerable candidate (improvisers have less difficulty *starting* vulnerable, especially if directed that way). This will sustain longer than a similar scene with less extreme characters, and may even include a possible end point, but it won't seem like a *story* unless somebody is changed. After quite a lot of platform, I find something apparently mundane, but new, said by the candidate, and I give the following instruction to the interviewer:

Put your head in your hands and start crying—now! Lose all your status at once!

Again, you may have to insist, but you should eventually get the interviewer sobbing furiously. "What's wrong?" is the natural question from the candidate. You *must* get an answer to this out of the interviewer, ideally referencing what was just said, or at least some element from earlier in the interview. Some interviewers lash out at or blame the candidate, but you must insist that their status dwindles to nothing. Some candidates twist the knife at this point, others patronize, some just sit there stunned—but their status can't help but creep up so we do have a status transfer, but one with a very different feel from those that preceded it.

While it's true that, most of the time, it makes sense to change little and often, you can create a stunning effect by playing all your aces at once. It's pretty much guaranteed to create interest in the audience, who perceive both the sudden and shocking vulnerability of the character and the *risk* taken by the improviser, and who will delight in both.

Once the Status Exchange has been mastered, set it as a pair-work exercise, perhaps supplying a location with plenty of possibilities, like a hospital or a church, so that students can invent their own characters and situations. This will make it clear just how powerful and flexible a technique they have on their hands.

SPEAKING IN TONGUES

Everybody up! It's party time. You've all come round to … Paul's house for drinks. You're going to mix and mingle. There's plenty of snacks, plenty to drink. There are old friends here, you're going to have a good time. But I want you to speak in an unintelligible, made-up language. It should sound like speech, it shouldn't just be the same two sounds over and over again. You act like you understand each other perfectly, but in fact you slarkit veto hubstent yerot plunch vrotil. Seebo? Sodar seebo? Pa, le, zooze!

Some people seem to require no training whatsoever in speaking gibberish (at least in terms of making a full range of sounds), and many others acquire the skill very rapidly, but some people are terribly anxious about making the "right" sounds and will persistently try to get by with "fah lah bah sah," or some other such weak-tea, often repetitive, sometimes consonant-free, version—or they will speak very hesitantly and sparingly and without the least bit of fluency.

There are at least two ways of dealing with an exercise that you pretty much *know* is going to be tough going for at least some members of the group. One is to introduce the game as "advanced." This may raise anxiety levels, but those who struggle with the game are absolved of their imagined shame of failure ahead of time. The other is to plough on with cheerful enthusiasm and hope that your sense of fun will lower anxiety levels sufficiently that even those to whom the skill does not come naturally don't feel that they have to try too hard. For gibberish particularly, enthusiasm and playfulness is key. So I just let my explanation segue into a demonstration and look like I'm enjoying myself enormously. Then I let everyone practice *en masse* so that people who are struggling can do so out of the spotlight.[23]

I pick someone who looks like they're having fun with the exercise and announce that they want to propose a toast or to tell a joke. With luck, the group understands that it's at least partly up to them to decide when the joke or toast is at an end, and they laugh together or try to agree on a word for "cheers."

Now the work begins. Have the improvisers make two lines (ideally of slightly unequal lengths), and get the people at the front of each line to step forward and perform a scene in gibberish that is exactly four lines long—

---

[23]Keith often supplies people who are struggling with gibberish cards—playing cards with gibberish sentences written on them—which they can use as a script, but with this approach there is generally no need for that. We try to avoid giving improvisers anything which distracts them from their partner, even as a temporary crutch. See the chapter on Characters for more of this.

two lines each. When the second improviser has spoken their second line, those two improvisers go to the backs of the lines, and two more jump up, ready to repeat the game. Encourage them to try out different "accents"[24] and in general to experiment. No doubt, some of these gibberish interactions will get quite a strong reaction from the rest of the group—a happy laugh of recognition or even a round of applause—whereas others will be greeted with silence. You may feel that the illusion of two people speaking a common language is quite strong in some cases (even if the actual gibberish spoken is rather different), but in others the lack of real communication will be entirely apparent. So, after about a dozen or so of these, depending on the size of the group, pause and share some of these observations. See if anyone can account for this difference, and feel free to try out any of the ideas they suggest.

Here are some ideas we have heard suggested by groups in the past, with comments on their chances of success:

- Use mime props. This can certainly establish place and situation more strongly, but it doesn't create the illusion of communication.

- Repeat the other person's words. This can work, and is a useful trick, but it isn't essential. It *is* useful to point it out as a counter to very slack gibberish with very few consonants. You should at least give your partner a chance to pick out words which they can repeat.

- Be filled with emotion. This again can be helpful, but isn't enough on its own.

- Make your meaning clear through gesture. This was Viola Spolin's approach. "Gibberish is a vocal utterance accompanying an action, not the translation of an English phrase," she writes in *Improvisation for the Theater*. She stresses that communication is achieved through the use of actions, but if taken too far these instructions result in the illusion of two people speaking a common language being completely destroyed, since if you knew what I was talking about, I wouldn't have to pantomime it out for you.[25]

- Understand what you are saying. Spolin would sympathize with this idea, which develops the previous one, but this puts the emphasis on you communicating with your partner. If you want your fellow

---

[24]Some people's "neutral" gibberish is very faltering and repetitive, but their Italian or German gibberish is marvelous. Deborah's always comes out a bit Swedish and Tom's often sounds Russian. Whatever works!

[25]The Marx Brothers' biographer Joe Adamson acutely points out that, for all the popularity of the scenes in which Harpo pantomimed a crucial piece of information for Chico—who found ingenious ways to misunderstand the most elementary mime—these scenes reduced Harpo from a character who *wouldn't* speak to one who *couldn't*.

player to understand what you are saying, why are you speaking in gibberish? This approach is almost never successful in creating the illusion of communication.

● Have a reaction to your partner's lines.

This last is the key to all work involving gibberish. This may come as no surprise in a chapter entitled "Being Changed," but the mechanism is subtle and easy to miss. Once the improvisers have cracked it, or they've got bored with their other ideas and you've told them the answer (and you should let them try out all ideas—they may discover something new!), you can demonstrate the effectiveness of reacting using the following procedure. Do a number of similar four-line gibberish scenes, but ask for the first line to be delivered neutrally. The second improviser picks an arbitrary reaction and delivers their second line, which inspires a reaction in the first improviser. Thus, players rarely understand what they are saying, but they *do make a choice about what was said to them*. This choice can be informed by the other improviser's tone, but what's crucial is that it affects you.

So, A approaches B holding a mime object and cheerfully says "Loksi laydo proot yub fitch." B accepts the mime object, but JOINS A, and in the same cheerful tone responds "Exsi laftoport yarral jee." A now has nothing to go on, and so continues in the same vein. The audience is completely lost, despite A's physical offer and initial emotional choice. Neither character has been affected, so nothing has happened. Because nothing has happened, and because their speaking in gibberish makes defining a platform difficult if not impossible, the improvisers have nothing to build on and nowhere to go.

On the other hand, let us suppose that A approaches B holding a mime object and says "Kulchi navarro goshi dest," in a neutral tone. B now makes a strong choice, seeing the object, clutching his face and howling "Veedo veedo teransi yewter! Ponsee goobal gerful!" in horror and despair. He snatches the object and clutches it to his breast. A becomes very somber and falteringly delivers more bad news: "Terkle zee damnink … kerslum…" B stares at him expectantly, and he finally finishes the sentence. "Pachoolit." "Pachoolit!" roars B, holding the object up and waggling it at the heavens, as grief turns to anger "Hooli jer futser pa damsi hinkle!"

Now the scene is gripping and involving. Everyone can make guesses about what is going on. Although much of the detail is obscure, the sweep of the story is perfectly clear and the improvisers find it easy to continue. In gibberish, if you want to know what you've said, look to your partner's reaction. If they look shocked, you just insulted them. If they look delighted and hug you, maybe you told them you are pregnant.

Once this idea is clearly understood, I set the following exercise, usually for the whole group to do in pairs.

For this game, everyone is going to begin speaking in English, but when I yell "switch" you will both switch to gibberish. When I yell "Switch!" again, you switch back to English and so on. You always understand each other perfectly—it should look like someone is cycling through the language options on a DVD. I'd like one of you to be a homeowner and one of you to be selling something door to door. Begin by knocking on the door, and you're speaking in English. Go!

I let them go for thirty to forty seconds, long enough for most pairs to have opened the door and struck up a conversation. Then I yell "Switch!" (or sometimes honk a horn if I need to save my voice). The change is often astonishing. The volume level goes up dramatically. People's eyes open wider and they start using their hands in very expressive ways. Their bodies become fluid and dynamic. The scene becomes physical, with lots of mime objects. After another thirty to forty seconds, I yell "Switch!" again, and listen to the volume drop and the body language return to normal. I let the scene play on, yelling "Switch!" at smaller and smaller intervals. Gradually, the distinction between the two modes starts to disappear.

Everyone returns to their seats and I get some feedback. What difference did they notice between the two modes? Chances are, most people have noticed the same thing as me: in gibberish, players are more expressive, more emotional, more physical and more committed. I ask if anyone demonstrated the thing they were selling. A few people indicate that they did. I ask if they began the demonstration speaking English or speaking gibberish. Often they began it while speaking gibberish. While speaking English, it feels far safer to talk about the item, and so we miss opportunities to make physical offers. In gibberish, we have to be physical or we may not add anything at all. Once the vacuum cleaner has been switched on, then it can suck up the family hamster. Once the encyclopedias are opened, the homeowner can discover a crucial error in the entry about her. If the aluminum siding is taken off the van, then it can fall and crush a valuable antique. But if the players just stand and talk, they'd better be amazingly funny or develop a fascinating relationship, or the scene is going to get awfully dull.

But of course, there's no reason why an improviser shouldn't display all the virtues of gibberish while actually speaking English (and this is what the best improvisers in fact often do). Switching rapidly between modes creates this effect, but it's a little bumpy.

This is only one of a number of English/gibberish "switch" games, but it is by far the simplest and best. Others include one person speaking English and one person speaking gibberish until the "switch" command whereupon they switch languages, one person speaking English and one person speaking gibberish and either person initiating a switch by electing to change language, or the "Battle of the Sexes" version, where boys speak English to boys and girls speaking English to girls, but boys speak gibberish to girls and girls speak gibberish to boys. Most of the time, these variants generate nothing over and above the basic version described above (except confusion), but you might want to try them for variety. The simplest version, of course, is to have someone speaking gibberish throughout and someone else speaking English throughout, which puts the focus squarely on who is defining and who is blind-offering. This is useful as a lead-in to Sandy Carroll (page 222) if the group is already happy with gibberish, but is less useful on stage.

What is not helpful, in our opinion, is translating the gibberish. Once again, only the safest and most limited version of a wonderful, exciting and liberating game is actually played anywhere! Improvisation is about taking a risk. The risk in speaking gibberish is that the illusion of communication will be destroyed and the improvisers will be unable to develop a story. Have the gibberish translated and the risk entirely vanishes, along with any reason to use the game. If that argument strikes you as a little too ideological for authors who earlier stated that their maxim was "whatever works," then let's consider what happens when you ask for gibberish to be translated. The standard game (often called Foreign Film Dub) has two players who speak in gibberish, while two other players provide English translations (sometimes just one player translates for everybody, which is no improvement). Apart from the pleasure of hearing people speak in gibberish (which is a minor and incidental one), this has none of the advantages of simply dubbing voices onto actors who silently move their lips.

In a dubbing scene, the vocal improvisers respond in the moment to the physical offers made by the actors, and these instant justifications are often very charming and funny. Likewise, the physical improvisers instantly embellish the lines of dialogue they are given, and a very positive feedback loop is created. The instantaneous reactions mean no one is quite sure who is coming up with what idea and so everyone is relaxed and happy to be obvious. Generating stories is usually effortless (see the section on Master/Servant Dubbing, which has many of the same benefits).

Get improvisers to speak in gibberish and they become loud, fast, physical, funny and excitable. But the wretched Foreign Film Dub game requires them to utter a line of gibberish and then stop—and for their partner to refrain from responding or reacting at all until the translator has supplied the English version. With one force encouraging them to react, respond, be emotional and be instantaneous, and another insisting that they stop, wait, pause and consider, it's no wonder that confusion generally reigns, and instead of being aware of the offers made and their implications for the story, the improvisers are stuck trying to work out whose turn it is to speak next. The solo version in which a single speaker delivers a gibberish lecture, translated by another player, does at least deal with this problem for the gibberish speakers and is therefore the least awful of the various ways of presenting this game.

If anything, life is worse for the poor improvisers required to provide the English translations. Clearly, the intent of the game is for the translation to pick up on emotional and physical offers made by the gibberish speakers, but that usually strikes most translators as dull. Assuming that everyone's been taught to play the game with pauses in the right places (you do workshop these games before you start playing them in public, don't you?), one of the actors lets fly a stream of gibberish, finds a place to stop, the other actor refrains from responding (which kills the illusion of communication, but let's not dwell) and suddenly the voice actor is the complete focus of attention. The pressure to be clever and funny and surprising is overwhelming. In most case, the actor abandons trying to build on the physical offers and looks instead for ways to block them, contradict them, purposefully misread them or just ignore them completely and continue developing their previous verbal offer. Audiences may laugh (because they enjoy seeing people thwarted) but you can see the gibberish improvisers visibly sag before they adjust their physical offers to match the joke, knowing that this too is going to be yanked away from them. In general, this approach puts all the emphasis on the novelty of the procedure, which means that variety is going to be desperately lacking.

No caustic description of the mechanics of Foreign Film Dub would be complete without mention of The Standard Foreign Film Dub Joke. This exists in two forms. The first is where the gibberish speaker drones on for paragraph after paragraph until finally pausing for breath, which Brobdingnagian utterance is translated into a Lilliputian "Yes" or "I know." The other is the same but the other way around—a very short piece of gibberish is translated into a lengthy English filibuster. This joke dates back at least as far as Charlie Chaplin's 1940 film *The Great Dictator*, and very likely much earlier than that. Comedians working from scripts have little excuse for exactly duplicating jokes from the Second World War, and improvisers have even less. BEING OBVIOUS does not imply repeating yourself. On the contrary, calmly noticing everything in the platform and YES ANDing the specific details will provide you with infinite variety.

In summary: The point of speaking in gibberish is to remove your ability to communicate and define. It makes no sense to give with one hand and take away with the other. If you want to do scenes in gibberish, do scenes in gibberish. If you want to do scenes in English (with or without some other restriction such as dubbing or speaking one-word-each-at-a-time), do scenes in English. If you want the best of both worlds, switch between modes. But don't have people translate your gibberish for you!

Our happy band of new improvisers knows nothing of this and is thrilled to continue exploring the delights of gibberish. Now that the group has gained confidence in speaking in tongues, it's time to put them to the test in front of the rest of the group. Begin with the English/gibberish "switch" game again and notice that as well as putting the improvisers in different states, there are different opportunities available in the different modes. That is to say, whereas improvisers may be more likely to make physical offers while speaking in gibberish but aren't constrained from doing so while speaking in English, there are things which they can only do while speaking in English and some things they can do with much greater freedom while speaking in gibberish. There are some close parallels here with the Master/Servant Dubbing game, but it's probably better to teach them on different days. These are vital lessons and require a certain amount of self-confidence to make them work. Such confidence is acquired slowly, so it makes sense to present the same ideas again with a different hat on, in a later lesson.

First and most obviously, while speaking in English, you can *define*—an absolutely crucial skill for improvisers, and a technique which always makes life easier, but which feels very risky at the moment of doing it. If a scene starts in gibberish, we may get some sense of how intimate or hostile the characters are, but it's only in English that they can define the relationship—by saying "I didn't ask to be born, Dad!" or "I'm so happy I get to share an office with you, I know I'm going to learn such a lot."

However, when speaking in gibberish, like the servant in the Master/Servant Dubbing game, the improvisers are free to take imaginative jumps into the darkness—suddenly producing mime objects, performing apparently unmotivated actions or (best of all) being emotionally changed. Part of the fun for an audience watching this game is the tension that exists between these two modes. The English segments may get repetitive and unimaginative if the gibberish segments aren't setting them up with blind offers in need of definition, and the gibberish segments will likely be extremely boring if they don't contain any physical offers or emotional changes, since they are otherwise content-free!

Also take care that offers which were crystal clear in gibberish don't get repeated in English. Speaking in English is an opportunity to define something new. If an improviser speaking in gibberish spills his coffee and begins frantically mopping it up, when we switch to English, it's a huge waste to say, "You just spilled your coffee." Much better to say something like, "There is just one way you can make this up to me..."

Once these ideas are understood, the story will race forward like a rocket:

> **Bob:** (*With an imperious air*) Snarkle fitch huptar hiptar?
> **Joanna:** (*Eagerly*) Juptif gab nid kreel. (*She begins frantically digging at his feet*)
> **Director:** Switch!
> **Bob:** Dig faster!
> **Joanna:** I'm sorry, sir, it's my first time on sand-castle duty.

Happy improvisers who are completely aware of everything their partner is doing and who are eager to make assumptions will have no problem making discoveries at this kind of pace. It's *your* job, as teacher, to get them into that kind of state!

One final note about playing this game in public: It's usually clearer and more pleasurable to have the switch take place in mid-sentence. We remember a practically show-stopping gale of laughter which followed the following exchange during a Micetro Impro show a few years ago. The situation was a woman visiting a pet undertaker to arrange for the burial of her cat. The undertaker was gesturing at his range of coffins while gibbering away.

> **Undertaker:** Wubbly prendergraf joot raffick porto. Gorbo throm hoy… *(Points at something)* Veerkle…
> **Director:** Switch!
> **Undertaker:** *(Points)* Medium… *(Points)* or large.

A more challenging game—but one that's extremely worthwhile—is the Scene in Gibberish. This emphasizes once again the primal importance of establishing a reactive relationship to create the "point" of the story. It is possible to make the scene engaging and interesting, even if some points are unclear by the end, if the characters are genuinely affected. It is rather harder to elegantly establish details like location, relationship, identities of mime objects and so on, but this also helps make the point that defining these things is tremendously useful, not only to stop the audience from worrying about them but to inspire your and your partner's imaginations.

A very interesting exercise for workshops, which can also be successful in shows, is just to set up a situation where two characters can sit and have a chat in gibberish. Try father and son at a wedding, old friends meeting at a coffee shop before one of them emigrates, the morning after a one-night stand. The characters don't need to undergo massive life-changing epiphanies. The audience will be delighted at the tiny details of the way in which the characters affect each other as well as by the success of the improvisers in sustaining the illusion of communication.

Gibberish scenes need a degree of both sensitivity and boldness to play well, and most groups will struggle at first. Persevere (if the group is relishing the challenge) and you will be rewarded with improvisers who have an exquisite sensitivity to their partner's offers and a tremendous willingness to stride boldly into the future.

One way to generalize this back to regular scenes is to observe that when your partner's words are unintelligible, a lot of other details become critical. If you imagine that everything your partner does, they do for a reason (which as we know also tends to be the audience's assumption), then all you need do is to notice their offer and act on it. As Patti Stiles used to put it to us: "Don't look for an offer, assume one has already been made." That offer can be a slight furrow of the brow or a tilt of the head, which makes the improviser look a little sad—giving rise to a breakup scene. A shifting of the weight from foot to foot makes the improviser look uncertain—giving rise to a secret diary scene. A confident air implies that the improviser is an authority figure—giving rise to a scene about a cruel military dictator. Improvisers can visualize themselves as detectives on the look-out for clues which they can act on.

Once this is understood and the improvisers realize that a lot of these "clues" are subconscious, they can also start thinking of themselves as active sources of clues. I don't just walk into my partner's scene, I bound in with a happy grin, or I creep in nervously, or I march in officiously. My partner notices my attitude and makes an assumption about who I am and what I'm doing there and—*boom*—the scene is off and running with very little effort on either of our parts.

One further use of gibberish is worth mentioning. We've written at length elsewhere about the nature of improv games, their uses and abuses. Gibberish provides an excellent litmus test as to the "worth" of a given game. Briefly, if a game is worth playing in gibberish, it is probably worth playing in English. If a game is not worth playing in gibberish, it is probably not worth playing in English. Sometimes the gibberish version will emphasize different things (gibberish Word At A Time is all about giving your partner a good time and committing to physicality without hesitation, and rather less about storytelling) but often it will illuminate the English version.

2.10

More on Masters and Servants

Overview

There are many ways in which improvisers can make us of the dynamic between a Master and a Servant and working with this stylized relationship can improve work on relationship scenes of all kinds.

The two Master and Servant games we've already seen are so much fun, especially the last one, that often if we set up a Master/Servant scene in an end-of-term Micetro show, the students will immediately gravitate toward Overconfessing, but a number of other excellent structures exist which the well-rounded improviser should be aware of.

As we've seen in the work on status, a great many stories, whether improvised or not, have a battle for dominance at their core. What isn't so often discussed is the difference between a STATUS RELATIONSHIP on the one hand and a POWER RELATIONSHIP on the other. If you are asked to play a scene in which you are two building site laborers on a lunch break, then you need to be aware that the scenario you have been given does very little of the "heavy lifting" for you. Being on a lunch break means you are spared having to perform complicated mimes involving cement mixers or ten foot girders, but also means that the building site location is unlikely to be much more than color since the activity you start with is eating sandwiches and pouring tea from a thermos, rather than carrying bricks or mixing concrete. Further, the implication of "two laborers" is that they are on an equal footing, they are JOINED, so it will be vital to discover something interesting about their relationship.

As we discussed earlier, characters like the fishermen in BassProv or Peter Cook and Dudley Moore's Pete and Dud characters can just sit and chat and the tiny status shifts, as well as their unique take on the world, make their conversation fascinating, but beginner improvisers would do well to avoid this kind of setup and given "building site" as a location, should strongly prefer to be foreman and laborer or property owner and laborer, because the power relationship makes it much easier for one of them to affect the other, and immediately gives them different stakes in the outcome of the building project.

Not only that, but now if they play a status gap, the power relationship throws that status gap into relief. If, as we expect, the foreman plays high status, we get to see him assert his authority, blame the laborer for every shortcoming in the project, make the laborer run menial errands for him and so on. We get to see the laborer's moral choice—whether to stand up to this overbearing tyrant or meekly go along with his over-the-top demands. A pair of laborers who have the same personal status as well as the same position in the hierarchy will find it very difficult to affect one another. Thus, the improvisers may feel compelled to look outside the NARRATIVE CIRCLE for something to start a story and may become trapped in melodramatic nonsense or improv absurdity rather quickly.

A pair of laborers who come equipped with a status gap will find it much easier to generate a narrative which flows out of their relationship—one is an old hand, the other has never set foot on a building site before; or one is the elder brother of the other, effectively acting as parent or babysitter; one finds fault with everything the other does; and so on. But note that there is no equivalent of playing the wrong status. As we saw when we first started playing around with status, you can make choices about positions in a hierarchy independently of choices about status and the scene will still make sense. You can play a Status Exchange using a job interview scenario and have either player begin High Status. And, it can be more interesting to play the power relationship one way and the status relationship the other.

> **Foreman:** (*head bobbing, hands clasped*) Hello there, Jim. Everything going well is it?
>
> **Jim:** (*without looking at him*) Fine.
>
> **Foreman:** Good, good, good. Enjoying your lunch are you?
>
> **Jim:** I was, yes.
>
> **Foreman:** What has Mrs. Jim put in there today? If it's Thursday, it must be ham. Am I right?
>
> **Jim:** No, it's cheese.
>
> **Foreman:** Ah well. A change is as good as a rest, eh?
>
> **Jim:** What do you want, Dave?
>
> **Foreman:** Well, Jim. I was just wondering if there was any chance of doing some … ah … work today…?
>
> **Jim:** Sure, knock yourself out.
>
> **Foreman:** Very funny, Jim. No but seriously. We are three weeks behind. On a two-week project.

Jim: Dave—I'm having lunch. Can I talk to you later?
Foreman: Yes, yes of course. Sorry to interrupt.

There's no equivalent choice to be made without the power relationship being defined, so when playing with status, it's good to include power relationships at the same time. Not all power relationships are clear-cut. In a job interview, the interviewer has power over the candidate, because the candidate wants the job which only the interviewer can provide. But what about a parent and child? The parent might seem to have the power, but when the child starts throwing a tantrum in public, then the power may well shift.

A Master and a Servant represent the archetypal power relationship and one which is very unlikely to ever change over the course of a single scene. Working on this relationship can be very useful in informing work on status and power relationships of all kinds.

If we are reintroducing the concept of Masters and Servants we might well start by getting the group to work together in pairs and just play around with some of the possibilities inherent in the idea of one human being owning another. Start by getting everyone to pair up and choose who is the Servant and who is the Master. Remind them that Masters should give their servants names and that Servants should call the Master "sir" or "ma'am." Using these forms of address helps cement the relationship, regardless of the status played.

Now get the Masters to train their new Servants. Begin with a fairly high status Master and a fairly low status servant. Have the Master give the Servant some orders and find fault with every little thing. The Master shouldn't wait for the Servant to screw up, whatever the Servant does should be wrong at first. If the Master requests a chair and the Servant brings it slowly and deliberately, then the Master should grow impatient: "Come on, come on. We don't have all day. You'll have to go a bit quicker than that if you want to remain in my employ." If, however, the Servant brings the chair very speedily, then the Master should react with alarm. "Careful, careful! Don't go rushing about like that, you'll break something." It's important that the Master be fairly consistent, and not keep changing whimsically, so gradually the Servant will learn what it takes to please this new employer and the scene will settle down. Try to call time before everyone reaches this stage and get them to do it again the other way around.

By "programming" the Master to criticize *whatever* the Servant does, the teacher absolves the improviser playing the Servant from any residual shame or guilt and Being Criticized becomes as much a game as Dishing Out Criticism, although in fact it's more usually the case that Masters aren't harsh enough, making the game safer but less fun (as ever). When everyone's had a go, make new pairs and this time have the Master get ready to go out. Once more have everybody pair up. This time, get each person to make a private choice of status and repeat the exercise. We may get a high status Master with a low status Servant as before, but three other choices also exist. The status choices shouldn't be too extreme, or—especially in the case of both playing high status—the battle for status may become overwhelming. Low status Masters are still able to criticize even high status Servants...

> **Master:** Jeremy, I'm terribly sorry but I think this is the wrong hat, isn't it?
>
> **Servant:** It isn't the hat you asked for ma'am, but this one is rather more fetching.
>
> **Master:** Is it? Is it really? Oh dear. It's just not as comfortable as the other one.
>
> **Servant:** I am most distressed to hear that, ma'am.
>
> **Master:** Maybe we could go back to the one I requested then? If you don't mind?
>
> **Servant:** Certainly, ma'am. It's entirely up to you of course.
>
> **Master:** Er, now, Jeremy?
>
> **Servant:** Oh I do beg your pardon, ma'am. I assumed you were joking. (*He goes to get the hat*)

And high status Servants are still capable of error. As before, allow the Masters to spend three or four minutes training and getting to know their new Servants. Once they are ready to go out and have established some kind of rapport, tell them they are going to a singles night, for lonely Masters to meet other Masters. The Servants can facilitate. Some may be sent on errands to pass on greetings to comely Masters on the other side of the room. Some may provide courtship advice or produce gifts for desirable Masters. Sometimes two Servants will be left alone together and may let their guard down a little. Servants should be very reluctant to talk to another Master, regardless of the statuses.

Having practiced the skills in these settings, students should be well-prepared to develop these kinds of relationships onstage in pretty much any situation. Two people wandering around an art gallery may or may not prove to be interesting, but a Master and a Servant wandering around an art gallery will allow the platform to be sustained for longer much more easily because the nature of the relationship will in itself be interesting. Sooner or later, someone may have to contrive a break in the routine of some sort...

> **Master:** That's a particularly fine painting, don't you think, Simon?
>
> **Servant:** That's not for me to say, sir.
>
> **Master:** Don't you recognize the figure holding the grapes?
>
> **Servant:** I don't think ... wait a minute. Is that *me*?
>
> **Master:** Yes, Simon.
>
> **Servant:** But I don't understand. When was this painted!?

The most interesting scenes are generally those which puts the formal relationship under stress. If the Master (who has power over the Servant) puts pressure on the Servant to relate in a less formal manner, then the Servant has to choose between disobeying orders or violating the "rules of engagement" and may very well feel damned either way. The struggle is fascinating and we will watch the improviser and the character caught between these two conflicting forces for quite some time.

> **Master:** Don't you like it?
> **Servant:** It's very flattering, sir.
> **Master:** It's my gift to you, Simon.
> **Servant:** Just working for you is reward in itself, sir.
> **Master:** Are you rejecting my gift, Simon?
> **Servant:** No, sir.
> **Master:** I'm rather offended. I thought we were rather more than Master and Servant, but perhaps I was wrong.
> **Servant:** No, sir.
> **Master:** Are you contradicting me!?
> **Servant:** No, sir—I mean...

See the next section for some more ideas about how to sustain the Servant's misery.

A few other structures are worth mentioning—two described by Keith and one developed at the Spontaneity Shop.

THE CHAIR GAME

This is a great game for younger, more physical improvisers and works very well onstage, but it probably shouldn't be used too often as it is a little limited in its scope. The Servant follows the Master around holding a chair. When the Master feels like sitting, the improviser in question should just start to sit, trusting that the Servant will be ready and will smoothly insert the chair under their lowering posterior. If they fail and the Master goes sprawling on the floor, then the Master should be furious and enact some kind of punishment (Keith likes to supply Masters with "airship" balloons to use as cudgels but we've found the right kind hard to come by in the UK).

The art here is for both players to understand what makes the scene interesting and funny and contrive ways to make the Servant's life harder. If they get it right, they will be collaborating beautifully while seeming to be totally at odds. If the Servant clings to the Master's side and never lets go of the chair, then even if the Master sits rather rapidly, it should be trivial for the Servant to insert the chair and the audience will never see the Master tumble (which they are itching to see of course). But equally if the Servant seems totally uninterested in whether or not the chair is provided in time, then there will not appear to be any jeopardy. So, Masters should quickly become irritated by Servants who cling to their shoulder, invading their personal space, and should order them to keep their distance. And Servants should take risks with the chair, especially in furtherance of the Master's orders.

> **Master:** Goodness, this place is untidy.
> **Servant:** I'm terribly sorry, ma'am. Let me tidy up.
> *The Servant temporarily abandons the chair and begins throwing mime garbage into a mime trashcan.*
> **Master:** That's better.
> *The Master wanders downstage and begins to sit. The Servant quickly returns to the chair and thrusts it forward just in time. The Master turns round to "see" the mime trash can.*
> **Master:** You've spilled it now. Honestly, I don't know why I employ you.
> **Servant:** No, ma'am. Nor do I, ma'am.
> *The Servant goes back to picking up garbage. The Master stands and peers at the ceiling on the other side of the stage.*
> **Master:** Is that a cobweb up there? Get rid of that at once.
> **Servant:** I'm not sure I can reach it, ma'am.
> *The Master looks pointedly at the chair.*

Many fine pieces of physical comedy are possible. We've seen servants sling the chair across the stage like a shot of whiskey flying down the bar in a Western and come to a stop at exactly the right point. More than once, Servants have used their own bodies as substitute chairs and we've seen countless Masters tumble to the floor. Make sure the improvisers aren't too reckless, ideally play these scenes on carpeted or sprung stages and you'll have a wonderful time.

This game is a more sophisticated version of Keith's Making Faces game which is worth briefly describing. Sit three improvisers in a row. The center player is the Master, equipped with two Servants. Give the Master something specific to be in charge of (a school, a library, a zoo etc.). The Master must interrogate the Servants but not send them away. If the Master struggles, suggest that each sentence begins "What about the…" and is then completed with something related to the school, or library or whatever it is. Encourage the Servants to snap out nice clear answer and allow the Master to ask a few follow-up questions but to keep moving to new topics.

> **Master:** What about the penguins, Karen?
> **Servant 1:** Bald, sir.
> **Master:** Oh really? Why is that?
> **Servant 1:** Mange, sir.

Master: Dear me. Will they recover?
Servant 1: They are on the mend, sir.
Master: That's a relief. What about the elephants?
Servant 1: Mating, sir.

And so on. Every so often, encourage the Master to switch to the other Servant. At this point, with the Master's back turned, I whisper in the Servant's ear, "Make faces behind the Master's back. Don't get caught." When the Master turns to face the first Servant again, I give the second Servant the same instructions. The Master is forced to split their attention between two servants, so someone always has the opportunity to make faces. Don't underestimate how funny groups will find this—we never tire of seeing an authority figure have their status threatened.

Servants will eventually start to take stupid risks and may be caught. If so, they can attempt to justify the bizarre rictus they were caught in, but Masters should be encouraged to fire insolent Servants (and it's particularly funny to see a Master regretfully letting a face-pulling Servant go, while the other Servant is furiously pulling revolting faces behind their back). They can be replaced by other improvisers.

This is good training for The Chair Game because it's easy for the Master to provide opportunities for the Servants to pull faces without being seen to be blithely permitting this insubordination (which is why there is little risk in providing the instruction secretly the first time). With The Chair Game, the Master has to be both more deliberate and more subtle.

You can also try this Face Pulling Game with five people: one Master with two Servants, each of whom has an Underservant. Underservants respond to Servants the way that Servants respond to Masters and Servants will sometimes (but not always) have to refer to Underservants for information requested by the Master. Underservants should pull faces behind the backs of their Servants and can be fired by Servants. Masters may notice Underservants pulling faces behind the Servants' back but are generally unconcerned by it, although they may want to point it out to Servants if it is particularly egregious.

FINGERSNAPS

Thom, you're going to play the Master. Phill, you're going to play the Servant. Thom, I'd like you to call your servant in and just gossip. Ask him questions, strike up a conversation but don't send him on an errand, and in fact don't give him any verbal commands at all. If you want him to do something, just snap your fingers. He has been in your employ for a very long time so all he needs is a prompt, not detailed instructions. When you snap your fingers, he will know exactly what you want and he is never, ever wrong. Phill, think of the power...

This game is worth discussing for a number of reasons. Firstly, it's fascinating to contrast the need for Masters to find fault with their Servants in the previous game with the need for them *never* to find fault with their Servants in this game. Once again, it's not that either is correct, it's understanding the effect you want to achieve and what actions are needed to bring that about. Secondly, when played well the game is amazing to audiences—in some ways it's a performance version of Hypnotist/Magician (see page 220). Finally, from the point of view of the teacher, this is a game which requires a bit of patience. In our experience, very few improvisers will understand how these instructions should play out (although audiences will often grasp the concept very quickly, so it falls into that awkward category of games which are harder than they seem—see Playing Games on page 254).

Let's start by looking at how this *should* work. Then we'll go through the problems it presents for many improvisers.

It's natural and easy for Masters to think of things for Servants to do, and many improvisers feel safe and in control when giving orders. Then, if they can't think of a new order to give, they can criticize the way that the last order was carried out. This keeps them in control and means they don't have to think of a new idea. For this reason, the Train the Servant game on page 163 is usually pretty easy. But neither ordering the Servant about nor criticizing the Servant is available in this game.

Beginner improvisers often get "tunnel vision." Asked to play a scene set in a coffee shop, they talk of nothing but coffee. Playing two teachers, their conversation is limited to GOSSIP about the last class they taught. Of course, we don't want to exclude the audience by ignoring their suggestions, but people meet in coffee shops to get a friend's advice about their upcoming wedding and teachers also talk about politics, religion, hobbies and sports. Asked to play a scene between a Master and a Servant, sometimes the only offers which seem "available" are those which relate directly to the nature of the relationship. The style of interaction used in Pulling Faces can be useful here so that the Master gets into the rhythm of asking questions rather than issuing orders.

Ideally, the Master and the Servant are able to sustain some kind of GOSSIP-y conversation about things which are happening offstage and every so often, the Master issues commands by means of a finger-snap (it may be necessary to prompt this). Anxious improvisers will also be unsure how to respond to this BLIND OFFER despite the reassurance that they can't be wrong. Coach them to do some normal and obvious things to start with, and make sure that the Master isn't tempted to issue any corrections.

> **Master:** Good morning, Franklin.
> **Servant:** Good morning to you, ma'am.
> **Master:** Did you sleep well, Franklin? *(snap)*
> *Servant mimes throwing open the curtains.*

> **Servant:** Oh yes, thank you ma'am. The cold flag-stones in the cellar are perfect for my back.
> **Master:** Well, that's good news. What's the weather like out there? *(snap)*
> *Servant pours tea into a mime cup and hands it over.*
> **Servant:** A little overcast, ma'am.
> *The Master drinks.*
> **Master:** Franklin—this is cold!
> **Me:** *No it isn't! The Servant is never wrong!*
> **Master:** Mm. Delicious.

And so on. Just seeing the Servant apparently "know" what the Master's intention is is fascinating for a while, but my last instruction to the Servant, "think of the power," is still hanging in the air. Just like in the Dubbing game, the Servant has rather more control over the scene than it would appear. Throwing open curtains and pouring tea are both pretty obvious actions, but the Servant can respond to the BLIND OFFER of the finger snap with a second BLIND OFFER. A perfectly fine response to the snap of the Master's fingers is to simply produce a mime object. Now the Master will have to name it—or even better find a way to use it. It's nice if the Master says "Ah my hat. Yes, I'll be needing that if the weather is bad," but it's nicer still if the Master simply takes the invisible object and puts it on her head while continuing the conversation.

It also helps to develop the story as well as taking the pressure off the improvisers if the Servant looks for ways to chain "orders" together. One finger snap can be interpreted as "pour the tea," the next as "lift the cup to my lips," the next as "remove the tea," and so on. Once a few pairs have got this working smoothly (and it might take several iterations), you can encourage the Servant to be even bolder. If there is *nothing*, *literally nothing* which the Servant can do which will make the Master unhappy, then that truly is power. If the Master can never criticize the Servant's actions, then the Servant can do things which no sane Master would ever want and trust that the Master will find a way of justifying these actions.

> **Master:** Well, if we're going for a walk, we'd better go sooner rather than later. *(snap)*
> **Servant:** Of course, ma'am.
> *The Servant mimes bringing in a dog.*
> **Master:** Hello, Alfie. You're a good boy. Isn't he a good boy, Frankin?
> **Servant:** Yes, ma'am.
> **Master:** Yes, he is a good boy. *(snap)*
> *The Servant mimes shooting the dog.*
> **Master:** It's no good Franklin. I still can't feel any compassion at all. We'll try again tomorrow with a kitten.

> **Servant:** Of course, ma'am. *(snap)*
> *The Servant mimes removing the canine corpse.*

Don't let them go up the ABSURDITY CURVE too quickly or the scene will be baffling.

This is quite complex stuff, combining a BLIND OFFER game with the formal Master/Servant relationship, the need to keep the main narrative moving forward, with the game itself accelerating. If all you get out of it is the fun of seeing the Master justify some crazy offers from the Servant, it might still be worthwhile. The very best of these scenes eventually manage to braid the various strands together. Students at one of our workshops once improvised a delightful version in which the Servant shaving the Master became more and more romantically distressed as he described his lustful conquests, until she eventually slit his throat with the razor.

We recently experimented with a variant on this, designed to get bolder behavior out of a group of particularly reticent students. In this version, a single Master was equipped with a retinue of Servants (typically about a dozen) who didn't wait for orders but looked for opportunities to help the Master out. We might cast the Master as working as a travel agent and send in a customer. Two servants immediately jump up to let the customer in. Another produces a chair and two more pour a drink. Hardly a word has been spoken. "Where were you thinking of going?" asks the Master. "Well, somewhere hot, ideally," replies the customer and instantly three servants mime stripping off his shirt and liberally applying sun-cream. Being part of a gang helps to reduce inhibitions since it's hard to notice how much any one person is contributing, and it doesn't matter whether only one, or a whole group, are inspired to intervene at a given moment.

MASTER/SERVANT DOUBLE HEADER

One more quick variation on the Master/Servant theme, this time developed at The Spontaneity Shop. Two improvisers play a Master and Servant pair awaiting the arrival of another Master/Servant pair who will be played by the same people, but the other way around. Thus one improviser plays Master A and Servant B, while the other improviser plays Master B and Servant A. Servant A hears the door and goes to answer it, coming back as Master B. Master A yells for his servant who doesn't appear. He goes in search, and comes back as Servant B and so on. A very pleasing farce structure can be developed very quickly and easily by this simple device, which also tests the improvisers' clarity of thinking and ability to transform themselves. It's nice if secrets are kept (maybe one Master wants something from the other, but talking to his own Servant, it becomes clear that a double-cross is planned). We should ideally see all possible combinations. Remember that Servants together behave very differently than if there is a Master around.

2.11

Twitching, Topping and Paperflicking

Overview

A simple procedure, very entertaining in its own right, gives rise to some important general principles about being changed, breaking routines and pacing.

In *Impro for Storytellers*, Keith describes a scene between a nervous but well-qualified job applicant and an interviewer with a twitch, of which the interviewer is unaware. As the twitch becomes more and more off-putting to the candidate, the interviewer perceives *him* as acting more and more oddly. A shame, as on paper he looked to be an excellent choice.

As with the Over-confessing game, which provided such a superb case study of JUMPING AND JUSTIFYING, here one simple game has proven to be an excellent vehicle to study some important aspects of improvising stories, especially improvising middles and, to a certain extent, ends as well.

Of the three variations which give this chapter its title, let's start with Paperflicking, also described by Keith. I give the instruction to the interviewer privately so that the audience and the other improviser are surprised in the same way as the other character. In theory, this should help to get genuine reactions out of the other improviser, but as we'll see, that's rarely the case. It's also fun to see one improviser denied knowledge that someone else is in on (which may explain the otherwise mysterious persistence of those wretched "endowment" games—see "Playing Games" on page 254).

Two volunteers please. Klaus and Neil, excellent. Neil, will you wait at the side for a moment? When you come back, you're going to be interviewed by Klaus for a job. One of you needs to name the job or you'll have nothing to talk about. Here, you can use this piece of paper as your CV. Klaus, come outside the room with me for a moment, I want to give you a secret instruction.

Once I have Klaus in private, this is what I tell him:

Be nice and polite. Neil looks like an excellent candidate for the job. But when he hands you his CV, I want you to start tearing strips off of it, rolling them into a ball and flicking them at him. You have absolutely no idea you are doing this. Okay, go and sit down and then call in the next candidate.

When the scene starts, both improvisers seem fairly calm and relaxed. Any anxiety Neil feels about my secret instructions to Klaus will be entirely appropriate to his role. With any luck, I won't have to coach too much as they establish the basic details of the platform: We will find out what the job is, how qualified Neil is, and any other details. The first break in the routine comes when Klaus first starts to tear the CV. Immediately all eyes are on *Neil*, the candidate. Everyone wants to know—how will he react? Believe it or not, there will often be no reaction at all. Improvisers get taught— including by us—to accept offers, and in general they hate to be changed, so the candidate takes this in his stride. Klaus balls up the torn-off strip of CV and flicks it at Neil. Again, the audience is agog to know what will happen next, but again there is no reaction. As the scene plays on, even the audience may be slightly mystified as to why they aren't enjoying it more. The guy interviewing the candidate is *tearing up his CV and flicking the bits of paper at him.* This is amazing! Why isn't it funnier?

We watch drama to see other people suffer, because that's more fun than suffering ourselves but more interesting than everything being nice. Neil is refusing to suffer because he isn't affected by Klaus tearing up the CV. He doesn't realize that when his scene partner does something extraordinary, he—Neil—becomes the most interesting person on the stage.

Let's just pause for a moment and ask why the scene is set up like it is. To understand this, you have to understand that the point of the scene is to make life difficult for the candidate—to make that person suffer. So, we begin by putting him in a situation where he has everything to lose: a job interview. This means that he is in an alien environment, whereas to the interviewer, everything is comfortable and familiar.[26] If necessary, the

---

[26]Giving the interviewer an instruction like "Tear up the CV" pretty much guarantees that they won't add anything to the environment, alas. Teaching improvisation is like trying to smooth out a sheet. As soon as you get one area nice and flat, wrinkles appear somewhere else.

candidate should also be coached to be desperate for the job. If they don't need the job, they can just get up and leave should the interview become too upsetting. Having a reason to keep them there raises the stakes. To also raise the stakes and for extra irony, we have the interviewer tremendously impressed with the candidate's CV. Now, we give the interviewer a quirk to put the candidate off—tearing up the CV. And it is *vitally* important that the interviewer is oblivious to the quirk, or the solution presents itself too easily and obviously. ("You're tearing up my CV." "Oh, sorry.") All of which careful work goes entirely to waste if the candidate won't be affected, which as we already know, they probably won't be.

So, once we've demonstrated that refusing to be affected won't generate much in the way of drama or comedy, we take the scene again. There's a chance (although not a big one) that this time, the candidate will call the interviewer on his peculiar behavior right away. This may seem bold, but is just another way in which the improviser manages to get the character off the hook—and we want them on the hook. We want to see them in a situation which they can't cope with. Yes, we may want the candidate to confront the interviewer, but not *yet*. That would squander a routine which the audience will be happy to watch for some time yet.

When the candidate manages to let the interviewer's actions affect him, even if only slightly, the scene leaps into life. The interviewer now has a technical problem to cope with: he has to mentally "edit out" his paper-tearing actions (since he is unaware of them) and perceive the candidate's reactions as if he were not provoking them.

Here's an example of how an early part of this scene might go, with both improvisers playing the game well.

> **Interviewer:** Well, I think we'd be lucky to get someone with your track record to work here, quite frankly.
> **Candidate:** That's great. I've been hoping to … (*Interviewer starts slowly tearing off a strip from the Candidate's CV. Candidate trails off.*)
> **Interviewer:** Yes? Hoping to what?
> **Candidate:** Pardon? Oh. Er, hoping to move on to a role like, er, like … (*Candidate is momentarily transfixed by the tearing*)
> **Interviewer:** Are you feeling all right?
> **Candidate:** Sorry, just thinking about something else.
> **Interviewer:** Well, you need a bit of focus in a job like this, you know. This is a very busy newsroom.
> **Candidate:** Yes, sorry. I was saying, I'm … (*Interviewer flicks the balled-up strip of paper at him. Candidate flinches as it hits him.*) Oh!
> **Interview:** What on earth is the matter with you?

Once this game is understood, it will probably generate a lot of enthusiasm in the players, and early versions of this game will be very funny. However, it will likely run out of steam eventually (whether or not the interviewer runs out of CV!) rather than arrive at a satisfactory conclusion. Time to generate some more variety. I get two more volunteers up, set up the same scene again, and take the interviewer outside with me to give them some secret instructions.

Carol, here's what I want you to do. Begin by repeating John's answers, as if you are considering what he has just said. Start accelerating the pace so you are repeating everything that he is saying. Then see if you can get it to the point where you are saying everything he says as he says it. Don't forget that you still have to speak for yourself and you are totally unaware that you are behaving in this strange way.

This is called Topping and is rather harder to do than Paperflicking, but it scores over Paperflicking in that it is rather easier to accelerate. A great offer, like an interviewer unconsciously tearing up a CV, will be squandered if it doesn't generate a reaction. But equally, the scene needs to *build*, and the same apparently great offer will outstay its welcome if it can't be developed.

Given an interviewer who can sustain the speaking-in-unison and remember to contribute their own lines and reactions to the candidate, and given a candidate who reacts to this behavior *and* remembers to speak in more or less complete sentences so that the interviewer can speak them simultaneously, the scene can be tremendously funny. The candidate must get more and more confused and upset, while the interviewer denies that anything is wrong. The effect is essentially impossible to communicate in print, however!

Hopefully, by now, the improvisers playing the candidate realize that their job is to be affected and to get into trouble. If they find a way to solve the problem, the scene is dead in the water, since it is the candidate's plight which is the main point of interest.

However, even given that this Topping procedure is funny in itself, even given that making the interviewer unaware of it increases the discomfort and therefore the interest, and even given that *both* the procedure and the reaction to it from the candidate can be amplified as the scene progresses—even given all of this, it is still unlikely that the scene will come to a satisfactory end. *Any* routine is capable of outstaying its welcome, and this one is no different.

Now is the right time for the candidate to say, "Don't you know you are saying everything I'm saying/tearing up my CV and flicking it at me?" Apart from anything else, the audience wants to know the answer to this question, and that means the candidate has to ask it. But saying it earlier squanders the candidate's discomfort. Remember that ideally, we break routines *just* before they become boring, and here the payoff for the apparent BRIDGING is the increased emotional stakes as the candidate gets more and more confused and worked up.

Clearly, almost any procedure will do for the interviewer. A simple muscular tic or twitch will do nicely. It has all the qualities required for this game: it's quick, it can be done at any time, especially when the candidate is talking (so it can interrupt their speech, which will be noticed by the interviewer) and it can be amplified. You start with a wink, then a wink and a grimace, then a wink and a grimace and a twitch of the head. By the end of the scene, it's a high-pitched yelp and a Nazi salute!

Once we've gone through these three (Twitching, Topping and Paperflicking), let improvisers choose their own, both in front of the group and in pairs. If they don't have anything, suggest that they pick one of these three. Obviously, some of these will be more initially entertaining than others. Twitches we've seen include sighing, making faces, blowing raspberries, singing opera and "freezing" in mid-sentence. One improviser swore under her breath with amazing fluency whenever the candidate began speaking, the effect of which was wonderfully funny and reduced the whole class to hysterics. But diminishing returns will almost always set in if you keep repeating the same thing. Even comedy sketches which rely on repetition (see "Finding the Game in the Scene" on page 228) usually have someone else reacting to the repetition, which reaction builds as the sketch goes on. In general, therefore, the twitch should build over the course of the scene (and improvisers should pick twitches which can build) and even if they don't or can't, the reactions should build.

As with Over-confessing, a pattern is emerging here. At first, everything seems normal. Then the interviewer starts behaving oddly but not acknowledging the fact. The candidate amplifies the interviewer's oddness by obviously noticing it and being put off by it (just as a skillful player amplifies the status choice of another player), and the interviewer notices that, which contributes to the candidate's discomfort. Both the severity of the tic and the candidate's reaction must now build to sustain the scene (although not necessarily at the same time or at the same rate). Sooner or later, the candidate must explicitly reference the tic. When the interviewer is baffled by the accusation, trouble for the candidate is maximized. Often, the scene reaches a suitable pitch of hysteria and we can yank the lights down without fully resolving the story.

If that doesn't happen, or we want a longer scene at this time in this show, or we want to practice resolving scenes, or we aren't satisfied with leaving loose ends dangling—how can we bring this to a satisfactory conclusion? This section picks up where our discussion on endings left off after Over-confessing.

The scene is a routine—being interviewed for a job. The routine is broken when the interviewer starts twitching (or whatever). This sets up the new routine of trying not to notice the twitch. This is broken and returned to several times as the candidate tries to maintain composure, with the energy building on both sides. Finally, the routine of trying not to notice is broken when the candidate acknowledges the tic. Some improvisers return to the routine when the interviewer denies all knowledge. This is fine if the routine still has anything left, but it should be temporary.

> **Interviewer:** Shrieking? What are you talking about?
> **Candidate:** Oh. I... nothing. Nothing. Sorry, what was the question?
> **Interviewer:** Where do you see yourself in five years' time?
> **Candidate:** Well, I'd like to have more...
> **Interviewer:** Yiiieeeeaaagghh!
> **Candidate:** ... er, responsibility, hopefully more money...
> **Interviewer:** Yiiiaaauuuuueeerrgghh!
> **Candidate:** Er, no, look, you are still doing it.
> **Interviewer:** Doing what?

More often, this sets up a new routine of trying to convince the interviewer, but that again doesn't end the scene (although it could prolong the middle very entertainingly). What does it take to bring this scene to an *end*?

Recall that when they are about to complete a routine, improvisers often feel uncreative. Completed routines at the beginnings of stories feel like introduction; it's when the routine is broken that the narrative kicks off. Here, the routine of being interviewed for a job has been altered but not abandoned. If we end that routine now, then it will feel like an ending and the audience will be happy because the hero will have been made to suffer. If the candidate runs off screaming or the interviewer calls security to have this maniac taken away ("Me crazy? *You're* the crazy one! You can see her tearing up my CV, can't you?") then we will be in no doubt that the scene has been completed. Likewise, if an element from the very beginning is reincorporated, that signals an ending to an audience.

But to *resolve* the story, we have to answer all the questions and justify the inclusion of all the elements. The huge outstanding question is *why* the interviewer is behaving in such a peculiar way. Improvisers' reluctance to confront this question speaks to their lack of courage in defining and in breaking routines, but also exemplifies the way that they sometimes don't question their assumptions. "You don't know you're doing it" is an instruction which I have given the improviser playing the interviewer. If this rule isn't in place, then life is much, much easier for the candidate (which means much less fun for the audience). If that rule remains intact, then there is very little likelihood of discovering the truth. But why isn't that rule up for grabs? No reason at all.

Really successful endings to this scene often violate some of the rules set up at the beginning, and this is true of many other scenes too, especially comedy scenes. The punch-line of many sketches, after all, effectively cancels the entire sketch. For example, Eric Idle's lascivious nudge-nudge man turns out to be a virgin or Mel Smith and Griff Rhys Jones turn out to be staking out a suburban home for hours on end simply in order to deliver a card reading "We called to read your meter but you were out." But you don't have to pull the rug out from under the audience in quite such an extreme manner—you just have to stop treating what has been established as sacrosanct, whether a coach or director told you to do it or not.

Once this is understood, then endings suggest themselves more easily. The interviewer admits that this was all an initiative test. The interviewer becomes ashen-faced: "It's happening again…" The twitch transfers to the candidate too—or abandons the interviewer for its new host: "Finally, I'm free!" Spotting endings is a skill in itself—and one that your lighting operator needs to acquire! It is possible to perhaps fill a whole three-hour class playing this game, perhaps including a Continue or Thank You element (page 237) later on to increase the pressure. This means that the audience becomes very jaded (which is useful) and so the players have to go through the beats of the scene more quickly in order not to bore them, but still making sure that each moment is sustained long enough to be effective. Despite the frantic energy of many improvisers, what tends to make middles difficult is that, having found what the scene is about, the improvisers get stuck there and fail to move on, so it makes sense to teach "moving to the next beat adroitly" as a skill. Moving to the *next* beat is key, though. Jumping from idea to idea at random is not recommended; the trick is to move one idea into the future—which is precisely what improvisers find so terrifying. Note that at the beginning of scenes, the problem is more likely to be one of improvisers tentatively exploring first one idea and then another, but not taking any one idea into the future. If they're being specific then this may be helpful platform-building, but more often than not it's just confusing. Playing What Comes Next again is a useful reminder of these points.

Some of these issues are developed further under "Breaking Deadlocks," which is in the next chapter.

2.12

Playing Characters

Overview

Rich characters are of tremendous value. Storytellers of all kinds, writers, performers, improvisers and many others put great store by the creation of characters, and that fits with the thesis we have been developing. But what *is* a character, and what tools are available for the improviser who wants to play lots of them?

WHAT IS A CHARACTER?

Before there was public improvisation, there was improvisation in rehearsal rooms and as acting exercises. Viola Spolin resisted the idea that any of her games could be performed in public. Stanislavski, along with his followers such as Lee Strasberg, popularized improvisation as an actor's route to discovering a character, and there followed a lot of actorly soul-searching about what a character was. Now it's certainly true that actors like Brando and De Niro gave more detailed, more naturalistic portrayals than many of those who preceded them, but does it make any sense to talk about a character existing *independently of the script* in the case of scripted drama?

Here's what we're fairly certain exists, or at least here are some things we can put names to and find uses for. Maybe one of them is what other people call "character," or (more likely) some combination of them is.

Characterization is the externals of an individual. These tend not to change much over the life of a scene and include matters such as age, accent, mode of speech, style of dress, way of moving and so on. It can be very useful for improvisers, who need to assume a character very quickly and without hours of searching, to adopt an "outside-in" *modus*, so being able to physically reinvent oneself is a desirable skill. It also provides variety in the (typical) case of a handful of performers and an hour-plus show.

Attitudes are the way an individual approaches things, their emotions from moment to moment. Attitudes vary also toward different things, so the same character might have a fondness for the comforts of home, a dislike of visitors, an excitement about model trains and an overall attitude of ennui. Unlike characterization, attitudes do (and should) change over the course of a scene. Status can be thought of as a particular kind of attitude. The word "attitude" is also used a lot by Chaplin describing his methods.

Choices or **Actions** are what the individual does. In the case of a scripted piece, these are—for the most part—given.[27] In the case of improvisation, players can use strong characterization and attitudes to inspire their imaginations and so make bold choices.

Talking about actions that are "out of character" suggests that there is some baseline against which actions can be measured, but we prefer to say that an action which is "out of character" is merely a choice that hasn't been justified. Great drama is about people doing extraordinary things, and great writers know the value of finding justifications for those extraordinary things. It's predictable to see a judge ruling dispassionately (or at any rate, it's platform), but how about a judge raping a nun? What has to happen for that action to be "in character"? (The answer, of course, is found in *Measure for Measure*.)

You could even go as far as to say, as Tom has, that **any character is capable of any action.** (Salinsky's First Law?)

Improvisers should study storytelling techniques so that they tend to build strong platforms, are changed by what's said to them, get themselves into trouble and reincorporate to provide structure and/or an ending. In populating the platform with characters, they should transform themselves, adopting a different posture, physicality, accent, register and so (and use costume pieces or props if that's appropriate). They should have strong attitudes toward the other elements of the platform, including the other characters, and they should be willing to change those attitudes and justify the changes. From these actions, the illusion of different characters will emerge. Sustaining a character also inspires improvisers; they get the sense that their character "knows" what they should do next. In our Level One improv course, which these chapters more or less follow, the two major improvements in the work tend to come in the fourth session, when we play Go Through An Unusual Door, and in the eighth session when we work on characters.

---

[27]In a scripted piece, you may be given some fairly clear directions about attitudes and characterization as well, of course. You can't play Sherlock Holmes without making the choice to take the case, but you will also almost certainly adopt a penetrating and arrogant attitude, speak with an upper-class English accent, wear a deerstalker and smoke a pipe.

Of these three components—characterization, attitude and actions—we have already looked at attitudes. Much of the work on JUMP AND JUSTIFY, using games like Over-confessing, made use of attitudes. Jump and justify with attitudes is also the preferred method for playing the servant in the Master/Servant Dubbing game and initiating a Status Exchange. In each of these cases, a change of emotion, or some other offer, precedes any understanding of what caused it, but the illusion is created that the character was changed by the last thing that was said to them, and a skillful (or at any rate prompt and comprehensive) justification enhances that illusion.

Here's a quick sample of the Emotional Direction game, which illustrates the power of this method (this is far superior to the Emotional Rollercoaster game, which is described in Appendix One: Games).

> **Frank:** Good morning, Andy. Your usual *Times* and pack of chewing gum?
>
> **Andy:** Yes, please, and a copy of *Private Eye* as well.
>
> **Director:** *Frank, anger.*
>
> **Frank:** *Private Eye*!? The issue with this shop plastered all over the center pages? The scandal! You could at least have bought a copy somewhere else, you contemptuous bastard.
>
> **Andy:** (*Opening the magazine*) Torrid orgy in corner shop. Frank's Papers used for all-night sex orgies without owner's knowledge.
>
> **Frank:** You've had your fun, now get out.
>
> **Director:** *Andy, love.*
>
> **Andy:** I…I'm sorry Frank, I can't. I wanted to gloat and jeer like all the rest, but inside my heart is breaking. I love you, Frank.
>
> **Frank:** Don't mock me.
>
> **Andy:** It's true. I'm sorry I was rude. Say you forgive me?
>
> **Director:** *Frank, boredom.*
>
> **Frank:** Oh, who cares?

And so on. Once the platform is established (and this very quick breaking of the routine means an enormous amount of platform must be assumed), the rest of the plot is developed simply as a means to justify the changes of emotion.

By way of illustration, here are those same plot choices with the emotional offers removed (a false example, since the plot choices were a product of the emotional offers, but hopefully instructive nevertheless).

> **Frank:** Good morning, Andy. Your usual *Times* and pack of chewing gum?
>
> **Andy:** Yes, please, and a copy of *Private Eye* as well.
>
> **Frank:** I see that scandal is all over the center pages.
>
> **Andy:** It certainly is. This place was used for orgies without your knowledge?

Frank: That's right. Bye now.
Andy: Goodbye, darling.
Frank: How dull.

This barely feels like introduction, and it certainly squanders a perfectly good offer. Story is one person being changed by another. Remove that element and all you have is jokes—if you're lucky.

This leads us to a second principle: **You can perform any action with any attitude** (Salinsky's Second Law?) which will be explored in more detail in the section on Shoe Shops.

CHANGING THE BODY

If we were giving a class on character, we would likely begin with *characterization*. Some people come to improvisation with a certain amount of vocal variety "built-in." These players are always willing to show off their range of accents and voices, and it is certainly helpful for a show to contain variety of all kinds. However, if this is the only kind of versatility that an improviser displays, it can become dull, and even a strong vocal characterization shows a marked tendency to drift back to neutral over the course of the scene, especially if the scene isn't going so well (since more of the brain is occupied with worry, leaving less room for the accent[28]). This leads to another endemic problem: improvisers making fun of other people's or (almost equally common) their own accent wobbles. The problem here isn't so much that the gagging destroys the story—although it does—it's that this is a very boring cliché of the genre. Cut it out.

Less common are the improvisers who make the choice to transform their body first, and this seems slightly less susceptible to the problem mentioned above. There is also less likelihood that the attitudes and actions will be impervious to the transformation. If Ed has a great Welsh accent that he can do, then chances are the character he plays will be Welsh Ed, who will have the same attitudes and make the same choices as "Vanilla" Ed would have. But, whereas it is possible to fret about your last line or plan your next one, your body is always in the present. This means that sustaining a different body image is more likely to keep improvisers "in the moment" and is less likely to be a source of anxiety for them—provided that they aren't self-conscious about transforming themselves physically.

The first order of business, then, is to get them transforming themselves. Exercises of this kind are hugely common in drama classes of all kinds, but it's not the techniques themselves that we're interested in at the moment

---

[28]This is also true of emotional offers, which is an even bigger problem, since if a scene runs out of steam, a change of emotion is often exactly what is lacking.

(although they are hopefully useful and interesting). It's just a way to get everyone moving around and using their bodies in novel ways. As usual, it's good to begin with the whole group working at once so that nobody feels too much "on display."

> *Everybody up and start moving around. As you walk, I'm going to call out different instructions which will change the way you walk. Don't worry about what anyone else is doing. There's no one right way to follow any of these instruction. If you happen to notice someone else taking a different approach, then fine. You just commit to what you are doing.*

As they walk, I give them some ideas. I do quite a lot of these, even to the point of boring the group slightly. If transforming their bodies is boring to them, then it isn't alarming them anymore.

- With each step you take you get a little older, until you are so old you can barely walk.

- With each step you take you get a little younger, stopping just before you start crawling.

- With each step you take you get heavier, until you are so heavy you can barely move.

- With each step you take you get lighter, until you are almost floating off the floor.

- Make your movements more and more jerky, sudden and spasmodic.

- Make your movements more *and* more smooth, flowing and sustained.

- Make a choice of either heavy or light and either sudden or sustained and do both together. Now do the opposite.[29]

- Pick a part of the body and have that part "lead." The impetus to move comes from there. (I start easy, with nose or belly, then make it harder. It's pretty easy to move from your forehead, rather harder to move from your knees. Or your elbows. Or the back of the head. You could instead add an adjective to the body part: happy ears, crafty feet, etc.)

- Pick an animal and let the physical qualities of that animal affect you—but remain human. I don't want you wriggling on your bellies if you pick "snake," I just want you to be sinewy, muscular and writhing people.

- Think of someone you know very well, who has a different body type than you, and walk like them.

---

[29]These are elements of a system developed by the movement theorist Rudolf Laban.

Many other possibilities exist. To use some of these body images in something that looks like a scene, try something like a waiting room scenario. (We try never to develop new skills in a vacuum. People don't learn to use a new technique until they've actually applied it *in situ*.) Stick some chairs next to each other in the middle of the playing area, and get the person sitting at one end of the group to wait at one side, ready to enter.

This is a waiting room and this game is going to be without dialogue. I don't mean it will look like we're watching it with the sound turned down, I mean that none of the characters will have anything to say. In a minute, Jo, you're going to enter, adopting a different physicality. You can use any of the techniques we've just tried, or anything else you want, but it won't look like you coming in—it will look like someone else. You'll come in, sit down and wait for your number to be called. When she's entered, the next person in line—that's you, Paulo—will also enter, and you too will adopt a different physicality, ideally something which will be a contrast to whatever Jo is doing. You'll sit next to her and you'll make eye contact. Then Jo's number will be called and she'll leave. Which means the next person, Tina, can enter with yet another physicality. And so on until everyone has had a go.

Like most silent scenes (see "You Can't Learn Mime From A Book" on page 213) this will likely be very slow and detailed, and therefore fascinating. The audience's interest peaks when a new character enters and whenever the two characters are affected by each other. It doesn't have to be a big reaction; a brief moment of connection is often enough. But there is a great deal of anticipatory pleasure in seeing what will happen when the hyperactive child enters the room in which the nervous old lady is waiting.

Transforming the body emboldens the improvisers, and both players and audience are keen to know what would have happened if the interactions had been allowed to continue. This is an excellent state of affairs.

HILARIOUS GEISHA

We will develop this into fully blown characters in a moment, but there's another game worth looking at which is fun and is particularly good for directors. It was taught to us by Jay Stern and Meg Sweeney-Lawless, late of the New York improv company Chicago City Limits.

One volunteer begins walking around in front of the group. The coach shows the rest of the group (not the volunteer) a description of a character, just two or three words. The group then has to "mold" the volunteer into the character given. Encourage the group to give instructions which the actor can follow easily, and avoid the use of props (mime or otherwise) or anything else that would give the game away, since part of the fun is asking the actor what they thought they were—once everyone's convinced they look just right. Given the description "tortured poet," it's pointless for both these reasons to give the instruction "try to think of a poem." Just as drama teachers wrongly assume that their students just "know" how to play a range of statuses, actors don't know how to play a tortured poet without dialogue. On the other hand, an instruction like "Pause and look into space, then scowl and keep walking," is easy to follow and will likely achieve the desired result. More subtle effects can be achieved by giving the actor mental procedures, although this should be used sparingly. Jay showed us "Count your money without touching it," which had a very pleasing effect on some people. Also, there is nothing wrong with one student reversing the effect of a previous instruction, provided there is general consensus that it isn't working. As teacher, don't let a tug-of-war develop. Be the one to decide what's working, and break deadlocks if need be.

The list that we use includes the following ideas. Students aren't necessarily cast according to type, or even sex, just whatever the coach thinks would be fun for them and for the group

- Famous acrobat
- Stern headmaster
- Pregnant nun
- Beauty pageant winner
- Member of a boy band
- Heroin addict
- Lonely child
- Energetic old person
- Sexy weightlifter
- Worried hunter
- Angry teenager
- Humiliated banker
- Charming slaughterhouse worker
- Gigantic toddler
- Exhausted dancer

- Hopeless concierge
- Furious wizard
- Sleazy theatrical agent
- Tortured poet
- Kids' TV presenter
- Dominatrix
- Restaurant critic
- Prisoner on a chain gang
- Circus ringmaster
- Frazzled film director
- Doorman at a grand hotel
- Store detective
- Naïve cowboy
- Cheesy nightclub singer
- Hilarious geisha

This last has become the name of the exercise, although we have never given it to a student to do.

As the instructions pile up and the picture starts to come in to focus, it's not uncommon for the actor to follow an instruction and for the whole group to suddenly laugh. The actor now looks just right and everyone agrees that we've got it. That doesn't necessarily mean that the actor will guess correctly what they were at the end of the exercise. Deborah remembers being given "boy-band member" and—while the whole group agreed that was exactly what she looked like—her best guess was that she was the Queen in prison.

What the audience sees may be very different from how you are feeling, and this can be a very important lesson for actors of all kinds, not just improvisers. Compare this exercise to Characters With Depth (page 208).

PRECONCEPTIONS AND BEING THE WRONG SEX

As soon as you step on the stage, the audience's mind fills with preconceptions about you. These can be based on anything: who else you remind them of, how you are dressed, the last thing they saw you do, how the other members of the group relate to you, how comfortable you seem onstage, how happy you are to address them directly, how your hair is done, how tall you are and especially what sex you are.

Unlike in premeditated theatre, and especially movies, and especially *especially* television, in improvisation actors are not cast according to type. As money increases and rehearsal time decreases, there is pressure on directors to cast actors who already look and sound like the part and who can therefore be relied on (hopefully) to show up and inhabit the role without too much tedious directing required. This is a useful skill for actors to acquire, needless to say, but the price you pay is typecasting.

In an improv show, the audience understands—in fact expects—that you will be playing whatever character the story demands of you. Tom, for example, is a slightly built Englishman standing no more than 5'7" but can play, say, a 200lb redneck Texan sheriff, if not perfectly convincingly then at least with sufficient commitment that the audience will suspend their disbelief. They understand the game, and they abandon their preconception of Tom (somewhere between Hugh Grant and Harry Potter) if he sticks his belly out, throws his shoulders back and swaggers on to the stage bellowing "Now see *hee*-yah, boy…" in his best Clifton James manner.

So, you certainly don't want to give the audience more to worry about if your show requires you to play many characters (as most shows do).

If you you're wearing a t-shirt with an obscene logo or your breasts are falling out of your top, then the audience may be distracted by this and find it harder to buy into the character you're playing, unless you're incredibly convincing.

Every couple of years or so, in the online improv community, someone comes up with the bright idea of Nude Improv, which they believe will solve this problem—and be a marvelous marketing ploy to boot. The latter might be true (if a bit desperate), but the former is almost certainly not. Susan Sarandon is an actor who knows a thing or two about nudity for the sake of art, or if not art then story, or if not story then money. She has pointed out in interviews that as soon as a female nipple appears on screen, the straight men in the audience stop listening immediately. A friend of ours told us that he got immensely frustrated watching David Lynch's *Mulholland Drive*, which has a rather impenetrable plot. But he said every time he thought he'd give up and walk out, Lynch would include a scene of two women kissing, and so he'd think "Well, I'll give it another ten minutes, then…"

Stripping is not the answer, and nor, we think, is dressing all the cast exactly the same. Audiences come to improv shows (although they may not know it) with the hope that the cast will reveal something about themselves, will express their personalities fully and completely. This is not that likely to happen in most shows anyway, but it's even less likely to happen if the improvisers look and feel like they are interchangeable members of the same family of clones. Just dress nicely but simply. You might want to wear contact lenses instead of glasses if you need them (so the audience can see your eyes), and choose subtle rather than ostentatious jewelry. Then you should be able to play pretty much any type, age, build or nationality.

What's wonderful about improvisation is that you can literally play anyone, anywhere, anytime. You can be anything you want to be. Remember, your budget is only limited by your imagination, and you do not have to spend hours in hair and makeup. However, if you do come on as a member of the opposite sex, make an offer which leaves the audience in no doubt whatsoever about your gender, otherwise there is a danger they will see you as an effeminate man or a masculine woman.

Notably, in our all-female show *Hell On Heels*, this was never an issue. Women frequently played male characters and there was almost never any confusion.

So, the students already understand the importance of attitudes (although many will need constant reminding to begin with an attitude and to be changed), and they have been emboldened to transform themselves physically. Both of these will encourage them to make choices which are "in character," but let's try another exercise to put the whole thing together.

CHARACTERS FROM A HAT

Everybody grab a sheet of paper and a pen. I want you each to write down half a dozen thumbnail sketches of characters you might find in a typical office. Write clearly and tear the paper so that each slip has just one character written on it. Things you might write include "angry boss," "gossipy secretary," "slacker temp." They don't have to be wildly original, just write down the first things that occur to you. I'll collect them in and put them in this hat.

What happens next is that two students at a time each pick a slip of paper out of the hat and then play a scene between those two characters. Picking up a thumbnail sketch like this gives the players a tremendous amount of "permission". Suddenly, actions which they would never have contemplated before seem "available" or even "obvious" but the additional cognitive load of remembering the character description is hardly great, certainly compared to having a list of actions to complete, and so players are still able to listen, respond, and be influenced. (Compare this to Being Andrew Willson under "Status" on page 98.)

We prefer the contents of the slips of paper to be kept private, even though that creates certain problems, since those problems are the sort that will come up when playing strong characters without slips of paper. If you wanted to, you could do some "training wheels" sessions with the contents of the slips revealed at the beginning—and even discussed!

Often we want the improvisers to screw up a new game a few times first—see Go Through an Unusual Door, for example—but here we want them to feel how useful playing strong characters is, and the problems are technical, not artistic, so it's necessary to preempt and warn them about the following issues.

- Play your own sex, *regardless of the apparent intention of whoever wrote the slip*. Yes, that means if you're a boy and you get "slutty secretary," you have to find the male version of that. If you're a girl and you get "lascivious salesman," you have to find the female version of that. This generates some wonderful characters!

- Your slip of paper may define your job, but your partner may endow you with having another job. The slip does not give you permission to BLOCK. Nor does the other person's slip give you permission to WIMP. Make assumptions about your partner and expect them to do the same. So, if the slip of paper says "nervous new boy" and you are endowed with being the director of the company, then you *are* director of the company. But your *attitude* is that of a nervous new boy...

- ...at least it is when the scene starts. You will almost certainly need to be changed over the course of the scene for it to sustain (although it is possible with two very extreme and very different characters that just watching them rub up against each other will hold our interest), and it's possible that you will be changed profoundly, or that the mask will drop away and we will find out something new about you. The slips of paper should be seen as imaginative spring-boards, not shackles.

I generally suggest that one player starts onstage and builds some kind of environment. Ideally I will have some chairs and a table—or better yet, a desk—which they can rearrange if they want. The second player should enter promptly, as soon as they've got some idea about who the first player is and where the scene takes place. You also need to encourage them to MAKE ASSUMPTIONS and correct errors created by sticking too closely to the slips of paper. The audience needs some fairly basic information to be established early on. Have these people met before? What is the hierarchical relationship between them? Whose space is this? Often, the audience will see the answers to these questions in the improviser's bearing, but it takes a little more practice before the improvisers themselves have this clarity of vision. Being specific right from the start is hugely helpful.

It helps if, as coach, you are a confident director. You will often have to prevent the improvisers from jumping from topic to topic (THAT'S NOT GOOD ENOUGH), from trivializing and from not being affected. You will often be able to see much earlier than the players what the scene is really about, but nevertheless these scenes are often tremendously entertaining and the players seem filled with inspiration, especially early in the scene. If you get two very similar characters, you may need to direct someone to be changed in order to make the story work. Get everyone to play one of these, only asking what was written on the slips at the end of each scene. Sometimes the players *will* make the error of not finding ways to make their description come to life in the form of actions. If necessary, you can retake a scene once you know what the description was.

What's key is the idea that if what we call a "character" does exist independently of the situation, then we expect different people to behave in different ways, even if placed in the same situation—but this observation is useless unless the writers or actors or improvisers find things to do which express that character in some way. In *Die Hard*, Takagi, the CEO, tries to out-status Alan Rickman and gets a bullet for his trouble; Holly Gennero tries to reason with him and mothers the rest of the hostages; Ellis, the sleazy salesman, tries to "sell" himself to Rickman, and also gets a bullet. Their different choices in the same situation provide character moments which space out the action set-pieces and build up the villain in different ways. Improvisers need to find ways of taking the adjectives used to describe the character and turning them into verbs. Descriptions must become actions for the words on the slip of paper to come to life. A "penny-pinching accountant" can't just be a bit grumpy and rude. We need to see them still using an abacus because they think computers are overpriced, trying to borrow money, insisting on turning off the light even though it's late in the evening and so on and so forth. Most improvisers will be inspired by the description, and in our experience, if this problem doesn't come up early, it doesn't come up at all.

The real message here of course is that it's *easy* to play a rich and committed character if some helpful teacher gives you a little slip of paper with a good idea written on it. But since the people who played all these characters also wrote the slips of paper, it should be possible to give yourself a note like that any time, just before your foot hits the stage. And then you'll have the advantage of being able to pick just the right character for this situation. To wean improvisers off this technique, try mixing in blank slips with the "real" ones, forcing the players to supply their own character note.

Two more approaches to creating characters follow. If you want to create character-and-situation comedy rather than gag comedy, shtick comedy or shock comedy, then this work will pay dividends again and again. Remember, audiences love story. What is story? A changes B. How interesting (and funny) that is depends therefore on who A and B are.

SHOE SHOPS

OVERVIEW

Improvisers don't always figure out what is most interesting about a given scene. Although the fact of the setting makes a promise to the audience, it's who the characters are and how they change which is most important. Put the emphasis on playing strong attitudes, and any setting becomes an inspiration. This section also explores the differences between blocking, deadlock-breaking, canceling and sidetracking.

It gets a little frustrating watching improvisers block in order to "make things happen." The scenes that result are rarely very interesting—just trivial conflict for its own sake. What would happen if the improvisers were compelled not to argue, and were put in a situation which didn't seem to have a lot going for it in plot terms?

I get a couple of improvisers up and get them to play a scene set in a shoe shop. One of them is to be the customer, the other the shopkeeper. I give them no further instructions. If these students are well-trained, happy and confident, they will be looking for something of interest to happen and—if I'm lucky—they will be content to be obvious.

I make a private bet with myself that they will *not* successfully buy and sell a pair of shoes.

Now, this wouldn't matter if the scene were any good. But nine times out of ten, the scene will get bogged down in pointless BLOCKING...

> **Hilary:** Do you have these shoes in black?
> **Sam:** I'm afraid not.
> **Hilary:** What about these?
> **Sam:** Those are for display only

...or will degenerate into BARGAINING.

> **Sam:** These shoes are actually mine.
> **Hilary:** I'll pay double.
> **Sam:** I don't think so. I really like them.
> **Hilary:** I'll pay triple.
> **Sam:** Maybe we could share them?
> **Hilary:** I'm not paying triple to share your shoes!

As the improvisers desperately try to create story (and hopefully comedy) out of the transaction, they completely gum up the works and the audience slides slowly into a grateful coma. The improvisers are terrified of creating a scene in which they buy and sell a pair of shoes because then (they assume) the scene will be over and it will have been dull. I demonstrate this by getting a couple more improvisers to buy and sell a pair of shoes as quickly as possible and without blocking. The fear of delivering this brief, event-free scene steers them toward the parade of blocking outlined above, and yet the block-heavy scene is no more interesting, and doesn't even have the virtue of being over with quickly!

I set the following challenge to the group. Can they improvise an entertaining scene which obeys the following rules?

- The scene is set in a shoe shop.
- One improviser plays the shopkeeper and another plays the customer.

- A pair of shoes must be bought and sold during the course of the scene, and it must be the first pair of shoes referred to.

- The two characters must be strangers.

If I pitch it right, the group is very interested in solving this problem, and they become very motivated and keen to have lots of goes. Maybe they will offer some theories as to how to achieve this. Assuming that they don't or their theories don't hold water (try everything they suggest; the results may surprise you), start to steer them toward the platform. Point out how little we know about either of these two characters or the space that they occupy. When these details are introduced, our interest in the scene goes up immediately. Remind them of Go Through An Unusual Door, if they've played that.

Good space work will help build the environment, and thus sustain the platform but that won't necessarily solve the problem of developing the middle, and it will be very hard for them to truthfully introduce a lot of personal background material. Even if they do this, the rest of the rules may screw them up. An improviser who raises the stakes on the shoes will find they still have to buy them and so there is no payoff...

> **Hilary:** I've been saving up for these shoes for the last year.
> **Sam:** Here you go. You've got just enough money.
> **Hilary:** Er ... thank you.
> **Sam:** Thank *you*. Call again.

But play the scene with strong *attitudes*, and ideas suggest themselves effortlessly.

I'll begin with an example which is almost bound to come up very early on (nothing wrong with being obvious). Alan, as the shopkeeper, sets up his shop with finicky care. Every box of shoes is in exactly the right place, all at perfect right angles, and the whole place is spotlessly clean. Here we synthesize the work done on attitude and physicality in Characters From A Hat with the work done on platforms in Go Through An Unusual Door. In Characters From A Hat, once you know that you are the fitness-obsessed marketing guy, then you might discover a small set of dumb-bells in the filing cabinet. In Go Through An Unusual Door, once you know you have a lot of abstract art, you might discover that you're a struggling artist. Here, both decisions come at once. "What is my attitude to this space?" also answers the question "What is this space like?" since it's your shop and it will be however you want it to be.

Creating a perfectly orderly shop makes a pretty explicit promise to the audience. Whoever comes through that door needs to bring chaos with them. What form this takes is up to the other improviser, but they have been given a huge "steer" by the shopkeeper's offer, making the process vastly easier than if the shopkeeper has no attitude. (Compare this to the difference between breaking the routine of "reading a book" and breaking the routine of "reading a book on hypnotism.")

Let's say that Terry elects to play a drunk Glaswegian wastrel, who practically falls through the shop doorway, knocking over several boxes of shoes. It's pretty much guaranteed that Alan will have some kind of reaction. Just as in Twitching, Topping and Paperflicking, when Terry makes this grand entrance, *Alan* becomes the most interesting person on the stage. Every member of the audience wants to know what Alan's reaction will be. Alan tries to throw him out, but I remind them that they have to buy and sell a pair of shoes. "Aye," moans Terry. "I need a new pair o' shoes." He flings himself in to a chair and thrusts his foot into Alan's face. Alan's fussy prissiness barely permits him to touch the foot, which he endows with being covered in sores and calluses and barely encased in a shoe which is falling apart.

What follows next is an exercise in timing as much as anything. As in Twitching, Topping and Paperflicking, we need to build up the tension and not squander the process of change, but sooner or later we need to see someone pushed to breaking point. Here it will probably be Alan who cracks first, but it could just as well be Terry. One more break in the routine will probably get them home. Alan feels guilty and gives Terry a free pair of shoes. Terry reveals himself as a mystery shopper sent by head office. Terry collapses in a drunken stupor and must be hidden from the next customer.

Of course, drunkenness is not the only obvious choice open to Terry. Terry could be polite and well-spoken but clumsy, desperately apologizing for the accidents while simultaneously causing three more. He could be breathlessly exuberant and energetic, flinging his arms about and declaiming wildly, while scattering shoes in every direction. He could be cold and high status, casually tossing unsuitable shoes over his shoulder. He can be even more prissy and OCD than Alan, finding even this ruthlessly geometrical shop hopelessly chaotic. The problem has gone from the very difficult, very open-ended "Make this interesting" to the much more focused "How can I upset someone who's very tidy?" to which a number of excellent solutions present themselves immediately.

Each shopkeeper makes their own promises. A truculent teenager should be confronted by an authority figure. An over-articulate aesthete should be confronted by a monosyllabic oaf. A depressive should be confronted by a dementedly cheerful elf, and so on and so on. Then those characters should be *changed* by the interaction. No matter how interesting and funny they are when they first meet, this is simply a routine which will need breaking sooner or later.

The other thing which is key here is that none of this has anything whatsoever to do with shoe shopping. Shoe shopping is a *substrate* on top of which a human interaction is placed. So while shoe shopping is the event, it becomes merely a detail in the story as a whole, just color. This is why shoe shopping scenes are often dull, since there is nothing inherently interesting about buying a pair of shoes (though if you write for *Sex and the City*, you might disagree). But the same problem occurs, and worse, if you pick something which, the players imagine, *is* inherently interesting.

The world of television drama, especially in the US, is filled with a tremendous glut of medical and legal programming. But an improviser asked to play a lawyer meeting a client may assume that *being a lawyer* is what will be most interesting about this scene, and this will likely panic them as they realize that they don't really know what lawyers do or say. So they put all their energy into trying to dredge up legal jargon and the scene becomes stilted, awkward and dull.

But this isn't a fly-on-the-wall documentary about a day in the life of a junior solicitor. The audience does not want to see a competent professional on a perfectly ordinary day and will not gasp in awe at your ready command of legal jargon (they likely know no more than you do anyway). They want to see two characters interacting, and if the situation becomes relevant and heightens that interaction, great. Here are some questions which are key and will be raised in the audience's mind straight away.

- Have lawyer and client met before?
- What is the case?
- How does the lawyer feel about the case/the client/the law in general?
- How does the client feel about the case/the lawyer/this process?
- Is the client in the wrong?

Playing *attitudes* is hugely helpful. A surly, potentially violent client stalking around his cell could be met by a physically smaller, very anxious man full of tics and twitches—or a deeply caring woman who tries to inappropriately mother him. A terrified teenager arrested for carrying marijuana could be confronted by a cheerfully cynical, seen-it-all-before old hack: "Got any plans for the summer? I shouldn't bother, you'll get eight months at least. Only joking! Now then…" Then, the fact of the legal situation may become relevant once we know who the players are.

> **Lawyer:** Poor baby. Do you want a lollipop, darling?
> **Client:** No, I want you to get me out of jail.
> **Lawyer:** Let's start with the lollipop and go from there. What flavor?

As the players get more sophisticated, they can play multiple attitudes within the same scene. Taking a cat to the vet, you could play sentimental to the cat but demanding to the vet. Since audiences like transitions, this will liven up the scene even more. Keith's Sexy Smelly Stupid game (see Appendix One) is great training for this.

Breaking Deadlocks

So, this is how to get an improvised scene off to a good start, but care must be taken that the good start is not squandered. Energy needs to build, the stakes must be raised and routines must be broken. By starting in "neutral," you make it easy to break the routine with an arbitrary change in emotion, but you may struggle to find the right trouble for the right hero. By starting with rich characters, vivid characterizations and strong attitudes, you'll find the right trouble quickly. But if the characters simply drift back to neutral over the course of the scene,[30] then the audience will feel unsatisfied. The characters need to be changed and/or take extraordinary action over the course of the scene in order to sustain the middle and find an ending. This is ground we have been over already under Twitching, Topping and Paperflicking, but now let's add attitudes and characterization into the mix.

When two characters pick strong, contrasting attitudes, this may give them strong purposes (good!) and maybe even Stanislavskian super-objectives. As these contrasts are brought together, a conflict develops which can certainly add to the drama. But as we've already seen, conflict sometimes develops emotional energy at the expense of stories moving into the future. A scene which starts in conflict will very likely never get off the ground.

Sometimes this problem comes up when working with TILTS (see page 113). The improvisers usually "get" how to build a platform very quickly. Let's say that Paul and Sally are building a "park bench" platform. Paul is writing poetry in a notebook. Sally is eating a sandwich and feeding bits of it to her dog. A stray soccer ball rolls past which excites the dog. Both Paul and Sally go for it at once, collide and apologize. Paul throws it back to the soccer players. Paul and Sally make a bit of small talk. Time for a tilt. Sally says "I'm your soul."

---

[30]A great note that Andy Eninger gave us was to "find the affinity." He, like Keith, identified negativity as hugely problematic, tending to close down narrative. Keith urges his improvisers to start positive, because a positive platform is easier to build than a negative platform, and that means that trouble, when it comes, breaks the routine easily. What Andy pointed out to us was that if you are in conflict or negativity, finding the affinity between the characters also provides a contrast (a break in the routine, in our terminology). The price you pay is sometimes a loss of energy, but if you get the timing right, it can be a very effective and moving way to end a scene.

If they've practiced tilting, Paul will resist, but Sally will be more and more convincing. Ideally, material from the platform is reincorporated (ideas have to come from somewhere, and improvisers in a relaxed and happy state are aware of everything in the platform). "When our hands touched over the soccer ball, didn't you feel the energy?" I direct Sally to establish a purpose. "We need to be rejoined," she declares. "You have to hug me now, as tight as you can." Believing that drama equals conflict, Paul declares "No—get away from me!"

Hopefully the analog with the Shoe Shop is obvious now. Paul can't say "Okay then," because then the routine is completed. But he can't say "No," because that will lock them into bargaining:

> **Sally:** You'll never be able to write poetry again.
> **Paul:** I don't care, go away.

Paul's refusal of this bizarre request makes more sense than his blithe acquiescence, and if he is changed by the interaction—his discomfort turning to panic as Sally pursues him—then the routine will be interesting for a time. But this is a routine which needs breaking. Unlike the twitch, there is no obvious way in which this can get more interesting by the repeat-and-amplify method, so good storytellers know when to set aside what the *character* wants and instead find a way to take the story into the future.

What's the most obvious way of breaking the routine of two people stating and re-stating what it is that they want? One of them gives up. Instantly you have something that needs justifying, and justification is easy to do and generates ideas. If Paul gives up (which is the most obvious course of action, since he is preventing the reunion from happening and the audience will be interested to know what will happen if he allows her to hug him) then, because this has been preceded by his fear and rejection, we sense that this acquiescence will come at a *cost*. This is a fundamental feature of many longer stories. In Joseph Campbell's classic Hero's Journey structure,[31] the hero is first confronted by the Call to Adventure, but does not immediately set off on a quest. Instead the next beat is that the hero Refuses the Call, only reluctantly accepting it when circumstances conspire to remove all other options. A weak choice can often be made stronger by adding a cost. One of the other defining characteristics of classic heroes is that they must *make moral choices*. If the "right" course of action is free of cost, then this is just another way of lowering the stakes and making the story dull.

---

[31]The template, whether consciously or not, for any number of adventure stories, including *Star Wars* and *The Matrix*, to name just two particularly conspicuous examples.

So Paul finds a way of justifying this complete reversal of his point of view. "My poetry *has* been pretty awful lately..." he muses. "Yes," cries Sally, seeing an opening. "One embrace and inspiration will return!" This is why character *must* be taught as something malleable. The cliché of the pretentious actor is to say, "My character wouldn't do that," but almost no action is beyond justification. Remember Salinsky's First Law. Any character is capable of any action. If the character does something new, then we will see another side to them. We will love to see the arrogant bully reduced to a forelock-tugging wretch by the one person in the world who really scares or impresses him.

Back to "I'm your soul." Once the characters break the deadlock and hug, we finally confront the issue of whether or not Sally's story is for real. This is a *binary choice*, and like most binary choices in improv, either will do, provided one or other character is affected. If Sally is for real, this should affect Paul in a profound way. You could tilt again here if you want, by having Sally be an evil demon, now possessing Paul and taking him to Hell. This is another way of dealing with the problem created by having a character get what they want—it turns out that they didn't want it after all, which adds a layer of irony.

If Sally is not for real, then her embarrassment and frustration may well be pay-off enough—it becomes a status reversal, with Paul being nice about it and Sally, who had earlier seemed so mysterious and powerful, trying to hold back angry tears.

But if Paul doesn't break the deadlock, then Sally has to. "Fine," she says, "I'll go. Just don't come crying to me when you can't think of a rhyme for 'perplexed'." This *weakens* Paul, making him wonder if he's missed out on something. Or, Sally drops her status. "Never mind, I'm not a very good soul anyway. The last person who used me was Sylvia Plath. You'd probably end up with your head in the oven." "You were Sylvia Plath's soul? Oh my god!" Again, you don't have to think through all the ramifications—the justification will come if the two of you commit to the reality of the scene and you're aware of the questions you are raising.

DISMANTLING THE SCENE

There's nothing whatsoever wrong with pulling the rug out from under the audience once in a while. It's the compulsion to constantly be original and the failure to justify the incorporation of those original ideas that does the damage.

But just because something is fine in principle doesn't mean it will always work, and there are definite distinctions between revealing character (good), canceling offers (bad) and gagging (awful). A very common "frame-breaking" device, beloved of improvisers who grew up watching *Monty Python* and similar fare, is revealing that the preceding events are merely part of a film or television program. This is only a short step away from "It was all a dream!" and is a way of escaping the need to develop the story into the future.

The question of what expectations have been raised is also important. If two fairly bland characters pass the time of day in a pub and then one of them jumps in fear and begins pointing frantically at the dartboard, then this generates a mystery which kicks the story off. If, on the other hand, one has been systematically bullying the other, humiliating him, making him run degrading errands and so on—and then the bully just suddenly stops and says "I say, I'm awfully sorry, let me get that for you," then this is beyond mystery and into total confusion (because it cancels an offer which has been made repeatedly). It's certainly preferable to endless repetition of essentially the same material, and the audience might respond very positively to the boldness of the choice, but the risk here is that the justification won't be enough to overcome the incongruence of the new offer. Far from revealing character, this may simply be abandoning it.

One group of improvisers we worked with fell into a pattern of setting up the details of the platform, establishing the characters and getting somebody into trouble—then, to achieve an ending, they would systematically dismantle the platform. "I'm sorry, there's no job anyway. This isn't even my office. I just walked in here off the street." "What a relief—everything on my CV is a lie. I was terrified you were going to give me the job and I'd have to do some of it!" Done with wit, this can be funny, and no doubt the improvisers thought they were being very bold and daring—which they were—but great stories follow the implications of their offers to the end of the line, and don't just pull reversals on the audience for effect.

It's a worrying thought that on some level, those improvisers thought they had found "the answer." One of the problems with books like this (not *this* book, you understand; books *like* this) is that they may be misinterpreted as—or even actually claim to present—recipes for success which need only be followed carefully to produce perfect results. Far better to have a diverse set of tools and fully understand their effects. CANCELING ends stories—when the woodcutter kills the wolf, the wolf is CANCELED—so CANCELING should not be used in the beginning or in the middle. But it isn't the only way of ending stories. Great improvisers and great storytellers make excellent use of a huge array of tools, and are always happy to find a new one.

In the shoe shop scenes, you have something else to play with. The strong attitudes give you something to hang on to and can provide a justification, which also heightens the emotional energy of the scene. Jess plays the shopkeeper and adopts a particular physicality. By clasping and unclasping her hands, rounding her back, bringing her chin up, bobbing her head and biting her bottom lip when she smiles, she creates the impression of a very nervous, obsequious character. She darts awkwardly from place to place in the shop.

Katherine comes in, very straight-backed and smoothly moving; at first she scarcely notices Jess. Offstage, both players are about the same height, but Katherine is lengthening her body and standing very straight, while Jess is hunched over and craning her head up, so it seems as if one towers over the other. Katherine finally acknowledges Jess's fawning presence and makes her request known: "Those, please." Jess raises the stakes on the shoes, and stammers out that they are the ones she is hoping to buy for herself, when she's saved enough money. Jess, an experienced performer, very successfully sells the conflict in herself: reassuring Katherine that it isn't anything important while her tics grow worse and worse.

If only because the rule states that Katherine must buy the first pair of shoes she sees (it's not an *entirely* arbitrary rule!), Katherine insists that she hasn't time to try on a lot of pairs, those look fine, will Jess box them up for her please.

If this seems familiar, it's because it's tremendously similar to the first bargaining scene we discussed at the beginning of this section. But the rich characters here are interesting to watch, so the fact that they are pursuing contradictory goals right from the start is not a problem. The problems will only begin if the bargaining doesn't go anywhere. Changing attitude can be very helpful. If Jess reasons, then pleads, then threatens, maybe that will inspire something else (enraged, she destroys the shoes: "If I can't have them, neither can you!"[32]) or maybe she will get through to Katherine and we will see some cause and effect.

It's clearly unsatisfactory for Jess just to say, "Okay, here they are," since the stakes drop to zero, the offer that she has her heart set on those shoes is canceled, and the routine of buying shoes is completed. It's even more unsatisfactory for Katherine to say "Never mind, then" since this has all the same problems *and* breaks the rule that shoes must be bought and sold.

---

[32]The scene ends when she frightens Katherine into buying the remains, so as to obey the rule that the shoes must be bought and sold!

Clearly, either of these choices could be justified—you can justify pretty much anything[33]—but do we have to start looking for a new offer? No, because our scene is built atop of a solid foundation—the platform—and that's where we'll find the answer to this problem.

What happens if Jess says "Okay, here they are," *without abandoning her attitude*? She says the line and wipes a tear from her eye. As she boxes up the shoes and rings up the sale, she becomes more and more upset. "You will look after them, won't you?" she pleads with Katherine. She is almost unable to hand the box over. "Can I just have a moment to say goodbye?" Suddenly the scene is about something—and even better, it seems like it was *always* about that. Skillfully done, a scene like this could be the highlight of an evening, combining high comedy with genuine emotion and accurate storytelling.

One of the biggest problems of storytelling is knowing when to give the audience more of the same, and when to vary it; when to give the audience what they are expecting and when to try and surprise them. Beginning improvisers need to cut their teeth just ensuring that cause and effect is preserved and that their stories make sense. Populating the environment and playing rich characters who are changed by what happens brings these skeletons of stories to life, and as their instincts become more finely tuned, improvisers will slowly develop these skills.

A great note to give to improvisers who are getting the hang of some of the structural elements of storytelling, but who aren't being affected enough, is to *make it personal*. It's not enough for you to be confronted by a talking mouse. As interesting as that might be initially, the audience will tire of it if you just end up fetching it cheese or chatting happily about politics. If instead, the mouse blames you for having trapped and killed her husband, then you've got a scene which can really move an audience, whether it's to laughter or to tears.

---

[33]This observation has led some improv companies of our acquaintance to stop judging each other's offers onstage in any way—which is madness. Yes, any offer can be justified, but it takes time. If, in desperation, you throw in a left-field offer just to make something happen (not a bad strategy, once in a while), the subsequent justification may unlock any number of narrative doors. But if before that process is complete, another left-field offer is made and then another, then they all get in each other's way and eventually all these offers in need of justification end up endlessly circling like planes unable to land. The point of throwing in one original offer is that it will refuel a story which has run out of energy. But you only need to do it once. Don't play THAT'S NOT GOOD ENOUGH.

OF MONSTERS AND MEN

Stories work by developing consequences of earlier actions so as to be true to the characters, but also you can also reveal more of those characters as the story progresses by repeating key elements. One reason why students playing the Word At A Time proto-story won't kill or be killed by the monster is that they assume that either of those two events ends the story. But if you complete a routine too quickly, it simply becomes an introduction which can be part of a bigger routine. Here's a quick sequence based on that proto-story...

- You go into the forest.

- You meet a monster.

- You fight the monster.

- You slay the monster.

- The villagers appear.

- You proudly display its head.

- They are appalled that you killed their pet.

- You try to apologize.

- They release another, slightly less fearsome monster to kill you.

- You kill this monster, too.

- Over time, the monsters they send to kill you get feebler and feebler.

- The last one is so pathetic that you adopt it rather than kill it.

- You become best friends

- One day in the forest, a brave knight kills your pet monster and proudly displays its head to you...

Having the villagers enraged pulls the rug out from under the audience, *but also the hero.*[34] I'm trying to get my hero into trouble and the

---

[34]This is what M. Night Shyamalan does not seem to understand (or at least take advantage of). "Twist" movies are fine, but the heroes have to be affected by the twist, since people go

monster hasn't done the trick, but I don't want to bring in something arbitrary, so I look for a negative consequence of killing the monster. It's natural then for the villagers to want to take revenge, and—again—I don't want to abandon my platform in search of new ideas, so I'll have them send in another monster. Having done this twice, it seems pointless to have this next monster defeat the hero (although, I guess he could limp away, find a Sensei to train with and return with better skills to take it on, but I don't like sports movies), so I'll just have him slay this one as well, and be terribly apologetic about it (it's important to keep the hero likeable). If they keep sending in monsters, I need to make the progression more interesting. The joke is that the monsters are no match for the hero, so I'll develop that by making them decreasingly fearsome (which makes sense—the villagers would put their fiercest pet on guard duty first), but this is just another routine that needs breaking (compare with Finding the Game on page 228). Befriending a monster now is obvious, so I'll have him befriend the last and feeblest one. I'm about to complete the last routine, so now I need an ending, which I achieve by reincorporating the beginning, but now with the shoe on the other foot.

You could get a good short film out of that, I reckon, or a book for children.

—*Tom*

---

to the movies (largely) to see one person changed by another. In *The Village*, the William Hurt character has to make two colossal decisions. Both are enormous moral choices with extraordinary implications which would make wonderful drama. But, because the entire structure of the movie has been distorted in order to hide information from the viewer (but not the Hurt character), the first decision—to wall up his family and friends in a fictitiously ancient village and never tell the children—is made before the movie starts and so we never get to see him make it. The second choice—to send his blind daughter to get medication and risk her safety and his secret—we do see him make, but we have no idea of the implications so the drama is absent. The payoff for getting through this structural pretzel ought to be our vicarious shock and catharsis when the Bryce Dallas Howard character realizes the truth. Except that she never does. Compare this kind of "twist" movie to *Fight Club*, where the revelation that the Norton and Pitt characters are the same person unscrews not just the audience's head but also the Norton character's. (If M. Night Shyamalan happens to read this, he may be able to find a crumb of comfort by counting his millions in his LA mansion.)

OPPOSITE, ARBITRARY, EXTREME

OVERVIEW

In pretty much all of the preceding exercises, we have put the emphasis on creating a physicality or playing an attitude in order to generate a variety of characters. Only in Characters From A Hat have we used actions as the basis for the character, and there we often find ourselves dealing in stereotypes. In this section we look at how a more experienced improviser could use their "second obvious" to come up with fresh characters.

Because we tell improvisers not to censor and to trust their obvious, if they're asked to play a teacher or a parking inspector, they too often go for the cliché—in this case stern and pedantic, respectively. A librarian always shushes people and a social worker is always touchy-feely. We don't want to encourage improvisers to try to be "wacky" and to spend time thinking things up to get away from their first idea, but we were bored of seeing the same characters played out again and again and felt the improvisers were getting into deadlocks in scenes because of being attached to stereotypes. Our problem was how to improvise characters with dimension, like classic characters in fiction that interested audiences; characters like people we knew in life. We know teachers who do drugs and librarians with loads of tattoos who are writing a novel, and there presumably must be kind-hearted parking inspectors.

Opposite

We developed this exercise so that improvisers could make quick decisions about characters and go beyond cliché without trying too hard to be clever. I introduce this game with the example of parking inspectors. First, I set up two students in a scene. I tell them that they are to play a parking inspector issuing a ticket and a motorist returning to their car. The scene normally develops into an argument between the inspector—who is usually pedantic and unrelenting—and the motorist, who is outraged and frustrated. This is something anyone in a big city can see any day of the week, so it doesn't seem very funny or interesting.

I stop the scene and ask the person playing the parking inspector to give me three adjectives to describe a parking inspector. They might say, "Unreasonable, rules-oriented and impolite." I ask them to tell me what they think of as the opposite of those adjectives. They might say, "Reasonable, not interested in rules and courteous." Then I ask them to play the scene again, but this time to play the parking inspector with the second three adjectives. Something like this might happen. The motorist comes back to her car…

> **Motorist:** Are you ticketing my car?
>
> **Parking Inspector:** Yes, I'm so sorry. Did you not want a ticket?
>
> **Motorist:** Well, I was just a few minutes late.
>
> **Parking Inspector:** You know, that's a good point. Tell you what. I'll tear up the ticket and say this never happened.
>
> **Motorist:** Really? That's very kind of you… Do you mind me asking why?
>
> **Parking Inspector:** It's my last week. I don't really care, you see. I've been a slave to this job for too long, and I fail to see why I should make any more money for the council. What have they done for me?
>
> **Motorist:** So are you just going to let everyone off?
>
> **Parking Inspector:** Everyone who asks. All this week.
>
> **Motorist:** Well, surely not *everyone*. Parking tickets are important. They stop people from parking in dangerous places.
>
> **Parking Inspector:** Not my problem anymore.
>
> **Motorist:** But it is, don't you see? For the rest of the week! I really think you're being irresponsible.
>
> **Parking Inspector:** Don't be so uptight. Live a little! (*He gets out a hip flask and takes a swig of whisky.*) To be honest, I'm really quite sloshed. Fancy a bit? (*He offers her the flask.*)
>
> **Motorist:** No I don't! You're a disgrace! And what's more, I demand that you issue me another ticket. I'm a law-abiding citizen and I insist upon paying my dues.

The scene becomes funny and interesting because it's not how we expect a parking inspector to be, and his unusual actions affect and change the motorist. As many times as we've played the parking inspector as opposite, the character's always been different and the story's never been the same. We've seen parking inspectors who applied for the job to overthrow the system. Parking inspectors who were high. Parking inspectors who were using reverse psychology, who were hitting on the motorist and who had just found god. These scenes are endlessly entertaining, and wonderful and effortless to play. Everyone's obvious here seems to be the cliché, but everyone's opposite of the obvious seems to be different. As long as the inspector's actions are justified, it's interesting to the audience. If they aren't, it just seems like improvisers trying to be clever for the sake of it, and it won't work.

The technique works just as well with the heartless midwife who acts like a sergeant major, the psychiatrist who doesn't tolerate complaining and the high court judge who wants to be liked and to fit in. Almost any scene you've played a million times before (strict parents and rebellious teenagers are a constant) can be given a new lease of life this way.

The above scene works just as well if the motorist plays "opposite" and is happy, accepting and complimentary. We've seen the scene played with the motorist as a "parking ticket collector" who's trying to collect all different varieties of ticket for his collection, someone so rich she thinks it's amusing to be ticketed, which aggravates the parking inspector, and as someone who says "It's a fair cop!" and commends the parking inspector on his fine work, which makes the inspector sob "No one's ever been kind to me before." The beauty of this technique is that it can be done in an instant. You just need to ask yourself "What's the opposite of my obvious?" and off you go.

Extreme

The second technique is similar. If we go back to the first exercise and the improviser says that a parking inspector is "unreasonable, rules oriented and impolite," I ask them how extreme they can be in embodying these qualities. Instead of reaching the stereotype and stopping, go further. The scene may go like this one, improvised by Mark Edel-Hunt and Matt Bannister at RADA:

> **Motorist:** Are you giving my car a ticket?
> **Parking Inspector:** Those who break the law must face its full wrath.
> **Motorist:** But I was only a minute late.
> **Parking Inspector:** The law isn't open to your interpretation. It's pure and precise and absolutely fixed.
> **Motorist:** You're crazy.
> **Parking Inspector:** That's a ticket for insulting a parking inspector. (*He writes another ticket*)
> **Motorist:** What? You can't do that!
> **Parking Inspector:** Arguing with a parking inspector. Another fine. (*He writes another ticket*)
> **Motorist:** Give me that! (*He tries to get the book away from him*)
> **Parking Inspector:** (*Shrieking with delight*) Assaulting a parking officer! That's a huge fine! An on-the-spot fine! (*He pulls some cash out of the motorist's pocket*)
> **Motorist:** (*Shouting and trying to get his money back*) I'm not assaulting you! You jumped up ticket jockey! I'm not paying any of these! You hear me?! Give me my money back!
> **Parking Inspector:** Refusing to pay! Refusing to pay! I have the right now to impound your car and sell it to pay the fines!

In a long-form, this gives the now-carless motorist a huge motive for revenge, but it can be used to just create a funny short-form sketch (see Finding The Game In The Scene). Taking the stereotype as far as it will go will yield scenes in which people really care. This approach will tend to create quite short scenes that race up the absurdity curve quite quickly, but they're lots of fun to play and the unreasonableness and determination of the characters will have audiences in hysterics.

Arbitrary

Ask the student to go through the alphabet in their head and then say "Stop" at random and ask "Think of the first word that comes to you that starts with that letter, but don't tell us what it is." Then ask the student to play the scene again, but this time the parking inspector or motorist needs to be inspired by or obsessed with this arbitrary word. If they stop at "D" they might think of "Dog" and play the scene like this:

Motorist: Are you writing me out a ticket?

Parking Inspector: Afraid so, sir. (*Looks down*) Oh, what a beautiful dog! I love Springer Spaniels.

Motorist: Thank you. He's got a lovely nature.

Parking Inspector: Hello there! (*Pats the dog and puts the ticket on the car*)

Motorist: In fact, the reason I was late back to my car was because I was kept waiting at the vet.

Parking Inspector: What's wrong with him?

Motorist: He's dying. Not long to live, I'm afraid. (*The motorist tries to suppress his emotion*)

Parking Inspector: Oh god! That's just awful. I'm so sorry. (*He looks at the dog and begins to well up*) Look, I shouldn't do this. (*He looks over his shoulder*) Don't tell anyone, but I'll tear the ticket up. (*He does*)

Motorist: That's very kind. I can see you really love dogs.

Parking Inspector: They're my passion.

Motorist: Look, what he really loves is to be outside walking every day, but I've got an office job.

Parking Inspector: Oh dear. Poor fellow.

Motorist: The thing is, as he's only got a week to live... You wouldn't take him, would you? Take him on your beat? He'd love it.

Parking Inspector: I'd be honored.

Motorist: Bye, Algie!

The motorist gets in his car and speeds away. The dog barks viciously and bites the parking inspector. He's very healthy, but an absolute menace. The parking inspector's been had.

Of course, dogs can inspire the scene in any number of ways. The improviser can decide her character will be dog-like, she can see a dog locked in the back of the car and try to free it, she can have a dog sidekick and when people complain about the tickets she sets the dog on them. What's important is that you do not forget to be a parking inspector, but you allow dogs to provide imaginative fodder for your character. Again, it avoids the cliché of the parking inspector who is obsessed with parking tickets.

Think about your favorite comedy characters and you will see that a lot of them have this sort of dimension. If we think of a hotelier as welcoming, organized and in-control, then ask ourselves for the opposite we get manic, contemptuous and frantic Basil Fawlty, spitting venom at the guests and charging around the hotel trying to ward off the disaster which he has brought upon himself. If we guess that a corporate CEO will be an alpha-male, well-dressed and capable then taking that to the extreme will create Jack Donaghy from *30 Rock* who when asked by Tina Fey's Liz Lemon why he is wearing a tuxedo in his office, replies, "It's after six, what am I—a farmer?"

The Janitor from *Scrubs* is an arbitrary character. We might expect a janitor to play low status to the doctors, and to be either a bit sour about having to clean, or helpful and willing, depending on his attitude. Instead, he arbitrarily takes a psychotic dislike to J.D. and makes his life hell. He's also randomly into taxidermy. Imagine this scene with the *Scrubs* janitor as the parking inspector.[35]

> *The motorist returns to his car as the parking inspector is writing the ticket. He slams it on the car.*
>
> **Parking Inspector:** I finally got you! Every day you come back with just seconds to spare. Well, you got complacent and now I've won. I've finally won!
>
> **Motorist:** I'm sorry. Do I know you?
>
> **Parking Inspector:** Oh that's right, pretend you're oblivious. You've been taunting me for months and I'll have my victory, Barry.
>
> **Motorist:** How do you know my name?

Sketch comedy uses these principles a lot. Mike Myers's sketch character Linda Richman is the most extreme version of a middle-aged Jewish New Yorker it is possible to think of (although he claims his mother-in-law is more extreme), and many of his other characters are extremes as well. *Monty Python* deals a lot in opposites. A politician is the last person we would expect to do a silly walk, so the Minister for Silly Walks is a classic.

---

[35]The janitor from *Scrubs* is played by Neil Flynn, who happens to be a brilliant improviser and ad-libs a lot of his lines. According to a behind the scenes documentary, sometimes the writers put "Whatever the janitor says here," rather than bothering to write him a line, because they know he'll come up with something better on the spot than anything they could contrive.

The Pythons also do a lot of arbitraries. The "nudge nudge wink wink" sketch is about a man who is arbitrarily obsessed with sex and won't let it go, to the consternation of the man he is talking to. He insists on taking everything the other man says as an innuendo, but this behavior is random and not encouraged.

We usually get the students to play with parking inspectors and motorists for a long time to see the variety they can get with these three techniques. Each scene will be unique, interesting and funny, even though the setup is always the same. When everyone has had one or two turns at this setup, we move on to other types of people we have preconceived ideas about like priests in confessional boxes, scientists and airline pilots. Most of the examples so far are occupations, but it works just as well with other members of the community. What assumptions do we make about grandmothers, newlyweds, college students or children? (*South Park* is all about challenging the idea of children's innocence, and has run for nineteen seasons at the time of writing.) You will never run out of stereotypes to subvert or alter.

One thing to beware of is mixing these two approaches together in a short-form improvised sketch, because it can overload the scene. This is especially true of two arbitrary characters meeting. If the doctor is obsessed with his screenplay and wants to talk about it during the examination but the patient can't stop talking about cats, then it's all Wonderland and no Alice. A "straight person" is important here, otherwise we have a wacky world but no way of giving the audience access to it. This is not to say that you cannot get very good results with the strictest teacher in the world and the slackest student who will really piss him off, or the uptight priest and the reluctant penitent. *Scrubs* juxtaposes these characters brilliantly, but playing a character who asks the questions in the mind of the audience is very valuable. *The League of Gentlemen*, for example, are brilliant at creating extraordinary characters and taking turns playing the bemused straight person. If you can see that the parking inspector is saying a little prayer over your car, then have fun being a normal person discovering an extraordinary character.

This is also a great way to deal with improvisers who insist on making crazy offers in every scene. If you can't understand the offers and try to YES AND them as if it's normal to make squirrel pants when you're in a donut factory, the audience won't get it and it'll feel too absurd. We've all been in scenes like these, doing ridiculous things which make both sense and story impossible. We feel we simply must say "yes, and" or we're letting our scene partner down. You'll actually do your partner, the scene and the audience more favors if you play the straight person. "Jenny, are you feeling all right? I know you like squirrels, but it's getting out of hand. We've got to make donuts or we'll be fired. And doesn't it seem a little crazy to you to think that squirrels would need pants?" You're saying what the audience is thinking and you turn this improviser who is trying too hard to be funny into an arbitrary character the audience can laugh at.

This whole section on character comes back to being affected. Arbitrary, opposite and extreme characters are likely to affect people in big ways. If we get a parking ticket, we're irritated and might get a bit cross, but ultimately we get ourselves together and make the best of it. Remember, Shakespeare did not write about irritated people who were putting on a brave face. He wrote about huge and irrational extremes of emotion, as did the Greeks, as do your favorite sketch and sitcom writers. Play characters that have unreasonable reactions or incite unreasonable reactions in others and you'll be playing characters worth seeing. If your partner is continually trivializing everything, be affected by that and you'll make them look good and also please the audience.

CHARACTERS WITH DEPTH

If a group has been working together for a while, it's interesting to ask them what sort of characters they see each other playing. Improvisers are always fascinated to hear what the group has to say about them. "Susan nearly always plays low status, young characters who are unsure of themselves." "David often plays goofy teenagers or high status angry people." This is a revelation in itself. Then I ask the group "What would you *like* to see them play?" Invariably they want to see what they haven't seen before: Susan as a femme fatale or David as vulnerable old man. I then sit the improvisers next to each other and get the audience to build their character one suggestion at a time. This character is not natural for this improviser and they may not be comfortable with it, so the group helps them go there. They need to give physical instructions that can be followed easily. There's no point saying to Susan "Be sexy," but "Cross your legs, tilt your chin up, smoke a cigarette and blow smoke rings" are instructions she can follow which will have the effect of making her look and feel like a femme fatale (compare this to Hilarious Geisha on page 183).

We give her a voice and a name, and then she says to the audience "My name's Violet," in her sexy voice with her new physicality. We then do the same for David, and these characters become two strangers on a park bench. These scenes often have more of a dramatic, theatrical quality, but they can also be very funny. They are often riveting. The improvisers tend to be surprised that they can so easily maintain a character that is unfamiliar and unnatural to them, but it usually works well because we've built it up step by step, and they've had time to make the character their own. Also they've been given permission, and in fact instruction from others, to "be sexy" or "be assertive" which is something they may feel embarrassed to try if it's their own idea.

After the whole group has done a park bench scene, we start mixing the characters around. The femme fatale goes to visit her father (the homeless guy from scene two) to give him money. The vulnerable old man goes home to his grandson (the hippy from scene four). Having seen all the characters interact with strangers, we now see them interact with friends, family and lovers. The improvisers really seem to inhabit the characters and it really helps them make a connection with new ways of being on the stage.

Then do an exercise where everyone must pick someone else's character and play it. We can usually guess who it is, but of course a different improviser, often of a different gender, looks different doing the same things. As the group has created all the characters, they now own about twelve characters they can do whenever they want. If they change the accent or the gestures or the attitude, the character will be new again. This is a great exercise in showing improvisers that even those who are uncomfortable about transforming themselves on stage can. They just have to do it. It's also great for improvisers who always play tongue-in-cheek characters: "I'm an old man *wink wink*." They can move and affect the audience far more if they really commit to it. If you don't sell it, the audience won't buy it. Commitment is two-thirds of your job done. It's our instinct to pull back when we feel silly or don't think things are going well, but we need to do the opposite. Push forward. Do more. Sell it. If you don't believe you're a Vietnam veteran with a limp, why would they?

CHARACTERS WITH DIMENSION

Screenwriting guru Robert McKee maintains that James Bond is a more enduring character than Rambo because Rambo looks like a killing machine and behaves like a killing machine, whereas Bond looks like a playboy but behaves like a killing machine. In other words, he looks like the opposite of what he is, and therefore he has dimension. Often in a short-form sketch we're seeing characters for such a brief period that we only get to see their surface. The first time we meet Dr. Cox in *Scrubs* he seems uncaring. It's only when we get to know him that we see a softer side. He cares more than anyone about the wellbeing of the patients, and when push comes to shove he is there to help the interns through the hard times, even though displays of emotion are difficult for him. This means a hand on the shoulder from Dr. Cox means more than a compliment from a doctor who is more effusive.

In a long-form or free-form show where we see characters repeatedly, we have an opportunity to show a touch of emotion from the sadistic school principal or a crack of sexuality from the pious nun. It's just another way of being changed. You are showing your character with a different emotional state, desire or action from the one the audience saw before so you will be more interesting. It is also a good way to move the audience.

Sketch characters usually only show their outside, not their inside. Sketches are usually drawn in bold strokes, so the strict teacher is unlikely to show that they're a person too, and in their youth they experimented with drugs and had their heart broken which led to less-than-exemplary schoolwork. This is something we would normally find out several episodes into a sitcom or halfway through a movie, not in a three-minute sketch. Improvisers quickly creating short-form scenes or short scenes during a free form often do the same. How can we create more dimension in our characters? If a policeman is getting ready and puts on his badge and gun, that's what we expect. But a nun who puts on her rosary and then conceals a gun in her wimple is immediately a character with promised dimension. If the gun is remembered and explored—she goes to confessional, confesses to a murder and shoots the priest in the head for fear he'll tell her secret; or is leaving the convent to take her revenge on the man who murdered her family; or is a nun as well as a part-time private investigator—the audience will be interested and, as long as it is justified, will feel it's a deeper character than they normally see.

Let's go back to the policeman. If he puts on his badge and gun, and then picks up a bunch of flowers to go out onto the beat, it will arouse the audience's interest. Is this a policeman in love? Is he going to give them to a woman on his beat? Are they for his wife's birthday? Answer the questions in the mind of the audience and they'll be pleased, plus you'll have created a character with some dimension. You're really just adding an opposite or an arbitrary here, but instead of rewriting the character from scratch, you are only adding one novel element. You can be a doughnut-eating, hard-nosed cop who has zero tolerance for crime, but today your mission is to ask that woman out. If you have to make an arrest while you're doing it, if you ask her out the way you'd normally question a suspect, if you end up finding drugs in her handbag and arresting her while you're in the process of telling her how much you love her, then the audience will have a wonderful time.

WHAT DO YOU WANT?

Another way of looking at it is to ask yourself what your character wants and what the consequences are of not getting it. You can choose an extreme, opposite or arbitrary goal. Let's say I decide to play a student taking an exam. If I make the choice that I want to pass because I don't want to have to re-take the test or get bad grades, that's a rational goal with medium-stakes consequences. If I'm a student and I want to pass the exam because if I don't pass I'm going to get kicked out of school, that's a rational goal with high-stakes consequences. I'm a student and I must come first in this test to beat my arch-rival or I will be humiliated and everyone will think I'm not as good as her, that's is an irrational goal with high-stakes consequences. It's important to remember that stakes are linked in the audience's mind with the emotional cost to the hero. If a kid doesn't pass the exam but finds it funny, the audience will not care because you haven't asked them to. It's not their exam. People fail exams every day. The audience are feeling for *you*, not exams, proposals, job offers or gold medals. There is no point putting the character in a situation that might raise the stakes for someone else but doesn't for them (compare with Over-confessing on page 131).

In other words, asking yourself what your character wants, and what it will emotionally cost them if they fail in their endeavor, is a good way of creating drama and comedy. The arch-rival and the rest of the class may be completely oblivious to the student's plight. This might make the character more ridiculous and funnier to the audience. (Think of Butters in *South Park* playing General Disarray—he thinks he's a super-villain but no one else knows or cares. We're amused and slightly touched by it because it matters to him so much.)

You can make the goal and its attendant consequences extreme, opposite or arbitrary. The student with the arch-rival is extreme. The student who wants to get expelled so he gets out of school by failing the test might be opposite and the student who believes herself to be the messiah and that all the answers will appear as a miracle might be arbitrary. (I went through the alphabet till I got to "g" for "god" and that's the first thing I thought of.)

As well as the cost of failure, a good question to ask is what is the price of success? In great fiction, getting what you want often costs you in terms of values, friends or moral corruption. Macbeth succeeds in getting what he wants but loses everything else in the process. Cartman gets his own private theme park, but it costs him so much he wants to get rid of it in the end. These "be careful what you wish for" plotlines can be improvised. What if the student beats his arch-rival in the exam and then rubs it in her face?

> **Student:** I did it! You thought you'd be number one twice in a row, but not on my watch.
> **Arch-rival:** (*a little sadly*) Congratulations, Mike. You did really well.
> **Student:** Oh sure! Congratulations? You're crushed, admit it!
> **Arch-rival:** Well, I don't mind about the test but I'm upset you hate me so much.
> **Student:** Oh, sure. Like you don't hate me! You've been my rival all year. You beat me in all those tests and ignored me.
> **Arch-rival:** No, no! I never even noticed that I got better grades. I wasn't ignoring you, I was just shy.
> **Student:** Why would you be shy of me?
> **Arch-rival:** Because…I was hoping you'd ask me out. You always seemed to be looking over at me in class. I guess I misunderstood.

> Student: (*suddenly uncertain*) Oh. I guess you did.
>
> Arch-rival: Well, I guess I'll go to the dance with Tony. He asked me but I said no because of you. But if you hate me...
>
> Student: Oh, well, hold on a minute. Don't do anything hasty. I mean, it's only a test. No need for overreaction.

The audience will enjoy the student's joy at having his victory robbed from him. If he loses the girl he could have his victory, but it would cost him a date with his intellectual equal. If he suddenly realizes he's been in love with her all the time and that's the cost of his obsession, the audience will laugh at this fitting punishment. If he changes and asks her out and she accepts, they'll still be pleased, because this episode has changed the student forever and has therefore been worth watching.

2.13

You Can't Learn Mime from a Book

Overview

Some handy hints and tips for improving your mime. If you really want to become a good mime artist, reading half-a-dozen pages of an improv manual isn't going to cut it. But you don't need to be perfect in order to tell the story.

The ideal improviser should bring a lot of different skills to the party. If you can do impressions or acrobatic tricks or juggle, if you can do sleight-of-hand, manipulate puppets, make faces, recite poetry or sing, then these will all add to your improv abilities. In particular, non-actors coming to improvisation will benefit from taking non-improv acting lessons or—even better—getting a part in an amateur theatre production once or twice a year. Of these skills, some will come up more often than others. In Tom's case, his hard-won sleight-of-hand skills get used on stage about once every five years, whereas he is constantly pulling faces to help him create characters. One reason to put some work into improving your mime skills is that they can be used as often as you want.

It's worth mentioning here as well that many improvisers like having toys to play with, and providing a table of props and costumes will inspire their imaginations in ways that mime props can't. A real prop can do things that a mime prop can't (like be seen sticking out of your pocket after you've shoplifted it), but many improv companies make do with—or *insist* upon restricting themselves to—four chairs and black drapes. That would be fine if they were excellent mimes—since it's also true that mime props can do things that real props can't (like get broken safely and inexpensively)—but most of the world's improv is primarily verbal.

We've already seen the advantages of learning to tell stories, and stories are about people being changed—so why should we worry too much about the physical? Well, in the first place, just because the characters are the point of the story, that doesn't mean that incidental pleasures can't be had along the way. More important, as we saw under Go Through an Unusual Door, a rich environment can reveal character and inspire improvisers' imaginations, and it can make finding the right trouble far, far easier. So, we only need to be good enough at mime that the audience understands the offers that we are making.

But that ignores how audiences react to seeing *detailed* mime—not excellent mime, but detailed mime. They really get into it! This is the most important thing to understand about mime: most audiences love watching it, but most improvisers hate doing it. Once again, anxiety is to blame. Improvisers, nervous about their ability to deliver technically perfect mime, hurry through it with deliberate lack of care, hoping to send the signal: never mind the physical offers, it's the words that are important. But little details added to the physical reality make the world richer, add variety and can delight the audience in and of themselves. It only requires that the improviser commit to them, not that the mime is technically perfect. Chris Harvey John, an improviser in The Spontaneity Shop who lives to mime, once played an improv scene in which he was lying in a hospital bed. As the scene opened, a nurse changed a drip in his arm and his friend came to see him. When, later in the scene, an argument developed and Chris, enraged, got out of bed, he remembered to wheel the mime drip stand around with him—to the audience's unalloyed joy. This is the same Chris who gave his name to the CJ SWEEP and the same technique is applicable here: visualize the imaginary world you are attempting to create, then you only have to notice, rather than invent.

Another thing to remember about mime is to take your time. Slowness is much more interesting than speed, and a piece of careful mime can be an excellent way of building a really solid platform, while also giving the improvisers a moment to focus and calm themselves—especially if the previous scene has ended in high-energy chaos.

Here are three concrete tips for improvisers who want to improve their mime, which happily arrange themselves in decreasing order of difficulty but increasing order of utility—that is to say, the most useful is also the easiest to do. We were first introduced to most of these techniques by Loose Moose improviser Shawn Kinley.

FIXED POINTS

Let's take the hardest and least useful first: fixed points in space. When a traditional mime does "the wall," it isn't the hands moving across an invisible plane that sells the illusion—it's that the hand stays still, apparently resting on the wall, while the rest of the body moves. Locking one part of the body to a fixed point in space while the rest of the body moves is a tremendously difficult skill to acquire, and luckily it's not required for most improvisers. The following exercise would improve the skill if you were to persevere with it, and it is worth doing once or twice just to appreciate the difficulty involved.

Stand facing a partner and imagine that there is a solid surface between you, like a desk or a shelf, at around belt height. Both of you rest your hands palms down on the surface to define this "shelf" (mime objects only exist while you are touching them). Now take turns slowly bending at the knees and lowering yourselves to the floor—while keeping your hands at the same level. Notice that your hands "want" to rise up off the shelf or sink through it; try and correct this and try to lock into your muscle memory what getting it right feels like. When you've both had one or two tries, just check—is the shelf still at belt height? Some pairs will find it has drifted by up to a foot!

Now try exactly the same exercise again, but this time the player moving should close their eyes, while the other player observes their level of accuracy and provides feedback. This is even more difficult, and many people will be stunned to realize how poor they are at it. Luckily, as I've said, this is not a skill that improvisers need, although confronting the difficulty can be helpful in making improvisers more aware of their bodies. A related skill is remembering where things are, which is worth putting a little effort into. Both because of their better view of the stage and because their senses are not deadened by the fog of war, the audience sees everything and remembers everything. They know where the mime fridge was, they know how big the car would be (a particularly difficult item to make real on the stage) and they remember which way the door opened.

In some cases, each improviser will carefully remember to open the door as they enter or exit—and if you're really lucky, they will remember to close it as well—but each improviser is opening and closing *their* door; none of them is in the same place as the others, and they all open and close differently. If you are lucky enough to be playing on a stage with a scratched and marked floor, or one where bits of tape and scuffed chalk marks represent the ghosts of departed productions, then you can use these marks as reference points to nail down your mime objects. One improviser of our acquaintance was forever opening doors as he simultaneously sailed into the room, creating the disquieting impression that the doorknob had slipped off in his hand, or that the door was made of rubber and was stretching into the room. He has since corrected the error, but it took some effort!

POPPING

The second tip is also technical, but is considerably easier to do. Begin by holding both hands up, palms away from you, at about head height. Let each hand in turn close into a fist and then *spring* open, fingers splayed.

The spasmodic motion should affect the whole forearm, all the way to the elbow, and should be as sudden as you can make it, as if you were receiving a brief electric shock. Keep springing open each hand in turn, but let the actual motion become less and less, and let the hand close less each time. Keep the idea of a shock to the forearm, but instead of having the hand spring open from a closed fist, just have the open fingers jerk a little, and then see if you can take it all the way down to a sudden, but barely perceptible, tightening of the muscles.

This is known as a "pop," and "popping" at the beginning and end of a motion can help give your mime a little extra snap and precision. Overdo this and you quickly end up doing the "robot," but used carefully, and particularly when object meets object, a pop can really help to sell the idea that you are manipulating real, solid matter. Go back to your shelf and try picking up and putting down a mime cup. Now do it again with a pop as your hand closes on the cup, and another as the cup hits the desk and your hand releases. The difference may be very striking. This technique also gives you another for free: mime demands precision, and that often means breaking actions down into discrete movements instead of—more naturally—letting each flow into the next or having them overlap. Popping introduces a stop at the end of each action, which will help you to arrange them consecutively instead of concurrently. Notice, too, the corollary of "mime objects only exist when you are touching them," which is that mime objects are *sticky*. You need to let go of them cleanly and deliberately.

MAKING NOISES

The final tip is terribly easy to do, but many improvisers are embarrassed to do it—not because it seems pretentious and "mimey," on the contrary, we suspect "real" mimes would loathe it—but because it seems childish. Things that you interact with have an aural reality as well as a physical one. If you add the auditory component, then you supply that extra layer. Try picking up a heavy (mime) suitcase and then putting it back down again. Now see what noises you can add. Obviously you can grunt with exertion as you pick the suitcase up, but you should also be able to make a satisfying "*shtooom!*" noise, or something similar, as it hits the floor. Yes it's childish, yes you might feel a little foolish and yes, it really helps sell the illusion. Remember, we *aren't* asking our audience to sit back and admire our physical dexterity; we want to make the world of the story rich and complete so that they can lose themselves in it—and so that we can too, to a certain extent. Improvisers who take their time over space work don't need to think up physical offers—they are aware of all kinds of physical details about the world they are inhabiting and need only make another one explicit to keep the story moving forward.

FURTHER DEVELOPMENT

We'll conclude by describing a few other helpful exercises to focus players on mime skills. First, have the players stand in a circle and imagine that a large circular table covered with objects is in the middle. Get them all to put their hands flat on it so they can agree where its surface is. Then, have one person pick up an item from the table and use it in such a way that we can all clearly see what it is. Be pedantic about correcting even some of the smallest errors, as students will often overlook vital details: an old Polaroid camera will have to be opened, readied for use, then the shot framed before the shutter can be pressed and the picture emerges. The camera must then continue to exist as the picture is withdrawn and begins to develop.

Once the object has been used and identified, have that player hand it to the person on their left. Make sure that the hand-over is performed smoothly and convincingly. If Sally lets go before John has closed his hand, then they've dropped it. But if Sally's hand stays closed as John's hand moves away, they've snapped it in two (or instantaneously cloned it). John now puts Sally's object back on the table (which is still at the same height) and picks up a new one. Challenge people to name details about the objects; they will know the answers *if* they are visualizing the objects. What color is it? Is it old or new? If they pause before answering then they are probably thinking answers up, but if they answer straight away then they were probably visualizing.

Although this kind of careful space work is fascinating, it's better to play the game in groups of eight to ten, so people don't spend too long watching other people play instead of actually performing their own mime. If you have a big group (more than twelve, say), split them into two or three circles so people don't spend too long standing and waiting for their turn to come (which, apart from anything else, will tend to inspire them to be "clever"— and that usually means stupid).[36]

Another, slightly more demanding exercise that *is* worth playing in front of an audience is the Scene In Slow Motion. Have the players speak … slowly … and … de-lib-er-ate-ly, but don't otherwise encourage them to sound like run-down tape recorders. Put them in an environment with lots of potential props (hospital, library or kitchen are all good) and encourage them to linger over every physical detail. At the end of a scene (which may have lasted many minutes), although all that has transpired is that one person has cut up an onion and another has mopped up a small spill, the audience will be transfixed and leaning forward in their seats,

---

[36]Experienced teachers may recognize this as a simplified version of another game which involves the additional element of transforming one object into another. This is a skill almost never required on stage, and the game takes too long as it is, so we simply omit it.

drinking in every detail. It's good for improvisers to feel the power of working slowly.

It's also fun to get improvisers to make themselves a mime cup of tea, which should take as long to make as a real cup of tea. Many improvisers get very engrossed in this, which is also good, but don't bother doing it in front of the rest of the group as it's more fun to do than to watch.

2.14

Control Freak

Overview

We look at what improvisers' preferences are with respect to taking control and being controlled, and how to develop the flexibility to happily do either.

Our work with a new group begins with the fundamental principles: say yes to your partner and trust your instincts (later refined to "trust your obvious"). Both of these immediately bring issues of control to the surface. Being in control usually means considering your actions before you take them, and protecting yourself from being controlled by others (sometimes by controlling them). If you say yes to your partner's ideas and don't censor your own, you are entering potentially dangerous territory. (At a recent open corporate event, one attendee was so freaked out by the loss of control she experienced playing Yes And that she burst into tears. Luckily our colleague, running the day, was able to comfort her and maintain his confident and calm demeanor so as to reassure the rest of the group.)

As other demands are placed on them (adopting a range of statuses, dubbing each other's voices, building platforms, breaking routines, miming, playing characters and all the rest), the pure joy of Yes And is sometimes lost, and people begin to adopt strategies for success. One way to identify these is to look at who wants control and who would rather be controlled. Word At A Time diagnoses these two states very rapidly and accurately. The next step is to start looking at games which require not just that control be shared (like Word At A Time, or Master/Servant Dubbing) but where improvisers can choose who has control and when.

HYPNOTIST MAGICIAN

This game seems very simple but when you watch it done well it looks rather extraordinary, almost magical. We probably wouldn't do it onstage, but the lessons it teaches—almost as a metaphor—are very valuable.

Start with that old drama school stand-by, the mirror game. Everybody finds a partner and chooses who is A and who is B. They stand facing each other, maybe about a foot apart. A imagines that they are looking into a mirror and B plays their reflection. A moves smoothly and slowly, not trying to catch B out. B keeps looking in A's eyes and continues to follow their movements. After a while, see if B can smoothly take over the role of leader, so they initiate the movements and A follows. Maybe there will come a point where nobody is quite sure who is leading and who is following.

Here's a more theatrically interesting version of the same idea. Once again, everyone finds a partner and chooses who is A and who is B. This time they stand about six feet apart. A will control B—not because B is a mirror image but because B is a like a puppet, magically controlled by A who is a sort of Svengali figure. A should grab hold of a bit of empty air which they imagine is connected to some part of B's anatomy. It's nice to add a "pop" to this action (see page 216).

They move their hand and B obediently moves their arm, as if A is holding a rod which connects to B's hand. When A releases the "rod," B's body stays in the last position. A can make B raise their knee, turn their head, bend at the waist and so on. Again the pace should be slow, the movements smooth and deliberate. After two or three minutes of this, I suggest that A returns B to neutral and they can try it the other way round.

So far so easy. Everyone finds new partners and this time I suggest that as A manipulates B, they start slowly walking around them. So when A moves the first couple of bits of B's body they are standing in front of B as before. Then A makes another couple of moves standing to the side. Then they try to keep playing the game standing behind B. Let them try it on their own. Maybe one or two pairs will figure it out, but most will admit defeat, or cheat by leaning right over B's shoulder or turning B's head to make sure that B can still see what A is doing.

In fact, it is perfectly possible to continue to sustain the illusion that A is puppeteering B even if A is standing six feet away from B and B cannot see a single thing that A is doing. Can you see how to make it work?

It's worth bearing in mind that the control that A has over B is just an illusion. B may believe that they are following A's lead and just obeying orders, but with six feet of floor separating them it's inevitable that A's physical offers will be ambiguous to a certain extent. So in part, it's B's *choice* which part of their body they move. Can you see how to make this work yet?

When the game starts, A sets the tempo and to a certain extent dictates what part of B's body should move. Once B can no longer see A, B can no longer wait for a visual cue from A because none will be forthcoming. But

B knows the rhythm which A is moving to by now and knows the kind of things to do. So, once A can no longer be seen, A must boldly grasp empty air *before* B does anything, trusting that B will make their own choice of which body part to move and will move in the rhythm which has already been established. Now as B lifts their left leg (or whatever) A follows B's lead, and keeps acting the role of puppeteer. They continue this process a few more times, as A continues to move around behind B. Eventually, A comes back into view and control passes back to them. As far as the audience is concerned, A has been in control all the way through. This kind of thing is easy to achieve with careful rehearsal and choreography (see for example Gene Kelly's "Alter Ego" dance number in the movie *Cover Girl*). To pull it off while improvising means having a great deal of trust between the players and a deep understanding of what "control" actually means.

DARTH VADER

I remember seeing a remarkable version of this principle in a totally different setting, many years ago at a workshop. We were being shown a pretty worthless game called Panel Show. Around four improvisers get the names of famous celebrities or fictional characters from the audience (yawn) and then the audience supplies some topic which they can all talk about (yawn yawn) and then the host interviews them and generates a discussion about the topic, filtered through these various personas. Being able to do perfect impressions isn't required, the task is just to channel something of that individual's attitude.

I have no recollection of the topic suggested, nor any of the famous names called out, save one, which was given to a new and rather anxious improviser—possibly someone who didn't have English as a first language. This chap was given Darth Vader as a suggestion and a few minutes in to the probably amusing, but no doubt trivial, discussion had failed to say anything. The very experienced improviser in the chair realized that this improviser hadn't contributed yet and so threw the next question to Vader. Sitting in the audience, I saw this young man shift uncomfortably and saw his mouth open and close. I realized that the combination of topic and persona had not inspired him in any way. Possibly he had no idea who Darth Vader even was. I desperately wanted the teacher to call an end to the pointless exercise.

But there was no need. The host came to the same realization as me, but unlike me he found a brilliant solution. After a second or two of silence, he suddenly began clawing at his throat, slumping in his chair and gasping for breath, crying "Forgive me Lord Vader! I apologize for my insolence!" At a stroke, he made this panicked improviser into the most powerful character in the scene. It's still the neatest, most elegant "save" I've ever seen.

—Tom

Without care, a group of new improvisers can fracture into the Clevers—who are very verbal, do a lot of planning (on and off stage) and who do all the work pushing the scene into the future—and the Quiets, who will happily follow their partner's lead but contribute very little of their own, even though they may come across as more intuitive and more appealing. With one of each, scenes may flow very well, but two Clevers will get in each other's way unless one agrees to play "quiet," and two Quiets will never get anywhere since they are both waiting for the other one to make a move.

The ideal improviser is wonderfully fecund when ideas are required, but perfectly happy to let their partner run the scene for a while if they look inspired. Because they don't need to be in control, they have no problem showing vulnerability on the stage. Because they know they can take control at any time, they never stand around foolishly, waiting for their partner to make the first move. How can we get both Clevers and Quiets to this happy state—not really a center ground, but able to express the positive aspects of both modes to their fullest?

In *Impro*, Keith wrote about having one improviser "work" another—in other words, to be responsible for generating the content while the other just goes along with their ideas. In *Impro for Storytellers*, Keith discusses a baffling popular improviser called "Sandy Carroll" in whom Keith could detect no talent at all beyond an appealing manner. Eventually, Keith turned his technique into a game, which bears the same name.

SANDY CARROLL

> *Two people up, please. Who would like to be Sandy Carroll? Okay, Jack. For the rest of this scene, you are restricted to just the following phrases: "Yes," "Okay," "Sounds good to me" and "I'll go along with that."*[37]
>
> *You can say any of them whenever you like and as often as you like, but you cannot say anything other than those four phrases. Alex, you can say and do exactly as you please.*

Now, give them a location or some brief idea of a situation, and run the scene for thirty seconds or so. Unless Alex is an absolutely neurotic Quiet, terrified of her own ideas, they can probably sustain a slightly gossipy platform, and it's not too hard to keep some kind of interaction going. Alex just has to avoid questions which can't be answered with "yes."

> **Alex:** Do you want vanilla or chocolate?
> **Jack:** (*Helpless shrug*) Er, sounds good to me!

---

[37]These are the "official" four, but in practice it's often easier to just use the first three.

Set the game in pairs and let it run a little longer. It's likely that the game will start to become difficult after about thirty seconds, and it protects anxious students if their early struggles are visible only to their partner and not to the whole class. In this case, Clevers asked to play Sandy Carroll may find the part horribly confining and will either start to become very obviously frustrated (not an ideal state) or will start archly using intonation and gesture to suggest a contradictory subtext.

> **Alex:** Do you want to play chess?
> **Jack:** (*With colossal sarcasm*) Oh, sounds good to me!

This makes them feel cleverer than the game, which is very rewarding for them, but it also protects them from anything the game might teach them, so it's necessary to congratulate them on their ingenuity and then ban this approach.

Quiets asked to play the other role will find it enormously daunting. Suddenly they have to do all the inventing and all the defining, with no help whatsoever from their partner. But even though some Clevers will report that while building the platform is no problem (because they don't have to deal with someone else's ideas getting in their way), it's tremendously difficult to break the routine and vastly difficult to generate conflict. This leads some improvisers to conclude that you can't get anyone into trouble in this game.

> **Alex:** Okay, that's it, you're fired.
> **Jack:** Okay.
> **Alex:** You're happy about that, are you?
> **Jack:** Yes.
> **Alex:** You're fired with no severance pay!
> **Jack:** Sounds good to me.
> **Alex:** Er...

As far as it goes, this observation is correct: Jack can't be negatively affected, so it's very unlikely that the scene will be about *him* getting into trouble. Very few improvisers are ever likely to play the scene and get *themselves* into trouble: the Clevers won't be vulnerable and the Quiets won't think of it. But if you point it out, they start to get the idea.

> **Alex:** I'm so sorry I'm late, sir. It won't happen again.
> **Jack:** Yes.
> **Alex:** Oh sir, please. You can't fire me.
> **Jack:** Sounds good to me!

It's worth doing a few of these in front of the group, and side-coaching them. This apparently simple trick goes against the grain, and many "free" improvisers will keep drifting back to trying to get a reaction out of Sandy

Carroll. Again, this is an issue of control. The improvisers who feel the weight of control pressing on their shoulders try to rise to the challenge by playing characters who are in control of everything. Learning to play Sandy Carroll well is an excellent way to learn to play scenes with audience members and make them look good.

Part of the skill lies in learning to make offers to which a "yes" response creates suffering.

> **Alex:** You aren't going to chain me to the wall and flog me with that knotted rope, are you?
> **Jack:** Yes!

Let's try some variations on this simple procedure. We begin with Negative Sandy Carroll, in which the Sandy Carroll character is restricted to "No," "Why should I?" "Fuck off" and "I'd rather die." Again, set this in pairs. It's only a bit of fun and the real lesson is: don't do this.

> **Alex:** Good morning!
> **Jack:** Fuck off.
> **Alex:** Have you finished repairing my car?
> **Jack:** No.
> **Alex:** Are you going to finish repairing my car?
> **Jack:** I'd rather die.
> **Alex:** Er...

At best, this game simply generates massive conflict straight away. At worst, Negative Sandy Carroll is simply blocking and canceling everything in sight, preventing anything from developing.

Let's try a more interesting variation: Diet Sandy Carroll. This game is similar to the "working your partner" exercise described in *Impro*, but the idea is easier to grasp if the group has already played Sandy Carroll. Both players can say anything they like, but the person playing Diet Sandy Carroll must let their partner take the lead. They can say yes to their partner's ideas, but they must stop at the point where they feel they would be adding something new. I generally let people play in pairs first, since this is one of the games from which people learn far more by doing than by watching. Here's the beginning of a mother-daughter scene in which Helen is "free" and Rebecca is Diet Sandy Carroll.

> **Helen:** Hi, sweetie, do you need any help getting ready?
> **Rebecca:** If you like.
> **Helen:** Your first real date, I'm so excited for you!
> **Rebecca:** Mum, you're embarrassing me.
> **Helen:** Why don't you wear that lovely dress we bought for you in Sweden last year?

> Rebecca: What, the red one?
> Helen: Yes … it makes you look so … chaste.

Rebecca adds little details of her own ("the red one"), and goes along with her mother's offers—both explicit and implied ("Mum, you're embarrassing me")—but she stops short of developing any of Helen's ideas, or introducing any of her own. Rebecca's actions are not too dissimilar to those of the typical Quiet, if in a happy and relaxed state (when anxious, they will be more likely to block). Helen understands that the onus is on her to make something happen and so she makes the choice to play an attitude to her daughter's sexuality.

What's particularly revealing about this game is what happens when I yell…

> *Freeze! Okay, everyone stay where you are. When I say go, you're going to carry on exactly where you left off, and you're playing the same parts. If you were doing a doctor/patient scene and you were the doctor, you're still the doctor and the scene hasn't changed. But the role of Diet Sandy Carroll is going to move to the other player. Go!*

Let's see the next "beat" of the mother-daughter scene, with Helen playing Diet Sandy Carroll. Rebecca is now free to drive the scene.

> Rebecca: No, I'm wearing that one. The slutty one.
> Helen: The what?
> Rebecca: The slutty one. You have to show a bit of tit and leg, mum, or boys lose their interest.
> Helen: I can't believe I'm hearing this!
> Rebecca: We'll probably come back here and have sex after.
> Helen: Here?
> Rebecca: Or a quick knee-trembler in the alley round the back of the chip shop.

Now Rebecca takes complete control of the scene, and Helen just plays shock and dismay. The rest of the scene will reveal whether Rebecca is just baiting her mother or whether she really is far more sexually precocious than had been supposed.

This really is a skill worth learning—taking and giving control smoothly and promptly and learning to be at home in either situation. This is a game worth lingering on. It's tempting as a teacher always to want to provide novelty (or what good are you doing?), but in this instance, deep learning can come from repetition.

If you do need more novelty, then Secret Diet Sandy Carroll adds another layer. In Secret Diet Sandy Carroll we bring the two modes even closer together and correct a possible problem that can crop up—that of not YES-

ANDing Sandy Carroll. This is especially likely with a Clever in the "free" role. Now, at first it seems unlikely that this problem will ever occur because, after all, Diet Sandy Carroll isn't meant to be making any offers. But just because they are not trying to make offers—or even trying not to make offers—that doesn't mean they aren't. Remember, don't look for an offer; assume one has already been made. Let's look at that first section of the Diet Sandy Carroll scene again:

> Helen: Hi, sweetie, do you need any help getting ready?
> Rebecca: If you like.
> Helen: Your first real date, I'm so excited for you!

Helen is focused on adding information, which is excellent practice for her if she's naturally a Quiet, tending to make meek and vague offers if she offers anything at all. But if she's a Clever, this stuff is easy for her. She needs to be aware of the offer that Rebecca is making. Rebecca's "If you like," is not a happy, enthusiastic yes. There's already an offer here that this is not a happy family. What happens to the dialogue if Helen looks to her partner for inspiration, while still making it her responsibility to do all the defining?

> Helen: Hi, sweetie, do you need any help getting ready?
> Rebecca: If you like.
> Helen: (*Beat*) Are you still upset with me?
> Rebecca: Yes.
> Helen: My mother sent me to an all-girls school and it never did me
>   any harm.

Playing Secret Diet Sandy Carroll, this is even more likely to occur. In Secret Diet Sandy Carroll, two players collude to decide in private which one of them will be Diet Sandy Carroll. This player should be fearless in *accepting* offers, but should refrain from making new ones. The other player should make just enough new offers to keep the story moving, thus making it as hard as possible for the audience to spot which is which. As an example of a full-bodied acceptance of an offer, consider a scene set in a school playground. Robert begins by looking around furtively, pulling out a mime object, reaching into it and putting an object from it in his mouth. Scott now enters and says, "Hey, you! Give me them sweets or I'll kick your head in!" Scott is doing an excellent job of accepting. He has accepted Robert's offer of sweets, and accepted his offer of the furtive glance by being the bully who Robert was hiding from. He has not added anything new. That's an exemplary Secret Diet Sandy Carroll.

I set the scene for the improvisers, I decide who will start on stage and I decide who will speak first. I don't know which improviser is which, but by having one on stage and the other speak first I can hedge my bets a bit. Without this instruction from me, the audience will simply assume that whoever speaks first *must* be the "free" player (and indeed, many Secret Diet Sandy Carrolls won't speak at all unless spoken to, despite my school bully example above).

Clearly there's no point playing this game privately in pairs. A big part of the game is whether the identity of Diet Sandy Carroll can be divined by the audience or not. In fact, much of the time there is one specific offer (usually quite early on) which gives the game away, and although I am interested in whether or not the audience can divine the identities of the two players—and happy for the players if there's doubt in the audience—what's more interesting is the state of the two players. Whichever role they are playing, the game and the need for secrecy strongly encourages the habit of developing your partner's ideas rather than thinking of your own, or feeling like you don't have any.

The procedure exploits the ambiguity which exists between introducing a new offer of your own, on the one hand, and spotting a low-key offer which your partner has made and making it explicit on the other. This makes Clevers connect their clever ideas to their partner's ideas, which helps to stitch the scene together and prevents two Clevers from getting in each other's way. It gives Quiets an endless source of ideas, while taking the pressure off them to be clever. It all comes back down to Yes And, but this version of Yes And is thoughtful, subtle, detailed and convincing. It lacks the euphoria of the original Week One version, but it has far more scope and substance.

More than any other, we recommend this procedure for those times when you feel rattled onstage. It almost doesn't matter which role you cast yourself in, but if you think you are a natural Clever, then play Sandy Carroll: tell yourself it's fine to take your partner's offers and run with them, but you've got to keep coming back to them for inspiration. If you think you're a natural Quiet, then tell yourself you are responsible for keeping the scene moving forward, but you can't let anyone see you doing it, so you must develop your partner's ideas—possibly in ways they haven't thought of—so as not to be "caught" controlling the scene.

This gets excellent, compelling work out of almost any improviser—a little slower than usual, which is no bad thing. Finish the session with something high energy and foolish just to remind them that being familiar with lots of different tools is the ultimate goal, not finding the One True Way.

2.15

Finding the Game in the Scene

Overview

Is the popular notion of finding the game as difficult as it seems? Easy or difficult, is it worthwhile? Is it the whole shooting match or just another tool?

"Finding the game in the scene" is akin to the Holy Grail for some improvisers, especially Harold players from Chicago. *Truth in Comedy*, the book most often cited for improvisers wanting to learn the Chicago way, makes no secret of this, and nor does the *UCB Comedy Improvisation Manual*. But the Harold approach provides a second way in which improvised scenes can gain "point" (nobody wants improvisation to be pointless). If a scene provides a moment, which is then juxtaposed with another moment, the scenes eventually mutually providing point for each other by the way they reflect each other—hence "Long-form" since point is found in the whole structure, rather than in the individual pieces.

In a short-form show, on the other hand, point is mostly discovered within a scene. A scene gets a point when someone is changed, often made to suffer, and then the situation is resolved. Once this is done, typically, we move on to something new. There may or may not be a "game" in the Chicago sense, but neither will there be a juxtaposition with a later or an earlier scene.

In a Keith Johnstone show, there very frequently will be a game structure for the evening as a whole however. This may be a show which incorporates a *competitive* element, and keeps interrupting the improvised content for scorekeepers, audience suggestions and the like. This can make for formats which seem less like theatre and more like light entertainment. Fascinatingly, Del Close, who began doing *cabaret* with the Compass Players, was responsible for generating a far more *theatrical* format, in which the only direct interaction with the audience is briefly at the beginning and thereafter the fourth wall is in place throughout, with scenes merging seamlessly into one another.

The effects of these choices are even more interesting. One of the "games" quoted in *Truth in Comedy* occurred during a show sponsored by Budweiser, during which the players discovered the "Name any beer but Budweiser" game—to the general appreciation of the audience. This is very cheeky and funny, but notice that it is not possible to appreciate the Budweiser joke without stepping out of the scene, so the improvisers end up *commenting on the scene*, rather than playing it for its inherent truth.

Maybe it's exactly because a Theatresports show includes "machinery" which keeps involving the audience and reminding them that the show is improvised, that "gagging" of this kind is frowned upon (and sometimes even severely punished). However an art form is set up, there will be a tension wanting to explore the opposite extreme.

What is potentially worrying is the "arch" quality that even the best Harold creates. In an episode of the American sitcom *Scrubs*, the hero, young hospital doctor J.D., is relaxing in the bath, listening to Toto on his iPod, luxuriating in his day off. Alas, the telephone rings and he is summoned in to work, where he finds the Janitor painting colored lines on the hospital floors to mark different routes. As he attempts to complete the task for which he was summoned, we learn that another young doctor, Elliot, has been bragging about her new-found knowledge of endocrinology. But an older, more experienced colleague has discovered her secret crib sheets and destroyed them in advance of the lecture she is due to give. Turk, the surgeon, is one of several given the task of persuading the father of a boy in a persistent vegetative state to donate his son's heart. The successful surgeon will get to assist in the transplant operation. Head nurse Carla, meanwhile, is frantic with worry that she will be a poor mother, and confesses that she is terrified of her own baby. As sympathetic as he is, J.D. just wants to get home.

As the various plotlines unfold, it dawns on the audience that whereas Elliot needs brains, Turk needs a heart, Carla needs courage and J.D. (and Toto!) want to get home. The four of them walk down the Janitor's yellow line to the exit to solve their problem together. The sudden insight gained from this revelation, that the whole episode is a *Wizard of Oz* spoof—and there are many other gags and references over the course of the show—is terribly funny. The achievement is jaw-droppingly clever, in the conception, in the execution and in the hiding it from the viewer until the revelation is ready. But as good as that is, it's the moments of humanity that live longest in the mind. The superstructure, which never affects the characters at all, inspires our admiration, but never moves us to laugh. Turk's moment of honesty with the father of the dying man reaches us on another level altogether.

The *Scrubs* episode above is far more subtle, clever and complicated than anyone could ever improvise, and even that would come across as dry if not for the depth of the characters and the reality of the situations sitting underneath it. This kind of thing is great and adds a really interesting extra layer to comedy of all kinds—but it's seasoning, not meat and potatoes.

Good meals need seasoning too, though, but for us a more useful word than "game" might be "pattern." Once again, this can refer to either the pattern of the show as a whole, or a pattern which emerges in a single scene. The "rule of three" is probably the most well-known of these patterns. The rule of three exists for a very simple reason: much of comedy has to do with both anticipation and surprise. These two support each other, and many improvisers struggle for surprise because they fear anticipation—they think that the audience will be ahead of them and so think less of their efforts. If you think back over the comedy you love, unless your taste is for the very surreal, you'll probably discover that anticipation can be funny without surprise,[38] whereas surprise depends on anticipation to be funny. If we are expecting X and then you give us Y, we may laugh out of surprise. But that means you have to contrive a situation where we are in fact expecting X. Otherwise, Y may seem simply arbitrary and this is likely to come across as more odd than amusing.

One way to cause an audience to expect X is to give them X. How many times is this necessary? Well, if you do something once, it's merely an instance. This paragraph begins with the phrase "one way," but that doesn't create an expectation that the next paragraph will also begin with that phrase, any more than any of the previous paragraphs' opening phrases did. If, however, the next paragraph also begins with the phrase "one way," then that sets up the possibility that this might be a rule. The third iteration is the first opportunity to violate the rule, therefore. It isn't that three is a magic number, it's that if you do X, X, X, X, Y, then Y may be funny, or at least surprising, because it breaks the established pattern. But for this to work, you have to do X at *least* twice before you do Y. The rule of three is simply the *most efficient* version of the general principle.[39]

To see this in action, we could consider any number of childhood jokes which present two "normal" iterations and then an abnormal one. We'll

---

[38] As for example, near the beginning of the second (and best) Pink Panther film, *A Shot in the Dark*. A murder is committed at the house of an important political figure, and Chief Inspector Dreyfuss is being briefed by his number two, who confesses that he did not realize the importance of the householder when he dispatched an officer to investigate. "Who did you assign to the case?" snarls Dreyfuss. "Clouseau," confesses his number two wretchedly. "Oh my god..." moans Dreyfuss. We cut to a magnificent push-in shot of Clouseau in the back of the police car, his impassive face pompously looking to the future. We already *anticipate* the chaos that is to come, even though Sellers has barely moved a muscle, let alone uttered a line of dialogue.

[39] Thanks go to writer and improviser Alex Lamb who first pointed this out to us. Counterexample: "Time flies like an arrow. Fruit flies like a banana." (Attributed to Groucho Marx.)

spare you the national stereotypes and offer this instead, half-remembered from a BBC kid's sketch show in the 1980s:

> **A:** I just accidentally drank some gasoline. I washed the taste out of my mouth with lemonade.
>
> **B:** I just accidentally drank some gasoline. I washed the taste out of my mouth with Coca-Cola.
>
> **C:** I just had a cup of coffee in the BBC canteen. Anyone got any gasoline?

Patterns are also strong features of classic stories such as *Goldilocks and the Three Bears* or *The Three Billy Goats Gruff* (there's that rule of three again). Children, discovering order in the world, look for patterns very early on and delight in seeing them (and, as we've already argued, story is a vital mechanism for humans to make sense of the world).

So, looking back over the examples we've seen so far, what do they have in common? The obvious feature—the thing that identifies a pattern—is repetition. You could say that the pattern of numbers "2, 4, 8, 16" contains no repetition, since no number is repeated. But what makes it a pattern, and what make "2, 7, 6, 9, 4" patternless, is that the first sequence repeats the action of doubling.

In a one-upmanship game, the players repeat the action of topping each other, as in the Monty Python "Four Yorkshiremen" sketch,[40] where four wealthy men attempt to out-do each other with stories of their harsh childhoods. In the Budweiser game, the players repeat the action of naming beers, calling further attention each time to their failure to mention Budweiser. In the first instance, there is no fourth-wall breaking, but the fact of the repetition helps to give the scene structure and provides a mechanism to accelerate the energy and absurdity. In the second instance, the game exists entirely outside the scene.

We do teach Finding the Game in the Scene, but we save it until the improvisers are more experienced, often with at least a few public performances under their belt. Not because the technique is difficult but because it's both *easy* and *limiting*. It's very unwise to give beginners an easy trick which may tempt them into thinking that learning how to tell compelling stories is rather too much like hard work.

If games depend on repetition, then find something you can repeat and you've got a game. We've already seen a version of this in the Twitching, Topping and Paperflicking scene (and probably others as well). It would be a downright peculiar choice for an improviser to tear a strip off

---

[40]All right, it actually predates Monty Python, having been written for *At Last the 1948 Show*, but it was a staple of the Python stage shows in the late 1970s and early 1980s and reprised by the remaining Pythons in their O2 shows.

the candidate's CV, ball it up and flick it across the room—and then never do it again! Remarkably, this, or something like it, is just what panicky improvisers are doing when they start playing THAT'S NOT GOOD ENOUGH.

Only a modest amount of skill and care is required as you decide *what* to repeat. As we've seen, repetition of content is not strictly necessary. Nor is this activity the same as REINCORPORATION, although it may be helpful to point out the difference between narrative reincorporation and "call backs." If, in a short-form show, a character from an earlier scene suddenly pops up in a later scene, violating the usual rule that the scenes operate in distinct silos, then the audience will laugh out of recognition, and they will laugh because of the violation. The pattern exists outside of the story and yanks the audience out of the narrative world, temporarily. Whether it *shatters* the narrative or not depends on whether the scene still makes sense if you entered the show late and didn't see the first appearance of the character (although note that it is unlikely to seem funny to you). This is akin to an "in joke," and since a primary reason why laughter exists at all is to bond people together, a joke that this group gets which another group won't is likely to seem particularly funny. Many catchphrases work in a similar way. The fact of the repetition may be funny within the sketch, but most importantly, we the audience know that the line has a meaning beyond the words themselves, because we already associate it with that character.

Reincorporation functions rather differently. A reincorporated element exists within the same narrative world and does not rely on any prior knowledge. Reincorporated elements are there primarily to add structure and bring about endings. If you are skiing and the devil appears, then the audience will be slightly baffled if he spirits you off to hell and the rest of the story is just about your damnation. But if the devil says "Hell has frozen over. Tell me the secret of snowboarding"—reincorporating the winter sports theme—the audience may or may not laugh, but they will understand what the point of the skiing was. Reincorporation is intended to provide "point," and might also be funny. Callbacks are intended to be funny and might (occasionally) provide point, sometimes even making an unfunny offer funny through sheer repetition.

I get two players up and give them a fairly bland scenario: two builders having lunch, a librarian and a customer, a doctor and a patient. Let's take that last example. I tell them just to play the scene and I will give them a direction.

> **Patient:** Have you got my results back?
> **Doctor:** Yes, yes I have.
> **Patient:** Is it serious?
> **Doctor:** No, no, no...
> **Patient:** Oh, thank god for that.

> **Doctor:** Well, actually it is quite serious.
> **Patient:** Tell me!
> **Doctor:** Have you lost your appetite lately?
> **Patient:** Yes, I have.
> **Me:** *Say "Does that mean anything?"*
> **Patient:** Does that mean anything?
> **Me:** *Say "No, no, no…"*
> **Doctor:** No, no, no…
> **Patient:** Oh, thank god for that.
> **Doctor:** (*Getting the idea*) Well, actually it does mean something…

Suddenly, the pattern for the whole scene is clear. It is possible that the Doctor's first choice, to suddenly change tack, will have made the audience laugh, because they enjoy transitions and they empathize with the difficulty in giving bad news, but appreciate the faint absurdity, since doctors should be experienced in this. The scene will sustain for quite some way now just on the repetition of this structure: the patient asks questions, to which the doctor responds "No, no, no" before immediately changing his mind. The pattern here is entirely blatant and dependent on the dialogue being repeated exactly. This is somewhat artificial, but it isn't enough to have mere indecision. The choice wasn't as interesting as all that, and so it must be made interesting by being repeated exactly.

Note again that once the pattern has been established and allowed to run for a while, the scene can be ended at any time by violating the pattern.

> **Patient:** Look, just tell me—am I going to be okay?
> **Doctor:** No, no, no.
> **Patient:** (*Pause*) Aren't you going to say "Well actually you are"?
> **Doctor:** No.
> **Me:** *Scene!*

It can be argued that *character* is an example of a scenic pattern, because we can tell the difference between two characters in the same situation since they react in ways which are easily foreseen if we know who they are. Notice that this may get in the way of having characters be *changed* (which is why we prefer to talk in terms of attitudes). Let's look at another, more subtle example of contriving a pattern in a scene as it progresses. I'll use a doctor and a patient again, for clarity, but you can do this in more or less any scene you like.

> **Doctor:** Right, let's listen to your chest. Cough for me.
> **Patient:** Is it my heart? Just tell me straight, I can take it.
> **Doctor:** You're twenty-four, Mr. Jenkins, and your heart sounds
>   absolutely fine.

> **Me:** *Suspect it's something else...*
> **Patient:** Oh god, it's MRSA isn't it? I've got the superbug!
> **Doctor:** You've never been in hospital, it's hardly likely to be MRSA.
> **Patient:** Is it my brain? My liver? Have I had a stroke? A brain
> aneurism?
> **Doctor:** Mr. Jenkins!
> **Patient:** I haven't made a will!

Here no words are repeated, but the action of "suspecting different diseases" becomes the pattern, creating a hypochondriac character. In Alan Bleasdale's masterly television serial *GBH*, which balanced human drama, high comedy and sociopolitical polemic like no television drama before or since, Michael Palin's low-status Jim Nelson is constantly badgering grumpy doctor John Shrapnel with cancer scares and the like. In the last scene between the two characters, Shrapnel insists that Palin palpate *his* abdomen. With bitter irony, the patient feels the cancerous lump in the doctor's body and is sent home, wracked with guilt.

This depth of feeling is rare in scenes which *depend* on the pattern for their interest, but primacy of pattern is commonplace in much sketch comedy, such as this from *Monty Python's Flying Circus*:

> *The door flies open and Cardinal Ximinez of Spain enters, flanked by two junior cardinals.*
> **Ximinez (Michael Palin):** Nobody expects the Spanish Inquisition!
> Our chief weapon is surprise—surprise and fear, fear and surprise.
> Our *two* weapons are fear and surprise and ruthless efficiency.
> Our *three* weapons are fear, surprise, and ruthless efficiency and
> an almost fanatical devotion to the Pope. Our *four*... No, amongst
> our weapons... amongst our weaponry are such elements as fear,
> surprise... I'll come in again. (*They leave.*)

Great sketch-writing employs two further techniques to prolong the interest. One we have already met and is referred to in Chicago as "heightening." Under Go Through an Unusual Door, we called it going up the ABSURDITY CURVE, and it was also emphasized under Twitching, Topping and Paperflicking. We have also referred more than once to RAISING THE STAKES. In our first doctor/patient scene, the patient should become more and more agitated and the doctor more and more blatant. Thus, the scene accelerates. This is relatively easy for improvisers to do, and is good advice even for scenes which don't depend on patterns. It's also why it makes sense to start with a calm platform—it gives you somewhere to go.

In some sketches, however, the pattern exists to provide a template into which jokes can be fitted. A peerless example is the *Not the Nine O'Clock News* "Constable Savage" sketch, a brilliant satire on racism in the police force, in which a new officer is given a dressing down by his superior for the ludicrous arrests he has made. It's easy to picture the writers all pitching new ideas for charges…

> **Atkinson:** Now then, Savage, I want to talk to you about some charges that you've been bringing lately. I think that perhaps you're being a little … over-zealous.
>
> **Rhys Jones:** Which charges did you mean then, sir?
>
> **Atkinson:** Well, for instance this one "Loitering with intent to use a pedestrian crossing." Savage, maybe you're not aware of this, but it is not illegal to use a pedestrian crossing, neither is "Smelling of foreign food" an offense.
>
> **Rhys Jones:** Are you sure, sir?
>
> **Atkinson:** Also, there's no law against "Urinating in a public convenience" or "Coughing without due care and attention."
>
> **Rhys Jones:** If you say so, sir…
>
> **Atkinson:** Yes, I do say so, Savage!

But the other mechanism is also used with great precision and elegance here. Not only do the charges get more and more bizarre as the sketch goes on, but the stakes are raised over the course of the sketch as it first transpires that Constable Savage has brought all these charges against the same man, a Mr. Winston Kodogo, and then further that the man has only been targeted because of the color of his skin.

This is a masterpiece of construction, but its existence does present us with a problem. We have discovered an important mechanism by which sketch comedy operates, setting up a pattern and repeating it. But improvisation is often a poor mechanism for generating high-quality jokes and worse at arranging those jokes in a perfectly accelerating order, let alone adding another accelerating element to bring the whole thing together. Improvised sketches are bound to fall short of this.

But, when was improvising facsimile sketch comedy ever our goal? For some companies, actually, that is the goal. The *UCB Comedy Improvisation Manual* reminds readers:

> We are not interested in the story of a Long Form comedy scene; we are interested in the Game. We are not creating a play with a story arc. We are not interested in finding a strong beginning, middle and end, and we aren't improvising to discover what is going to change about our characters. We are improvising comedy sketches, not stories.

This is no doubt a useful skill to acquire, but we question the wisdom of limiting the scope of improvisation so drastically. Why not explore what else the form is capable of, in order to have more variety within a single show, or to create shows which affect the audience in ways other than having them admire the cleverness of a Game?

And that's key, we think. With some notable but rare exceptions, sketch comedy has no power to *move* and is drastically limited in its storytelling power. One of the most powerful story weapons in the Johnstone narrative arsenal is BREAKING ROUTINES, which is very easy for improvisers to do. It is also the exact opposite of Finding the Game. Now, this doesn't mean you have to make a choice as to which rule you are going to swear permanent allegiance to. Both are tools, and both can be put to good use, but they can be hard (although not impossible) to combine in the same scene.

Remember that the audience is waiting for "point." Once they fully know the point of the scene, it is likely that it is coming to an end. So, we build a platform to create the world of the story, break the routine to provide "point" initially, maybe do so on subsequent occasions and then can use reincorporation, canceling or completing routines to end it.

Let's say we begin with a man admiring a painting in an art gallery. We break the routine by having him spot the artist (and the audience thinks, "That was the point of the art gallery"). He talks to her, but they disagree about the meaning of the painting, which changes both of them (and the audience thinks, "That was the point of them meeting"). Eventually, she becomes so enraged by his analysis that she yanks the painting off the wall and smashes it over his head (and the audience thinks, "That was the point of the painting"—it is also now canceled). Security guards drag her away, not believing she is the artist, and the routine of "talking to the artist" is completed, ending the scene. But often, as soon as you start repeating something, *the repetition becomes the point of the scene*, and it can be frustrating for the audience if the transition between a pattern-segment and the rest of the story is not carefully managed. The scene above could possibly be punctuated by a very light pattern which sits on top of the structure (he always mispronounces something and she keeps correcting him?), but in finding-the-game scenes, the game *is* the structure. Thus, if Finding The Game is your goal, it isn't hard to do, but you drastically curtail the scope of your improvised scenes. Devoid of human feeling, robbed of the power to move the audience and all the same as each other, pattern scenes may be very funny if the improvisers are witty and inspired, but they will almost never ascend to theatre.

Possible counter-examples include plays like *Waiting for Godot*, which spread a pattern out over the whole piece, allowing the characters to breathe in the gaps.

2.16

Continue or Thank You

Overview

A key game for developing storytelling technique, which is also dependent on accurate feedback from the rest of the group.

This is a game we developed so that students could be sure they were interesting the audience. If you play this game enough in your group, you could become brilliant at both entertaining and satisfying audiences.

Students' ability to estimate the length of a scene depends far more on how much they are enjoying it (from the stage or from their seat), so start by asking them to improvise scenes which are exactly two minutes long. Shout out to let them know when they have thirty seconds to go, but other than that don't interfere. We usually let the whole group do scenes and then analyze them at the end. We typically include this game around six or seven weeks in to our beginner's course, and so many of the scenes will stall early on and start very negatively or suffer from the problem of having no one who was affected strongly.

Now I set up a pair to do a scene and tell them that after a minute I will freeze the action and say to the group "Continue or thank you?" If the group wants to see more, they should say "Continue"; if they've seen enough, they should say "Thank you." I explain to the group that it's very important that they say what they really feel, otherwise they will train each other to be boring. Also, improvisers know when they're in a bad scene and will be relieved to get out of it if it's really going nowhere. I tell the improvisers that most people do not get a "Continue" the first time around, to lower their expectations and make a "Thank you" normal rather than disappointing. After sixty seconds I freeze the scene and poll the group. If the majority say "Continue," the pair continues. I freeze the action again this time after thirty seconds and ask the audience "Continue or thank you?" From then on I freeze the action every thirty seconds until the audience says "Thank you" or the pair finishes their own scene. When the majority of the group says "Thank you," the pair sits down and we ask the group "Why did you say thank you?" i.e., why did you not want to see any more?

Typically, the group will say "Thank you" the first time around, and when I ask them why, they usually say, "It wasn't going anywhere. It didn't look like anything was going to happen." In other words, the improvisers *hadn't promised us anything.* Sometimes even though the sixty seconds they have seen has been highly entertaining, they still say "Thank you" because nothing further is imminent. It looks like we're going to see more of the same. If we let the improvisers try again, they will usually learn from this and make a platform full of promise and the group will shout "Continue!" Even if the first minute is fairly dreary but just before the minute is up one of them says to the other "I've got something I need to tell you," the audience will want to see more.

This is a valuable revelation for improvisers. The audience doesn't have an incentive to keep watching because you've just been funny. They want to keep watching if they think something good is to come. Having made an enticing promise in the first minute, the improvisers need to deliver on it in the next thirty seconds. If they waffle and bridge (as they often do), the audience will say "Thank you." They now lack faith that you will deliver on your promises. You look like you've teased us, but now you don't have anything. The crucial learning point here is that anything will do. You just need to deliver on your promise and then make another one, and the audience will keep shouting "Continue" until you're ready to finish the scene.

FRUSTRATING THE AUDIENCE

If you get audience suggestions, that in itself is a promise you need to deliver on. I remember improvisers once taking the suggestion "Casino," and then delivering a scene about a man trying and failing to get change so that he could buy chips to play blackjack. The audience shouted "Thank you!" I asked the improvisers why they thought an audience member might shout "Casino" as a suggestion, and what sort of things they might be hoping to see. The improvisers realized that anyone who suggests that is hoping to see the sort of high stakes situations that are in films like *Casino, Ocean's Eleven* or *Indecent Proposal*. They were not hoping to see a man get change for a twenty, so no matter how amusingly that is played out and how much witty wordplay the scene contains, the audience will be disappointed.

During a RADA graduate workshop I remember the actor Tobias Menzies was annoyed that the audience continually said "Thank you" to his scene after the first minute. "They need to give us more time," he said. "It's impossible to be interesting in the first minute." I told him he could either argue with the audience that they really wanted to see more of him even though they said they didn't, or he could learn to be so compelling they'd beg to see more. He laughed and said he wanted them to beg for more rather than imploring them to watch him. He cracked the game that night by making promises and delivering on them and had them shouting "Continue!" every time. It wasn't long after that that he became a really wonderful performance improviser and someone everyone wanted to work with.

—Deborah

Any group that plays this regularly and is really honest in their feedback will begin to be riveting performers. It's really crucial to get the feedback as to why the audience said "Thank you," though. Deborah once dropped by a rehearsal a group was having and they were playing this game, but when the audience said "Thank you," the improvisers skulked back to their seats looking depressed, and never asked why. Played this way, it's just a downer and you're not learning anything. Sometimes people don't know why they said "Thank you," they just felt they'd seen enough. That's fine, but if you're the performer, at least ask. Usually someone will be able to deconstruct it, and for the most part people know, even if it's as simple as "You said you were going to show her the painting and then you just stood and talked." At the end of a sequence, it's also helpful to go back and ask the audience why they said "Continue"—this is better than breaking the flow and asking them at the time. Usually they say something like "I had to know whether she would go into the cellar and what was down there." They want to see a promise delivered on.

This is a game that even nervous improvisers can play. They're doing a regular scene and the responsibility for a "Thank you" is shared. A "Thank you" can mean "We enjoyed what we saw but now we want to see something new," and it's not unusual for a group to laugh hysterically, say "Thank you" and mean it. It's the audience saying "Thank you, you entertained us. Can you do another one because this one has gone as far as it can and it looks like we'll just see more of the same?" It can be just as valuable at teaching improvisers when to *end* a scene as how to do a scene.

Games like this require improvisers to approach performance without the traditional artist's ego. The more the group can see an exercise as a "group Sudoku" (a problem to be solved collaboratively), the more they stop seeing their go as reflecting on them and taking its success or failure to heart. If we have sixteen students in pairs taking turns to play Continue Or Thank You, the work will get better with every round because the group is teaching itself. If someone has just told a fellow improviser "I got bored because you stopped making the cake and started talking about the big race," then they've felt it for themselves and are far more likely to follow their own advice. The group begins to crack the problem together, and people jump up to have a go when they think they're starting to see the light. They rejoice when they get even one "Continue" and run back to the stage with the attitude "This time we're going for two!" rather than "This scene has to be perfect or it will reflect badly on me." The more you can encourage this spirit of group problem-solving and point out how the work gets better as this group makes discoveries, the more the students will have a wonderful time and forget themselves, which will make them better improvisers.

One way to think about it is to approach the challenge of keeping an audience enthralled the way a scientist would. Scientists are forever doing arbitrary things, and are interested to see the results. They see themselves as observers, recorders and discoverers, and remove their own biases from the situation as much as possible. When improvisers are more in this state, jumping up to try it this way or that way to see how the audience will respond, then the atmosphere is fantastic and they can put themselves into the highest possible state of learning and discovery.

2.17

Agree, Agree, Agree

Overview

Some extra exercises and ideas to help slightly more experienced improvisers maintain their instinct to agree and help mitigate against the tendency for an ever-increasing bag of tricks to erode the fundamental principle of YES AND.

As a new improviser grows in confidence, begins to acquire some technique, maybe performs in a few shows, it's quite natural for that initial happy spirit of YES AND to be in part replaced by one or both of two other approaches. Some improvisers, who have responded strongly to the storytelling and What Comes Next work, will now be trying to process all of the rules or principles they have learned, while the scene is in progress. It will be very hard for them to really attend to their partner because they are constantly attempting to judge the effect of the previous offer, or speculate on the possible effect of a possible future offer.

Other improvisers, with more confidence and less anxiety, will start to feel that YES AND was nothing more than a crutch for beginners who hadn't yet got to grips with pushing narratives into the future or bringing the funny. They effectively imagine that their partner is perpetually playing Sandy Carroll and ignore or block any offer they don't like the sound of. Obviously, this approach won't get the best out of the improviser who is forced into playing second fiddle, but it won't get the best out of the improviser determined to get the upper hand either. Remember that the audience pays to share your moment of inspiration. If you are turning an improvised scene or game into a solo stand-up performance, if no audience member can see where your ideas are coming from because the process is entirely internal, it just isn't as much fun.

It's often valuable for a relatively new practitioner to go back over the most fundamental and primitive exercises to shore them up—piano players who have been taking lessons for several years should still practice their scales—but for improvisers particularly, a return to the basic principles should be a constant part of the learning experience, probably forever. Here then are a couple of exercises which are a bit demanding for beginners, but which return to the concepts we would introduce in the very first session. One exercise is designed to remind improvisers of the huge importance and tremendous efficacy of *just saying yes*. The other looks in a bit more detail about exactly what is and is not a BLOCK, and has in turn become very valuable for us in teaching one of the most challenging performance games we know. We'll also use this as an opportunity to discuss our approach as teachers in more detail.

WHEN HARRY MET SALLY

Two people up please, and have a seat next to each other. Have you seen the movie When Harry Met Sally? *Okay, you remember those interviews with different couples you see at the beginning? I want you to improvise one of those "how we met" stories. I'm going to make it a rule that you both remember the story very well, and you both remember it the same. We can do a scene about a couple who remember the same events differently, or who argue with each other, on another day. Today I want you to agree with everything your partner says. Try and create the illusion for us that you have told this story many times before, that you're used to telling it, and that you enjoy telling it.*

Unless you give this exercise to very inexperienced or anxious improvisers, this is unlikely to create a lot of problems. Possibly one improviser will leave it to the other to do all the work—they will agree but not add much—or one improviser will get "on a roll" and not leave any gaps. If possible, try and correct this as the scene unfolds. The whole story likely won't take more than a couple of minutes to tell and it's great for the audience to watch the process whereby one or two arbitrary offers early on are developed, justified, and YES ANDed into a complete narrative.

Here's a fairly compact example of how it might go.

> **Me:** So, tell me how you two first met.
> **Milly:** I did not like him when I first met him.
> **Thom:** It's true, I made a very bad first impression.
> **Milly:** I was just out of university, and going out to work for the first time. I'd got a job in a mobile phone shop and it was my first day,

and I was really anxious. And my first sight of Steve was him just buried—buried... *(Milly may or may not have something but Thom jumps in in any case)*

Thom: ...under this pile of boxes. I was thrashing about like a trapped animal. It was a prank which the other guys in the shop had played on me, but I saw Juliet and...

Milly: *(They've got a good rhythm going now, there's no obvious pause, but Milly takes over smoothly)* ...he blamed me! I'd been there less than two hours. He was calling me such terrible names!

Thom: The other guys started laughing and I realized this new girl had had nothing to do with it and I was so embarrassed.

Milly: You're so sweet when you're embarrassed. *(She gives him a quick touch on the leg, emphasizing their intimacy)*. Then he asked if he could buy me lunch to make it up to me.

Thom: We ended up going to the cinema together that night.

Milly: And that's—how we met.

They both look very pleased, and quite relaxed at the end of it. Neither feels as if they've had to do all the work, but equally they feel as if this was a story they created together which—simple as it was—neither of them could have created on their own. It will probably be rather difficult for them to reconstruct who contributed which element and when—which is how it should be. By treating the material created through improvisation as "ours" rather than "mine," by seeing it as generated by the team, rather than the individual, we can start to separate the ego from the work, and put the emphasis on the process rather than the content. This means that the content likely will be rather better, but it also means that an audience watching will get to see a good process. So even if the content is a bit bland, the audience will have had the pleasure of watching two improvisers throw away their preconceptions, egos and desire to stay in control and just take it in turns following the other's lead.

After you've done a few of these, try some larger groups. Ask three people how they put the band together, or ask four people what happened at last night's party. The party scenario is particularly tricky for people who would rather contradict someone else's account (because then they can stay in control) or escalate that disagreement into an argument (because then they can stop inventing) because both of these strategies can be concealed under the perfectly reasonable story offer of "I drank so much I can't remember." In fact, sometimes people will profess complete amnesia. As with couples who remember stories differently, it isn't that this never happens or scenes of this nature can't be improvised. It's that the rule "always agree" shouldn't be too difficult to follow for 120 seconds. It's the improvisers who *can't* follow this rule who are limiting the kinds of scenes they can create.

If you are improvising a scene in which you disagree, or remember events differently, there needs to be an underlying, unspoken agreement between the improvisers which keeps them bound together, even as the characters diverge. The golden rule, as ever, is to give your partner a good time.

> **Phoebe:** I looked through the window, and guess what I saw?
> **Vicky:** Daddy stealing money out of Mummy's purse?
> **Phoebe:** No, guess again.

If the whole story has been building up to this revelation of parents thieving from each other, then Phoebe's offer becomes a BLOCK, or at least CANCELS Vicky's obvious and necessary offer. But if it's relatively early in the scene, and Phoebe thinks it will be fun for Vicky to effectively play New Choice with her a few times (see page 265) then the audience will have a marvelous time as Vicky has to guess again and again and again what it is that Phoebe has seen. If she ever eventually gets it, the scene will very likely be over. The real challenge is not to make the right offer, or always to play characters who agree with each other. The real challenge is make offers which inspire your partner. And one of the best ways of doing that is to get inspiration from the last offer they made to you.

PHOTO ALBUMS

This hinterland between BLOCKING and not-BLOCKING can be productively explored using this next game. Whereas for When Harry Met Sally, it's best to do all examples in front of the group, so that the teacher can instantly identify any trivial BLOCKS or WIMPS and remove them, this next exercise tends not to be quite so interesting to watch and it's also harder to screw up, so it's more efficient to just get everybody to play in pairs.

> *Everybody find a partner and call yourselves A and B. A, I want you to pretend you have a large photo album, full of pictures of you and your family, going back to your childhood. You are showing these pictures to B who is very interested to see them. Point a picture out to B and start telling them about it. B ask questions, and find out more. Both of you adopt a* YES AND *attitude so that an audience watching you can believe that there really is a photo album there and you are looking at the same picture. Keep moving to a new picture so you don't get stuck. Away you go.*

This is not a particularly challenging game, and it's unlikely anyone who's done even a few improv classes will struggle with it. After two or three minutes, get them to switch roles and play the same game the other way around. If you listen in on pairs playing this together, you should hear something like this (Sarah is A and James is B).

> **Sarah:** This is a picture of me and my mum.
> **James:** Oh, that's soo cute. How old are you here?
> **Sarah:** About five. It's my first day at school.
> **James:** Hence the uniform.
> **Sarah:** Exactly.
> **James:** Did they make you wear those straw hats every day?
> **Sarah:** Every day of the week. I kept losing mine.
> **James:** That sounds like you. Who's in this picture?
> **Sarah:** That's my little brother.
> **James:** What's he standing on?
> **Sarah:** My older brother.
> **James:** Oh yes!

Making the photo album Sarah's generally puts the onus on her to add information, which she's often happy to do. Sometimes James asks her direct questions and she answers ("How old are you?"). Sometimes she just volunteers information ("It's my first day at school."). But James makes offers of his own too, sometimes BLIND OFFERS ("What's he standing on?") and sometimes he "notices" things in the picture like the straw hats. Neither player feels any particular stress and both probably feel happy to have generated so much material so easily.

As a piece of scene-work for a performance, this is a fair enough way to establish a bit of platform, but it's smooth and easy as opposed to playful, and there's little likelihood that anyone is going to be changed or affected, so after a couple of minutes, an audience could easily be forgiven for wanting to see a pretty spectacular BREAK IN THE ROUTINE to pay off this—perfectly amiable—but rather waffly opening.

It's possible that the players' experience won't have been quite as smooth as that. As they ask and answer questions, as they add detail to the imaginary photograph, essentially performing a modest CJ SWEEP (see page 112), it's possible that what is "obvious" to A, may have been entirely unexpected to B. The feeling, and the impression, of smoothness comes from the same kind of easy acceptance, the same kind of instant and automatic YES AND-ing which we made use of in the previous When Harry Met Sally Game. Let's try a version now which makes a permanent feature of this occasional need to reconfigure the fantasy photo in the light of the new information added by your partner.

Okay, everybody find new partners. Again, call yourselves A and B, and again A has a photo album which holds pictures of A and A's family. A, start showing the pictures to B and B you can ask questions. Last time, I asked you both to play Yes And, and to make the process of building up information about the pictures easy. But it may have been that—without meaning to—B asked a question which caught A by surprise. This time

I want B to ask those kinds of questions a lot. Endow A with having contradicted earlier information, or with being at odds with the photo. Put elements into the photo that seem unlikely or unpredictable. But take care! We have to believe that you are looking at the same picture.

It may be helpful to give a few examples. If A starts by saying, "This is a picture of me and my brother," then in this version of the game, it will be excellent for B to say, "I thought you said you were an only child," or "Why is he dressed as a clown?" or "That's just you holding a rabbit." A must now JUSTIFY, saying perhaps, "I am an only child, but Barry was like a brother to me," or "We were a circus family but I ran away," or "That's right—we called our pet rabbit Mybrother." There's a totally different energy in the room this time round. People seem much more engaged, demonstrative, and many people—sometimes everybody—seems to be having more fun. Get them to switch roles ("revenge!") before debriefing further.

Polling the group, many people report that the second version was more fun and that they generated much more imaginative and interesting material the second time around. Having a partner, B, who doesn't just blandly accept what they say, maybe adding something super-obvious, but who instead makes them think, react, jump through hoops, inspires them to new heights.

There are two very important points to make at this stage. One is that as fun to play (and probably to watch) as this second version is, that does not imply that immediately contradicting your partner's offers should become your primary improvisation technique! You will derail a lot of perfectly good scenes and piss off a lot of good improvisers quite rapidly if you do that. Rather the point is that a contradiction or a left-field offer—especially early in the scene—can be made *safely*. It isn't something you need to or you should do all of the time, but it is not something which must be avoided at all costs, provided your partner understands that they have to help justify this new offer.

Especially in longer form improvisations, where a lot of plot has been established, improvisers may get in a funk about adding new information for fear of contradicting something which has already been established, and so the narrative grinds to a halt. A better strategy is to add something new when the plot needs a kick without stopping to think about it too much, because the very worst that can happen is that you create a contradiction, which as we have just seen, is more likely to inspire your partner than confound them!

The second point is that when we talk about BLOCKING we're really talking about two different things, of which one is far more important than the other. If I say, "This is a picture of my father," and you say, "Why is he wearing a clown outfit?" then I may *feel* blocked. I had some cool story ready to go about my father taking me and my little wooden boat to the local pond and now I won't get to tell it, because we're off on some kind of circus story instead. But you don't have to be deliberately trying to ask difficult questions to create this feeling in another improviser—you can do it quite inadvertently, and often will. It's an inevitable, in fact a delightful feature of improvisation that your "obvious" is not the same as mine and so I don't have to be playing mischievous games to YES AND your offer in a way that you weren't expecting. That's precisely why teaching accepting of offers is so important and why we do it so early on.

And as far as the audience is concerned, no block has occurred yet. But if you say, "Why is he wearing a clown outfit?" and I say, "He isn't, he's wearing a suit," then that's a massive BLOCK. Not because I have rejected my partner's clown outfit, but because it is now *impossible for the audience to believe that we are both looking at the same photograph* and so the reality of the scene is now falling apart. It's only when I deny the existence of the dress that the audience is in any way bothered. It's me that's not keeping the promises which we are making, not my blameless partner.

JUSTIFY *THIS*

One of my favorite improv memories is a scene I did with Deborah in a workshop. We were rehearsing for a season of shows and had just come back from a coffee break, so the room was littered with Starbucks cups. Deborah and I jumped up and began a scene from nothing. I was onstage, sitting in a chair, hunched over a mime laptop. Deborah entered the scene and because she was holding one of the Starbucks cups at the time, incorporated it into the scene. "Here you are darling, I've brought you a coffee." I made the character choice to play distracted and ungrateful. This is perhaps not the best, most open-ended choice available, but it was my instinct in the moment, and I felt it made sense of the physical offers I had made so far. I didn't realize how problematic the exact form of words I used would be. "Just put it down there on the table," I muttered, waving at empty air, but this presented Deborah with an almost insoluble problem, since even the most skilled improviser or technically proficient mime artist, cannot set a real coffee-cup down on a mime table.

Deborah looked at the cup, looked at the non-existent table, looked at me, and looked back at the table again. Then she finally said "There isn't a table there." This is the archetypal BLOCK, denying the reality established by one player. This is not simply putting them in a BAD STATE, but actually preventing the story from moving forward. But what choice had I given her?

If I agree that there isn't a table there, then that cancels everything, so I had to insist that there was, and Deborah began treating our differing versions of reality as a pathology. I insisted that the room was filled with various objects—a lamp, a filing cabinet, the desk I was sitting at, the computer I was working on. Deborah swept through the space I had endowed with being occupied with desk and pleaded with me to leave my fantasy world and come back to reality. In frustration, I pulled a gun out from my desk drawer (all mimed of course) and told her that if none of the objects in this room were real, then nothing would happen if I pulled the trigger. When she insisted that was true, I fired the gun, and she collapsed wounded. I panicked and tried to revive her. When I was unable, I grabbed for the telephone (mimed again) and tried to call for help, but now the telephone melted through my hands. As I realized that the phone and the desk it was on weren't real, Deborah came back to life, saying "You're cured."

The room burst into spontaneous applause, but what I find so telling about the scene is that even though neither of us really knew what was real and what wasn't, and even though the narrative momentum of the scene had forced us (or really I had forced Deborah) into the most outrageous of blocks, underneath it all, there was a shared agreement and a commitment to justify the offers made so far and end up with a coherent reality for the audience. It was quite a circuitous journey, but I think we got there.

—*Tom*

So, to get the best out of your partner, you want them in a good state, and that won't be achieved by heedlessly tossing their offers aside and substituting your own ideas instead. But if you think your partner will find it fun for you to make them run the gauntlet a bit, or you have a strong reason for wanting to steer the scene in a new direction, or because your partner has simply given you no choice in the matter, you may end up not making the offer that your partner expected or wanted—not to mention the great many times you will do this entirely inadvertently. But the audience only cares when the scene stops making sense or when they aren't given something which they feel they were promised. It's blocking in this second sense which we should really care about. The audience out-ranks all of us.

Returning to the photo album game, from the point of view of a hypothetical audience, the second version will likely be a little more interesting. We get to see the improvisers work a little harder, especially A, and the content generated will be fresher and less clichéd. But this is still likely to seem a little flat, a little dry after only two or three minutes. Let's try yet a third version.

I pair everyone up again and get them to use the same mechanism again—A will show B photos from an album. This time, B is not only permitted to ask challenging or unexpected questions, they are also allowed, in fact encouraged, to become suspicious or even accusatory. This time around, the scene might start something like this.

> **Kitty:** This is a picture of me and my mum and dad. We're all on vacation together.
> **Flinn:** Really? Because that just looks like an ordinary living room to me.
> **Kitty:** It's a bed-and-breakfast. We couldn't afford anything fancy.
> **Flinn:** A bed-and-breakfast? Where is it? By the sea-side?
> **Kitty:** Er, no, it's here in town actually.
> **Flinn:** Wait a minute, I recognize that lamp.
> **Kitty:** Oh, have you been there too?
> **Flinn:** That's my lamp!
> **Kitty:** It's a very popular make. Ikea, I think.
> **Flinn:** Hang on—this is my living room.
> **Kitty:** No it isn't.
> **Flinn:** Yes it bloody well is. When was this taken?
> **Kitty:** Oh, years and years ago.
> **Flinn:** It couldn't have been that long ago—look you're fully grown-up in this picture.
> **Kitty:** All right—last summer.
> **Flinn:** Did you go on holiday in my house last summer!?
> **Kitty:** Well, you weren't using it. You were in Cyprus.

This *does* feel like a proper scene. Not just platform, but we already know what the scene is about, and the narrative has largely been generated by Flinn, not because he's trying his hardest to think of good ideas, but because he's looking for ways to keep Kitty "on the hop" and enjoying playing this suspicious attitude. Both players have to take care that the information which is being added to the world remains consistent, but the need to agree and add doesn't mean you can't play characters who lie.

"That looks like an ordinary living room" is possibly a BLOCK in the first sense, wrenching away whatever beach/cultural/intrepid vacation Kitty had in mind, but because of the way the scene has been set up, Flinn is perfectly safe to do this, knowing that it won't put Kitty in a bad state. When Flinn asks "Is it by the sea-side?" Kitty's response, "No, it's here in town," possibly risks being a BLOCK in the second sense, denying the audience the sea-side they were briefly promised. But saying it's very close by, which is not the usual choice for a vacation destination, pays off the earlier and more interesting promise that there's something wrong with this vacation.

When Flinn says "This is my living room," and Kitty responds "No it isn't," this might seem like the muddled realities kind of BLOCKing—the most destructive of all—but Kitty knows she's lying and Flinn knows that if he now agrees with Kitty and withdraws his offer, then between them they will have canceled the delightful offer that Kitty's vacation picture is his own living room. He has no option but to insist that he is correct, and when he does so, the audience is in no doubt about what is shown in the photo.

For a scene which apparently contains so much disagreement, negativity and conflict, in fact the improvisers are in total agreement throughout, However because they take care not just to introduce potential contradictions, but also to resolve them, the audience is never left floundering, and because the characters are being affected by the interaction, it feels like we're there for the story. The story isn't the time that Kitty vacationed in Flinn's house without his knowledge—that passed off without incident. The story is the day Flinn found out about it. To resolve the story properly, I'd like an answer to the question: why has Kitty given the game away by showing him the pictures? It doesn't matter which improviser sees the need to tackle this problem. It's probably more natural for Flinn to demand an answer out of Kitty, but if Kitty feels that Flinn isn't going to put her on the spot like this, she can just start confessing. As is so often the case with justifications, the improvisers shouldn't wait until they have the whole thing figured out—they should just start talking.

It's possible that this last iteration of the game reminds you of another game—a famously difficult game described by Keith Johnstone in *Impro for Storytellers* and apparently beloved by audiences at the Loose Moose. If you don't know this game, or can't yet identify it, let's see if it will help if we change the situation of the game while keeping the mechanism the same.

Everybody find a partner. Call yourselves A and B. A, have a seat. You have been arrested and B is interrogating you and showing you the evidence against you. B, you have a series of photographs showing A and various other people and things connected to the crime. Show the prisoner the photos, have them describe what's on them and ideally incriminate themselves. If you want, you can kick-start the process by saying something like "What are you doing with these tins of tomatoes?" as you produce the next picture, but there's nothing wrong with just saying "What's this a picture of?" either. If A's answers are not sufficiently incriminating, you can get more aggressive and demand to know the truth, but A, you are very guilty and very scared—you should be eager to confess and get it off your chest.

Pretty soon the room is full of noise and clamor. Eavesdropping might reveal a conversation along these lines...

> **John:** What's going on in this picture?
> **Philip:** That's me. I'm in an art gallery.
> **John:** Oh yeah, art lover are you?
> **Philip:** Not really. I'm casing the joint.
> **John:** Who's that next to you?
> **Philip:** Um, no one.
> **John:** Who's that *there*, next to you!?
> **Philip:** John, my twin brother. It was all part of the plan.
> **John:** I see. (*Produces another mime photo*) Why are you both dressed as pirates?
> **Philip:** Disguise?
> **John:** In an art gallery?
> **Philip:** If you look completely incongruous, people don't notice you.
> **John:** And why are you both holding water melons?
> **Philip:** We hollowed them out to hide the paintings we stole.

And so on. The practice they've had with the various versions of the Photo Album game should mean that no matter how challenging the questions from B (John), A (Philip) manages to justify and maintain the coherence of the emerging picture. And B is less likely to panic and jump from question-to-question without ever properly pursuing any one line of enquiry. The scenes which result are much more interesting than the early Photo Album scenes, partly because the new scenario has automatically raised the stakes, but mainly because both players are so emotionally engaged. B is furiously trying to prove his case and A is desperately trying to confess in the hope of leniency.

Sometimes the material generated by this process still gets a bit confused. Let it run for more than two-or-three minutes and there's a danger that A will have confessed to half-a-dozen different misdemeanors and will have justified any number of bizarre disguises, secret rendezvous in different remote locations, not to mention accomplices, weapons, hostages and so on. If you suspect that the content has started to unravel for at least some of the pairs, you can ask the B's to end the scene by saying to A "Okay, let's recap." B now summarizes the main content generated in the scene so far and attempts to mold it into some kind of coherent narrative. You and they may be surprised at how much more sense everything seems to make when recapped in this way!

Improvisers first attempting to extemporize long-form narrative plays would do well to employ a narrator to link the scenes together for similar reasons. As well as clearly identifying characters, setting the locations for the next scene and pushing the plot into the future, narrators can subtly streamline the storylines in a way which appears not to deny the improvisers any credit. Writer Ian Rowland, in his amazing book *The Full Facts Book of Cold Reading*, advises those who wish to appear to have psychic powers that toward the end of a reading, they should recap what has transpired. The supposed psychic uses this to emphasize all the things they got right and craftily takes credit for much of the information actually supplied by the sitter. The process also affects the sitter's ability to remember just who said what and when. Rowland refers to this as "reprising with gold paint" and narrators of improvised plays can do they self-same thing when they sum-up the story so far. Thus when the interrogator says "I see—let's recap..." and reels off the evil plan which has now been foiled, they may essentially be playing the Join the Dots game (page 74) but the material sounds familiar enough that the audience can't help but think it was their fault for not following it the first time!

Readers familiar with Keith Johnstone's classic game "Boris" will almost certainly have seen the resemblance by now. For those who aren't, here's a quick description. Boris is an interrogation game for two players. One is the interrogator who fires questions at the prisoner, often (but not always) rather arbitrary ones. The other is the prisoner who spits out answers which JUSTIFY the questions. The prisoner is very eager to confess, because also in the room is the eponymous Boris, who is usually merely imagined by the players. Boris is an eight-foot-tall monster whose job is to hurt prisoners who are uncooperative. Having Boris be invisible means that he can inflict massive and exotic pain on the prisoner with no risk at all to the improviser. It's more fun if the interrogator merely asks for Boris's help rather than specifies what Boris should do. Then the improviser playing the prisoner can elect to have Boris twist an arm or deliver a blow to the abdomen or whatever they like.

Keith gives brilliant examples in his book and describes audiences chanting "Boris! Boris! Boris!" until they agreed to play it, but it's a game which causes all but the most verbally dexterous of beginner improvisers to falter. Some young male improvisers are captivated by the idea of Boris being able to physically abuse them and are eager for the interrogator to set the monster upon them, whereupon they fling themselves enthusiastically about the stage. This is usually quite safe (although Keith does report that an "uncaring" Boris once broke his victim's collarbone) but it's also safe in the sense that it can't fail. In the best Boris scenes, Boris himself is a constant threat, but his physical intervention may never in fact been needed.

Other improvisers may find that being the interrogator is a very difficult role, partly because of the supposed need to keep coming up with more and more surprising questions. As they over-tax their imaginations, eventually the pace slows, which not only robs the scene of much of its energy and power, it gives the prisoner far too much time to think which means that the answers provided tend to be duller and, once again, safer.

But in fact, making every question completely unpredictable is not necessary. It can stop the game from ever developing into a narrative— despite the "let's recap" get-out-of-jail-free card described above.

> **Interrogator:** Tell me about the chess set.
> **Prisoner:** I stole it from my best friend.
> **Interrogator:** And what about the country cottage in Ireland?
> **Prisoner:** I burnt it down!
> **Interrogator:** What does this have to do with the Modern History Faculty?
> **Prisoner:** I've never been there.
> **Interrogator:** Boris!

This kind of interaction is typical of people who have managed to get past the stage of stopping-and-starting due to imagination-funk but nothing is being developed here. It's more like the quick-fire round of a game show than an interrogation. This can't be reprised with gold paint; the interrogator will virtually have to invent the criminal plot from scratch.

To specify when the interrogator should follow a single line of questioning, when they should throw in an arbitrary offer, when they should reject an answer and call for Boris, is very difficult for a teacher to conceptualize, and providing guidance for the prisoner is almost as tricky. But by using the Photo Album game as an on-ramp, it's possible to get students playing quite good Boris games in about half an hour.

If your students find something difficult, the solution may not be for you to continue to describe more and more idealized versions of what the game or exercise should look like. Nor may simply giving them LOTS OF GOES be enough. Often, a relatively new improviser will be so overwhelmed by the many different demands of a new game that they become discouraged. Then they face the same game again with less confidence and so are less successful. Eventually, an otherwise splendid game gets relegated as "too difficult" and so falls into disuse.

What we try and do as teachers is to construct a pathway, which begins with a very easy—possibly even unrecognizable—version of the exercise, and then we add small elements one by one, so that each iteration is not so very different or so very more difficult than the last, but after a short time a very challenging game has become relatively straightforward. We are not always lucky enough to find as smooth and easy a learning curve as we eventually found for Boris, but this approach informs all of our teaching. Our eight-week Level One course starts with Pointing At Things And Saying What They Are Not, and ends with The Guest Game (see *Impro For Storytellers*) in which the same ability, to be able to produce a new idea out of thin air and commit to its inclusion, is required—along with numerous other skills as well—but by this time, the habit of confidently committing to a series of arbitrary offers has been quite deeply ingrained.

Playing Games

Overview

Many manuals of improvisation are little more than lists of games, often sorted into neat categories and difficulty levels so that teachers can easily assemble a class schedule. Many public performances are just so many games arranged end-to-end, and websites abound with lists of dozens—sometimes hundreds—of improv games, all of which have presumably been played somewhere by someone. What we think is required is greater selectivity—picking games which serve a particular purpose—and that means understanding the point of playing games at all, instead of just playing open scenes.

THREE WORD SENTENCES

A class of improv games which will be familiar to even fairly new improvisers is the two-in-one game, where two people have to cooperate very closely in order to build a single entity. Examples include Word At A Time, Arms Through and Dubbing. Another very popular class of game is the **verbal restriction**, where some things cannot be said or must be said. Three Word Sentences is a particularly interesting example of this type of game. The rules are very simple: everything you say must be exactly three words long, no more and no less. Once you've said your three words, it's your partner's turn. (So it should really be called Three Word Utterances; you can't string together multiple three-word sentences in order to still speak in paragraphs.)

You are not permitted to mangle the grammar in order to cram your thought into three words, either. ("Can I have some of your ice cream?"

thinks the improviser. "Want your ice," is what stumbles out of their mouth. This should be corrected.) Nor may you tail off in mid-sentence. ("The thing is…") Each utterance must be a complete three-word sentence. Contractions count as one word.

On its face, this seems like a significant constraint to work under, and that is one of the reasons for playing games, especially in public. If there is a task that must be accomplished with a very clear and obvious success/ failure outcome, that adds an extra layer of interest. Of course, if you are improvising an open scene, the task is to make sense and not be boring or stupid, but that's a bit more subtle, and the moment of failure harder to spot, compared to the difference between saying three words and saying four. You can think of these as hoops the improvisers have to jump through, or bars they have to clear, and we sometimes refer to games which provide nothing more than a challenge of this kind as "hoop games."

Watching even fairly inexperienced improvisers play Three Word Sentences, however, is often a revelation. A lot of anxious improvisers tend to gabble, desperate to fill all the silences, but they talk half an inch of meaning to every fifty feet of noise, and frequently talk over each other. In Three Word Sentences, they make every word count. If the scene "wants" to be funny, it very likely will be—and if the improvisers don't want to "spin their wheels" by restating the same information again and again, the scene will shoot into the future. It's also very common, even in a workshop, for *every line* to be followed by a happy wave of laughter—even though the lines may be nothing special in themselves. The audience is delighted at how successful the improvisers are in working within the constraint, and they laugh out of pure pleasure. There is nothing negative about these laughs (as opposed to the laughs one gets from blocking one's partner or gagging a potentially interesting scene into an early grave), and they should be cherished.

Often the game generates a useful and pleasing economy of dialogue. It may also be that the improvisers are unable to follow their instincts because the line that their brain gives them cannot be easily boiled down to three words, and so they have to come up with something else. This doesn't necessarily fly in the face of the imperatives to "be obvious" and to "be spontaneous." There isn't one obvious offer which only the most skilled or experience improvisers can find, rendering all other offers "unobvious." Nor is it the case that their second or third choice will be less spontaneous. It can prevent the improvisers from repeating clichés, and so their offers seem fresher and more surprising, both to the audience and to them.

However, on some occasions, the improvisers may be momentarily stumped. If you're coaching, it may be helpful for you to prompt them, at least to start with (you are more likely to be able to think of something, since there's no pressure on you), but this very faltering can also be advantageous!

Let's get two more people up, and this time I want to see a scene played for real drama. Karen and Michael, can you play a recently separated couple for me? Karen, you're still living in the marital home. Michael, I want you to come to pick up the last of your stuff. Remember that you can still make physical offers. Just because you have three words at your disposal, you don't have to use them straight away. Also bear in mind that if you can't think of what to say, it's possible that your struggle to construct a three-word sentence may be interpreted by the audience as the presence of deep, churning emotions.

Provided that Michael and Karen can sustain the reality and integrity of the scene, their acting will likely be very gripping. As Michael glowers and Karen's eyes flick down, a tremendous sense of emotional power is generated. The silences become absolutely compelling, and again, a very few utterances are really made to count. Many improvisers can be tremendously impressed with the potency of scenes such as this. It's good to get them intoxicated with this stuff; it will stop them always playing in the shallow end. Coach Michael to say "I love you," and whether Karen melts or— more likely—continues to regard him coldly, the result will often be rather moving.

The audience's laughter at the end of each line (which was an expression of their appreciation at seeing the improvisers succeed in the task) will likely be eliminated in this version, but the audience will be gripped and will often tell you how engaging and true-to-life it was. This is such a useful procedure that it can even be worth adopting covertly, while a scene is in progress, in order to generate a change in energy, or if you feel you are running off at the mouth.

Before we look at some more games, let's just digress briefly to discuss a feature of playing games in front of an audience, which is often overlooked by novices. As a coach, you also need to be a good MC and make sure that your audience (the other workshoppers) have everything they need in order to be able to appreciate the game. Many groups go in front of an audience for the first time never having practiced explaining the rules of the game they are about to play. Often they are very pedantic about getting the name of the games right ("The next game is called Expert Double Figures"), despite the fact that the name is meaningless to most audiences and that most games are known by different names in different countries. However, the procedure of the game is often reduced to a sort of "word salad" as they realize that they haven't had to conceptualize the game since it was first taught to them.

Some people have the knack of doing this naturally (they make good teachers) and some don't, but there's no problem with getting improvisers to learn a few sentences that succinctly describe the game if that relieves their anxiety. Whatever works. A particular problem is that in games which involve a rule to be obeyed, it is sometimes not made clear to anyone (including the improvisers) what should happen if the improvisers fail in this endeavor. Taking the Three Word Sentence game as an example, the following are all possible answers to the question "What happens if an improviser doesn't successfully restrict themselves to three words?"

- They must take the sentence back and try again.
- Another improviser takes over for them.
- They lose a "life."
- The other team gets penalty points.
- The scene ends and they have lost.
- They endure a token punishment, such as having wet sponges thrown at them.

All of these have different effects. Some are helpful but some, like the wet sponges, can be very destructive. Audiences do this to the judges in some countries where Theatresports is played, which is somewhat foolish, since we want the audience to take the competition seriously and we need the judges to be high status authority figures. It would reduce any theatre game to a Saturday morning kids' TV show, however.

Connected to this is what the audience must do. Is it their job to spot infractions or will the host/director/judge do this? In No S (see Appendix One: Games), it's fun to have the audience hiss at improvisers who use a word containing the letter S. In Alphabet (also discussed later), it's fun to ask the audience to shout abuse at the improviser who got the letter wrong—provided that abuse begins with the omitted letter!

Some thought should be given to how the scene will play out and which instructions for improvisers and audience are going to get the best effects. For Three Word Sentences—which most improvisers find fairly easy to sustain—we recommend that the host calls errors and has the line re-taken. For Scenes in Rhyme—which many improvisers find very difficult—it's great to have the lifeline of substitution by another player as soon as you stumble.

ANOTHER GAME "COMPLEXED-UP"

By this stage, it will probably come as no surprise to learn that the excellent Three Word Sentences game also exists in distorted forms which destroy much of what makes it so special. Give improvisers a hoop to jump through or a bar to clear and they will quickly wonder whether the hoop can be made smaller or the bar higher. In theory, there's nothing so wrong about this—improvisation is about taking a risk, after all—but the consequences can be dire.

A misguided attempt to add variety and/or difficulty to Three Word Sentences has led to the game X Word Sentences, which exists in two equally pointless forms. In the first version, which is suited to a larger cast of improvisers, say three to five, every member of the cast gets a number from the audience. That number is the number of words they can speak per sentence. In the second version a "caller" freezes the action periodically to call a new number, which then becomes the sentence length for everybody. In either version, some poor soul usually has to speak in 27-word sentences, which they will have to count on their fingers. The audience laughs at their plight, but the existence of the game now completely swamps the action, so different iterations of the game all look the same as each other. The improvisers feel safe because, despite increasing the apparent risk, provided they can count, they have found a way of distracting the audience's attention away from the story (which they don't know how to develop) and on to their supposed cleverness at being able to improvise sentences of particular lengths. Pretty soon, because the game is always the same (whereas story games have inherent variety because people never get bored of stories), it is abandoned and replaced by a new, even stupider game. So it goes...

QUESTIONS ONLY

We now move on to a second classic improv game, which also presents a verbal restriction: the players may only ask questions (see The Rules on page 301). Despite the apparent similarity of the two games, playing this game results in very different effects. Knowing that most people are going to struggle, it's best to set this game in pairs first (possibly after a quick demonstration), so that at least the suffering is a little less public.

Again, a few technical points. Each utterance must be one sentence, and that sentence must be a legitimate question. You should not allow improvisers to get away with sentences such as "I'm going to tell the boss what you just said...okay?" Insist that any sentence which is not a question is struck out and replaced by one which is (the other improviser can police this if necessary). After a couple of minutes of this game, the room will be rather quiet and still, full of furrowed brows and a general air of gloom and frustration. Whereas the Three Word Sentence game seems to inspire many improvisers and generate scenes of great economy and power, the Questions Only restriction apparently makes it impossible for the scene to ever get off the starting blocks.

In front of an audience, the best way to play this game is probably to acknowledge that it's hard and treat it similarly to What Are You Doing— as a game worth valuing for its difficulty alone rather than for any other qualities it might possess. So have your whole team ready to play, and replace anyone who hesitates for even a moment as well as anyone who actually utters a statement. Some people will be better at the game than others, and people may get competitive about it. With just a little wit and an awareness of how the game is being perceived, this might make a nice break from an evening of stories, if you keep it short and snappy. Mixed in with a lot of other games, it'll probably seem a bit uninspired and silly. Whereas Three Word Sentences is worth adopting covertly, you'd be insane to adopt the Questions Only procedure unless the audience was very well aware of just how difficult you were making life for yourself.

So why even bring this game up? It's not like there aren't plenty of idiotic improv games out there. Well, "game rehabilitation" can be a very interesting exercise in itself. Try making a list of the games you most dislike and experiment to see if they can be salvaged. We spent several workshops doing just this, and out of this process came this game's position in our current workshop program. We think it has at least three uses.

1 Learning to play Questions Only well (and it is possible) will help you play all sorts of other games well, and it refocuses improvisers on what is really important about improvised scenes, with or without similar "handles."
2 Playing Questions Only in workshops can make you more sensitive to waffle versus story offers while on stage in open scenes.
3 Contrasting Questions Only with other apparently similar games reveals some interesting answers to the questions "Why do we play improv games at all?" and "Which games should we play?"

These are all aside from the general point that workshops are places to do the things you aren't good at. Some games are worth playing *in workshops* just because, although pointless, they are also daunting! The 185 game— where you have to make up joke-book jokes to order—is a good example of this. It has nothing whatsoever to do with theatre or character or story or any of the things which we find interesting, but it takes balls and wit to do it, and it's great to get new improvisers to "run the gauntlet."

How to Play the Game Well

The usual problem with Questions Only, and the reason that the improvisers look so depressed while playing it, is that the scene doesn't go anywhere.

Put two improvisers in a flower shop, and this kind of sequence will likely occur:

> **Joe:** What would you like, sir?
> **Sital:** What would you recommend?
> **Joe:** Well, what do you like, sir?
> **Sital:** What do you mean by that?
> **Joe:** Would you like some roses?
> **Sital:** Do I look like the kind of person who buys roses?

And so on, and so on, round and round, with nothing of any consequence happening and an uncertain feeling that they are simply chasing their own tails. You can break the log jam by ADDING INFORMATION. The scene stutters forward a little when Joe suggests roses. Unfortunately, Sital can't find a way of accepting this offer without making a statement. Let's try the scene again with this principle in mind.

> **Joe:** You here for your usual, Norman?
> **Sital:** Do you have any roses?
> **Joe:** Roses? What do you want roses for?
> **Sital:** Can you keep a secret?
> **Joe:** Is the Pope Catholic? (*They are allowed to do this joke exactly once—then ban it!*)

Immediately, they are MAKING ASSUMPTIONS and ADDING INFORMATION, and so the scene contains something of a platform. Let's go back and see how Sital could have accepted Joe's earlier offer. As we've seen, the bedrock of all improvisation is YES AND. Let's apply that here. Sital has been asked a yes-or-no question. It's a very useful strategy to mentally answer that question "yes," and then ask the next obvious question.

> **Joe:** Would you like some roses?
> **Sital:** (*Yes I would.*) How much are they?
> **Joe:** Didn't you read about our special offer? (*Adding information*)
> **Sital:** (*Yes I did.*) Why do think I'm here?
> **Joe:** (*Making an assumption*) You want my whole stock?
> **Sital:** (*Yes I do.*) Can you deliver them by four o'clock?

Another way of accepting offers and of making new ones, without worrying too much about questions, is to make *physical* offers. Obviously you shouldn't let the scene degenerate into mime or you'll look like you are *avoiding* the restriction—and you've promised the audience that you will confront it. But if you want to see if you can tell a story under this restriction, this is an excellent way to keep it moving into the future.

> **Sital:** Can you deliver them by four o'clock?
> *Joe nods happily. Sital opens his wallet and hands over the money (mimed, of course).*
> **Joe:** Would you like to take one bunch with you now?
> *Joe proffers him a (mime) bunch of roses, which Sital happily accepts. Sital takes a sniff and sneezes.*
> **Sital:** Is there an antioxidant on these?
> **Joe:** You aren't allergic, are you?

The final element has been creeping in as we've been "improvising" these little segments, and it should come as no surprise: add emotional reactions. As we've already seen, what the audience perceives as story is dependent on one person being changed by another, and this is no less true if you are speaking only in questions. Let us put all of these aspects together and try to improvise a short scene, taking all of this advice. This one is set in a doctor's office.

> **Doctor:** It's Mrs. Jenkins, isn't it?
> **Patient:** (*Suddenly suspicious*) How did you know my name?
> **Doctor:** (*Consulting her chart*) You're on Provanon-P, aren't you? Did they warn you about the paranoia?
> **Patient:** Are you one of *them*?
> **Doctor:** Would you like me to give you something for the mood swings? (*She mimes taking out a syringe and approaches the patient*)
> **Patient:** What happened to the other doctor?
> **Doctor:** You mean Dr. Sanders?
> **Patient:** (*Yes I do.*) What have you done with him?
> **Doctor:** "Done with him"? Whatever do you mean?
> **Patient:** You killed him for his parking space, didn't you?
> **Doctor:** (*Dropping the pretense. A rueful silence.*) How did you find out?
> **Patient:** (*Pulls a mime object out of her pocket, all paranoia gone*) Recognize this?
> **Doctor:** My new pager?
> **Patient:** Did you know we bugged it?
> **Doctor:** What's going to happen to me?
> **Patient:** Do you like prison food?

No one's claiming that this is a work of art, but it *is* a story, albeit a pretty hasty one, and it would probably hold an audience's attention. However, the game is of more use in front of audiences for its difficulty, rather than because of the stories that the game inspires you to tell.

Waffle vs. Story

It is very common for improvisers to spend a lot of time onstage talking, while actually saying very little. This is especially true when they can see the next step coming, and rather than get there quickly, they luxuriate in the safety of seeing it in the future and taking their time getting there—usually to the frustrated boredom of the audience.

The difference between waffly offers and story offers can be very subtle, but in Questions Only—especially before all the foregoing strategies have been outlined—story offers are often so rare that they stand out like shining beacons in the dark.

> **James:** Going anywhere nice on your holidays, Tony? (*Not a strong opening offer, but passable*)
> **Ivan:** Why do you ask? (*waffle*)
> **James:** Are you saying I shouldn't ask? (*waffle*)
> **Ivan:** What's that supposed to mean? (*waffle*)
> **James:** What's with all the attitude? (*The emotion is helping, but this is still waffly*)
> **Ivan:** Do you want to come with me, Tony, is that it? (*Aha!*)

Playing Questions Only can sharpen awareness of what is and is not a waffly offer and help to keep improvised stories sleek and free of fat.

Why Do We Play Games at All? Which Games Should We Play?

The first point to make, and it may seem obvious, is that not all games are created equal. Some games will suit different people, some are more appropriate for some performing situations than others, but often game selection seems to us to be entirely random, or at least arbitrary, and many improvisers seem to have little idea as to which games bear repeated performances and which rapidly outstay their welcome.

Here is a short list of possible reasons why one or other game might be played.

- To strengthen a particular muscle (in a workshop). If you never make big emotional offers, play It's Tuesday. If you are too controlling, play Master/Servant Dubbing.

- Because the challenge presented by the game adds an extra layer of interest, distinct from any story which might emerge (see "Two Stories," page 23). Thus some games are worth cherishing simply because they are difficult—although this must be handled carefully in front of an audience.

● Because the procedure is inherently amusing. This might apply to games like Arms Through (see page 269) and, to some extent, the various "Emo" games (see Appendix One: Games). It is rarely a good enough reason on its own to include a game, and leads to idiocy such as the Spit Take game where the players speak all their dialogue with a mouth full of water and so spray each other the whole time. Pointlessly stupid, but it might make drunk people laugh. Then again, you can make drunk people laugh by saying "penis" and that requires even less practice.

● Because the game provides a framework within which the players can demonstrate their wit and/or skill. Games like Genre Rollercoaster or Same Scene Three Ways (which is a very clear example of the retreat away from narrative) are entirely worthless unless the players are inspired and very witty.

● Because the procedure inspires the players to make offers which are different from the offers they would have made if they hadn't been playing the game.

● Because the procedure enforces a behavior which would be desirable whether the game was being played or not.

Consideration of these different reasons (and there very well may be others) will help us to pick the games we want and to have some idea about the effects they will have on the audience and the improvisers. It should also be clear to see now that the reason Three Word Sentences is so much more effective than Questions Only is not that it is an easier procedure (Word At A Time, a vitally important game, and one beloved of audiences, is tremendously difficult), it's that it does something *other* than providing a hoop to jump through. In particular, it enforces otherwise desirable behavior—economy of dialogue.

Some games can account for a great many of these reasons, and some very few (or none). More than that, consideration of these reasons will help you pick the right game for the right moment in the right show performed by the right players. There's simply no point playing a game which shows off the players' wit and joke-making ability if their strengths are in playing characters and telling stories. But don't ask the gag-merchants to play narrative games, either!

You can also pick games which are going to put the improvisers (and the audience) in a particular state, and which will provide a contrast with what has gone before. After a hilarious clown game, play a dramatic Three Word Sentence game, because another funny game will be compared unfavorably to the clown scene which preceded it. Following an epic which dragged on and on, play a "quickie" or a high energy game like Half Life. Following a scene where the improvisers didn't do their best work, get them to play a game which they know and like and which is a crowd-pleaser.

With this list in mind, we'd like to mention a workshop that we would usually save for a slightly more experienced group, but all the same issues are brought up here. Lists of improv games are easily found on the Internet, but just from the name and the description it is not always easy to tell the difference between a mighty game which will delight audiences time and again and a feeble novelty which even the group who developed it only played twice before abandoning it—but the list was compiled between the first and last attempts!

After twenty years or so of The Spontaneity Shop, we've played or seen a fairly high proportion of the games that are out there, and an even higher proportion of the worthwhile games, and we've developed some pretty firm opinions about what works and what doesn't. We want to share our (sometimes passionate) opinions with our students, not so that they will inherit our tastes wholesale, but rather so that they will develop critical thinking where improv games are concerned.

We therefore present them with a list of improv games, divided into three columns: Good Games, Dumb But Fun and Never Play. We generally retype the list, without reference to previous versions, once or twice a year, and we notice that games do tend to shift from column to column. The Dumb But Fun column always ends up longer than the Good Games column, and the Never Play column always ends up the longest. We bring three or four copies of the list to the class and pass them around. Anyone who is curious about a particular game may call out its name and have it described. The anyone who wishes can play the game (if this is practical, sometimes the list includes games which require special props). We sometimes do multiple iterations of the same game, with advice in between, and we discuss any issues which the game brings up. If a debate develops over the categorizations—great! That critical thinking is beginning to develop.

Our current list is not reprinted here, although the categories are indicated in Appendix One: Games at the back of the book. Instead, we'll just discuss a few games which typify these categorizations.

GOOD GAMES

Most of the games under this heading would crop up naturally over the course of a syllabus like this in any case, since Good Games are very often precisely those games which, like Three Word Sentences, enforce good habits, and which therefore can be used to "train" particular improvisation "muscles." Almost all of these games make for excellent work onstage, since most of them also involve an element of storytelling. Even improvisers determined to only ever play games should learn to tell stories. Without this, every game must be learned as a new skill, but with it many challenging games can be unlocked—as we saw with Questions Only: find a way to make assumptions, add information and be affected and the game works fine.

New Choice

How to Play

The game is for two players, plus a "caller." The players play as normal but every so often the caller announces "new choice." The last player to speak must replace their last line of dialogue with something new. The lines which are "edited out" are assumed to hit the metaphorical cutting-room floor—they make no further impact on the scene.

Here's an example, set in a vet's.

> **Geoff:** Good morning, how can I help you?
> **Peter:** It's about my cat.
> **Caller:** *New choice!*
> **Peter:** It's about my dog.
> **Caller:** *New choice!*
> **Peter:** It's about your dog.
> **Caller:** *New choice!*
> **Peter:** It's about four o'clock.
> **Caller:** *New choice!*
> **Peter:** Got any animals you don't need?
> **Geoff:** I'm sorry?
> **Peter:** You know, any abandoned animals you don't want.
> **Geoff:** Certainly not!
> **Caller:** *New choice!*
> **Geoff:** Yeah, all the time…
> **Caller:** *New choice!*
> **Geoff:** Did Mary send you?
> **Caller:** *New choice!*
> **Geoff:** Does it matter if they're unwell?
> **Caller:** *New choice!*
> **Geoff:** If they're infectious?
> **Caller:** *New choice!*
> **Geoff:** If they're dead?
> **Caller:** *New choice!*
> **Geoff:** I've got a tortoise.
> **Peter:** Will you gift wrap it for me?

Experienced players will be able to keep the story moving forward, while beginners are likely to just generate trivia. But the exhilaration, the genuine feeling of on-the-edge improvisation by the seat of the pants is very hard to beat, and it toughens improvisers up in a very useful way.

How to Play the Game Well

Geoff, above, has discovered a way to eliminate some of his thinking time (good) by letting early parts of his sentence be assumed rather than laboriously repeating them ("Does it matter if they're unwell?"/"...if they're infectious?"). It's not a disaster if improvisers repeat the first part of the sentence while groping for the final word, but using this procedure, Geoff is more likely to genuinely surprise himself. This game should be no different and no more difficult than Pointing At Things And Saying What They Are Not, since any foolish choices will be removed by the caller—and if they aren't, it's the caller's fault—but in practice, the same "freezing up" can occur in the first few attempts as the improvisers strain to think of something good and discover that the pressure crushes the imagination out of them. Great improvisers just open their mouths and blurt things out, waiting for the caller to spot something that they like and stop saying "new choice."

The difficulty of this game should not be ignored. Especially when a game presents an obvious hoop like this, *it's good to let the audience see you sweat a little*. The audience is there to see you take a risk, so they don't always want to see you saunter casually through without a single hair out of place. Of course, they don't want to see you panic or fall apart either—it should be an exhilarating ride for you, but it shouldn't necessarily look easy all the time. Good callers know this and sense when improvisers are running out of ideas—and that's when they keep barking "New choice!" Sequences like this are common:

> **Bob:** Would you like to come in for a coffee?
> **Kate:** No thanks.
> **Caller:** *New choice!*
> **Kate:** Yes, please.
> **Caller:** *New choice!*
> **Kate:** I'm not sure.

That's the three obvious choices out of the way—Kate isn't pushing herself at all here. A good caller would certainly want to "new choice" her at least three more times!

The players also need to bear some of the technical demands of the game in mind. Obviously if they babble, speak in paragraphs or—worst of all— talk over each other, it will be impossible for the caller to clearly intercede.

The players need to keep in mind that "New choice!" could be heard after each of their utterances and after each of their partner's, and make sure that there is space; half a second is enough. It's also clearest to see the game in action if arbitrary choices are made. The caller will often be waiting for a player to say something like "A glass of port, please," because that can easily be new-choiced into "A pint of beer, please" or "Champagne for everybody." But the caller also should not forget that the audience has heard this game described and wants to see it played. They need not wait for a perfect line before interceding, and they certainly should not take the pressure off because "the scene is going really well."

Because this game does depend to some extent on the novelty of its procedure, we suggest you keep it short. We also suggest that you don't take too long to set it up. It's easier to demonstrate than describe and it generates its own content, so you don't need an elaborate setup. You don't even need to get an audience suggestion if you don't want to; you can just start from nothing, since it will be perfectly obvious that you are improvising, and the necessary inspiration will come from having to keep coming up with "New choice!"s.

What's the Game Good For?

In workshops, this is an excellent game to introduce if players are getting too bogged down and trying to find the "right" offer. The drawback with learning to construct and deconstruct stories is that some players can feel like they are being asked to solve crossword puzzles instead of developing an artistic feel. The reality is that there is probably never one and only one right *decision*, but instead there are many good *choices*. Although there are more poor choices than good ones, an unobvious, stupid or otherwise "out-there" *bold choice* can probably be justified. A weak, vague or empty choice does not even give you that possibility. This game can be a wonderful exercise for reassuring improvisers that they genuinely do have bottomless wells of imagination that will never run dry. As mentioned previously, part of the fun of the game (and many games) is to let the audience see you sweat a little, which is also a useful antidote to improvisers who always want to do their best.

In shows, this is a great high-energy game which will often give a flagging show a "lift," although that is rarely how we would deploy it. An audience can't laugh their hardest for more than about twenty minutes, but if you can manage the trick of being funny early, then the audience relaxes, confident that you know what you are doing. This gives you the freedom to choose not to be funny, or even to take a risk that doesn't come off at all, without fearing that the audience will give up on you.

Easier said than done, you may be thinking—and you'd be right—but with this strategy in mind, we've found that New Choice is an excellent *opener*. It doesn't require a huge amount of concentration from the improvisers, so it helps them to settle down. The procedure itself is funny, and it pretty much guarantees funny results (unless the improvisers start trying to "force the pace" and saying stupid things straight away). But even more than that, it very clearly and very economically "sells" the idea of what improvisation is to an audience. The fourth wall is torn down for them, the effort that the improvisers are putting in is clear and so is the risk they are taking.

Obviously, as an opener to a thoughtful, Harold-like piece or an improvised play, this would be wildly inappropriate, but we recommend it for pretty much any short-form show. Happily, it also bears repeated viewings.

Variants and Spin-Offs

- Ring a bell instead of saying "New Choice." This contrasts slightly with the game Dinner At Joe's, in which an audience member's family dinner (or some other such occasion) is enacted with the audience member ringing a bell for an accurate choice and honking a horn for an inaccurate choice (which then has to be re-taken, as in New Choice). You could also give the bell to an audience member. This denies you the possibility of shouting "New [something else]" however, which is occasionally appropriate: "New noise!" "New facial expression!" and "New dance!" are all examples we've heard (or said).

- The game is also called "Shouldasaid" (should have said) in which the caller says that instead of "New Choice." We prefer New Choice for the reason mentioned above.

- Edinburgh University troupe The Improverts plays this game as a finale and has the *audience* shout out "New choice," which worked better than we would have expected. Players need to be especially good at leaving pauses for the "New choice" to be inserted, and bear in mind that audiences are not likely to new-choice the same offer more than once or twice.

- A spin-off of this game which Tom invented for a Micetro show has proven to be quite popular. Called "Perfect Pitch," it is for two improvisers plus an audience member. The audience member is given a big jacket to wear and ideally a desk to sit behind. They are asked to play a Hollywood movie mogul and the two improvisers play writers who are coming to "pitch" a movie. The audience member is told they have just two lines, but they can use them as often as they like. Those lines are "I love it!" and "I hate it!" Between them, the writers describe the plot of their movie, pausing for acknowledgment every so often. If they hear "I love it," they carry on, but if they hear "I hate it," they have to revise their idea. Whereas in New Choice, the "failed" lines are edited out of existence, here the writers must also justify why they said what they did: "The hero is very young…" "I hate it!" "Er … young-looking for his age. He's sixty-five."

- While writing this section, it occurred to us that you could play a version of this which resembles The Removalists (page 466) or Yes Let's/Nope (page 479), wherein either player could new-choice the other—not to torture them, as in this version, but simply to express dissatisfaction with an offer and try to get something better out of them.

Arms Through

How to Play

A "classic" game which Keith apparently saw in a Laurel and Hardy film. One person stands behind the other and thrusts their arms forward. Their partner's arms go behind their back, or otherwise out of sight. Now one improviser is responsible for dialogue and the other for gestures.

How to Play the Game Well

This simple procedure is quite well known and yet it contains many subtleties which are often not appreciated. A number of different variations exist and exactly how you set it up will have significant ramifications on how the game plays out.

It's an obvious close cousin to the dubbing game, and both are versions of the two-improvisers-create-one-character sub-genre. Our preferred version of the dubbing game is the Master/Servant version described on page 128 but the two-people-off-stage-dub-two-people-onstage version is fine too and both that game and this one can teach many of the same lessons. The Arms game is slightly easier for beginners however, and contains a number of useful lessons as well as being a fascinating procedure for an audience to watch. If we're called upon to do a "learn to improvise" team-building day for a corporate group, we always include Arms Through. Corporate groups laugh hysterically watching each other play this game.

With dubbing, it's quite clear to what extent the non-speaking parties can make offers. They can enter, exit, sit, stand, produce mime objects, gesture, change their expressions and so on. The key questions with Arms Through are: what offers can the "arms" make? And what offers *should* the "arms" make?

The physicality of the game can be a little awkward. It's best to start training the game with the "body" seated. Then the improviser providing the arms can kneel or crouch behind them. This eliminates difficulties associated with improvisers of differing heights and also makes the positioning of the two improvisers a little less intimate which can help beginners. Keith suggests that the "arms" touch the face of the other improviser and/or adjust their clothing. This helps to break down a few inhibitions and begins integrating the two players. Sit two of these "arms" creatures side-by-side and have them meet as strangers on a park bench (a very useful scenario).

Improvisers playing the arms generally fall into one of two categories: those who let their hands dangle limply, apart from the occasional twitch, waiting for some signal or other from the body which never arrives; and those who gesticulate wildly almost as soon as the scene starts, desperate to contribute and to be seen to be contributing. Similarly, improvisers playing the bodies will also tend to miss the target, either waffling away without really noticing what the arms are doing, or constantly being surprised by how they behave and adjusting their approach mid-sentence (a form of GAGGING). Maybe because of this, the most popular form of the game is with audience volunteers providing the arms, since it's not likely they will feel out-of-their-depth in this role and if they do screw up the improvisers' intentions then the audience will find that funny.

To start correcting some of these problems, it's first necessary to remind the improvisers that the goal is for both players to work together to sustain the illusion that the speakers' arms are under their own conscious control. This may seem like a curious thing to have to point out, but it's absolutely vital. To witter on and ignore the arms is trivial. To keep changing your mind based on what the arms do next is funny (briefly) but hardly a challenge. What makes the game interesting is the seeming difficulty of two minds operating as one. That's where we can truly see that precious moment of inspiration.

So, you may need to encourage some arms to be active. When we did a puppetry workshop (for a corporate *Avenue Q* spoof some years ago) we were taught that even when a puppet isn't contributing to a scene, it needs to be "breathing." The puppeteer must constantly keep the puppet alive with small movements or it will lie there like a lifeless doll. Similarly, the arms must keep making gestures, even quite small ones, which are suitable for the emotional temperature of the dialogue. But arms absolutely shouldn't pantomime what the body is saying, for the same reason that this is unhelpful for scenes in gibberish. Nobody furiously gestures at their watch, holds up an index finger, mimes drinking from a glass and then puts both hands together next to their head while saying "I think we've got time for one more drink before we go home to bed."

If the arms keep doing little things which relate to what the body is saying and the body is aware of the need to create the illusion that the arms are theirs, then a tight feedback loop can be generated quite quickly, and even if the gestures made by the arms aren't doing very much to push the story into the future, the audience starts to be aware of the silent conversation going on between the two improvisers and may begin to laugh out of the sheer enjoyment of seeing this close collaboration. "That's a good point, you're very perceptive," says one improviser, wagging an approving finger. "Me? No one's ever said that to me before," replies the other, putting her hand on her chest. No one's quite clear whether her verbal response told the hands what to do, or whether she chose the line because of the gesture, but we're delighted to see them working so closely together. Even without doing anything very overt, the arms are beginning to influence the story.

And then, of course, you can do more overt things, once everyone has found a happy rhythm. If the arms produce mime objects from the pockets, suddenly start doing "jazz hands" or making fists, then the body will have to justify (Tom once grabbed both the ears of the improviser he was working with, who brilliantly turned this into an offer involving him using his powers of mind-control) but these should be occasional flourishes, not the main point of the scene.

A few other details. Two person scenes work best and it's helpful to provide some kind of relationship. Think about power relationships, family relationships and status. You may need to remind the improvisers that turning sideways wrecks the illusion (such as it is) and if you are playing the game standing up, this will be a particular temptation. Having one person deliver a lecture is a good way of focusing on what the arms are doing, since the content of the lecture can be dictated by what mime objects the arms pick up, but this tends to lead back to the "arms" PIMPING[41] the "bodies" and/or the "body" being overly concerned with thinking of funny things to say.

What's the Game Good For?

Obviously the game *is* good for hearty yucks in bars and comedy clubs with audience members flailing around as the arms and improvisers making jokes at their expense, but handled with care in a workshop, it's a great way of developing those elusive skills of complicity, listening, cooperation and what Del Close called the "group mind." Presented like this, it reminds improvisers that they can contribute to stories in a variety of ways, and that playing an apparently minor role can still be critical to the success of the scene. And don't forget how funny and charming the stage picture is to people who haven't seen it before.

---

[41]The improviser's term for making an offer which the other improviser would prefer not to say "yes" to (or so the audience imagines). For example: "You know a song about that, don't you?"

Variants and Spin-Offs

As usual, this game is often presented as an interview with an expert, which adds nothing except an unnecessary safety net and a gnawing sense of familiarity. Versions with a table full of props or a coat with pockets full of objects are unlikely to be anything other than stupid. On an early episode of *Whose Line Is It Anyway?* Ryan Stiles had an entire brie stuffed into his mouth during this game. It's amazing that he came back for more.

DUMB BUT FUN

Games under this heading are "guilty pleasures"—games which have a utility, but possibly also teach improvisers bad habits. Despite our heroic efforts to rehabilitate it, and despite the possibly valuable lessons one could learn from playing it, Questions Only is still far too pointless to go anywhere other than "Never Play."

Half Life

As improvisers the world over retreat from the problem of successfully improvising satisfactory stories, games are devised which could create something else to fill that gap, while providing either the illusion of storytelling or a morsel of narrative to temporarily quell the audience's hunger pangs. This has given rise to the sub-genre of "repeat" games, the most obvious of which is Same Scene Three Ways. A short scene is improvised and then the same basic plot is re-played with a twist: a different emotion, a different genre, a different period in time and so on. It's crucial to understand that this game does very little of the "heavy lifting" for you. It provides an opportunity for the improvisers to exercise their wit within a given template, so while easier than the ever-popular Genre Rollercoaster (see Appendix One: Games), it's very far from sure-fire.

Our preferred version of this game is Half Life, which is also about as close to sure-fire as you're ever likely to get. If repeating the same basic plot with a twist represents a retreat from the challenge of improvising stories, then this game represents a complete surrender! But it's so joyous and such an audience-pleaser that we're compelled to mention it. The *modus* is very simple: A scene is played in exactly sixty seconds. Then the exact same scene is repeated in only thirty seconds, then again in fifteen seconds, then again in seven, then in five, then in two. By the final iteration, the scene has completely deteriorated into a furious burst of running around and shouting, and the audience is typically very happy.

How to Play the Game Well

The caller needs to make it very clear when the time starts and finishes, calling "Go!" and "Time!" crisply and clearly at the start of each time period. You can make an audience member responsible for this, although that's not always helpful.

The initial sixty-second scene should be fairly simple and should include a small number of big physical offers. As the scene collapses and the fat is stripped away, these (and possibly some key verbal offers) will become the "tent poles" that the game depends on. Improvisers should be happy to take risks with what can be achieved as the game speeds up. At one show where we were lucky enough to be provided with a large supply of costumes and props by the theatre (improvisers like toys to play with), Tom discovered a rather ratty old wheelchair. When this game was called, he gleefully stuck his fellow improviser in it and wheeled him across the stage, to their increasing terror and the audience's increasing delight, as they were forced to re-enact it faster and faster.

In some companies, the improvisers take obvious shortcuts within the story of the scene in order to achieve the reduced running time, but we find that the game is more fun if you try your hardest to pack everything in. Once more, the audience likes to see you sweat a little. Oddly, most improvisers seem to require next to no practice to get the timings about right (and the caller should be happy to cheat the times a little, rather than leave the improvisers hanging or cut them off—that's why it may be inadvisable to give this role to an audience member who may delight in exposing the error).

The relationship between the caller and the players can also be exploited here to give a little more appeal to the game. There's no point explaining everything that the audience is about to see—after all, the first sixty-second scene might be terrific, in which case you want the option to end there. It's nice for the caller to be a little critical of the initial scene and request that a new version be performed with less flab on it. The improvisers can affect being a little put-out by this, but agree to go along with it, and then after the thirty-second version, go back to their seats ready for the next game. Then the caller can insist on a fifteen-second version—to the improvisers' disbelief—and so on. This all sounds a little contrived, and it is, but we're recommending this game for occasional use when a show needs a boost or a big finish. If the improvisers are anxious, having made this rather mechanical game work will calm them down and they will be much better able to take risks and improvise with daring and élan.

Variant

More than once we've experimented with playing the game in reverse—starting with a dementedly manic ten-second burst and then working up to a more leisurely sixty-second version, "adding back" the supposedly "missing" details each time. This almost never works. Another version, devised as part of an "invent a new game" workshop, where a simple scene is made more melodramatically elaborate with each iteration, was fun, but it was crucial to retain elements from the second iteration in the third. We did it with three different casts as well, instead of having the same players repeat the action.

Musical Emotions

As noted elsewhere, games involving emotions are very popular because they "program-in" one of the key things which will tend to elevate improvised scenes: being changed by what is said to you. Emo Party and Emo Rollercoaster games in which everybody in the scene adopts the same emotion can be fun but don't quite capture that sense of one person being altered by another because everyone in the scene is permanently JOINED. Games like Emo Caller (see page 180) are preferred because emotions can be applied to individual players. Musical Emotions can seem to have a very similar issue, but actually it plays out rather differently.

How to Play

Set up the scene however you like, and begin it without any particularly strong emotion (in order to build a platform) but have the emotional content of the scene switched every so often by music which can be supplied either by a live musician (or musicians) or via prerecorded music from a laptop or iPod in the control booth. As the music changes, the improvisers must adapt the story to suit the tone.

How to Play the Game Well

Like Emo Caller, if the emotions switch too rapidly and violently, the scene can take on a rather disjointed or even slightly psychotic quality. For bar-prov settings, the fun is just seeing the improvisers have to adopt and then justify rapidly changing emotions. This version is a bit more theatrical and because the change in underscoring is not quite so intrusive as the offstage order to "be angry," it can be played more subtly. The improvisers should shift what they are doing to suit the music rather than violently altering their behavior. This is partly to make sure that the story doesn't go off the rails, but also because you can trust the music to do more of the heavy lifting for you. The same line said with very different musical accompaniment will sound very different despite the actor doing little or nothing to alter the delivery.

Note too that although the scene takes on a romantic, sinister, scary or joyful quality—that doesn't mean that both players need to adopt the same tone. If the music becomes sinister, that implies that one improviser should become threatening and the other should become *scared*, so this game does a much better job of creating the illusion of narrative action than the Emo Rollercoaster game it superficially resembles.

Having skilled musicians as part of your ensemble means you can include songs or even whole musicals if your team has the ability to do so, but we actually prefer pre-recorded music for this game, since a much greater variety of sounds and styles is possible. But note that songs are not suitable since the lyrics will fight for attention with the dialogue spoken onstage. Creating a playlist of twenty or thirty contrasting pieces of music can help and movie soundtracks are particularly useful.

Variants

The Booth Hell game where the lighting and sound operator can do anything in their power to screw up the improvisers is the PIMPING version of this game, and will seem very samey if played every week.

NEVER PLAY

The list of pointlessly stupid improv games is no doubt growing by the day. To avoid boring you with too much more opinionated ranting, here are just two examples—one apparently innocuous game and one class of games which is very widely disliked but mysteriously popular with some improv companies (we've no evidence that it's popular with audiences).

First Line/Last Line

This game barely needs a "how to play"—you get two lines of dialogue from the audience and you begin a scene with one and end with the other. To understand what's so awful about this game, it's really necessary to play it. Just as the gulf between Questions Only and Three Word Sentences is only really apparent when you see them both in action, so it is with this game. After all—if the improvisers can work together to develop a satisfying improvised story, why should they not be able to begin and end at a predetermined point? Most decent improvisers can give you something of value with pretty much any first line—you can quite safely get this from the audience. It's the last line that's the problem.

What is the nature of the challenge here? What is the problem confronting the improvisers and what is the promise that has been made to the audience?

The audience has been promised an entertaining and interesting story which happens to begin with the first line and end with the last line. During the middle of the scene, the fact of the game is of much less importance, but as the scene starts to come to a close, the question of whether they will be able to end on the last line or not becomes key.

But the *actual* problem for the improvisers is rather different. Endings of stories need to make perfect sense in the light of what has gone before, but ideally they also need to be surprising (being obvious isn't the same as bridging). It is pointlessly easy to get from line A to line B with some semblance of coherence. Most improvisers could do that in twenty seconds if that was the only goal, but then the game would be no fun. So instead, the usual advice is to strike out boldly from the first line and ignore the last line completely until late in the scene, at which point it is suddenly remembered and a hasty banging of square pegs into round holes ensues.[42]

Neither of these versions is typical, however. What is much more usual is that the improvisers make sure that they give themselves the *possibility* of credibly uttering the prescribed last line very early in the scene (at around the thirty-second mark, or sometimes earlier) but don't *actually* say it for many minutes, which makes the majority of the scene a slow, joyless plod to an obvious endpoint.

What's striking here—and will become an even bigger problem in the next game considered—is the disconnect between the desirable outcome of the game and the behavior that the game actually generates. The game is almost *guaranteed* to produce the kind of hesitancy and bridging which would be undesirable in any case. The chances of the last line being slotted in triumphantly against all the odds are essentially nil—time and again it's a feeble anticlimax.

How to Play the Game Well

It's almost impossible to play this game well. About the best you can do is to make it a competition to see which pair of improvisers can get from given first line to given last line in the shortest time or fewest lines. This follows the general rule that if a game is getting in the way of your storytelling and improvisation ability, you may be able to solve the problem by magnifying

---

[42]If you're lucky, that is. We have seen versions of this game where the scene reached a triumphant conclusion, the lighting improviser slammed the lights down, and then there was a sort of stunned silence as it eventually dawned on the improvisers what the audience was well aware of: their scene, good as it was, had not reached the end line given, or anything like it. Here the improvisers had forgotten the very existence of an end line. In yet other cases, we have seen improvisers realize they have forgotten what the end line is altogether, and then panic about it.

the importance of the game, thus eliminating the story altogether, which deals with the problem that you can't tell a *good* story within the confines of the game. It should be pointed out that this is the nuclear option and condemns the game to occasional use to add variety.

Endowments

In an "endowment" game, the audience decides on information which one player is kept ignorant of. They then have to guess this information during the course of the scene.[43]

One of the peculiar things about reading improv game books is the way in which multiple procedures are combined to make a new game, which is then given a name all its own ("Expert Double Figures"), and the way that same game is written up again and again with only minor variations. "Endowment" games do exist in a few different forms, but the basic version can also work (to the extent that it works at all) in multiple settings. Because some of these settings have become standardized, they get written up as different games. But we, or you, or anyone could sit down and come up with a dozen possible settings for an endowment game in ten minutes, so there's really nothing special about these.

Endowment games probably began life as workshop exercises in which one or more players had to endow another player with various qualities which had been secretly decided for them ahead of time. The version most commonly played now is generally referred to as Interrogation Endowment and goes something like this. One player is sent out of earshot. The host tells the audience that that player is a murderer and asks them to name a famous person who will be the victim. Next, the host asks for a murder weapon, and then finally a location where the crime took place. The absent player is returned to the stage and a police interrogation is staged during which time that player has to guess the three pieces of missing information, with the audience *ooh*ing when they get close and applauding when they get something right. One or sometimes two police offers threaten and cajole the killer while dropping hints as to what response is required. If the guesser is particularly slow, an extra improviser, often referred to as "Constable Obvious," can enter with an even easier clue.

---

[43]The term "endowment" is also used to refer to any offer which adds a detail to another character or object, as opposed to offers which relate to you. If you look up and say "Doctor!" when your partner enters, you have endowed them with being a doctor. This is an excellent technique and should be encouraged. Ironically, so-called endowment games often omit this feature entirely, with the hidden information having nothing to do with the character played by the improviser in the role of guesser, and indeed sometimes being offstage (what part of the world a disaster is taking place in, for example).

The scene begins with a vague attempt to play the story as set up, and then rapidly degenerates into nothing but a procession of desperate clues which the guesser either gets or doesn't, until finally the wretched thing comes to an end and the audience applauds with relief. In other variants, the "naïve" player is a politician addressing a press conference, or a news reporter out in the field, or a suitor on a first date and so on. Other more elaborate versions exist, such as Party Quirks or the Dating Game, both popular on *Whose Line Is It Anyway?* (the British and American versions, respectively).

The popularity of these games (among players) astounds us. No kind of story is ever likely to emerge. One player is faced with having most of their offers blocked (whenever they guess wrong), and the need to complete the task rapidly overwhelms anything else of interest that might be going on. Typically, these games outstay their welcome—often by some minutes.[44] Clearly, no one who is interested in creating improvised *theatre* would dream of including anything remotely resembling this (they should consider things like Three Word Sentences, though, if only for variety), but this is too worthless and too problematic to be considered even for a cabaret setting.

The problem inherent in playing parlor games in front of an audience is how to make sure that they are having as much fun as you are. Younger readers or those in other countries may be baffled to learn that the parlor game Charades was shown on British network television in an early-evening slot for thirteen years. It wasn't exactly gripping stuff when it began in 1979, and today it would be laughed off the air (unless they could find a way to include audience voting).

The Endowment Game presents an even bigger problem in that it isn't even a *good* parlor game. Being unable to speak makes it genuinely difficult to communicate *One Flew over the Cuckoo's Nest* in under two minutes, but the improvisers in endowment games are under no such restrictions, and could no doubt communicate the identity of, say, Jack Nicholson very easily, without using the words "Jack" or "Nicholson" even once. But that would be "no fun," and so they resort to the most obscure clue they can think of

---

[44]*Tom*: The worst night I ever spent in an improv theatre was dominated by a First Date endowment that went on for approximately twenty-five minutes (out of a sixty-minute show), due to an inexperienced Micetro director who was asleep at the wheel and a guesser who was an invincible moron. When finally this monstrous fool had guessed all three items correctly, and I believed that I was finally to be released from this monotonous hell, he had to recap all of them—the players, all students, had obviously been drilled in this pointless exercise. However, as he began the recap we realized that the game had gone on for so long that he had forgotten the first item. Not to worry, the other players began offering more clues! I genuinely thought at that point that I would never escape. I had always thought that endowment games were pointless, but never before had I experienced that kind of pure improv torture.

so that it isn't over with too quickly, and so the thing drags on and on and on. It's appalling theatre, lousy cabaret and it isn't even a good game—no improvisers would ever play it just for fun, offstage for example.

How to Play the Game Well

A number of strategies exist, although probably the best strategy is never to play them ever, ever again. It's very unlikely that your audience will miss them.

1. If you are only interested in jokes and have a ready supply of them, then this formula might permit you to rattle off a few good ones. Put a time limit on the game, and don't worry about making your clues either obscure or obvious, just make them as funny as possible. Ninety seconds should be enough time for three clues, and end it as soon as the last clue has been guessed—don't bother recapping them all; nothing could be more dull. Notice that even on *Whose Line Is It Anyway?* the host usually called an end to the scene and then asked whether or not the guesser knew the answers. They wouldn't dream of letting it crawl painfully on until they were all guessed.

2. The "Guess the situation" version is very useful in workshops for looking at clarity and elegance of offers. One player has to guess information secretly agreed by the rest of the group such as "You are a surgeon coming in to an operating theatre to perform a heart bypass on your own father," and is faced with three or four other improvisers who will play other characters in the scene—but they all speak in gibberish. It's worth giving different improvisers goes and conveying the same information to the same person if the first team is unsuccessful. Groups often laugh a lot playing this game and it's very educational, but it's not really worth doing on the stage.

3. The Three Canadians, an amazing street theatre and cabaret group out of the Loose Moose who enjoyed phenomenal success in Australia, played this as a Master/Servant game in which the servant is guessing and finds that the task completely defeats him. As the clues get more and more obvious but the poor Servant remains entirely baffled, the Master gets more and more enraged and beats him with a foam "pool noodle." Here, the guessing-game structure is simply a device to get a Master physically angry with a Servant, which is almost always worth watching. The hugely successful and very slick Boom Chicago players adopt a similar strategy of deliberate stupidity, although without the Master/Servant relationship. I worry that they have been encouraged in this by the huge cheers that go up when the last piece of information is finally guessed. (We were cheering out of sheer relief.)

4. During our show "Imagination" we developed a version of this game which does allow a genuine scene to be improvised, relegating the guessing game to an incidental feature. We sent a player out of the theatre and then asked the audience for a rumor that might have been heard about her. When she returned, we played a scene in her place of work and had one or two other players drop hints about the rumor. This worked because the audience appreciated that they knew something that at least one other player did not, and because the player's state of mind and the character's state of mind were beautifully aligned. If or when the player guessed what was being rumored about her, interest in the scene dropped sharply, so a big offer was required to keep it going, or we had to end it promptly. We don't play it any more.

5. The Chain Murder version is even more wretched. Google it if you really want to know.

LET'S SCREW WITH TOM

During my visit to Improvention in Canberra (where I had a marvelous time and was generously looked-after by Nick Byrne and the Impro ACT team) I had the delightful opportunity to assemble a team to play in a Gorilla Theatre show at the beautiful Street Theatre. The show was going great when Eric Heiberg told the audience that I was to be sent out of the room while he got some secret information from the audience. I left with a cheerful smile, inwardly cursing the fact that an entire scene was going to be effectively wasted playing a pointless endowment game.

I returned to the stage and began making as many offers as possible, but the scene quickly spun out of any semblance of sanity or control. To the best of my recollection, one improviser was clutching on to my leg while another was whispering obscenities in my ear and a third was conducting an imaginary orchestra while Eric (and the audience) were killing themselves laughing. Every so often, one of my offers got something like a reaction from the audience which might indicate that I had come close to guessing the secret information which had been decided.

Eventually, the scene came to an end and Eric explained what he had *actually* said to the audience when I had left the room, which was that this was not the Endowment Game I surely thought it was, but in fact a game of his own devising called "Let's Screw With Tom" in which the audience would make no decision at all about any secret information, the improvisers were just going to do random stuff and the audience would "oooh" or applaud any time they felt like it. It was a hilarious lesson in expectations and assumptions.

—*Tom*

FREAK SHOW GAMES

There are a few games which defy easy categorization, and where the fact of the game is of absolutely overwhelming importance and the nature of the risk changes utterly. There are very few examples in the "canon," but here are two.

Bucket of Death

Game for a group of improvisers: five or six, say, plus one bucket of water, ideally standing on a stool or chair at the side of the stage. The rule of the game is very simple. Once the scene has begun, at any time all the actors but one must be on stage. The actor not on stage must wait at the side and can only enter when another actor leaves. This offstage actor must plunge their head into the bucket of water prepared for the purpose, and leave it submerged until the exiting player taps on their shoulder and relieves them of their watery burden. Those who enter must also justify why their head and hair is soaking wet.

Clearly, once this game is begun, no sane audience member will be remotely interested in the details of the scene being improvised. Nothing is more interesting here than the plight of the improviser with their head submerged and the time which elapses between each change-over. Whereas it usually makes sense to increase the pace as the game goes on, here you want to leave people in the bucket for longer and longer periods, since that's what will freak the audience out. If you *really* want to freak them out, then observe that the first few people to dunk their head will displace quite a lot of water. That means that the fourth or fifth person may very well be able to put their head quite a long way into the bucket and still breathe. After ninety seconds or so, this person can start stamping their feet, slapping the side of the bucket and so on, apparently in a pre-drowning panic—and then if they really want, just slump over the bucket as the other players continue the scene, seemingly oblivious to their death.

We have never played this game (or wanted to, to be honest) but we have seen it done. Keep the water lukewarm.

The Mousetrap Game

Whereas the preceding game is pretty obviously a joke, what makes this next game such a freak show is that it seems all too real. For The Mousetrap Game, you will need twenty to thirty mousetraps, depending on the size of your stage. You should demonstrate setting and then triggering one to an audience member, who will no doubt yelp a little when it goes *SNAP!* near them. Have a couple of improvisers spread the mousetraps around the stage, carefully setting each one, while two more improvisers *remove their shoes and socks and don blindfolds*.

The blindfolded, barefooted players then play a scene (sometimes daring each other to dance or run across the space) or possibly play a Hat Game. (Other players should act as "spotters" and make sure the blindfolded players don't blunder into the scenery or fall off the edge of the stage.) With each step that they take, the audience gasps. When they disturb a mousetrap, it will likely go *BANG!* and jump a foot in the air—and the audience will *scream*. Again, you should keep this game short, so as not to let the audience get used to this bizarre spectacle, and again the audience's interest lies entirely in the mousetraps and not at all in the content of the scene being improvised.

The truth of this game is slightly more mundane. Yes, if you get your little toe in exactly the right place, the mousetrap will snap shut on it and that will hurt. But the rest of your foot is just too big to get caught, although you can set the mousetraps off with just a nudge. So the apparent risk is enormous, but the real danger is only slight.

Do not play this game with rat traps, or you will break a toe. The magicians Penn & Teller do a similar routine with bear traps and the like. We have no idea whether it is faked or done for real and have no plans to find out by personal experiment.

The Spontaneity Shop has played the Mousetrap Game only three times in its twenty-year history, always on "special occasions" and always with Tom as one of the barefooted players. Credit for its invention goes to The Three Canadians, who played it in the streets to gather a crowd.

DIFFICULT AND EASY GAMES

One final aspect of games before we leave this topic. As discussed, some games are, in general, easier than others. Everyone is different and some people will find some games easier and other games harder. Nevertheless, it's a fairly safe bet that a given group will find Questions Only harder than Three Word Sentences. Some games, as we've said, should be valued simply for their difficulty, but before we take them public, we should ask the question "How difficult do they *seem?*"

It's a seldom-mentioned fact that games which look difficult to an audience don't necessarily present a particular problem to most players, and—more problematically—some games that look perfectly straightforward to audiences present huge problems for most players. This gives us another way of categorizing games: games which are harder than they appear to be, games which are easier than they appear to be, and games which are about as hard as they appear to be.

For work in front of an audience, games which are easier than they appear are very useful. The audience want you to take a risk, but they also want you to succeed, unless the game's interest lies in seeing you screw up (Hat Games, No S). A game like Alphabet (each line of dialogue must begin with the next letter of the alphabet) is fairly easy for most improvisers—providing they are prepared to JUMP AND JUSTIFY—but looks very difficult to most audiences, so it's a quick win, and there's some chance of being able to tell a story, so you get some variety, too (it's dumb but fun). The corollary of this is that if you do happen to be somebody who finds this game hard (about one in twenty gets completely confused by it), you should probably not play it in public, as the audience will not understand what is screwing you up. They have come to an improv show to see things they do not believe they would be capable of. They want to see you being more daring, imaginative, playful and relaxed than they ever could be. They don't want to see you failing at something which they think (rightly or wrongly) they could do with ease. That said, if you remained tremendously cheerful while leaving out "K" for the fourth time, the audience might enjoy themselves quite a lot.

So, care should be taken when considering a game which looks *easier* than it is. This isn't to say that such games should be avoided, or we'd throw out some excellent games. Remember, some games are worth cherishing for their difficulty but others inspire improvisers in fresh directions, or enforce positive behavior or teach improvisers good habits, and so it's worth persevering with them—you just need to get to a certain level of comfort before you take them public.

A particularly tricky example is Scene In Rhyme. Verbal improvisers will often have little trouble with this game and only require modest practice, but more visual or emotional improvisers will often find the game dreadfully difficult. A common fault is to neglect the rhythm and struggle to find anything which rhymes with anything else. But it's the rhythm of rhyming poetry which tells us what is intended to rhyme with what. Try reading this aloud:

> Way back in the days when the grass was still green
> And the pond was still wet and the clouds were still clean,
> And the song of the Swomee-Swans rang out in space...
> One morning, I came to this glorious place.
>
> —*The Lorax* (Dr. Seuss, 1971)

The stress falls perfectly on the end of each line, setting up the rhyme that is to come. Panicky improvisers just try and come up with a rhyme as soon as possible and ignore the pattern of vocal stress. But an audience listening to the first line quoted above knows that the goal is to find a rhyme with "green." They may not even notice a rhyme with "back" or "grass." Reading poetry aloud is an excellent way of developing an ear for this. Edgar Allen Poe's famous poem "The Raven" is so pleasurable to read aloud that often Tom can barely resist reading out the whole thing, and we certainly can't resist quoting the first verse.

Once upon a midnight dreary, while I pondered weak and weary,
Over many a quaint and curious volume of forgotten lore,
While I nodded, nearly napping, suddenly there came a tapping,
As of some-one gently rapping, rapping at my chamber door.
"'Tis some visitor," I muttered, "tapping at my chamber door
                                        —Only this, and nothing more."
                    —"The Raven" (Edgar Allen Poe, 1845)

No improviser could ever (or should ever try to) duplicate Poe's complicated structure of internal rhymes, alliteration and repetition,[45] but spoken aloud it makes perfect sense. And this is the real problem for improvisers attempting to work in rhyme: most audiences are used to hearing poetry, or at least song lyrics, and *they* can hear the rhythm perfectly. Should an improviser screw it up, the error is immediately apparent and so the audience becomes frustrated: "Why can't they just get it right?"

In this case, it's not that the audience necessarily believes that they could do a better job (audiences often finding sustained rhyming scenes very impressive, which is also a reason to include them), it's more that they don't expect you to fail, which is why we categorize rhyming under harder than it looks. But we don't *just* play games because we want to show off to an audience. Rhyming often pushes improvisers into areas which they would never have gone to if it had not been for the need to find a rhyme, and so is an excellent way of generating fresh material. You just need to be good at it before you do it in public.

Perhaps surprisingly, singing brings with it a lot of other issues. It's a very different proposition from rhyming. Music has a power to buoy up an audience that's very hard to match, and some groups contain a great deal of musical talent, which it's nice to be able to show off. But whereas (non-musical) rhyming strikes audiences as an impressive but familiar skill, improvising both melody and lyrics simultaneously, in collaboration with a musician and sometimes other singers, strikes most audiences as ludicrously impressive. In some cases they can't get over the fact that you are doing this at all—and we're right back to the SKATEBOARDING DUCK.

The truth is that, even for someone as musically limited as Tom, improvising a mediocre song just isn't that difficult (although doing so excellently requires more dedication and musical experience). This means that the audience reaction and the difficulty of the task are particularly disproportionate. Couple this with the "lift" that even a fairly amateurish song can give a show, and you can be left with a group that is forever dragging out singing games to prop up a crumbling show—but this too will become old, and it becomes another version of the retreat from risk and the retreat from storytelling.

---

[45]It's written principally in trochaic octameters, if you really want to know.

Groups who really have singing "chops," who have a great musician (or more than one), who can work in a variety of styles, whose skill with improvising melodies matches their ability to extemporize lyrics, can sustain a whole evening with one improvised musical, because that has become the nature of the risk they are taking. And groups interested in story should certainly learn to improvise good songs, because they represent an excellent way of adding variety to a show.

But anything which you see as a safe option, anything which "always works," should be regarded with deep suspicion and mistrust. When the audience overpraises something which "always works," then the problem is even worse. Remember, no matter how much they like it, they don't have an insatiable appetite for more of the same. The beauty of storytelling is that stories contain infinite variety.

Word At A Time, one of our favorites, is about as difficult as it appears— which is to say fairly difficult—but that makes it an excellent choice, since an audience can appreciate a less-than-perfect version, especially if the players look happy and relaxed.

GAMES YOU LIKE AND DON'T LIKE

It is also worth asking yourself what games you personally enjoy playing and why—and which you dislike. With a game you dislike, it's worth considering: does it have any value? A game which will only ever generate stupidity, which teaches improvisers bad habits and which bores audiences can be discarded without a second thought. On the other hand, if you recoil from a particular game which you think (or even suspect) might have something to teach you, then—hurrah!—you have discovered a weakness in your technique. This is tremendously good news, since you now know exactly what you have to do in order to make yourself a better improviser. You should grit your teeth and play that game at every opportunity, although ideally not in front of audiences until you feel your antipathy for it wane.

If a coach tells a top tennis player, "It's your back-hand that needs work," that tennis player doesn't say, "But I hate hitting back-hands," and look for ways not to do it. On the contrary, they may do little else but practice back-hands until the problem has been fixed. Nearly all improvisers *avoid* what they can't do, and so problems often go untackled—even unacknowledged—for months or even years.

2.19

Final Thoughts

Overview

We review the tools we have developed for looking at improvisation, and consider where to go from here.

The preceding chapters represent a version of our eight-week beginners evening course in improvisation, with a few other exercises suitable for more experienced players slotted in. As discussed under How To Use This Section, we have had several audiences in mind, both teachers and students as well as those with a less practical interest in the subject.

Eight weeks is simply not enough time to turn a complete novice into an expert improviser, and many other terrific games and procedures exist which can help to strengthen existing muscles and add depth and variety to improvised performances. But we believe that the ground we have covered here represents an excellent foundation on which improvised performances of almost any kind can be built. Rather than trying to find the One True Way, we have looked to provide a range of tools suitable for different purposes, so that improvisers can stage a wide variety of shows, and sustain variety within those shows. Almost anything is worth doing very occasionally as a change, even the Never Play games in Appendix One (most of them). In this last chapter of the "How to Improvise" section, we will review these core skills, suggest ways to diagnose improvisers who are struggling and look at how to improve. We will also touch on how to direct and how to be directed.

So, what should an improv show be? It should be an expression of good nature. This is first because, happy, positive people are a delight to watch. Note that many amateur stand-up comedians play negative, aggressive versions of themselves (because they feel that "protects" them from the audience), but as you go up the ranks, it is the positive characters that tend to dominate, with only a very few of the very best sustaining a negative outlook—because it's so difficult to do!

Second, improvisation is fundamentally about *process*, and the process is made far easier when the players are in a good state. This means that the process will be more satisfactory to watch and the results are more likely to be worthwhile. Once the players are in a good state, they will be happy to take *risks* and happy with the possibility of failure. Ideally, some mechanism exists to account for failure as part of the show, but some excellent formats do not permit this, so risk must be judged and used appropriately. The improvisers need to bear in mind the *two stories* they are telling and be aware—across the whole show and moment to moment—which should be given more emphasis.

Lastly, improvisation by its very nature is a *storytelling* medium. Ignoring the presence of story is futile. Most attempts to remove story put something less interesting in its place, such as physical theatre effects, comedy shtick, back-referencing, hoop games, shock tactics or wisecracks.

Out of these elements—positivity, risk-taking, storytelling—great comedy can come, but comedy need almost never be an overt goal in workshops. Most great comedy is an expression of an individual's personality, and that personality can only be coaxed out; it can't be cut out and stuck to a board. The joy of a great improv show is seeing those vibrant, authentic personalities reflecting off each other and creating something genuinely fresh.

In order to accomplish these feats, various individual skills must be acquired. By far the hardest is learning to tell spontaneous stories, since many of the sub-skills go so thoroughly against the grain, but the most important is being in a good state (since most audiences would far rather watch a happy improviser's story go down in flames than a guarded improviser deliver a technically perfect story without a trace of daring or elation). For this reason, we begin by exposing the anxieties that novice improvisers are likely to feel, and trying to make those feelings part of the conversation between teacher and student.

Then we start to move the students into a relaxed and happy state, getting them acquainted with their own imaginative powers and what tends to screw them up. We also stress collaboration, but this isn't so much a skill that must be acquired as a process, albeit one which feels threatening to some people. Sharing someone else's idea means abandoning control of the future. It is vital to be in a relaxed and happy state, to enjoy your partner's ideas and to let them know how much you enjoy them, so that a positive feedback loop can begin. Those who doubt the value of their own ideas need to be shown that they have the power to inspire their partner. Those who doubt the value of anyone else's ideas need to be shown that if they allow themselves to be inspired, rather than working in a vacuum, the resultant synthesis will be even better than their own solos.

Once we have a positive process, we can put it to whatever use we wish, and as we've argued at length, we want to put it to the use of telling stories. Stories are about a hero who is made to suffer. Therefore, the first question is: who is the hero? Or, more generally: what is the world of the story and what does "normality" look like in this world? Once we know that, then we can recognize the extraordinary when we see it. Again, relaxed, happy improvisers have no problem putting specific details into the world of the story—the PLATFORM—especially when the utility of this is made clear to them.

Stories happen when routines are broken and when A affects B. Although both of these (related) things are more likely to happen when the improvisers are in a relaxed and happy state, ready to accept ideas, they both have to be specifically drilled, since they don't come naturally and their usefulness is not often realized. Some actors will be affected without much training. Few will break routines in any more general way. Comedians and writers may "get" breaking routines very quickly, but will often want to remain aloof. Great improvisers relish getting into trouble and have a built-in timer that warns them to move on to something new—yet connected—before they start "spinning their wheels."

Stories are generally wrecked through too much originality. Panicky improvisers reject all ideas, or hop from idea to idea, or clutter the narrative with ideas it doesn't need. Improvisers need to understand that surprise in stories is necessarily a rare commodity and be relaxed enough to accept the "obvious" ideas their brains give them. One special kind of "obvious" idea is reincorporation, which also can happen just because the players are relaxed and fully aware of the world they have created, or because they have learned the technique and are applying it more or less consciously.

Much of the rest is essentially superficial: remembering to be physical, playing a range of characters and "tricks" like speaking in rhyme or parodying different genres. All this can be useful in impressing and entertaining the audience, but without the core skills, the work might dazzle but won't move or linger in the mind. More likely it will seem cold or glib, whereas the best comedy often seems rich and warm.

Further training beyond the point where the importance of these skills is realized and their development has begun consists of three things: continuing their development, broadening the range of devices and just being on the stage without a script. The ideal situation, we believe, is to spend some time working with a coach, some time working with a group of people you like who are at about your level (but with no coach) and some time in front of an audience. Try to teach yourselves and you'll likely end up reinventing the wheel (and you may forget the axle). But depend on a coach and there's a risk that you'll be intimidated in their presence, or always rely on them for guidance. Rehearse without them sometimes and it's also less likely that you'll end up a poor copy of your coach.

Going in front of an audience is vital if you really want to know what skills you have successfully mastered. Your first show will be a revelation— far less frightening than you feared, and you will rise to the challenge in many ways, although other skills will desert you completely! That's when you know what you *can* do and what you *can't* do, which is excellent, since you then know how to improve.

If you are the coach, you need to be clear about what your goals are. We offer public workshops, essentially to anyone who will pay us. We attract a wide range of people looking for a wide variety of things. Some will be trained actors, experienced comedians, successful writers. Others will be younger, less experienced. Some will be professionals hoping to find insights which they can use to improve their networking skills, presentations and the like. Some will have no interest in performing as anything other than a hobby. Some will have an accurate appreciation of their level of ability, others will be less self-aware.

Having agreed to take their money, we have to commit to being able to help them improve, regardless of the fact that only some will be arriving with performance talent, or a well-developed comedy sense, or a boldness of imagination already in place. Even someone with little or no acting ability can learn to make good choices and commit to those choices, and that can make them a very credible improviser, at least as far as fringe theatre is concerned. On the other hand, some talented performers can "coast" on their performing abilities and neglect some core skills, so while they seem very able at first, they plateau very quickly.

Our aim is to provide a place where those that want to play and explore this strange art form can do so in a relaxed yet focused atmosphere, and where those who have a drive to improve can be pushed and encouraged without these two goals interfering too much. More about running workshops is under "How to Make Improvisation Pay." If you are casting a company of improvisers, life is very different. Subsequent chapters will explore this in more detail, but—although you will want to get the best out of those you work with—you are under no obligation to work with people who don't want to do the work you want to do, or who you don't enjoy working with, or who you don't think are up to snuff. If you put the money in and you invite people to be a part of your company, you also get to say goodbye if it's not working out.

So, the question of how you help someone get better has to be preceded by asking the question "Should you try?" Some people have positive qualities— possibly which could not be taught to someone else—which make it well worth putting time into tackling their flaws. Assuming that you do want to help someone, the next step is diagnosis. We here describe some common problems, many of which have cropped up in the main text, and outline the kind of work which can be done to tackle them.

Almost all problems come down to either fear or ego. If this is borne in mind, the teacher won't go too far wrong.

PROBLEM: WIMP

SYMPTOMS: Improviser is reluctant to enter a scene in progress, and reluctant to commit to offers when they get there. Will often WIMP outrageously, making only vague offers and struggling to make choices either in character or as an improviser. They may play scenes very slowly and wait for the other improviser to lead. They are never happier than when they have a clear endpoint in sight which they can pick their way toward with agonizing slowness. On one occasion, we remember a typical Wimp coming out with a brilliant opening offer at the start of a scene, which got a huge reaction from the audience. This so threw her that she barely made another offer until the scene was over!

DIAGNOSIS: This improviser lacks the conviction that their ideas are worthwhile and believes that choices have to be carefully considered. They imagine that other people's brains work faster than theirs and that their "disability" has to be taken into account. In extreme cases, improvisation seems very stressful for them and appears to make them so miserable, many would question why they want to do it in the first place. This is a version of the "quiet" tendency discussed under "Control" (page 222).

CURE: Improviser must be placed in a safe, supportive atmosphere and then *pushed* to do exercises which demand that they act quickly and spontaneously. Useful games include Standing Wave, New Choice, Over-confessing, Master/Servant Dubbing. Although the improviser appears to be miserable, it does them no good at all to be cosseted, as this will only reinforce the idea that they require special treatment. Make them do the things they claim they can't do and show them that they can; don't punish them for their failures.

PROBLEM: JOKER

SYMPTOMS: Improviser has a compulsion to be funny all the time. This also manifests itself as an ironic detachment from the scene—editorializing rather than emoting—or as a desire to force the pace of absurdity of a scene. Such players are rarely changed by what is said to them, preferring to contrive exotic plot choices to sustain interest. They may also steer scenes very rapidly toward taboo subjects such as sex, scatology or worse. Part of the problem that Wimps have is that they often want to be Jokers. The worst player of all is the Joker who isn't funny. Funny Jokers can be useful in some kinds of shows, but unfunny Jokers are very difficult to work with.

DIAGNOSIS: Improviser believes that it is *their* responsibility to make the scene funny and that how funny it is is all that matters. They may think "All this story stuff is fine for workshops, but an audience just wants to laugh,"[46] or they

---

[46]This is sometimes true, but it is also a self-fulfilling prophecy.

may genuinely believe that stories are worth telling and want to move, delight, awe and chill an audience as well as generate laughter—but then they panic when they're actually out there, and fall back on GAGGING. They may be personally uncomfortable with certain emotions or emotional situations and so minimize them by making fun of them.

CURE: Teacher must have a zero tolerance for unnecessary GAGGING, but more than that, the improviser must find success through other avenues. We once put two student improvisers, neither of them egregious jokers but both with a weakness for GAGS, into a scene in a Micetro Impro show as two horribly shy teenagers who fancied each other at the end of a party. They both committed totally to the characters and played the scene with agonizing slowness and awkwardness. Despite being almost dialogue-free, it was crucifyingly funny— easily a highlight of the show—and we think they will remember that success and want to build on it. Games which require close observation of partner will be useful, as reacting instantly to someone else's offer may short-cut the "find-a-joke" mechanism. Also try It's Tuesday for big reactions.

PROBLEM: YES-SAYER

SYMPTOMS: Improviser blandly goes along with any idea, no matter how ridiculous or shocking. Rarely plays unpleasant characters, finds solutions to problems which prevents middles of stories from taking off. May be very charming on stage (which is hugely important), but can neither play an effective "Alice"—since they are not affected—nor an antagonist, since they never create trouble for others.

DIAGNOSIS: Improviser has learned the skill of accepting offers very quickly, but is not focused on dramatic situations, which they are much less comfortable with. In life, they may be people-pleasers, eager to go along with whatever the prevailing view is and wanting to solve problems. Wanting to please the people they are working with and the audience, this same behavior pops up on stage, even though an improviser who says "I'm leaving you," hopes and expects to hear "No, don't go," instead of "That's probably for the best."

CURE: Feedback games such as The King Game, Yes Let's/Nope and The Removalists (all described in Appendix One: Games) will go some way to reminding this improviser that dramatic offers will please and delight their partner and the audience. They can solve the problem of the scene being boring and pointless by failing to solve the problem of the stolen watch (or whatever).

PROBLEM: SHINER

SYMPTOMS: Improviser always strives to be the focus of attention, even if they initially enter as a minor character. Often very verbal and also often very controlling, they will block offers that don't continue to make them the hero. In some cases, the Shiner is Teflon—offers slide off them. This kind of Shiner almost always plays high status, is unafraid to be negative and is never affected by what happens. A more subtle version of the same complaint can exist in an improviser who is a skilled storyteller and does not appear to be controlling—who certainly very rarely blocks—but who somehow always manages to wrap the story around their character so that they become the focus. They are also fond of soliloquies, solo scenes, introducing games and hosting shows.

DIAGNOSIS: Improviser believes that they are the best and that the show requires them to be on stage and in the limelight again and again and again. The Teflon, negative version, is driven by fear and by ego: "I must not allow the possibility that better improvisers exist." The more subtle version is driven just by ego: "I am the best and, for the good of the show, I must lead the way."

CURE: Improvisers need to be reminded that the best work comes from collaboration, and that even their genius can be stimulated by working with others. If they reject this, then a glittering career as solo writer, stand-up comedian or straight actor (possibly) exists, but an audience comes to an improv show to see performers collaborating in the moment. The actions of the Teflon Shiner are clearly destructive, but the actions of the subtle Shiner less so. Although they may be among the audience's favorites, for the good of the group they need to treat the improvisers whom they perceive as inferior to them instead as their equals or betters, since faced with a strong presence, some Wimps and Yes Sayers may accept their lot as second banana, which is fine until a show crops up which the first banana can't do. Teachers and directors are especially likely to be Shiners. We both have been guilty of this in the past.

PROBLEM: RANDOM

SYMPTOMS: Improviser makes very unusual offers, which is not in itself a problem if it only happens occasionally. But unusual offers must be either *justified* or *treated as unusual* (or both), and these things take time. If the unusual offers come thick and fast, then the story loses coherence. If the unusual offers are treated with equanimity, then the story loses interest because the character is not affected. Can go unnoticed if the Random is surrounded by improvisers happy to be Alice.

DIAGNOSIS: Improviser may either have a genuinely unusual mind, or—more likely—is constantly straining for effect, which is a version of THAT'S NOT GOOD ENOUGH. They simply don't believe that, waiting at a bus stop, the audience will be happy to see a bus arrive. So, they have a cabbage arrive (or something else intended to be funny). What could be funnier than a cabbage at a bus stop? Why, calmly saying "The Number 24 cabbage is usually quicker than this." The audience may laugh, if only out of sheer confusion, but the stories are limited to surreal, dreamlike narratives which will all blur into one another.

CURE: Improviser should be put in the situation of responding truthfully to other people's offers and must learn to appreciate that peculiar offers are required sparingly. They should be challenged to play Boring or Truthful scenes (have a panel of judges throw them off if they make an interesting or false offer) and may be astonished at how interested the audience is.

PROBLEM: HARD WORKER

SYMPTOMS: Improviser may be able to do some good work, but wears a near-constant frown and operates at a slightly slower pace than more intuitive improvisers. Will often justify destructive choices with reference to some rule or other. Hates to lose even trivial games like No S or the Hat Game, and makes no secret of their displeasure.

DIAGNOSIS: Improviser may or may not have a high opinion of themselves. Wants to get better, but believes (wrongly) that the harder they work, the better they will do.

CURE: Needs to be surrounded by happy, playful people and rewarded for enthusiasm rather than technique. Play intuitive games like Word At A Time and don't put too much work into the narrative side of things. Praise them for glorious, spirited failures. It's great to have an improviser that wants to improve, and the first thing they need to improve is their outlook. An improv show should be a joyous explosion of creativity, not the product of fierce concentration and careful thought.

* * *

This list is not intended to be comprehensive, but covers a lot of problems which we have encountered. It should not be read as a list of types but as a list of behaviors, and some people slip from one to the other, over long or short periods of time. Some people are capable of more than one, sometimes simultaneously. As teachers, we begin with the assumption that everybody can improvise. Some people might have less in the way of acting chops, a less flexible body, a speech defect or a mind easily lost in the fog of war. But we begin with the assumption that they can do it—make strong choices to tell a story with a partner—and we try to figure out what's stopping them and to gently move it out of the way.

One way which we find very helpful, and which has been referred to implicitly many times earlier in the text, is to side-coach: shout out instructions which the improvisers can follow immediately. Many teachers would never do this, and some students who aren't used to it can be very put off by it. At least two alternative strategies exist, both of which we do use from time to time. One is to wait for the scene to reach a natural end and then volunteer notes. This is generally your only option if you are directing a show which you are not in. The other is to freeze the action and to discuss the error at that point, and then either resume the scene or start over.

The first option can lead to the workshop becoming a depressing place because much of the work isn't good. The second strategy can be equally frustrating, since so many scenes get cut off in their prime, and it increases the ratio of talk to action. Students who are used to being side-coached don't generally object to it, and those who aren't used to it can get used to it quickly enough once they stop perceiving it as a threat to their creative egos. It has the virtue of pointing out an error on the horizon, in the making or just made, and correcting it instantly, so that the student still appreciates what (nearly) went wrong, but also experiences the successful version. More experienced students generally need as much side-coaching and so should get less in order that they don't come to rely on it, and so that they don't end up aping the teacher—both significant traps for the unwary.

Since side-coaching and public directing are both essentially the same thing, it makes sense to come on to talk about the role of director in an improvised performance. From here on, when we talk about directors, we are generally talking about someone whose direction occurs in front of the audience while the show is in progress. The pre-show pep-talk and the post-show "notes" are the function of a different kind of director, one who may be just another cast member as far as the audience is concerned, but who more productively just sits quietly in the audience like the director of any other kind of theatre show.

Many popular improv formats include a person, or more than one, whose job it is to not merely set up a scene or game, like an MC, but to actively work to improve it by shouting advice from the sidelines, just like in a workshop. The utility of this public direction is hard to over-estimate. The fog of war can be dense and all-encompassing, robbing improvisers of sight, hearing, orientation, common sense and taste. A director, although still in the public eye, has a clearer view; they see the scene in progress from a vantage point much closer to that of the audience than any of the improvisers. Their input is tremendously valuable. Our Level 2 students doing their first Micetro Impro shows (with two of their teachers directing) may do much better work than our Level 3 students doing their first shows of whatever kind, but without a teacher sharing the stage with them. This isn't simply because we are telling the Micetro players what to do, it's also—maybe mostly—the security that comes from knowing that we are there.

So, whether your "directing" is in front of a paying audience or whether you are simply using side-coaching in workshops as a tool to speed up the learning, it's important that, having taken the role on, you are genuinely going to make the work better. No point having someone sitting at the side of the stage or workshop space perpetually screwing the work up. Here are some quick notes about how to direct a show like Micetro, which also apply to side-coaching in a workshop setting.

Speak up: The other players/students are depending on you. If the scene is going badly, you need to say something, you need to intervene. The responsibility for improving the work is on your shoulders, and likely through your choice. At least if you pitch in, the pain is shared, even if you can't solve the problem. Sit back with your arms folded and you can think, "I have no part of this," but the truth is that you do, and the other players won't trust you to direct again after displaying this attitude.

Shut up: If the show is going well, the director should be seen and not heard. It isn't about you (see Gorilla Directing vs. Micetro Directing), and you must content yourself with improving the work of the others and making them the stars. Ideally, your contribution is forgotten by the audience (see How to Be Directed), since your interventions may pull them out of the story for an instant. Don't pad your part.

Be bold: Push the story into the future, deliver the promises that the improvisers have made, whether they know they have made them or not. If a woman says "yes" to a marriage proposal, cut to the honeymoon. If a chef remarks on how sharp a knife is, have someone impaled on it. This is especially true when it comes to dark, risky or taboo material. Improvisers, especially beginners, often shy away from material of this kind, but if the story is heading in that direction, don't be afraid to get it there. If the story is dull and you can liven it up by adding a little spice, then do. You don't have to perform the taboo action, so you can suggest it safely. The improvisers only do it because they are told to by you, the audience knows that and the improvisers know the audience knows that, so a lot of daring can be released this way.

Be obvious: As an experienced improviser/teacher/coach, your sense of obvious should be quite well developed. You should know from past experience that what strikes you first tends to work well, and there's no reason to doubt that instinct now that you are telling other people what to do. Be the one to keep the story on track and get them to justify peculiar choices. But "being obvious" is meaningless unless context is considered, and a major context here is what the other improvisers have established already. *Be very careful you are not simply substituting your obvious for theirs.* If the audience gives them a teacher and a pupil in detention, and your first thought is for the pupil to be sexually precocious but the improvisers quickly establish that the teacher envies the pupil's daring, then the scene is no longer about sexuality and you do not help by getting them to perform a U-turn. Not an experienced improviser/teacher/coach? Then what are you doing in that chair? Someone else should be directing you. Which brings us to...

Get it right: Make sure you have the experience and the temperament to succeed in this role. Directors who are asleep at the wheel, or who are yanking the improvisers around the stage like puppets, or who panic and throw in random material that muddles the narrative, or who stick only to their pet topics, or who imitate other directors they have worked with, do no good at all.

Make mistakes: The only way to learn to get it right is to start doing it and make mistakes. And since you are improvising too, don't expect always to do a perfect job. We tell our students before their first Micetro that, as directors, we usually screw up around one scene per show, and if that's your scene then we apologize. Actually, our strike rate is nearer to one scene every four shows, but us screwing up two or three scenes is not impossible, and it's good for us to calmly and happily give ourselves permission to screw up in front of the students. We suck and we love to fail. Having heard horror stories in which Micetro directors have been given enormous and absurd thrones to sit in and made the star of the show, or companies where the most experienced players have all the power and want all the stage time and so make the most junior players "direct," we have generally made our direction fairly colorless and unobtrusive, unless the players are being mischievous and naughty (good!—see "How to Be Directed"). Lately, we've begun to find the freedom to inject just a little of our personality into the show, without drawing too much focus off the players. After all, the audience is hoping that they will see the mask fall and discover something personal about the players—why should we be exempted? In general, though, this kind of thing should be kept for Gorilla Theatre.

GORILLA DIRECTING VS. MICETRO DIRECTING

In Gorilla Theatre, directing is not just an important element of the structure, but the whole point. In this show, around five improvisers take turns directing each other, with the audience punishing or rewarding the director at the end of each scene. Thus, directing in Gorilla Theatre has two purposes, which relate directly to the Two Stories discussed under "What a Good Improv Show Should Be." In the first place, having a director there and having that outside eye can improve the work. This is especially useful with improvisers who tend to GAG and whose GAGS tend to be funny, if destructive. In a Gorilla Theatre show, you can GAG "safely," since a horrible GAG can be removed by the director. Thus, you can have the best of all possible worlds: The audience appreciates your funny joke, and then the director repairs the damage. This doesn't change the fact that GAGS are destructive and that the best improvisers can reign in the impulse to GAG when it is going to be more destructive than funny, but it provides a way of incorporating GAGS and doesn't risk neutering the comedy instincts of a genuinely funny performer. In this way, the director can nurture, protect and encourage the first story—the story that the improvisers are telling.

However, the mechanism of taking turns assuming the role of a director who struggles to achieve their vision on the stage has other benefits as well. The struggle—the second story—may be more interesting than the story the improvisers are telling. This may be because this first story is fundamentally uninteresting, or because the improvisers are wimping, failing to commit or not being obvious—or because the setup was incompetent or ill-advised. Whatever the reason, good improvisers playing Gorilla Theatre understand this and shift their attention to the struggle instead. Directors become demanding, players become mischievous and deliberately misunderstand what is asked of them. One player is fired and the rest walk off the stage in protest. "Right, I'll do it myself!" announces the director, who is then plunged into darkness by the lighting operator.

In training people to play Gorilla Theatre, we've found it useful to make a distinction between Micetro directing and Gorilla directing. Micetro directing exists to make the scene more successful. Gorilla directing exists to draw attention to the directing process. This usually (but not always) makes the scene worse, which is excellent, since a crash-and-burn failure can be terribly funny and entertaining but a scene which limps pathetically into the night will only inspire apathy and boredom. Micetro directing should be learned first, and then the players encouraged to explore the possibilities of Gorilla directing. Likewise, a Gorilla Theatre show should begin with Micetro directing, so that the audience understands the form before they start to see some of their preconceptions challenged (build a platform, break the routine).

Improvisers should never confuse being rewarded with a banana as "success" and having to pay a forfeit as "failure." The only question you need to ask is, "Was the audience entertained?" If they happily roar "Forfeit!" at the tops of their lungs, you are on the right track. If they mutter "Forfeit" as if they really couldn't care less, you are almost certainly not.

HOW TO BE DIRECTED

Let's finally look at this issue from the other side of the equation. For some improvisers, especially those introduced to the concept of directing and side-coaching later in their careers, having a director there who can tell them what to do threatens their identity as creative individuals—and, more important, as ostentatiously creative individuals. They want to be seen as entirely responsible for the choices they make on the stage. While understandable from a psychological point of view (fear and ego), this is a little peculiar set in the context of theatre in general and improvisation in particular.

In regular theatre, the actor is very far from autonomous. Although the actor works hard to contribute to the illusion enjoyed by the audience that they are voyeurs observing spontaneous behavior, the reality (which the audience is fully aware of, intellectually) is that an actor is reciting memorized words and enacting behavior agreed upon in rehearsal, if not actually dictated by a director. In some mega-bucks touring productions, such as *The Producers*, even star names may simply be drilled to replicate the performances of the actors who originated the roles. Do they rebel and announce that their identity as an actor is predicated on their creativity, and that they must be allowed to rewrite the script and perform the role exactly as they see fit? No, of course not.

But hang on, goes the argument, that's precisely what makes improvisation exciting and special for me and for the audience. When I'm improvising, I'm not mechanically replicating any pre-ordained dialogue or actions; I'm making it all up as I go along. Well, this is of course true, as far as it goes. But you are not improvising in a vacuum. The audience is also there to see *collaboration*. If you enter the scene intending to play my employer, but are greeted with a cry of "Mother!" then you have become my mother, whether you like it or not. Blocking may get a laugh, but it is not recommended, no matter how good your employer offer is. Not to spare your partner's feelings, not to protect some idealistic notion of what improvisation must be, but because it yanks the audience out of the story to no purpose whatsoever.

Most improvisers understand this very well, and have no problem at all with YES ANDing offers of this kind. So…if you are happy to be *endowed* with being my mother if I'm onstage with you, why are you complaining so bitterly about being *instructed* to play another improviser's mother by me when I'm sitting at the side of the stage or in the front row?

Well, comes the retort, for the same reason that you told me not to block the offer: It yanks the audience out of the story. Ah, well that poses a new question then doesn't it? The problem is not that I'm directing you, it's that my direction is calling attention to itself. What if I were a narrator? Then I'd still be adding information to the scene which you would have to accept, but you wouldn't object to that, would you? You're right, good direction does not call attention to itself, as we've discussed, but you have your part to play in that, too. If a director gives you an instruction, do it. If a director gives you a line of dialogue to say, say it. Don't wait. Don't contemplate. Don't work up to it. Do it. Say it right away and say it word for word.

Improvisers who feel that a director threatens the audience's perception of them as independently creative will often rewrite lines the directors give them.

> **Him:** Angie, what are you doing here?
> **Her:** Oh, er…I…
> **Director:** *Say "I'm pregnant."*
> **Her:** Tony, the thing is…I think I'm…going to have a baby.

All the audience can think of now is "Why didn't she say 'I'm pregnant'?" Rewriting the line (you wouldn't feel you had to paraphrase every line of *The Crucible*, would you?) only draws further attention to the fact that you were directed to say something. If a director gives you a potentially funny line and you say it straight away, word for word, then you will get the laugh. It's funny if the character says it in context because then, and only then, it's part of the story.

Some improvisers make matters even worse…

> **Him:** Angie, what are you doing here?
> **Her:** Oh, er…I…
> **Director:** *Say "I'm pregnant."*
> **Her:** (*To director*) I was just going to. (*To him*) Tony, the thing is…I think I'm…going to have a baby.

If the director gives you something to do which you were about to do anyway, then various possibilities exist.

- *Everyone* knew you were about to do it, and you had been "about to do it" for a while and needed a push.

- You and the director are so in sync that the same idea occurred to you both at the same moment. Clearly, this is a very good thing indeed, and no cause for complaint.

- The director is padding their part and interfering unnecessarily.

Even in this last case, complaining about it on stage in front of the audience doesn't solve the problem (although it might be the beginning of an entertaining feud in a Gorilla Theatre show), and in the first two cases there is no problem. If you really feel that the director is getting in your way, then have them replaced or omitted and see if the audience enjoys the show more without them. The only way to find out if something works is to try it.

FINAL WORDS TO STUDENTS AT THE END OF A WORKSHOP OR SERIES OF WORKSHOPS

Close your eyes and remember a moment in the workshop that was awful for you. You really got it wrong and you felt bad about it. Maybe you even cringe to think of it. Have you got a moment like that? If not, you don't need to worry. If you do, I want you to play that moment back now…and then let it go. Breathe it out. If the moment haunts you when you're lying in bed or walking down the street—see it and let it go. Generally, other people can only remember your good moments and their bad moments, so unless you continue to play it back, it will be gone forever. It's disposable.

Now think of a moment when you really had it. You were great! Maybe something you did or said made the audience really laugh or lean forward. Maybe it was a personal revelation about something. You felt talented in that moment. Okay—you've all got a moment like that. Now play it back. Play it back. Play it back. When you go home tonight, lie in bed and construct a Greatest Hits Tape of all your best moments and play it over. By doing this you reinforce your own talent, and when you come to improvise again, your brain will remember it as something you love to do because you have a talent for it. You must reinforce your own talent because this is a tough business and you can't expect anyone else to do it for you. Never let a teacher, director or other performer make you feel untalented. One way to do this is make a Greatest Hits Tape in your head, add to it regularly and play it back often.

Deborah invented this mental exercise for performers because playing back events again and again is the way we create memories. By playing back our bad moments, as human beings are inclined to do, and forgetting our good moments, we can seduce ourselves into thinking that an activity is scary and beyond our ability. At the beginning of the RADA Summer School, which we used to teach on every year, we tell students to make a Greatest Hits Tape in their head of all their work throughout the month: Shakespeare, stage combat, voice work, improvisation. That way at the end of the Summer School they'll have a lifelong memory of being brilliant at RADA. It will be a huge confidence boost for the rest of their life. They can play it back right before an audition or an opening night to give themselves courage.

Also we point out that it will be a wonderful souvenir for their old age—imagine sitting in your dotage and having a clear montage memory of being at RADA in your youth. It's in your power to create it. Most people will obsess over the time they forgot their lines or froze up and then take some photos in the pub and those things will become their long-term memories. The great thing about this technique is that you can add to it all your life. As an improviser you'll have good and bad moments every week. We still find ourselves on public transportation thinking about terrible scenes we did in the early 1990s and want to cringe and shudder. We've taught ourselves to let them go and play back our Greatest Hits Tapes instead.

The Rules and Why There Aren't Any...

We are often mystified by what some improvisation teachers tell their students. It is certainly true that there are principles that help people learn to improvise, and technique can always help even an experienced improviser out of a tricky situation. However, a slavish obedience to rules that were originated as training wheels for beginners but have taken on a sacred connotation is one of the factors that may be keeping improvisation stagnant. In cinema it is obvious that practitioners continually asked the question "Why is that rule there and what would happen if we broke it?" Wherever you are improvising and whatever stage of your improvisation career you are at, please ask yourself that question regularly.

NEVER ASK A QUESTION

For example, some teachers tell their students never to ask a question. Perhaps this rule has some effect on the students offstage and makes the teachers feel they themselves will not be questioned. If we may break the rule ourselves—why? Improv teachers will say that it is to stop the improvisers from robbing the scene by asking the other improviser to provide all the information, that an improviser who never asks questions is bold and imaginative. But of course an improviser can ask a question that can be the motor of the scene: "How would you feel if I told you I'd never loved you?" and another can make a statement that's vague and adds nothing "I like some kinds of jam but not others."

The first thing that strikes us about the no-question rule is that it eliminates so much *drama*. We dislike improv rules that make improvisation somehow above the principles that apply to all the rest of the comedy and drama in the world as if we are somehow immune to the challenges that great playwrights, sitcom and sketch writers face, and therefore above their insights. If you are an improviser who subscribes to this idea of "no questions" improvisation, it is probably because you were taught that by someone else, and we often hold on to the first things we were taught because they are comforting and feel right. But ask yourself, what is the most famous line in the history of theatre? "To be or not to be? That is the question." The second most famous is probably "Romeo, Romeo, wherefore art thou Romeo?"

Shakespeare knew that questioning characters were characters who were not in possession of all the information and therefore sometimes unsure, and that this made them vulnerable. Improvisers do not enjoy being vulnerable because people do not enjoy being vulnerable. If we don't enjoy being vulnerable offstage we are unlikely to welcome the feeling when a crowd of people are looking at us. We, as improvisers, are in the unique position of having to *choose* vulnerability to create great comedic and dramatic situations. Playwrights and screenwriters will play god and force actors to go to all sorts of emotionally and physically terrifying places, and actors will go there because they are pushed by writers and directors. Improvisers have to choose to ask "Will you marry me?" knowing that the answer could well be "No," which will make their character (and therefore, to an extent, them) feel awkward, embarrassed and upset in front of an audience. It feels better, then, not to ask, to already know: "So, honey, I know we're getting married on Thursday, so I've got the rings." "Yes, and I've organized the flowers."

If you want to create great comedy then you need to ask yourself "What comedy do I enjoy?" If you love *Frasier*, *Friends*, *South Park*, *The Simpsons*, *Scrubs*, *Fawlty Towers*, *The Office*, *Monty Python* or any other sitcom or sketch show, watch an episode and see how many questions they ask and how many times they are not in possession of all the information. Fair warning: do not turn it into a drinking game or you'll be unconscious within ten minutes.

KNOW THE OTHER PERSON

While you are watching, examine how well the writers and performers are following other improv rules. One such rule is "Always know the person you are talking to for at least six months." *When Harry Met Sally* would have to be *When Harry Had Already Known Sally for Six Months* if it followed this rule. *Annie Hall* and *Four Weddings and a Funeral* would similarly be out. It actually rules out pretty much all romantic comedies, because the audience wants to see lovers meeting for the first time. It also rules out every episode of hospital shows because new patients are always coming in and having to establish trust with the doctors. It also rules out all detective shows, legal shows or sketches about these subjects. It means we can never improvise something like *Monty Python*'s dead parrot sketch or one of the many brilliant first-date scenes in *Seinfeld*.

NEVER ARGUE, ALWAYS AGREE

Deborah once taught some improvisers at a workshop in New York. They were doing an exercise where a man took a woman back to his house—Go Through An Unusual Door. Through their offers, they established that the house was underground, in some sort of mine, and there were little picks and shovels—and that the dwarves would be home soon! The man told the woman that he had brought her here for a purpose. She was to be their new Snow White. She would never be leaving.

The audience was laughing a lot because of the way this information was delivered and her gradual realization that this was no ordinary first date. What was her response to this momentous revelation? "Okay, that's fine." The audience was disappointed and they stopped laughing. Deborah directed her to be frightened and try and get away from him. She answered "But then I'd have to have an argument with him." Why this was a problem wasn't at all clear until the students said "We've been taught not to have arguments. We should always agree." That was truly astounding. Deborah side-coached her to try and fight her way out—react like he's the madman he is. Then the dwarves come home and they're so excited about their new Snow White.

There are many ways for this scene to go from here. He could offer her an apple and she could make him eat it. She could knock him out with one of the dwarves' picks and become the new leader of the dwarves. She could get away and liberate the dwarves in the process. No doubt you can think of others, but all of them require conflict and arguing and the characters disagreeing. There is probably no piece of drama or comedy in the world where the two characters interact and always agree and are never in conflict. It is possible for the improvisers to agree while their characters argue: they YES AND each other's emotional state.

Of course, we don't want to watch people bickering over trivialities. We can get that at home and don't need to go to the theatre to see it. What we want is to see improvisers being truly affected and having big reactions. Think of the wonderful fights in *Frasier*, *Seinfeld* and *Friends* ("We were on a break!"). Watch all the comedy you can and see if you can find any examples of people who always agree. If you do, the comedy will probably not be very well known because it will not have a very wide appeal.

AVOID TRANSACTION SCENES

Some improvisation teachers tell students never to have a scene in a shop or a store. This is said to help the improvisers avoid "transaction scenes," as if the only interaction that can happen in a shop is someone paying for goods and then leaving (see our Shoe Shop game on page 190 for a definitive refutation of this idea). When rules for improvisers start to limit the locations of scenes, they show a real lack of trust in improvisers. There are whole sitcoms and comic films set in bookshops and supermarkets. Is *Monty Python*'s Cheese Shop sketch a dull transaction? No, because the customer is affected, changed and put out by the lack of transaction. The film *Employee of the Month* follows a slacker who wants to become employee of the month to win the title from the store's overachiever, all the time hoping to impress a woman. It is a film of countless questions and arguments, and is all about what happens in a store when someone no one's met enters and changes their world. It is about people going through change and making themselves vulnerable, sometimes to their detriment.

Another often-repeated rule is to never have a teaching scene. This is to avoid repetition: "Do it like this." "Like this?" "No, like this." But rather than eliminating these scenes and narrowing our options, why not learn to do them well? What makes comedy and drama set in schools or classrooms, or where one person teaches another a skill, work? What principles are they using? Can we use them?

Dirty Dancing is one long teaching scene, but because of the lessons, the characters are changed and affected (albeit in a cheesy 1980s way). Baby teaches Johnny how to stand up for himself, while he allows her a sexual awakening. Ostensibly he's teaching her how to dance, and if it didn't go any deeper than that, it wouldn't have been a successful film. It's only a classic because the real learning is far more profound.

An episode of *Frasier* where he and Niles go to auto shop class to learn how to look after their cars gets its comedy from the brothers struggling to learn this mechanical skill and being poor students (something they are not familiar with), and eventually becoming the "slacker kids," who sit in the back and giggle through the class, for the first time in their lives. This works because the teacher is highly affected by their bad behavior and throws them out of the class. It also works because Niles and Frasier go through so many different emotional states throughout the episode.

If you're still not convinced, think of the amount of hours you have probably spent watching scenes set in the classroom at Springfield Elementary or South Park Elementary. On the whole they are pure comedy, and they always involve people being changed and affected. It is a good exercise to list all the improvisation rules you have been taught and analyze them. Do they make sense to you? Do the comedy writers and performers you love abide by them?

If you're an improviser who's always WIMPING and leaving the defining to others, it might be great to go into a scene and decide to build an environment and establish a platform without letting yourself ask a question. When it comes time for the climax of the scene however, you may wish to allow yourself to be affected by someone else. If they pull a gun out and you say, "Ah, I know that gun! It's a Smith and Wesson. I've got one just like it," and pull out your own, whereupon the two of you agree what lovely guns you've got, the audience will not be as pleased as if you say, "Mike, what are you doing?" and beg for your life.

If you're an improviser who always finds yourself bickering and arguing at the outset of the scene so that it can't go anywhere, decide that you are going to agree with your partner to build a platform and be an excited, positive character up until the point where your partner says something that could affect you, and then allow yourself to be changed negatively. Most of these rules are attempting to iron out bad habits, but surely they need to be exercises that strengthen improvisers' skills rather than rules which limit improvisers' actions long-term. Some improvisers who have learned with these rules have said to us that there is a time when you are so experienced that you can break them, but is always said in a bit of a whisper as if it is almost a heretical idea. Anything that is worth teaching a beginner as a rule or principle should stand them in good stead for the duration of their career. There are countless exercises that can be used as training wheels in the interim.

START IN THE MIDDLE

Deborah was teaching a workshop at a festival in the US and doing some exercises on building a platform. The improvisers found a lot of success in establishing an environment and a world and were producing great work which was very funny, but they were looking skeptical and confused between scenes. Deborah asked them why they were looking so uncertain, and one of them confessed that this seemed like a sacrilegious thing to be doing because they had always been taught to start scenes in the middle, to avoid beginnings which tended to be uninteresting explanations. The quality of the scenes started at the beginning was throwing them for a loop.

One of them said "It seems so wrong. It's going against everything I've been taught. But now that I think about it, it does make sense to start at the beginning." Several times we had people come up to us during the festival to talk in hushed tones about how the idea of starting at the beginning could help them, but they seemed genuinely uncomfortable discussing it in public. It felt a bit like they were betraying someone by learning a new technique which expanded their view of improvisation. We always encourage students from The Spontaneity Shop to go abroad and work with different companies. It can be very liberating to see things from a different angle, and it is highly possible that if they have plateaued working with us, then another teacher will say something that will unlock them. We hope they wouldn't feel that there was any sort of cultish reason to adhere to our way of working if something else was producing better results or making them enjoy improvisation again.

SCRIPTED VS. IMPROVISED COMEDY

Most drama is about people having big reactions to serious situations. You've encouraged your husband to kill the king so he can inherit the throne. You're now living with the guilt and the subsequent murders which need to be done. He sees the ghost of one of his victims and is terrified. You drive yourself mad and commit suicide.

Most comedy is about people having big reactions to everyday situations. You and your gang of friends are arguing over whether or not the boys know more about the girls or the girls know more about the boys. You, the girls, have a much nicer apartment, and you make a bet that if you know more about the boys in a trivia quiz, you will switch apartments. You are very confident about this. The boys win and you go crazy in fury about your perceived unfairness of the quiz, your own hubris and recklessness in engaging in this bet and the apparent unkindness of the boys in their intention to actually make you leave your beloved apartment. No one is really hurt, and leaving the apartment is an inconvenience more than anything, but it feels like the end of world.

Most improvisation is about people having trivial reactions to serious situations. You're pouring your mother a cup of tea when you knock her in the head with the teapot and kill her. You shrug and claim that she was old anyway and continue to drink your tea. The ghost of your mother rises up but you're not fazed—she's come back to tell you off for breaking the teapot. You have a trivial exchange with the ghost about how you hated the teapot anyway and in fact you don't even like tea. No one mentions that you have killed her and no one seems to care. You feel no remorse and she feels no hurt or anger. The most either of you experience is irritation, but mostly you are apathetic.

Sometimes you will go to an improv show and the audience is laughing but somehow the improv feels unsatisfying and nothing ever really takes off. Then an improviser steps on stage and they somehow seem great. Everything they say and do seems brilliant and the scenes they're in seem to go somewhere. The reason is usually that they are having big reactions to everyday situations, which makes their work seem genuinely funny and meaningful. The other improvisers are probably getting laughs from bathos—constantly trivializing serious situations and being apathetic about everyday situations. They often make wordplay which is mildly entertaining, and most audiences will laugh a little if you gun down everyone in your office and then sit down to check your email, because it is absurd.

George Bernard Shaw once wrote in a review: "When I go to the theatre I want to be moved to laugh, not tickled to laugh." Often we are tickling our audiences, who get used to making little laughter-like noises at whatever improvisers do. We could be moving them like great sketch, sitcom or screen writers and performers do. The secret is that we must genuinely be affected. We must be as outraged as Frasier when he finds out Niles is trying to buy their father a better birthday present, as devastated as J.D. when Dr. Cox ostentatiously withholds his affection, as vengeful as Basil Fawlty when he discovers "Lord" Melbury has only been pretending to be an aristocrat, as delighted as Cartman when he gets his own theme park and has the power to shut others out, and as unreasonable as he is when he needs to let others in to make money and as hysterical when he loses everything in the end.

If your grandmother dies and you cry, that is dramatic, and if you do it with conviction and the audience has had a chance to get to know you and your relationship with your grandmother before it has happened, they will probably feel for you. If you rail at God for taking her and destroy her things because you are angry with her for leaving you, they will not want to look away because your actions seem almost insane and certainly somehow blasphemous or dangerous. The audience will probably expect to see you changed again quite soon. You will probably look at the remnants of her Bible that you have ripped apart and cry with remorse for what you have done. Perhaps God's voice will reprimand you or you will become cold and cynical and never love again. You are certainly promising some big emotional change here, but it will probably not be funny. We understand that grieving people can go a little insane and you are reacting emotionally to something that is tragic to you.

If you come home and find that someone has erased your TiVo and now you cannot watch your favorite television program which you have been looking forward to all week and you react the same way, the audience will probably find it funny. If you smash up the TiVo and shout "Why, God, why?" and swear off the program forever because it has let you down, they can laugh at this because you are acting as if a tragedy has occurred although it has not. It is your own unreasonableness that is causing this great emotion, not circumstance. They know the feeling. They have also lost it over something small and understand your frustration. As an adult, most of the time they try and keep a lid on their irritation, so they enjoy seeing someone let go. Audiences revel in big reactions which seem insane in adults and are more befitting to toddlers. It is a way of allowing an audience the catharsis of great emotion—which is the basis of all theatre—without them having to empathize with a genuine tragedy.

Think of how irrational Frasier would seem if he were your brother. You might suggest he go to anger management classes. *Seinfeld* and *Curb Your Enthusiasm* are probably the apotheosis of this—an enormous and neurotic reaction to something as simple as buying soup or the fact that you don't know where to put your cocktail stick at a party. Every great comedian knows the power of childish and extreme reactions and how they move an audience.

Think of your favorite comedy characters and ask yourself "Are they usually rational? How would they respond if you parked in their parking space or sat in their seat and wouldn't give it up?" Would they shrug, say, "Whatever, these things happen," and move on? Or might they fight their corner and try every possible strategy to get what they want? Use this knowledge on the stage when improvising. Allow your characters to be truly affected by small things.

This makes improvising easier, not harder. Your scene partner can say, "Want to go to the beach?" and you can choose to have a big reaction to that. "Why do you taunt me when you know I have a phobia of sand!? Oh god, just the suggestion makes my skin crawl. I feel it on my skin. Talk me down! Talk me down!" Your partner can then apologize and be changed; he was being thoughtless. Or he can make it worse—perhaps he brought it up to torture you because he read your diary and knows you're in love with his girlfriend.

Don't let other improvisers get away with trivializing everything. Call them on it. The audience will enjoy it. If your mother comes back from the dead and scolds you for breaking the teapot, point it out. "Mother, I killed you, and you're worried about the teapot?! What kind of unfeeling person are you? Even as a ghost you can't get in touch with your emotions. Please say that you love me. Please say that you forgive me!" If the ghost refuses, you have made something of their offer to trivialize and the audience will be delighted in your pain and devastation at your mother's refusal to emotionally engage with you. If the ghost agrees that she's being unfeeling and apologizes and reaches out to you, you will have caused her to change, creating drama and pleasing the audience, while the absurdity of the situation makes it funny.

There's a reason why Shakespeare didn't write "Hey Romeo—what do you think of Juliet?" "She's okay. I wouldn't kill myself over her." Or "Hey Macbeth. Want to be king of Scotland?" "Maybe. Sounds like a lot of work." Shakespeare's plays have thrilled millions of people for hundreds of years because they're all about people who care, who are changed, affected, vulnerable, hysterical, insane, angry, joyful and desperately in love. We can learn from that.

HOW TO IMPROVISE A SCENE THAT INCORPORATES ALL THIS ADVICE

Try this as a way of proceeding. Go onto the stage. If you've got anything in your head, keep it there, but it's not what you're going to do. Instead, start physically building an environment. Look around you and see what's there. If you don't see anything then do something physical—open a door and go through it or open a cupboard and take something out. Keep doing things at random until you have established where you are, or at least that there are certain things in your environment.

Try having a positive attitude about what you're doing. Are you pleased to be relaxing and watching television and eating snacks? Are you excited to be exploring a laboratory you shouldn't be in? Are you thrilled to be in a waiting room anticipating your turn? Are you nervous but drawn with wonderment toward a golden bird in a cage in your master's bedroom? You may not even be sure what you're doing but you will be establishing something in the space. If you can encourage other improvisers not to come on immediately but to allow this environment to be built, when they do enter you will have a little playground to explore. When the other character enters, build on each other's ideas positively until you have established your relationship and the environment. Are you two roommates enjoying your longed-for night in? Are you trying to be polite to your mother as she inadvertently ruins your relaxing evening? Does your lab partner enter to help you steal the lab rats? Does the mad scientist enter and mistake you for his new assistant? You can easily extrapolate further on these examples.

When you have established an environment and a relationship and we know what you want—to have a relaxing night in or to set the lab rats free or to meet the scientist you idolize—then allow yourself to be affected. The easiest way to affect a character is to thwart their desire. If the relaxing night in is ruined or you are caught with the lab rats and locked up with them or the scientist realizes you are an imposter and experiments on you, the trouble will please the audience because you have delivered on your promise.

This will only work if you are really affected. If you are only vaguely irritated that the television has exploded or your roommate is eating all the snacks or your mother talks through the climax of *Breaking Bad*, then it will feel unsatisfying. If you are truly emotionally—even unreasonably—affected by these things, if you are Frasier affected, Cartman affected or Withnail affected, then the audience will be satisfied and will laugh hard. If you change your attitude toward lab rats and realize they are necessary to cure the disease you have now been injected with and beg that they sacrifice the rat to save you, or if you scream in horror as the Nobel Prize winning scientist you adore sends you into the future to stop you from telling the world that he has invented a time machine—the audience will love it. If you can look back and reincorporate something from the beginning of the scene—the Coke can or remote control you first picked up, the skeleton key you broke into the lab with—the audience will think you are a genius as they had forgotten it, and it also establishes that the scene as over.

These same principles govern nearly all the famous comedies and dramas you can think of. The writers and performers establish a stable environment and let the audience know where they are and what the hero wants. Sooner or later the hero is denied what they want or getting what they want affects them negatively. They are truly affected and changed and the story ends with some sort of reincorporation. This is a shape—not a set of rules. These are principles that can help you—it is not a formula. In an hour-long show, we want variety. If we have just had one scene which looked like this, we might start the next scene with two people on a bus talking. The principles of starting positive (or at least stable), being changed or affected and ending with a reincorporation can help you especially if you feel uncertain or uninspired. If something else wonderful is happening, abandon this.

You might start with the most misanthropic old man in the world digging his own grave with his daughter. This could be a fabulous start to the scene. It is two people doing something negative and starting in the middle of the action. It doesn't follow the principles above, but it does make a promise and it is showing people who are emotionally affected. It poses questions which the audience will enjoy seeing answered. Why are they digging the grave when the man is clearly alive? Is he going to kill her and then himself? Does he assume his death is imminent and not want to leave her with the heavy work? Any way that we answer these questions will satisfy an audience. It is just important that we answer them. They will prefer in general an answer which raises the stakes. We don't want them to dig the grave and then go home and have a cup of tea. A grave promises death, so we will probably want to deliver one even if it is just the family pet dying, which makes the man see the reality of death up close and change his mind. If the end of the scene is them burying the dog in the grave and going home more hopeful people, the audience will feel satisfied because they have seen a long-lasting emotional change.

In other words, we can "break" any improv "rule" or storytelling principle. We just need to know that people come to see people changed and emotionally affected. If your character doesn't care then why should the audience care? They might giggle or make some empty laughter-like noise, but they won't care or really laugh from the gut. If you're okay with tickling your audience and feel you're entertaining them, then it's fine to allow your characters to remain invulnerable. Just know that in doing so, you're departing from the experience of generations of dramatists and comedians, and what the audience is laughing at is the fact that you can make up anything at all on stage in an instant. It's the SKATEBOARDING DUCK. They are also laughing at the bathos—it's kind of funny that someone will kill their mum and not care; it shows a callous disregard for life that they don't relate to. They are laughing at your audacity. No one in *their* life would be like that. That's why the laugh is more of a giggle.

If you show them people they do understand, who are as angry as they are when their TiVo is wiped, and then who act out the revenge that the average audience member would dream of but not be brave enough to see through, then they'll laugh out of recognition and admiration. They'll laugh for the same reason they laugh at a great moment when Cartman is thwarted or Joey is devastated that Rachel has broken his much-loved armchair. If the examples we're using are not to your taste, examine your own favorite comedy and create your own examples. If you feel that the comedy you love operates to different principles, adopt those and create your own improvised comedy that identifies with your sensibilities. That way you know why you abide by the principles you do and why you're making the choices you make in scenes, rather than following random rules and freewheeling while the audience giggles. Know why you do what you do and be ready to make an intelligent argument to defend it.

How to Improvise in Public

3.1

Feel the Fear and Do It Anyway

Overview

From workshop to stage. What can you expect and how should you cope?

Whether you are running your own workshop program and teaching yourself and your compatriots to improvise from scratch, or attending casual drop-in workshops run by a lone improviser, or you are taking classes at a huge improv academy, there must come a day when you appear in public for the first time. Otherwise, it's all foreplay and no orgasm. This stuff was meant to be performed! There's no point learning how to please an audience if you never put yourself in front of one.

If your first show is set up for you by your teachers, then you should be in safe hands. Do invite friends and family to see you perform. You may feel like you don't want them to see you fail, but you don't want to try to perform comedy of any kind to a meager audience. If you invite lots of people and so do all the other students, you will have a nice full house, and a big audience renders everyone in it pretty anonymous, so you won't have to worry about spotting a familiar face in the crowd.

Don't shrink from a chance to perform, especially with the company that's training you. You can trust them to know that you are up to the task, to be supportive if it should happen that you struggle and to give you a good time on stage. If you wait until you are sure you are "ready," you will never do your first gig. The only way to be "ready" for an improv gig is to have done lots of other similar gigs in the past. So you start the process of getting ready for your hundredth gig by doing your first (and you start the process of getting ready for your thousandth gig by doing your hundredth).

This goes double if you are starting a new group and you have to decide when the whole group does its first gig. Get them out there in front of an audience. Don't leave it a year, or two years. Get in front of an audience while you are still green. Three months is plenty of time to learn to improvise well enough to keep a friendly audience interested. Pick a good format and try it out. If you can perform for ten or fifteen minutes and then leave the stage to a more experienced group, that's good too, but don't feel you have to put in months more practice if you can't. Get out onto that stage and start improvising, because that's when you start learning.

You will probably feel some anxiety before your very first gig, which could be anything from excited anticipation to outright terror. Try to remind yourself that these fears are fundamentally an illusion. You cannot come to any physical harm performing an improv show, whereas you take your life in your hands every time you cross the road. What you are afraid of is the loss of status you will experience if you can't think of what to say next or if your scene makes no sense. This is why we teach you I Suck And I Love To Fail first. If you screw up and stay happy, the audience will love you and you will have a good time.

Your first time onstage will almost certainly be much more fun and far easier than you thought it would be. That means that your second time may be more of a struggle, because now you have something to live up to. But an important principle to bear in mind is that nothing in particular is riding on *this* show. This show will not be the last show you ever do. In fact, for all intents and purposes, you have infinitely many shows stretching out in front of you. Don't worry too much about *this* one. (This is also advice we would give to people complaining about why they haven't been cast in a particular show.)

Here are some other tips to help your first time on stage go as smoothly as possible.

Get there promptly. You will want time to get used to the space, warm up with your fellow players and generally acclimatize. You don't want to fall through the door in a panic ten minutes before you go on stage. Be organized, know where the theatre is, leave an extra half hour for traffic problems or public transportation snafus.

Don't give yourself too much free time during the day. Assuming the show is in the evening, don't spend the whole day planning, fretting and worrying. To do your best work, you need to walk onto the stage and see what shows up. Any plan you make will only get in your way, and fretting about what the show might be like is entirely pointless. Arrange to do distracting things during the day to take your mind off the show.

Know your strengths and weaknesses and give yourself one thing—and only one thing—to work on through the show. Tell yourself: "I'm going to say 'yes' to offers" or "I'm going to fail and stay happy" or anything else you think will help and that you can do easily. At the end of the show, check to see if you achieved your goal. You probably will have done so—great! Any other criticisms you have of yourself or that anyone else furnishes you with can be dealt with at a future show. Maybe you feel that you just want to *get through* this first show, without giving yourself a hurdle to clear. That's fine, although don't underestimate the calming effect of giving yourself just one thing to accomplish. This strategy can be useful throughout your first year of improvising, and probably long beyond that.

Don't drink before the show. That one pint to steady your nerves will only dull your senses.

Have fun. Nobody *has* to perform improvised comedy shows. You're here out of choice. Take it all in and enjoy it. And be good to work with, too.

If you are setting up your own group (more on this in the next section), then you have another job to do: rally the troops. Before the show, tell them you love them and you'll look after them tonight. Onstage, treat them like marvelous talents and great friends. When the show is over, congratulate them and buy them all drinks. It's best not to have notes after your very first show. You could save up a few observations for the next rehearsal. Introduce notes casually three or four shows in.

After the show, just check out the space again before you leave. Notice how much smaller it looks now than when you first came in. When you are improvising, you own this space. Now you have conquered it and it holds no fear for you anymore.

See you at show number two...

3.2

Starting a Company

Overview

Practical advice about starting, running and developing your own improvisation theatre company.

The first thing to do is to try putting on a show. This probably sounds daunting, but honestly, if you can throw a party, you're overqualified. When you're hosting a party you just break the evening down into smaller jobs. You need to decide on a venue, invite people, make a list of food and drink and buy them, maybe choose a theme and put up some decorations and then be there to let people in and make them feel welcome.

Similarly, in producing a show, you need to decide what sort of show you want to do, find a venue, invite a cast, design a flier and poster and spread the word in as many ways as possible. If you are on a campus or in a town with only a few shows competing, you will definitely find an audience if your show is watchable. If you're in a big city with lots of competition, you'll have to work harder to develop a following.

Once you have a venue, decide who you want to cast in the show. If you're already working with a group of friends, this part will be easy; otherwise, you'll need to cast some people you know from workshops. If there's no workshop program in your town or university, you'll have to get a group of interested people together and hire a teacher or assign a workshop leader to take the group through some of the exercises in this book.

You now have a choice: You can either establish a democracy or a benign dictatorship. We would recommend the latter. Democracy is a great way to run a country, but rarely produces great art. That's why theatres employ directors and producers rather than just hiring a group of actors, giving them a copy of a play and letting them work it out. Still, the choice is yours. If you choose the democratic approach, you give every member an equal say and you need to vote about what sort of show you will do and how you will rehearse and publicize it. This can cause problems if someone continually doesn't show up at rehearsal. The question will be asked: Do they get to be in the show? The obvious answer is "no" but they might have a great reason for not being there and you might decide they're one of the stronger performers and want them there anyway. Others may disagree. It can, and will, instantly become political.

The upside of a democracy is that people have to share the workload when it comes to production. You can break down the jobs that need to be done and people can volunteer to do them. If you have a website designer in the group, it makes sense to have her do that rather than handing out fliers in the street. Some people won't do their jobs and someone will need to project-manage to check that everyone's on it. If you're reading this section—bad news—that's probably you. If someone can't do their job, it's better that they own up rather than hiding out. It's best to make a rule that people need to find their own replacements. If they just call you, you'll end up doing everything. Same goes for dropping out of a show—people need to call around and replace themselves, so make sure everyone has a full contact list or is part of something like a Facebook group.

If you're going for a benign dictatorship, then you get lots more control. You're running the show, so you get to include the people you want, to do the sort of shows you want and you don't have to justify your decisions (although you will be asked to continually and so probably will). The downside is that people will complain about you and to you. Most people who are drawn to improvisation are not businesspeople. If they are good at improvisation, they are probably not very organized. Most improvisers are either like hippies or children or a combination of both. Improvisation is inherently collaborative, playful and imaginative, so it stands to reason that the people who are drawn to it and have time for it are going to have the best and worst qualities of stoners and kids.

You are probably not very organized or very naturally business-oriented either, but you are reading this section so you are probably motivated, and that makes up for a lot. Your problem is that you, a disorganized person with an overdraft, are going to try and marshal together a group of people whose qualities make them ideal for building on offers and pretending to be vampires and taxidermists, and therefore not so ideal for being places on time with the right stuff and remembering to hang up posters and tweet about the show.

We're obviously speaking in generalizations. There are some improvisers that find this sort of stuff natural, but they're few and far between. You will screw up and so will they. They will get disgruntled and so will you. You will think they are ungrateful because they don't understand how much work you put in and they will feel that they're doing you a favor for performing in your show. If you do not want this to happen, don't start an improv company. Just don't.

If you're fairly thick-skinned and really, really, really want to perform improv and have a vision that simply must be realized, then do it. Just know that we all have a tendency to criticize those who are doing things. If you stay home and watch Netflix, who's going to judge you? If you put on a show and cast five people, then there will be four others who are furious you didn't ask them. You might decide to do a Theatresports show which two of your cast think is a bad idea. They find the Harold more comfortable. Maybe the first show is okay but there are some bad moments. The two people who want to do the Harold will talk in the pub about what a dumb decision you made. If they were running things, the show would have been better. They have no desire to run things, but they do think they would do it better. (Also be aware that if you had done the Harold, there would have been different problems and the others would have shaken their heads and said that they always said Theatresports would be better.) In reality, these are not matters of right and wrong but matters of taste—although people will argue them as if they're imperatives rather than opinions, and you'll want to defend them in the same way.

No matter what side of the fence we fall on, we are human beings and will behave this way. You may, right now, be thinking of starting your own company because you are dissatisfied with the one you're in. Most new improv companies start because someone is disgruntled with an old one. If we hadn't felt we weren't getting enough stage time at London Theatresports, the company where we were workshopping, we wouldn't have started The Spontaneity Shop. To her credit, the AD of that company, Natalie Haverstock, always encouraged her students to produce their own shows if they felt they wanted more experience that she wasn't providing.

The biggest thing to learn in running a company is not to try and please all of the people all of the time. You will end up pleasing no one. The best advice we can give you is to put on the show that you want to do and insist on quality. It's really best to have an outside director who can give notes to improvisers without having to perform with them. If you can't do that and you're planning on running rehearsals and being in shows, make sure you take turns being the outside eye so you can get notes as well as give them. Have more performers than you need for any one show if you can. Assign a note-taker to each show and have them hold a five-minute notes session as soon as the show is over. When Keith Johnstone was with us in London, he showed us how to do a fabulous notes session. Let the note-taker go over the scenes and give their opinion without further discussion. It's only an opinion, after all. They're not god. Don't allow arguments about who blocked whom and why. If you must have further discussion, do it in the bar. Many a fun show has been ruined by a notes session that has turned into an endless debate and left everyone pissed off.

There's a tricky balance to be had in finding friends you want to work with and turning your company into a social club in which people can't give each other notes because it seems too personal and you can never part company with anyone when it just isn't working. If we work out how to do that, we'll let you know. If you're still reading this chapter after we've tried so hard to put you off, you probably are going to start an improv company no matter what we say. Congratulations! You are the right person for the job and it will be one of the most rewarding experiences of your life. When you're very elderly and can barely move, you will not think, "You know what I regret? Starting that improv company. That wasn't fun at all. I didn't meet any great people or have any great moments on stage. I really wished I'd watched more TV and just thought about producing some improv shows." We wouldn't trade the years we've had running The Spontaneity Shop for anything. We could have made more money doing something else but we wouldn't have any of the extraordinary experiences we've had teaching people to improvise, traveling the world, being continually blown away by the talent of our fellow improvisers onstage and building up a wonderful group of friends with whom we got to play every week.

So few adults really get to play or have the lack of self-consciousness required to do it. It's a real gift to improvise regularly. Furthermore, to stand in a theatre and see an audience come in and a group of excited performers backstage and think, "None of these people would be here if I hadn't produced this. They'd all be somewhere else, somewhere less exciting, if I hadn't done this," is a lovely moment. We've had this experience many times, but other people who produce shows or films have reported this experience to us independently. It's the producer's rush. It's your reward. Take time to enjoy it. Just for a few seconds every show, think, "I made this happen." Then listen to people complain in the bar about how you got it wrong.

3.3

Nuts and Bolts

Overview

Having looked at the broad sweep of putting together an improv company, we now go into some of the finer details, from choosing a venue to ending the show.

Okay, so you've got a group of people together and decided to put on a show. The following list of questions will help you to go into this process with eyes open and to avoid, or at least think about, some of the more obvious pitfalls. Rest assured that we have blundered into most of these problems ourselves. Our hope is that you can learn from our mistakes.

We have tried to arrange these into a fairly logical order, but some depend on others, and some have to be decided in parallel. Here goes.

WHAT SHOW?

A fundamental decision to be made is: What show are you going to do? While some companies do manage to put on a pretty generic impro show (one game followed by another game, one scene followed by another scene or a Harold) and make it successful, this kind of show can be hard to sell, and you may not really be getting the best out of your team.

These are questions which need to be considered together. If you like interacting with each other out of character and you like the idea of competitive improvisation, then a format like Gorilla Theatre could be good. If you want to do improvised theatre, then a format like TellTales might work for you. But you also need a hook for the audience. TellTales was one of our best-loved formats by our regular audience, but it's hard to describe it without it sounding rather dull and worthy. Our show DreamDate promised and delivered a romantic comedy based on the lives of two audience volunteers, and it perfectly played to our strengths as comedy storytellers.

WHAT NAME?

As well as picking a name for your show that describes some of what the audience is likely to see, thus making a good promise, you will also need a name for your group. Pick a group name with a very strong association and you may limit the kinds of shows you can do. If you call yourselves "The Serial Murder Comedy Hour," you won't get asked to do many children's parties. On the other hand, if you call yourselves "Fluffy Bunny-prov" you may struggle for "cred" in comedy clubs and on the comedy circuit generally.

Picking a name which makes a pun on "improv" or related words seems almost irresistible. The Spontaneity Shop was originally The *Old* Spontaneity Shop, a play on Dickens which thankfully seems to have been overlooked by most people. "Improv" names, however, are hugely easy to come by. Among the shows we have seen and the companies we have worked with, we can name The Impronouns, Improverts, Improvedy, Improfessionals, Improvology, Improbable, Chimprov, Mission Improvable, Stanford Imps, Oxford Imps, Roving Imps; not to mention Spontaneous Combustion, Scared Scriptless (two or three times), Scriptease and countless others. It's a fairly safe bet that any improv pun you come up with has probably been thought of already. If you come up with one that your whole group falls in love with, make sure you Google it before you print off 5,000 fliers or buy twenty domain names.

FREQUENCY OF SHOWS

This is another key criterion. Most groups want to stage a weekly show, but why should this be so? Sure, it makes sense to be able to say to your audience, "We're here every Thursday," and it beats scrabbling around for gigs all across the country the way that stand-up comedians do, but a weekly show can become a burden if you are also busy teaching workshops, doing corporate jobs or working behind a desk somewhere, leaving you very little time to rehearse and innovate. For a new company just starting out, a monthly show gives you more opportunity to practice between shows and also to build up an audience. If successful, it's easy for a monthly show to go fortnightly and then weekly, if the demand seems to be there for it. Another option is to book a theatre and do a run of shows, performing nightly for anything from one week to five or six weeks. This gives you the benefit of down time between "seasons" for you to rehearse and innovate, a focused marketing push for your new idea and a brief, intense period of performing, followed by a breather. Very few improv companies take this option, but whenever we've done it, it has been very successful for us.

REHEARSAL SPACE

Much of this is covered under workshop venues (see page 343), with the exception that workshop attendees will cover the cost of the workshop venue in their fees. With show rehearsals, you will have to pay for the rehearsal space out of the show takings, so finding a cheap space becomes even more important. Don't be tempted to use somebody's large front room, though. It's very hard to keep focused on the business of creating improvised theatre with TVs easily to hand and sofas to lounge about on.

FINDING A VENUE

You will have to decide whether you want to do a cabaret show (with tables for the audience to sit around) or a theatre show with the audience in rows. Theatres are generally easier to play, as the audience has nowhere to look but the stage so it's easier to keep them watching. Theatres are very rarely dark except for Sunday or Monday nights, and then they are dark for a reason: Those are tough nights to get an audience out. Look around and explore all your options. You may be able to put some seats, lights and a stage in a room above a pub or bar, which may suit your needs as well as a theatre but give you more flexibility in timing for shows and rehearsals. Otherwise, you might find a theatre that'll give you a late night slot, which can be great. Smaller "black box" theatres may have more flexibility and you may be able to get odd nights here and there, or even a weekly residency.

COMEDY CLUBS

Another option is for your team to perform as part of someone else's show. In an evening of sketch comedy or a showcase for actors, or a variety night, an improv team can be a nice change of pace. Less successful, and certainly more daunting, in our experience, is taking your improvisers into a stand-up club and doing ten minutes of Arms Through or Animal Expert for the audience. We've known companies that have made this work, and it can be a good means of reaching a bigger audience, but the difference in expectation and energy between an improv show and a stand-up show is hard to overestimate. Improvisers who don't take this into account may get eaten alive in that often-hostile environment. Of course, some clubs are friendlier than others, and if you think you will be warmly received, go for it.

Be prepared to take some technical/logistical problems into account also. You may not be heard without a mic, and you may have to hold the mic in one hand or remain behind the mic stand in order to accomplish this, both of which drastically constrain your ability to make physical offers. A good compromise, if you are keen to tap into the stand-up audience, is to try and get a friendly stand-up club to give you a show-length slot once a week or month. The Stand Players in Edinburgh did excellent improvised comedy, accurately giving the rowdy stand-up crowd exactly what they wanted, but did so with tremendous wit, daring and charm. It's not exactly theatre, but it kept that audience very happily entertained on a regular basis.

FLIERS AND POSTERS

All right, you know what you want to do and where you want to do it. Now you need to think about selling your show. Even in this digital age, fliers and posters can be worth having and the price of printing is falling all the time. Where we live in the UK, it's now possible to get thousands of color fliers for less than £100. This is well worth doing, although often fliers act as little more than an aide-mémoire. A good photograph of the team is worth getting, and worth spending a bit of money on—a good set of photos can be reused almost endlessly—but try to resist the temptation to make faces, clown around or wear silly costumes unless you've got a strong idea for a particular show. If there's someone in your team who can use Photoshop or InDesign, then now's the time to use their talents. If no one in your team is so equipped, almost certainly you will be able to find a friend or friend-of-a-friend who is. Let them get on with it, and trust them if they tell you that the design works. They know more about it than you, or you would be doing it yourself.

If at all possible, include a map on the flier showing how to get to the theatre. Also, do a quick check before you send the file to the printer that you have included all the key information, such as how to book tickets, how much they cost, when the show starts and so on. Have several people proorfead teh flire for spellign mistakes. When you take delivery of the fliers, encourage everyone on the team to have some on their person at all times, and think about how you can get people to see them. Some ideas include: paying to have them included in local papers, leaving them in local shops and restaurants, paying to have them placed in racks around town, handing them out near the venue, leaving them on seats at other shows (with permission), handing them out to workshop students, handing them out to people leaving other shows.

Posters are less useful, but it's good to get a few done for the venue itself at least, and they make nice souvenirs. Many copy shops in the UK will do A3 (poster size) color copies from digital files for a pound or two, and this is a very cost-effective way of making attractive color posters, assuming you have some good artwork to begin with.

INTERNET

As well as these more traditional, old-fashioned ways of promoting a show, the Internet brings many marketing opportunities. Again, try to make use of any in-house (or near-house) expertise you might have, and don't think you have to spend a lot of money. In the UK, you can get your own domain name (web address) and web space for about £20 a year. Your own domain name is important and should ideally be nice and short with no punctuation (advice we didn't heed, but we're stuck with www.the-spontaneity-shop.com now). If you don't have website-building skills in your arsenal, then services like Squarespace or WordPress can create very professional-looking pages for you in minutes and as your experience (and budget) increases, you can customize them further and further.

Once you have a website up and running, keep it up-to-date with news of where you are performing and what other events you have. Give your audience the opportunity to talk back to you and you will keep your site dynamic and active. You can also try and persuade other websites to link to you. If you have a links page on your site, you can offer "link-exchanges." This will also help you to rank higher in Google and other search engines.

Social networking sites like Facebook and Twitter are hugely important. These give you another route to promoting your improvisation shows and should not be overlooked, both for creating communities and for paid-for advertising. This can be quite highly targeted and can be very useful. You can also include a link to your website in your email signature, even in your regular emails, if that's appropriate.

Creating podcasts and YouTube videos using your improvisers is another way to spread the word about what you are doing. Without a great deal of care, it won't be possible to recreate the excitement of being at a live show, and the art of creating effective pre-recorded improvised productions could probably fill another book, but using the same team to create comedy sketches, or taking clips from shows to create trailers are both excellent and very cost-effective marketing strategies.

You should also compile an email list of your existing workshoppers and show attendees, and send an email once a month or so advertising your upcoming events. Your website should include a way to sign up to the mailing list, ideally on every page. Services such as MailChimp now make these sorts of lists very easy to set up and maintain.

PRESS

Just about any press you get is worth having, even (or perhaps especially!) "Ban this filth now!" Obviously you can pay for advertisements, but unless you have star names or a particularly brilliant hook, this is unlikely to pay for itself in ticket sales. Most towns have some kind of listings magazine or similar page in the local paper, but as print is slowly forced out of business by the Internet, these pages have less and less space and tend to be less and less useful. Readers in the UK should also be aware that the Press Association runs a listings "clearing house" known as PA Listings which provides listings material to many other publications, who then select the most interesting. Submitting to PA Listings is well worth doing, but it needs to be six to eight weeks in advance of your show date.

Reviews and editorial are the very finest kind of printed advertising you can get, not just because people will read them when they come out and want to see your show, but because you can endlessly quote and recycle them for years afterwards. A good quote on your flier adds a tremendous amount of legitimacy, and you should save press clippings for this purpose. Again, personal connections will be hugely helpful. If you don't have them, try and make them. Call up the comedy editor or theatre reviewer at a local paper or magazine and see if you can talk to them. Send them short, well-laid-out press releases from time to time, and stress what's different about your show.

We have found that doing shows themed for Valentine's Day, Easter or Halloween are fun for audiences and a great way of getting press. Often the story or picture editor is looking for something seasonal to run, and a show called "Cupid's Last Stand" or "The Trick or Treat Comedy Hour," with a picture of your company dressed in appropriate costumes, is something easy for them to put front and center, especially when the comedy editor is normally dealing with pictures of men behind mics.

SELLING TICKETS

If at all possible, have a mechanism whereby people can book *and pay for* tickets in advance. You may have to give up a percentage of each sale in order to take credit card payments yourself or through an agency, but it means your audience will be much less diminished if it suddenly pours with rain an hour before your show starts, and it means you will know before the day of the show whether or not you need to call up all your friends to fill spare seats because tonight a reviewer is coming. We've been using ticketweb.co.uk, which has proven to be very worthwhile, but several similar services exist. If you are using a theatre space, they will very often have a fully functioning box office that you can use, but check whether their box office phone line is a real ticket booking line or just an answering machine on which people can leave messages requesting tickets. As well as selling your own tickets, you may also be able to arrange an allocation of discounted tickets via services such as YPlan or LastMinute.com and these can be very useful extra marketing avenue for you.

If there is no box office, make sure that it's somebody's job to turn up to the venue with a cash box—with sufficient change in it—and with a book of cloakroom tickets or similar. Make sure also that a count of the cash box is done at the start and the end of the night and that the number of tickets available and sold is recorded somewhere. For less than £100 you can also get a credit card reader which connects to your smartphone so you can take card payments on the door.

STARTING THE SHOW

Be a little wary of coming out to pumping rock music and laser displays, even if you can afford them. Such an over-confident, high status presentation gives you very little room to move in terms of success or failure. Slickness and showbiz is the enemy of risk and can lead to very formulaic work. But having a charismatic host who is happy to talk to the audience and welcome them to the show can be very helpful—just don't let them dominate the whole show.

Like setting up a game, if the audience needs to understand the show's format in order to appreciate it, then you need to explain it quickly and clearly. But there's no point wasting time telling them things they don't need to know. Instead, a good host will make them laugh happily, give them practice shouting things out (if necessary) and create a friendly mood. A show like Theatresports benefits from having a single dedicated host throughout, but in other formats, it may be appropriate to share the business of setting up games, keeping the show moving, sending the audience out to the bar at intermission and so on. Encourage as many people as possible within your team to interact with the audience as "themselves" so that they can happily take over main host role if need be.

If your show is more theatrical and less cabaret, then it may scarcely need a host at all, so don't include one just because you think it's the thing to do. Always ask yourself what your show needs.

MUSIC AND LIGHTS

Your show will need technical support of various kinds. Whether or not you have a musician on the stage with you, you will want to have music playing in the venue when the audience enters, for atmosphere. Some companies create musical accompaniment for scenes purely by means of recorded music. While this is nowhere near as flexible as working with a musician (improvisers need to understand that it is their responsibility to fit their actions to the music once it has started), it can give more breadth in terms of styles and sounds. This kind of musical accompaniment was pioneered at the Loose Moose in the 1970s when it meant juggling hundreds of cued-up cassette tapes. With iPods, it's possible to have near-instant access to thousands of tracks. We've compiled playlists with an eclectic selection of music, biased away from lyrics which can compete with the improvisers' dialogue. More sophisticated software like the excellent GoButton or Q-Lab can also be used to sequence tracks and automate fade-outs.

Depending on how the tech booth is arranged, one quick-off-the-mark operator may be able to run both sound and lights for you, but it may be that the two panels are on opposite sides of the room, or that it's just too much for one person to accomplish at once. In either case, both lighting and sound operators need to be bold and fearless. "Is this hell?" wonders one of the improvisers. Suddenly the stage is suffused with red and the low rumble of distant volcanoes booms out of the speakers. This kind of coordination can't be accomplished by technicians used to working from a cue sheet or who wait for explicit instructions before acting. The very best technicians are usually improvisers themselves, which can create problems if everybody wants stage time. Very few in-house technicians have anything like the boldness required for the role, although most will grow into the role if given some encouragement and will start to enjoy the freedom and creativity it affords them.

ENDING SCENES

The best, most elegant and simplest way for a scene to end is for the lights to come down, ideally accompanied by a burst of music from somewhere—musician or sound improviser. This means that the lighting improviser has a considerable amount of power, not just spotting endings, but actually *creating* endings. If the pace of the show is sluggish, a portion of the blame should be directed to the tech booth.

However, even if the agreement is that scenes end when the lights come down, that doesn't mean that the improvisers can't end scenes themselves. In directed formats, it's easy for the director to call "scene" or wave the lights down with a gesture. Players on and offstage can also be encouraged to give this kind of signal. In one company we know, players slap the stage when they feel the scene has come to an end, which is especially pleasing if more than one person does it at the same time, but not as elegant as having the lights fade around them.

Some formats allow one scene to blend into another without any input at all from the technician, but that doesn't mean that they can't use the other resources at their disposal to add to the show. Trust your technician and that trust will often be rewarded.

Some shows also include specific mechanisms for ending scenes. Australian Theatresports shows always used to include time limits for all games (which can be very restricting, especially if the scene is over but the available minutes "must be used"), and most versions of Theatresports include the Horn For Boring, which if sounded means the improvisers must leave the stage. Clive Anderson and Drew Carey had a buzzer they could sound to bring scenes to an end. Pick whatever works for the kind of show you are performing, and don't be afraid to experiment.

GETTING SUGGESTIONS

A fun part of many improv shows, but not essential. Australian Theatresports, which was wildly popular in the 1980s, had all the suggestions in sealed envelopes, written by committees before the show began. In *Whose Line Is It Anyway?* almost all suggestions came from the host and were written by the producer, or selected from ideas written by audience members before the show began. If you are getting audience suggestions, here are some useful points to bear in mind.

Common "ask-fors" include: a place to be, an object, a profession, a relationship, a professional relationship, and all of these will work fine. But, for variety, why not try to come up with new ones for each show? Audiences often give the same responses to the same ask-fors; dentist seems to be the most favored profession, for example. So why not ask them for something more unusual, personal or eclectic? "What was your grandfather's profession?" may get you a more interesting response than "Can someone name a profession?" It's also a more personal way of connecting to the audience.

Another common problem is that an improviser asking for a location is hoping to hear "cemetery" or "library" but will more frequently hear "Botswana." To cope with this problem, some groups ask for "a non-geographical location," which is a potentially confusing phrase, and may not solve the problem at all, since the presence of the word "geographical" puts the idea of countries into their heads. One way to deal with this is to ask the person who shouted out "Botswana" to tell you something about it which you can then use, but if you suspect they know nothing about it, then this is a bit too combative. Another strategy is to give examples of the kind of thing you want, which you can also use to "knock-out" answers you've heard too many times before. "Can we have a suggestion of a profession please, like dentist or police officer?" However, if you try to "knock-out" crude suggestions, you may find that *you*, and not your audience, are dragging the show into the gutter: "Can we have suggestion of a location please, like lavatory or brothel?" The phrase "Can we have a suggestion of a place where two people might meet?" seems to provide many fewer cities and countries as answers. You could also try asking for "a place of work."

In general, you shouldn't take suggestions that don't inspire you (such as famous people you've never heard of!) but equally you shouldn't waste time suggestion-shopping, since this makes you look uncertain. It's particularly frustrating to hear an improviser solicit more suggestions after hearing one, and then six or seven later, finally agree to take the first one given.

Bear in mind that taking a suggestion makes a promise to the audience. If you take the suggestion "doughnut" and you finish eating a doughnut before taking your dog to the vet, never mentioning doughnuts again, then the audience will feel cheated. Equally, your *question* should not be what inspires the improvisation. If you ask for, as suggested above, "your grandfather's profession" and get "brush salesman," then the scene should be about brushes and selling them—*not about grandfathers!* If you ask for something you might find down the back of the sofa, the scene which follows should not even feature a sofa.

Always repeat a suggestion once you've accepted it: for clarity, for volume and to reinforce your control of the stage. Also, don't forget to thank the audience for their contribution. We train our improvisers to say "Brush salesman, thank you," and look happy.

If you always get audience suggestions, try doing at least one show without them. If you never use them, see if you can incorporate them. How will you know what works if you don't experiment?

USING AUDIENCE MEMBERS

Not always appropriate, but can add an extra layer of interest to many improvised shows. Be aware that rest of the audience is on the side of the volunteer you have on stage with you (unlike in a stand-up club where somebody heckles, when generally the rest of the audience is *not* on the heckler's side). You must therefore treat them with respect and kindness, make them the hero of the story, raise their status and make sure they get a round of applause for their contribution. Never get unwilling volunteers, and think twice before taking people being "volunteered" by their friends, anyone who looks drunk or anyone you know (or what's the point?).

ENDING THE SHOW

Once your show is over, get off the stage. A quick bow and a thank you and then just get the hell off. If you have other shows to promote, it's far better to plug them right after the intermission than to let the energy of your big finish drain away as you read out a long list of your forthcoming attractions. Put fliers on people's seats and try to get all announcements out of the way long before the show is winding down. And make sure that your technician pumps out happy music as soon as you have left the stage, or even as you are leaving.

THE NEXT SHOW

Once you've had your congratulatory drink in the bar, it's time to start thinking about the next show. Especially when starting out, some kind of notes session is advisable. This can either be a free-for-all among the cast, or (better) you can give one person who did not perform the job of scribbling down observations as the show is in progress, and these can then be shared with the cast, either directly after show or at the next rehearsal. Try to avoid these becoming shouting matches—separate the ego from the work.

One particular thing to be aware of is that as improvisers in one company start to find their feet, they can develop into specialists. Physical performers will look for opportunities to do their physical shtick. Verbal comedians will stand at the side of the stage, commenting on the action. Story-heads will knit everyone else's random offers together into a coherent narrative. This is a very positive thing—it means that confidence is growing and that the group is sufficiently diverse to have expertise in many areas.

But as time goes on it may be a problem—a particular scene requires your physical performer to be verbal and they "refuse the jump." Or worse, your player who always ends scenes can't play tonight and so scenes never end! As you develop as a company, while each of you will doubtless have "favorites," you should all be trying to broaden your skills. Have the specialists lead workshops so that each of you can acquire a bit more of that specialization and the group as a whole becomes better able to cope with shows of all kinds.

You may also find, if you are doing a weekly show, that press is harder and harder to come by. "Improv Company Performs Same Show as Last Week" is hardly a gripping headline, and so you will need to keep generating variety. Doing new formats with fun names, themed shows (as mentioned previously) and inviting special guests to play with you can be very useful for reinvigorating the promotions business.

FESTIVALS

Once you've found a show you like doing which gets an audience, you may want to take your show on the road. Taking a show on tour is probably beyond the scope of this book, but getting invited to festivals is not difficult and often means that other people—the host company—are responsible for much of the foregoing. The Edinburgh Fringe has an entirely open-door policy and is (thus) the biggest arts festival in the world. If you can afford it, you can book a venue and take a show there, but it's very easy, even for a foreign company (exotic!) to get lost in the shuffle; there are around three thousand shows performing there for three weeks.

Improv-specific festivals tend to be smaller and friendlier. Companies that play Theatresports are especially likely to want to invite international teams to play with them, as the format makes the process of combining companies on one stage very easy. Check out the list of licensed teams on the ITI website (theatresports.org) and keep an eye on Facebook groups for companies looking for teams to come and play. Put together some YouTube clips so those hosting festivals can get an idea of the quality of your work. Of particular note is the Chicago Improv Festival, which runs every year, usually around May–June. The artistic director is Jonathan Pitts, who is keen to encourage new shows and international groups. Visiting companies to CIF can often perform to big audiences, teach and attend workshops and be assured of a fine welcome.

Most companies will do what they can to help you pay for your airfare, but some may be able to do little more than suggest you book early. You can reasonably expect to be put up—at least in a local improviser's spare room—and given well-attended shows to perform, often workshops to teach and always a friendly guide to the nightlife afterwards. You are part of an international improv community, so why not take your part on the international stage? You can have a wonderful time and learn a lot from this cultural exchange. Also taking your team to Amsterdam for a week can be incredibly bonding in itself.

The Paradox of Improvisation

Improvisation is the only art form that can't be edited.

Live theatre or concert performances also have this feeling but, in general, are scripted, so you only get to see moment-to-moment decision-making on the rare occasions that something goes wrong. In improv shows you get to see it all time, including when everything's going right. One of the reasons that improvisation is so difficult for some people, and why the results are so often unsatisfactory, is that most people maintain a fiction that there is a "me" which is in control and which takes careful, measured decisions to ensure our best interests. Competing for control with "me" is a rolling, boiling, dangerous, libidinous, reptilian force called "the unconscious." If this is allowed to have control over me, I fear I will become childish, psychotic or worse.

A little introspection reveals that, to some extent at least, this is illusory. Yes, sometimes we will make very careful, measured decisions over matters such as which house to buy, whom to marry, whether to start an improv company of our own. But it's entirely false to suppose that this kind of detailed, conscious decision-making is operating all of the time. Of course, at the other end of the scale, there are purely instinctive actions. The jerk of your knee when a doctor taps it with a little mallet is not something you could control if you tried. If you put your hand on a hot surface, you will yank it away *before* the pain registers. But in between these two extremes, a lot of very good, very automatic decision-making is going on. Whether to go around this person to the left or to the right. Whether to say "goodbye," "cheerio" or "laters" at the end of phone call. Whether to sit cross-legged or put both feet on the floor.[1] No doubt we could invent reasons for these things, but the latest results from neurology show that rationalization is a separate process which post-dates actions. First, we act, *then* we work out why we decided to, in order to be able to keep telling ourselves the story that "I am in control up here."

The pain and suffering which accompanies bad improv scenes is *nothing* compared to the possible injuries people risk on skiing holidays, sponsored parachute jumps or even crossing the road. But concealing your feelings is also an important survival skill. We must not let the libidinous monster have its way, or people will judge us. Public loss of status, to some people, is more frightening than death![2]

Inspiration is the friendly face of the reptilian unconscious. And if you use your unconscious inspiration to paint, sculpt, write or compose, then your conscious decision-making mind can come in afterwards and edit. Often what it will remove is anything which reveals something we'd rather went unsaid. Improv's strength—and its weakness—is its ability to reveal the unconscious mind. At best it can be daring, exciting, truthful, human and hilarious. At worst it can be self-indulgent, idiotic or pointless. Inability to edit can mean that the audience feels all is revealed and they are watching a dangerous process where anything can happen, but it also means that a lot that would be edited as sub-standard in another art form is presented as the best we can do in improv.

However, it isn't the case that editing is always a negative process. Read first drafts of any great screenplay, novel or other famous work and you will very often see that errors have been corrected, focus has been restored and it is only redundant material that has been removed. One reason for this is that most such art forms are generally the province of soloists. Great writers, artists and composers work alone, or occasionally in two-person teams. What has often happened between first draft and final version is that a second mind has entered the picture, even if this is the original creator some time later.

In 1986, a television serial called *The Singing Detective* was broadcast on BBC1. It was written by famed television writer Dennis Potter and is widely considered to be his finest work. We consider it one of the greatest things ever written for British television, if not *the* greatest. The complex,

---

[1] Many people report that, especially on a familiar route, they can drive themselves home and have no recollection of the journey: they were "on automatic pilot."
[2] Or so people say to researchers conducting surveys.

multi-layered story depicts an embittered crime novelist, Philip Marlow, played with heart-rending sincerity by Michael Gambon, who is confined to a hospital bed with a crippling case of psoriatic arthropathy which seizes up his joints and covers his skin in painful blisters. As he lies on his back, swapping caustic remarks with diligent nurses, other patients and his ex-wife, he fantasizes or hallucinates childhood memories, bits of his current novel and a morbid waking dream about his ex-wife's betrayal— all set to 1940s show-tunes. Over six hour-plus episodes, the different plot strands touch, mingle and intertwine until the shocking denouement, which demonstrates in a single brutal yet cathartic image just what Marlow has to give up in order to rejoin the human race.

The serial was directed by Jon Amiel, who has gone on to a good career in Hollywood (*Entrapment*, *Sommersby*), but he was in awe of the script when he first read it, and his only hope was that he wouldn't fuck it up. He and Potter had lunch to talk about the script, and Amiel sang its praises. But, he said, he did have some notes for Potter. Nobody gave Dennis Potter *notes* in 1985! Potter bridled, but Amiel persevered. Amiel wanted the detective story to continue through the serial rather than be only a feature of the first episode. He wanted the role of Marlow's ex-wife expanded and deepened. And the ending, he opined, was clever, but it didn't have the emotional punch required. After five-and-a-half episodes of Marlow's suffering, the audience needed a bigger pay-off than Potter had supplied. The current ending was like the solution to a crossword puzzle: intellectual but not emotional, all head and no heart. After this and another meeting, a furious row developed between the two men, with Potter hurling foul insults, and Amiel considered withdrawing from the project.

After a third, more productive meeting, Potter called Amiel and told him: "I'm rewriting it. I'm rewriting the whole thing." By this time, pre-production had begun and Potter (like his creation, suffering from psoriatic arthropathy) wrote in longhand, sometimes with a pencil strapped to the outside of his buckled fist. Nevertheless, the new scripts arrived (just) in time to be shot, and if the previous draft had been dazzling, the new version was a masterpiece. After the first full read-through, it was Potter who broke the silence. "Jesus, I didn't realize it was quite so close to the fucking bone."

The Singing Detective got huge ratings[3] and won countless awards[4] and is still regarded as a landmark piece of television. But Potter refused to work with Amiel again. His next major TV serial, *Blackeyes*, he directed (and

---

[3]The final episode recorded viewing figures of almost 10 million. The controversy of the sexual content of some of the episodes no doubt helped. Tabloid newspapers somehow knew the content of episode three before transmission. Many suspect that Potter himself tipped them off, or if not him then another member of the production team.

[4]Among them, best actor BAFTA for Michael Gambon, and a Peabody Award in 1989. It was ranked number 20 on the British Film Institute's list of the 100 Greatest British Television Programmes in 2000.

narrated) himself. Many of the discarded ideas from *The Singing Detective* crop up there, including the "crossword puzzle" ending. Whereas *The Singing Detective* was widely regarded as a work of genius, *Blackeyes* was thought to be derivative, indulgent and misogynistic.

Great creativity frequently requires collaboration to be most fully developed. The best artists combine a pure faith in their creative powers with a ruthless self-discipline to remove whatever doesn't belong or isn't working. Most people's artistic expression can be improved by collaboration, but few people are natural collaborators—fear and ego get in the way. Improvisation, on the other hand, barely exists at all without the notion of collaboration. You don't need to have all the answers at once, you don't need to spot the implications of your own ideas, you don't need to decide for yourself what of the various options you have given yourself is the most interesting. You are onstage with other talents who can help you to take these decisions, and do it all in an instant.

More often than not, though, throughout the performing arts, performers face the audience with armor on. In theory, improvisation should be the most revealing art form, but the performers are aware of this and so put on more armor than usual. Actors can draw on their unconscious inspiration in rehearsal, but they usually create a performance throughout that process and so are largely in control of what they choose to show the audience (although great actors will often access that in-the-moment spirit on the night and then the audience can feel they've seen something special). Because improvisers feel their unconscious might reveal the breakup they're going through right now, their political opinions, their childhood secrets, the things their mother used to shout at them—they don't always trust themselves to freewheel.

Actually, the audience would love to see these things represented in stories, through characters, and would sense they were truthful without knowing they were personal. What is truthful about your adolescent fears of sex is probably shared by the audience, and if not they will relate to it in some other way. Unless you've actually got a body buried in your garden, you are probably safer than you feel when improvising.

We're not suggesting that you use improvisation as some kind of cheap therapy, rather that great playwrights and screen and TV writers—whether writing comedy or drama—are revealing their own secrets, as well as those of their friends and families, all the time. Great writers often talk about the models for their characters and relate how they took real situations and "tweaked" them to create inspiring drama or hilarious comedy. Compare this to those formulaic sitcoms that fill airtime for a season before they're canceled. They're full of implausible situations and cheap gags which the writers simply don't care about. These writers aren't revealing anything of themselves here because it's a workaday job for them and they're saving their personal revelations and experiences for their own sitcom or indie screenplay.

Most improv companies are the same. They're not giving you anything of themselves, just some tricks they've learned and recycle weekly. The slicker they are, the truer this probably is. The best improv shows we've seen or been in are a bit messy around the edges. Think about the sort of improv show Salvador Dalí would host. It probably wouldn't start with World's Worst and end with a cleverly rhyming song, with everyone taking one line each.

Of course, you can't let an unsupervised unconscious out onstage—it'd be unwatchable. But a retrained brain that's learned narrative technique and some skill in presenting stories through some understanding of status and character that's then let off the leash is in a different league—almost a different medium—from a series of improvisation games performed by technically skilled joke-tellers.

Making Improvisation Pay

4.1

Performing?

Overview

How hard can it be to get paid to improvise? You put on a show, you sell tickets, you make money. We look at when this is true and not true before considering alternatives.

Some towns are theatre towns, like London, New York and Chicago. Some towns have only one or two theatres—or none at all. But being in a theatre town—even being in a comedy town—is no guarantee that there will be a ready audience for your improvised performances.

In Chicago, there is a huge audience for improvisation, that audience probably containing a high proportion of improvisers, but no more appreciative and available for that. At iO, and other institutions like it, you can also get encouragement to form your own "team" and get playing time on their stage and in front of that built-in audience. Successful teams can then go on to have a highly successful life outside of the "mother-ship." We regard this as an excellent model for assisting improv students to make the transition from learning to doing.

However, our assumption, if you are looking to make money out of improvisation, is that you are having to go it alone. We've already looked at putting a group together, finding the right team and the right space. But in almost all cases, the kinds of venues that we've looked at will struggle to make any kind of money at all, even if your show is wildly popular. Companies that have made real money out of improvisation—such as The Comedy Store Players in London and Boom Chicago in Amsterdam—do so only after huge investment in premises and promotion. And of those two, only Boom Chicago is a dedicated improv venue. The Comedy Store is a regular stand-up club five nights a week and only presents improvisation on Wednesdays and Sundays.

The economics of fringe theatre are such that if you can only take fifty people per night, once you've paid for the theatre, the advertising and the rest of the materials for the show, most of the door money will be gone. Dividing that up among a company of six to seven, plus musician, plus technician, leaves next to nothing per person. Putting it in the company coffers means that the cast doesn't get paid and so have to take other jobs besides. It would be nice if those other jobs were improv-related, hence this section of our book.

Of course, this ignores the possibility that what begins as a money-losing fringe show will explode into a phenomenon. This is not impossible, but it's not exactly a sound business plan either. For every *Jerry Springer: The Opera*, there are countless other fringe shows which—while they might thoroughly entertain the audiences that see them—never become anything more than what they were when they began. Part of the problem is that, for promoters, a one-person stand-up act is more saleable, more portable, more economical and more profitable. It is not just tradition or accident which has given the stand-up comedian dominance in the fringe/comedy genre. There are sound fiscal reasons for preferring to take one man standing behind a mic around the country, and selling his personality to audiences.

Other models are certainly possible, but improvisation, which combines the unwieldy bulk of sketch comedy with the inherent uncertainty of scriptless comedy, is often fighting an uphill battle. Shows which have succeeded have usually done so by virtue of an ingenious "hook" or by being the only game in town. Our firm advice is to devise improvisation shows you love doing, work with people you adore working with, perform your shows to audiences that enjoy them and let all that be a reward in itself. A show cynically constructed to be a success almost certainly won't be, as your heart won't be in it. If you do a show for love and you *do* love doing it, then you are ahead of the game already. If it does slay all before it at an international comedy festival, or gets picked up by a big comedy promoter or gets on the TV or radio, we'll be right there to crack open the champagne with you.

And that brings up another way to make money out of improvisation. It's not impossible that, although your style is too theatrical for other mediums, your show is too expensive to tour and your concept too hard to sell, your talented cast may very well find other acting, comedy or even improvisation work through your fringe performances. Many members of The Spontaneity Shop have been asked to lend their talents in various ways to unscripted or semi-scripted TV, radio and West End shows of various kinds, through their improvisation work in smaller venues. Your fringe show can be an excellent showcase for the individual talents in your company. Just remember, there's no particular reason why the talent scout in the audience should pick you just because you put up the money, or came up with the idea for the show or encouraged the rest of the cast to turn up for rehearsals. Be happy for their success.

4.2

Teaching Workshops

While doing and teaching are undeniably different skills, many people who have learned to improvise can teach it fairly effectively—even if all they do is replicate the lessons they learned. If you care about the medium and you enjoy sharing your experiences with others and seeing them improve, you will no doubt be able to run an effective workshop program of some kind. This is something which will almost certainly make you money if you have any ability at all in this direction. Although probably not enough to live on, the money you make can supplement your other income, or be ploughed into shows, and your workshop students will provide an audience for your shows, just as your show audience may want to sign up for your improv workshops.

All you need for an improv workshop is a space in which to run it and a bunch of willing students. Many big cities have dedicated dance studios and rehearsal rooms, and many theatres have rehearsal rooms which can be hired out. If these are too expensive, then arts centers, community centers, church halls or pub function rooms are cheaper alternatives. It's worth doing a little bit of poking around to find something nice and big with some natural light which isn't going to break the bank.

Next, you need to let people know that the workshop exists and figure out a price for it. Look around on people's websites for local market rates and decide where to set your bar, depending on the quality of the teachers you have, their experience levels, the length of the workshop, cost of the room and so on. If it's your first time teaching, you may decide to run classes for a nominal fee, which will just cover the cost of the room and some tea and biscuits, until you have more experience. As a general rule, we suggest that you set an upper limit on attendees—say sixteen—and then aim to break even, having paid for venue, advertising and all other expenses with half that.

Contributing to existing communities on Facebook and other such websites can be a good way to spread the word, and advertising on Facebook, Google and Twitter is inexpensive and can be very effective, but it requires careful monitoring to get the best results. And don't underestimate the power of printing some fliers and leaving them in local coffee shops, and especially fringe theatres and arts centers.

You also need to decide if you are offering a one-time workshop, a consecutive series or casual "drop-in" sessions. While we know other London improv companies which have thriving drop-in workshops, the model has never worked for us. In the first place, it is quite hard to teach a very mixed-ability group, and the nature of a drop-in session is that there will be a constant stream of total beginners showing up. Having to teach them not to block every week will bore and frustrate the more experienced players, who will drift away. It is also near-impossible to plan effectively if you are collecting fees on the night, since attendance is likely to fluctuate wildly.

A possible compromise is to teach a beginner's workshop every so often, and then run a weekly drop-in session for "graduates" of the beginner workshop (or, at your discretion, any more experienced improvisers who come by). This fixes one of the problems above, and if you find that you regularly get a quorum, then you're done.

As the student body grows larger, and people keep coming back for more, the other problem inherent in running drop-in workshops returns. Sooner or later, a burgeoning improv academy needs to kick out the most experienced students or introduce some kind of streaming. In many companies, the best and most experienced students get "kicked out" into the main performing company and, if handled sensitively, this can be an excellent way both of finding new performing talent (replacing those who have been poached by TV?) and of satisfying students' needs for fresh challenges and more stage time. The risk, however, is that it turns every workshop into an audition. If you are taking money to teach people to improvise, you need to make sure that, for the duration of the workshop, you are focused on helping them to improve their skills. We eventually relaxed our once-hard-and-fast rule that we would never cast people in our shows from our workshop program, but early on it was very important to us to keep this separation in place.

The other option is to stream the students. This also means that you can take all comers, but teach those with natural ability, especially natural performing ability, separately from those who find the prospect of standing before an audience more daunting. Teaching inexperienced performers to improvise means *both* imparting improvisation technique and dealing with the fundamental being-looked-at-by-strangers anxiety. Teaching experienced performers typically means much more of the former and much less of the latter. Most of the cast of The Spontaneity Shop's performing company was recruited out of workshops we taught for graduates of RADA, which were kept entirely separate from the public workshops we were teaching at the same time.

Currently, we have an open beginners' workshop, which runs over eight evenings, known as Level One, which can also be covered over two weekends. Decent attendance at Level One gains admission to Level Two, which concludes after another eight weeks with an end-of-term Micetro Impro show. Entry to Level Three is by invitation only, and Level Three students program their own shows, with our supervision, over the course of each term. This structure seems to be working for us at the moment, but who knows when we might see the need to change it again? Some kind of streaming is almost certainly required if you want to grow the student body. Ultimately, students are going to leave your workshop program, and our goal at the moment is to give them the encouragement that they need to start their own company, so that they don't need to sever relations with us, but nor do they continue to be dependent on us.

Having established your credentials as teachers, you may be able to offer your services to local drama schools or drama societies. Teaching improvisation as an acting skill is somewhat different from teaching it as an end in itself, but it can certainly make actors more responsive, more immediate and less risk-averse. Many actors are also asked to improvise in auditions, especially for commercials, and so you may be able to simply teach it as its own skill. Combining teaching your own evening classes with paid drama school work, it is certainly possible to earn some sort of a living, and it's a great way of gathering a group of like-minded people around you who can then appear onstage with your existing team, and help out by running box office, delivering fliers or operating lights for shows—possibly in exchange for workshops.

4.3

Corporate Entertainment

Another route altogether is to pursue one-off opportunities to perform essentially your basic show to corporate audiences (assuming your basic show is fast-moving and funny as opposed to gentle, slow and unfolding). Any bar-prov experience you have had will stand you in good stead here. Corporate entertainment generally means a group of businesspeople outside their normal environment at some kind of conference, convention, sales event or similar. Many use it as an excuse to eat and drink (especially drink) to excess, and then *you* come on!

You want to do your easiest, fastest, simplest, most crowd-pleasing stuff, but—as tempting as it may be—we recommend you steer clear of sex, scatology and so on. Any suggestions you get are likely to steer you in that direction, but once you head down that road, there's no going back. Just as easy and more effective is to stock up on company in-jokes. Find out what new software has just been installed that's driving everyone crazy, what the personalities are in the company, what problems they've been having with the building and so on. Drop these into your improvised games and scenes and the audience will go nuts.

You should also be prepared for some resistance to the idea of improvisation at all. At one of our first corporate entertainment jobs (a rather more civilized one than those just described), we were hired to be strolling players at a Shakespeare-themed garden party. We pitched a series of improv games performed in a Shakespearean style, but the client couldn't bear the risk of an entirely unscripted performance and so we compromised on three rehearsed Shakespearean extracts during drinks and then one improvised Shakespearean game between the main course and dessert. The rehearsed extracts took some time to prepare, but the al fresco sound system we were provided with was hit-and-miss, and the guests watched politely. The improvised Shakespearean Day In The Life game, however, was a huge hit (and we were asked back the following year to do more improv).

So you may be asked to provide written comedy sketches—possibly around which you can improvise. If you have this talent in your group, then this can be a very good compromise: giving the client security but giving you the freedom to improvise your way out of trouble if it looks like you're losing the crowd.

4.4

Corporate Training

We had not been teaching workshops for very long before one or two of our students started telling us how useful they found the skills we were imparting in their business. Great improvisers are fearless imaginers, powerful performers, expert storytellers, bold leaders, sensitive followers, happy team players and charismatic presenters. These are all qualities in great demand in business. Many improvisation companies have been successfully able to repackage improv skills as business skills, and it provides much of our income today.

A key question that needs to be answered as you enter this market is: are you on the outside looking in, or the inside looking out? There are some extremely successful corporate trainers, including ex-actors, who made a decision a long time ago that in order to really help top executives in the financial sector to be better leaders, communicators and presenters, they needed to understand the business as well as their clients did, and—even more important—look and sound like one of them. As a result, they are liked and trusted in that world and can talk the language.

Other trainers using theatre skills make their main selling point that they are presenting something which cannot be found in the business world. They are successful precisely because they seem to come from somewhere else, and because they don't duplicate abilities which can already be found within the company.

Whichever approach you take, you need to bear in mind that is rather less true today than it has been in the past (at least in the UK) that training and teambuilding are seen as desirable ends in and of themselves. More and more attempts are being made to take intangibles such as "distinctiveness," "client rapport" and "presentation skills" and to measure them before and after training has taken place. In some instances, this is very easy to do: If you are hired to give a sales team more impact, then their sales records can be examined before and after the training and you will likely get credit for any improvement. If there is no improvement, however, then you won't get re-hired!

Corporate training can be very well paid—you can get much more for a half-day's corporate training than for an evening's corporate entertainment—but you need to be very focused on delivering value to your client if you want a successful career, even a secondary one, in this area.

The following is a short list of training services which an improvisation company might be able to supply to corporate businesses of various kinds. This is by no means an exhaustive list, but should give you some ideas.

Presentation skills. If you can coach a performance out of a nervous improviser, and direct a performance out of an actor, you can do the same with a formal presentation. Very few businesspeople enjoy the process, and if you make the workshop fun, you may see some big improvements in their confidence, and therefore their skills.

Creativity/brainstorming. Most corporate brainstorms are ghastly experiences, choked with fear and ego. Improvisers can generate ideas easily and can share them happily. Passing this skill on, and running a brainstorm in a positive way, is not hard for an improv coach with a bit of personality and experience.

Teambuilding. Nothing brings a team together like a crisis, and having to do an improvised performance in a few hours' time is a huge crisis to most bankers, architects and middle-managers. However, if you are confident in your abilities to lower anxiety levels, you can teach them to play Arms Through and New Choice and they will find that they feel marvelously clever and funny. More important, the process of learning to cooperate, share ideas and act on their instincts may be very significant lessons they never forget. This is the clearest example of the Outsider approach.

Customer service/sales training. A YES AND attitude is not just a vital part of improvisation, it's a seductive trait which some people possess naturally. Passing on this skill can be of tremendous value to many kinds of businesspeople, especially those in customer service and sales. Understanding the business clearly is very important if you are going to pull this off—you need to be an Insider.

Role playing. While this can be an important element in training of all kinds, it is also possible for you and your improvisers to get employment from other companies who specialize in delivering training which requires the presence of actors to play certain roles. This will not likely leave much room for your comedy skills, but can be fairly well-paid and responsibility-light.

The kind of corporate training work you go after and get will be determined by the talents you have in your team, what you feel you can happily and successfully deliver—and the kind of work you get first, since you will get recommended for more of the same if you do well.

4.5

Corporate Events

Sitting between corporate training and corporate entertainment is corporate events work. Whereas the typical corporate training job involves you and a dozen or so executives in a conference room or studio developing a new skill, and the typical corporate entertainment job involves you and a few hundred well-lubricated executives in a hotel developing a distended liver, corporate event work generally means the same noble intent as corporate training, but the same large audiences as for corporate entertainment.

Events work can include morning "energizers," motivational speaking, break-out sessions where you deliver an abbreviated version of some of your training, acting as host or interviewer for other guests—or even more elaborate work. We put together an entire musical puppet show for one client, in which we carefully concealed some of the important business messages they wanted to communicate.

For many of these services, big names from TV and the comedy circuit are sought, and so you may find this kind of work hard to come by, but it can be a very successful blend of your abilities to teach and to entertain if you can get the job.

Related to this kind of work is promotions work. This is one of those archetypal out-of-work-actor jobs. At its worst, it involves standing around in an animal costume handing out fliers on the street, and getting paid a pittance an hour do to so. You don't need to be an experienced or inspired improviser to do this job; you need to be fit and healthy, have a low boredom threshold, not mind the smell of your own sweat and have an underdeveloped sense of shame. However, more elaborate work does exist, and some companies will approach improvisers where interaction with members of the public is concerned (sometimes called "invisible theatre").

Generally, the point of setting up your own show is artistic fulfillment, and if you can pay yourself, that's a nice bonus. With corporate work, the opposite tends to be true. You are hoping that the job will be well-paid, and if it happens to be artistically interesting, or even just not humiliating, then that's a nice bonus. Promotions work is almost always humiliating to a greater or lesser degree, so you need to make sure you are getting very well paid for it. Don't be afraid to pass on work of this kind which looks like it's going to be long hours, or dreadful costumes, or lots of travel for not much money. Put the time instead into building your reputation in other areas, and better-paid work you can be prouder of will come your way.

A CORPORATE LOWLIGHT

Our worst day ever of this kind of work must have been the time we were employed by a newspaper to satirize a political party conference. We ended up on the beach in an almighty sandstorm having our photos taken by a tabloid photographer. I can just remember one of the improvisers turning to me and shouting through the sand "I'm suffering, but I'm not sure it's art!" We went for coffee and found ourselves surrounded by autograph hunters because Gary Turner, one of our longest-standing company members, had just come out of a stint on the popular soap opera *Emmerdale*. He had been playing a heartthrob so there were all sorts of hysterical fans wanting to touch him. The next minute, the photographer decided Gary should clamber into a nearby skip (dumpster) to show just how washed up this party was. I remember thinking "The Spontaneity Shop has gone as low as it can go. We're actually in a skip." I was wrong. The next minute a man came out of a shop looking irate and shouted "Get out of my skip!"

This seems to be a perfect metaphor for show business. One minute you're signing autographs and the next you're being evicted from a skip.

—*Deborah*

4.6

How to Get Corporate Work

Whereas you will probably get a dozen or so students to your improvisation workshop simply by putting a few ads on Facebook and leaving some fliers in a fringe theatre, corporate work is often much harder to come by. Very few companies will employ you without a recommendation, especially for corporate training where they have to be able to trust you enough to tell you where they are going wrong. Once you have been in business for a while, you will have collected testimonials which can adorn your website. Once potential clients see a few famous brand names associated with praiseworthy comments, they will relax considerably.

But to get started, you will probably have to use a different strategy. You need to get a recommendation from elsewhere, either by partnering with an existing training provider or by getting your contacts to provide you with an introduction. Even better: combine the two.

We were lucky enough to be teaching actor Alex Khan at one of our RADA graduate classes who had also worked as an athletics coach. It transpired that the runner Roger Black credited this actor with encouraging him to give up soccer for athletics, which was of particular significance to us, as Roger was now making a killing on the motivational speaking circuit, and partnering with his brother Alistair who was running a corporate training business. Alex insisted we meet Alistair, who agreed to try us out at the end of a telecommunications conference, where we played Yes And and Pointing At Things with seventy-odd men who looked like they hadn't laughed in twenty years. At the end of the event, they were darting around the hotel lobby like children and our corporate training careers were off and running.

Women in Improv

By Deborah Frances-White

Since we wrote the first edition of the book, much has changed in gender politics in both the wider world and in improvisation. In the United Kingdom, most of the well-known and more successful improv companies have a great gender balance—and if anything, more women than men. I rarely hear complaints of women being relegated to always playing secretaries and girlfriends (nothing wrong with either!), while men insist on playing CEOs and doctors. If your company still has this problem, seek out groups that don't. Watch them. Ask their improvisers to guest in your shows and try to get rid of that problem. If you're an all-male group and can't find women to play with you, ask them why they don't want to and listen to their answer. I've cut most of this essay for this edition of the book, because I feel it's dated. And I'm really happy about that. I've left just what's below in case anyone is still feeling a pervasive sexism in improvisation in their part of the world. I think the next thing improvisation needs to tackle is frankly how white it is. This was parodied brilliantly by Key and Peele in their "only black guy in the college improv troupe" sketch. Talent scout and invite people of color into your company. Comedy is meant to reflect the human condition. Only a part of this condition is white. A minority of human experience is white, straight and cis-gendered male. If your group can only reflect this experience in an increasingly villagey globe, that will probably be reflected in its ticket sales.

* * *

Members of companies which only have men have told me rather defensively—although I haven't asked—that women don't want to improvise, are not funny or are simply not good enough to cast. These companies are normally creating a competitive environment on stage. Sometimes they have a token woman who is constantly endowed with being a sex object or a secretary or both. Women who don't want to be treated like they are in a 1950s film simply leave and find another group to play with or something else to do. Apart from the obvious old-fashioned sexual politics at work here, it is artistically and comedically limiting for the women on stage to be always the nurse and never the doctor. It is my opinion that women leave more often because they are bored than offended. I saw a scene at a festival recently where some men waited nervously in a waiting room for a meeting with the big boss of a corporation. A woman entered the room and they immediately endowed her with being the PA and she went along with it and brought them coffee and told them the boss was running late. As they were out of improvisers, the whole scene became about the men waiting and the audience never got to see the meeting. The scene was one long, tedious putting-off of the future.

Under these circumstances, it is not a block for the woman to say, "Why do you assume I'm the PA? I'm the CEO." It feeds the scene and it contradicts the assumption of the characters, not the big offer on the table that the improvisers made—that they had a meeting with a CEO. It pushes the action on and puts the characters in trouble. Female improvisers can train the people they work with by coming out and making strong offers and playing strong characters. Start a scene as the surgeon, the police chief or the president, and within a few weeks that will become normal.

If your group can only find one or two women who will agree to perform in your shows and you suspect that you are fostering a competitive, aggressive environment, it is possible that the women you have are happy to play that way. If you want to change that trend because you find it destructive and wish to attract different women to the group, you have to go back to basics. It is impossible to play collaboratively, YES AND each other and be generous if you are encouraging an atmosphere of every "man" for himself. A simple way to breed collaboration out of competition is to make a competitive game out of it: first to block loses, or anyone who GAGS at the expense of the story is tagged out, for example.

In only a few cases have I witnessed or experienced real bullying. In one improv "jam" show at a festival, I was on the stage with half-a-dozen men and I was the only woman. I was a very experienced improviser and had often performed in large male-heavy shows, so to be honest, I didn't really notice. When a scene was glorifying domestic violence in what I thought was an inane way, I played a character who objected to these views. This went down well with the audience, but very badly with the other performers. After that some of the men on the stage ganged up on me during and between scenes. My strategy was to make them look good because I figured that they wanted status. They sarcastically insisted I set up a scene so they could do things my way, so I set up a kung fu spoof because I knew they were good at it and I didn't enter the scene.

The hectoring continued and I figured that treating it as good-natured banter was the way to go, but laughing it off seemed only to exacerbate it. When one of the improvisers turned some sharp-legged chairs upside down and announced we were going to play a game where improvisers pushed each other onto the spiky legs, I made a joke and left the stage. I realized I was a person first and an improviser second. If someone offers me a part in a scripted play I can read the script, and if I feel its values are wildly different from my own, I can turn it down. Sometimes, if you improvise with people you don't know, you can end up in a show you don't want to put your name on. Leaving the stage is an absolute last resort. I've never done it before or since. I came back for the finale, and afterwards some of the improvisers apologized that the "teasing" had got out of hand. I explained that I wasn't upset or emotional about it—just surprised. At the point I didn't want to be in the show anymore, I realized that nothing was keeping me there.

Our company revels in good-natured banter, and once we had a whole Gorilla Theatre show which became a battle about gender politics. It's one of my favorite improvisation memories because it felt playful and intelligent and exciting to the players and the audience. We cross-cast scenes and revisited them from the point of view of a man and then a woman. However, in this case I respected the values and views of those I shared the stage with. The show I did at the festival was an unhappy experience because it seemed that some of the people on stage really didn't like sharing the stage with a woman (at one point I was physically restrained and at another, publicly stopped from speaking), and maybe that's why they were an all-male group.

I wouldn't see a scene glorifying domestic violence or blatant misogyny in any company I respect because both the men and women in those groups are clever, decent people. It simply wouldn't occur to them to put those views on the stage, so it's never been an issue. They wouldn't shy away from playing a reprehensible character but they would know that their partner in the scene would thwart them in some way or they would lower their own status and be changed.

Regardless of whether you are a man or a woman, work with people who you like and whose views you respect. If you notice in their actions or their conversation that you don't like their values or opinions, then don't work with them. This is not true of scripted work, but in improvisation those opinions will be aired on the stage and you will be complicit. If you are a woman and you don't feel respected on stage, it's probably because you are not respected offstage. That's lose-lose. Leave and start your own group with people you like. If you're a man and feel that your group would be better if there were more women in it, but women don't want to play with you, work out why. If you can't fix it, then start a new group and invite women you think are fun and talented in from the get-go. Groups that are co-founded by women seem to rarely experience these issues.

Improvisation is predominantly straight and white, too. This certainly isn't true of theatre and it's not even true of stand-up comedy any more. It's probably as well that we start to analyze why and make our workshops more accessible and welcoming to different sectors of society. Not out of any worthy, liberal motive, but because if we are to reflect society in any meaningful comedic way, we need to reflect the views and values of that society. Most film and TV comedy has extended its range of characters to be inclusive of a modern, cosmopolitan society. It's probably time we caught up. Talking about it won't make it so, but it's a start.

Talking to Improvisers

5.1

Keith Johnstone—The Innovator

Keith Johnstone invented many classic improv games both in London in the 1950s and 1960s and in Calgary from the 1970s onwards. His books are seminal texts. He still teaches improvisation in Calgary and internationally.

What are the most important things for an improviser to know?

I would say to help the other person, to give the other person a good time. Try and give the other improviser what they want. Also don't try to be clever. Be obvious. And be audible.

What do you think are the most common blocks for improvisers?

Fear—which often comes across as arrogance. We want improvisers to look humble and courageous. Your job is to sell good nature. You can't be good natured if you're terrified.

What do you think is the future of improvisation?

It would be nice if people were interested in being truthful rather than funny. Because truthful things are funnier.

What do you think of Del Close's work?

Del Close got me to Chicago in 1982, I think. He read *Impro* and phoned me up and got me down there. It was the first time I realized my attitude was a bit different. We worked together for about two weeks. We were basically trying to do the same thing, but his origins were in cabaret and mine were in theatre. Also my interests were in storytelling, which is why our work is different. I would watch the shows with him and Del would be furious if the improvisers were just screwing around. He'd say "They're fucking around again!" I didn't mind because I hadn't seen it before and I'll watch people do anything for twenty minutes if people look happy.

I can't imagine Del Close saying "You can't ask questions." He might tell one person that, but then so might I, if that's all they were doing or if there were a good reason for it. Del's much better than that. I sat with him every night at Second City. He showed me two Harolds. I couldn't think why he was doing it. I think he was trying to get it to have some point. David Shepherd showed me two as well. I think probably what Del was trying to attack was to stop it being a total waste of time. But how does starting from one word do that?

Why do you think you see so much presentational acting in improvisation?

In life, showing emotion is natural. It just happens. You only try to show emotions when you're lying. For example, you might try to convince your lover you're still interested when you're not. Sometimes in life we pretend to be more upset than we are to score points but it's an unnatural state and we don't generally enjoy doing it. Waiters aren't trying to show you what they feel. They're trying to hide what they feel. They don't want to pretend they have extra emotions; they're trying to pretend they're not irritated with you or trying not to show that they're thinking about their break up.

Improvisers always try to show you their emotions, which is the opposite of what most of us are doing in real life. Fighting your emotions or letting the audience see you try to hide them makes you more vulnerable than displaying them ostentatiously.

What separates good improvisers from great ones?

In improvisation rules are for beginners. Great improvisers, like great actors can really be in the moment—almost in a trance state. Drama is one person changed by another. Otherwise it's not drama. It's just literature. If you don't enter the trance state, if you're not really there and really changed, it's probably just literature.

It's natural not to want be changed while we're being looked at. Most people prefer to look busy, unattainable or cross to avoid change, but great improvisers are open. They have learned to enjoy being changed while an audience watches. If you have had a wonderful night improvising and you are very open and available on stage, the audience will want to take you home with them. I recommend you do not go with them but that is how they will feel. They're not used to seeing people so open and available and playful.

Why do you think it's so hard to be open and available?

Because people are watching. You might be able to make a perfect omelet, but if a thousand people are watching you'll try to do it better and you'll fuck it up. No ape likes being stared at. It makes them feel threatened. That's why making theatre can be terrifying.

Improvisers often look scared at the start of the show or tormented at the start of the scene. But where's the pleasure in tormenting you if you already started that way? Start with charm, confidence and courage. Then screw up and stay happy. Enjoy being bad. It's better to have a good time being bad than a bad time being good.

In martial arts, before they let you fight, they teach you how to fall. Before an improviser learns anything they should learn how to fail and stay happy. It's not that bad improvisers are untalented. It's just that they're using their talents to produce consistent behavior and stay out of trouble. Improvisers don't like sharing control because dangling off a cliff by your fingertips doesn't feel as dangerous as someone else dangling you off it.

What's the cause of unimaginative work or times when improvisers feel uninspired?

Sometimes improvisers feel they don't have ideas. They do have ideas. The trouble is they have ideas that *stop* the car moving. It's a long and painful process teaching people to move into the future. Improvisers need to be an expert in knowing what the other improviser wants. Make an offer. Does your partner light up? Sometimes an idea isn't good or bad in the abstract, but the problem is an improviser attaches ego to their idea and won't let it go, even if it doesn't inspire anyone else or move the scene on. When I'm directing, I try to come up with lots of ideas until I find one the improvisers like. Sometimes in Micetro I'll ask an improviser "What kinds of stories do you like?" They might say, "Rags to riches" and then I'll know how to please them. The problem when you're directing is if the actors start planning the next bit you can't work with them. In scripted work, actors underline their own lines in the script. Really they should underline the other actors' lines because it's by them they can be altered.

Why do you think the form of improvisation hasn't developed much beyond Theatresports and the Harold, whereas film has moved on so much in the same period of time?

Any idiot can get up and do it [improv]. Film is Darwinian. To some extent, if they're no good, they won't make money and they won't be asked again. That's why Micetro is better than Theatresports: because the audience can eliminate. Often improvisation attracts people who want to be the center of attention.

Sometimes in notes at The Moose I'd say, "The audience had a wonderful time. The show was fine. But was it worth doing?" It would shock the visitors to the Summer School. For me, everything has meaning. Every sequence of events has implications, and often I don't like the implications. The audience is often sadistic, of course. Fear plus pressure from the audience turns it into light, harmless entertainment. But the idea of doing theatre games based on audience suggestions is not exactly demanding.

I think unless your work in public is better than your work in rehearsals, there's something seriously wrong. Then you're confronting the problem. We need to solve that problem.

5.2

Neil Mullarkey—The Comedy Store Player

Ex-Cambridge Footlights President Neil Mullarkey founded the Comedy Store Players with (among others) Mike Myers and Paul Merton in 1985, and he still performs with them, usually twice weekly. He also runs "improvyourbiz" workshops with many different organizations.

Tell me about Mullarkey and Myers and how you started improvising.

I met Mike Myers at The Gate Theatre in Notting Hill Gate. He was writing some sketches but had nowhere to perform them. I thought he was really funny and told him he should be doing "alternative comedy." That's what was happening in London at the time (1985). So we started working together as a sketch double act [Mullarkey and Myers]. We got a "try-out" gig at a dodgy pub in Chiswick. We had to do five minutes but we only had three minutes of material, so we had to improvise for two minutes. I was terrified. After that I went to do a workshop with Desmond Jones. Around that time we met Kit Hollerbach, who had learned to improvise in San Francisco and had worked with Robin Williams. Mike and Kit got some comedians together and taught some workshops.

Before I did that I'd never seen people improvise, so I assumed that they'd got a suggestion from the audience and then gone to a sketch they'd already written. When people ask me now if we secretly prepare sketches, I always tell them that we're far too lazy to do any such thing.

Why was Mike Myers in London in the first place?

He'd toured Canada with Second City. He was the youngest male ever to join Second City. His parents were English, so he had a British passport and loved British comedy. He just decided he'd go and live in England.

How did The Comedy Store Players start?

I'm not sure whether The Store approached Kit or she approached them. Our first show at The Store was in October 1985. The first half of the show was stand-up because no one thought people would come to see improvisation on its own. After three months we were allowed to do the entire show.

By October 1986, Don Ward, who owned the Comedy Store, said, "I'm not making any money on this, I have to take a door split." Within about six weeks our door split was more than he'd been giving us before. Somehow it built, and then *Whose Line* came along and we were much more part of the zeitgeist.

In Westminster there was a by-law, in Leicester Square you had to charge £5 a head and nobody else in comedy was charging anything like that much. So we had to persuade people to become members and have two for the price of one. We used to give a prize for the best suggestion, which we started doing again at our thirtieth anniversary. People like it.

What's the prize?

Two free tickets.

How much is it now?

£17 and £12 concession. What a bargain!

How much of the audience is repeat business and how much is new?

I'd love to know. Recently, I've been saying to the audience at the end of the first half, "Okay, it's the interval but I'm just going to find out who's been here before, once, twice, five times, more?" There are quite a few people for whom it's the first time. "Who was even alive on 27 October 1985?" I ask. And there are quite a few. As well as youngsters who can only imagine what life was life before the internet...

If Mike came from a long-form or Harold background, why do The Comedy Store Players do short-form games?

Mike had done lots of short and long form at Second City. I think games are the easiest thing to teach beginners, and we were just starting out. The show worked, so we never really changed it. Also, although we play games, in a way it's like one long two-hour game because we have so many callbacks (or "re-incorporations") from earlier in the show.

Were you ever tempted to try other things?

Once the Sunday show was selling out, we decided to start a second night on Wednesday. Originally, the plan was to try something edgier but then when we got there, there was a queue around the block and there was pressure to put on a good show, so we did many of the "Sunday" games. Then we just got used to doing the same games both nights. Now we'd be uneasy doing anything else.

But some of you do different shows elsewhere.

Oh yes. Lee [Simpson] does shows with Improbable, both scripted and improvised (such as Animo, with puppeteers and prop-makers and musicians, which are very inventive). There are Paul Merton's Impro Chums, the Stephen Frost All-Stars and Josie does The Glenda J Collective. At The Store we're far too set in our ways. The advantage is we're experienced at what we do.

Do you always do exactly the same thing?

We do the same running order, yeah, but I wouldn't call it doing exactly the same thing. Each show is unique. Last night I played a donkey.

Do you never get bored?

No. Those are the games that work on that small stage in an environment where you can't be as theatrical as you would be with a more theatrical space with wings and so on.

Do you never find you're repeating yourself?

We do Freeze Tag every show, and when the energy needs a bit of quick boost of energy, we'll come on and say something like, "I'm milking a huge cow or reading a paper." But we try not to do that too much, even though much of the audience hasn't seen that before.

They don't care.

They don't. In a way, as Jim Sweeney once said, "It's a show about six people putting on an improv show." What he means by that is we will dimp and pimp, but that's the game. We know we can do it. And the basic trust we share is not lost within that. In a way it's sort of beyond an impro show. It's a sitcom with six people who know each other very well. There's a meta-text: "I'm blocking at this moment, but in an interesting way, because I know you can make an offer."

"Dimp" and "pimp"?

That's Mike Myers's jargon, maybe from Second City. "Pimping" is making someone do something difficult. Like saying "That South African guy with a limp will be here in a minute." "He speaks in rhyme, doesn't he?" "Yes, that's right." One of the other improvisers has to come in and play that guy, and the audience is on their side if they have a go and don't wimp out of it. "Dimping" is dissing another player, I suppose. Like pointing out that their accent isn't all that Welsh or that they've just walked through a mime table. The audience love watching us tease each other, as long as it's still in the right spirit of attentive playfulness.

Now of course, you might say, there is the Keith Johnstone game, which is the blocking game, which is I'll block you and you block me. "Hey, I'm Stella, I haven't seen you for ages," "No," "Yes you have."

"Yes you have, I passed you in the street yesterday. You ignored me."

"I ignored you, yes. Because you ignored me." I don't know, that was an accept, darn it! But the thing is, when the game is to block, the offer is the block. It's to find a creative way to get around the block. So the block is an offer in disguise.

We're blocking in an offery way. Because the audience are now going to be interested into why we're ignoring each other.

We know the game, yeah. There's a guy called Robert Poynton. He wrote a book called *Everything Is an Offer*. He was part of On Your Feet which have done various things, applied improv stuff, like I do now. I met them through the Applied Improv Network some years ago. And their definition of an offer is "something somebody gives you which you can do something with." Which is beautifully open and helpful, because even what feels like a block, there's something you can do with it.

Is this in life or just on stage?

Well, both. Robert's book is about how improv might apply to places outside the theatre. So it was his journey as a marketing man to learn improv from somebody who'd done improv who then got into business with him. So they came from their different worlds. They have a little example of, "Let's paint the room blue." And the big Yes And is, "Yes, let's paint the entire house blue!" But is the offer blue or paint? Or let's change the décor? All of the above? And the big block would be, "No, I hate painting, and I hate you." That's clearly a block. But in between those two, there's a huge area for negotiation. Which is, "I like painting, I'm not sure blue would work here," or something like that. So what's the offer?

If you said that to me on-stage, my immediate response would be "Do you know it's a boy?"

Oh yes, great! Hurrah!

"You said we weren't going to find out." "I have found out."

Yeah, there you go, you see. But there would be nothing wrong with that. It might not have been the offer the other actor was thinking of giving. But the audience just likes watching the game we're playing with each other. They like to see us having fun. It's like a six-person double act, as Brian Logan of *The Guardian* said. We may pimp each other and the audience love to see us rising to the challenge. We didn't know it would last this long. And we are realizing we may be in danger of being a bit samey. But actually the audience likes what we do, so our innovation is pushing the form, so stepping out, breaking the fourth wall, enhancing the sitcom element. In the end, though, we still do pretty good improv, dare I say it.

Is it like a band now though? Because you've been going so long, people don't want anything from the new album, so you can't experiment.

We couldn't do anything too experimental. We have to provide comedy, we're at the Comedy Store. Many people have never heard of our "band," they've been brought along by their friend. There's a group outing and some of them might not even know it's improv. On the other hand, there are some people who've travelled from around the world. They saw *Whose Line* years ago, or they've seen the re-runs on Dave and they want to see these people. So we're catering to a broad range of expectations, but we have to keep still supplying the funny.

It would be hard for you not to be funny now though, I think.

Probably yeah.

Did you have ever a flat show where things aren't funny?

No. Occasional moments. I say we're always been between seven out of ten and 9.9 out of ten. The audience who come intermittently or for the first time wouldn't know the difference really.

But in your head you can see the difference?

The seven is probably Wednesdays before Christmas. We have a full house, but many people have had no investment in the show at all. It's an office party, they've been drinking, they've come to the Comedy Store, so they've got there early for Happy Hour. And so they're drunk and/or some of them are thinking, "Why are we here?" "I want to get off with Dave from accounts." Or "Why aren't we at a restaurant?" Or "Why aren't we dancing? Why aren't we having Jaeger Bombs somewhere else? Why are we having to sit in silence while people talk to us?"

So the audience's focus is lost. And our focus can be lost. When you're improvising, although it looks like you're just coasting, you're actually concentrating a great deal and I think it's much more fragile than doing a tough corporate gig where you're, kind of, steaming through your set with occasional ad-libs. This is much more fragile, you're creating theatricality, you're creating a fourth wall, you don't know what you're going to say next. And the moment somebody over there starts talking, you lose the focus. So those three Wednesdays in December we dread a little. But we often come off and go, "That wasn't as bad as we expected," since we had low expectations. Those shows give less opportunity to use finesse and grace moments, pauses and silences, and true genre points.

There are the times when you think, okay, this is one of those nights where we're not going to surf the audience's good will, they'll enjoy us going on flights of joyous fancy and imagination, we have to keep it going, keep the pace up and the rhythm of comedy and a laugh every thirty seconds or so. Which probably, in a more theatrical environment, and with the purists in Chicago, you don't have to worry about too much.

I think that's a very specific problem when you've got corporates because they are a large group that knows each other. I think it's like music festivals; you have to make it all about them because that's all they care about.

That's why I developed my alter-ego L. Vaughan Spencer (www.succeedy.com) because then I can plumb in all of that stuff about them into my existing script. So I've got 90 percent script and the 10 percent is stuff they give me before the show starts or that emerges on the night. In that corporate environment where the client gives you a bunch of stuff, which is funny or not, it's harder to bring into an entirely improvised show like the Comedy Store Players. Especially when there are five of you doing it. Whereas I can slot it in to my alter ego's script quite easily, as well interact with the audience. So if somebody says something that night, I can use that. So I can do everything about that group and especially if I've said can you put three or four people at the front, everyone knows and likes. And I then tease them as if they're complete losers. So I've got much more ammunition. Whereas if we're creating scenes and scenarios set in a garage it's harder.

When the Players do corporate things occasionally, we do a musical about A Day in the Life of somebody in the crowd, and so that's when we can do all of that in-house stuff. Those are quite scary, because at the Comedy Store we have mics, we have sound, we have bouncers. When we're doing a corporate after-dinner gig they may be expecting Kriss Akabusi or Bjorn Again or Derren Brown or third-rate versions of those. And we come on and say we haven't got a script and can we have a suggestion, please. Whereas at the Comedy Store they kind of roughly know or they begin to learn, okay when we say "Give me a musical," don't just say Mrs. Thatcher's bottom or something like that. They try and think of something...

I feel like we're now thirty years ago with Mrs. Thatcher's bottom. It feels like you really are remembering 1989.

That's very bizarre, yesterday somebody suggested at Mrs. Thatcher's funeral as a location.

Oh my god.

And also these days, occasionally you get as a location, Tinder. As a location.

Did you do it?

We didn't, because we didn't know what Tinder was, or some of us didn't. We didn't do it. Maybe we should have done.

I would have thought all the Comedy Store Players are on Tinder now?

No, but I'm shocked to hear that the protocol with Tinder is that we're having a date, I've met you on Tinder, it's not going that well, I go to the toilet, I go on Tinder. Who's nearby? Click left, click right. I come back saying, "Oh, I'm not feeling too good," and I go next door and there's somebody else there. You can have many Tinders in one night.

You can multi-Tinder. Is this the Comedy Store Players getting hip, getting down with the kids?

Kind of not. We had to explain to Paul Merton what hashtag meant the other day.

Stop it.

Hashtag awkward.

There's no way he doesn't know that, he's on Have I Got News for You. *How can he possibly not have heard of a hashtag?*

He kind of knows what it is, he's heard of it.

He literally has never hashtagged.

But he reads the papers. So his work, his TV job, is reading the papers and he will buy newspapers. He doesn't have email or a mobile phone.

Do guest players change the way you improvise?

If we have guests playing we don't do pimp and dimp with them unless we know them well. Like when Mark Rylance came to play with us, we didn't do it to him. He's an actor so he really listened to our offers. He's since won an Oscar. I'm sure that it's in large measure to do with what he learned from us... If Phelim McDermott [from the innovative theatre company Improbable, which he shares artistic directorship of with Comedy Store Player Lee Simpson] comes to play with us, he uses the whole space. He may even go into the audience. And he plays wonderful characters. After he's been I'm always conscious to do that, but to be honest, we may be prisoners of our own success. When I've done other things like Animo with Improbable I've really enjoyed it. But what we do has become comfortable. There are six of you and it's like your own home and you can do it even when you're a bit tired. But for a show-off like me, there can't be many more satisfying things to do.

When stand-up comedians come along, do they normally play more your way?

They can do both. Marcus [Brigstocke] is brilliant but he knows theatre, he's a great listener. He can create a character, he can play the genre, he'll pick up threads, story. Phill Jupitus, Miles Jupp and Dave Johns ditto. There aren't many stand-ups who play with us, though.

Those four are all actors as well.

Yeah, then they want to be seen as actors, not just stand-ups, so they appreciate the importance of listening and being generous…They love being part of a gang, as well.

Why does improvisation appeal to you?

When you go to stand-up or other comedy shows it's rare for the whole audience to laugh all at the same time. There may be a few people who aren't getting it. But when you go to an impro show, the whole audience are on the edge of their seats laughing together. Other forms of comedy are more demographically dependent perhaps, but everyone loves impro. People always ask me "What do you do when you can't think of anything?" But watching someone struggle to think of something can be wonderful. Freud said that pleasure is the relief of pain. And improvisation is a sort of exquisite pain. The audience are always so relieved when you do come up with something, and there's a pleasure in fearing you won't and being relieved.

But bad improv can be painful to watch. What's happening there, do you think?

Ah yes. That's when improvisers are trying too hard, not listening and saying too many things. Saying nothing or repeating what someone else has said can often be funnier.

Is that because an audience would rather see someone be vulnerable than someone trying to be clever?

Yes, I'm sure that's true.

When was the thirtieth anniversary show?

Sunday, October 25, 2015.

Was it sold out?

Yes. We did a month of celebrations because we found that everyone wants to come to that particular show. The anniversary shows are always sold out ahead of time. And so we found some old pictures of ourselves looking very young and rather more beautiful than we do now. And we have a slide show before the curtain up showing these pictures, which is quite nice, isn't it?

How long will you go on for?

I don't know. It's a good question. Until we die, really.

Do you think you'll make a fiftieth anniversary?

I don't know. I'm sure they'll be some people still doing a show called the Comedy Store Players in twenty years' time.

Do you have any kind of succession planning?

We have allowed some people under forty to play with us occasionally. Cariad Lloyd, Joseph Morpurgo from Austentatious, Pippa Evans and Ruth Bratt from Showstoppers. The thing is, we want people to have a good time so you have to sort of feel that when they come into the dressing room they know at least two or three faces, and they're not overawed by the whole thing. Lee's advice is always keep up the volume, don't do jokes. Which means don't try too hard, but when you're nervous you dip a bit in projection.

How do you decide who guests with you?

There are people who've been helping us out regularly for many of those thirty years (apart from the names I've mentioned so far) like Stephen Frost, Steve Steen, Niall Ashdown, Phelim McDermott, Suki Webster, Steve Edis (and Greg Proops and Mike McShane when they are in the UK) and others who we like to give a slot to when possible. Sometimes, there are hardly any berths available at all. Because we six have first refusal. So if Josie's not off doing a show, or Paul Merton is not touring somewhere or doing a TV or radio, there are hardly any gaps

But if in fifty years' time...

In fifty years' time, one of us will be dead. Probably. So one of those six berths will be taken by somebody else.

In fifty years' time, one of you will be dead!?

Well 100 percent of us might be dead!

I don't want to be pessimistic here so I'm going to ask you something else. What does your improv do for the rest of your life?

I think I probably do say "Yes And" more in life. Most of my work now is teaching in the corporate environment, teaching improv, leadership, creativity, teamwork, or doing talks at conferences or coaching. So, I use improv every day in my work.

Now, was I drawn to improv because I was a Yes And person, or do I look now at life and think "What can I Yes And?" Discuss. But just the simple idea of an offer, so everything is an offer. You can easily write the book on "everything is a block," it's just how you frame it. "That wasn't what I was expecting to happen, oh no, my idea has gone." Anyway, so I do see things as offers. But is that because I was brought up or born that way? I don't know. If something goes wrong, I'm thinking well that means it's an opening to the other possibilities. There's a Yes But there, but that means the other thing is the thing to follow. Or what can I learn from that setback? I do look for that.

I would say that the Comedy Store Players have, of the probably all the other groups in world that I've seen, one of the greatest spirits of play. How did you get so playful?

I don't know, that's interesting. The playfulness is the willingness to step outside the genre and break the fourth wall and so forth. So the playfulness came gradually, I suppose. Kit Hollerbach and Mike Myers, both of them were very proper improvisers but not at all dogmatic nor po-faced.

Mike was never one to tell us you can't do this or that, for example, ask questions of another character in a scene. He would ask if that question was really an offer, or was it "commenting" and not committing to the scene. Maybe it was a block, not justifying the other person, a question which stopped the action. And also he'd say teaching scenes don't tend to be the strongest, because you tend not to have somewhere to go. So you want to find some emotional connection over and above teacher and student.

The smallness of the stage, the fact that it's a Comedy Store, it's not a theatre affects things too. I think the playfulness came to the fore over time. You couldn't really justify much theatricality because you see everything there, you see the performance at either side of the stage. So sometimes we wink to the people off stage. There's a deft sense of Music Hall rather than Shakespeare.

Some other improvisers would say hang on a minute, that isn't helping the scene. And there are times we probably go too "playful," and the story gets lost. The story works because it's both funny and has some narrative momentum. The audience does want closure, even at the Comedy Store, even with short form. They do want some sense of story and we do a half-hour narrative that has a sense of story and if it gets too clunky we all feel frustrated. We walk a dangerous line between playfulness and story.

And the nights that it gets too playful, do you get frustrated?

I think the playfulness sometimes inhibits what I think the audience really do want, yet they may not know it. Which is, let's go for the story, let's invest in these characters. All the things that the purest improviser would certainly agree with. Our best moments are when we come from playfulness and step back into the story. And then the playfulness actually informs the story. It's most satisfying when the playfulness, the naughtiness, then somehow becomes involved in the story. A wayward comment, a throwaway aside, could become the spine of the story.

What's the best thing, or the most important thing, you think that you learnt from Kit and Mike?

Establish a reality. Clarify what and where, who are you, what are doing, where you. Without those three basic building blocks you just have two commenters. And Mike would often say something like this, the worst kind of improv scene, is "Oh hello, who are you? Look there's a thing happening over there. Yes, it makes me angry." The thing must be between you and me, it must be here. And Mike would say, "Why have the gods of improv chosen this scene, today, here, now?" Like William Goldman's advice to start the scene as late as possible. It's who are you, what you are doing, why are you here? You can never stop answering those simple questions.

5.3

Randy Dixon—The Synthesizer

Randy Dixon is regarded as one of the most experienced improvisational artists in the northwest United States. He was a member of the legendary Seattle improvisation troupe None of the Above. In 1983 he was a founding member of Unexpected Productions, and he has served as the company's Artistic Director since 1988.

What do you think an improviser absolutely needs to know? If someone had never improvised before and was going out on stage for the first time, what things would you tell them?

Trust your partner, the audience is already on your side, and above all else…listen.

Improvisation is about fifty years old in its current form—why do you think so many groups are still doing some version of Theatresports or the Harold and looking back rather than innovating?

Well, with improv being new to many people over the years I think they start with the basics which are these forms. Most groups learn the games, then want to organize the games, so along comes Theatresports. After a while, improvisers want to do longer work, so they turn to Harold, which was created around 1967.

I think another reason is that these forms are taught in many cities. It's amazing with almost a hundred long-forms that Harold is still a basic block. I call it the "bouillon cube" of long-form because there's a little bit of Harold in everything.

There doesn't seem to be a lot of groups building on those schools or rejecting them and breaking out into something new. I ask this especially of you as I know you and your group are big on innovation. Why is this a goal of isolated groups rather than movements? Or am I wrong about this? If you think innovation is a trend, where and how?

Well, one is that many of the masters are still with us. As long as they keep teaching, we will still have these camps. I think people find their way into the woods with a teacher and then just stay on that path. What I don't understand is the complete rejection of other paths. Improv should be inclusive, not exclusive.

I think I first made my mark breaking down these walls for myself. The "Keith says…" camp versus the Del Heads, versus the Spolin, versus … I thought that everyone was talking about the same thing but with a different emphasis. So, I began studying and working with all of them and contrasting the philosophies. I really think the "camps" are getting old and too dogmatic. It's along the same lines of the short-form versus long-form discussion that has been going on for decades. It's a waste of time if the goal is storytelling, because that encompasses all work.

I think groups don't innovate because there is less reward for innovation. First off, the most popular forms of improv we have seen on stage and on TV are the safest forms. Festivals are organized and everyone comes and plays their greatest hits rather than really bringing something new. Then everyone sees the latest "Oh, they are doing styles or they are using puppets!" and they return back to their cities and pretty much reinvent the wheel. I have been around long enough to see these cycles return again and again.

In Seattle we try both, we try to do the most entertaining Theatresports that we can muster *and* also try to push the forms further. We have our own space, which helps, and do lots of shows. I think Unexpected Productions has been successful at innovation because any of our improvisers have a long history in the field and want to do something new. Also because in Seattle we are doing improv as an art unto itself because no one is trying to parlay their work directly into a TV career, etc., that you have in many larger cities. Improvisers who see the improvement of the art form as the goal are easily inspired to innovate.

After an individual has improvised for a few years with success, they often get stuck or plateau. What would you suggest they do to get out of a rut?

It will happen many times along the path. Improvisers need to make a choice in these moments. Keep improvising through it, or stop improvising altogether. I have seen improvisers go both ways.

The best way is through and not around, because the payoff is always great. I think the plateau really is an indication of a rebirth as a performer that wants to happen. My suggestions are to try things differently for a while. Change up your game choices, your warm-ups, your characters, the clothes to perform in, the route to the theatre … everything! The change will come anyway if you stick to it, but the changes will expedite the process. In a way, the plateau is an artistic cocooning where the performer feels much more limited than before during this period, but much more liberated when it lifts.

What's the secret of being a good improvisation teacher?

Having a lesson plan, but always being willing to toss it out the window in favor of what's happening in the room. I think also setting up the exercises to aid the students in teaching themselves, serving more as experienced guide than expert. Let's see … teach with a beginner's mind…

I also think having a point of view is important. It gives something for the students to either agree or disagree with, and in that friction learning happens. I also think it is important to know and give credit to where exercises and ideas come from. Knowing that something comes from Spolin or Johnstone, etc., helps to unpack the lesson in light of the philosophy which created it. It also helps in creating your own work.

What do you think is the future for improvisation? And what do you hope it is?

I think that improvisation has an uphill battle against the status quo we find ourselves in. The types of forms you allude to are here for a while. But I do also see innovation slowly happening and doors opening up. Currently it's hard to see, but it is there.

You're someone who has brought Keith and Del's work together. What do you think are the merits of each? How do they best mesh and why do you think there's a trend for the schools to be kept apart when they have so much in common?

I think Keith is the best observer I have seen. He can find the root of a scene in no time. I think Keith's strength lies in giving improvisers tools to create productive scenes. Del was much more interested in why we do it, how it can affect an audience and how the performers could utilize themselves in their work. Much more about the expression of the artists and how they move an audience.

When improvisation is bad or mediocre, what do you think keeps it that way? When improvisation is wonderful, what makes it that way?

Misunderstanding games, concepts, philosophies. Oftentimes you are watching the copy of a form which is the copy of a form, which has been changed, which is a copy of this … Because this is an oral craft passed down, I see many times improvisers doing or teaching things without all the instructions or understanding. I certainly have seen it in the interpretation of my work. I think the other part of what keeps it mediocre is a lack of vision from many groups. I spend a lot of time in workshops now asking improvisers and groups why they do it. It's amazing how few have actually thought of it beyond a chance to perform. I think everyone really needs to understand themselves as performers before they can improve their craftsmanship beyond a certain technical level.

As far as what makes improvisation wonderful, it's when you are sitting in a room that has been opened and accepting of the people in it. The actors onstage, the audience, everyone is of the same mind and know exactly what's going to happen next. This requires trust from everyone, it requires confidence, and it requires being in the moment. Time is on hold for art!

Is there anything else you'd like to say to improvisers?

Be generous.

5.4

Jonathan Pitts—The Impresario

Jonathan Pitts is one of the co-founders of the Chicago Improv Festival, which has become America's biggest and most prestigious festival devoted to improvisation.

What do you think every improviser needs to know—if someone was doing a show and had never previously improvised, what would you tell them?

If you are doing your first show, relax as best you can. Everyone says "have fun," and it is true, performing is play time. Remember: it is improv, there is no real-life consequences, there is no junta waiting outside to kill your family if you fail, so play, connect, listen and respond.

Another thing I'd say about your early stage experiences is that soon you will learn that onstage improv time happens much faster and slower than time passing in the audience. It's a weird thing, but true. I'd also say that you may rock the stage on your first couple times out, but it will take about a hundred shows before you become a rock star. It's all a learning curve, so play, play and play.

Improvisation in its current form is now about fifty years old. Why do you think most groups are still doing some version of the Harold or some version of Theatresports? Why do think there are not more movements of innovation? Or do you think I'm wrong and there are?

Yes, the masterpieces of cinema were done in the 1950s, but what was the average movie like? I'd say that we're probably on a similar scale of improv masterpieces to improv averageness that the movies were, or really any art form after fifty years. I do see that there are people who are or have worked on creating new forms, ideas, philosophies that are different than the main vocabulary of current improvisation. People such as Todd Stashwick and Shira Piven with organic improvisation, Mick Napier and the Annoyance Theatre, Chris Johnston's experimental improvisation, Jeff Wirth's multimedia improvisation, my work with Storybox, as well as improv artists around the world with specific shows.

The problem is that improv is ephemeral, so that really great shows don't get showcased on a worldwide level to create newer vocabulary for the mainstream improvisers. Then the struggle is to have the shows become training centers so that the new ideas can become codified for new students as it becomes part of their artistic curriculum. I'd also point out that Todd does have a training center in Los Angeles [Hothouse Spontaneous Conservatory]. It takes a lot of work becoming an institutional training center to then reach out to new students and alter the mainstream improvisers and audiences, and most improv artists just want to do their show and move on to the next thing.

What's the function of the Chicago Improvisation Festival?

The function of the Chicago Improv Festival is to be able to showcase many different expressions and styles of improvisation from a local, national and international perspective. We are an audience-centered festival, and we want to expand the audience for improvisation in Chicago, while at the same time showing audiences the wide varieties of improvisation and showcase improv artists from all over the world. We also offer workshops to improvisers to learn more of not only how Chicago teaches but also how improv teachers from other parts of the United States and the world teach as well.

Last year we began having an Apprentice program for improv teams, and that went incredibly well. We worked with five teams, they all got private coaching, free tickets to see shows, artistic and business consultation and a chance to perform as guided by their private coach.

Two years ago, CIF became a not-for-profit organization. That has allowed us to create year-round educational outreach programs, and we also now have a Teen Comedy Fest and a College Comedy Championship.

What's the best thing about bringing so many improvisers to one place?

The best thing about bringing so many improvisers to one place is the joy that develops as improv artists share who they are and they all find out what they have in common. Plus the parties and the playing.

What kind of groups or shows are you looking for at CIF?

We always look for groups that can show us another way of creating, playing and performing improv. We look for teams that are from other countries, as we are an international arts festival. We also look for ensembles who demonstrate overall excellence in what they do.

There are only three main schools of improvisation to know about—Close, Johnstone and Spolin—whereas in other disciplines there are many more. Why do you think there's not more interest in mixing these schools?

My short answer: I don't know.

My long answer: I've been influenced by Del, Keith and Viola, as well as Martin DeMaat, Charna Halpern, Mick Napier, Paul Sills, David Shepherd, Todd Stashwick and many, many others. As an artist, I open myself up to as many influences as I can find, and attempt to synergize them together to create my own understanding and performances. As a producer, I present and understand as many of those artists and schools as possible. As a teacher, I teach the principles of all the schools. As a director, I use every resource I can. Other artists will only do what they get excited by and from what they want to achieve. I'm powerless over everyone else and what they do or don't do. My choice is to go and experience what is in the various improv communities.

I've seen that the process of improvising is the same, regardless of the artistic discipline or expression; we just agree to focus on different pursuits within that process. There are many ways up the mountain, they all work well, and the view is the same once you hit the mountaintop.

Is there anything else you'd like to say about improvisation?

I've been doing improv for all of my adult life. It has shaped me in several ways. It has taken me abroad and helped me meet people from around the world. It has introduced me to life-long friends. It has given me another language to speak than the one I grew up with in the suburbs. It has been another paradigm to experience the process of life by. It has given me a strong theatrical training base which has guided me to create and discover from. It has taught me to access my intuition, to become a better listener, to be more compassionate, and that it is okay for adults to keep playing and keep learning.

There's also been several laughs and awe-inspiring moments along the way, too. I'm grateful for improvisation theatre.

5.5

Charna Halpern—The Keeper of the Harold

Charna Halpern co-founded the world famous ImprovOlympic Theatres in Chicago and Hollywood with her late partner Del Close. Her book, *Truth in Comedy*, which she co-wrote with Del, is regarded as the "bible" of Chicago improv.

What would you consider to be the most important things for an improviser to know?

It isn't about trying to be funny. It's about trying to take the work seriously. Play at the top of your intelligence. The humor comes out of that. I think people come with the misconception that they have to try to be funny, but when you do that, it's certain failure.

What do you mean when you say play at the top of your intelligence? That's something Del used to say, isn't it?

Yes, it means bringing your real brains to the work. Never pretending to be stupid. Knowing what you know. Never playing down to the audience. Being the best that you can be onstage. And also being a smart game player. Knowing that the humor comes from the connections, the callbacks, the recycling of the information that your partner used. I might bring something back that my partner did twenty minutes ago, which takes on more information and brings more energy to the piece. We're teaching you to be intelligent game players. We're showing you where the laughs come from.

We're not trying to make a joke. It's the kind of attention that a chess player needs to pay to play a game of chess.

Do you ever think that puts improvisers in their head?

It doesn't put them in their head. It's freeing for an improviser to know that they don't have to invent. You just have to listen and remember. You don't have to make a connection, you just have to notice them. It's where the group-mind comes from. As a group, we're seeing where our ideas come from and weaving them together.

What are the most common problems today? How would you change improvisation today?

In Chicago we don't have a lot of the problems that people have in other cities because we're playing so well together. The problems I used to see are people not listening, people not agreeing, but now we're doing it great here and the work is extremely sophisticated. My biggest problem is that there are so many people doing amazing work and I can't get rid of anyone. I don't see too much improv from outside, but when I do it's a matter of people not listening, playing beneath their intelligence, playing stupid characters, like children who are dumb. We always teach if you're going to play a child, play the smartest child in the world, because children today are on computers, they're doing incredible things, they're not dumb.

Do you ever see groups moving beyond the Harold?

The Harold that I wrote about in my book, three scenes and a game, is just a training-wheels version. Now we've taken off the training wheels because we've understood that it's now about a number of scenes that connect in different ways with the group games and monologues that may connect as well. It's a lot freer. It is already happening and forms are being developed.

You can have A story line, B story line and C story line and how do they connect together—like a movie. Del and I hoped that would happen eventually. It's like learning the notes in the musical scale—you don't have to sing the same song every time. One of my top shows here is improvised Shakespeare. It's hilarious but it's a linear two-act play. There's tons of stuff being created. Musicals. The art form is getting better and better all the time. I'm thrilled with it.

What's your history with Del and the Harold?

Del had already started working on the Harold when I met him. Then it was a long thing that never worked with no structure. When we met, I had a little game theatre that was like a Theatresports-type thing, which I had got tired of even though it was successful. I thought there had to be something more for improvisation. So Del said "I've been working on a form that is basically unteachable and unplayable, so maybe if we put our theatres together we'll be able to come up with something together and use some of your games." One of my games was a David Shepherd game which was a three-part scene, so we thought that could be the basic structure foundation of the Harold. We thought "We'll do three three-part scenes and then we'll put some ImprovOlympic games in between and have an opening and a closing." So that's how we came up with the Harold. After that it became much more free. Sometimes I see people who knew Del in the 1960s and they say "Oh, I hated the Harold," but that's because it was an earlier version they remember and they have no idea what's happening now. If they saw it now, their teeth would drop out.

Do you think the quality and the substance of the work is better now, or was it better when you started out?

It's better now. I'm seeing beautiful things now. Harolds that are touching and where the improvisers are revealing mysteries. We were pioneering things in the 1970s and 1980s and none of the work was that great. But back then we were still discovering the rules and tools. Like I can remember Del telling me about sitting round in his kitchen with improvisers who were depressed after a bad show and one of them said "What are we going to do? How do we make it better?" and Del said "Well, for one thing, we have to start agreeing with each other and stop arguing so much." They started to develop rules and tools while they were doing shows. In my book I refer to these as the kitchen rules because they came up with a lot of them in their kitchen.

What do you do with a student if they're agreeing at the expense of drama? If one person tries to hold up a store and the other person says "Sure, take everything," and doesn't show any fear?

Well, that's where people get it wrong. The agreement is not with the character, it's with the actor. The agreement is not "Sure you can rob me, take everything." That's not agreeing. That's just losing your integrity and not getting on with the scene. The agreement is with the actor and what the robber says. So if the robber says "Give me the money," you can still have the tension of "Please don't rob me."

Do you remember when Keith Johnstone came to play with Del—do you remember that?

No. I sat in on a class Keith taught at a festival in Houston. I left during the break. He kept interrupting the scene. And I couldn't really understand what he was doing. I found it confusing.

Basically, when we've traveled doing improvisation, we've found that most people are doing some version of the Harold or Theatresports. Why do you think there's not more cohesion between the schools?

I feel there's really only one way to do it. That's why I wrote my book *Truth in Comedy*. You listen to what the person wants and then you give it to them. How many different ways are there to play baseball? You hit it and you run to the base. It doesn't seem to me there should be a lot of different ways to do it.

With filmmaking, people draw from a lot of different influences, so there's a lot of cross over in genre. Why do you not think there's more cohesion between these two big schools of Del Close and Keith Johnstone?

What is Keith doing?

That's what interests me—why isn't there more understanding between those two school? Keith feels he and Del were trying to do the same thing but that he came from a theatre background and Del came from a cabaret background. You certainly see a lot of amazing work done at the Loose Moose, which I think you would like.

That's great. I haven't seen any of Keith's shows, just this one workshop. I know there are a lot of fights about whether short-form or long-form is better. I tell the short-form people that all that happened is Del and I created a meta-game which ate short-form. It's still there. You still see it turn up. No one needs to fight and say what's better or worse.

I agree that there's a place for everything. We don't limit other media like that. We don't say "I don't like movies—I only watch sketch shows." We like both those things, plus we like novels and plays and stand-up.

All those short-form games turn up in the Harold. Like you might have a scene where people are watching a foreign film and then you can use your subtitles translation game. Those things happen all the time. You can narrate in a Harold. All of these things turn up. It's all in there.

Would you think there's still a place for short-form shows?

Sure, people still like it.

I wonder why we're not embracing variety more rather than trying to homogenize it. For example, you'll see Mike Myers doing Saturday Night Live *no and then he'll go and do* Austin Powers, *which I think has a lot of the facets of the Harold.*

He loved the Harold. People used to say "Are you mad about *Whose Line Is It Anyway?* because it's just games that are fifty years old?" But I'm not because it got the word out about improvisation to people. People like my mother. So now people are asking "What's next for the form?" which is great. It got people understanding what improvisation was. I think that what we found in Chicago is that the performers would rather do long-form because it's more fun and challenging. And we're better at long-form at iO because we're not good at getting up and making quick jokes.

What would you like to see for the future of improvisation?

Right now I'd like to see more TV. We have a great group in LA called Opening Night who do improvised musicals. They're so good they could be on Broadway. I'd like to see more improvised sitcoms like *Curb Your Enthusiasm*. I'd like to have TV give more of us a chance for long-form shows. It's hard for me to plan because I live my life as an improviser, that what happens is more interesting than what's planned.

How long has iO been going now?

Twenty-six years. On our twenty-fifth anniversary all the stars came back on their own dime. Mike Myers, Andy Richter, Tina Fey, Neil Flynn, Tim Meadows, writers from *The Daily Show* and *MadTV*—and that's because this is their home. There's a reason that they come home. It's because they love each other.

My friend Kevin, who works as a writer on *Conan O'Brien*, called me recently and said "You'd be really proud of us because we wrote this bit for *Conan* which was too close to one of the movies that had just come out, so he asked us if we could write something else. So we all huddled in the corner and came up with something new and it was brilliant. And Conan said 'How did you come up with this in five minutes?' And we said 'We're an ImprovOlympic team. We say yes to each other.'" They got behind each other and said yes and believed in each other's ideas. You don't normally get that in the real world. People fight for their ideas. Some people bowl, but some of these TV stars—on Saturday night they do an improv show, then drink beer and laugh together. You can't get in to see the show, it's so crowded.

Can you describe what kind of teacher Del was? He's got a reputation as both charismatic and inspirational, but also quite scary at times.

There were a lot of sides to Del. I am proud to say he's my mentor. He would always take the unobvious choice. If I don't know what to do, I think "What would Del do?" because he'd always do something unexpected. But if he had something to say to you he wouldn't put icing on it. This is a tough business and he'd tell it like it is. It didn't mean he hated you. Most of the time he was very supportive and he'd put things in a very humorous way so you could laugh at yourself. But sometimes someone would do something and he'd be angry, but you had to be rude to people onstage or do something like that for him to be like that. It depended on his mood. This was his temple.

One time someone brought a friend who wasn't in the class. So he hinted that people couldn't come into the temple just to observe. The person ignored him so he said once again "Without asking the high priest, we do not have visitors in the temple." And the guy still didn't move, so he looked at the guy and said "Fuck off, turkey." He tried to be as polite as possible, but it wasn't getting across.

Another time this guy was onstage with other newer players and Del said to him "Do you think that you're funnier than the other people you're onstage with?" and the guy said "Yeah," and Del said "It shows." So sometimes he'd say something that would stab you in the heart. But sometimes we would leave flying high because he'd given us the secrets of the universe. Because we knew nothing until we were working with Del. Because the idea of being truthful or honest onstage was new to us. And to play intelligently. He'd say "What are you trying to do—be stupid?" He had a lot to say. He'd work on something he was reading from Freud or *Drawing on the Right Side of the Brain*—he was very well read—and he'd inspire you. You'd tell everyone "I made Del laugh. Oh my god, I made Del laugh."

When we teach people who've been trained in the Chicago way, they've often been taught not to ask questions, so they can't say "Why did you do that?" or "Will you marry me?" which we find minimizes drama.

That's people getting it wrong. Improvisation works when I tell you something, you tell me something. You don't take information, you add information. But people get confused. Of course you can say "Doctor, what's wrong with me?" because that gives information about the relationship. Your partner now has some information that there's something wrong with you. "Will you marry me?" carries information that you're in a relationship. Of course you can ask a question if it adds something. People get hung up on rules.

It's hard to be an improvisation teacher because one minute you tell them not to do something and then the next minute it's exactly what they have to do. The whole basic idea is you have to give them information. That's the yes-and principle. If you just ask questions like "What are we doing? What's happening?" then you're not giving the scene anything. But if you ask "How are we going to find food now that we're stranded?" then you've given your partner something—you know you're stranded. There are bad teachers. So many people come to me and I tell them that the agreement is between the actors and not the characters, and they're relieved but also angry that they've been taught by bad teachers who've told them they have to say "yes" to the offer even when the offer is "Kill yourself." The first rule is that there are no rules.

We find no matter where people have been trained they have a tendency to trivialize and not be affected. Is that a problem you see?

Yes, it's a big problem, people not reacting. Listen and react is one of the most important things. Someone in a scene can say "I'll pay for dinner" and their scene partner will say "I don't want you to pay for dinner because I don't want to owe you anything." And the improviser will say "No, no, I want to pay." And I'll say "Did you hear what she said? She was really saying 'No sex tonight.' React to that!" And then they'll say "What? Do you think I'm trying to get you into bed?" which is what that offer was really about. It is a big problem I see in beginners—not reacting. Part of the problem is that they think they know what the scene is about. They're already thinking of their next line.

Is there anything else you'd like to say about improvisation?

What Del said to me on his deathbed is "Tell them we've created theatre of the heart." In improvisation, people take care of each other and make each other look good. That's why we have the problem that no one leaves. We treat each other as a group of geniuses, artists and poets. When you do that, bonds form that last forever. And without getting too hokey, in this corner of the world we create better people. It's something to live by, not only to do on the stage.

5.6

Mick Napier—Power Improviser

Mick Napier is an actor, director, teacher and author living in Chicago. He is the founder and artistic director of the Annoyance Theatre and an award-winning director of The Second City. He is the author of the book *Improvise: Scene from the Inside Out*.

What do you think an improviser absolutely needs to know? If someone had never improvised before and was going out on stage, what things would you tell them?

An improviser absolutely needs to be invited to make choices. It's not good enough to go along in the scene and make sense of it all, you must make choices that surprise from within your point of view. Otherwise, it will probably be boring.

When film was fifty years old, there were whole movements and we'd already had Citizen Kane *and* Casablanca. *Why do you think improvisation as a medium is stuck in terms of innovation?*

First, I don't believe there's an apt comparison between the evolution of film and the evolution of improvisation. Film is a medium in which many different tools are available to express various styles, points of view, narrative, etc. Improvisation is a concept: making up content on the spot, as you go along. So the way in which you do that is derivative of that one simple truth. You could improvise in film or video or live on stage or through puppetry. It's a way to communicate, not the medium *in which you* communicate.

Then, to answer the question, I believe that people are innovating. But as I said before, it's derivative of the simple concept of making things up on the spot. Groups are innovating that, but it only comes in the way of forms. Improv forms, as innovative as they are, are sometimes hard to distinguish. They can all look like another short-form or another long-form, because we stupidly define our art form in regard to time: long or short. So TJ and Dave create an hour-long piece that is real and acted and funny and one scene, and we chalk it up to another long-form. Long-form gets the credit, not TJ and Dave's innovation. So there's a lot going on, it's just hard to get past the labels. iO, Second City, The Annoyance, Theatresports, ComedySportz, all have mainstay shows that allow them to finance innovation in the shadows. But it does occur.

What makes Annoyance special? What do you think will be its/your lasting contributions to the art form?

Well, Annoyance is rather anti-art form. We used to have a big sign on the back of our theatre that read "Theatre Sucks." Our meaning was "Often theatre, in the way you think of it, is boring. We're going to just fuck around in a non-pretentious, funny way." What makes Annoyance special is that we truly invite our people to create whatever they want to on our stage. There is very little intervention from me or the production entities of the Annoyance during a rehearsal process. We help as invited and support as needed. Another thing that I am proud of with Annoyance is that we were the first comedy theatre I know of to create a schedule with a multitude of shows each week. Traditionally, a theatre would have the show that they would run, and that's it. Right now, the Annoyance has fifteen different shows a week, with an ensemble of actors overlapping in multiple shows. Other theatres here in Chicago do that now, but I believe we were the first. As far as training, the Annoyance distinguishes itself in that we provide very individual critique. Whereas a lot of improv schools center on the power of supporting the partner and ensemble, we encourage the improviser to support themselves: the power of the individual within the ensemble.

When we visited Chicago, many improvisers told us that they were actively avoiding storytelling onstage. Why do you think this is? What does "storytelling" mean to you?

I think the concept gets convoluted. There's storytelling, telling a story, going into story, story theatre, telling your story ... The word "story" gets bandied about so much. I think storytelling in Chicago means "Showing, not doing." And to be honest with you, I don't even know what the fuck *that* means, at this point. I think it means don't talk about what you're doing, but do it.

But sometimes a scene is about talking *about* what you are doing, if that's what you declared it to be. If the lights come up onstage, and I declare, as a pirate, to my partner, "Let me tell you a story about when I..." then what I am doing is declaring that I'm telling a story. It gets all fucked up. It gets a bad name in the improv world here because when weak improvisers get freaked out, they start talking about the future or the past, in the form of a weak "story." "We could go shopping or we could go to the museum or we could…" [is] talking about something they could do in the future or something that they did do in the past in the form of a story. There could be a context for a show in which all of the actors tell stories one at a time à la Spoon River, and that would be acceptable, even in Chicago. But then are they storytelling, or story telling?

What do you know of Keith Johnstone's work? What have you seen and what did you think of it?

I don't know much. I saw Micetro once. I liked it okay, but it's a lot of judgment and competition to improvise well with. Does Keith improvise? I'm not sure. Anyway, I know that *Impro* was a very inspiring book when I first read it. I like the sense of play in it. I believe that my book, *Improvise*, is not *the* way to learn improvisation. I believe that it is important to have a very strong point of view about the way to do anything when you write a book. I believe that any student of improvisation should take from all that is offered, and not overly protect any school of thought. That is the way to a well-rounded, open-minded approach to this work.

What was Del Close like to work with? How do you think his personality shaped the work still done at Second City and iO today?

I respected Del as friend more than a director or teacher. His stories were inspirational and fucked up. The stories made you excited to be an "artist," whatever that is. To experiment and live life in the dregs or in the limelight. I personally don't think Del liked teaching. His class would be an hour and a half of him talking, and then a few scenes. I did enjoy Del as a director. I was in one show he directed, *Honor Finnegan vs. The Brain of the Galaxy*. Del was a bit mean at times, but also surprisingly supportive and grateful. I believe his heart was in the right place, but his social skills were askew. One of things I liked most about him was that you would be in the middle of a conversation with him and he would just walk away mid-sentence. I often do that as a bit. It's fun.

After an individual has improvised for a few years with success, they often get stuck or plateau. What would you suggest they do to get out of a rut?

If you're in a rut as an improviser, as I have been a million times, do anything you can to trick your adult brain. The reason we get in ruts is because of patterns which create safety in our improvisation. One needs to break those patterns, and we're not going to do it by obsessively thinking about it. That's why I say trick your adult brain, the part of it which rationalizes, etc. How? Start a scene with a sound, lead with an odd body part, start in the middle, have a thought ahead of time and change it when the scene starts be an animal, whatever the fuck it takes to constantly challenge the rational side, and stimulate the child and the play and the "fuck it."

5.7

Dan O'Connor—West Coast Legend

Dan is co-founder of LA's Impro Theatre and a co-founder of four other American Theatresports companies, including Bay Area Theatresports. He performed in the Improbable Theatre's OffBroadway production *Lifegame* and in the TNN television series of the same name. He co-created the NBC/PAX television improv comedy show *World Cup Comedy*.

What do you think every improviser needs to know? If someone was doing a show and had never previously improvised, what would you tell them?

That's it's not life and death. That part of the fun of it is your failure and failing good-naturedly. That a great part of it is failure in a good way, and the more relaxed and excited you are onstage the better, and that trying to be funny is getting in your own way. Just try to get out there and react to what's there and have fun. When you try to be funny, you get into your head. The audience likes to watch people in challenging situations where at any moment the thing may go wrong, but they also want to know that the actors are going to be okay and won't run weeping from the theatre. The worst improv shows are when people are trying to be good and failing, and the audience starts to feel bad for them or uncomfortable. Be relaxed and happy regardless of what happens because it's only improv and it'll be over in two hours.

When improvisers become regular performers, what are the trends that make improv mediocre or bad?

They forget about the audience, which make them indulgent. They sit and pull from their bag of tricks, they start to plan. "I know I'm good at this so I'll set it up so I do that." They'll do "Mad Lib" improv, so they ask for suggestions to get something they're good at. They play with the same people all the time so there's no danger of being surprised onstage. They get bored. They're good enough to phone it in.

Improv is fifty years old, but people all around the world are still doing Theatresports and the Harold—why do you think they're not innovating?

I've never quite understood that. I think there's a certain tribal aspect to following certain teachers, and people have always said "Short-form's not challenging—it's just gagging." I've always thought that most of the East Coast companies started doing Theatresports and have ended up doing improvised plays, and that comes from Keith's work. The same skills you use doing short-form, you use doing long-form like The Harold. The Harold is made up mostly of short scenes.

I would define Theatresports games as short-form, plays as long-form and the Harold as free-form. We've taken to calling our shows "unscripted theatre." I think lots of good short-form shows will have thematic links and recurring characters, like the Harold. The Harold is like jazz—when you put all those scenes together, they're one song. But they're all short little pieces. You're finding the game of the scene to have the runner that goes through the show. It's semantics, long-form, unscripted theatre, whatever you want to call it. Good Theatresports scenes—if we let them go, they could be a play. Bad short-form is when people are repeating gags.

I don't understand the rift and I think Spolin, Close and Johnstone are all great and there are wonderful teachers teaching new stuff now. We tell our students to learn wherever they can, take classes wherever they can. There's no such thing as too much information. You take what you want and leave the rest.

When film was fifty years old, there were whole movements and we'd already had Citizen Kane *and* Casablanca. *Why do you think improvisation as a medium is stuck in terms of innovation?*

People like their gurus and will defend them with religious fervor. I've never understood people so zealously defending their guru. Often someone will argue that Theatresports is competitive and that's a bad thing, but then you'll ask them if they've ever seen a Theatresports match and they'll say no. They won't realize that the competition is for the audience in professional groups. I do think that on the West Coast people will bring in teachers from Chicago and mask teachers and mime teachers and try to be well-rounded. I think that's less the case in Chicago. You would think that since the nature of the art form is to make things up, you would constantly want to be making things up—including how you make things up. Maybe because improv's so fluid, we hold on to the formats because they're more stable.

Randy Dixon and I taught at a festival a year ago in Melbourne, and there were teachers from all over the world. We all got to do a show in a format we wanted to do. We did about ten different shows. I think there is innovation. It's a new art form. I think when opera started, it was done the same way for a long time, and when someone wanted to change it, it was probably seen as sacrilegious by the old guard. Maybe because improv hasn't learnt to walk yet, people are unwilling to try new things or to get outside their comfort zone. Because it is a very terrifying thing to do, to get on stage and make things up. Once you get comfortable with one aspect of it, you don't want to go back to feeling like that again.

You don't want to revisit the discomfort that you felt when you were first learning?

Yes, I think that's true for some people. I know when I was in my early twenties, as a young improviser, I just wanted to do what I was doing and I didn't really want to hear about anything else. I understand it in young improvisers—there's a certain amount of "Sharks and Jets" feelings. But once you've been doing it for a long time, you need to try new things so as not to atrophy. In LA there's a whole bunch of gigs around town for people to do. Although it's glacial in its pace, I think there is a move for new things. I think when people are young they want to be onstage and do whatever it takes to get onstage. In LA, people want to be able to invite casting directors.

Do you think for too many improvisers it's a means to an end, like sketch or film, so they don't really care about the art form of improv?

Yes, I think that's true. I think improv got a bad reputation among casting directors because they were invited to so many bad shows with people who were inexperienced. It wasn't till *Whose Line* that people realized that improv could make money. There are people who are doing innovative things. Lifegame is the most amazing theatrical improvisation I've ever seen or been part of. It's the culmination of so many things. You have to be a good actor and a great improviser.

Where do you see improv going?

More in the theatrical, unscripted play direction. If I'm a theatre producer and I have four plays in rep that are heavily costumed and have lots of props, and I have one play that has very little or no costumes or props that's going to save me a bunch on production but is just as visceral and exciting as the others, then I'm going to want that fifth show in the mix—which is what the Colorado Shakespeare Festival did a few years ago with people from LA and Seattle. Also there'll be more hybrid shows as well, like *Curb Your*

Enthusiasm, where you're getting the best out of the writers and the best out of the actor/improvisers as well. I think *Curb*'s just the tip of the iceberg.

When did Impro Theatre start doing genre narrative shows?

LA Theatresports had started genre shows in the 1990s with Triple Play (created by Forrest Brakeman) a play, a movie and a musical in three acts each. We were very ambitious and initially took suggestions on the night for the genres from the audience, i.e. Shakespeare, Spielberg and Sondheim. But we started getting suggestions like Sam Shepard which only half the cast had a clue about! So, eventually we started to program the styles ahead of time which allowed rehearsal and for more ambitious stuff like Gabriel Garcia Marquez, Noir and the Weavers (American Folk music) or Brendan Behan, Scorsese and Fifties Doo Wop. Eventually we evolved into full-length plays inspired by one author, the first of which was Shakespeare in 1999 at the Globe Playhouse in West Hollywood. We then started down the road of soap operas, musicals and formats that were narrative-based.

When we started improvising plays, a few things happened. First we had to rehearse like a theatre company by diving deep into the subject matter. Not just tropes and parody but honest-to-goodness depth. We rehearsed for three months for a new show. We joked at the time we were going full Moscow Arts! Secondly we realized that we were able to move people to tears by playing the story straight when needed. In an early Tennessee Williams UnScripted, one of the characters was a fragile young man who was "thrown" from a second-story window and the audience burst into tears to see his tragic end, as he lay dead in the aisle.

Now if we had written this moment and performed it as a scripted play, the type of engagement we had with the audience would be one step removed from the story. They would become observers as opposed to participants. Because they gave us the suggestion, they are not just an audience; they are stakeholders in the writing of the play that is happening in front of them in real time and are part of the creation.

There is something about improvising that is dramatic and allows for greater emotional possibilities because it is happening in the moment. We found in developing this kind of theatre that we embraced all those things we learned in drama school but had not really accessed that much doing years of Theatresports and bar-prov.

When we became Impro Theatre in 2006, our goals included trying not be indulgent or wanky and not relying on improv audiences but building a theatre audience. We choose to use the unscripted genres of famous writers as a way to inspire theatre audiences to come see an improv show. We have become a gateway drug for "serious" theatregoers to experience improv for the first time. We want to pay tribute to the writers, not parody them. The plays are still inherently comedic because they are improvised and mistakes in the moment are bound to happen but the goal is to perform a play that Williams or Austen or Shakespeare never wrote but might have.

It is a different play every night which is terrifically exciting. We've taken this work to theatre venues (Oregon Shakespeare Festival, the Pasadena Playhouse, the Broad Stage and others) that are looking to explore the definition of theatre as well as engage the next generation of theatregoers as the traditional demographic is aging. We are looking to be part of that expansion and growth.

How has improv made you a better actor?

I'm still striving to be as comfortable on film as I am when I'm improvising. But onstage I feel really relaxed because I'm an improviser. A good improviser is present and really listens. That's what every acting teacher I've ever had has told me is the secret of good acting. It's the same skill set.

Do you have any advice for people who get stuck?

If you're getting to the point where you're not looking forward to coming, don't come. Take a break for six months. Going away and doing something else, like a play or writing, is very healthy. Do new things to re-energize yourself. Or if they're a young player who hasn't been doing it that long, start working on specifics like characters or endowment work. Also make it less about you. Look after your partner. Challenge yourself.

Is there anything else you'd like to say to improvisers?

Keep doing it, but know when to stop. Not entering a scene is just as important as entering a scene. Keith says the sign of a good improviser is that people like playing with you. If you find yourself not asked to play among your peers, then there's something you have to work on. So ask your peers what you need to work on. Learn as much as you can and do as much as you can. Even rehearsing a format you never intend to do can give you more skills. You should learn from everyone you can, unless a teacher is destructive. Get as wide a skill set as you can.

5.8

Patti Stiles—Our Teacher

Patti began improvising at Keith Johnstone's Loose Moose Theatre Company when she was a teenager. She went on to be artistic director of Edmonton's Rapid Fire Theatre and is now artistic director of Impro Melbourne in Australia.

If somebody had never had an improvisation lesson and had to go out on stage to perform, what would be the things you would tell them? What is the minimum requirement for an improviser to know?

What I would say would vary depending on the person, how they seemed to be (confident, over confident, nervous etc.), the type of show they are going to perform in or type of performance space (pub, theatre). Some of the things I would say would be…Don't worry. Improvisers are trained in making their partner look good so everybody there is going to be looking after you and taking care of you. It's all about having fun. Aim to be average. Listen to what people are saying, accept their ideas and go along with them. Just be charming and relaxed and look like you're having a good time on stage. The audience wants to have a good time and they don't want to have to worry about you. If you are trying too hard or looking really nervous, they will. Let's hope you make a ton of mistakes, then you will really have an opportunity to learn something and all of these pre-performance nerves will be worth it.

What do you think holds improvisation back and keeps it mediocre?

It's not all mediocre; I've seen some amazing work. Unfortunately the majority of the work out there is horribly mediocre. Our conditioning to survive in this world and be accepted in our "pack" holds us back. We spend so much time trying to fit in, impress and succeed it is hard to let go of that conditioning. It is all around us and starts from a very early age. As a result we carry a lot of fear—fear of revealing our inner thoughts, honesty, intimacy, abandonment, rejection, so much fear we carry with us. Fear of being on stage in front of people makes matters worse. What if I get it wrong? What if I look bad or stupid? What if I reveal something about myself? Those fears, mixed with ego and with how society conditions us, lead us towards making bad creative choices. The improvisation work starts to become based on success, on building our own ego, on impressing ourselves and others, and all of those choices hold back the improvisation work and our ability to push to the next level.

In many ways it's a contradiction. You can go into a company's workshops and the company will be talking about being positive and accepting ideas and making each other look good and then everyone walks on stage and it's a fight for survival. Notes sessions are all about stroking each other's egos. All of that is actually giving in to the fear. If you spend notes just stroking ego then people get a false sense of themselves in their work and they start doing it for this empty—and often untrue—gratification, instead of doing it for the creative risk and joy. You have to love the failure. You really have to go out there and be fearless, constantly questing for what haven't we done, where haven't we gone? The minute you start asking those questions there's fear. If you've never done a scene in a Bedouin tent you don't know whether or not it will work—which is exactly why you should do it.

If we don't keep pushing the form and challenging ourselves, then the whole form gets repetitive and monotonous because we're just recycling the same work we've done again and again and again. I'll bet there's still a billion places you've never done an impro scene. But if a first date is called for then more than likely you're going to end up in a generic restaurant. Or if you are more advanced, an Italian restaurant. We don't even do first dates in Chinese restaurants or Thai restaurants—we're always in Italian restaurants!

"I'll have your best bottle of Champagne!" In a way, that's a wimp. If you've been improvising for five, ten, fifteen years, a generic "best bottle" is still wimping. Because I'm afraid of saying "I'll have your Moc Chedon," because some people will know I screwed up "Moet et Chandon." So what? My verbal mistake could be a fun offer. The wannabe try-hard, the date where it just never goes quite right. We don't allow these possibilities, these natural offers and potential gifts. Instead we go into templates—the generic waiter, the generic girlfriend, the generic home environment, the generic restaurant, the generic first date. We've got those templates from all the movies and sketch shows we've seen—but we don't push beyond that. We recycle what we've seen work and then we try to make something unique, clever and amazing happen half way through.

If you don't have a director, or a teacher, or a group mentality that keeps pushing you past that, then you'll begin recycling. We learn how to tell stories, but we don't push ourselves past our own limitations and that's why the work around the world is becoming repetitive. People get out on stage and they find safety in this, they find a level of achievement in surviving this way, they get applause laughter, dates—so why would you want to change? Being liked and adored by the audience, why would you want to change *that*? So people settle for mediocre because it is safe, comfortable and feels good to them.

When film was fifty years old there were whole movements and we'd already had Citizen Kane *and* Casablanca. *Improv is fifty years old but people all around the world are still doing Theatresports and the Harold—why do you think they're not innovating?*

The people who moved the film genre forward, the people who innovated film were not the people on film. They weren't concerned about everyone knowing their face in relation to that work. Innovation comes from a desire and a need to explore. In improvisation, people start exploring when they need to impress others or build a larger audience. When you observe a group discussing inventing a new format, inevitably within the first half hour they are talking about what the audience will like, how it could be sold. So they're not actually talking about what they want to do, say, create, explore as a creative artist but how they can be more popular and successful.

Art is often a statement *against* something. And sometimes when things are innovated it's in opposition to what's there. A lot of groups do improvisation as a launch pad to something bigger they are hoping that someone will come and discover them so they can be on *Saturday Night Live* or *Whose Line Is It Anyway?* People don't see improvisation as an art form in itself. So why innovate when you are just stopping by?

Tell us about your new show, Mr. Fish and His Spooky Library of the Impro Macabre.

Derek Flores [one third of the Three Canadians, a group formed out of the Loose Moose in 1994] came over to Australia to work with me. A big part of the reason that we did that show was because Derek and I were saying we're so sick of doing the same thing in impro. This is not the way it was at The Moose. You didn't feel like you kept regurgitating the same work. And so we needed to play with someone who understood us at our basic level. We needed someone who got our creative headspace and we needed to take a risk and create something. We only did three shows of it, but other improvisers who watched it were coming up afterwards saying they had "show envy" and they'd never seen anything as ground-breaking. Both Derek and I said to each other: we know how to make an audience laugh. We want to terrify them. We want to spook them, set them on edge, feel uneasy and still entertain and tell good stories. How do we do that? And how do we do that without having a show that's always static and slow and cliché. How do we use that genre, use a lot of different theatrical styles and forms and improvise? It was a success and a really interesting experiment. We want to keep developing it.

Our process was simple. We went into the rehearsal room, Derek, myself, Lliam Amor and Rama Nicholas. We admitted to each other where we are in our work what we feel stuck in? What do we want to be challenged with? Where do we want to be pushed? What are we craving to do in the work? All four of us had a discussion about that and then we started looking at the actual genre and the different elements of the genre—actually did some research. Read *Shockheaded Peter*, read Edgar Allen Poe, looked at the different forms of horror so that our whole information base wasn't just film or television. Then we got up onto our feet and tried, failed, played, laughed, failed, paced around, explored and finally hit some 'ah-ha' moments.

My friend Meg in New York has a joke. How do you hide information from improvisers? Put it in books. And there is some truth in that.

Yeah, there is. Funny, the people who I know who are the most well-read are the original Loose Moose gang. However, a lot of improv work right now is recycling sketch comedy and sitcom. Nobody does stories from newspapers, or scenes on politics without doing gag impersonations. There's nothing wrong with having some sketch/sitcom popular culture, it is important in the variety and diversity of your work. But if that is all you're doing you're limiting yourself. However, the majority of the improvisation world thinks that all we do is comedy, so why read classic plays, Freud, Nietzsche? How will that be helpful in getting the laugh? I see improvisation as a form of theatre that creates stories. Comedy is one form of story work we can do. For me it is important to work with improvisers who have something they want to say, question, reveal. We discover a lot about ourselves through our responses to literature, art, politics, world events.

Does it make you want to go into a different medium? Does it make you think screw it, I'll write plays? Or does it make you want to try and change it?

No, I'm way too stubborn and passionate. I don't believe in giving up, especially on something I love. When you're part of a group, like the Loose Moose, that produces shows like Keith's *The Last Bird*, you're picking up on work that challenges, so that becomes a part of your fabric, and I think that's why Moosers are a bit different than other improvisers—not to make us sound like an elite, snobby group, I don't mean to do that—it's just when you're performing Theatresports on a Sunday night and the night before you've just watched one of Keith's plays that has Death and Christ come in and argue about who gets the grandfather in front of the grandfather's child, then you go into rehearsal for a children's show and you are questioning the roots of a fairytale and how to make it relevant to the eyes and ears of a five-year-old, then you are working on or performing in sketch shows that would often explore surrealism or absurdist humor—you learn there's many different storytelling possibilities and ways to entertain an audience. You are being exposed to it daily. So, you start absorbing and your boundaries are pushed and your eyes opened to other this amazing limitless potential called improvised theatre. I can't let that go. It is way, way too exciting and there is so much left to explore and create. I've only just started, I'm not going to give up.

Some other improvisers we've met from the Loose Moose seem to us to have picked up not just Keith's techniques, but his content too.

It's normal for people to repeat what they've seen work and what they've done. It's normal for an improviser to have a bag of tricks, whether it's their own or someone else's—or someone else's that becomes their own—and I don't think that having a bag of tricks is unhealthy. It's only unhealthy if that's all you ever do, or know how to do. Fear will come into play as will someone's ability. Not everyone from Loose Moose is going to be a brilliant improviser, good teacher or director. There are techniques used by Keith that help move the narrative forward, if you are using these then I think that is good because the technique does not dictate the story or content. If you are trying to repeat scenes you've seen him do, then that isn't good. Find your own stories.

There is a lot of pressure in coming from Loose Moose. People judge you differently and expect a special magic. I suppose we all fall into doing Keith tricks, I know I have, I'm human. But when you train with people it's normal to pick up their ways and their styles, from how they would direct to how they would teach to even how they would stand. I've noticed that I've picked up a Keith-and-Dennis-ism [Cahill, current artistic director and co-founder of Loose Moose] with how I hold my hands when I'm teaching certain games.

When Keith and I were teaching for you guys last year, I told Keith after the first day how nervous I was, knowing that the group I was working with in the morning would be working with him in the afternoon. I started getting incredibly insecure, thinking what if all these years I've been doing it wrong and I'm about to be found out as a fraud? What if I've got this horribly wrong and then they go and work with Keith and it's all much better? And he looked at me and said "Hmm let's hope so. It could promote some interesting discussion."

What advice would you give an improviser who has hit a plateau or a rut?

Again, my approach would depend on the person. However, one thing I often say is sit down and write out a list of games or scenes that you love to do and then write out a list of games and scenes that you dislike doing or avoid doing. It's through that list of games that you avoid and dislike that you'll find the skill areas that you need to challenge yourself in. I had an awakening once at Loose Moose where I realized I was avoiding doing Word At A Time, Typewriter and Story Story Die. Anytime those were called for, I didn't want to go up and do them. Interestingly, all three of them are narrative. They're all about the narrative and I was enjoying being a passenger and not having any responsibility for the narrative in any scene. Well, no wonder I plateaued. Because I'm just following. So it wasn't until I started tackling those areas and pushing myself in those areas that I opened up a whole other level of my improvisational work.

I'd also say sit down and ask yourself who are the people who most inspire you? Another player, an international teacher, a local teacher—seek them out, either as a teacher or as a fellow performer. Observe them, work with them, find what inspires you and nurture it. Question what in the work do I love and what in the work don't I love? What do I want to do? Am I enjoying doing pub-prov or am I doing that because it's the only show available? Okay, if it's the only show that's available you can still do it, but why not get two or three people together, get a room and jam other ideas? Create your own opportunities. Improvisation isn't about following rules. If you belong to a company, that doesn't mean you can only workshop when that company is workshopping. Get people together and jam! Try other things. Do mask work. Do clowning. Do other forms that will help challenge your improvisational skills. It's up to you to keep the fire alive and you're only going to do that by actually asking yourself those questions.

It's also worthwhile asking questions and connecting to other impro groups and forming those discussions with people. If you're a director of a group and you're feeling absolutely exhausted and like everybody is depending on you, contact other directors from other impro groups and you'll have someone to chat through and bounce ideas off of. Don't feel that you're isolated.

Do you think it's helpful each time you go out on stage to decide you're going to work on one thing?

I think it's good to have personal challenges and be aware of your work and say here's areas I could develop and work on. But I think it can be destructive if your only point of focus is your own work and you're not available to what's actually happening. I do think it's really helpful to have areas you want to work on that develop you and the work. Tonight I will really listen. This makes you more present, available and supportive. Tonight I will take time, in creating platforms. This allows you to gift yourself. If we take time with that detail and the attention to things, then we're setting up better narratives. We've got a beginning so we've got something to make a middle and we've got a place to go for an end. If you don't have a platform it's very hard to end a scene. Watch scene after scene and again and again they start right in the middle and they've got nowhere to go and it becomes a nothing. If you start with a platform, the endings become obvious.

I often find what I need to work on through post-show notes. I will ask other players to give me notes and I am always fascinated by someone's perception of my work. Ask someone in the group to be your pal, mentor whatever term you want. Someone who is going to give you direct and honest notes. Then take them—don't argue! This will probably be more enlightening then a generic note to self "I will do a new character tonight." You need to build how people take notes in training. This is something I've been doing a couple of years now and I didn't really realize how important it was at first. In the classes, I am now giving very direct notes, as if it were show notes. The first couple of times doing this, there are a couple of nervous people and I can see people are taking notes and going home and beating themselves up and doing all the things that we do, because we're human and we do those things but what it's actually doing is starting to get them to focus more on the work. And now when they get together and jam, they're actually starting to direct themselves and each other and starting to question the work and look at it differently.

Sometimes we worry so much about hurting people's feelings. But isn't that a contradiction to what we're teaching in the work? Shouldn't that just be a given—that we all trust each other and we all know that everybody's going out with the best intentions and sometimes we'll soar and sometimes we'll fail. Do we really need to be building each other up in notes? If someone does something extraordinary or there's an amazing character that presents itself or something happens, well yeah. But do we constantly need to be giving each other permission or are we just giving in to our fears?

If you need to give permission and validation in your notes, then something isn't right in your training and approach.

I am completely off-topic again aren't I?

5.9

David Fenton—Theatresports MC Down Under

Improviser David Fenton was a regular MC at Brisbane Theatresports in the late 1980s. He is now a theatre director and academic.

Theatresports at the La Boite Theatre in Brisbane in the 1980s was a phenomenon, with queues around the block from a genuine fan base. Why do you think it was such a success?

There are a few different reasons why those years feel like a bit of a golden age, a combination of critical mass and the space itself [a theatre in the round in downtown Brisbane]. La Boite has now moved from that space to a much larger space, and a lot of people yearn for the days when you could actually fit something like 250 people in there. It's something to do with the distance between the players and the audience, the sense of arena, of coliseum, but really an intimate one, which was really important to that kind of critical mass at that time.

The Brisbane theatre community was small and so you could easily get critical mass in the sense of community, because the majority of people knew each other—I'm talking about the performers—and that spiraled out into the audience. Almost everyone in that audience knew someone involved on the stage at a certain point during that period. They'd either been taught by someone on the stage or knew them personally in some way.

I think that there was a legacy that we were tapping into that came through from Toad Show. They were early 1980s political theatre/musical theatre satirists and they created these great big community musicals. I think they started with a Western version of *Jesus Christ Superstar*. Sean Mee, who's currently the artistic director of La Boite, was part of the groundswell of that, along with Brian Kavanagh, who was the MC before me. There was a real groundswell of community support around Toad Show, and a lot of that spilled into this other kind of community outlet which was Theatresports, because Toad Show by then was winding down their production house for live performance.

Having been an improviser yourself, did you enjoy the role of MC?

Twenty minutes before I went on stage, I was usually close to throwing up and mortified, thinking "I can't do this. My voice is going." And of course, my voice would be gone by the end of the night, which is stupid enough. But I often went on thinking "I can't do this." Having that mandate to be the one that gets us all on the same page and sets the tone of the space was an interesting challenge. I remember early on being very dark and being a bit kind of black and sardonic and a bit too sarcastic, and I recall making a gear-change in the way that I went about controlling—or engaging with—the audience. The only way that I could get away with being a bitchy queen was to then turn around straight afterwards and say "But I mean that in a loving and kind way," which is a classic lift from Dame Edna.

What's interesting is how young I was. I realize now that I hadn't officially come out at that time, and yet there was a strong tacit understanding in the room that I was gay and that the acceptance of that as a persona was quite liberating. It was almost like doing drag.

Did you ever want to improvise more?

Well, the money was good for hosting and the players didn't get paid. I'd improvised for three years before becoming the MC. I started in '86 and our team, Macbeth and The Bed Wetters, had won a championship the first time we competed. We took on Mental Floss—and Mental Floss and Bananas in Pyjamas were the teams that you needed to beat—and we won the championship. By the time I was asked to host, I'd been improvising for not just two years but all the time before then, because I was also teaching at La Boite with the youth theatre. I suppose, as a performer, the opportunity to MC was like one very long stand-up improvisation, so I was actually getting my jollies through the entire community relationship in that space, as opposed to just with the two other people on my team. But also I had lots of time out to think while they were playing. I could read things and look at stuff and there was a sense of structure to it, whereas I remember going into improvising sometimes being so scared and wanting to plan and structure, and then knowing that all of that was going to be thrown out the window. I think it's the difference between a long throbbing tension and a short sharp tension, and I think I preferred the long throbbing tension of MCing.

Do you still teach or have anything to do with improvisation?

I do. It is the whole basis of my teaching. I've just finished my PhD, and a lot of the work I've been doing has been group-devised work in contemporary performance, and so that involves a lot of openness on the floor, and so improvisation is very much the core of—actually it's been the foundation of my directing, the tenets of improvisation as opposed to the nuts and bolts of it. It's the openness, it's the acceptance of play and spontaneity in the space which has created the foundation of what's been a really strong directing career here in Australia. It's only been in the last couple of years that I've veered off into academia because I've started to enjoy the intellectual challenge.

Is it something that you would like to see some kind of renaissance of in Brisbane, or in fact in Australia?

Absolutely. I'm restructuring a unit at the moment, and the reason why I'm restructuring it is because we get through the practical aesthetics at the end of the unit but I realized there was no scaffolding at the front end. They don't know how to play. So when you get to practical aesthetics, which is rigorous but also quite logical in the type of questions which it wants you to answer, you can't actually do it unless there's a creative sense of play underneath that kind of logic. There's no way you can teach practical aesthetics without there being a really firm foundation of people feeling confident with playfulness, spontaneity and improvisation in the space.

Theatresports is still strong in Sydney, and of course after Theatresports there were several improvisation troupes, one of which I'm involved in professionally here through the university, which is much more akin to applied performance or applied theatre, which has a much more Boalian basis to it, so that's pretty much what I'm operating in professionally at the moment, and we're doing large corporate gigs for business process management and that type of stuff.

When film was fifty years old, we'd already had Citizen Kane *and* Casablanca. *Improv is fifty years old, but people all around the world are still doing Theatresports and the Harold. In the 1950s no one was wondering what the Lumière Brothers would think of their movie, but people still argue about what Del and Keith would say or think. Why do you think they're not innovating as much as they could be?*

I think it has got stuck because, of the two different forms you are talking about, one is based in an ephemera and the other is captured, studied and commodified. So the thing about film is that you can go back to it, look at it, study it and work through it and analyze it, and it can be disseminated throughout the globe quite easily now, and people can quite easily build on that body of knowledge, and this is why your book is really important. The problem with improvisation is that the very core notion of it works against it being as easily analyzed or disseminated or commodified, and that's a good thing but a bad thing. We want to keep things spontaneous and fresh, within a kind of theoretical structure that should be rigorous. The problem is that when we capture it, it has a tendency to look like people just mucking around, but that's actually its strength.

Do you think we hold on the formats and the gurus' ways of doing things because it's all we have? Because the rest of it is so ephemeral?

Yes, we don't record it often, we don't disseminate it often—which I actually think is part of its strength as well. You're comparing one form that is that based in spontaneity and ephemera and another which is highly structured, first non-matrixized, then matrixized through editing, disseminated and captured potentially digitally for all time, so the mere fact you can go back and use the Lumières as an example is interesting, as opposed to the so-called "first moment" of improvisation in the 1950s. That moment might have been written about, but has not been captured; it's gone forever. It's actually a double-edged sword, the improvisational form, the fact that it embraces ephemera but at the same time the ephemera works against it, with regards to disseminating practical and theoretical knowledge of it.

When improvisation is bad or mediocre, why do you think that is?

Because people don't understand that it's an artificial form, just like drama is an artificial form. It's not real life, although it can mimic real life incredibly well. Drama is a construct. Time is condensed. There are issues of dramatic action. Everyone has something to do and it's life sped up. So that's part of the problem: People confuse improvisation with real life. Often when they go into improvisation, they don't really understand on any genuine level the elements of drama themselves. They don't understand that whole idea of dramatic tension—issues of time, space, focus—all of those dramatic elements. And so they go and think "If I stand around and say some funny things and talk over other people and pull focus, then surely I must be improvising." And in some respects they are, they're just improvising badly.

The great thing about Theatresports and Johnstone and all the other theories that well up around improvisation is that they acknowledge it's a dramatic form and that it has a structure, an internal structure and logic to it, which demands that the player has to pull out those skills that adhere to dramatic rules. So I actually think the reason why there's a lot of poor improvisation out there is not because people don't have the skills, but because they don't understand dramatic structure.

I understand what you're saying, but I think I see people who do understand the theory who still don't put it into practice. Is it because improvisers are the only people in the world who have to choose to make themselves vulnerable? Actors working on text will do it because writers and directors have led them there, but no one naturally likes to choose to be vulnerable.

Yes, but no level of vulnerability is going to get you through a scene that needs a story told, unless you actually understand that there's a story that needs to be told and how to tell a story. I'm wondering whether that type of vulnerability that you're talking about has some type of intuitive connection to a strong practical understanding of dramatic form. That there's some type of bridge between being open and vulnerable that can actually facilitate people's innate understanding of dramatic form and storytelling. I think there's a connection there between both our points of view that there's no point in understanding dramatic form theoretically unless you can apply it, and often the only way you can apply it is to be open to it falling apart on you in the space, or somehow being able to personalize it in the space. For example, I suspect Robert McKee [screenwriting guru, author of the screenwriting manual *Story*] would probably be a terrible improviser. He'd fall back on rules and structure instead of letting those rules flow through that moment.

5.10

Tobias Menzies—The Actor

Tobias graduated from RADA in 1998 and took improvisation courses with The Spontaneity Shop as part of a RADA graduate program. He has since appeared in the Complicité show *Light*, the James Bond film *Casino Royale*, as Brutus in the HBO series *Rome*, Edmure Tully in *Game of Thrones* and Black Jack in *Outlander* among many others.

What first drew you to improvisation after drama school?

I'd always been pretty interested in improvisation since reading Keith Johnstone's *Impro*. I remember that being a seminal read. That would have been early on in RADA, or just before RADA. We had done some improvisation at RADA, but it hadn't been that successful and we didn't really feel like we had got to the bottom of it. Our improvisation teacher was a really interesting and charismatic man, but he'd get us up and we'd do something and it was quite difficult and not very good, and his reaction would be "Wow, improvisation's really difficult, isn't it?" He'd say "That's interesting, because that wasn't very good was it? What wasn't very good about that?"

So he had an element that it was okay to fuck up and that was nice, but you wanted to get beyond that at some point and learn some skills and feel like some progress had been made, and that never really occurred. We just spent a lot of time going "That wasn't very good, was it?" We'd just do that each week.

What do you remember from the workshops that you did with The Spontaneity Shop?

I remember the workshops being very, very energizing. It was very exciting. When you first come to impro, that first time you experience building a story with someone else, accepting an offer and building on it, doing all those different basic building blocks of impro for the first time is a real buzz and a real rush. I remember that very clearly. Quite basic impro things, but being told about them and then getting up and doing them and them working and you going "God, yeah, we've made something that wasn't there before and it wasn't really either of us, it was both of us."

Are there any elements of impro that you found helpful for acting?

I feel very strongly that working in improvisation made me a much better actor, made me more open to other actors. It also helps you to understand the structures of drama a bit more. I had a cleaner, clearer appreciation of what makes drama and what makes scenes work. It makes you more sophisticated, more accurate as an actor, in fulfilling the role that your character is performing within the structure of the scene. Part of your job is to stand up for your character and fill that particular niche—you have to partly trust that the drama will take care of itself, but I think it really helps to have an outside eye so you can ask: What is it that you are contributing to the story here? What does the story need from me? That was something I learned through improvisation. I remember gags kill narrative. I remember that as one of your catchphrases. Things like that are very apposite to performance—the choices you make. To choose to go for a gag on something, you have to understand that that will interrupt the story. If it's a good enough gag then maybe that's what the moment needs, but it's still a careful balance.

Improvisation gives you a confidence and a flexibility—a lack of reverence for the process. You can dive off the edge of the cliff and still be okay because you've done it in improvisation. You've been in situations where there's nothing—no script, no costumes, just you and somebody else. I think certainly that stood me in good stead for the rather hairy situations in filming when you don't really know what's going on, you're shooting out of sequence, you've only just turned up on set, there are millions of people milling around....I gained a lot through doing improvisation purely because it was something I found quite scary to do, and I think you always learn a lot from doing what scares you.

Having experienced successful and unsuccessful teaching, what would you say it takes to make a good improvisation teacher?

You have to take genuine pleasure and have a real interest in seeing people develop and grow. The great teachers I had from The Spontaneity Shop appreciated the underlying belief and passion in the improvisation message. They have a broader understanding of what Keith Johnstone wrote than just being able to accept an offer in the context of a funny impro scene. Keith's book is really about life.

Would you recommend improvisation to other actors?

I would definitely recommend that all actors do it. It made me grow hugely as a performer. If an actor can improvise, it will make them a better performer. It won't make a bad actor into a really amazing actor, but it will maximize any potential they have—largely because it goes such a long way to reducing fear. Fear is the enemy of a good performance. Improvisation really, really helps.

5.11

Jeffrey Sweet—Illegitimate Grandfather of American Improv

Jeff is a playwright, journalist, director, lyricist, occasional performer, and theatre historian among many other things. He got involved in improvisation in Chicago and New York via writing *Something Wonderful Right Away*, the first book to draw attention to the pioneering work of Paul Sills, Del Close, and David Shepherd. He then began applying what he learned to creating plays and training others in how to write scripts based on improvisational explorations.

Something Wonderful Right Away *was one of the first ones we read when we began preparing our book. How did you come to write it?*

I grew up in a suburb of Chicago, and my family would take me to see Second City when I was in high school. I came to New York for college because I wanted to get into theatre and film. I started noticing that a lot of the plays and movies that appealed to me included the significant involvement of people who connected to Second City or its predecessor, The Compass. I saw *The Graduate* and I thought, "Huh, Mike Nichols, that's an interesting guy." And I saw *A New Leaf*, starring and written and directed by Elaine May. And Alan Arkin was directing plays by Jules Feiffer off-Broadway and I asked myself "What is it that all these people have in common?" Of course, when I looked into it I found that they'd all found their voices in the city that I had fled!

What was it that was so appealing about the work that they were doing? How was it different from what other people were doing at the same time?

There was a sort of cheerful insolence to it. It's hard for people to remember, but once upon a time mainstream comedy was not very adversarial. It didn't challenge institutions, it didn't challenge government or business or the military, or any of the other things that are now pretty common comic fodder. When I say "challenge," I don't mean joshing, like in Bob Hope service comedies. I mean material that attacked the very bases of these institutions and power centers. David Steinberg pointed out to me that in those days most comedy was based on a personal eccentricity or quirk. Lucille Ball wanted desperately to get into show business, so we laughed at her. Jack Benny was stingy, so we laughed at him. Bob Hope was brash with women but was essentially a coward so we laughed at him. None of these things had anything to do with larger institutional failings, or failure of anything in the American dream. These were all personal failings or foibles.

What started happening in the mid-1950s (and improv was a branch of this), comedy started to train the guns away from the humor of personal failings to the humor of institutional failings, corruption, and hypocrisy. And it seemed that the people who were most consistently addressing these satiric issues were people who'd come out of Second City. I thought, "Oh, I wanna read a book about these," and it turned out that nobody had actually written one. So with the logic of youth, I said "Oh, nobody's written it? Then I'll write it!"

I had stumbled into interviewing freelance for New York papers and magazines, and one of the people I had interviewed along the way was the great satiric cartoonist and playwright Jules Feiffer. When it occurred to me that there was a book to be done about the people who'd come out of Second City and The Compass, I thought of him because he'd worked with many of these people. I told him what I was thinking of doing, and he said "That's a swell idea, and yes I'll put you in touch with Mike Nichols, but the first person you should talk to, actually, is a guy named Sheldon Patinkin."

Sheldon had been Alan Arkin's assistant on an off-Broadway production of Feiffer's play, *Little Murders*. Jules said, "This guy has been there for almost everything and he will give you the overriding arc of the whole story. And then as you talk to other people you can fit that in within the larger context that he'll provide you." So I call up Sheldon, and he says, "Have you ever improvised?" And I say "No." And he said "No." And I say, "Excuse me?" And he says, "No, you're not fit to write this book because how the hell are you going to write this without some experience of actually improvising?"

Then he says, "This is what's gonna happen: I'm teaching improv in New York for a little while and you're gonna come to that." And I said, "Oh, you're going to let me observe?" And he says, "No, schmuck! Observe? Jesus Christ! You're gonna get up and you're gonna do it." And so I did. I remember we were in a studio in downtown Manhattan, and indeed he taught me the basics—what scenes are based on and characters pursuing objectives and how objects can be used and all the rest of this stuff—that all fed into my playwriting and made me a better playwright.

Then I went running around for a few years, talking to everybody who would talk to me. The key thing was that Mike Nichols talked to me. Once he talked to me, then almost everybody except Elaine May would talk to me. Elaine wouldn't talk to me. In fact, Elaine for a while was calling people up and telling them not to talk to me!

Many years later, I had formed a group called the New York Writers' Bloc, which was a group of actors and writers who developed and tested material in the sessions. Donald Margulies, who won the Pulitzer Prize, came out of that, Jane Anderson who recently won the Writers Guild and Emmy awards came out of that. Also in that gang were Jerry Stiller and Anne Meara and their friends, who were in Compass, Mark and Barbara Gordon. It was quite a group of people. Many years after *Something Wonderful* came out and the Bloc had ended (after running for eleven years), I was at a memorial service for Barbara Gordon. Elaine May was there. At the end of the evening, Elaine came over to me and she said, "Everyone was talking about this marvelous group you had. Is it still going?" "No," I said, "that ended a while ago." And she said, "Well, if you ever get it started again, I'd be interested in joining. What's your name?" And I said, "Jeff Sweet," and she said, "Oh, I tried to ruin your book!" I said, "Yes Elaine".

Anyway, that's the reason why I did it, because there were all these people who were creating work that I responded to on a deep level. Part of it has to do with fact that I'm part Jewish and this material, to a great extent, has roots in Jewish humor, the ironic perspective we kids who were brought up with Jewish parents bring to the world.

Okay, here's another story. Second City had its fiftieth anniversary back in 2009, and there was a big party in Chicago. It lasted three or four days. And a lot of the alumni came and performed. Steve Carell and Stephen Colbert did a great scene that they had done together at Second City. And Fred Willard was there and David Shepherd was there, and Andrea Martin and Martin Short and a lot of others. It was an extraordinary assemblage. And we all had a lot of fun and there were lots of performances and late night sessions and lots of drinking and swapping stories.

The day after this was over, I got on a train to come back to New York (I like trains). And I was reading an article online in the *New York Times* about the party, about the anniversary, and nowhere in the article was there any mention of Paul Sills or Viola Spolin. In an article about the fiftieth anniversary of Second City!

So I start working on a letter to chew out the *Times*, saying that to run a piece about the fiftieth anniversary of Second City and to not mention Paul

Sills or Viola Spolin is like, you know, running an article about the Bible and not mentioning Moses or Abraham! (See, Jewish humor.) And as I'm writing this article I get an email from Mike Nichols: "Did you see that fucking article in the *Times*?" And I said, "Well, yes I did." And he says, "Did you notice that they didn't mention of Paul or Voila, or me or Elaine, or Barbara or any of the rest of us?" And I said, "Yes, I did notice that." And he wrote back saying, "Well what are you going to do about it?"

And for a moment I thought of writing back: "You're Mike Nichols, you can do whatever you want about it. If you write a letter, they're going to publish it!" But I assumed he was trying to get me to go into the field, to defend everybody's reputations without him looking publicly miffed. And I finished my letter and I sent it in, and they didn't print it.

So I thought, well, how do I get this out? I'd written that book a number of years before. But there was more story to tell now. So I decided to do a solo show called *You Only Shoot the Ones You Love*, about my dealings with the community over the years. It's stories of Paul and Mike and Elaine and Del Close, and it's also on a larger level about where this stuff came from.

If you take a look at a lot of the early people, a huge number of them are from Jewish families who fled Eastern Europe. Mike had the distinction of having relatives who had been killed by both Stalin and Hitler. So you have a lot of people whose parents or grandparents had fled anti-Semitism in Russia or Europe, and they've managed to make a life in a country where still there was a fair amount of anti-Semitism but they could get along. As I say, this is part of my background too—my grandmother was nearly killed in a pogrom in Polotova.

And then after the Second World War, up pop Joseph McCarthy and Karl Mundt, and Richard Nixon, all supposedly hunting communists, but whenever they call people to browbeat and bully in front of HUAC, somehow magically most of these people turn out to be Jews. So the blacklist and the McCarthy era were seen by Jews as being an excuse for more anti-Semitism. Joseph Papp, who had founded the New York Shakespeare Festival, his name was originally Papirofsky, so they insisted on pointing out that he had changed his name so as to hide his Russian-sounding origins. And Judy Holliday's real last name was Tuvim, which means holiday, and these apes made a big deal about that. And they went on and on, emphasizing the Jewishness of a lot of the people that were being called in front of HUAC.

My theory is that this bullshit made the smart, well-educated children of people who had fled Tsarist Russia and Hitler's Europe say to each other: "Well, fuck this. Let's nail these bastards." Within about four or five years of that time there was an explosion of satiric humor. That's when we got Lenny Bruce and Jules Feiffer, and Phillip Roth and Herb Gardner, and Mort Sahl, Mel Brooks, Carl Reiner, Tom Lehrer. There was an explosion of all these, mostly Jews, responding to this crap—responding to jerks in Washington and then looking at other targets in society that deserved their attention.

I believe that was part of the impetus behind The Compass and Second City. I'm not saying everybody in The Compass and Second City was Jewish, but most of them were. (The non-Jewish people tended to be the straight people. Andrew Duncan was sort of the square WASP. Mina Kolb was a nice Catholic lady; part of the joke of what she did was her cluelessness.) I think you can't overestimate the influence of the ironic Jewish sensibility. When people keep wailing on you, you may not have the power to turn around and knock them on their asses, but as they're beating you up, you can make some pretty devastating ironic comments under your breath. Only now they were making these comments out loud, in theatres and night clubs, comic strips and fiction.

So Del Close, who started with Second City, ended up going off and doing his own thing. What can you tell us about that?

Del was one of the rare non-Jews. He started in the St. Louis Compass and he was briefly partly of a group that tried to get launched in New York. But when Second City moved first to Los Angeles and then to New York, they needed people who could step in and keep the show going in Chicago. Del was part of that second cast.

One of the directors Paul Sills hired to help in Chicago was a man named Alan Myerson. Myerson and Sills fought. Myerson was more overtly political than Sills was. Sills was mostly interested in people's general alienation from society, and Myerson was more interested in attacking specific institutions and people like Lyndon Johnson and Richard Nixon. So Sills basically said, "If that's what you're interested in, why don't you start your own fucking theatre?" And Myerson went to San Francisco and started The Committee. Myerson had also fought with Del Close when Myerson was directing at Second City, and Myerson always joked that Del was one of the people who drove him out of Chicago. So Myerson is working with The Committee in San Francisco and he's now the boss, and he calls up Del and he says, "You helped drive me out of Chicago so I'm dragging you to San Francisco." Where the logic was in this I'm not entirely sure, but Del did indeed come to San Francisco, where he not only performed but began to experiment and direct.

What did he see in Del? Why did he want Del's involvement?

I think he saw Del's talent, his raging intelligence and his anarchy. I think that he respected that. Del rather swiftly started teaching workshops and directing, and then there was a time when there were Committee theatres in both San Francisco and Los Angeles. A branch of The Committee was in LA on Sunset Strip and Del used to live under the stage. Del established a reputation and did a lot of experimenting with the company at that point. And then he was brought back to Chicago to direct at Second City. He would direct and then get fired, and then get re-hired and get fired and so on…

What was the reaction when your book was published?

It had one effect which I had not anticipated. People read it and said, "I want to do this work." So, for instance, Mick Napier was a college student when my book came out, and he read it and he told me that's the reason he came to Chicago. He indeed ended up directing at Second City and then he started his own theatre, The Annoyance.

Charna Halpern told me that she started iO because she read the book and said, "This is what I want to do." Because David Shepherd was in my book, she originally partnered with David Shepherd, apparently ignoring everything in the book that had said he was not the world's greatest person to partner with. And eventually she realized he was great in terms of inspiration but not all that practical in terms of follow-through. So she showed him the door, and then she said, "I want someone who's really gonna contribute." She was taken by Del's chapter in my book, and it was on the basis of that that she called up Del. Del met with her and, you know, as he reflexively did when he was in a situation when he didn't know somebody, he began by insulting her. And she said, "Okay, you can act this way if you want, but I'm the person who's going to make it possible for you to take your work to the next level, so you might wanna rethink this." There came a point where it was apparent to Del that the kind of work he wanted to do was not going to be supported by the Second City format and that Charna was actually giving him an institution within which he could do the explorations and the research that he wanted to do.

There's a sort of ideological split, isn't there, with Second City slightly denigrating improvisation as a performance medium, whereas Del and Charna really wanted to show audiences improvisation happening live in front of them?

That Bernie Sahlins and Del Close split. Bernie, who was the owner-producer of Second City for years and often directed, was less interested in improvisation for its own sake but more as way of developing new material. Whereas Del always wanted to get improvisation to the point where paying audiences would show up knowing that everything was going to be made up in front of them, and they would still pay to see people who had such skill that they could trust that their money would be well spent.

I think that the final vindication of Del's perspective was TJ and Dave— TJ Jagodowski and David Pasquesi. They perform once a week in Chicago. Whenever they come to New York to do four performances, all their producer has to do is announce to the community that TJ and Dave are here and—without any advertising whatsoever—they sell out all four shows. That's because everybody knows how good they are. Whatever happens will be worth watching.

So my book ended up having something to do with the founding of The Annoyance, and iO. And of course Upright Citizen's Brigade came out of iO, and out of UCB came the Magnet Theatre and The People's Improv Theatre. My joke is I have inadvertently become the illegitimate grandfather of all these troupes. And you know kids: they never write, they never call...

Do you still use the work? Does it still influence your playwriting or your other works? Do you still improvise?

Oh yeah. Every summer, for the past five or six summers, a very nice couple lend us their beautiful summer house on Cape Cod. And I invite a group of improvisers who are also writers, who are working on projects, and we spend the week improvising based on each other's premises. We record the improvs. If I improvise based on your premise, whatever I do is a gift to you, and if you improvise based on my premise, whatever you do is a gift to me. This is absolutely understood going in so nobody will argue over who owns what.

There is an actress-writer I was very fond of named Catherine Butterfield. I invited her the first year. And there is an improvisational writer-director named Ron West who also came the first year. And they've been together ever since. They met at that. Dan Castellaneta and his wife Deb Lacusta have been fairly regular participants as well. They did an improv for Catherine that turned into the first scene of a play that she later had produced off-Broadway. And Catherine, Ron, Dan, and Deb continue to work this way. They're based in Los Angeles and they now have a regular group that meets weekly, developing stuff.

So this is a community that continues to develop material this way. I'm not one of these people who sits firmly in one pew when it comes to improvisation. There are some people—like Del—who are absolute purists. It's got to be absolutely in the moment, you can't polish and refine stuff later. And then there are other people at the other end of the spectrum—more in the Bernie camp—who say, "Oh this is a great way for developing finished material." I think it's all valid. All of it is in pursuit of doing something worth watching on a stage. If I lean towards one end rather than the other, it's because I'm not as good an improviser as TJ and Dave!

I remember reading this one book—it was a fairly terrible, mean book—but it contained one fairly smart observation which almost redeemed the otherwise hideous quality of it. (I'm purposely repressing the author's name.) But she observed that when you talk about people going to their first impulses, frequently the first impulse is to go to stereotype and caricature. You're not going to get very fresh stuff if, as soon as somebody says "Catholic priest," the first thing you get is some creepy guy threatening to abuse children on stage. That's become a standard-issue, automatic response.

The cliché is the first impulse that almost everybody will go to. Del sometimes would talk about doing a bank shot, which was go to your first impulse and then bounce off that someplace else. There are people now who do bank shots automatically. There's been a big emphasis on the idea of saying "yes and" to everything, which of course is an important idea. But sometimes if you say "yes and" to your first impulse, you're going to go straight into caricature and cliché. So sometimes instead of instantly embracing the first thing you feel or you think of, it's better to recognize that you're heading into the trap of cliché and then put a hop on the ball and see where it bounces next. So take the second bounce, not the first.

A lot of the people who are trying to do work like TJ and Dave are what I call "first bounce people"—they just give you the obvious. (Did I just coin a term, there: *first bounce people?*) I believe in second bounce improvisation—not taking the first impulse, but taking the second, because the first is usually something a lot of other people have already done, but the second is often oblique and provocative.

But also, you can only improvise based on what's inside you: what you've experienced or understand, or what you've learned about. And if you aren't curious about the larger world, then what the hell are you going to comment on or satirize? There are a lot of people who are going into it now whose highest aim is to get onto *Saturday Night Live* and then do franchise movies. That's why you see an awful lot of these films that claim to be satiric but actually have very little genuine satiric comment except about showbiz conventions. The early Second City people had studied widely in literature, philosophy, and history, and they knew a lot of shit so they commented on a lot of shit. If you have people who are going into this and all they know is show business, it's going to be pretty repetitive and pale stuff. How many parodies of commercials can you do? How many parodies of game shows can you do? It's so often just the same old tired crap.

I'm a great believer in people coming at it with a deeper reference level. That's what was distinctive about people like Mike Nichols and Elaine May—they had read everything. This is why Shelley Berman felt so insecure around them! They would be talking about what they had read, and Berman would hear the names of philosophers or novelists—people whose names he had never encountered before—and, panicking, he would run off and start reading all of this stuff so that he would be able to hold his own in these conversations. Shelley had not gone to the University of Chicago. Actually, neither had Elaine. She would attend classes, but she never enrolled. Still, she was part of that community and was ferociously well-read.

But there are an awful lot of people who are doing this who don't know much about anything except comedy and show business. So the content isn't fed by very fresh springs. There's a metaphor for you! But one of the things that's on the highest end is *Curb Your Enthusiasm*, which is all showbiz humor. It's very good, but if I don't watch it regularly it's because I have a low tolerance for too much showbiz humor.

That's something we've written about, too. When improvisers are thrown on stage and just told to make stuff up, if there's any anxiety in them at all then they may retreat into trivia because that feels safe. They won't reveal anything about themselves because they won't have to confront anything uncomfortable.

Well, there are two impulses. One is to go into autobiography, which Del went into a lot. And the other is to go into the journalist mode, which is to be very interested in people and structures and institutions and conventions outside yourself. If you do too much autobiography it risks becoming masturbation and pleading for approval or sympathy. But if you get really interested in other people and other institutions and revealing the secret mechanisms of society, then I think you can go a pretty long distance. The world is endless and inexhaustible. Your own resources, your own autobiography—they're not inexhaustible. Certainly Tennessee Williams ran out of stuff to write. You can never run out of material drawn from the larger world. I think curiosity about the larger world is vastly important to having ongoing careers in this area. You have to be interested in something outside your own little enclave, otherwise you're just going to end up recycling the same bits.

5.12

Dylan Emery—Starter of *Showstopper*

Dylan is a performer, teacher and director of improvisational theatre. He co-founded *Showstopper! The Improvised Musical*, *Grand Theft Impro* and *The School of Night*. *Showstopper* had a 10-week run in London's West End in the autumn of 2015, for which it won the Olivier under the Best Entertainment category. It was the first improvised show ever to be nominated for (and therefore also the first to win) an Olivier.

Hi Dylan. Let's start with you. How did you get into improvisation in the first place?

An ex-girlfriend of mine was working for Camelot, the people who do the Lottery, and she was in marketing and branding and so on. They had brought in an external expert to do some improvisation workshops, a guy called Alan Marriott. He turned out to be a world-class improviser and one of the big creative forces behind the growth of impro in the UK. She didn't know it at the time—she just thought it was so much fun, and so different from the way that she learnt to be creative in the corporate world, that she asked whether she could do classes with him. By chance, he had just started doing weekly drop-in workshops down in the Chrysalis Theatre in Balham. After she started doing the classes, she called me and said "This is really your kind of thing—you should come." And so I did.

And did you see it straight away and go, "Oh, this is it, this is what I want to do."?

Yes, I immediately thought this is incredibly compelling and fun. It was the spark that kept me excited about life. I did it for a year or so doing workshops and occasional shows at the theatre in front of our friends, and then Alan said he was going to get a couple of his old veteran impro friends who hadn't been doing very much performing in recent times—there wasn't much regular impro going on at all at the time—and set up a regular public show. He asked me if I wanted to be in it—but also, because I was reasonably well organized (I wasn't a performer by profession, but a financial journalist so good with deadlines) I offered to help produce it. That's how Alan and I started up *Grand Theft Impro*.

You know when you start doing short-form impro and it's incredibly exciting and people laugh a lot? That might be because you've come up with a line or two, but mostly it's just because they are impressed that you're doing it at all. The audience are mostly people who have a reason to be generous—your friends, other improvisers and so on. That is a nice and nurturing environment to start performing in—that's how it had been at the shows we had done at the Chrysalis.

However, *GTI* was a commercial show in the middle of Soho aimed at ordinary comedy-goers. There were some people from Alan's workshops that came but mostly it was non-improvisers. If it wasn't funny, they wouldn't laugh. Instead they would stare resentfully, the unspoken question being "Why are you wasting my precious evening out with this bullshit?"

The most important lesson I learned was that I had no idea what I was doing. Alan was very nice about it, Phil Whelans (another founder member of *GTI*) was much more direct, and between them they created the crucible in which I learned.

The two shows that I think of you being most involved in are those two: Showstopper *and* Grand Theft Impro, *and what I find interesting is that they are very different.* Grand Theft *is very short form—loose, funny, playful. And although* Showstopper *has that playful element, it's much more focused on narrative, characters and of course the musical numbers themselves. Did you have any kind of reaction to that? Are you keen on as broad a church as possible? Are those the two things you think improvisation is good at? How have you ended up doing two such different shows?*

This is one of the things that I have recently become increasingly interested in, in people's training. I think nomenclature is limiting people's improv. They find it very hard to say "short form" without saying "short form game," and of course those two are completely different—games are the structures you might use in a short form, but you can do short form without any games (I'm not talking about the game of the scene, but games as in Emotional Rollercoaster, Arms Through Expert, etc.), you just do a short scene. Similarly, just because you have been doing long-form shows doesn't mean you can do narrative impro.

Grand Theft has always done some of the traditional impro games, but the heart of it is open scenes—get a suggestion from the audience and see where you end up—don't impose a pre-set structure. You might introduce all those tricksier "gamey" skills you've learned like gibberish, switch/change and so on—but only if the scene seems to call for it.

Showstopper is very different because it came out of *The School of Night*, a theatre show revolving around improvising in the styles of poets, novelists and playwrights, the core being improvising "lost" Shakespeare plays. It was founded by Ken Campbell and, like everyone who had contact with him, he had a profound impact on me as a performer and director.

The first show I ever did with Ken was at the Royal Court theatre. We were improvising Mamet, Pinter, Beckett, John Osborne. I was the musician for the show at that point. None of us really knew what we were doing, including Ken. But Ken, as has been said many times, was a seeker. Once he'd found out how to make something consistently successful, he generally lost interest in doing it. Not for his one-man shows, I should say, which were honed to micrometer exactitude. But for all the stuff he did with us, he restlessly pushed us into his next experiment in theatre.

What was interesting about that training is that Ken didn't really know much about impro or how you might improvise, but he absolutely knew everything about theatre and what makes an interesting show. And he was a master of the dynamic between audience and performer. He used what we call the "goader and rhapsodes" technique, in which he would give us a series of apparently impossible challenges to see if in the attempt we managed to surprise both ourselves and the audience with something really worth watching.

In my experience, most comedy-orientated impro doesn't make good use of the space it's being performed in. Often it ends up with two performers facing each other in the middle of the stage for three minutes as they try to think of funny things to say. And that's down to the training, which often stops after "how to improvise comedy sketches." Ken wasn't interested in a couple of folk wittering on while people watched. He wanted extreme emotion, extraordinary feats of prowess, amazing stage pictures, blood-curdling plot-twists, exquisitely impossible mental contortions.

So when Adam Meggido and I (and the rest of the founder members) were creating *Showstopper*, it didn't occur to us to create improvised sketches with some songs dropped in. We automatically went for the whole theatrical experience. All improvisers should remember that they are not just comedy writers and performers—they are also actors, choreographers and directors—and don't forget lighting and sound design. If you don't work on those skills and use them, you're missing out a huge chunk of what might make your performance interesting to the audience.

So how did Showstopper *emerge from* The School of Night?

When *The School* first started, almost no one in the group had any formal impro training. They had done improvisational exercises at drama school, of course, but the idea of being able to improvise something that people would pay to watch wasn't part of the training of the vast majority of drama schools. That's still the case today. Part of Alan Marriot's training was how to improvise songs. And as I was resident musician with the School of Night, I suggested that we improvise songs as part of our set. Ken immediately embraced the idea and we started doing it straight away.

Now *The School of Night* had started out as a competitive impro format. It was formed in 2005—this was before my time—when Mark Rylance (then artistic director at the Globe) asked Ken to come up with something to celebrate Shakespeare's birthday. Ken created what was basically Elizabethan Theatresports with games like "best wounded messenger," "most boring lords" and so on. One of the games he created was essentially a modification of emotional rollercoaster, but characters would switch between the four humors instead—sanguine, melancholic, choleric, phlegmatic. It was always a winner—and, as with anything that seemed to be working, Ken wanted to test it to destruction. He asked: why not get people to sing their humors? And why not make each humor have its own unique style?

So he created this insane part of the show, which reached its peak in 2006, when we went up to Edinburgh to do a show called *In Pursuit of Cardenio*. By the end of the run, the last chunk of the show consisted of a musical Elizabethan humor roller-coaster. There were eight actors each with four unique musical styles they would sing in depending on which humor they were in. I had these thirty-two different styles written on bits of paper in front of me, and I had keyboards and guitars and percussion around, and as they were doing scenes, they would switch between different humors, and I would have to switch to different styles of music on the whim of the actor. Completely manic and bonkers, but I guess it was interesting to watch, and it was certainly fun.

At that point, I talked to Adam (who as well as a cast member of *The School of Night* was the artistic director of what is now called Extempore Theatre) about creating a narrative Shakespeare show. I said I thought the Shakespearean scenes were extraordinary, but no one knew how to end a scene because every scene ended with Ken saying "Right, enough of that. Next!" And these musical bits-and-bobs we were doing were really interesting, but no one could ever finish a song. It was a by-product of the goader and rhapsodes technique.

Adam wasn't that interested in a Shakespeare narrative show, but as a musical theatre performer and writer, he was very interested in the idea of taking all the song stuff we'd been doing and turning that into a show. The thing that really triggered it, that actually got us busy, was when we did a Halloween show with the *School* in 2006 at the Union Theatre in London. And Ken thought we would end the thing on a musical, which basically meant he could sit down and watch the last bit. And he said, "Let's get a really dark suggestion for the musical." And so the audience gave us Dennis Nilsen the serial killer.

The whole group was full of people who could actually act and sing and move, even if they weren't hugely polished improvisers at that time. Adam had taken the protagonist role, playing Nilsen himself and I was on keys. And we found this very Sondheim/*Sweeney Todd* moment where he sang about the man he loved while cutting the throats and strangling a series of men on Hampstead Heath. It was horrific and extraordinary and really good theatre.

So after that, Adam and I said, "Okay, so now we have to do something." Adam suggested we do a week-long residency—essentially a training course—at the Actors Centre in London. We would spend an intensive week with whoever booked to come on the course—and at the end of it we would improvise a musical in front of an audience. Ken came in to take a few sessions, but the bulk of it was me and Adam experimenting on the people in the workshop, asking them to do things, realizing it didn't seem to be working, tweaking it, reversing it, and eventually throwing it out and trying something new. I imagine it was probably like being on the crew of a galleon in the middle of a storm with two clearly insane but energetic captains shouting contradictory orders. But at the end they did a show and it was thrilling to watch and we realized this thing had legs. Now we just needed to find a cast to turn it into a professional show.

The thing I really admire about Showstopper *is the care that everyone seems to take and the commitment to quality. And that's a weird thing to refer to when you're talking about something that's improvised, but I think it is important. One of the reasons to do an improvised comedy show is that a good improvised comedy show stands a fighting chance of being funnier than a scripted comedy show, and that's the reason to do it.*

One of Ken's memorable quotes was "There's no point in doing it unless it's going to be better than the scripted stuff." And one of things that impro does better than scripted stuff is allowing the audience to see the moment of creation. Often the most memorable bits of a stand-up routine are often the unscripted bits of banter with the audience. So, one choice we could have made would be to do a show that encouraged as much of that as possible. What you would end up with is a show that asks this question: "What would it be like if we asked a bunch of funny improvisers to do a parody of a musical?"

There is a lot of fun to be had with that notion—it generally pushes you towards underlining the clichés of musical theatre, overacting, making wild story choices. However, the question we asked ourselves was not that one. We asked this one: "What would it be like to watch a bunch of talented actors actually try to improvise a great musical?" It's a lot harder to make that show work. As Carl Reiner put it: "A brilliant mind in panic is a wonderful thing to see." We are not letting the audience see that. You don't get characters struggling to sing their songs in a scripted musical, so we've trained to be able to improvise fairly sophisticated songs with a high degree of skill and confidence. But then we are in danger of the show becoming earnest and dull, so then Adam and I have to inject more creative excitement and more whimsy—but the danger then is that it loses emotional resonance and becomes trivial and throw-away and forgettable. We are always riding the wave between those two outcomes.

However, when it works, it's great. Having sincere, well-acted, beautifully constructed scenes that make the audience cry—followed immediately by hilarious dicking about. That's our aim. Another of our mantras is that we of course want to make the audience laugh. But what's better is if we can make them cry. And what's the best is if we can make them gasp. We are aiming to extract from musical theatre what makes it a great art form, not just what makes it recognizable.

It's the same with *School of Night* when it does theatre styles: "What would it be like if Mamet had written another great play?" rather than "What are the three parodic elements you can do in a short form sketch about Mamet?" If you think about why he was a great playwright, then it occurs to you it might be a good idea to improvise in the style of Mamet even if the audience had no idea you were doing it—your scenes would just be more interesting.

The problems of approaching an idea from the point of view of "how would I improvise it?" as opposed to "why is it great?" also applies to narrative impro, which I see a lot of groups struggling with. For instance, let's talk about story structure. An awful lot of people learn improv by doing Harolds—or some other free-wheeling montage style. If you go from a Harold into a pure narrative show, the natural thing to do is to modify the Harold into a story-form. A typical outcome of that is to have the first three scenes being in totally different worlds with different characters. Then the troupe spend the rest of the show trying to knit the three worlds together. Now, that is certainly a way to make a show feel like it has an ending, because by simply weaving one world out of three you create the story diamond: starting from nothing, you break it out, you reach the mid-point and stop creating new stuff, then you just keep tying things together until it comes back into a point. And it will feel, to the audience, like that's definitely the end because you've brought the strands together.

However, look at great musicals and plays and very few are structured like that—instead they more or less stick with the protagonist and a few other major characters who are closely connected to the protagonist from the start to finish. If your central characters take two-thirds of the play just to meet then it's going to be hard to create tight, emotionally packed, economic narrative. I see a lot of groups that try to create narrative shows out of Harolds and they struggle because they are, in my mind, wearing roller-skates to go rock-climbing, as it were.

However, you can get trapped in other ways as well. Another popular route to narrative is to look at the Hero's Journey (coming out of Joseph Campbell's *The Hero with A Thousand Faces*)—it's a massively popular way to analyze films, books, plays. We spent our first few years churning out Hero's Journey style musicals—and we got pretty good at them. But eventually Adam and I got frustrated with the limitations of that form. We asked the question: would we ever naturally improvise something like *Into the Woods? Merrily We Roll Along? The 25th Annual Putnam County Spelling Bee? Cats?* No! If you use the Hero's Journey as a way to create, you'll never get those stories.

So, we started looking at musicals that had different forms. The first was romantic comedies—we analyzed them and worked out structurally how to improvise them in rehearsal and then started doing those in shows. Then we looked at multi-plot epic musicals, whodunits, book club musicals (what we call a show with a bunch of characters in one place each telling their story) and so on—and we worked on each of them until the cast were sick of them, but had worked them into their bones. Now when we start a show, we don't need to have any particular pre-set structure or style. The cast works out which of those—or which mixture of those elements—grows out of this particular show.

So, the system is: remove most of your creative freedom, work on a whole series of small skills until you are very comfortable with them, then give yourself your freedom back. We've recently been working on multiple time line structures—a difficult, disciplined form because you can't be messy with who does what where otherwise you'll never tell a coherent story. So now we've done that work, it's available to us if the show demands. It's just like learning impro game skills and then playing open scenes and using the game forms as it occurs you to do it, rather than forcing it.

So that is, essentially, the way that we've eventually learnt to do *Showstopper*, which is why the shows can be very varied. Most people who sees the show assume there must be a structure to the show, and they ask us what it is. Well in fact they are not wrong—there is a very strong structure to every show of ours that's any good, it's just that we didn't know what the structure was going to be before we started.

And we do the same also with music. Again, you start by going, "Okay, how do you make it sound like Gilbert and Sullivan?" So you identify a sub-style of Gilbert and Sullivan songs—and you work out a highly controlled set of guidelines about kinds of tune, harmony, lyrical content, pace, pulse and so on. It will also be rather stultifyingly limited, but it is repeatable and it completely sounds like Gilbert and Sullivan, because it's kind of an amalgam of three or four well known songs in the sub-genre.

And then you go, "Right, now let's identify another subset of songs from Gilbert and Sullivan"—trios, patter songs, or whatever. And then once you've done three or four or five different sub-styles, you then say, "Now, let's just sing a Gilbert and Sullivan song without saying which type it is and see what happens." And suddenly you end up genuinely just exploring their musical world, able to create a song that totally sounds like them but isn't a parody of any particular song or set of songs.

Can you talk a little bit about how your role on stage has developed over the years?

Yes, it's changed a lot. The reason why there is an on-stage director at all is because the first time we did it at the Actors Centre, neither me, nor Adam, nor our cast had any very clear idea what was going to happen but there was a show to do and an audience to be entertained. And we are very audience-minded, as Ken was. It has to be compelling for the paying public. We're not interested in shows in which the cast have a better time than the audience. We thought it was advisable for one of us to be an on-stage director, to push the story on, move quickly on if any bits of the show collapsed, re-iterate plot calls that not everyone might have clocked and generally make sure the show was fun even if it fell apart. I'd done onstage directing before so I took the job.

Well, nine years and 730 shows later, my job is very different from what it was at the start. At the beginning I would often more or less call the entire show—including plot developments, emotional reactions, calling songs. Now I don't need to do any of those things. Our cast can manage scene and story-work themselves. We don't need a chair any more to keep the show on track.

However, it turns out there's a lot of fun to be had with a chair even if you don't need one. There is a unique three-way relationship between chair, cast and audience, which doesn't exist in any other show that I know. The high-status chair is under pressure trying to create a musical. He has very little creative power himself—so he needs the audience to give him ideas, which then the cast implement. The chair takes credit for good work and takes the blame when things go wrong. He has ultimate power over the cast—they will try to do whatever he says without question—but it won't always come out as he (or anyone) expects—the audience can cheer one moment and throw him a curveball the next. So his status is constantly being raised and then lowered. It's an interesting roller-coaster to ride.

Another one of the chair's main jobs is to make sure the audience is as integrated into the show as possible—we want them to realize it is their show—without their ideas, nothing would happen. So, we get the setting and the title from them—but also we get plot twists, big protagonist decisions and more. There are a great many impro shows that get a single word from the audience at the start and then it's a case of "Sit back and watch us be brilliant for 45 minutes." That's not for us.

Another thing the chair did from the very first show was get musicals from the audience—and we'd do songs in the styles of those musicals in the show. I think it came out of our genre music work that we'd done with Ken—and our keyboard player James Lovelock could do a few different styles. However, getting audiences to shout out musicals has become a big part of the workload in rehearsing for the show because we have to be able to improvise songs in the styles of all of the hit shows of Broadway and the West End and a big chunk of the lesser-known ones.

One part of the chair's role has never changed and that is the idea of re-writing the contract between actors and audience. When an audience comes to an impro show, they generally have the attitude that this is a comedy show, and therefore when someone says, "shout out suggestions," they might think the funny thing is to shout out stupid or vulgar suggestions. In a short form show, you can deal with that by simply accepting it, doing a two-minute scene and moving on, until eventually the audience realizes they are enjoying the scenes set in The Palace of Versailles and 20,000 leagues under the sea and Wall Street more than the ones set in toilets in Scunthorpe.

But in *Showstopper*, or in any kind of long-form show, there's just the one audience decision which lasts all evening. So, the first ten minutes of the show are spent really trying to get the audience to understand that we are trying to create a genuinely great musical here, and if they play along and suggest things they actually want to see, then everyone can have a better time. A big part of the fun is leading audiences into the world of musicals. We still get people shouting out something because they think it's funny—but I will simply not take it. I will absolutely turn down certain suggestions, even if I know we could do it really well—because I want to reward the audience for their ambition rather than their wit.

The last thing I want to talk about is your amazing recent achievement of getting an improvised show into the West End—one of about two or three I can remember in thirty years. How did that come about?

It came about partially because *Showstopper* itself had grown into a well-known brand over the years. We tend to sell very well in Edinburgh, we tour all over the UK and other countries as well. And for a show with no celebrities in it, that's pretty good. Actually some of the cast members are now quite well known for their other work on stage, radio and TV—people like Pippa Evans, Ruth Bratt, Lucy Trodd, Sarah-Louise Young. All that gives potential investors in a West End run some confidence. But even established shows packed with celebrities fail in the West End—it's a very hard business.

So when it comes down to it, the reason why we got into the West End is because hard-bitten industry veterans fell in love with the show and were prepared to risk losing substantial amounts of money to see something genuinely new. There were many contributors but the main ones were Keith Strachan—our long-term backer and one of the directors of the production company; Ray Cooney, who knows everyone and has supported us for years; Nica Burns, who owns the Apollo Theatre and really pushed for us to get in there. It needed those very special people because the vast majority of typical theatre investors wouldn't touch something like this.

They want to see a script, they want to come to a reading, they want some kind of guarantee of quality, which you can provide through your training and dedication, but you can't provide it in the form that backers are used to.

Yes, exactly. They come from traditional theatre and traditional theatre doesn't have much to do with improvisation. But it's not just backers that are conservative—theatre-goers are as well. The kind of person who can afford top West End seat prices has probably little free time and wants a guaranteed good night out. An improvised show doesn't sound like a guarantee.

Convincing mainstream audiences that they should come and see the show has always been a challenge. I think it was Sondheim who said one of the roles of the opening number was to convince the audience that they had made the right choice in buying a ticket. So one of the earliest things we worked on was to make our opening numbers tight, impressive, structured, so non-impro punters could relax in the knowledge that they were in the hands of people who knew what they were doing. By the time we got to the Apollo run, we'd gone through many iterations of our process—Adam and I were confident our cast would always deliver something good—so now we encourage the cast to be as creative and daring as possible from the moment the lights go up.

And how was the Apollo run?

It was great! The quality of the shows was the highest we'd ever consistently achieved. Although it was also quite sobering to realize the scale of the challenge. In Edinburgh in 2015 we were in the Pleasance One—a big venue for the Fringe. For a sell-out run, across the whole month, we would sell 8,500 tickets or so. That would fill the Apollo for just two weeks of our ten-week run. And the amount you have to spend on marketing is huge. You can spend £100,000 over a ten-week run just to have posters on a handful of tube stations covered. It's absolutely insane.

You've got a big cast to manage as well haven't you?

Yes. There are eleven people in one of our big shows—seven on stage, a band of three musicians and a lighting improviser. So, there's a lot of people to manage, the cost is pretty high, but the marketing is the real killer.

Was it a big transition from bigger fringe theatres to the Apollo?

The most important thing was that we could set up our sound from scratch, using pro equipment, so the monitoring was exactly what we needed. I mean, our show has got the weirdest, most awkward monitoring you can imagine. For every other musical, how you do good musical sound design is you have almost nothing on stage, there's piano and people can hear their own voices, because that's all they need. However, we can't do that, because you have to be able to hear everyone else constantly so you can improvise harmonies, sing counter-melodies and so on. Everything that the audience hears has to be heard on stage. The feedback issues alone mean you shouldn't do it if you have a choice. But we have no choice.

We had this guy called Tom Lishman, who is a very experienced West End sound designer, and he came in and created a beautiful on-stage sound, we could hear everything with crystal clarity. We also had our own lighting rig and set—having your own dedicated space meant we felt really comfortable.

On opening night, the question was, "Can we step up and make this space not look like a fringe group have hired it, but like this is the *Showstopper* theatre?" And that was the most exciting task. Could we do the ultimately audacious thing, which is take this rag-tag fugitive fleet of improvisers who for years had been starting their show pretending to get a call from Cameron Macintosh who needed a musical to go into the West End, actually go into the West End and get away with it?

And so what next with Showstopper? *Will there be more West End runs? Bigger theatres? Bigger touring? Is it going to change? What are your plans?*

We're going to go back to the Edinburgh for our ninth year, and we are now moving up the Pleasance Grand. That's a big risk for us, because we are producing it, so we could lose out. It's more than twice as big as the Pleasance One. We are also taking it earlier—6:00 p.m. instead of 10:30 p.m. So, the question is: Will more mainstream people, regular people, be as keen to see it as everyone else? We're hoping yes, because lots of people did come to see it in the West End, so hopefully they will come to see us there.

It's hard to go back, that's the problem. Once you've had something that looks as great as it did in the Apollo, you then don't want people to see a show with substantially lower production values. So there's that, there's bigger touring venues and there's quite a few possibilities doing international tours around the place. There's a few theatres out in Hong Kong and Singapore which we've been to before which will probably happen again.

And we're always looking to see if anyone in the States is interested. How would be we do on Broadway? It seems to me, having gone to the States quite a lot, and Canada, and done a lot of impro there, the one thing that *Showstopper* has which is different from a lot of British impro is that a lot of British impro is verbal and talky and sarcastic. American impro on the whole is big and loud and positive and naïve is some senses, and our show is the same.

If an audience member spends most of their time assuming that there is a trick—some secret way that we are making it easy for ourselves, then they are not going to enjoy the show very much. You have to embrace it. So that will be interesting, trying to find out whether American audiences would say, "This is just great, these guys are really trying something insanely ambitious!" Or, whether they instead they will say, "What do these Brits think they are doing to our art form?" We'll see...

5.13

Paul Rogan—An English Actor and Improviser in LA

When we first started showing up to improvisation classes in London, Paul was one of the teachers who would lead workshops, and we consistently found that his workshops were some of the most useful and enjoyable. Now he's one of the leading lights of LA Impro Theatre.

How did you get involved in improvisation in the first place?

In the 1980s I used to go to Battersea Arts Centre a lot, and one day there was a show there called *Omelette Broadcasting*. It was Jim Sweeney, Steve Steen, Peter Wear and Justin Case, two double acts who had come together to form an improvising team. And they performed the fishbowl: an audience writes suggestions for a scene using the word "Meanwhile…" and then they're put in the fishbowl so that there's no cheating, "Look, we didn't stuff this in advance, you can see." And one by one they performed these improvised scenes, some longer, some shorter, some just as gags, and that was the moment that changed my life, seeing that show. And at the end, Jim Sweeney said, "So hands up if you had one of your scenes done," and half the audience put their hands up, including me.

Can you remember what your scene was?

No, I don't. Wouldn't that be a great thing? But I went up to Jim Sweeney afterwards and I said, "This is amazing. How can I do this?" I had already been doing theatre at university and I was at a theatre company in Fulham called The Lost Theatre, directing and acting, but I'd never seen improvisation before. Never heard of it even. So, Jim said "There's a book called *Impro* by Keith Johnstone, that's what you need to get." So, I got it, and within a week or two I was teaching it at The Lost Theatre to try and get other people doing it and within a few more weeks we were doing a 24-hour all-night improv marathon as a fundraiser for the theatre.

Was it something that came relatively easily to you?

Yes, it was a natural home because I'm sort of quick-witted, and also shallow and lazy! Plus, I have natural inclinations towards story and character. So my style has always been character improv based. Funnily enough, I'm currently teaching a narrative class for Impro Theatre in LA, and one of the things we're looking at is Dan Harmon's story circle. And we're specifically looking at the first quarter of the story circle, which is the normal world, and what we're trying to do is slow everybody down because everybody starts off with a rush to story. And part of the theory of this is you have the whole quarter, the whole first quarter of a show, to build the normal world of your character and their wants.

The more naturalistic you can make it, the more you can create a hero character who is relatable, who is likeable, who has hero qualities, whatever they may be, in the genre and tone that you're doing, the better. And so we work on status to adjust to the hero and then we play with "Could you pass off the hero to another character in this scene?" And we're using "want" monologues a lot because that's something that Jo McGinley has drilled into us. Want monologues. Instead of just getting to the point where you've got an opening scene and it's starting to go towards trouble, want monologue and that will give you the entire long form.

Not long after that I saw a thing in the *Evening Standard* about Kit Hollerbach and the Comedy Store Players so that was my next step. That's where I met a whole bunch of people—including James Gaddas, who became my first double act partner in the Sean Connery Brotherhood, an improv-based double act; and Luke Sorba, who led me to Alan Marriott and the Theatresports people who were just about to start up at the Donmar Warehouse. And Theatresports is where I met you guys and also Dan O'Connor visiting from the States.

Then when I went to LA ten years ago, I followed up the connection with Dan O'Connor because the Theatresports locally there was the obvious home for me, and I went to see some of their shows, talked to Dan about doing the courtroom drama, which I did with Pete Wear of the original *Omelette Broadcasting*. But I was watching the Masterpiece Theatre Jane Austens thinking "Why on earth is nobody improvising Jane Austen?" And so I proposed that to Dan and the Jane Austen became their best-selling show, and still is. Dan, by the way, is a tremendous and inspirational company leader, and would be a CEO somewhere if he wasn't the AD of Impro Theatre.

Were they already doing genre narrative shows?

I saw them doing Dickens and I also attended a workshop where they were doing Shakespeare. They had already done Chekhov which is, to my mind, the single best improv there can be, improvising Chekhov, and I'll explain that later.

Let me ask you quite a fundamental question about this: there are two related questions and they come back to the same thing, why do this? On the one hand why improvise it? If you have an insight into the world of let's say Austen and you can generate a really charming pastiche Austen, why not write it and guarantee that it's as good as it can be through iteration? And, at the same time, as improvisers, why subsume yourself into a previous genre; why not create stuff from scratch?

These are great questions. First of all, I mentioned the laziness thing, but that's not really it. There's a maxim in screenwriting, or any kind of playwriting, that you shouldn't tell anybody what you're writing because as soon as you've done that, you've told the story and you will no longer have the desire to actually sit down and write it. By the same token, if you're an improviser, it's very hard to pull yourself out of that world and go back and write because you are telling new stories every night, so the impulse to sit down and write it seems much more tedious and time consuming. Which is not to say that improvisers don't make great writers. The ones with story instincts really do.

But also, there are people who have come to see our improvised plays hundreds of times, because we can do a different one every night. There are Jane Austen addicts who will come and see our Jane Austens over and over again, in the same way that they would otherwise be consuming Jane Austen fan fiction.

Why do this in the first place? Well, I don't really know why we do this. We just do. If you look at it from outside, it seems like a really odd-ball thing to do, to study an author academically and break down how they tell story, how their characters interrelate and how to—it's a unique process for every author.

From the audience's point of view, to what extent does it look like an adaptation of a Jane Austen book they were unfamiliar with, and to what extent does it look like an improvised comedy show?

We are aiming for it to look like a theatrical adaptation.

Do you get any initial suggestion from the audience?

Yes. For that particular show, and it's unique to every genre, the ask-for is, "Could we have a suggestion of a trivial topic of conversation?" Jane Austen is a mistress of the small things. So, that was my notion of having a trivial conversation. Whatever that is, perhaps it's leaves, becomes a way in which you can differentiate the world views of—if it's a two-sister show, the two sisters and how they are different. So, leaves mean something outdoorsy and wonderful for one sister because it means I can rush through a country afternoon, kick up the leaves, but to her sister they are those awful things that clog up your shoes and get your dress all wet, because I prefer to be indoors reading a book. It started just as a way to start a show, but now we use it to create a world-view because to us one of the models for Jane Austen is bonding with shared values, that's the key phrase.

Then we get a second suggestion after the interval—usually "which two characters would you like to see together in the next scene?"—just in case anyone thinks we're using the time to pre-plan the second half. In fact what we're doing, as well as just having a break, is going over character names and wants.

And you have costumes?

Yes. And they become better and more authentic as the years have gone by.

Isn't there a danger that if you put all the emphasis on story and character and theatre that some of the sparkle will go? Is that something you talk about or do you find that you are able to keep that playfulness without having to work at it?

It's very carefully thought through. I said our shows look like a theatre show but that's our intention. It never quite makes it that far because our performers have comedy instincts which take us to comedic moments, as long as we don't break the reality of the piece.

Your intention almost is not to quite succeed.

Yes, exactly. For example, our Tennessee Williams can get very much like a play, and it's a huge debate and one we have with our students all the time. Our main company consists of people who have done thirty years of comedy, and so they cannot but help but find riffs and gags. I have a thing about playing the game of the character. We have students who've trained at UCB and iO, Improv Olympic, and they all use that phrase "finding the game" differently, so it needs to be very carefully parsed in order to work out what it means. But to me it is; it's finding a gag, it's finding a character note and riffing it. But increasingly my thought is your hero character is like Seinfeld who is the one that everyone dances around.

But our students came to us a few years ago and said the work we're doing is great, and it's beautifully narrative, but how do we find the comedy, like you guys? And it is something we have taken on. We've re-introduced Theatresports as a show in order to help people have fun and hone those comedy instincts. And I've just reproduced The Fishbowl in the last few weeks, and that's going to be happening in the autumn for exactly that reason, to teach students about comedy.

I think Theatresports in particular is great for that spirit of play and that spirit of "everything is an offer," all the machinery of the show is an offer.

And that's what we're going for. The key difference for us with the Jane Austen was when we started doing it and realized that towards the end, after all the laughter and the fun of telling these stories, that there was a proposal or a romantic moment and we would hear the audience go, "Ohh…" and realizing that we were capable of producing in an audience the same emotional effect as a play. And that was a transformational moment in the company because we realized that you didn't just have to do comedy; there was a serious level of emotion you could tap into. If you go and see an improv show and you laugh and it's fun, you'll go, "Great, I've seen that now." But if you go and see an improv show and you cry, then you are going to love that company forever and that was our transformational moment.

There has been an explosion of our improv community in the last two years. It's astounding! There is a whole generation of nerdy twenty and thirty somethings who have found a home with Impro Theatre. Last night they were doing another "nerd night" where they do their *Star Trek: The Next Generation* improvised. There's an all-girl company called Ripley (as in the lead girl in *Alien*), and their intention is to do girl, all-girl genre improv, and they are currently doing YA dystopia which I've seen and it's tremendous.

Because they've had our training, the storytelling is immaculate and they stay rigorously in character, but they have the sense of fun because they are smart and funny performers. And there's a Dungeons and Dragons team who have actually come down from Minnesota, moved to LA, and wholesale now moved into our community and are taking classes and helping shape the future of it. So it's from beneath there's this volcanic pressure of young fun improvisers.

Our theatre is becoming the natural home for people who are interested in story, who have maybe done their initial training at Improv Olympic and UCB but who want to do something different. Ours is more woman-friendly, for example. There's been a whole thing recently about sexual harassment because there were a couple of incidents at other companies. You teach an improviser they have to say yes, so someone says "Hey bitch, suck my dick," and somebody might feel they have to pretend to do that on stage. There are certain people who don't want to be around improvisers like that, and that whole thing is being addressed as a thing we can't do.

I've been looking at the list of genres you've covered. I can see that tapping in to the repressed relationships of Jane Austen-type characters would get a lot of out good improvisers, and I've always thought that improvising in the style of Shakespeare was great for getting people to play with bigger emotions and more creative use of language. But among your shows was an improvised Twilight Zone. That seems to me to be an impossibly difficult task.

It is very difficult. I could talk for half an hour just on that. It's a shorter form, so it's three or four twenty-minute episodes whereas the Jane Austen show is a full length play, two forty-minute halves. That's usual for us. Everything is like that except the Dorothy Parker we've just started doing which is more like a Harold, it's a patchwork based on the short stories. But Twilight Zone is three or four twenty-minute episodes.

Do you get a new ask-for for each one?

Yes, but we found ... this is again Jo McGinley's influence. I came up with the phrase "slow improv," or I thought I had, but it turns out it's a worldwide movement. And it's all about slow it down, get the character as built as possible so that you have a totally real, totally relatable character. We try and do that with Twilight Zone as well; totally play the reality of the scene and do not ever force the what we call "portal moment" because as soon as you start forcing it, what you've got is something that is not as valuable as the moment that appears organically. You've got a shallow idea. The difficulty with the Twilight Zone is Rod Serling could sit down in advance and plan what their conceit was, but we can't. We have to discover it and it's hard. I find it personally a very hard thing to do.

I think there are two different Twilight Zones, aren't there? They are all kind of mood pieces which is something that improvisers can do, but they are either ones that start with an extraordinary premise, or everything seems normal for most of it and then there's a shocking punch line.

We are usually doing the latter and finding that portal comes out of a typical improv slip, a wrong word somebody said or something like that. We are experts at not just pouncing on it but subtly picking it up and going "what's that?" and building the mood. It's all about the mood. But it's a constant debate, that show, because Jo McGinley is all about identifying particular themes, so Rod Serling's themes of humanism and anti-war, liberal stuff, that's where she's going with it. You would be amazed at the work, the rigorous work, that goes into this kind of thing.

This is why, though, Chekhov is the best show improvisers can do. Chekhov is again a full length play, and we break them into four acts. The first act is exploring the world and the characters, the second act is developing that, the third act is building towards the climax and having the climax, and then the fourth act is the aftermath.

The other thing is you don't have to worry about story. It's all about characters. Why it's perfect for improvisers is that you have self-contained ego-bubble characters who each have equal weight in the story, so it's not that pressure of that one lead character that I was referring to earlier which we're having a problem with teaching because not everybody wants to and is capable of being endowed to being the hero character in a single character narrative. Whereas Chekhov, by comparison, has six or seven people of equal weight and the chain of relationships—A loves B, B loves C, C loves, D loves, E loves F, and nobody will ever get who they want. We never turn the lights out and you find your own exits, and it's a set of two or three or more characters together, and by the end nobody has what they want. And so it's incredibly easy by comparison to Twilight Zone.

Ditto Tennessee Williams where we struggle for tone a lot, but Brian Lohmann, the director of that show, is really working hard to help us with tone because it can get very serious very quickly, and how you find the comedy and yet keep it as a serious involving piece is amazing. I watched *Tennessee Williams Unscripted* the other night, because I'm not in this current run, and the ask-for was a family heirloom and they got a chamber pot, and the brilliant Lisa Fredrickson towards the end—somebody smashed the chamber pot and she tried to commit suicide with the broken pieces of the chamber pot cutting her wrists and was later being wheeled around in a wheelchair with her wrists wrapped in a scarf. That's sort-of where the tone is.

I would have thought that the expectation of the audience coming to see one of these shows would be that they are going to see a spoof.

It's not a spoof. It's a homage. Or a pastiche. It's somewhere between homage and pastiche. But it's a genuine attempt to answer the question: if that author was still alive, what would they be doing? Michele Spears, who co-directs the Sondheim with Dan O'Connor, said an interesting thing when we were doing it last summer. *Sunday in the Park with George* is about the struggle of the artist, Seurat, and how much of his life he had to sacrifice in order to produce this work. But Michele in a moment of semi-despair said "You know what, if Impro Theatre wrote *Sunday in the Park with George*, it would be about whether they'll get the painting into the summer exhibition." Our gestalt common mind is not the same as Tennessee Williams' or Sondheim's darkness. We are much more comfortable with Austen and Chekhov because we can identify more closely with that comedy-influenced yet highly intelligent creative mind.

Is there a genre or more than one that you attempted but never made it out of the rehearsal room?

No, we will always do it. We will always do it.

Because you learn in front of the audience as well as in the rehearsal room?

Yes. With Jane Austen, we had never done a full-length one before we got in front of an audience, because the audience helps shape the story. Their response helps you direct the story. Our process is usually: start. Start, start, start, start, start. And getting off on the right track and finding what you need to get off on the right track.

What are the other things you're developing at the moment?

Our teaching genres have become more filmic so we're doing Romantic Comedy at the moment and Buddy Cop. When you introduce filmic styles into improv, you have to work a lot more with the vocabulary of film. So, shorter scenes. I used to talk about the opening scene in Jane Austen but now I talk about the opening sequence; it does the same job but you can skip to they're outside feeding the geese or whatever, but you are still getting the same character information. But by nature improvisers will stand in the same place talking to each other, unless you tell them otherwise or unless you tell the lighting person to end the scene. So I make a point personally as an improviser to march off stage at the first opportunity; as the director I have to set a good example.

One of my themes at the moment is the unreliable character. So it's like the unreliable narrator and it's how you show trainee improvisers or improvisers who are learning long form the difference between your Johnstone training and advanced narrative. When somebody says something you're supposed to say yes, and accept it, but with long form there are two stages. First of all, somebody can say no to you and it's yes. "Will you marry me?" "No." And that's the set-up for the whole show. "Then I shall win you!" With the unreliable character, if somebody says something to me and I'm supposed to accept it, but that may be a complete lie and it's up to me to endow whether it is or not. The person telling me that thing could be a cad, if it's Jane Austen, for example. Maybe he's already married. The story can choose to make that a piece of unreliable information. It's not a fact just because a character said it. So it's those kinds of things that we have little themes and moments.

One of the other things that we're working with is that fun of working with sub-text. Where we will have people act out at a scene: you're a woman, you're a man, you're meeting for the first time in twenty years, when you were forced to reject him. He has never stopped loving you but you don't know that. You've never stopped loving him but he doesn't know that. And you're just going to talk about the weather. The point being it doesn't matter what you say. It's about how freighted each line is by the emotion and when you play it subtly, an audience will laser focus on what's going on.

But are you going to ever do any of these shows anywhere near us? Are you going to come to Edinburgh or a European tour?

There's constant talk about doing, for example, Tennessee Williams in Edinburgh but the cost of it is enormous and the money could go elsewhere. We're doing our Los Angeles noir show at the John Anson Ford which is a 1,100-seat auditorium in October.

What's it like doing an improv show in a room that size?

I don't know! We haven't done it yet.

What is the biggest audience you've done?

We went to Austin, Texas and played 600 people and it was like playing in their living room because the whole place was rocking with laughter. We did

Austen there, we're going back to do Dickens at Christmas, and we're going to be doing the main stage Pasadena Playhouse, we understand, playing on their set on their dark Monday nights. We've realized that as long as you've got amplification and you've worked carefully at that thing where you don't talk over each other—and we don't, it's amazing. As long as you don't talk over each other and you take your time, and you have so much more time in a big room because the laughter will give you more time. Playing a small gig is tougher. You would think it's easier but it's tougher. And people scale up their performances. We've already done a Jane Austen in a 500-seat and people scale up their space work accordingly.

It's become obvious to me that improv is scalable and we didn't think it was. But it totally is.

5.14

Mike McShane—Transatlantic Improviser and Actor

Mike McShane was one of the crop of American improvisers who were recruited into *Whose Line Is It Anyway?* in the 1990s. Since then he has continued to improvise in the UK, America and elsewhere and has also appeared in countless films, TV series and theatre shows as an actor, improviser and sometimes singer.

So, Mike, how did you first discover improvisation?

I was in a Shakespeare festival in Berkeley California, struggling. I hadn't had any training and I was among really dedicated and experienced actors—Annette Bening being one of them, and Andre Braugher who were both apprentices then. These guys had some training but I had none. I've always been truly an apprentice, I picked it up by getting a job, holding a spear and all that stuff. But I was getting really uptight about scansion, about the poetry, about rhetorical devices, all those things. I was becoming an awful, stiff, uptight actor. I knew something was going wrong. When I got my teeth around something comic, I was okay. I felt more confidence in myself—because I'm a cut-up. But I wanted to do Shakespeare and I wanted to do it right, whatever "right" was, I didn't want to just blunder in.

And then, a guy I went to school with at San Francisco State, Greg Proops, he called me up. We were buddies and he said "You know, we're going to start up again this improv group that we had at school, called Faultline." And I did one show with them. I didn't get hooked then, I had a great time but I didn't get hooked. Mostly I played with Greg, so I had a great time.

And you felt comfortable doing that straight away?

Yeah, because I think the first time I saw anyone else perform, it was sketch comedy. And so the idea of a sketch actor being allowed to be looser and freer, more comic in its style of gesture—that seemed familiar. I went—oh, okay, I'm not scared of that. I'm not Being An Actor, you know. That's what I wanted, of course, that prestige!

You didn't miss the safety net of the script and the rehearsal process?

No, although one of the things I noticed about myself, which lead me to think that I might want to be a professional actor, was when I was doing shows in junior college and I would get a script, I'd play around with it acting-wise. I would try different things, because I knew that's what you were supposed to do in rehearsal. Whereas other people who were more am-dram weren't that interested in the kind of exploration. And I would generally come up with something good, especially with the more comedic parts. So I knew that something within me could generate something without, it didn't have to be just on the lines.

Greg asked me to join the group, just to mess around and to get involved in it and I did. And right as that happened, San Francisco discovered Keith Johnstone. So Greg, Brian Lohmann, Reed Rahlmann, Sandee Althouse, Cathy Arcolio and I were the company members. Keith's book *Impro* appeared and the rest of those guys had had Second City training, and this book I think knocked everybody for six. Because it was an actor-friendly book about impro. Keith was talking about narrative and status and daring to be ordinary.

I kind of got the idea that doing ordinary stuff in a particular way had its basis in humor. You didn't have to be loud—even though I am a loud, brash, comic person. I was a huge fan of Stan Laurel when I was a kid. Ollie would leave and Stan would occupy the frame on his own, doing very ordinary, very stupid things in a little sequence. A little cognizance dance with his face and his eyebrows. I remember just being fascinated by that and realizing that this is just a guy figuring shit out in front of you. Just going "Oh, I've got it. I'm thick," and then moving out of the frame. I was fascinated by the small stuff that he did.

Anyway, so, I got into improv. There were a number of improv groups in San Francisco because it was one of the homes of improv in the States— Robin Williams lived there and so on. So we already had a good audience out there who could have confidence in what we were attempting. And we dolled it up by dressing like Madness. We had suits, black ties, that's how we were different. We were the New Wave Improv Group.

We'd do half sketch, half improv games and scenes, a bit like Second City, but unlike Second City, we wouldn't use the improvisations as the basis for sketches which we'd later write. Greg and I already had a job writing for a radio DJ called Don Blue. We had a pretty good writing relationship, Greg and I. It was a mix of really stupid stuff and really smart references. Greg is like the Library of Alexandria of cultural references. If you went inside Greg's head for a walking tour, it would take you a year.

We also embraced absurdism—absurdism for its own sake—which San Francisco shared as a comic attitude, Robin Williams being one of the greatest purveyors of it, a bit different from the attitude in Chicago. Greg was the stand-up of the group, that's what he'd always wanted to do, he was doing that while he was doing improv with us. The rest of us were writers and actors. And that's when I realized this was a place where we all could meet. It was a tree where we all could gather, all these different disciplines which might otherwise have been pitted against each other in a strange way, especially in Hollywood. And that group ran for about five or six years.

Tell me about how Whose Line Is It Anyway? came into your life.

Around 1987, Dan Patterson started trawling the various cities in America to find improvisers. I don't remember my audition that clearly, but this is the story that Dan told me when I asked him why he picked me, you know there were a lot of good improvisers in town. He said "I asked you to do *Star Wars* and you didn't do a light sabre. Everyone else did a light sabre. You did a narrating scene as Greedo, talking in gibberish and then providing the subtitles."

You get inspired, you get encouraged, so if something works I want to go further with it, especially if someone else is with me, running along. I don't work well by myself, I know that. That's maybe why I chose never to be a stand-up. When I was a little kid, I used to be on the phone with this other kid named John Wilson. We'd call each other up, ostensibly to do homework, but after about twenty minutes of homework, we would start just doing sound effects on the phone and going on imaginary adventures. My dad would be going "What the hell? You're on the phone for an hour and a half!" He'd be losing his mind about it. I've always wanted to find that guy again and go "Thank you. You have no idea how important you were to me." Because he gave me the confidence just to go off into nonsense with somebody. That's a big part of it, just "catching" with somebody.

So, around the same time, Dan must have hired Greg and Ryan?

Greg was on the road the year I first auditioned, but he got picked up the next year. Then he found Ryan and Colin together after that. My first episode I was really nervous, really intimidated. I had done no TV work before that, of any kind. I was a San Francisco actor so I had no movie or TV experience. And then I mistook a side comment by Tony Slattery as a slam. During a film dubbing scene, he said something about "stupid Americans" and I confronted him about it. I said "What did you say that for, man?" And the minute I said it, I saw Tony's face and I went "Oh no. He's actually a really nice guy." And I just went "I'm stopping what I'm saying and I'm apologising to you because I was about to say something really stupid." And then we had a bunch of drinks and it was fine. The English solvent.

But when you began improvising in front of the cameras and the audience, you were...

I was right back in that playful groove, yeah. The audience was up for it, Clive guided it very well, and I was on stage with some brilliant people.

What's the difference between improvising in front of cameras in a television studio and the live shows you were used to doing?

There would sometimes be second goes, depending on the producers' needs. Sometimes the show recordings would go very long, and the law of attrition would start working against you. You'd be bluer and more outrageous and the audience would be less liable to laugh at you because they were tired. Dan could get people to stay in the studio all night long. When he tried to do that in New York he almost got killed! The crew would be like "Are you kidding? I've got to drive across the bridge tonight, get this fruity English guy outta here."

He was looking for sketch and charades. He wasn't going to explore improv in a way that was "more richly rewarding for the performers." But I went, you know, it's richly rewarding for me in the pocket book, this is amazing! I never thought I'd make *money* doing this! It's like William Holden. "How do you get started?" "Be lucky enough to be *in this show*." Otherwise, I don't know what I'd be doing. I mean, I'm an okay actor, but, Christ, that show broke me for people. Like any success, it creates its own momentum. You attach yourself to that momentum and ride it out for as long as you get to ride it, which was some time for me.

In your second year on the show, you had Greg to work with?

Which made me more comfortable because he's a mate, and we're both Anglophiles, to a degree. That second year is also when I met Paul Merton, and Paul would set me and Greg down in front of a VHS machine and show us tapes of Morcambe and Wise and Tony Hancock—because there would be these references which meant nothing to us. You know, John Sessions would glibly announce "I'm going to do Mervyn Peake," and Greg and I would be looking at each other like "Who the fuck's Mervyn Peake?"

At that stage, we were all still finding out how this thing was going to work. We all came from different backgrounds, or even different continents. One of the reasons why they brought Americans in was because of course it had started on the radio. This is what I was told, anyway, the producers felt that British improvisers were the best in the world—from the neck up. But from the neck down, well you had Robin Williams, you had guys like us who could be a bit more physical with it. For TV, that's what you need. I think that's blended to the middle now.

I remember watching those early episodes and you especially coming on as this whirlwind of physical energy, with the cameras barely able to keep up with you.

I think we did bring that, yeah. I know people have some very mixed opinions about the producers of that show in the improv world, but the fact is Dan saw our strengths and definitely played to them. I think in the long run, he had to find a more cohesive group, that I wasn't a part of, when it went to America. I don't know how long he'll keep doing it. He's become a sort of master at taking parlor games and jokey political fun and making shows out of them. And more power to him. He was very helpful to us.

Just as important as Dan was the guy who directed the episodes, Chris Bould. Chris was a really keen director and really understood our comic energies, so he could cut to us before we acted. He could sense where we might go next—so much so that Denise O'Donoghue and the producers asked him to shave that off so it looked more unplanned. And of course, he's going "So you're asking me to subjugate my instinct as a creative person to make it look more off-the-cuff!?"

So, you're earning money and you have some profile, certainly in this part of the world. What do you do with that?

I did another improv show on TV with Tony Slattery called *S and M*, which was an improvised sketch show. At the time, we got lambasted for it, but now it enjoys a weird cult following. We're seen as the first guys to do this thing—with varying degrees of success. Dan put Tony and me together, I think because we're both a little blue, a little crazy. I think he tapped into our hidden Catholic sub-world. Tony was a great partner for me, so giving and so friendly and he worked really hard.

Then I did a spin-off with Sandi Toksvig, a traditional sitcom called *The Big One*, a sort of romantic comedy between two unlikely-looking people. Hat Trick banked on me two or three times. *Whose Line* opened the gates for me to an area that I never thought I would have access to. You know, I was a repertory theatre actor, I had a nice career working in a San Francisco theatre called ACT, but after that show I could do film and TV and theatre without having to go to LA. I always had ambivalent feelings about Los Angeles, and still do even though I live there now. I liked San Francisco, and I liked London. I liked how art went here. You know, you guys have been doing theatre ever since somebody picked up a lyre and went "Here's a little song about Beowulf!" It's part of the culture, it's not considered a frippery or an excess. In America we suspect anything that's…that's…intelligent!

I got to work with John Gielgud! I got to play scenes with one of the greatest actors in the world. I did a thing called *A Midsummer Day's Dream*—Rosemary Harris, John Gielgud, it was just an amazing cast of people and I was in the middle of them. I would pinch myself. I would go home saying "Karen, I spent the afternoon acting with Sir John Gielgud!"

That voice, that timbre. The hairs would stand up on the back of my neck when I heard him talk. And he was a lovely man.

Of course, I did go to LA. I did *Robin Hood* in LA and the producer wanted to show me this shot of an arrow going into a tree, looking at me and nodding like D.W. Griffith just showed me *Birth of a Nation*, going "Huh? Huh?" I'm sorry, it's just hard to hold up against Gielgud, or doing a TV movie with Jeremy Irons about the first Europeans in Hollywood. I guess that makes me a snob. That's unfortunate, but I think I am a snob when it comes to this kind of thing.

I love the process of making a movie, I love the technical aspects, the organization of it, but I'm a theatre guy. I like the live. I like connecting. And finding an audience here in the UK that I could connect with was great. I hung to it for as long as I could and I'm still trucking my tired ass over here and getting away with it.

I've got a real soft spot for this country because people here accepted me no matter how I looked. People here were like "Are you funny? Okay then." That was it. I could be as fat as I was, and people were just "Yeah, all right."

When I went to LA, first thing they said—you know I have a birthmark here on my temple—and they said you should think about getting some surgery. And I said "There's no surgery, it's a birthmark. It's called make-up." Hollywood's like a fascinating, beautiful hostess's party and you're having a great time when all of a sudden you open up a door and you see her snorting up a line of coke and smacking the servant. "Oh! Oh! Momma's ugly!"

Throughout this time, you continued doing improv shows of various kinds. On the spectrum of styles of improvisation from the short form games of Whose Line *at one end, to the longer more sustained narrative pieces at the other, with short form scenes somewhere in the middle, is there a place which you prefer to be?*

I have a sort of salad bar mentality when it comes to improvisation. I think there are lots of things to pick from. I do enjoy the challenge of a long form narrative. I just finished a run of improvised Tennessee Williams with Brian Lohmann and Paul Rogan and those guys. And sometimes when we're rehearsing, to get into the groove of it, we'll stay silent in a scene for five or six minutes. That won't happen on the stage, but it helps to build that muscle. I enjoy that. It slows me down, calms me down, helps me listen. That can only happen if you move slow and low on the ground, I think.

But you still enjoy going back and doing Paul Merton's Impro Chums for example?

Absolutely! Because it's high-end mucking about. And I get to enjoy being with Richard [Vranch]—I owe a lot of my success to Richard's abilities. Paul and I get along real well, I know how to play with Paul. We share a liking for silent film, and for absurd stuff. He was always, from the beginning, just a nicely uncomplicated gracious guy. And like Greg, he's got this voluminous mind and a capacity to use it—they're both very similar in many ways.

It's like sitting in with a band. And the band does this kind of music, and you know this kind of music. We do the bucket, because that allows us to do short jokes, puns, scenes, songs. And it's great for the audience because they see their written material become live right away, but it gives us the width to play with it how we will. Paul and Lee Simpson will do a scene that will go on for five or six minutes, just them mucking about with some weird dialect thing. And they're great at it. Lee's like the ninja of the group, the guy who can do everything really well and some things superbly. We've all got these chops now, because we're older, Paul and Lee and Suki and I, and Richard and Lee. And I enjoy being in that group a lot, I do.

A lot of people who are successful improvisers also teach. Do you?

I don't do it well. I've learned to demonstrate less and listen more. I think I'm a pretty good beginning teacher. I do try to impart one of the things you talk about in this book which is creating a place where you can learn to fail. One of the points I make is that this is a stress-inducing act and that's why people have all of these defensive techniques. They go straight to the toilet, or blue material, they joke, they get anti-social, because they're protecting themselves. So the first thing you've got to do is to find a place where you don't need to protect yourself. And that's an isolated place. It's not part of the real world, it really is a bubble. But you must create that bubble for yourself.

Eventually you learn that's just your reaction—that's neither good nor bad, you're not a good or a bad person, you're not a good or a bad improviser, you're just an effective or a less effective improviser depending on the instincts that you cultivate. So most people have to find some place out of the firing line. I didn't! I went right up to the firing line to learn! Fortunately, I was with Brian and Greg and Cathy and Sandee and Reed and we all knew each other from school and we liked each other, we all supported each other. And being in San Francisco, you didn't feel career failure as much as if you were in LA. LA's all about career success, it's all around you.

That's what I try to get across to people, to be calm, so they can just sit with a scene. I'm big right now on small physical offers. There's an improviser in LA called Stephen Kearin who can hand you a cup six different ways and you know exactly what's in the cup, what it's made out of, why he's giving it to you. It's such a complete offer. All you've got to do is be there for it and you can start a scene. And I think that's great, because that adds more to the "How do they do that?" thing about improv. The magic of improv is that there's all this information and cooperation and listening running underneath this scene that's about two people trying to dig themselves out of a hole. And the audience sees that part and enjoys it and occasionally there are these flourishes of technical brilliance that they see, but all the time, we're handing each other code and building mutually. It's just a good way to operate as a human being. That's the old hippie in me, I guess.

Are there any trends which you're noticing in improvisation at the moment?

There's a book called *Whose Improv is it Anyway?* And I saw that on the shelf and I thought "Well I've got to have a look at this." And the question in the book was: in an art form which is based on co-operation and goodwill, how come there are so many bitter, isolated jerks in improv? It's turf wars. I don't know. It's probably economic. It's a small pool of cash, and I need to get it all, that kind of mentality. When you build a group it becomes "Oh those guys don't do this form. They don't do the *Ohio form*," you know, and when I see that I just want to get a big slapping stick and run around and whack people. It goes against something in improv which is so positive and good. I know it sounds Pollyanna-ish to say that but if you learn how to cooperate with people and let yourself off the hook and fall and fail.

When I was a kid I took judo. I was getting beat up a lot, and my dad said "Okay, let's nip this in the bud. We'll take you to Mr. Kim and you'll learn judo." But what I learned was falling. It's the first thing you learn. How to tumble, roll and get up. I'm a fat guy. It's like Shakespeare: I am the cause that is wit in other men. The stupidest lout in the world can make a joke about a fat guy falling over. It's one of the basic food groups of comedy, fat people falling over. And when you're young and you fall over and people laugh at you, you don't like it, you feel miserable. So I learned how to fall over *great*. And get up again and fall over again and fall over kicking my legs up in the air, like Oliver Hardy. I will shoot this arrow over your roof and have your attention.

I thank my dad for taking me into that class, because I was okay at judo, but I could *really* fall. And I liked falling. I liked falling so much I have artificial hips now. And the sooner you learn that, the sooner you get that coincidence. Not the stupid confidence like "Where's my trailer?" But the confidence of being able to play with people and share and create things with people. That makes you a good player and people want to be with good players.

5.15

Tom Salinsky Discusses the Improv Show *Voices in Your Head* and Its Spin-Offs with Deborah Frances-White

Between 2012 and 2015, Deborah directed a number of improv shows, all of which used the same fundamental mechanism to try and push improvisers further, creating richer worlds and deeper characters. As we finished putting this book together, we talked about those shows.

Hello Deborah.

Hello Tom.

Tell me how the original idea for Voices in Your Head *first came to you?*

Well I was doing the London Storytelling Festival and I thought that we needed an improv show. I asked myself "What do I really love about improvisation?" And I thought "I love watching people genuinely be in the moment." When people first improvise they are often really immediate. And then they get good and you can see they're comfortable up there, but now they're a little bit ahead of themselves, they're planning, they know where they are going. Often they learn a routine, a game, a format and then they're slick. They work with people they know, nothing surprises them. And what I love is that immediacy, that in-the-moment quality which the great improvisers seem to maintain throughout their careers. But even then, once you know what you're doing it's fun to be on stage and it's exciting but you don't often get that "Whoa, I'm right here!" feeling any more.

And the other thing I love about improv is story. And that often goes by the wayside because improvisers are anxious and they over-complicate things. There are so many minds all in the moment that the plot gets very convoluted. So I thought: what's a format that will allow story, allow change, but also force improvisers to be in the moment? And I came up with this very experimental idea that I would sit in the dark and I would prep the audience a little bit and invite some people to come and play and say to them I'm not going to tell you anything about the show. So, I asked five people: Thom Tuck, who is a comedian and improviser; Jana Carpenter, who is an improviser and actor, Matthew Crosby who is a sketch comedian; Martin Dockery who is a storyteller and...was there somebody else?

Me I think.

Oh, Tom Salinsky! And I said to them I don't want to tell you anything about it, I just want you to go into the dressing room. And I was amazed that everyone said yes and didn't want to know more about it, but they were very trusting.

On the way to the gig I got a call from Matthew and he said "What time am I on?," and I said "Well, you're on for the whole show," and he replied "What? It's a storytelling thing," and I said, "No it's an improv thing at a storytelling festival." He hadn't really read the email. He'd just seen "storytelling festival" and thought he was telling a story. He said "I'm not an improviser, I've never improvised on stage ever," and I said "That's great. Because you won't have a bag of tricks, you will be in the moment." He's a brilliant mind, he's a brilliant sketch comedian, writer, performer and I thought that's really ideal. So he said, "Okay, but I don't know," and I said "Well nobody else knows either so this is perfect."

I sent all the improvisers back-stage and got a stagehand to go and knock on the door and let them out. When they came out there was a chair with their name on it and the improvisers all looked at each other like, "I guess we sit down on these chairs." Then I said "Thom Tuck to the stage please," and Thom Tuck came out and he couldn't see me, he could only hear me. I said, "Thom, there's a girl in the audience, she likes you, she's smiling at you." And of course the whole audience starts to laugh, he doesn't know where she is. He eventually narrowed it down to who it was and she gave him a present, wrapped in birthday paper. He opened it up and it was a very cheesy, touristy, statue of Big Ben, with neon sparkly colors—almost psychedelic. And I said "This isn't the first time you've opened this present is it?" and he said "No." And I said "What was the last time?" and he said "My mother gave it to me, it was from my real father and I never met him."

The whole experience was designed to throw him into a weird world where someone's coming out of the audience and giving him something. A situation where he can't see the director, where he doesn't know what's going on. And then starts answering the questions in a more truthful way than he might have otherwise. And then when we have some information out of this interview with "The Voice," I can say, "Martin Dockery, you are his father," and we can see a scene played out.

We had a scene where Jana Carpenter had a little box and I was asking her what was inside. There was actually nothing inside, but I got it from a charity shop and it had lots of little compartments in it and I asked her what were in the drawers and she said hair. And it was quite a dark scene; her grandfather had been a serial killer of prostitutes and she knew that and the hair was in the drawers was from the women he'd killed. Through the interview we learn that Jana's character is devastated by this knowledge and carries huge guilt on behalf of her grandfather, so one night a year she goes out to give a sex worker the night off and takes her place as penance. And so this is the night. And I say "Martin Dockery, you're the John." And they start to talk and it becomes clear, very slowly and horribly, that he's going to kill her and we don't want this to happen and we're all watching it and willing it not to happen. It's like a terrible thriller.

Before the show, I had told the audience—quite arbitrarily—that if I said "Let us go," then another person in the audience should say "Let us go," and then someone else should, until the whole audience is chanting "Let us go." And I realized that's what it was for. I didn't know if I was going to use it, I didn't know where it would come in handy. And so it was really freaky for Martin and Jana when the audience started chanting because they're just not used to that. There are these voices coming out of the audience saying "Let us go" which I've never seen in any other form of theatre. And we realize, we just know that it's the souls of all the women her grandfather has killed and Jana is fueled by them and she rises up and she kills the John—and she sets the souls of the women free in that act. And that's the last time she ever needs to go out and do what she was doing. We know the point of it now. She was always meant to save that woman she covered for that night to atone for what her grandfather did. And I don't think any of us would have written that. I wouldn't have. I don't think Jana or Martin would have and the audience certainly wouldn't have but somehow it's this gruesome, ghostly story about the sins of the fathers and what we all live with if we come from a family with a violent history and women in the sex industry and the violence they live with and what society says their lives are worth and the powerlessness of women. That was super dark for the first show but some of the audience really loved it and came up to tell us they'd never seen anything like that before. It wasn't funny—it was compelling and terrifying and improvisation rarely does that.

We played another scene where Sara Pascoe was a character who lived in a snow globe and couldn't remember how she'd got there. She'd been there forever locked in a beautiful magical world and everyone in the audience blew bubbles onto the stage when someone shook the globe. It felt very magical for the improvisers because something coming out of the audience like that is such a rarity. The audience love playing like that. It feels so remarkable for them to be part of the theatre and to help create the show. When I tell them code word is "blow" for the bubbles they have no idea what the story will be and neither do I most of the time, so it's wonderful when we find meaning all together.

So what happened after that first one-off show?

I think, I said to my producer Ant Butler from So Comedy, who was taking my live stand-up show to Edinburgh, "Shall we try this out in Edinburgh as a late night show?" and he got excited and got us a great deal on this late night venue. It was huge and I was thinking, "Oh my God, we're not going to fill this." We didn't have any particularly famous people doing it, and I thought we're going to have thirty people in a space for a 150, but by the third show it started to sell out because the word got around. The audience just loved being involved. They loved that they got to participate but it wasn't "audience participation." They got to be involved but it wasn't about them. The audience were very, very keen to help because they saw that they were not in any way being ridiculed, it wasn't patronizing. It's that the audience were in on a secret.

It took me ages to realize that I had to come out in person at the beginning of the show. Not be "The Voice" to them, but conspire with them as a host and say, "Okay, we're going to give them an experience together." And that really made a big difference.

Different players respond to The Voice very differently. I remember Hannibal Buress doing the show and he plays it like a stand-up comic—because he's a brilliant one. The audience love watching Hannibal do the show because part of the story is Hannibal's resistance to being changed by The Voice and it's wonderful to watch that. He'll answer the questions with genius answers, but if I push him to be vulnerable he won't. And so sometimes I'll say something like, "Are you in love with Tina?" And he'll say, "No," and be really cool about it and I'll say "I read in your diary that you were really in love with her," and he'll respond, "Why are you reading my diary? Diaries are personal," and he'll get really angry about that and the audience will take that as vulnerability and it'll be sign that he is in love with Tina and he's denying it, which is very funny.

The first time he ever did the show, I said the code word "seven" (which was planned before the show) and six people in the front row of the audience got up and they all had a garden gnome which they put around him so he was in a garden of garden gnomes. And someone put a little hat on his head and then they all sat down. And I said, "Hannibal, why do the other garden gnomes hate you?" And he said. "Ambition. They want to keep a gnome down. They want you to do gnome stuff like hoeing and fishing and I've got dreams." And it was so great, not just because it was such a funny answer. It was hysterically funny because he was obviously much taller than the actual garden gnomes around him. But after a while, what became apparent to the audience was that it felt like he was talking about being from a down-town neighborhood and now being on television, so when he goes back to that neighborhood, that ambition can sometimes separate you from your people. I don't know if that's true, I never asked him that, but it felt like that's what the scene was really about.

To test this, many shows later, I gave the same set-up to Tom Bell, who is like a British indie comedian, much more low status. I said, "Why do all the other garden gnomes hate you?" And he said, "Hate's a strong word. I mean, it's just banter, isn't it? It's just teasing, it's just good fun, we all tease each other." So his response was as if he was talking about being bullied at school and pretending he was in on the joke so as not to cry about it. And what I discovered was if you ask anybody a question like that, and they're in the moment, and they've just had this weird experience of being dressed by the audience, and they don't have their bag of tricks, they don't know what the scene's about, they haven't decided on the fun game that they know how to play—they will tell you the truth about why they suspect people hate them or have done at a certain time in their life. This is my assumption. I'm not sure about it—but their answers were so truthful and like no others I'd ever seen in any improvisation show. And although the answers are truthful and sad it doesn't play as poignant, it's very funny (with just a lovely touch of pathos) because the juxtaposition is they're playing a garden gnome.

So I played with those tropes a lot, you know, tooth fairies and magical realms, but also sometimes just runaway children and sad, loner people, recluses, all sort of things. And you can really get into their heads and it was really exciting.

As you did it over that and then subsequent Edinburgh Fringes, how did the structure of the show evolve?

When I first did the format, almost every interview turned into a two or three player scene, but I discovered the part the audience liked, which was different from other improv shows was the part where an improviser got interrogated by the voice, so it ended up being more of that. I'd do an interrogation scene with everybody in turn, and then I'd get all four improvisers out and give them all something like an LP that I found in a charity shop. They would all have some association with the LP they were holding. So if it was a double act with guitars like Smiling Joe And Randy Sing The Blues, I'd say "You used to be Smiling Joe, didn't you? What happened?" And they have to tell me the story of Randy and what happened to the double act and why they weren't "smiling" anymore. Then for the next person it would be their image that had been wrongly used for the soundtrack for the Berlin Olympics or whatever.

There was one person who was remarkable in a way that nobody else quite was. That was Phill Jupitus. He was the first person to ever talk back to The Voice and endow The Voice with being a character. I got the audience to put a load of their own possessions into a canvas bag and said that he was on a train and asked him to explain why these things were in the bag and where he was going. I said something like, "Why can't you love again?" and I remember him looking up into the tech booth and saying, "As if you don't know, Jocasta! You of all people!"

He endowed me with being an ex-lover, with whom he was having this imaginary conversation. Like how you might have a conversation in your head with someone like an ex-boyfriend or girlfriend you haven't seen for a long time and imagine what you would say to them now. At the end of the scene, he actually ripped his shirt off and I remember him jumping over the seats, making people in this packed house get out of the way, shirtless coming through the crowd to me. And I was shocked, I genuinely didn't know what to do. It's my job to be in charge of the show because they're so in the moment usually. They're almost in a trance state sometimes, so I've got to be on it. I mean the content is an interplay between the two of us, but I've got to be the grown up, like you would be if you were doing mask work. And he was the first person to turn that around on me. I remember that being a very exciting moment and so that's how we then decided to do *The Phill Jupitus Experiment*.

Doing the original *Voices in Your Head*, I would never know who was going to turn up, so I would just come with a bag of props and the producer would say "Felicity Ward's on tonight," and I'd think "Oh, she'd make a great French spider!" But if it was just going to be me and Phill, I could plan much more, I could get other actors in and we could make a much more structured show out of it,

So for that show there would always be a PowerPoint slide that would come on at the back of the stage, telling him who he was, what year it was, where he was, and I would always start and end with Phill playing himself but usually at a different time in his life.

So one character was the Tsar's beekeeper on the eve of the Russian revolution and I remember he turned it into a metaphor about the queen bee and what was happening to the government. Then he was playing a father who hadn't spent Christmas with his children for some years because his wife had left and there had been a lot of problems. He was really excited and he was wrapping the presents—I'd given him real presents to wrap and a real Christmas tree, so it felt very real.

For that scene, we had Russell Tovey come in. Russell is a very good looking, charismatic actor, who I thought Phill probably hadn't met, but would recognize from the television. I've prepped Russell to play a cool music producer who's the kid's new young, handsome stepdad. Russell tells Phill he has been offered an amazing opportunity over Christmas to go to Euro Disney. There's going to be this big concert for all the kids of rich music producers and there's this huge party being thrown by Disney and One Direction are going to be there, and, various other legends that eleven-year-old girls would want to see. He tells Phill his daughters are invited but they'd have to miss Christmas with him. And of course he's going to have to say either "No, I don't want my children to go and have a wonderful time," or he's going to have to let them go and have Christmas alone again. I remember that being incredibly funny but also really poignant and heartbreaking.

The last scene of the first show I did is still one I'm most proud of. I put Phill in a psychiatric unit as himself on his birthday one year in the future and I played a therapist character and I asked him what he used to do for a living. He tells me he used to be a comedian—because he's playing himself and it's one year from the date we're doing this show. And I tell him we've got to go back to the beginning, we've slipped back a little bit in our therapy and I remind him he's worked in the Job Centre for twenty years. And he protests: "No I worked in a Job Centre for two years," which he really did, I researched that, "and then I left and I became a professional comedian." This is true to life.

I said, "No Phillip, you've had a very important job, you've helped a lot of people at the Job Centre, but we've got to make this line between reality and fantasy a little less blurry. We all imagine things don't we? We all fantasise. Some people fantasise about being a popstar or, you know, a film star or a footballer and that's fine, that's normal, but it's when we start to think that it's true, that's when it's a problem." And Phill started to get angry and say "No, I was the team captain on a very famous British comedy panel show, *Never Mind the Buzzcocks*, for 17 years" (which is true). And I said "No, Phillip, you were in the studio audience for *Never Mind the Buzzcocks* over seventeen times. That's not the same. And you were asked not to come back. You were banned from coming to the show. Do you remember why you were asked not to come back?"

And it becomes clear that he has fantasied his whole career and when those fantasies kicked in he started to act in erratic ways and make trouble. We discover that he got into a fight and pushed someone off the roof of the Groucho Club, which is why he's been sectioned. And I'm trying to get him to realize his life is not as he believes it is and he's getting angry because of course that's a very disorienting thing to do to someone.

And he's saying "No, I was a comedian," and I'm saying to him, "Phillip—that's in your head." And he's saying "No—it's real." And eventually I say, "Phillip, sometimes you tell me you can hear an audience laughing." And he said "Yes, I can." And I said "Can you hear that audience laughing now?" And he said "Yes, they're laughing." And, of course the audience at the show *is* laughing. And the more we talk about this, the more they laugh. And I say, "Phillip, you're never going to be well until that audience stops laughing." So he starts shouting at the audience to stop laughing and of course they can only laugh more and more. And the end of the show is him in a fetal position giggling on the sofa, sort of laughing and crying at the same time and it's really remarkable.

We did it at the Edinburgh Fringe and doing it every day was much more challenging because he would start to know what to expect. So I had to start mixing it up and trying to make it more like one long life journey. So in one show, he had hit someone with his car that day leaving Edinburgh to go to Glasgow. And then he would then play all the characters of the people that he'd met that day and end up back being interrogated by the police, things like that. And then I'd think, this is it, this is it, I've got it now! And then of course, that was predictable and we'd have to mess it up again.

So the challenge became having to change it so Phill wouldn't know what was happening. We always had a safe word in that show, because I was messing with Phill's real life at times, and we had to make sure he was happy to go into the territory I was taking him into so I could take risks. The safe word wasn't a word really, it was always a line from a song, like "There she goes just walking down the street," or "Coocoocachoo, I am the walrus," or something like that, so he couldn't accidentally say it. He used it twice I think, because he didn't want to go wherever it was we were going but it was also exciting for the audience to see a show with a safe word.

I often used to ask the audience if anyone is a waiter or a nurse or whatever if we needed a waiter or nurse to be in the scene. And they were the best people because they how to wait tables or be a nurse or whatever because they're not pretending, they're doing their job, so they never showed off, they just tended bar, they waited tables, they took temperatures. This one night, the first thing that happened was Phill being arrested for a kidnaping. I found this big Scottish real-life security guard in the audience and I told him to march Phill in, and sit him down and then lean in and whisper in his ear "There's no fucking safe word tonight."

And Phill was genuinely angry, he was furious, he was like "You can't do that," but it was to try and make it exciting again. And because he was so furious the show was great! It was proper theatre with actual anger on the stage. It was very funny and also scary at times. There was another night where he really wanted his safe word because I was making him apologize to Jeremy Clarkson (for a hit and run), and Phill has no love for Jeremy Clarkson and he wouldn't apologize to him, but he couldn't remember the safe word and he was begging the audience to help him and they wouldn't. That was hysterically funny.

So, after the Edinburgh Fringe, did you feel you had mined Phill's life for everything it had to give?

For the time being anyway. We've talked about bringing it back for one offs sometime. But if we do it, I want to surprise Phill, so I organize it with his agent, but he doesn't know, so he's in that excited state again and I have time to plan something incredibly theatrical. I've shelved *Voices In Your Head* for a while for the same reason. We got into a routine so that people who did it regularly who were well-known and brilliant at it would go, "Oh yeah, I know *Voices*, I know how this works." And they were amazing at it but it didn't have that "anything could happen" feel anymore because I got into a rut with the possibilities and they knew the drill. I'd like to do it in different cities with brilliant improvisers like Jim Libby and Jacob Banigan in Vienna or Dan O'Connor and Paul Rogan in LA or Impro Melbourne—Patti's company—because they're incredible but they haven't seen it yet so it'd be new again and I'd be inspired to do new things.

A while ago, I wanted to mess up the format again for myself, as well to be more playful. So I did a show called *The Beau Zeaux* that originally was just a two-day workshop to play around with ideas. I thought actually we're getting these lovely deep characters and this could be a great way to create characters who felt like they were from an independent film. I actually wanted to make indie films in first instance.

I have to say that first two-day workshop we created some remarkable things, very dark, but like something between Christopher Guest and League of Gentleman in its flavor. I'd originally gone for Wes Anderson style stuff, but being improvised it's always a little bit more absurd. The one that really sticks out for me was Marcus Brigstocke, playing an Argentinian nanny. She was in her sixties, and when she was a young woman she'd nannied for this child and he was a sociopath. He pushed his nanny down the stairs and now she was paralyzed. And Marcus was playing this woman, this nanny, and talking about her love of taxidermy. She said she was new to it, she said she was an "amateur stuffer," which was very funny in this Argentinian accent but also delightful because it was a new passion for her and she wasn't very good, but she was really into it. It's always lovely to see improvisers play enthusiasts.

And I said, "you've fallen in love recently haven't you?" And the nanny said, "Yes, with this man, a young man at my class." And I sort hinted and together we kind of got there that this young man was making her promise in her will that when she died he could stuff her. He really wanted to stuff a human being and that's why he was seducing her. I remember that being my obvious and I was asking questions going that way and then Marcus came back to me with, "Well yes, because my legs are paralyzed, I haven't felt anything from the waist down for many years. I mean we've agreed he can start stuffing just that part." Her paralyzed legs were being stuffed as she was alive and were going septic. I mean, that's remarkable, that's an incredible thing—I didn't see it coming at all—and that was improvised on the first day.

The cast was Thom Tuck, Brendan Murphy, Marcus Brigstocke, Ed Coleman, Pippa Evans, Milly Thomas, Rachel Parris with me directing. They were a terrific cast. They really committed and always surprised me. A mixture of actors, improvisers and stand-up comics which I did for a reason. Sometimes people guested with us. Russell Tovey guested a few times. He's an incredible actor but also very funny.

So you're generating these characters by the same mechanism: you're a voice in the dark. But they're no longer self-contained scenes?

Right. Marcus would start playing his nanny character then someone else would a play a character who was an animal rights activist or something and then we would see how they connected. So the animal rights doctor would turn up and the Argentinian nanny would be his mother or his sister or whatever. So we find these connections and sometimes they would meet for the first time. Maybe someone would have an antique shop and someone would come in. Sometimes they'd have pre-existing relationships, and we would discover that the respectable banker would go and visit his brother in prison.

The challenge was to get the improvisers not to talk about what we'd already seen but play out that reality that day and engage on that level. We decided to do a show, again at the Edinburgh Fringe, and the excitement was we didn't know what we were doing and it was more challenging than any of us anticipated. Sometimes it would just be incredibly brilliant and amazing, breathtaking, moving, sometimes the audience would cry, sometimes I cried at things. There was a scene in Edinburgh that Rachel Parris improvised, playing a little girl, that I couldn't even tell people about without crying. And then other times, it would be improv chaos.

Sometimes it was too dark for an afternoon show, but to me that's what was originally exciting about it. The first rehearsals which we were jazzed about were the darkest stuff. People trapped in basements. A French DJ who collected screams in his basement because he wanted to capture the sound of pure terror for his music. I think doing it every day for a month at the Fringe was too much. We learned a lot, but it was too dark too often and the performers got tired of the tone and I got locked in and didn't know how to get out. We were all doing other shows and were tired. It was a great experience though, a great run, and audiences always loved it.

Even so, I think improv formats get samey when you do them every day. You need to constantly mix them up so they're fresh and I find that really challenging as a director. I start to try to control it—which is my weakness. And you can't. It's exactly the time you need to relinquish control. It's coming from a good place of wanting to support the improvisers and not leave them hanging but it's the opposite of what you should do. I talked to Dylan Emery at Showstopper about this and he said he had exactly the same problem learning to direct that show. He said when things aren't going well or the improvisers seem uninspired he'd try to take the wheel and after the show they'd complain he was doing too much but sometimes he'd let them take it and nothing would happen and then you end up feeling like you're not doing enough or you're leaving them out there. It's a super tough balance. It comforted me that Dylan, who is so brilliant, felt the same pressures as I did. His show has been going much longer and has recently won an Olivier so there's always hope you can find the balance. The brilliant Patti Stiles came to direct us and worked with me on releasing control and when the show is working, of course, that just happens and everyone is excited about and it just feels effortless.

The whole deal that we made with each other was that we would make it a playground for us, but it was almost always entertaining for the audience. We wouldn't always reach our goal of making this an actual piece of theatre that would haunt you, that would remember the characters, like those independent films, but it was nearly always entertaining. And there are a few characters I really remember and won't forget and would want to turn into an independent film. There was some amazing moments and amazing interactions and it was really worth doing.

So how would you sum up your experience doing these three different versions of a show in which you directed improvisers from the darkness?

With *Voices* it's nice to create the touchpaper, that's exciting. It's nice to be able to create exciting worlds for the improvisers so they're starting from nothing, but you can have little secrets, you can have little things, costumes or things hidden in the audience like little time-bombs ready to go off. Voices is playful and fun because people are turning up to do one off shows and are not invested in the production in the same way so it's easy. Sometimes I worked with performers I'd never met on that show. They first encountered me as a voice in the dark. It's pretty exciting.

With *The Phill Jupitus Experiment* it was nice to get to know one very talented performer very well and push it to new places you'd never dare go with someone who didn't really trust you. The Beau Zeaux—we learned how to create narrative with this format. And it was nice to watch the group dynamic build.

In The Beau Zeaux, *you're part of the same team, but there is a sense in both* The Phill Jupitus Experiment *and* Voices in Your Head, *that you're on opposing teams, isn't there?*

Yes, on those shows, it was my job to excite and inspire and surprise. With *The Beau Zeaux*, we were collectively creating worlds for the audience and that was different. Ultimately that show worked better if I interviewed people at the top and then pulled right back. Actually as the run went on, I realized it was better to back off. But to be honest with you, when I did back off it became more like a normal improv show, which satisfied me less, although it was a very entertaining hour for the audience.

I think I never really got the precise balance between that flavor of an amazing arc and me backing off enough. I felt like whenever I backed off, it was a very playful, delightful, wonderful show, but probably a little bit more in the genre of most improv shows. Occasionally we'd get it just right then it was like watching an incredible independent film that appeared before your eyes that you had a stake in and was really magical when it could happen.

And I'm sure if we toured it we'd mix-and-match the cast and have different directors. And if we decide to take *The Beau Zeaux* forward, that's what we'll do, we'll sort of reinvent it I think. We'll start again with a new name. And my big thing is I want different people to be The Voice. Actually my writing tone isn't particularly dark, but my tone on that show was quite dark and I wanted other voices, other tones to come in, other improvisers to play that role and see what those voices would be.

Would they be lighter? Would they be faster? Would they be more Tarantino or would it be more like a French film? What other things could be done if different people were sitting in the driving seat? And I've become very busy with podcasts and other things in stand-up comedy, but I think at some point I will revisit it and that's what I'd like to do: train other people to be the voice—or in fact just get other people to be the voice and see if they do it their own way.

AFTERWORD

Improvisation is an art form which survives in the moment. It lives because audiences and performers want to see and feel the instant of creation. When improvisers are in the present—not planning for the future or recreating what they have seen or done before, but truly in the present—it can be the most magical, beguiling art form in the world. Perhaps because those moments are rare and elusive, improvisers become addicted, always searching for another glorious exchange, scene or show.

In our search for innovation while writing this book and conducting interviews with some of the international leading lights in improvisation, we have asked the question, "Why has film changed so much since its invention but our art form is still creating variations on a theme more often than not?" The truth is that film's first efforts were not stories but documented moments. Improvisation explored story from its inception. In some ways, because it requires so little in the way of accoutrements, its birth was more like a foal that walks on the first day, rather than a baby which takes months to hold up its own head.

Our mission now, as members of the improvisation community, and one we surely must choose to accept, is to raise the bar. We need to address the quality of our work and then ask that it is given a platform as theatre rather than relegated to rooms above pubs. We need to make the chemistry between the players a high priority, but not if it means casting friends no matter their ability or attitude, and then fearing that post-show notes will offend them. We need directors who are prepared to miss performance opportunities to work as an outside eye on shows, to challenge those who perform to strive beyond the gag and to remind the improvisers that we can hear the audience laugh but we can't hear them being disappointed when we sell out the story.

Improvisation requires practitioners who are students of narrative in a variety of disciplines. We can read new, form-breaking novels and bring their narrative voices to our work. We can be influenced by innovative theatre and television—not just by parodying genres, but by being genuinely inspired by its form, structure and daring content. We can create brand new procedures and forms that are unique to improvisation, remembering that we have freedom from the constraints of scripted disciplines. If we want to see genuine change, we can't just read about it and talk about it. We have to organize rehearsals, cast our net widely for talent, come to workshops with new ideas to explore and—as our good friend and great improviser Gary Turner always says—"Leave our chewing gum and attitude at the door." We could do it this week, this month, this year. We just need a room and some willing, talented people. Both will be available in your area. Improvisation is a collaborative art form, so getting a group together, sharing your vision (even if your only idea is to do something "new") and creating a form that your whole team will feel responsible for is a wonderful way to work with enthusiastic innovators.

Finally, we must escalate the collaboration between companies and groups, and attend and create festivals with the goal of sharing our innovations—both our failures and successes. We can use improvisation networking sites like yesand.com to air problems, questions and discoveries, and avoid bickering about details or arguing over preferences for forms that others have created. We owe Johnstone, Close and Spolin a lot, but now we must stand on the shoulders of giants and be the innovators and creators of our own generation. This is our moment, and we must be in it.

APPENDIX ONE

Games

As discussed under "Playing Games," we divide games into three categories.

Good Games have something to teach you, promote good habits or sustain endless variety in themselves.

Dumb But Fun games are not actively destructive, and while they may not have much to do with the real business of improvising stories, they are not likely to insult the audience's intelligence either.

Never Play games are destructive or pointless or both, and survive on novelty value or because they crudely mimic some of the key mechanisms of theatre, or because they exist as a means for improvisers to show off how clever they are.

We have also provided a list of warm-up games for the beginning of a workshop.

GOOD GAMES

A short list of recommended games not described elsewhere in the text.

Animal Expert

Expert scenes are a skill in themselves, which is why games which graft the "expert" scenario onto some other restriction are rarely satisfactory. Keith's formulation, which recalls some of the Peter Cook dialogues, is to ask the audience for an animal and a sport, hobby or activity. The improvisers then stage a television interview in which one party is an expert in teaching, say, dolphins to play snooker.

The promise that the game makes is not kept by experts who tell us how they grew up with a dolphin and had a fascination for cue sports of all kinds from an early age. This is just WAFFLE. It isn't paying off the promise of the suggestions. What's interesting about a dolphin playing snooker are questions such as: How does it hold the cue? How is the table kept dry—and indeed is it? Do they play against each other, or do they play humans? Details specific to both the animal and the activity make the scene especially interesting. Inventing properties for the animal which solve the problem for you ("Dolphins are innately attracted to large green rectangles, it calms them down. Nobody knows why.") robs the scene of almost all its interest.

Train experts to start answering right away, even if they don't know what their initial one-or two-word answer means. Weak experts waffle and weak interviewers let them, but stronger interviewers make the expert confront the absurdity of the proposal and JUSTIFY it. They may not feel like it, but by asking tougher questions, they are being very GOOD TO WORK WITH since they get better material out of the expert. If the expert is unconvincing, they can be accused of fraud. If the techniques are cruel, have an animal liberation group burst in.

Once—just once—in a workshop, we got as our suggestion the sport of "horse riding" and the animal "horse." The scene that followed was pure absurdist bliss!

In performance: Use it to follow a broad physical scene, or for an audience hungry for jokes, but not when attention spans are short.

In workshops: Use it to train BOLDNESS, MAKING ASSUMPTIONS, JUMPING AND JUSTIFYING, avoiding WAFFLE.

Variations: The same principles can be used to interview anyone about anything.

Death in a Minute

Two improvisers must complete a scene in sixty seconds, no more and no less, during which time one must kill the other. Beginners misinterpret these instructions and begin a fifty-nine-second bridge toward a murder. Daring players kill the other player at the twenty-second mark. The very best way is just to drop dead at around the ten or fifteen second mark. This forces the other player to justify *how* the murder was committed as well as *why*. Then, if time remains, they can dispose of the body.

In performance: Useful for shows like Theatresports where a "challenge" is required, but not a particularly entertaining procedure for an audience.

In workshops: Excellent for "unfreezing" planners.

Dubbing

Typically two players onstage have their voices dubbed by two more players offstage. If necessary, give the offstage players mics. Many variations exist.

Having audience members as the bodies can be successful if (as always) the audience volunteers are dealt with respectfully and kindly. Having one person dub the voices for several characters can also be fun, if the dubber has the necessary quickness of mind and vocal versatility.

Four-way dubbing (A dubs B, B dubs C, C dubs D, D dubs A) is almost guaranteed to be a train wreck, and that would probably be the only point of playing it (to teach "failing and staying good natured," or to deliberately earn a forfeit in Gorilla Theatre).

Fight for Your Number

An easy game for demonstrating how status works, and it models families very well. Get four people up and cast them or have them choose roles within a family. Then get each of them to make a private choice of number: 1, 2 or 3. Number 1s are head of the family—what they say goes. Number 3s will do whatever the others want. Number 2s are looking for a Number 1 they can look up to and a Number 3 they can boss around. The players must "fight for their number," although with four players and three numbers, there will obviously be a clash for at least one "slot." Excellent for sustaining platforms, but hard to tell a story because people will tend not to be changed.

In performance: Use it if you can set it up clearly and keep it short.

In workshops: Good introduction to the idea of status, maybe to follow Status Parties.

Handbag

Short-form game which was originally invented by Deborah for TellTales and which she now sometimes uses for Voices in Your Head. Borrow a handbag from someone in the audience. Ask the person who donated it for her name (and ask her if there's anything she wants to take out before the game starts). Explain that one of the improvisers will play this person, using the contents of the handbag to inspire a character. Set up a scene with another player where they can sit and talk (meeting a friend for coffee, that kind of thing). The handbag player plunges into the bag and removes items whenever they need more inspiration, justifying whatever they happen to bring out. Good players don't allow the character to be surprised by what they find (because it's supposed to be *their* handbag). The other player plays the scene straight and helps to justify if need be. As well as offering the sight of an improviser genuinely in the moment, this also makes audiences laugh because it feels gently invasive of the audience volunteer's privacy. Put on their makeup, open their diary, use their phone—but don't be cruel. Having both players use handbags tends to overload the scene.

Hat Game

Two players perform a scene, both wearing large floppy hats. Each tries to snatch the hat off the other person's head. A successful "grab," ending with your hat in my hand, wins me the game and the scene ends. An unsuccessful attempt loses me the game; hence, you can win by tempting me into making a grab at an ill-advised time. A perfect illustration of the possible primacy of the Second Story, since no improvised scene, no matter how brilliant, can possibly distract the audience's attention away from the goal of snatching the hat. A wonderful tie-breaker for any "competition" show. The Hat Game has no connection to Keith's Hat Stealing game for clowns described in *Impro*. Lyn Pierse's book *Theatresports Down Under* conflates the two games into one, rather missing the point of both.

It's Tuesday

An "over-accepting" game which *can* generate story, but which is more useful to break down inhibitions about strong emotions and to have as an "in case of emergencies" tool. One player makes a dull offer such as "I've put the cat out," or "Did you want cornflakes?" or "It's Tuesday." The other player picks an arbitrary emotion and has a lunatic overreaction to this news, repeating the offer in terror, joy, confusion, rage or whatever they've chosen. They then JUSTIFY why this offer created this reaction, and so the story lurches forward. At the end of their rant, they either make a dull offer back or their partner uses their last sentence as an offer to start the process again. In performance, you would tend to simply remember that doing this once will help to kick a moribund scene into life. Otherwise, not really a performance "game."

Laugh and Leave

An elimination game in which any improviser who makes the audience laugh has to leave the stage. Audiences are perverse, and if told they must not laugh will find almost anything funny—except improvisers who try to be amusing. Play this on a good night when the audience is in a giggly mood.

No S

A brilliantly simple way to screw up verbalization—players must speak without using the letter S. If they do use an S, they must leave the stage. A good tie-breaker for the end of a competitive show. Also an excellent way of exploring issues of risk-taking and good nature. Clearly, you could win the game by never speaking, but the point of playing the game is to entertain the audience, and ultimately the way to do that is to say an S so the audience can laugh at you. For this reason, the game is usually played with five or six players so we get this pleasure multiple times. If the game threatens never to end, some players will suicide (but hopefully make it look good). In practice, all that is needed if you are too good at the game, is to speak in paragraphs, make emotional offers and try and commit to the story. Pretty soon you will say an S without having to contrive it.

For variety, try No T, No N or any common consonant. Using rare letters is pointless and using vowels is too hard. S is a particularly good choice because it knocks out key words like "yes," "is" and singular verbs, but still makes dialogue possible. Another related game is "No I" where the personal pronoun "I" is banned. You can set this up as giving a prize to the "least egotistical player on the stage," if you like.

GAME HARDER THAN IT LOOK, NO?

I have a very happy memory of playing this game as part of a Theatresports match with another company. Our scenes and games tended toward narrative and relationships, and their scenes and games tended toward jokes and one-upmanship, which actually meant a very strong show with a lot of variety. We had challenged to a No S game, played with two of them and two of us, with points going to the team who won. Two of players were eliminated fairly quickly and we were down to Jana Carpenter for The Spontaneity Shop and a member of the opposing time.

This improviser had begun the scene adopting a thick Slavic accent which meant that inconvenient words like "is" could just be eliminated as part of the dialect and this had got him a lot of laughs for his cleverness early on, but he started to become less and less interesting as the scene progressed because he had "solved" the game. In a pause in the action, Jana looked at him and asked, "Tell me...where are you from?" There followed a very, very long pause and a gale of laughter as he tried to answer the question without using an S. Eventually he came up with "Georgia!" and was so pleased with himself that he said an S almost immediately thereafter and was eliminated.

The audience might have perceived Jana as undermining her opponent (and to a certain extent she was) but I see her as playing very generously. She found a way to make his choice work against his chances of success and not for them. She returned the element of risk to his playing and made him much more interesting to watch, just when the audience was starting to tire of him.

—Tom

The Removalists

A workshop game which can be used to develop a sensitivity to what your partner wants from you, and to realize when a scene is better abandoned. Each player is told that if they are unhappy with the way the scene is going they can blame their partner. A finger-snap at the moment of unhappiness is a signal for two more (burly) players to enter and physically drag the other improviser off the stage—who should protest the injustice of this: "You can't do this to me! This is totally unfair!" etc. A more subtle and interesting version of the King Game where a servant who does not please the master is killed by a finger-snap.

Sexy Smelly Stupid

Another good "platform extender" and a great antidote to a lot of character work which may make improvisers terribly introspective. Get four people up and tell them all to look at the other three and privately pick one to find sexy. Then they pick another to find smelly and yet another to find stupid. There is no one sexy person; it's about how people treat other people. Have one of them host a party and the others arrive as guests. Experiment with playing the reactions very broadly and very subtly. Try different qualities: fragile, dangerous, funny, boring, weird, aggressive, sarcastic, cold, etc. This often makes for very funny scenes, because it enforces transitions and gives people goals, but again is hard to create a strong narrative with. Not really a performance game, but a good lesson in creating a rich world.

Small Voice

An onstage player has an interaction with a tiny creature, too small to be convincingly portrayed by an actor, whose voice is supplied from offstage. Beginners won't dare name the thing, regardless of which role they are playing (the audience, as usual, doesn't care who names it as long as they get the information promptly). Coax them to come up with something and they'll name something inanimate. This is very unhelpful. If you finally get them to admit that it's a snail, then you can help it find a new home. If it's a moth, you can save it from mothballs. Keith recommends you add an arbitrary detail to the creature: instead of a worm, have a transvestite worm; instead of a flea, have a flea in a wheelchair.

In performance: An excellent story game which also allows the audience to see a new procedure. The onstage player *must* physicalize the animal and know where it is and what it's doing. They must *not* look at the offstage player.

In workshops: Good for strengthening narrative muscles, not WIMPING, creating characters with purpose, playing a resistance.

Speak in One Voice

Another Keith Johnstone procedure for avoiding planning. A group of improvisers stands in a tight bunch and improvises dialogue, speaking in unison, each of them trying to avoid leading the group but all happy to break deadlocks by making a noise and to complete a word they think they know. It isn't necessary to go very slowly (mistakes are part of the fun) and it isn't necessary—in fact it can be distracting—for the group to all be able to make eye contact. This is often presented as another expert game, rendered entirely tedious if the expertise is a suggestion supplied by the audience. It's more fun to have two such creatures interacting. On a good night, the audience can play this game *en masse*.

Speed Dating

A "medium-form" lasting about twenty minutes, invented at The Spontaneity Shop. A team of six or eight players, equal numbers of men and women, each get one suggestion from the audience to inspire a character. The men line up on one side of the stage and the women on the other. Man one and woman one enter and play a short scene as if at a speed dating event. When a bell rings, their place is taken by man two and woman two, and so on until we have seen everybody. Now the men cycle around, and so on round two we see man two and woman one. This process continues until we have seen all the possible combinations.

As well as getting a series of pairs of characters together and having them talk about themselves, this structure has two extra pleasures. First, we get to see how these people are changed by their interactions. The macho Italian Stallion is humiliated by the karate teacher and so is cowed and anxious when meeting the librarian. Second, after the first iteration, the audience starts to anticipate. "I can't wait until the wine-taster meets the truck-driver!" they think.

Twins

A procedure for creating bizarre characters which bypasses the instinct to check an impulse by "yoking" two players together. Two players agree to the same bizarre characterization and gang up on a third who plays the straight person. The "twins" (who should generally be of the same sex) stick physically close together and often repeat each other's dialogue (affirming that the other improviser made a good choice). If they are changed emotionally, they are both changed in the same way. They are never in conflict with each other. This game was inspired by the *Fast Show* "Suit You" sketch and some of the work of The League of Gentlemen, like Tubbs and Edward.

Variations: Several ways of beginning this game exist. One player adopts a characterization and is then joined by their twin; both players make a face at each other, and then they both try to make the same face, then twist their bodies and add a sound that fits; both are inspired by a suggestion from the audience and fit the characterization to mirror their partner's.

In performance: A high-energy, high-stakes scene which shouldn't be allowed to linger for too long. Get the straight person into trouble. We usually set them in a shop, and have the straight person come in to buy something.

In workshops: Can release very bold offers in the twins. Also good training for being "Alice"—the normal person who needs to react truthfully to being in the same room as these two lunatics.

Typewriter

One player becomes the "typist" and narrates a story, while pretending to type it out. Improvisers jump up to be the various characters, and control is shared between typist and actors. Beginners tend to tell wildly overcomplicated stories given this structure. Coach them to establish a hero with a goal, then make the hero suffer in pursuit of that goal. Typists need to be aware of mechanisms they have for moving the story on, but not to treat the improvisers like mannequins to be pushed around the stage.

In performance: Excellent for a more sustained piece toward the end of the evening.

In workshops: Good practice for narrative skills, sharing control, multi-person scenes.

DUMB BUT FUN

Some personal favorites. If not a comprehensive list, then certainly a useful sample.

Backwards Scene

Keith prefers "Forwards/Reverse," where at the signal of a director, the improvisers repeat the lines of the scene in reverse order until the signal comes to go forwards again. This seems to us to be a purely mechanical skill, whereas improvising an entire scene backwards is genuinely impressive and fun, and is also open-ended (or open-beginninged). The mechanism is the same, though: The lines are (apparently) spoken in reverse order, so the scene is constructed from the last line all the way back to the first line. Some excellent blind offers and jokes are possible, although this game does put more emphasis on the improvisers' cleverness than is possibly ideal. Begin by teaching (or practicing) a backwards TV interview, since this falls neatly into answer, question, answer, question, and is easy to start ("Mr. Jenkins, that was fascinating. Thank you for talking to us.") and end ("Today we are lucky enough to have Mr. Jenkins with us in the studio."). Then try and liven it up with big emotional choices. From here, try Murder In Reverse, where you start (end) with a dead body on the floor. Then you should be ready to do an "open" version.

Clap Switcheroo

An example of a game which has the potential to be a story game, but which includes a gimmick if the story gets boring. Begin with one or two players and add more as the scene develops to build the pace. When one player claps their hands, everyone picks someone else's character and takes it over, assuming the other improviser's position on the stage, physicality and characterization—so big characterizations really help. Then the scene re-starts. Not a game you'd want to see too often, and it needs to be done really well, but it isn't destructive and can inspire players.

Variation: Switch Change. Two players onstage and two players waiting in the wings, one on each side. The first two players start improvising. On the command "change," the players in the wings change places with the players onstage and, as above, take over the characters and continue the scene. On the command "switch," the players onstage switch places with each other. On the command "switch left" the two players at stage left switch places. On the command "switch right" the two players at stage right switch places.[1]

Da Doo Ron Ron

An elimination game in which a series of improvisers attempts to sustain a version of the well-known Crystals pop song, sustaining the same rhyme until one of them flounders and is thrown off. Typically, after each elimination, the MC gets a new name from the audience for the improvisers to rhyme with, the first line always being "I met him/her on a Monday and his/her name was [BLANK]." Here's an example performed by three players.

---

[1]Jim Libby, an American improviser who has lived and worked in Vienna for many years, showed us this version which he learned from Matt Alden Dykes of Rapid Fire Theatre in Edmonton, and for the moment, there the trail ends.

A: I met him on a Monday and his name was Jack.
All: Da Doo Ron Ron Ron, Da Doo Ron Ron!
B: He was lying in a field, flat on his back.
All: Da Doo Ron Ron Ron, Da Doo Ron Ron! Yeah!
C: Alas and alack!
All: Yeah!
A: We went back to his shack!
All: Yeah!
B: I'd forgotten to pack!
All: Da Doo Ron Ron Ron, Da Doo Ron Ron!
C: Three weeks later, he gave me the sack.
All: Da Doo Ron Ron Ron, Da Doo Ron Ron!
A: The thing was, he … er…

A is eliminated. To make the game tougher, have one improviser do all three "short" lines. Practice this before playing it to make sure everyone can sing the group lines with gusto, and keep rolling around to a new verse without pausing, to keep the pressure up. If an elimination game is needed, we prefer this to Die, because this doesn't pretend to be a story game.

ID Cards

Ask for a couple of pieces of photo ID from the audience—driver's license, passport, library card or the like. Hand these to two onstage improvisers and tell them not to look at them yet. Set up the rest of the scene (get a suggestion if you like) and then have them glance at the card and try and make the face which they see. On a good day, the face will be quite extreme and will generate a pair of quite rich and strong characters. On a bad day, the improvisers may have to exaggerate what they see a little (bear in mind no one else can see the ID card). For the scene to sustain interest, the improvisers still need to be changed, but the ID card provides a baseline, and the audience finds the procedure amusing, as well as gently invasive in the same way as the Handbag Game (see page 463).

Inner Monologue

Two improvisers play a scene, while two more supply their inner thoughts at various intervals. Can be successful if the "inner thoughts" improvisers understand that they have to provide a counterpoint (or even a contradiction) to the spoken dialogue or what's the point. Not a great improvement on just having the actors speak their own inner thoughts to the audience, except that the former version looks more like a "game."

Variation for drunken and indulgent improvisers after a show: Play a scene and have two other improvisers supply the *improviser's* inner thoughts: "Jeez, do I have to play another scene with this guy? I just know I'm going to end up making all the offers. Okay, I'll give him one shot to define something, but after that I'm just going it alone."

Variation to avoid: Inner interpretative dance-alogue. Really. People play this.

Variation to avoid like the plague: In general, piling up procedures to make a super-duper game is a terrible idea. Tom remembers being trapped onstage once, a guest in someone else's show, and made to translate a gibberish poem while two more improvisers staged a genuinely appalling interpretive dance version. Ghastly beyond belief.

Panel

Barely a game at all, this simply presents a panel of three or four people who will hold forth on a subject, probably suggested by the audience, and which discussion is moderated by a chairperson. Can tend toward jokes but is also an opportunity to play big characters. The TV studio setting and reassuring presence of a chairperson makes it feel very safe, and we'd prefer something more open-ended, but this could be a nice way to inject some variety into a performance and to play a game that lasts a little longer. It's also a good way to get improvisers from different groups all playing together.

Variations: The panelists can be inspired to create characters in any of the ways which already exist for the purpose: a word from the audience, costume pieces, borrowing an identity card from an audience member and making a face like the one on the card, being an animal. Some groups get the audience to give them famous people to play, which we don't recommend unless you have brilliant impressionists in your group.

Paper Chase

Have the audience write lines of dialogue on slips of paper and supply improvisers with a small number of such slips in their pockets or somewhere on their person. Every so often, they must read their next line from a slip of paper and then attempt to justify this random line's inclusion in the narrative. Try to avoid pre-justifying the lines of dialogue with phrases like, "Well as my mother always used to say to me..."

Variant: in a workshop, try giving people non-specific relationship-altering lines like, "How dare you say that to me?" Or "That's why I love you so much."

Variant: We saw a Second City show in which the lines of dialogue were written on the backs of sticky Post-It notes which meant spare players could scurry up to the onstage improvisers and stick a new line of dialogue on their shirt which they could peel off and read when it was convenient.

Pillars

Two people, usually audience members, stand at the side of the stage and contribute a word or two to the dialogue of one of the improvisers when touched, or when the improviser claps their hands or gives some other such signal. It's best to tell the audience volunteers that they have to "finish the improviser's sentences," and try to provide them with sentences which are just missing one word. If you say, "Seeing you dressed like this makes me want to..." then the volunteers will probably be able to come up with an appropriate word quite easily. If you give them something more open, like, "I'm afraid that..." then their job is much harder.

The improvisers *must* repeat the word they are given, first, because the audience doesn't perceive it as having been spoken until it is spoken by the character in the scene, and second, just to make sure the rest of the audience has heard it!

Sound Effects

One improviser, or possibly two, acts out a scene, while another makes sound effects into a microphone. An amusing procedure, which doesn't have much to do with improvisation but can provide a happy give-and-take between sound effects person and actor.

Variation: Have the audience make the sound effects. This is even less of a challenge, but the audience like to be involved, so it can be useful for generating a feeling of good nature.

Thumbs Up Thumbs Down

A politician is interviewed on TV but has brought along a spin doctor who gives a thumbs up, a thumbs down or an equivocation gesture before each answer. Again, the TV interview situation feels safe, so it's up to the spin doctor to make life difficult for the politician. The interviewer should ask yes/no questions to make the procedure clear: Thumbs up means a "yes" answer, thumbs down means a "no" answer. Interviewers should also be quick to spot apparent contradictions and try to make the politician justify.

Variation: Yes/No/Maybe. Get a pack of playing cards and, with a permanent marker, write YES on the back of fifteen or twenty of them, and NO on the back of fifteen or twenty more. On the remaining cards, write other possible answers to Yes/No questions such as "I'll never tell" or "How did you find out about that?" Let a member of the audience shuffle the pack, and then they can use the cards as a script to answer questions from the improvisers. We usually stage it as a press conference and have the improvisers be the press.

NEVER PLAY

A random assortment, barely scratching the surface.

Die

Yes, putting Die under "Never Play" is harsh, but it's become an improv cliché. There are Dumb But Fun games which get seen less often, so the overused ones should get relegated to Never Play for a while.

A collection of players, four or so, line up and tell a story, with the role of storyteller moving when a director points at a new player. If a player falters, the audience shouts "Die!" and that player retires. Eventually there will be a winner. A few years ago this might have made it into Dumb But Fun, but familiarity breeds contempt and mediocre versions of this game seemed to plague almost every improv show we were at. It isn't a very interesting game, it doesn't generate very interesting content and all the variations available make it worse. Something like a tap-out monologue would be much more fun if you wanted a shared narrative. Something like Da Doo Ron Ron or Laugh And Leave or No S would be a better elimination game, since there is no pretense at storytelling in those games.

Variant: The eliminated player commits suicide, usually with a household object suggested by the audience. Risk-free, variety-free and essentially pointless.

Variant: Each player has their own genre. This does not improve matters at all, and fogs the issue.

Variant: Instead of telling a story, players must name items which fit a particular category. Passable parlor game, but of little entertainment value to the spectators.

Variant: Instead of telling a story, players must invent brand names for a particular product. Harder than it sounds. Less fun than it sounds.

Entrances and Exits

Each player is given a trigger word which, when spoken by another player, causes them to enter or exit as appropriate. A boring exercise in PIMPING which audiences tire of rapidly.

Freeze Tag

Two players begin a scene and continue until someone else yells "Freeze!" The players hold their positions, and the person who yelled "Freeze!" replaces one of the existing players, adopting the same posture. This tableau now becomes the starting point for a new scene, and so on. A classic game, a mainstay of many workshops and some groups even play it in public, but we can't see the point of it, and it perpetuates the habit of killing off scenes in the middle instead of finding resolutions. In general, beginning by justifying a position does not seem to inspire many improvisers (which is why this stricture is so frequently ignored), so why do it?

Genre Rollercoaster et al.

A particularly important Never Play game because of its huge influence and popularity through *Whose Line Is It Anyway?*, to the point where "in the style of" practically became a watchword for improvisation in general. In this game, a scene in progress is switched into different genres over the course of its life. Plot elements established in one genre should continue into the next.

Let's just look at the kinds of promise made by this game. The apparent challenge is to keep the story moving forward while taking the different genres on board, but the audience also expects improvisers who take offers of genres from them not simply to replicate the genre but to *satirize* it. This puts pressure on the improvisers to come up with arbitrary genre jokes as quickly as possible. If the jokes are funny, this is probably the best outcome, since the chances of the given genre and the story so far meshing perfectly, yet surprisingly, are almost nil, and so if the game becomes nothing but a series of arbitrary genre jokes, then we're okay with that if the jokes are very funny and the game is kept short.

But improvisation is not the best procedure for inventing a string of jokes, and since audiences tend always to suggest the same genres and the genre material fights for dominance over the plot, the same jokes tend to come up again and again and again.

Other variations tend only to make matters worse. Emo (emotional) Rollercoaster substitutes emotions for the genres, which is thought to put the emphasis back on storytelling. It enforces transitions, which is better than having the improvisers refuse to be changed at all, but because everyone in the scene takes on the same emotion, it's hard to experience this as one person changed by another. It also encourages JOINING. Much the same can be said for the "emo" games which have spun off from this (Emo Date, Emo Party, etc.), which the interested reader can look up for themselves.

Of Accent Rollercoaster, the least said the better.

Sign Language Translation

A sketch appropriated to be an improv game. One player is (yawn) interviewed by another. A third player provides a simultaneous sign language translation of both sides of the conversation, ideally incorporating many visual puns. We have seen this played well, but never as well as it could have been scripted—so what's the point?

Superheroes

Given a life-or-death situation, a superhero named by the audience summons further help, each hero naming the next as they enter. So Captain Narcolepsy cries "Thank god it's you, Always Talks In Song Lyrics Girl!" as the next improviser enters, who then responds "I just called to say 'I love you'" or some such nonsense. The superheroes then peel off again in reverse order, ending the scene. The temptation to pre-plan a funny superhero name must be overwhelming, and if you got better results that way then fine. Again, the game nails the improvisers down rather than inspiring their imaginations by having a strict order of entrance and exit built in to it, which also locks you in until the sequence is completed, regardless of a perfect punchline appearing half way through. We did see a splendid example in which a suicidally demented improviser at The Stand in Edinburgh played "Never Touch The Floor Boy" with total commitment, while everyone around him gasped in horror. Great energy, wit and daring can save pretty much any game, but we would have loved to see that same improviser working without the shackles of silly games like this one.

WARM-UP GAMES

Again, a small selection of some of our favorites, useful for backstage preshow and to kick off a workshop.

Bibbity Bibbity Bop

A very firm favorite, especially with children (who can play it non-stop for hours). One player stands in the middle of a circle of players and has various strategies they can use to get someone "out," who must then take their place. The first two are to point at someone and say "Bibbity bibbity bop" (the person you point at must say "Bop" before you say "Bop" in order to survive) or to point at someone and just say "Bop" (the person you point at must say nothing at all in order to survive). All the rest involve a count to ten during which time the person pointed at and the ones either side must arrange themselves in a particular configuration. Examples include "Elephant, 1, 2, 3, 4, 5, 6, 7, 8, 9, 10!" (person pointed at is the trunk, people on either side are the ears), "James Bond, 1, 2, 3, 4, 5, 6, 7, 8, 9, 10!" (person pointed at is James Bond, people on either side are the Bond girls), "Monkeys, 1, 2, 3, 4, 5, 6, 7, 8, 9, 10!" (the three people must be the three wise monkeys) and many more, which often vary from group to group. It may not sound like much, but try it!

Big Booty

Suitable for a group of about five to ten. One person is "Big Booty," then they number off clockwise. Everyone clicks a rhythm and then Big Booty begins by chanting "Big booty, big booty, big booty. Oh yeah! Big booty number x." Number x must then respond "Number x, number y," sticking to the rhythm. If anyone screws up, the group cries "Oh shit!" and while Big Booty starts up again, they go to the final position, causing other people to be re-numbered.

Variations: Replace the numbers with words.

Electric Company

Stand in a circle and whoever would like to start begins by saying a one syllable word. The person on their left adds a second word to complete a two-word phrase which the group then repeats: "Fly." "Trap." "Fly-trap." The person who said "Trap" now begins the sequence again with a new, unrelated word. Once everyone has got the idea, play again, this time with everyone clapping out a rhythm. Encourage people who struggle to come up with the "right" word or a "clever" word to just spit something out and to hit the rhythm. Their choice will be validated by the group repeating the two-word phrase anyway, even if it's "Roof-aargghh!"

Fling Shoo-Ey

The group stands in a circle and everyone takes off one shoe. Everyone puts up one hand and then one person throws their shoe (a gentle under-arm toss is all that is required) to someone with their hand up. That person throws that same shoe to someone else with their hand up and so a sequence is established, coming back to the first person, who throws it to the same person again, repeating the sequence. When one shoe is making its way happily around the group, try adding a second, or a third, following the same pattern. Some groups can manage as many shoes as there are people.

There should be no risk provided that people don't *hurl* the shoes, but you may want to remove enormous heavy hobnailed boots from play. This game was taught to us by Shawn Kinley, but the name we call it by is due to Bob Hanson.

Greetings

We often use this with a group of improvisers from different backgrounds, or sometimes as a corporate ice-breaker. Have everyone march around the room, introducing themselves and shaking hands with people. Then have them do it in different styles. Some of our favorites:

● A little *too* enthusiastically

● As if you are at a funeral

● As if you've just noticed someone more interesting over their shoulder

● As if you're trying not to let anyone see how drunk you are

● Very flirtatiously, but without touching

● As if you are bitter business rivals, trying to be polite

● As if you are hyperactive children

I Am, I Am, I Am, I'll Take

One person stands in the middle of a circle and announces what they are: "I am a king." "I am a dog." "I am a wall." Something like that. They then adopt an appropriate pose. A second person joins, adding to the tableau. A king might be joined by a crown, a throne or a queen. Again, the second person adopts an appropriate pose. Finally, a third person joins and completes the tableau. Perhaps the king sitting on his throne gains a cushion. Now the first person announces which of the other two they will remove. "I'll take the throne." The king and the throne leave together and the remaining player restates their role ("I am a cushion") and so the sequence starts again.

This is a great YES AND warm up, which also allows people to be funny if they want to. Prioritize speed and playfulness over wit, however, and be on your guard for people who come in third and ignore the second element.

More Stories Like That

Three or four improvisers tell a story, taking one line each at a time, according to the following sequence.

- Once upon a time there was...
- And every day...
- Until one day...
- And because of that...
- And because of that...
- And because of that... (*repeat as necessary*)
- Until finally...
- And ever since then...

If anyone stumbles, either over the template or the content, the whole group shouts "Yay!" and three more people rush up to have a go (this is part of the fun, so don't give people too much time to memorize the sequence). If one group gets to the end, everyone yells "More stories like that!" and then three more people rush up to have a go.

Sevens

The improvisers stand in a circle and count off numbers from one to seven, then start at one again. Each improviser touches either their left shoulder with their right hand or their right shoulder with their left hand. Touching their left shoulder indicates that the person on their left should say the next number in the sequence, and touching their right shoulder indicates that the person on their right should say the next number. The person who says "seven" makes a sort of "Olé" gesture with one hand pointing over their head and the other hand pointing the opposite way across their middle. The position of the top hand indicates who should continue by saying "one." Anyone who makes a mistake is "punished" by doing one lap around the outside of the circle while the game carries on. Huge fun, and taught to us by Jacob Banigan.

Variants: Try with days of the week or letters from A to G, or switching sequences, either at the end of a run of seven, or at any time ("One," "Two," "Wednesday").

Spotlight

A beautifully simple game. The group stands in a circle. One person stands in the middle and starts singing a song (not an improvised song). As soon as another person is reminded of another song—or if the person in the middle looks like they're in trouble—they tag out the singer and start singing a new song. Insist that everybody has a go, although if you play for long enough, even people who look aghast at the beginning will be singing along with everyone else, and taking their turn in the middle, too. A great pre-show warm up, as it's all about bonding and fun and you can't get it wrong.

Yes Let's/Nope

In twos, one person makes suggestions about how their story should continue ("Let's explore this cave"). Their partner responds "Yes let's!" if they want the story to continue in that fashion, in which case both players act out the suggestion. But if they don't like the suggestion, they respond "Nope!" brightly and cheerfully, in the hope of inspiring a better suggestion. Remind the suggestion-makers that their partner is responsible for quality control. If they suspect the response is always a bland "Yes let's" (to be nice) they should try getting a "Nope" deliberately.

Variant: A player who says "nope" becomes the suggestion-maker.

You

One of those games which exists in many forms. This one was taught to us by Shawn Kinley. Begin, as with Fling Shoo-ey, by establishing a pattern around the group. Everyone puts up one hand. Somebody begins the pattern by pointing at someone and saying "You." That person points at another person who still has their hand up and says "You." This continues until everyone has been pointed at, with the last person pointing at the first person to complete the circuit. The "you" pattern is repeated several times until everyone has got it.

The procedure is repeated using a category, such as capital cities, farm animals or favorite foods, but a new pattern is developed. So the first person points to someone and says "London." That person points to someone who still has their hand up and says "Rome," and so on until everyone has pointed at someone. This pattern is practiced until everyone has got it. You always say "You" to the same person, and you always say the same capital city to the same person, but typically you say your capital city to a different person from the person you say "You" to. Once the capital city pattern is up and running, start the "You" pattern and try to sustain both simultaneously. Unlike Fling Shoo-ey, it is the responsibility of the sender to make sure the pattern is continued. If I say "Rome" and you don't notice, I should continue to say it—politely—until you notice, and pass it on.

Once the group can sustain two patterns simultaneously, we add a third. Again, everyone puts one hand up, and the first person crosses the circle and touches someone on the shoulder, replacing them in the circle. That person crosses the circle and replaces someone who still has their hand up, and so on. You always walk to the same person, and you still say "You" to the person you said "You" to before, no matter where they happen to be standing, and the same goes for your capital city. Now try to sustain all three patterns together. This is a good exercise for panickers—it calms them down because the game doesn't get easier if you panic.

Variation (due to Melisande Cook): For the middle pattern, use "Names of people in the room" as your category, but when you point at Jeff, you say "Peter" and so on. This is wonderfully confusing.

APPENDIX TWO

Syllabus

This is an outline of our Level One syllabus. Each class is taught over three hours. The first four classes are also offered as an intensive weekend.

DAY ONE: SPONTANEITY

- Pointing At Things
- What Are You Doing?
- Yes And
- Word At A Time
- What Comes Next?

DAY TWO: STATUS

- Low Status Clowns/Still Heads Same Dialogue
- Status Parties
- Fight For Your Number
- Status Ladders
- Status Competition
- Happy High Status

DAY THREE: WORKING TOGETHER

- Tug Of War
- Standing Wave
- Speak In One Voice
- Arms Through
- Master/Servant Dubbing
- Over-confessing
- Status Exchange

DAY FOUR: TELLING STORIES

- The Narrative Circle
- What Comes Next (committees)
- Join The Dots
- Go Through An Unusual Door
- Tilts

DAY FIVE: BEING CHANGED

- Gibberish
- Dubbing
- It's Tuesday
- Twitching, Topping and Paperflicking

DAY SIX: DEFINING

- Death in a Minute
- Small Voice
- Photo Album (and sometimes Boris)
- Animal Expert

DAY SEVEN: FAILURE

- Hat Games
- No S
- Continue or Thank You

DAY EIGHT: CHARACTERS

- Mime Skills
- Transforming The Body
- Characters From A Hat
- Sexy Smelly Stupid
- Twins
- The Guest Game

GLOSSARY OF TERMS

Absurdity Curve The principle that a scene which gets progressively more absurd will hold the audience, whereas the absurd offer which comes at the end of that process would not be acceptable without that build-up.

Accept Embracing an offer, the opposite of blocking. In Chicago, the term "yield" is sometimes used. See *Offer, Block*.

Ask For A question you ask the audience to solicit an idea to inspire an improvised scene or game. Also, the answer to that question. See *Suggestion*.

Blind Offer An offer which leaves some information conspicuously un-said allowing the next person to define.

Block Preventing an action from continuing or denying the reality of an offer. Used by anxious improvisers to maintain control or to make audiences laugh, but it kills the story. In Chicago, the term "deny" is sometimes used. See *Offer, Accept*.

Break in the Routine An event which prevents an action from being completed without *sidetracking* (qv) away from it.

Bridge Taking your time to achieve an obvious end-point.

Callback Referring to an element from earlier in the show (typically from another scene) as a joke. A form of *Reincorporation* (qv).

Cancel An offer which undoes the effect of a previous offer.

Circle See Narrative Circle.

Close, Del Influential improvisation performer and director who is credited with the creation of the *Harold* (qv)

and who is associated with the Chicago improvisation movement.

The Committee The theatre company which Del Close was a part of in San Francisco in the 1960s.

Compass Players An influential improvisation theatre company which flourished in Chicago in the early 1950s.

Competitive Format A format which includes some element of competition as an extra point of interest for the audience.

Deny See *Block*.

Direct/Director While this can refer to the usual actions of a theatre director—rehearsing the show, giving notes afterwards and so on—in an improv context, this usually refers to live public direction during the show. See *Side-coach*.

Endowment (a) Adding a detail to someone else's character or another element in the scene. (b) A class of improv games in which one or more players has to guess secret information.

Finding the Game See *Game*.

Fog of War The idea that improvisers are easily distracted by the stress of the situation and will fail to see or hear things that are easily noticed by the more relaxed audience.

Format A mechanism for packaging improvisation for public consumption, e.g., Theatresports.

Fourth Wall (a) The imaginary wall between the performers and the audience, assuming a standard Proscenium Arch architecture, or something like it. (b) The usual procedure in theatre of never directly acknowledging the audience, since they lie beyond the imaginary wall. Improvisation often involves "fourth wall breaking" to some degree—the opposite procedure.

Gag A laugh at the expense of the story.

Game (a) A formal structure imposed on a scene before it starts, also known as a *Handle*. (b) Any pattern which occurs within a scene.

Gorilla Theatre A Keith Johnstone competitive format controlled and licensed by the International Theatresports Institute in which a small group of experienced players take turns directing each other.

Gossip Talking about people or things which are offstage: in the past, in the future or elsewhere.

Halpern, Charna Del Close's partner, now running iO following Del's death.

Handle See *Game*.

Harold A Del Close format wherein a single suggestion inspires a variety of improvised scenes which are ended and begun by the improvisers themselves. Ideally the whole piece gains extra structure as elements of earlier scenes are reincorporated later on.

Heighten A Chicago term which roughly equates to raising the stakes or going up the absurdity curve.

Hoop Game A formal game or *handle* whose main point of interest is whether or not the improvisers will achieve the task.

Impro The British English variant for "improv." Improvisation.

ImprovOlympic The theatre company founded by Del Close and Charna Halpern following their departure from Second City. Now known as iO.

Instant Trouble A way of killing stories by having dramatic events occur before the platform has been established.

ITI International Theatresports Institute. Body established by Keith Johnstone to control licenses for his show formats and to provide support to companies holding those licenses.

Johnstone, Keith British theatre director and improvisation teacher, inventor of many improv games and exercises regarded as classics, now living and working in Calgary.

Join Two improvisers adopting the same attitude or the same emotional state.

Justify Make sense of an offer, or put it in context after it has been made. NB: Mick Napier uses the term rather differently, as a negative, to mean essentially apologizing for an offer.

Life Game A format invented by Keith Johnstone and controlled by the International Theatresports Institute wherein a single volunteer is interviewed about their life on stage and their answers inspire a series of improvised scenes. At the time of writing, Life Game licenses are no longer being issued by the ITI.

Long-form A kind of public improvisation which sustains over the course of a whole show, or much of a show, instead of being split into distinct, unrelated chunks.

Loop A part of a story which is repeated, usually unnecessarily.

Loose Moose The Improvisation Theatre founded by Keith Johnstone in Calgary.

Micetro Impro A format invented by Keith Johnstone and controlled by the International Theatresports Institute wherein two directors set up scenes for members of a large pool of improvisers. The audience scores the scenes and low-scoring players are gradually eliminated until only one remains. (Also "Maestro.")

Mime Creating a physical world through manipulating imaginary objects—not necessarily without speaking.

Montage A variant of the *Harold* which puts less emphasis on show-wide structure.

The Moose See *Loose Moose*.

Narrative Circle A way of thinking about the audience's expectations. Given a particular set of story elements, some further elements seem very likely also to be included (inside the circle), and the audience will be pleased if they in fact are. Elements from outside the circle should not be included without justification. (Given a circus, clowns are inside the circle. Vampires are not.)

Obvious An offer which could have been predicted by earlier offers. Generally, a sign that things are going well (yes, really).

Offer Any new idea brought into an improvised scene, whether a line of dialogue, gesture, mime or whatever. See *Accept, Block*.

Open Scene A chunk of improvisation with no other handle or game to play. See also *Scene, Handle, Game*.

Original An offer which has no relation to earlier offers. Generally a sign that things are going badly.

Pimp An offer which sets a supposedly difficult task for your fellow player. The point of such an offer is to make your fellow player squirm, which the audience will hopefully enjoy. An example of *Second Story*, but also an example of a *Gag*.

Platform The stable situation which exists at the beginning of the story.

Promise An offer which foretells another offer. Making promises and keeping them draws audiences in.

Raise the Stakes A strategy used to make a story more interesting. Anxious improvisers often do the opposite in the hope of getting a laugh—a form of *Gagging*.

Reincorporation Feeding earlier elements back in to a story to give it structure.

Scene A discrete "chunk" of improvised theatre, often telling a complete story, but almost always taking place in continuous time, and usually around two to five minutes. Can be used to differentiate an improvised segment with no overt game from one with a game. See also *Open Scene, Handle, Scenework, Game*.

Scenework The art of creating open scenes.

Second City A theatre company which evolved from the Compass Players. Second City now uses improvisation principally as a sketch-writing tool.

Second Story The theory that an audience at an improv show is relating to not only the story the improvisers are telling (the First Story) but also the story of them telling it (the Second Story).

Sills, Paul Son of Viola Spolin, who was happy to teach his mother's improv games to actors who wanted to perform improvisation to audiences.

Shepherd, David Founder of the Compass Players, probably the first North American theatre company to present public improvisation.

Short-form A kind of public improvisation which consists of short, discrete scenes or games.

Side-Coach Directing in a workshop: calling out instructions for students to follow while a scene is in progress.

Sidetrack An offer which takes the story off in a new, uncalled-for direction. A version of *That's Not Good Enough*.

Space Object A mime object.

Spacework The art of manipulating mime objects.

Spolin, Viola The earliest improvisation practitioner, whose improv games were taught to The Compass Players (qv) by her son Paul Sills.

Stiles, Patti Improviser who trained at the Loose Moose and who taught the authors of this book when they were just starting out.

Suggestion An idea from the audience, solicited by an improviser or MC during the show.

That's Not Good Enough Unconscious strategy adopted by anxious improvisers of hopping from idea to idea instead of pushing one idea into the future.

Theatresports A format invented by Keith Johnstone and controlled by the International Theatresports Institute wherein two teams challenge each other to improvised feats. Usually scored by three judges.

Waffle Talking without doing.

Wimp, Wimping Failing to define.

Yes And Accepting a fellow improviser's idea and building on it.

Yield See *Accept*.

THANKS

The authors would like to thank...

Keith Johnstone. We are not so much standing on the shoulders of giants, but in the shadow of one. (Have you met him? He's enormous!)

Patti Stiles, who opened our eyes.

David Barker, who commissioned the first edition for Continuum.

Jenny Ridout, who commissioned the second edition for Methuen Drama.

John O'Donovan, who made sure that the second edition was actually published.

Bob Hanson, who introduced us to David Barker.

Our teachers over the years, especially in London: Natalie Haverstock, John Voce, Paul Rogan, Luke Sorba, Phil Whelans; and overseas: Dennis Cahill, Shawn Kinley, Dan O'Connor, Andy Eninger, Charna Halpern, Gary Austin, Steve Jarand.

Lloyd Trott, who introduced us to RADA.

Brian Walter for the kiss and the slap.

All those who have from time to time been members of The Spontaneity Shop "core company": Justin Rosenholtz, Richard Doyle, Jane Elson, Ojan Fletcher, Chris Harvey John, Belinda Cornish, Kevin Tomlinson, Matt Watts, Jacqueline Haigh, Philippa Waller, Gary Turner, Jeremy Finch, Jana Carpenter, Melisande Cook, Stephanie Kasen, Sonya Vine, Natalie Richer and especially the indefatigable Alex MacLaren.

Our office companions Rebecca Coleman, Francesca Hunter and especially Gina Decio whose services as Miss Moneypenny constantly went above and beyond the call of duty.

All our interviewees for their generosity with their time and their ideas, and especially Mike McShane for the foreword.

The other two members of the Secret Impro Group, Chris Gibbs and Alex Lamb.

Friendly improvisers overseas who have given us workshops to teach and shows to be in, or who have come and visited us: Randy Dixon, Jim Libby, Jacob Bannigan, Jay Stern and Meg Sweeney-Lawless, Hans Guykens, Girl Clumsy, Greg Wah, Dan Beeston, Mark Meer, Jonathan Pitts, Naomi Ikegami, Rebecca Northan, Zachary Quinn, The Three Canadians, Sue Walden, Rama Nicholas, Eric Heiberg, Lisa Ricketts, Rob Lloyd, Timothy Redmond, Nick Byrne and no doubt many more— and Brook Sinclair who produced our international tournament.

Those who helped us make money at this: Richard Chapman, Richard Garnett, Mark Weston, Alistair Black, Alex "Fuzz" Khan and all of our corporate clients.

All of our workshop students, and all of those who came to see our shows or played with us as guests.

You, for buying this book. We *love* you. Why not buy another for a friend or relative?

BIBLIOGRAPHY

Adamson, Joe. *Groucho, Harpo, Chico and Sometimes Zeppo*. W. H. Allen, 1973.

Barkow, Jerome H.; Cosmides, Leda; Tooby, John. *The Adapted Mind: Evolutionary Psychology and the Generation of Culture*. Oxford University Press, 1992.

Barnes, Alan; Hearne, Marcus. *Kiss Kiss Bang! Bang!: The Unofficial James Bond Film Companion*. Batsford, 2001.

Besser, Marr; Roberts, Ian; Walsh, Matt. *The Upright Citizens Brigade Comedy Improvisation Manual*. Comedy Council of Nicea, 2013.

Campbell, Joseph. *The Hero with a Thousand Faces*. Fontana Press, 1993.

Carr, Jimmy; Greeves, Lucy. *The Naked Jape: Uncovering the Hidden World of Jokes*. Penguin Books, 2006.

Carroll, Lewis; Gardner, Martin (Ed.); Tenniel, John (Illus.). *The Annotated Alice*. Penguin Books, 1970.

Chaplin, Charles. *My Autobiography*. Penguin Books, 1973.

Close, Del; Halpern, Charna; Johnson, Kim Howard. *Truth in Comedy: The Manual of Improvisation*. Meriwether Publishing Ltd, 1994.

Coleman, Janet. *The Compass: The Improvisational Theatre that Revolutionized American Comedy*. University of Chicago Press, 1990.

Collet, Peter. *The Book of Tells*. Bantam Books Ltd, 2004.

Dawkins, Richard. *The Selfish Gene*. Oxford University Press, 1989.

Dennett, Daniel C. *Consciousness Explained*. Penguin Books, 1993.

Gilbert, Stephen W. *Fight and Kick and Bite: Life and Work of Dennis Potter*. Hodder & Stoughton, 1995.

Gladwell, Malcolm. *Blink: The Power of Thinking Without Thinking*. Little Brown and Company, 2005.

Goldman, William. *Adventures in the Screen Trade: A Personal View of Hollywood*. Macdonald & Co, 1984.

Goldman, William. *Which Lie Did I Tell? More Adventures in the Screen Trade*. Bloomsbury, 2001.

Gottman, John; de Claire, Joan. *The Relationship Cure: A Five-Step Guide for Building Better Connections with Family, Friends and Lovers*. Crown Publications, 2002.

Griggs, Jeff. *Guru: My Days with Del Close*. Ivan R Dee, 2005.

Hayes, Kevin (Ed.). *The Cambridge Companion to Edgar Allan Poe*. Cambridge University Press, 2002.

Holt, John. *How Children Fail*. Penguin, 1990.

Holt, John. *How Children Learn*. Penguin, 1991.

Johnson, Kim Howard. *The Funniest One in the Room: The Lives and Legends of Del Close*. Chicago Review Press, 2008.

Johnstone, Keith. *Don't Be Prepared: Theatresports for Teachers*. Loose Moose Theatre Company, 1994.

Johnstone, Keith. *Impro: Improvisation and the Theatre*. Methuen Drama, 1981.

Johnstone, Keith. *Impro for Storytellers: Theatresports and the Art of Making Things Happen*. Faber and Faber, 1999.

Louvish, Simon. *Monkey Business: The Lives and Legends of the Marx Brothers*. Faber and Faber, 1999.

Martini, Clem; Foreman, Kathleen. *Something Like a Drug: An Unauthorized Oral History of Theatresports*. Red Deer Press, 1998.

McKee, Robert. *Story: Substance, Structure, Style and the Principles of Screenwriting*. Methuen Drama, 1999.

Napier, Mick. *Improvise: Scene from the Inside Out*. Heinemann, 2004.

Ondaatje, Michael. *The Conversations: Walter Murch and the Art of Editing Film*. Bloomsbury, 2003.

Pierse, Lyn. *Theatresports Down Under*. Improcorp Australia Pty Ltd, 1993.

Pinker, Steven. *How the Mind Works*. Penguin Books Ltd, 1999.

Poe, Edgar Allan. *The Raven and Other Poems and Tales*. Little Brown and Company, 2001.

Rowland, Ian. *The Full Facts Book of Cold Reading*, 4th ed. Ian Rowland Limited, 2008.

Rudlin, John. *Commedia Dell'Arte in the 20th Century: A Handbook*. Routledge, 1994.

Seuss, Dr. *The Lorax*. Wings Books, 1971.

Spolin, Viola; Sills, Paul. *Improvisation for the Theater*. Northwestern University Press, 1999.

Sweet, Jeffrey. *Something Wonderful Right Away: Oral History of the Second City and the Compass Players*. Limelight Editions, 1987.

INDEX